Sacred Kingship in World History

Sacred Kingship in World History

Between Immanence
and Transcendence

Edited by A. Azfar Moin
and Alan Strathern

Columbia University Press

New York

Columbia University Press wishes to express its appreciation for assistance given by the University of Texas at Austin and the John Fell Oxford University Press Research Fund in the publication of this book.

Columbia University Press
Publishers Since 1893
New York   Chichester, West Sussex
cup.columbia.edu

Copyright © 2022 Columbia University Press
All rights reserved

Library of Congress Cataloging-in-Publication Data
Names: Moin, A. Azfar, editor. | Strathern, Alan, 1975– editor.
Title: Sacred kingship in world history : between immanence and transcendence / edited by A. Azfar Moin and Alan Strathern.
Description: New York : Columbia University Press, [2022] | Includes bibliographical references and index.
Identifiers: LCCN 2021040025 (print) | LCCN 2021040026 (ebook) | ISBN 9780231204163 (hardback) | ISBN 9780231204170 (trade paperback) | ISBN 9780231555401 (ebook)
Subjects: LCSH: Kings and rulers—Religious aspects. | Religion and politics. | Immanence (Philosophy) | Transcendence (Philosophy) | Monarchy—History.
Classification: LCC BL65.K55 K56 2022 (print) | LCC BL65.K55 (ebook) | DDC 201/.72—dc23/eng/20211207
LC record available at https://lccn.loc.gov/2021040025
LC ebook record available at https://lccn.loc.gov/2021040026

Cover design: Milenda Nan Ok Lee
Cover image: Priest King, Mohenjodaro, copyright © J. M. Kenoyer/Harappa.com. Courtesy Department of Archaeology and Museums, Government of Pakistan.

*In Memory of David Graeber and
Marshall Sahlins*

Contents

Preface and Acknowledgments xi

1. Sacred Kingship in World History: Between Immanence and Transcendence   1
   A. AZFAR MOIN AND ALAN STRATHERN

2. Kings Before Kingship: The Politics of the Enchanted Universe   31
   MARSHALL SAHLINS

3. Immanence in the Andes (1000–1700 CE): Divine Kingship, Stranger-Kingship, and Diarchy   53
   PETER GOSE

4. Gods and Kings in Ancient Mesopotamia   72
   NICOLE BRISCH

5. Pharaonic Kingship and Its Biblical Deconstruction   94
   JAN ASSMANN

6. King, Divinity, and Law in Ancient Greece   111
LYNETTE MITCHELL

7. Humanizing the Divine and Divinizing the Human in Early China: Comparative Reflections on Ritual, Sacrifice, and Sovereignty   137
MICHAEL PUETT

8. Caliphal Sovereignty or the Immanence of Transcendence   162
AZIZ AL-AZMEH

9. Neoplatonic Kingship in the Islamic World: Akbar's Millennial History   192
JOS GOMMANS AND SAID REZA HUSEINI

10. Hobbes the Egyptian: The Return to Pharaoh, or the Ancient Roots of Secular Politics   223
ROBERT A. YELLE

11. Ancient Apostasy, Modern Drama: Henrik Ibsen's *Emperor and Galilean*   249
NICOLE JERR

12. The Last Hindu King: How Nepal Desanctified Its Monarchy   271
DAVID N. GELLNER

13. A Caliphate Beyond Politics: The Sovereignty of ISIS   299
FAISAL DEVJI

14. Sacred Kingship: A Synthesis   323
A. AZFAR MOIN AND ALAN STRATHERN

....

Bibliography   *351*

Index   *381*

Preface and Acknowledgments

"We have no right, in the present state of our knowledge, to assert that the worship of gods preceded that of kings; we do not know." With this quintessentially striking observation in his book *Kingship*, the pioneering anthropologist A. M. Hocart put his finger on the analytical difficulty of prying politics apart from religion. Indeed, to solve the enigma of organized politics is to unravel the riddle of institutionalized religion. *Sacred Kingship in World History: Between Immanence and Transcendence* is a collaborative and interdisciplinary exploration of this multifaceted puzzle. It shines a light on the constitutive bond of religion and politics from behind, that is, from a historical perspective of the very long term, via a comparison on a truly global scale, and by an anthropology of elementary forms. Our point of departure is the concrete institution at the core of large-scale politics until modern times—sacred kingship.

This does not reflect a lack of interest in secular modernity—far from it. Our intention, however, is to provincialize it. The problematic we refer to has drawn a prolific amount of interest, most notably in political philosophy, where heuristic concepts such as "political theology" and "sovereignty" attempt to bridge the secularist politics of the nation-state and the religion-dominated rule of earlier empires. Similarly, genealogical approaches to the problem have led scholars to scour the past in an attempt to unmask the way categories of politics and religion were produced and deployed in modern times. It must be noted, however, that much of this work has proceeded under the sign of modernity. Thus, the conclusions it reaches rarely escape the disenchanted teleology of secularism that it sets out to critique. We seek to resist this teleological pull. In arriving at our answers, we want to explore the deep past as more than just a foil for a criticism of the present and to take serious account of the experience of non-Western and nonmodern humanity.

Our collaboration on this book began in the fall of 2018, when A. Azfar Moin received an invitation to give the Radhakrishnan Memorial Lectures at All Souls College, Oxford. Since the three lectures were to be held in residence at Oxford the following summer, when Alan Strathern's *Unearthly Powers* was scheduled for release, we decided to organize jointly a major conference on sacred kingship at Oxford. However, rather than just issue a general call for papers, we wrote a programmatic paper entitled, "Sacred Kingship in World History: Between Immanence and Transcendence."

We sent this framework paper to a set of scholars from the disciplines of anthropology, history, Egyptology, Assyriology, classics, religious studies, and literature, all of whom had published widely on sacred kingship. Our intention was to generate a more focused and intensive form of intellectual collaboration among scholars than is typical at conferences. Our paper offered a conceptual framework and theoretical vocabulary to enable a coherent conversation across multiple disciplines and regional specializations. It was offered in a deliberately provocative, condensed, and abstract manner, and now stands, with a few alterations, as chapter 1. To gain an overview of the book, we recommend reading the first and last chapters, with the latter containing our reflections on the key arguments of all the chapters.

The most salient aspect of our framework paper, which is here presented as chapter 1, was a heuristic definition of religion that considered its evolving and dynamic relationship with sacred kingship. At its foundation lay Strathern's suggestion in *Unearthly Powers* that the term *religion* is impossible to define without first recognizing that this term encompasses two opposing tendencies, that of immanence and transcendence.

To oversimplify, immanentism implies an enchanted universe populated by what Marshall Sahlins calls metapersons—spirits, ancestors, gods—and where the primary goal of religion is to sustain the flourishing of life. Because the flourishing of life in these cultures depended on the constant ritual effort of building relationships between humans and metapersons, chiefs and kings monopolized this ritual role. In short, in immanentism, rulers were assigned priestly roles and, indeed, ruled as "cosmic" kings. Religion conscious of itself as serving a distinctively salvific end took shape with the rise of transcendentalism in the first millennium BCE, an era sometimes referred to as the Axial Age. This eventually gave rise to religions organized around canonized sacred texts, which could now be abstracted from politics and indeed provide a platform for criticizing or even rejecting that politics. Transcendentalist religions tried to reform and constrain sacred kingship by ethicizing it. A king could be tolerated only insofar as he upheld and propagated transcendentalist ideals enumerated, collated, and canonized in scripture. Transcendentalism produced the ideal of "righteous" kingship.

Our project was also emboldened and influenced by the most important recent study of the immanentist imagination of politics, *On Kings*, coauthored by the late Marshall Sahlins and the late David Graeber. We were very fortunate to benefit from Graeber's presentation and comments during the conference, but he sadly passed away before he could complete his essay for inclusion in this collection. Sahlins provided a paper that was discussed at the conference, a version of which sets a foundational tone for the volume as chapter 2, fleshing out the politics of the immanentist imaginaire by drawing on a huge range of material from Africa, the Pacific, and the Americas, among other regions. We feel honored to dedicate this book to Sahlins and Graeber, as two of the most iconoclastic and inventive thinkers in anthropology and politics.

Peter Gose's analysis of divinity and foreignness of rulers in the precontact Andes is a clear-sighted examination of the internal dynamics of an immanentist system. Michael Puett performs a vital role by situating the case of China within the Axial Age paradigm—something the framework paper had not attempted—thereby generating a series of insights on the changing role of ritual and salvation. David Gellner's chapter explicitly extends the analysis to the Hindu world, as part of his illuminating exploration of the fate of the last Hindu kings of Nepal.

We were privileged also to include a chapter by Jan Assmann on the birth of kingship in Egypt and its deconstruction in the Hebrew Bible. Assmann is not only one of the most distinguished Egyptologists but also a major thinker on the origins and meaning of monotheism and a theorist of religion. Covering many of the same foundational themes for ancient Greece, Lynette Mitchell offers a highly original argument on the evolving relationship between law and kingship. Nicole Brisch, on the other hand, offers a perceptive treatment of the variety of relations between gods and kings in Mesopotamia.

Islam receives the best chronological coverage of all transcendentalist religions. Aziz al-Azmeh, who has written the definitive work on early Muslim kingship, provides a fresh analysis of the paradoxically immanentist nature of the classical caliphate in Islam. Jos Gommans and Said Reza Huseini present what happened to Islamic kingship after the rise of the Mongols and their destruction of the classical caliphate in a new light through an illumination of its Neoplatonic character. Faisal Devji, a historian of modern Islamist politics, resolves the conundrum of the short-lived ISIS caliphate in twenty-first-century Iraq and Syria.

Last but not least, Europe features in the volume in two markedly creative essays that attempt to get beneath the disenchantment of secular modernity. Robert A. Yelle, a historian and theorist of religion, unmasks the "Egyptian" or pagan proclivities of the founder of modern political philosophy, Thomas Hobbes. In a related fashion, Nicole Jerr, a scholar of literature, explores why the Norwegian playwright and pioneer of modernist theater Henrik Ibsen was fascinated with Julian the apostate, the fourth-century Roman emperor who had tried to revive paganism.

Our last chapter integrates reflections on all the chapters to show how they have deployed, developed, critiqued and enriched the model proposed in the first chapter, what we call our framework paper. The last chapter provides a panoptic synthesis of their cumulative implications for world history.

ACKNOWLEDGMENTS

We wanted a broad scholarly audience for this book, taking in all disciplines mentioned here. Our goal was to combine breadth of coverage with tightness of argument, given the sheer range of cases, and therefore we encouraged the contributors to eschew the usual concerns of specialist literature in favor of serving the larger arguments. We are also grateful for the contributions of many learned colleagues during the conference for their interventions that have shaped this volume.

All of this was made possible by financial and institutional support provided by Brasenose College, Oxford; the John Fell Fund and the Oxford Centre for Global History; and the College of Liberal Arts at the University of Texas at Austin. We offer sincere thanks to their administrative leadership and staff members, and to our doctoral students: Natalie Cobo in Oxford for her help in organizing the conference, and to Blake Pye in Austin for organizational assistance and also finalizing the book manuscript.

Sacred Kingship in World History

I

Sacred Kingship in World History

Between Immanence and Transcendence

A. AZFAR MOIN AND ALAN STRATHERN

WHY SACRED KINGSHIP?

Kingship, a form of politics in which a venerated leader is set apart from and above the group and imbued with extraordinary power (a power over life and death), has been, for much of history, the default form of organization in societies large enough to sustain a state.[1] Marshall Sahlins has pointed out that even small-scale societies without the rudiments of a state or even a chief in sight were often encompassed within a "cosmic polity" in which a divine hierarchy of "metapersons" (ancestors, spirits, gods) fed and nurtured or killed and threatened at will, thus keeping order and commanding respect.[2] The transcultural pervasiveness of sacred kingship in human and metahuman forms makes it a fundamental concern not just of history but also of anthropology and religious studies.

What, then, about modern times, in which sacred kingship seems so conclusively marginalized? Out of sight, however, does not mean out of mind: kingship was not simply abandoned; it was repressed. As such, it continually springs back—in Freudian speak, returns—making its presence felt in distorted forms, a mélange of the familiar and spectral, liberal and totalitarian, enshrined in constitutions and magnified in charismatic breaks from the law.[3] One could even argue that the most gnomic of pronouncements made by modern political philosophers—on sovereignty and law ("Sovereign is he who decides on the exception"),[4] on sovereignty and theology ("All significant concepts of the modern theory of the state are secularized theological concepts . . ."),[5] on sovereignty and power ("It can even be said that the production of a biopolitical body is the original activity of sovereign power"),[6] on sovereignty and violence

("Divine violence, which is the sign and seal but never the means of sacred execution, may be called sovereign violence"[7])—make sense only against the embodied performativity of sacred kingship. In arriving at these conclusions, contemporary thinkers draw upon a Western and Christian experience of sacred kingship that was, in comparative terms, tame and restrained. It is probably time to sharpen these theorems and corollaries against the whetstone of a broader empirical reality.

WHY WORLD HISTORY?

A conversation on sacred kingship that is as broad and encompassing as the phenomenon itself must be held under the aegis of world history—or global history, to use the term more commonly employed in recent years. The potential liberation from the typical scale of analysis offered by the global turn presents an opportunity for rapprochement with other disciplines: sociology, philosophical history, anthropology, religious studies, comparative literature, political philosophy, and even psychology, evolutionary biology, and cognitive science. A number of these disciplines have never really abandoned a taste for the robust generalization to which we are advocating a return.

Recently, however, the great majority of global history scholarship has taken the form of "connected history," in which the viewpoint follows flows and entanglements across far larger expanses of space than the nation or region. There is much more profitable work to be done in this way, but that is not the primary aim of this project. Some of the most important debates in global history have depended on a quite different method, that of comparing distinct cases in order to gain deeper insight into large-scale questions of causation. The most famous question addressed by these means thus far has been that of the "Great Divergence": why it was the West that rose to industry-fueled global dominance in a century or two.[8] Religion has been conspicuously absent, however, in comparative global history.

One reason religion has been avoided as a category of analysis is that postcolonial and anti-Eurocentric impulses have tended to body forth in a deconstructive and genealogical vein. This resulted in a major criticism of master concepts used by past scholars—"religion," "world religions," "salvation"—and of their association with colonial and imperial hegemony. These much-needed critiques certainly added sophistication and subtlety to monographic research, but, at the level of analytical macro history, they have also led to a form of conceptual stasis.

Thus, Robert Yelle's wide-ranging and comparative work, *Sovereignty and the Sacred*, is a timely intervention that offers a bold synthesis by setting European intellectual history in dialogue with developments in other world regions and ancient religions.[9]

Anthropology meanwhile has been more acutely affected by poststructuralist and postcolonial anxieties than history. Nearly all social and cultural anthropological writing is at least implicitly comparative, if only because of its foundational regard for relativism.[10] But more far-reaching or global forms of comparison in anthropology have suffered by association with the prefieldwork era epitomized by James Frazer and A. M. Hocart. It is encouraging, however, that the latter two have been undergoing something of a mild and late renaissance—and they also, of course, happened to have both spent their careers obsessed by the puzzles of sacred kingship. In particular, Marshall Sahlins and David Graeber invoke both figures in their recent book *On Kings*. The publication of this book is a landmark event in the field because it helps establish the respectability of a modern form of comparative anthropology in which it is taken for granted that the sophistications of recent specialist literature may be duly respected.[11]

Closer inspection of recent historical writing indicates that it too has continued to yield collaborative attempts to understand sacred kingship from time to time, such as in the conferences and resulting publications edited by Nicole Brisch and by Lynette G. Mitchell and Charles Melville.[12] One reason why sacred kingship might continue to be a favored topic of comparison is because it is striking in terms of its ubiquity without being banal in its familiarity: there is a strangeness to it that the modern (disenchanted, naturalist) mind is still liable to regard as a knot that needs unpicking.

It is true that any comparative endeavor is liable to flirt with banality. But even ubiquitous patterns may be disarmingly nonobvious, as Sahlins has shown with his work on the repetitive materialization of the stranger-king or David Graeber on the logic of the association between clowns and kings.[13] Genuine universals surely invite us to pursue them even into the realms of psychology and cognitive science. Sahlins rests his analysis on a truth of human nature, after all: that people intuit that they are not authors of their own fortunes, that every good or bad thing that happens to them is the result of forces beyond their own capacity.[14] However, this invites the simple question: why have all societies conceived these forces and conditions in terms of personlike entities?

On the other hand, neither does the comparative impulse amount to a fascination with lowest common denominators. As Marc Bloch realized, rather than dragging us toward the denial of cultural and temporal specificity, it should be seen as a means of establishing particularity on a much more solid footing.[15] It is all too easy for the specialist to become bewitched by the apparently unique in whatever she studies; only by having some grasp of the full run of cultural variety will it become possible to appreciate what uniqueness properly is. Indeed, in more general terms, the comparative method should help to wash away some of the sedimented habits of thought that collect in pools of specialism unperturbed by other streams of scholarship. For example, the work on European Christian sacred kingship has some admirable qualities: the sheer quantity of source material and its accumulated depth of scholarship means we can reconstruct narratives of its vicissitudes and internal tensions and dwell on the role of individuals or conscious debates.[16] But very rarely have these yielded to attempts to conceptualize the overall contours of European sacred kingship, and that is surely because of its curious isolation from the rest of scholarship. One result is that it is difficult to assess how peculiar the European monarchies were. Should we in fact see them as unusually unsacralized when set against a global backdrop? Or is that merely a reflection of divergent scholarly approaches?[17]

Comparison does not require us to squash our reasoning into predetermined categories. Doing it properly should challenge the concepts that we start with, allowing us to dispense with those that make sense only within the confines of Western political thought, for example.[18] Nor does comparison involve the artificial isolation of static systems to serve as cases. Instead, it may take as its subject movements and processes rather than systems, as Michael Puett and J. D. Y. Peel have explicitly argued.[19] Indeed, any one monarchical tradition will play host to plural discourses, impulses, and imageries as it moves through time, weaving together or pulling part.[20] Nevertheless, when placed in a global context, such internal plurality and dynamism within any one tradition may still be seen to be contained within some distinctive pattern of the longue durée. It is equally true that patterns may emerge that seem to pay little heed to cultural variation. One suggestion emerging from the collection edited by Nicole Brisch is that explicit claims of self-deification tended to be rather ephemeral or "punctuated" in nature and clearly linked to moments of crisis or unusually rapid expansion of imperial forms[21]—in other words, in contexts unusually suited to the generation of charisma on the part of ambitious rulers. In addition, Strathern has suggested that such claims may also reflect determined moves on the part of rulers to centralize authority by establishing their dominance over the priestly sphere.

Indeed, the bird's-eye perspective of the global historian also draws us toward a much bolder approach to diachrony and to consider how to make sense of changes across thousands of years rather than the decades of the typical field of specialism. Naturally, this flies in the face of the skepticism toward grand narrative that historians now consider to be their scholarly responsibility. It can only be done by handling the disciplinary conceits of continuity and change in a very particular way and as ever entwined. One simple means of picturing this is simply through the accretion of layers. As in the works of Robert Bellah, Jan Assmann, and others, the old forms are never lost—rather, they are bundled into new forms, both retained and reconfigured.[22]

The two great transformations signaled here are both taken from historical sociology. The first is the Axial Age—and in particular the eruption of transcendentalism—and the second is secularization. The latter is far more often criticized than endorsed today, for obvious reasons, while the former remains a distinctly minority taste among historians. That is only natural: it is only when we adopt a truly longue durée and global vision that they become indispensable. In both cases, the claim that nothing ever happened here is as implausible as the claim that, after these watersheds, everything was different.

Since we have selected world history as our way in, it is the Axial Age that we must turn to first. Although mostly referred to these days by Weberian-minded historical sociologists, the Axial Age—whether as a historical event or as a type of sociological phenomenon—is helpful in providing a common vocabulary for a global history approach to religion. It is notable that Joel Robbins, in particular, has championed its comparative potential among anthropologists.[23] At its simplest, it offers a dichotomy—immanence and transcendence—that we will use below to reconstruct a working definition of religion.

WHY BETWEEN IMMANENCE AND TRANSCENDENCE?

One reason why establishing a coherent definition of religion—and its relationship with the enchanted sphere of politics that we are calling sacred kingship—has proved so elusive is that the phenomena typically associated with this category arise from two distinct and contrasting tendencies, that of immanence and transcendence. Our first task then is to state what we mean by these terms and explain why, despite their distinctiveness, they must be discussed together. The following account of immanentism does not recount Strathern's depiction of its ten characteristics but rather takes a different tack by exploring its foundations in the psychology of religion.[24]

Immanence

Before there is religion, there is immanence. Not all societies have a sphere of culture that they might separate into something equivalent to "religion," but none exist without a tendency to imagine unseen forces and beings at play in the world with whom humans must interact in order to flourish. This predisposition can be found everywhere because it arises from higher mammalian emotional capacities and human cognitive and symbol-generating capabilities.[25] No amount of disenchantment—modern or otherwise—can permanently rid humans of the propensity to make anthropomorphic and anthropocentric assumptions about the cosmos.[26] Indeed, if there could be such a thing as an entropic state of culture, it would be that of immanence. That is, humans would populate the cosmos with metapersons; they would interact with these metapersons via nonordinary realms of "play"; and they would organize these realms primarily on the basis of rhythm and affect (ritual) and secondarily on the basis of cognition and language (myth).

We use the term *play* here in a highly specific sense.[27] Even though this play typically occurs in a "relaxed" state—once there is food enough to eat and security enough to dream—it does not mean that it is not serious and productive work. Consider, however, its affective yield. Psychological approaches to religion have typically focused on one of two poles of human emotions. At one end is a cluster of positivity—most notably joy—that dissolves or heals the self and generates communal bonds (collective effervescence and *communitas*). At the other end is a mosh pit of negativity—most notably fear—that culminates in disgust and aggression (taboo and sacrifice). These diverging emphases split those theorists who privilege the positive potential of "empathy" and those who emphasize the neurotic defense of "projection."[28] The latter stems from the human inability to come to terms with anxiety and trauma and, when given free rein, yields to the psychotic desire to derive pleasure from pain and death.[29]

The immanentist tendency to harness empathy and joy, via ritual and concrete means, for healing, nourishment, and community becomes the basis for an implicit quest for the "good." It affirms egalitarianism and espouses equality, a felt shared morality—what is sometimes theorized as "invisible religion" because it is common to all.[30] But a broadly experienced positivity is difficult to monopolize. It is useless for imposing hierarchy and marking boundaries—the elementary acts of political life. To engender status and sustain identity—to establish the basic markers of difference such as gender, caste, race, clan, and so on—requires not only a common bond and sense of belonging but also the collective projection of fear and disgust, the association of paranoia and pain with persons, places, and times. When these contradictory immanentist impulses—compassionate and cruel, egalitarian and hierarchical, uniting and differentiating—begin to be institutionalized in society, it produces the "enchanted" building blocks of both religion and politics.

Yet immanentism operates primarily in terms of "play," that is, rhythmic gestures of body and concrete structures of narrative. Put another way, immanent forms are not founded on contemplative or disembodied thought and do not depend on the latter for their efficacy.[31] It is true that immanentism could take a more rationalized and institutionalized form, as we see in the temple religion that pervaded many ancient societies. The temple was organized as an ontological continuum of gesture and space, primarily given structure by "purity" taboos. Cosmology, or a knowledge of metapersons, might come later. What comes first, in cognitive terms, is a gesture or, more precisely, an "empty" ritual that generates sheer difference in an attempt to "parcel out" perceived reality into discrete segments.[32] With such a basis in the "science of the concrete," temples have little need of philosophy.

If religions of the book hinged on doctrinal truth, religions of the temple turned on ritual purity. Purity, or more specifically the pure/impure distinction as opposed to the true/false distinction of scriptural religions, is fundamental to the power structure of societies where rationalized forms of immanentism predominates: the sacred is pure, and the profane, polluting.[33] We may define *purity* more elaborately as a tactile quality inhering in a body, object, or space that is set apart from profane and everyday reality by taboos; it is a quality that imparts sacredness (Durkheim) or charisma (Weber) to its possessor. Most significantly, it is a quality that must be created, manipulated, and destroyed by ritual means. Sacrifice—a rite that must be performed in a purified space; with means of a purified implement; and by a ritual specialist in a state of purity, that is, the priest—is the dominant patterned act of temple religion. As a corollary, legitimate violence, or its parallel immanentist form, ritual violence, is simply that which is deployed to purify a person, place, or thing.

The predominance of purity and sacrificial rituals in immanentist religions has little to do with morality.[34] To be sure, ritual may generate a kind of morality in the Durkheimian sense of a shared feeling of purpose and obligation toward the group. These rituals, unlike rites of purity, are not empty and neurotic, as Freud called all rites, but instead depend on empathy and joy. More complex moral problems, such as those of suffering or the "immemorial misdirection" of life, require a narrative mechanism to resolve them or to work through their intractability.[35] Whether the mode is performative or narrative, immanentist cultures seldom strive to provide or preserve universal answers to such existential problems. The concrete and embodied morality of immanentism is difficult to translate into abstract categories or enumerate in lists of ten.

Nevertheless, a degree of abstraction could be achieved as it was in the highly literate culture of ancient Egypt. There, as Assmann shows, hymns and wisdom tales advocated a common morality and salvation justice "from below" to sustain the social order, while the cosmic order was overseen by an elaborate pantheon arrayed in a status hierarchy.[36] Yet these efforts very rarely moved beyond mythospeculation;[37] that is, they did not break permanently the bonds of culturally embedded ritual and myth and produce the one cure-all doctrine of "truth," which would dominate with the rise of transcendentalist traditions.

It would help the discussion to outline a schematic model of what immanentist "religion" might look like if it were to be heuristically isolated within culture. The left-hand column of figure 1.1 depicts a loosely structured hierarchy with three fields in descending order of cultural priority: rites, morality, and cognition. The field of rites is one in which humans interact with metapersons. As mentioned earlier, it is set apart from everyday life by purity taboos and can be accessed primarily via the purity specialist—the priest—and in a pure space, such as the temple. In this field, people's relations with metapersons are defined not by morals but by power, by the giving and taking of life.[38] Simply put, the field of rites is deethicized. It does not function as a foundation of morality.

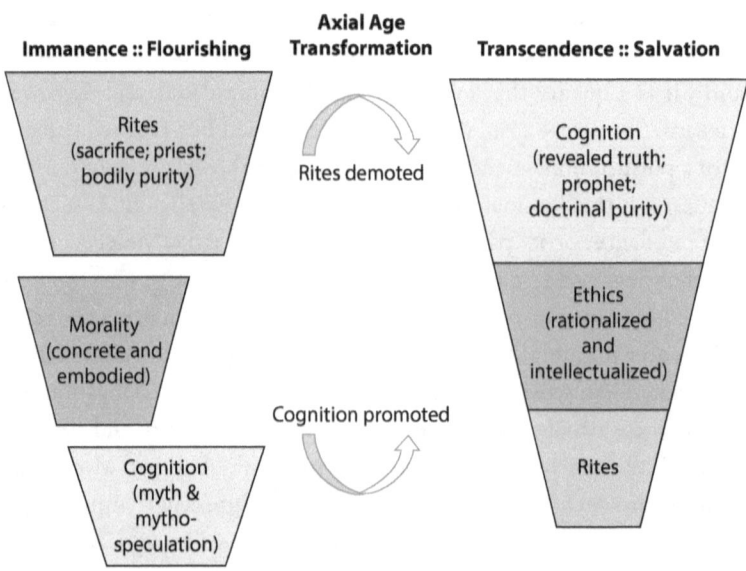

FIGURE 1.1 Axial Age transformation: from immanence to transcendence

Morality is the next field, below the field of rites in cultural priority. Here, matters of justice, sharing, nurturing, and concern for the greater good are worked out. It is at best integrated loosely with conceptions of purity. The priest does not preach morality, but he does maintain the general notion that disorder in cosmos and nature—that is, impurity—is linked to disorders in communal life and thus is ready to prescribe ritual, and sometimes violent, countermeasures.[39]

Below morality in significance is the field of cognition, where knowledge of metapersons is processed. In immanentist traditions, religious knowledge is supple, contained in malleable narrative and plastic myth. It is expected to change, to produce multiple variants. There is seldom a concern with determining the one "true" myth or the one "correct" belief held to with all of one's heart. Truth—what becomes faith in biblical monotheism—is not at issue. Immanentism easily sustains a variant set of myths about the same metaperson in a culture area and wastes no effort in preventing these stories from changing to keep pace with historical events and social needs. There is no equivalent in emic terms to the notion of religion, or a religion, because there is no sense in extracting relations with or knowledge of metapersons from the normal run of life and making it the basis for a distinct form of ascription. Instead, equivalent status or, given the right circumstances, even the translatability of different metapersons could be assumed across culture areas. Nor was there, in emic terms, a supernature as something divorced from nature (these terms are only used here in a highly etic way).[40] Wherever there appears a loosely structured hierarchy of rites, morality, and cognition, however, it begins to look like what might indeed be called—or mistaken for—religion. This, at least, was the state of affairs in the world before transcendence made its dramatic entrance.

Transcendence

One way of understanding the emergence of what we refer to as transcendentalism is to view it as a reaction to certain alarming apprehensions of relativism in which the very given-ness of the status quo was somehow undermined.[41] This was indeed part of a larger historical phenomenon that many scholars have come to refer to as the Axial Age, a concept that attempts to capture what various philosophers, teachers, ascetics, and prophets in first millennium BCE Greece, Israel, northern India, and China may have had in common. In all these cases, to varying degrees, features of immanentism were queried, rejected, or at least considered insufficient. In the Indic and West Asian cases, however, transcendentalism proper began to emerge in the form of the Indic traditions of Upanishadic Hinduism, Buddhism, and Jainism, and successive iterations of monotheism. These were distinguished by the way they set to one side the entire raison d'être of immanentism of attaining worldly well-being and ordering the world via a scheme of ritual interaction with metapersons.

Indeed, just at the moment in which immanentism attained its most elaborate and hegemonic form in the temple-and-king complexes of late Bronze and Iron ages, transcendentalism entered history in an attempt to flatten this worldview. If immanentist power had weaponized material "purity" in its pursuit of a flourishing earthly hierarchy, transcendentalist insurgents countered with the purity of "truth" and claimed monopoly over all the paths that led to morality and the "good." As Hocart put it, most bluntly, about India: it is now "better to be good than to be healthy and wealthy."[42] In a similar vein, Assmann observes, "The most important compliment that monotheism has ever paid itself is that it is the religion of justice."[43]

It is still a puzzle why the core intellectual foundations for these developments were all laid down in the middle centuries of the first millennium BCE in the settled cores of Eurasia, and then subjected to important forms of institutionalization and coalescence in the early centuries CE. A fundamental element must have been the invention and spread of democratic forms of writing that bred a bookish culture of argument and debate, producing an age of criticism as well as an age of canonization.[44] Nonetheless, what all the transcendentalist traditions shared was the capacity to criticize priestly rites and sacrifice as mere ceremony or misguided magic and to promote instead a codified form of knowledge as indispensable doctrine. Thus, priestly knowledge of how to communicate with the divine was subordinated to divinely revealed truth or philosophical insight. In other words, "purity of the body" became less of a concern than "purity of the conscience." The result was an inversion of the immanentist hierarchy. Transcendentalism promoted the centrality of cognition, that is, of an exclusive, canonized, and sacralized truth. Doctrinal truth not only gained high cultural significance with the rise of transcendentalism, it also brought morality and ritual under its firm dominion (see figure 1.1). Accordingly, the central figure became that of the prophet, philosopher, and teacher who preached or taught how to live a humble and ethical life. From this arose the transcendentalists' claim that the source of ethics and justice was not the king but a much higher divine reality or cosmic law. What had been a diffused and concrete morality now became an intellectualized ethics governed by revealed truth.

In transcendentalism, the point became to escape the human condition rather than to ameliorate it. As a result, salvation became Salvation, something total, almost inconceivable—truly transcending not only the mundane realm but also the capacity of the mundane mind to conceive of it. This new vision rested on a kind of ontological breach by which existence was separated into two domains, and crossing from here to there became the overriding objective.[45] The promise of transcendentalism was located in the afterlife, and it was therefore granted a kind of immunity from empirical evaluation in the here and now.

Transcendentalist religiosity was not, like its immanentist counterpart, a matter of bodily participation, immersive affect, and performative imagination. It did not depend on making features of the landscape or effigies or people or temples vehicles for metapersonhood and power. Rather, such forms were profoundly encompassed and reframed as they were subordinated to soteriological and ethical imperatives that were enshrined as Truth. This was the case for the existing field of metapersons, which was either wiped out and replaced by a drastically simpler set (as in monotheism) or subordinated and redescribed (Indic versions). This was also what happened to the ubiquitous forms of interacting with metapersons, through ceremony and sacrifice. Indeed, now any such techniques employed to access immanent power might be devalued as magic, superstition, idolatry, or, at the very least, profoundly missing the point. This amounted, in an extremely specific sense, to a form of disenchantment.[46] Previously vital rites that had upheld the flourishing of a community might become mere ritual, an impediment to authentic salvation seeking, as in Paul's reprehension of Jewish circumcision in favor of the circumcision of the mind, or in the Pali scriptures' injunction against clinging to rules and rituals. Put another way, as rites lost their efficacy and were declared inert, cognition gained efficacy and was affirmed as active.

Under transcendentalism, the realm of play was relocated away from the arena of public action—the sacrifice in the temple courtyard—to the shadowy interior realm of mental and emotional struggle—the contemplative prayer, or "sacrifice of the lips," in the enclosed hall of the mosque, synagogue, or church. The self—not the social group—now took on the burden of responsibility for its liberation. Indeed, these traditions exhibited a distinct anticommunal quality, as expressed in the shocking repudiation of kinship claims in certain Buddhist and early Christian texts. As a form of individualism emerged, so too did a form of universalism. Therefore, morality too moved from a matter of communal flourishing to one of codified and explicit ethics founded on the Golden Rule and aiming for universal applicability. The good, a common morality that had previously been ritually experienced and communally felt, was now hitched to truth or, what was the same thing, the purity of conscience. Faith became the font of ethics.

The overall ethical vision of transcendentalism was indeed idealized to the point of utopianism: self-sacrifice, rather than ritual sacrifice, became the order of the day. A minority of people were even induced to attempt to live out this utopian morality in a very real way: monastics and mendicants who operated as soteriological virtuosos on behalf of the masses. "In the immanentist mode one may become sacred by approximating the qualities of metapersons: amassing power, success, brilliance. In the transcendentalist mode one does it by denying the quest for power, success, brilliance."[47]

Transcendentalist traditions are distinctive too for the way that they are rooted in the teachings of specific historical figures whose lessons, admonitions, actions, or life story become the source of universal truth. This entailed a certain containment of revelation because the validity of future prophetic and philosophical insight could always be measured alongside the overriding authority of the original insights. That act of containment was only possible because of the way that literacy—or forms of oral transmission that mimicked the text in their stability—preserved the integrity of past revelation.[48] Now it was ideas and the writings that contained them that became truly sacred, much more portable than the specificities of person and place.[49]

When transcendence, in its most intense form, became distilled truth (faith, prophet, scripture), just as immanence had become the essence of purity (sacrifice, priest, temple), doctrinalism emerged.[50] This threw tremendous social power into the hands of a "clerisy": the exegetes and guardians of the texts in which truth was now enshrined. The Church, the Sangha, or the Ulema therefore became a source of ineradicable moral authority and a primary counterorganization to the state. These professional literati ensured, too, that their tradition would come to exhibit profound forms of intellectualization, the systematic ordering and testing and elaboration of doctrinal propositions and narratives.[51] Even the notion of bodily purity was transposed onto the mind. Transcendentalism made purity a matter of conscience, of disciplining the self through realizing the truth, by the manipulation of thoughts and feelings, reading or listening to texts, restraining one's instincts, and cultivating the proper emotions. This was harnessed to the mission of spreading the one true doctrine. The world could now be divided between the soteriologically pure and the impure. As such, all transcendentalisms may be understood as "offensive" systems, to borrow a term from Ernest Gellner, insofar as they set out to assault all other claims to comprehend reality.[52] We recognize this most readily in the monotheistic traditions, following what Assmann calls "the Mosaic distinction," by which all other cults and pantheons were rendered inherently false or evil and all internal difference of opinion banned as heresy and apostasy, even, at times, on pain of death. But Buddhism mounted a no-less assertive claim to be the vehicle for profound truths that otherwise lie veiled. Equally implicit in this revolution is, of course, the potential for identity construction, for something like religion to be extracted out of—indeed in opposition to—the mass of normal life, and to become the reference point by which new affinities and sentiments of belonging are constructed.

However, it is vital to note that the above description *represents no religious tradition as it has ever existed in history.* That is because all the diverse developments that we sum up under abstractions such as Islam or Buddhism are in fact profound amalgamations of immanentism and transcendentalism. This is so for a host of reasons, the most important being that the underlying cognitive, emotional, and psychological underpinnings of immanentism never disappear. After all, the Hajj pilgrimage to the ka'ba, by doctrine the purest space in Islamdom, remains the key annual ritual for Muslims, even though it is required only once in the faithful's lifetime and only if she can afford it. Yet the Hajj features last on the list of Islam's five pillars, the first and most foundational of which is to hold in one's conscience and bear witness in public to the testament of faith that "there is no god but Allah." Even in the most avowed moments of transcendentalism, the drive for bodily purity remains ever present, repressed and encrypted as ritual, waiting to resurface in distorted forms, just as a concrete and felt morality continually tries to wriggle out of the straitjacket of enumerated ethics and doctrinal rules. Indeed, transcendentalism can only ever develop and embed in culture in a meaningful way through a tension-filled accommodation with immanentism, which finds ways of suspending its truth claims and monopoly over morality. In addition, it makes recourse to immanentist techniques of purity to propagate and preserve itself, the most ironic case being the use of taboos to sanctify and canonize the books containing doctrinal truths, treating them like a type of "speech-temple."[53]

As any transcendentalism works it ways from the margins of a society to its center, it must take on the Durkheimian functions that all religious systems serve—far from questioning hierarchies, kinship, or mundane prosperity, it must become their fundamental guarantor. To clarify: immanentist aspects are discernible from the start of any one transcendentalist tradition and are then liable to proliferate and deepen in certain ways over time. In particular, the process of expansion produces strong incentives to develop vehicles for the deliverance of supernatural power—most obviously in the cult of the saints in Christianity and Islam. And yet all such developments may in turn become vulnerable to the castigations and reformations of movements reasserting transcendentalist principles. This tension is a major structuring principle of the history of societies that have enshrined transcendentalist traditions (figure 1.2).

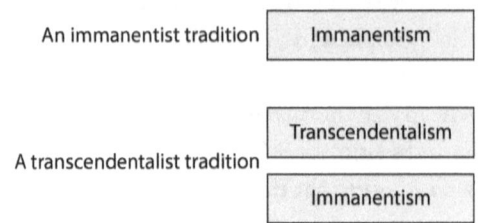

FIGURE 1.2 Makeup of immanentist and trancendentalist traditions

SACRED KINGSHIP IN WORLD HISTORY: BETWEEN IMMANENCE AND TRANSCENDENCE

What does all this mean for sacred kingship? In the immanentist mode, the ruler is sacralized through *divinization*; that is, they are treated as if they were a metaperson, that they are close to the ancestors, spirits, and gods, or descended from them, or share in their power or incarnate them at times. This does not quite adhere to the most straightforward understanding of divine kingship, in which the king is simply understood "to be" a god.[54] Rather, surveying a very broad range of cases, one finds scholars repeatedly grappling with a generic sense of ambiguity.[55] Indeed, this is often a cultivated ambiguity because kings are "in-between" things: already and evidently human, they are pushed part way into the sphere of the divine in order to intercede on our behalf. This elevation occurs through rituals of the empty or neurotic kind in the sense that they that impart "sheer difference" to the king's body.[56] The more emphatically the king is divinized, the more he must be stage-managed into a denial of his humanity and mortality—hence a whole series of prohibitions on seeing the king eating or sleeping, for example. His person is imbued with same taboos and status markers and is approached with the same modes of play and purity that are employed for metapersons. No wonder, then, that Hocart remarked, "[W]e have no right, in the present state of our knowledge, to assert that the worship of gods preceded that of kings; we do not know."[57] Their status as liminal beings is what allows the paradoxical tendency in certain immanentist societies for kings to even become scapegoat figures.[58]

To provide further analytical purchase on the diverse ways in which the business of divinization may proceed, Strathern has suggested that sometimes it will help to break it down into two subtypes, heroic and cosmic.[59] In the heroic guise, the king acquires an unusual, unnatural status because of his accomplishments, on the battlefield above all; his access to the supernatural wellsprings of all good fortune is therefore advertised in an immediate and concrete manner and invites veneration. Such eruptions of charisma, as Weber realized, may be entirely transgressive and may breach typical conceptions of the boundaries between the mortals and the gods, seen especially in the breaking of everyday moral strictures against arbitrary godlike violence.[60] The heroic mode does not preclude the king from mixing with his subjects in a relatively free and open manner.

Cosmic divinization, on the other hand, is sustained by ritual performance rather than achieved by "transgressive" godlike deeds. This is because cosmic kingship is an attempt to overcome and resist historical change by the repetition of rites (to use Lévi-Strauss, by constructing a structure out of events), while heroic kingship, which introduces and encourages historical change (by producing an event by means of a structure) is an effort to gain status by refusing to play by the rules of ritual restraint.[61] Given that, in the immanentist *imaginare*, the biological, social, political, and cosmological realms are relatively undifferentiated and subject to the operations of supernatural power, the figure of the king may be established as the central pivot of all of them. He therefore becomes the focus of communal hopes for the coming of the rains, the banishment of disease, or simply the continuing order of the universe. In this way, his body becomes loosely linked to a general notion of nurturing, sharing, and justice, that is, morality. But this also tends to entail a determined effort to dehumanize him, to turn him into a cult object, to constrain and stylize his movements, to obscure him from view, and to isolate him from the rest of society. Consider table 1.1.[62]

These subtypes cannot be pushed too far—indeed it must be stressed that they are sometimes distinctly unhelpful. Nevertheless, one reason for experimenting with them is as a way of capturing what seems to be a recurring dynamic in the monarchies of immanentist societies. Indeed, it bears a strong resemblance to

TABLE 1.1 Divinized Kingship (the immanentist mode)

	Heroic	Cosmic
Achieved through	Deeds	Rites
Relation to society	Exposed	Isolated
Status	Creates (event)	Sustains (structure)
Stability	Brief	Enduring
Archetypal location	Battlefield	Temple
Normativity	Transgressive	Ordered

a table of ideal types of kingship independently arrived at by Jeroen Duindam, as a means of conceptualizing the cycles of charisma (associated with itinerant kingship) and *Veralltäglichung* (associated with its fixed form); Duindam notes that the former typifies the rule of empire founders while their successors acquire more attributes from the second column (see table 1.1).[63] As Weber also realized, the heroic form is inherently unstable. As reigns wear on, as misfortunes accumulate, as less successful successors succeed to the throne, as bureaucracies develop around the court, as *celeritas* gives way to *gravitas*, the more natural it becomes to comprehend and assert the elevated status of the king in the cosmic mode. This may be a strategy of the dynasty, but it may also be a strategy of lesser elites who wish to detach the ruler from the levers of power. As expressed in many diarchic forms of kingship worldwide, ritualization and political efficacy are not simply mutually constitutive: the pursuit of one may damage the other. At one extreme then, rulers may fall—or be pushed—into the ritualization trap, or what Graeber and Sahlins refer to as "adverse sacralization."[64] The goal of this sacralization is to remove all "heroic" agency and to render the king static. This indeed happens in its most perfect form when rulers have died, when they are finally and truly voided of problematic humanity. For the Incas, their bodies then became cult objects in a most literal sense, albeit treated as if they were still ruling in one sense. Note, however, how direct the connection is between their past heroic achievement and their postmortem cosmic potential. As Peter Gose observes: "dead sovereigns were worshipped only to the extent that they had conquered in life" and were therefore able to remain a source of oracular wisdom, fertility, and prosperity.[65]

Graeber and Sahlins also dwell on the transgressive aspects of what they call "divine kingship," meaning a kind of untrammeled assertion of the king's inherent and superhuman superiority.[66] Indeed, it makes sense that the immanentist imagination would allow the king to be sacralized through an appreciation of his negative powers, his capacity for arbitrary violence, and the deliberate breaking of convention. It allows for this because, of course, the whole field of relations with metapersons is not ethicized in a transcendentalist manner. Considered from the viewpoint of the heroic mode, such transgression may merely signal an exceptional degree of power; while from the viewpoint of the cosmic mode, kings, like gods, were participants in cycles of mutual fructification and destruction. But it is important to note that *allows* does not mean *necessitates*. The bulk of the material on the noneuphemized qualities of kingship comes from African examples—as does, for example, the scapegoat form—and it is perhaps less a general feature of immanentist royal divinization as it is an intriguing regional variation of it.

Note that the entire discussion thus far has taken place in terms of the immanentist mode of royal sacralization—and indeed, Graeber and Sahlins's *On*

Kings may be understood as fundamentally concerned with the exploration of immanentist logic.⁶⁷ The transcendentalist mode of righteous kingship, however, requires a different approach to that of the immanentist mode of divinization.

Under the transcendentalist paradigm, it is neither the essential and pure being of the king nor his ritual intercession that matters but rather his subordinated role within an overarching soteriological order. His status now depends on his responsibility to establish the conditions within which his subjects might attain salvation. To be righteous, he must uphold the truth—scriptural truth, to be precise. There is no room whatsoever for a dark and transgressive register of royal sacralization for kings as sacred monsters, as scapegoats, as the embodiment of arbitrary violence, as at war with their people, or as the conductors of the rites of human sacrifice. This is perhaps the most important reason why the Eurasian traditions of kingship (especially Christian, Muslim, Buddhist) might seem to belong to a different world than those explored by anthropologists of many other regions. "When kings are divinized, it is their human mortality and weakness that must somehow be obscured; when kings are made righteous, it is their human immorality and violence that must be effaced."⁶⁸

In making kings heroes of the salvific quest, transcendentalist discourses also thereby idealize them in terms of their impossible ethics. By this means, a principle of self-government was lodged in the psychology of the righteous ruler: now, at least in theory, the king was not tamed by ritualization (as in adverse sacralization) but by his ethicization, reducing him to the level of other beings concerned for their own liberation, as constrained by the iron laws of God or karma.

Indeed, the transcendentalist desire to make the king righteous by strictly subordinating him to scripture is analogous to the immanentist desire to make the king divine by strictly constraining him by ceremonies. If immanentism idealizes the immovable cosmic king—swathed in purity rites—then transcendentalism idealizes the rigid doctrinal king—hemmed in by scriptural truths. In short, the most extreme forms of righteous kingship also seek to eliminate all the ruler's agency and personal charisma. Thus, the Bible orders the king to read scripture "all the days of his life, so that he may learn to fear the Lord his God, diligently observing all the words of his law and these statutes, neither exalting himself above other members of the community nor turning aside from the commandment..." (Deuteronomy 17:19–20). In the same vein, the Qur'an records God's warning to King David: "Lo! We have set thee as a viceroy in the earth; therefor judge aright between mankind, and follow not desire that it beguile thee from the way of Allah. Lo! those who wander from the way of Allah have an awful doom, forasmuch as they forgot the Day of Reckoning" (Qur'an 38:26, Pickthall's translation).

Indeed, who would now want to be king? It is no accident that none of the transcendentalist religions began as cults of state but rather as movements outside major imperial centers. Most recently, Aziz al-Azmeh has described this process for the emergence of Islam in Late Antiquity, in which transcendentalism, in a self-consciously bookish manner, emerged slowly but surely in desert Arabia, the last kingless reservation of paganism in the Near East.[69] Thus the Qur'an's strident insistence that kingship belongs only to God, and that earthly rulers—Adam and David are the two it mentions—can only ever be deputies (*khalifa*).

No less consistently, however, transcendentalist traditions would go on to be co-opted by the great Eurasian empires of antiquity—by the logic of legitimation, the repudiation of power sucked in power. But in keeping with their origins, transcendentalist traditions at the very least implied a certain relativization of politics—just as with kinship or ritual—and an assertion of the inherent subordination of earthly government to higher objectives. The result was not a secularization of power, as Shmuel Eisenstadt put it, but rather a certain potential for its disenchantment or chastisement.[70]

When Graeber, following Carl Schmitt, says that "to say a state is 'sovereign' is ultimately to define its highest authorities as beyond moral accountability," this is presumably not intended to apply to the transcendentalist *imaginaire*, which encompassed and relativized the state no less surely than any other area of life.[71] Theoretically, the ruler was always held accountable to an ethical vision oriented around a set of imperatives that greatly surpassed his own being; and institutionally this vision was given reality and authority in the form of the clerisy. Church, Sangha, or Ulema acted as a counterweight to the state and ultimately reserved the right to pass judgment on whether the exercise of sovereign power was legitimate. Henry of Huntingdon's account of the old English story about King Cnut ("Canute," r. 1016–1035) expresses it well: "Let all the world know that the power of kings is empty and worthless, and there is no king worthy of the name, save Him by whose will heaven, earth, and sea obey eternal laws."[72]

Yet this does not imply that there is absolutely no room for heroic deeds under transcendentalism. Rather, a restricted form of transgressive action is permitted and even encouraged. The king can go off to war, loot, burn, pillage, enslave, and rape—even at times kill "anything that breathes" (Deuteronomy 20:16)—but only if these massive ethical lapses are committed in the service of truth or, what is the same thing in biblical monotheism, in the name of God. The hero in transcendentalism is the holy warrior and martyr, a phenomenon unthinkable under immanentism, where the king either acts like a god, calls on the gods to aid him in battle, or attacks the sacred space of his rival—to break the enemy's link with the gods—but, as a rule, he does not fight and conquer in the name of truth.

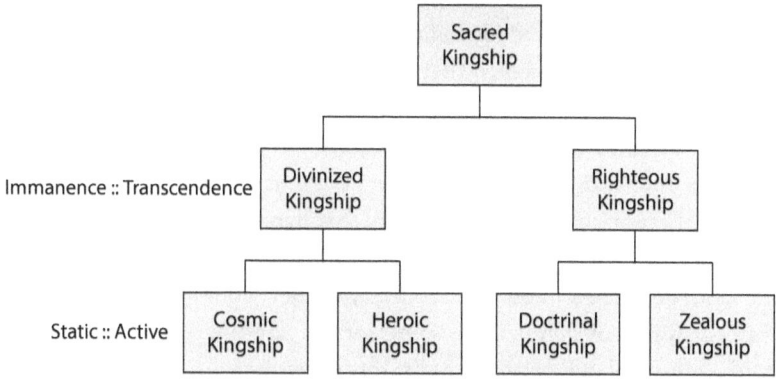

Figure 1.3 Types of sacred kingship

In a word, heroic kingship under transcendentalism is allowed only as zealous kingship.[73]

Figure 1.3 lays out the schema developed so far, dividing sacred kingship between immanence (divinized) and transcendence (righteous), and further subdividing each based on their static (cosmic or doctrinal) or active (heroic or zealous) natures. Figure 1.4 is an attempt at visualizing how these categories were

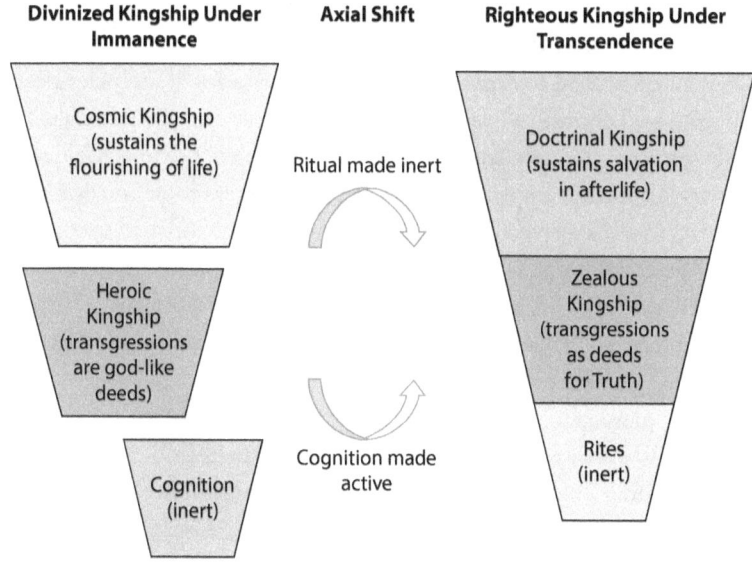

FIGURE 1.4 Sacred kingship between immanence and transcendence

produced and transformed by the Axial Age shift, which devalued purity down to mere ritual and promoted instead the active primacy of doctrinal truth.

It is certainly true, however, that the potential devaluation of sacred kingship under transcendentalism was, for long periods in nearly all places, largely suppressed or suspended. The central reason why is, once again, the inevitable tendency for transcendentalist understandings and immanentist forms to combine. There were many reasons why this happened. As chiefs and kings converted to Christianity or Islam, for example, they tended to stretch the immanentist elements of these faiths as far as they would go in order to allow traditional forms of divinization some sort of afterlife in the new dispensation. The powerful pull of immanentist forms gave newly or partially converted rulers confidence that they could simultaneously serve all functions, old and new: be the cosmic pivot, the charismatic hero, and uphold true doctrine. As Moin has noted, the classic case of adverse sacralization in Islam would be that of the Abbasid caliphate from the tenth to the thirteenth century in which the powerless Caliph became a "relic" of sovereignty, a cosmic pivot, whom Muslim rulers from all over Asia had to "touch" to become kings.[74] Much of this took place because of the agency of neo-Muslim rulers, many being Inner Asian warlords and slave-soldiers—classic transgressive "heroic kings"—who collectively invented a ritual of caliphal investiture, simply ignoring the cries of protest from the ulema. In this vein, the work of Jos Gommans has highlighted relevance of the frontier zones of Eurasia, especially of Inner Asia and India, where nomadic and settled peoples interacted and shaped such patterns of heroic kingship over the long term.[75]

When rulers wished to break the intolerable authority of their clerisies, they could just as well choose to insist on their own cosmic centrality or stake heroic claims by enacting morally transgressive godlike violence. Moin has described how powerful Muslim emperors of the post-Mongol era took on cosmic astrological titles in clear disregard of scriptural norms—no Christian monarch ever did so in Western Europe—and enacted the most transgressive rites on the battlefield.[76] In the Indic variants, meanwhile, where the whole field of metapersons was far less problematized to begin with, there were few barriers toward the maintenance and elaboration of forms of divinization.[77]

It is worth pausing to underline this point: the dynasties of societies shaped by Christianity, Islam, or Buddhism could draw on elements from both sides of the diagram in figure 1.4. Indeed, this was a principal generator of the pluralism and the tension-filled dynamism of their forms of royal sacralization.

This modal hybridity was one of the reasons traditions such as Christianity, Islam, and Buddhism were able to induce kings and emperors to convert, even when they occupied positions that had already been elaborated in divinized terms. Indeed, one pattern that becomes discernible from the vantage point of the longue durée is the way that *purely* immanentist systems and the divinized forms of kingship they sustained were so inevitably devoured, one by one, by traditions that combined transcendentalism and immanentism. We may speculate too that the universalizing tendencies of transcendentalism, its unusual capacity to trample over the culturally particular (and the underpinnings it provided for the monopolization of the legitimate use of violence), also proved attractive to rulers bent on expansion and empire. Finally, there is the problem of whom to take seriously in the written record, the immanentist king who sets out to become a charismatic hero or the transcendentalist scribe who describes his heroism as activist zeal for the faith.[78]

Subsequently, there were undoubtedly features associated with emergent modernity that helped to sustain and even enhance the divinized element of royal sacrality. The increasingly impressive feats of empire building and political centralization attempted by rulers across early modern Eurasia, and their battles with their quarrelsome clerisies, for example, might propel them toward pushing claims of their ritual centrality. And yet from the seventeenth century, in the Christian and Islamic realms at least, such claims started to become vulnerable to voices appealing to transcendentalist principles. The more exclusive the hegemony of righteous conceptions of kingship, the more that disenchantment itself might be the result. Certainly, the tension between transcendentalism and immanentism became more visible, more acute. James I of England (VI of Scotland), for example, began his reign afflicted by deep Protestant anxieties about the traditional practice of the royal touch, by which the monarchs of England were endowed with the capacity to heal scrofula. Yet he bowed to popular demand and ended by healing hundreds of people a year.[79]

INTO MODERNITY

Still, in the long run, such qualms would simply grow into plain common sense. As Charles Taylor and others have argued, therefore, there is a principle of disenchantment—a relegation of the role of immanent power—lodged in the transcendentalist vision from its inception.[80] Nonetheless, it was not until the nineteenth and twentieth centuries that sacred kingship entered into crisis on a global scale, and, when it did so, it was both the divinized and the righteous forms that started to seem anachronistic. Placed against the long-term vision of politics sketched above, this development looks momentous indeed and can only reflect some powerful process of secularization.

It is true that secularization theory is often invoked today only to be reprimanded. We would also like to participate in fruitful erosions of the distinction between the premodern and the modern by inviting speculation about how some of the patterns we have described have afterlives in the contemporary world. Thus, Nicole Jerr has written about the "counterrevolutionary" tensions evident in modern theater that has had difficulty conceptualizing sovereignty without a kingly figure.[81] More broadly, an appreciation of the deeply popular wellsprings of sacred kingship help explain how communist and fascist leadership ineluctably took on its forms. These were given intellectual ballast by conservative thinkers such as the infamous but still widely cited Nazi collaborator and Catholic jurist Carl Schmitt, who led the philosophical assault on the Enlightenment's attempt to rid the world of miracle and liberalism's move to contain the exceptional status of the sovereign.[82]

However, even when secular liberalism had won the war by the mid-twentieth century—if only after exercising an inordinately illiberal and "divine" scale of violence—the intellectual battles continued. Now, the sallies came from the far left as postmodern philosophers launched a dark critique of modern politics. For instance, Agamben, building on Foucault and others, insists that beneath the modern liberal façade of human rights and equality under the law lies a deep structure animated by a pernicious will to dominate and destroy. This will spawns, in the normal state of things, the mass production of disciplined bodies and, in the state of emergency, executes their destruction on an industrial scale and under the full gaze of a deethicized medical science. This literature on biopolitics—the modern state's uncanny desire to care for, control, and cull populations—has turned to examples from the premodern past to sort out the enigmas surrounding the ritual handling and extralegal treatment of the body of the sacred king. These quandaries involve how to preserve and take care of the sacred body of the sovereign; to transfer its purity from one bearer to another; and finally how to desecrate, eradicate, and dispose of it.

Is it possible to frame the political trends of the twentieth century in the analytical categories developed for sacred kingship in world history? If so, it might look something like this: another Axial turn, a powerful rationalization and disenchantment, did away with millennia-old cosmological and ritual means of dealing with the conceptual dilemmas and moral ambiguity of sovereignty. This led to three major reactions: a liberal attempt to reproduce a righteous, doctrinal kingship in restrained, time-delimited forms via constitutions and elections; a conservative pining for the heroic king in transgressive and unconstrained form via fascism and totalitarianism; and an anarchist lament that the king's body had not been destroyed but instead atomized and cast around the globe to seed the most ineradicable, if spectral, form of cosmic kingship that humanity had ever experienced, which has been called biopolitics. To be sure, the last analogy is not intuitive to grasp. The point, however, is to underscore the highly deethicized yet bodily and disciplining nature of both cosmic kingship and biopolitics, the former directed at the sovereign ruler and the latter at the sovereign citizen. This parallel might become clearer if we consider that radical resistance to such a deethicized and diffused regime of power might just take the form of an equally diffused but ethicized zealous response. In this vein, consider Faisal Devji's provocative suggestion that al-Qaeda's acephalous global network, which brought together utter strangers only to transform them into holy warriors and martyrs, produced an "accidental universe" in which jihad displaced politics by ethics.[83]

In actual fact, modern politics are an amalgam of all the reactions above. This is because none of the forms—liberal/doctrinal, conservative/heroic, biopolitics/cosmic, and most certainly anarchic/zealous—is stable in itself. All forms tend to morph and mutate into one another. For instance, where the style of leadership echoes transcendentalism in its restrained, ethical, and normative ideal, it is vulnerable during times of perceived collective crisis to the more transgressive charisma of the heroic king—or even to the clown, as noted by Graeber. To give a recent example from the theater of sovereignty in the United States, Barack Obama an austere, "no drama" professor of constitutional law (a doctrinal king) was replaced, in a moment of perceived crisis, by a philandering, know-nothing, orange-haired reality-TV star who provoked both fear and laughter (a heroic clown).

In some areas, and particularly outside the West, recognizable forms of sacred kingship may persist in a more straightforward way into modern times. Consider that the largest shrine in Pakistan, built on the mesmerizing scale of the Taj Mahal, belongs not to a Sufi saint but to a "martyred queen," Benazir Bhutto (d. 2007), whom the Western world knows as the Harvard- and Oxford-educated, left-of-center, democratically elected prime minister of Pakistan.[84] Her political party launches its annual convention on the day of her death—as if it were the annual jubilee of a saint—and invites tens of thousands of her devotees to the festivities in the sprawling courtyard of the shrine. When the festival ends, the saint-queen continues to work her miracles, which is to bless newlywed couples who come from across the province of Sind to ask for sons. Electoral politics might look like the staidest form of transcendence until the next twist of the kaleidoscope reveals dazzling immanence.

This state of affairs, however, does not negate the fact that something massive has changed. Of course, it is now routinely acknowledged that religion is still of tremendous importance in the public sphere. But where kingship has remained, it has tended to lose most of its sacred qualities and nearly all of its political power.[85] And as for leadership in general, it has tended to retain qualities that only vaguely invoke a transcendentalist ethos; that is, incumbents win popularity by brandishing their commitment to truth claims and ethical norms. It is only in a long-term and global perspective that we can understand how different this is to those societies in which the political order was truly "determined by the religious basis"—that is, by immanent power.[86] Is it necessary to state the obvious? In most parts of the world, we do not submit to rulers because they are the incarnations or lovers of deities, because their ritual intercession is the most basic condition for successful agriculture or our physical protection. Their authority does not really come from embodying the will and the power of the divine. We require instead that, through the ballot box or through their deeds and rhetoric, they embody the will of the people—a cause and a consequence of a certain disenchantment of politics.[87]

NOTES

1. David Stasavage, *The Decline and Rise of Democracy: A Global History from Antiquity to Today* (Princeton, NJ: Princeton University Press, 2020), reminds us that forms of broadly "democratic" governance could be found around the globe in premodernity, but once state structures and larger polities arose, they ineluctably lost out to more autocratic forms. One of David Graeber's functions at the conference was to remind us of how insistently societies have sought to curtail or resist monarchical power.
2. This is to follow Marshall Sahlins and to use his term *metapersons*, which helps us avoid questions of translatability afflicting terms such as *gods*. See David Graeber and Marshall Sahlins, *On Kings* (Chicago: HAU, 2017).
3. See, for example, Eric L. Santner, *The Royal Remains: The People's Two Bodies and the Endgames of Sovereignty* (Chicago: University of Chicago Press, 2011).
4. Carl Schmitt, *Political Theology: Four Chapters on the Concept of Sovereignty*, ed. and trans. George Schwab (Chicago: University of Chicago Press, 2005), 5.
5. Schmitt, *Political Theology*, 36.
6. Giorgio Agamben, *Homo Sacer: Sovereign Power and Bare Life*, trans. Daniel Heller-Roazen (Stanford, CA: Stanford University Press, 1998), 6.
7. Walter Benjamin, "Critique of Violence," in *Reflections*, ed. Peter Demetz (New York: Schocken, 1986), 300.
8. Kenneth Pomeranz, *The Great Divergence: China, Europe, and the Making of the Modern World Economy* (Princeton, NJ: Princeton University Press, 2000).

9. Robert A. Yelle, *Sovereignty and the Sacred: Secularism and the Political Economy of Religion* (Chicago: University of Chicago Press, 2019).
10. "Relativism" here means a concern with establishing cultural divergence, which is an implicitly comparative exercise.
11. Graeber and Sahlins, *On Kings*. Also note the important volume, which draws on African material in particular, Declan Quigley, ed., *The Character of Kingship* (London: Routledge, 2005). There are signs of a renewed esteem for comparison among certain anthropologists of Christianity, in particular Joel Robbins, as in "Transcendence and the Anthropology of Christianity: Language, Change, and Individualism (Edward Westermarck Memorial Lecture)" *Journal of the Finnish Anthropological Society* 37 (2012): 5–23.
12. Nicole Brisch, ed., *Religion and Power: Divine Kingship in the Ancient World and Beyond* (Chicago: Oriental Institute of the University of Chicago, 2008); Lynette G. Mitchell and Charles Melville, eds., *Every Inch a King: Comparative Studies on Kings and Kingship in the Ancient and Medieval Worlds* (Leiden: Brill, 2013). Further back, David Cannadine and Simon Price, eds., *Rituals of Royalty: Power and Ceremonial in Traditional Societies* (Cambridge: Cambridge University Press, 1987), is an important volume bringing historians and anthropologists together, while monographic works to note are Aziz Al-Azmeh, *Muslim Kingship: Power and the Sacred in Muslim, Christian and Pagan Polities* (New York: I.B. Tauris, 1997); and Francis Oakley, *Kingship: The Politics of Enchantment* (Malden, MA: Blackwell, 2006).
13. Sahlins's writings on the stranger-king are now well represented by Graeber and Sahlins, *On Kings*. For an application of the stranger-king idea to Sri Lanka, see Alan Strathern "The Vijaya Origin Myth of Sri Lanka and the Strangeness of Kingship," *Past & Present* 203 (2009): 3–28.
14. Marshall Sahlins, "The Original Political Society," in Graeber and Sahlins, *On Kings*, 23–64.
15. Kenneth Pomeranz and Daniel Segal, "World History: Departures and Variations," in *A Companion to World History*, ed. Douglas Northrop (Chichester: Wiley-Blackwell, 2012), 13–31.
16. That is, much in the manner that Michael Puett, in *To Become a God: Cosmology, Sacrifice, and Self-divinization in Early China* (Cambridge, MA: Harvard University Asia Center, 2002), advises for China.
17. Jeroen Duindam, *Dynasties: A Global History of Power, 1300–1800* (Cambridge: Cambridge University Press, 2015) is unusual in the extent to which it integrates Europe into a global vision.
18. Consider the way that the Great Divergence debate involved breaking down the terms of comparison from West versus East to certain regions of Europe and China. For an example of the comparative method as a disruption of European normativity, see Sheldon Pollock, *The Language of the Gods in the World of Men: Sanskrit, Culture, and Power in Premodern India* (Berkeley: University of California Press, 2009).
19. J. D.Y. Peel, "History, Culture and the Comparative Method: A West African Puzzle," in *Comparative Anthropology*, ed. Ladislav Holy (New York: Blackwell, 1987), 88–119.

20. We may be looking at arguments and oscillations as much as assumptions and norms: Michael Puett, "Human and Divine Kingship in Early China: Comparative Reflections," in *Religion and Power*, ed. Nicole Brisch (Chicago: Oriental Institute of the University of Chicago, 2008), 207–20.
21. Nicole Brisch, "Introduction," in Brisch, *Religion and Power*, 1–11; Piotr Michalowski, "Mortal kings of Ur: A Short Century of Divine Rule in Ancient Mesopotamia," in Brisch, *Religion and Power*, 33–45; Puett, "Human and Divine Kingship," 207–20.
22. Robert N. Bellah, *Religion in Human Evolution: From the Paleolithic to the Axial Age* (Cambridge, MA: Belknap Press of Harvard University Press, 2011); Jan Assmann, *The Price of Monotheism* (Stanford, CA: Stanford University Press, 2010); Jan Assmann, *Cultural Memory and Early Civilization: Writing, Remembrance, and Political Imagination* (Cambridge: Cambridge University Press, 2011).
23. Robbins, "Transcendence and the Anthropology of Christianity"; David Graeber, as in *Debt: The First 5,000 Years* (New York: Melville House, 2011), 22–50, is another important example.
24. Alan Strathern in *Unearthly Powers: Religious and Political Change in World History* (Cambridge: Cambridge University Press, 2019), Chapter 1, defines *immanentism* in terms of ten characteristics and *transcendentalism* in terms of fifteen, but the discussion here represents our collaborative thoughts.
25. Bellah, *Religion in Human Evolution*, 44–174.
26. Stewart Guthrie, *Faces in the Clouds: A New Theory of Religion* (New York: Oxford University Press, 1993).
27. This model, in which the mammalian capacity to play holds a central role, is taken from Bellah's discussion of the evolutionary processes that shaped the development of human culture and religion, especially before the spread of democratic writing and philosophy, in Bellah, *Religion in Human Evolution*.
28. A survey of literature on the psychology of positive emotions and empathy that links with the work of William James and Carl Jung is George E. Vaillant, *Spiritual Evolution: A Scientific Defense of Faith* (New York: Broadway, 2008).
29. Religion as neurosis and projection is, of course, the famous thesis of Sigmund Freud. The intense focus on eroticized and deethicized violence is in Georges Bataille, *The Accursed Share: An Essay on General Economy* (New York: Zone, 1988).
30. The concept of invisible religion is that of Thomas Luckmann and is discussed in Jan Assmann, *Religion and Cultural Memory: Ten Studies*, trans. Rodney Livingstone (Stanford, CA: Stanford University Press, 2005), 31–37.
31. Merlin Donald's evolutionary scheme, in which the human brain and culture coevolved, lays out the layers of culture as mimetic, mythic, and theoretic, which is used in Bellah, *Religion in Human Evolution*.
32. Jonathan Z. Smith, *To Take Place: Toward Theory in Ritual* (Chicago: University of Chicago Press, 1987), 96–117. Smith builds upon Freud and Lévi-Strauss and gives the example of italicizing a word as a way of creating "sheer difference" without adding symbolic content.
33. As opposed to the true/false distinction, which becomes the basis of transcendentalist and especially monotheistic traditions. Assmann, *The Price of Monotheism*, 23.
34. Assmann, *The Price of Monotheism*, 50–60, passim.

35. Bellah, *Religion in Human Evolution*, 155.
36. Assmann, *The Price of Monotheism*; Assmann, *Of God and Gods: Egypt, Israel, and the Rise of Monotheism* (Madison: University of Wisconsin Press, 2008).
37. Bellah, *Religion in Human Evolution*, 241.
38. These relations could become decidedly transactional, even antagonistic. Indeed, immanentism often yielded a rather empirical, pragmatic, and experimental mentality: particular rites, and ritual specialists and spirits were expected to produce tangible results and, under certain circumstances, could be set aside if they failed to deliver.
39. Mary Douglas, *Purity and Danger: An Analysis of Concepts of Pollution and Taboo* (New York: Praeger, 1966).
40. For the immanentist traditions, a whole series of anthropological injunctions against the inapplicability of the default concepts and dualisms of the West have most force. For the dualisms appropriately warned against, see Graeber and Sahlins, *On Kings*, 19–20.
41. The account of the transcendentalist mode of religiosity in Strathern, *Unearthly Powers*, Chapter 1, underscores the different forms it took in Buddhism and Christianity, which cannot be brought out here; nor is there space to present anything like a proper historical account of the different forms that transcendentalist traditions took or how they emerged.
42. A. M. Hocart, *Kingship* (Oxford: Oxford University Press, 1969), 72.
43. Assmann, *The Price of Monotheism*, 43.
44. Jan Assmann, *From Akhenaten to Moses: Ancient Egypt and Religious Change* (Cairo: American University in Cairo Press, 2014), 79–94. The causal power of literacy may have to be qualified in the case of Axial Age India, where there is great uncertainty over the use of writing before the third century BCE. It may be that certain forms of disciplined memorization and oral transmission could mimic the stability of the text. "Book religions" here strictly refers to scriptural religion. Also note that Jack Goody's observations on religions of conversion as religions of the book amounts to a good description of transcendentalism; see Jack Goody, *Literacy in Traditional Societies* (Cambridge: Cambridge University Press, 1968), 2.
45. This language needs to be handled with care when it comes to Buddhism. It works best as an account of Christianity and monotheism, but it is not intended as a proper historical account of the evolving currents of Judaism. In addition, transcendentalism has the paradoxical tendency to collapse into a special form of monism at one level. Hence the stress on monism in Richard Seaford, ed., *Universe and Inner Self in Early Indian and Early Greek Thought* (Edinburgh: Edinburgh University Press, 2016).
46. In this vein, a subtle treatment of the Weberian concept of disenchantment and its intellectual roots in early modern European as well as early Christian polemics against the ritualism of Jewish law can be found in Yelle, *Sovereignty and the Sacred*, 37–73. Also note Marcel Gauchet, *The Disenchantment of the World: A Political History of Religion*, trans. Oscar Burge (Princeton, NJ: Princeton University Press, 1999).
47. Strathern, *Unearthly Powers*, 58.

48. The process of canonization, which may take place over many centuries; see Guy Stroumsa, *The End of Sacrifice: Religious Transformations in Late Antiquity* (Chicago: University of Chicago Press, 2009).
49. The only really sacred things under transcendentalism are the canonical words of truth, a new "semiotic ideology" to use Webb Keane's term, which continues to have a long life as evidenced by Protestant Christian missionaries in our day; see Webb Keane, *Christian Moderns: Freedom and Fetish in the Mission Encounter* (Berkeley: University of California Press, 2007).
50. And hence the doctrinal mode of religiosity as in Harvey Whitehouse, *Arguments and Icons: Divergent Modes of Religiosity* (Oxford: Oxford University Press, 2000).
51. The Axial Age in general has been characterized by the eruption of second-order thinking, reflexivity, and competitive intellectual argumentation.
52. Ernest Gellner, "Notes Towards a Theory of Ideology," in Ernest Gellner, *Spectacles and Predicaments: Essays in Social Theory* (Cambridge: Cambridge University Press, 1979), 117–32.
53. Assmann, *Cultural Memory and Early Civilization*, 78.
54. Our approach here agrees with Sahlins's "Original Political Society," in Graeber and Sahlins, *On Kings*, 64.
55. This comes out well in several contributions to Brisch, *Religion and Power*.
56. See note 32 for the very specific meaning in which rituals may be "empty" and "neurotic." Do note that these are not at all pejorative terms.
57. Hocart, *Kingship*, 7.
58. Luc de Heusch, "Forms of Sacralized Power in Africa" in *The Character of Kingship*, ed. Deccan Quigley (London: Routledge, 2005), 25–37.
59. There is a certain resemblance—but not equivalence—between the heroic/cosmic distinction and Graeber and Sahlins's (*On Kings*, 7–9) distinction between "divine kingship" as elite will to power and "sacred kingship" as communal entrapment.
60. This is what Walter Benjamin referred to as mythic violence or lawmaking violence. Benjamin, "Critique of Violence," 294–95.
61. See the discussion on the difference between games and rites in Claude Lévi-Strauss, *The Savage Mind* (Chicago: University of Chicago Press, 1966), 30–33.
62. This is based on the table in Strathern, *Unearthly Powers*, Chapter 3, but has been adjusted through our collaboration.
63. Jeroen Duindam, "The Court as a Meeting Point: Cohesion, Competition, Control," in *Prince, Pen, and Sword: Eurasian Perspectives*, ed. Jeroen Duindam and Maaike Van Berkel, vol. 15 of *Rulers & Ethics* (Leiden: Brill, 2018), 119. See table 2.1, "From personal valour to institutional consolidation: models, types or phases of rulership."
64. The ritualization trap is described in Strathern, *Unearthly Powers*, 186–189; compare David Graeber, "Notes on the Politics of Divine Kingship: Or, Elements for An Archaeology of Sovereignty," in Graeber and Sahlins, *On Kings*, 403–19. Graeber tends to describe this in terms of a broader communal chastening of the king, while Strathern emphasizes subroyal elite strategization. Note that there are times when one would want to distinguish between the ritualization trap and the immanentist logic of cosmic kingship per se—the former can also happen in contexts where the latter is not evident. This may apply to certain examples given by Graeber and

Sahlins, *On Kings*, 418–19, including the Ottomans, and, we could also adduce, the Safavids. It is worth noting, however, that both dynasties began with spectacular military achievements (opportunities for heroic charisma), but by the seventeenth century, their emperors had withdrawn from the battlefield.

65. "Thus, there was not even an incipient sense in which the Inkas approached a Hindu-Christian distinction between secular politics and religious transcendence." See Peter Gose, "The Past Is a Lower Moiety: Diarchy, History, and Divine Kingship in the Inka Empire," *History and Anthropology* 9 (1996): 407.

66. David Graeber and Marshall Sahlins, "Theses on Kingship," in Graeber and Sahlins, *On Kings*, 7–9, and David Graeber, "Divine Kingship of the Shilluk: On Violence, Utopia, and the Human Condition," in Graeber and Sahlins, *On Kings*, 65–138.

67. This certainly goes for their major cases (Kongo, Mexica, Shilluk, Madagascar) and most but not all of the examples. David Graeber, in "Notes on the Politics of Divine Kingship," (417–8, 425–6), explicitly says that *On Kings* does not address the implications of the Axial Age for kingship, with just a few hints here and there of what these might be.

68. Strathern, *Unearthly Powers*, 197.

69. Aziz al-Azmeh, *The Emergence of Islam in Late Antiquity: Allah and His People* (New York: Cambridge University Press, 2014).

70. Shmuel N. Eisesnstadt, "Introduction: The Axial Age Breakthroughs—Their Characteristics and Origins," in *The Origins and Diversity of Axial Civilization*, ed. Shmuel Eisenstadt (Albany: State University of New York, 1986), 8. Secularization would imply that kingship is either removed from the sphere of the religious/sacred or held there at the expense of its political and societal significance. Disenchantment would signal a devaluation of the role of immanent power in describing and constituting the king.

71. Graeber, "Notes on the Politics of Divine Kingship," 399–400. We could say that the king no longer advertises his capacity to create society by his *transgression* of it, but instead by his *transcendence* of it, by virtue of his association with the transcendentalist project. Germane here are Erik Peterson's criticisms of Carl Schmitt, drawing on Augustine, on which, see, György Geréby, "Political Theology versus Theological Politics: Erik Peterson and Carl Schmitt," *New German Critique* 105 (2008): 7–33.

72. Henry of Huntingdon, *The History of the English People 1000–1154*, trans. Diana Greenaway (Oxford: Oxford University Press, 2002), 369.

73. On the notion of "zeal" and its relationship with violence in monotheism, see Jan Assmann, "Total Religion: Politics, Monotheism, and Violence," in Assmann, *From Akhenaten to Moses*.

74. A. Azfar Moin, "Sovereign Violence: Temple Destruction in India and Shrine Desecration in Iran and Central Asia," *Comparative Studies in Society and History* 57 (2015): 467–96.

75. Jos Gommans, *Mughal Warfare: Indian Frontiers and Highroads to Empire, 1500–1700* (London: Routledge, 2002); Jos Gommans, *The Indian Frontier: Horse and Warband in the Making of Empires* (New Delhi: Manohar, 2018).

76. A. Azfar Moin, *The Millennial Sovereign: Sacred Kingship and Sainthood in Islam* (New York: Columbia University Press, 2012).

77. This should resolve Graeber's puzzle in "Notes on the Politics of Divine Kingship," 420, as to why "Hindu kingdoms, which have the strongest priestly castes of all, are also most likely to have sacred and divinized kings."
78. Moin, "Sovereign Violence."
79. Marc Bloch, *Les rois thaumaturges: étude sur le caractère surnaturel attribué à la puissance royale particulièrement en France et en Angleterre* (Strasbourg: Istra, 1924); Marc Bloch, *The Royal Touch: Sacred Monarchy and Scrofula in England and France* (London: Routledge & Kegan Paul, 1973).
80. Charles Taylor, *A Secular Age* (Cambridge, MA: Belknap Press of Harvard University Press, 2007). Robert A. Yelle also notes, "Disenchantment, although it is a narrative indebted to earlier theological polemics, can no longer be dismissed as 'mere narratives,' nor as the byproduct of temporary political upheavals. On the contrary, there is every reason to believe that the disenchantment of a sovereign deity was one of the key moments in the political constitution of modernity, as well as in the developments that we label collectively as 'secularization.' " Yelle, *Sovereignty and the Sacred*, 72.
81. Nicole Jerr begins with Alain Badiou's lament that since "great theatre of the revolution is so rare . . . we must conclude that the theatre avoids the revolution." See Nicole Jerr, "Exit the King? Modern Theater and the Revolution," in *The Scaffolding of Sovereignty: Global and Aesthetic Perspectives on the History of a Concept*, ed. Zvi Ben-Dor Benite, Stefanos Geroulanos, and Nicole Jerr (New York: Columbia University Press, 2017), 340–64.
82. Christopher Duggan, *Fascist Voices: An Intimate History of Mussolini's Italy* (Oxford: Oxford University Press, 2013). Schmitt, *Political Theology*.
83. Faisal Devji, *Landscapes of the Jihad: Militancy, Morality, Modernity*, Crises in World Politics (Ithaca, NY: Cornell University Press, 2005), 13–14.
84. Rizwan Tabassum, "Commemoration or Deification? Pakistanis Honor 'Martyred Queen' Benazir Bhutto," *NBC News* (2013), http://worldnews.nbcnews.com/news/2013/01/02/16283955commemorationordeificationpakistanishonormartyredqueenbenazirbhutto?lite.
85. There are, of course, some very minor exceptions. The Thai monarchy may be the closest we have to a monarchy elaborated in both divinized and righteous forms, and also still has at least some kind of political influence.
86. Graeber and Sahlins, *On Kings*.
87. Naturally there are huge global variations in the extent to which this applies and the form it takes.

2

Kings Before Kingship

The Politics of the Enchanted Universe

MARSHALL SAHLINS

Allow me to begin where I left off in the coda to a recent article on "The Original Political Society."[1] After I had completed the piece, I discovered a text by Thorkild Jacobsen in which he described Mesopotamian civilization of the third millennium B.C. BCE as "merely a part of the larger society of the universe": a "cosmic state," populated and dominated by a host of divine figures.[2] The cosmic state of the Sumerians was essentially similar to the "cosmic polity" I had discussed for the traditional societies of the Central Inuit, certain Amazonians, Aboriginal Australians, and Min and Hagen peoples of New Guinea, among others. Most of these were classically "egalitarian peoples;" many were hunters; and, notwithstanding all were "tribes without rulers," they were subordinate to cosmic authorities with life and death powers over them. Taking the social and political order in its cosmological entirety, the state of nature had the nature of the state.

Indeed, the so-called animists were subject to cosmocrats such as Sedna of the Inuit or the Sky People of the New Guinea Melpa; whereas by Jacobsen's telling, Anu, Marduk, and the other great and lesser gods of Mesopotamia were ruling an animist world in which "every stone, every tree, every conceivable thing on it was a being with a will and a character of its own."[3] The implication is that from hunters to high civilizations, all these peoples were hierarchically encompassed and ruled by a multitude of beings of human character and ultrahuman powers—"spirits" in the common acceptation, "metapersons" as I have called them.[4]

The suggestion that follows is that historical kingship is the humanization of divinity. Of course, in the common average social science functionalism, it's the other way around: spirits in general and gods in particular must be the imagined forms of the social realities. Yet in the relatively undifferentiated societies at issue, there is no proportionate relationship, either in structure or power, between the politics of the cosmos and the human social and political order. There are kingly beings in heaven even where there are no chiefs on earth. Given the locations of many of these societies, far from any earthly regimes of great kings and high gods, it is highly unlikely that their own versions of a "cosmic state" were diffused or otherwise transmitted from some existing civilization. It is more likely that the reverse has been the historical course: that the ancient civilizations inherited hierarchical cosmologies of the kind long and generally established in human societies. The human kingdom was already prefigured as a cosmic polity. The kings came from heaven to earth, rather than the gods from earth to heaven.[5]

HUMAN FINITUDE AND THE SPIRITUAL MULTITUDE

The Hagen people of the New Guinea Highlands worship Kor Ngenap, the Great Woman, "in order not to die."[6] "The Manus put a price upon their devotion to the dead, but it is an impossible price. They want life, long life, and no accidents."[7] People are not the authors of their own life and death. If they were, they would not die. Their vitality, mortality, and prosperity depend on forces and conditions beyond their ken or control. The basic human condition is a kind of existential finitude, and accordingly a dependence on extrahuman powers of people's fate. Durkheim famously argued that God was an expression—or more exactly, a misrecognition—of the power of society: people knew their actions were constrained, but they did not know the source. But it is better said that divinity is an expression of the limitations of society. Whatever the supposed disenchantments of modernity, the hierarchical encompassment of human societies by a host of greater and lesser metahuman powers has been the common finding of anthropologists, from Aboriginal Australia to Amazonia, from southern Africa to northern Asia.

As Simon Harrison reports from the middle Sepik region of New Guinea, Avatip people are well aware that to cultivate yams successfully, they have to be planted in the right kind of soil and tended properly while growing. These skills are everyday common knowledge of adult men and women. They know *how* yams grow. "But Avatip religion," Harrison says, "poses and answers a different question: *why* yams grow successfully and to whom the social and political credit is owed." Inasmuch as they neither made nor control the relevant processes of photosynthesis, let alone the qualities of the soil or the weather, Avatip people do not *produce* or *create* the yams; rather, they *receive* them from the ancestors in remote villages who are responsible for their growth—that is, "from beyond the world of sense and inaccessible to practical, uninitiated knowledge."[8] The credit and prestige thus do not go to the cultivators so much as to the clan authorities who hold the secret ritual knowledge by means of which yams are released from their ancestral sources. The alienation of labor was not a modern invention.

That the political dividend of material success accrues to the ritual specialist rather than the apparent "producer" prefigures the main argument of this essay. The main argument is that, in the great majority of societies known to anthropology, the human polity is appropriated from an enchanted cosmology. By various means and forms of hubris, humans of privileged status or charismatic attributes assume the functions of divinity in the midst of society. But first, the more proximate implication of the Melanesian ethnography is that the propagation, growth, decline, and end of life are effects of processes and forces of which humans are not the authors—no more of their plants and animals than of themselves.[9]

A host of sources of human fortune and misfortune are not of human causes, including sickness and health; all sorts of accidents, good and bad; the rain, sunshine, and other climatic conditions upon which people's livelihoods depend; not to neglect war, trade, and other such fateful reliance on the skills and wills of external others. In a well-known text, Malinowski argued that the spirits entered into human affairs specifically where the undertaking is hazardous and the outcome is uncertain, as in the deep-sea fishing of Trobriand Islanders, or gardening at the risk of bad weather.[10] But in the Trobriands, as elsewhere, it is the spirit powers that make the gardens grow in the first place: the outcome, good or bad, is always their work, and their intervention must be ritually solicited for crops to grow anywhere, even where there is little or no risk of failure.[11] As it were, the whole economy runs on spirit power.

Such spirit powers form the preconditions of human existence in the sense that the metahuman others are the essential sources and agents of human welfare and "illfare." The gods, ghosts, and ancestors, the indwelling persons of plants and animals, are structurally pre-posed to the action that they potentiate, engaged beforehand by means ranging from spell and sacrifice to the ministrations of spirit-possessed shamans or divinely inspired kings.[12]

In a wide array of societies, people are surrounded, outnumbered, and subordinated to an eternal cosmic population of metahuman beings endowed with life and death powers over them. As is reported from the New Guinea Highlands, it is common anthropological testimony that "the spirits rule the life of men.... There is simply no profane field of life where they don't find themselves surrounded by a supernatural force."[13] It should become apparent in the discussions to follow that the various cosmic denizens are not only interacting with the human population, but often in certain ways with each other, even as all operate in a unified field of divine life and death force—of the kind sometimes known as *mana, manitou, nihialic,* and the like. The entirety forms what could be called a cosmic polity.[14]

SPIRIT OWNERS AND MASTERS

Of the various metapersons of the cosmic polity, some living a cultured life as people in their own communities, the human population itself is among the lesser or least of beings. As such, the people may well be engaged in hierarchical relations of domination and submission, of which they are innocent among themselves, in their own society. Prominent among these hierarchical relations is the concept of a spirit "owner" of the lesser beings of its dominion. Actually, the notion is polysemic: it involves the sense of "master" as well as a strong sense of possession, and it often explicitly supposes that the dominant personage is the parent, mother or father, of the beings it encompasses—although for all that, the usual descriptor of ethnographic report the world around is "owner."[15] "Spirits are the true owners of things and goods of this world," so famously claimed Marcel Mauss; "it is with them that exchange is necessary. It is from the gods that we must buy, and they know how to repay the price of things."[16]

The dominance of a species master or game master over species upon which humans subsist effectively puts these people also under the spirit owner's control because they will have to negotiate their access to the desired animals as well as obey the master's rules regarding the respectful treatment of the remains—in Native America, typically with a view toward reincarnation of the animal via preservation of its soul. Peoples who would not themselves tolerate one man putting himself above and controlling the others—Northern Algonquian hunters such as Salteaux, Montagnais-Naskapi, and Cree; Siberian peoples as Chukchee and Yukaghir—nevertheless live in a larger hierarchical society where just such submission to authority is a matter of existential necessity and normal experience. In 1924, an older Naskapi man, adopting the voice of Mesanak, the moose-fly, master of the fish, explained to Frank Speck what his powers entailed: "Mesanak, I am called, the one who is master of the fish. I support them. You Indians will be given fish . . . you who do as is required are given fish, not him who wastes them."[17]

How is it that these peoples know and submit to relations of dominance that they do not practice among themselves? I am almost tempted to speak of

Levi-Straussian inherent properties of the human mind, or at least of human symbolic capacities. In its elementary form, the species-master or species-owner concept is at once a common category logic and a hierarchical social structure. It is in part a matter of philosophical realism, the reality of the class, the species, as such. In another part it is the hypostatization of the species in an "owner" or species being who is sometimes an outsized version of the species type, sometimes a human or other person who thus represents the class. As the paradigmatic species being, and notably as the parent of the class, the species master is a distributed person who thus encompasses and is instanced in the individual members of the species. Otherwise said, this is a structure of the one and the many—and more particularly of the one over many—which, however difficult or problematic in human social relations, is a common practice of symbolic thought.[18]

The categorical logic of the one over and including the many is a highly productive form of cosmological order. I speculate one reason is that spiritual being is unitary, as is spiritual power, morphological differences among the cosmic host notwithstanding. In his well-known study of Nuer religion, E. E. Evans-Pritchard formulated the principle succinctly:

> It is in the nature of the conception of spirit . . . that what is distributed in a number of beings is, though different, yet the same, and though divided, yet a whole . . . *Deng* [the spirit] has several forms, but they are all the same *deng*, and *deng* may be in a number of different prophets at the same time, each of whom is *deng*, without *deng* being in any way divided.[19]

The principle may be compounded through several orders of inclusiveness, the universe as a whole dominated by cosmocratic gods who are "owners" of the world or large realms of it, within which lesser spirits such as species masters or lineage ancestors rule subjects of their kinds. In the cosmos of the nineteenth-century Bakongo kingdom as described by Wyatt Macgaffrey, the living and dead were arranged in a hierarchy, of which the paradigmatic spirit, Nzambi Mpungu, was "the highest Nzambi," and the lowest, also *nzambi*, was any human being. Although the most general spiritual entity, Nzambi was rendered less remote by being implicit in all the others: "he participates in and is presupposed by all lesser forms or entities, the 'spirits,' the dead and the living."[20] Perhaps unsurprising in an African kingdom, the existence of a metahuman world hegemon might also be known to so-called egalitarian peoples like the Salteaux. Their universe, reports Hallowell, is roughly stratified in a hierarchy of celestial to terrestrial peoples, of whom Kitchmanitoci, "the 'owner of the world' is both the most remote and most powerful of beings."[21]

HIERARCHY AND POWERS

Myth allows the Kwakiutl to believe that the spirit animals are the primary owners of powers [nawalak]. There is no explicit higher source or original dispenser. They have their independent world in which they contest with one another, and from time to time with human ancestors. . . . The Kwakiutl concept of cosmological worlds and of realms of beings serves to define the distribution of nawalak *and poses the problems of its acquisition. Supernatural power . . . must come from an outside realm, from an outer cosmological realm or from another type of being. This principle of acquisition is pervasive and fundamental. It lies at the foundation of Kwakiutl lineage exogamy, of ritual exchange and antagonism, and it lies at the heart of the shamanistic Winter Ceremonial [where initiates repeat the original acquisition of powers from animal spirits by human ancestors] . . . In fact, we are dealing with a Kwakiutl version of a universal principle of acquisition of powers.*[22]

Like the original Kwakiutl spirit animals who accorded the first human ancestors their powers (*nawalak*), life-giving and death-dealing potencies emanate from the primordial origins and the divine summit of the spiritual hierarchy. As a rule, however, they are conveyed by immediate ancestors, species masters, and other such metapersons in direct communication with the human population. The lesser spirits typically act with the referred powers of the greater. As Dinka say, "Divinity is one."[23] It is a question, Viveiros de Castro wrote of the Amazonian Araweté, whether the gods had shamanic powers or the shamans, divine powers. Bogoros said essentially the same of Siberian Chukchee: the great host of evil spirits know the shamans as evil spirits. The powers of divinity may be explicitly hypostatized in forms such as the Polynesian *mana*, the Souian *wakanda*, or the Malay *semangat*, or they may remain an implicit aspect of divinity in its various manifestations. In either case, their ultimate sources are the sovereign gods of the cosmic hierarchy, so the common notices of these gods as *deus otiosus* are often misleading. It is more appropriate to say, as Hallowell does of the Ojibwa Manitou, that the ruling god is at once the most remote and the most powerful.

High gods vary in number, one or many. Ethnographic reports of a sovereign god are as often contested as they are made, on suspicions of Christian influence. Less problematic are the accounts of a primordial generative pair, male and female, typically celestial and terrestrial, respectively, such as Rangi and Papa of the Maori, Lahatala and Puhum of the Huaulu, and Chibo and Ama of the

Jukun—not to mention Uranus and Gaia. Indeed, like the Greeks, the primordial pair may give rise to a family of deities, of whom some of a later generation, like Zeus—or Tu, Rongo, Tane, and Tangaroa in New Zealand—become the eternally active arbiters of the human fate. As a general rule, the summit of the cosmic polity is occupied by a collection of gods: one typically being *primus inter pares*, with more or less influence on the others, like Sedna, generally acknowledged to be sovereign deity of the Central Inuit, ruler of land and sea but known to act through Sila, god of the atmosphere, the celestial Moon Man, and even earthly ghosts and demons.

As a general rule, the highest gods are not human. They are persons in their own right, but for good reason they differ in some significant way from ordinary humanity. Either they were never human; they are ex-humans who were translated to divinity; they were born of nonhuman parents, they are part human and part animal; and/or they are aliens, migrants from some distant and exalted spirit land. The good reason is, again, human finitude: the sources of vitality, mortality, and prosperity are external to humanity. The gods come from and convey the metahuman sources of human existence. It only need be added that the sovereign divinities originate in a primordial time, so-called mythological time, likewise extrahuman in quality, notably for the miracles of creation and transformation that the gods accomplished.

The godly hegemons of the cosmos encompass it in three different ways: temporally, spatially, and potently. Originating in primordial time, they are pantemporal, eternally present, controlling the human destiny directly or indirectly through lesser beings of their inspiration. Spatially, the ruling spirits are situated or originate in an inclusive territorial realm, most often the heavens or surrounding oceans, while their consorts and lesser metahuman powers, located above, below, and around the human population, complete its encompassment. Completing a triple encompassment, the vital powers of the cosmic rulers envelop the beings and entities of the world, usually through the mediation of the lesser metapersons in frequent and direct contact with human persons. From the human perspective, the overall effect is a cosmos constituted as a great force field of life and death powers—as, for instance, Mark Mosko's recent description of the powers that be in the Trobriand cosmos.[24]

At once unified in power and differentiated in structure, the cosmic regimes of the Trobriands and others considered here are complex societies, marked by interactions among the several kinds of metahuman beings as well as their respective relationships with the human population. Missionary and anthropological accounts of the Melpa and their Highland New Guinea neighbors of the Hagen area describe a systematic organization of spiritual labors in the maintenance of the human order.²⁵ The dead are always present, shaping the fortunes and misfortunes of the living, but their powers are only "handed down" from great spirits and other sky gods of extrahuman origin and nature. As a rule, then, the supreme gods are remote and powerful. But as they are ultimately responsible for the human fate, at critical moments they may well remain present to the living. In the face of extraordinary events, especially personal or collective misfortune, Hagen people do not hesitate to attribute their lot directly to "Himself, the Above," a personified form of the sky people as a class. Strauss reports a number of circumstances in which "Himself, the Above," or simply "the Above," is alleged to be the primary agent: bad deaths of individuals, unexpected defeat in battle, epidemic mortality among children, drought and famine, among others. Considered closely, however, what some of these incidents reveal is the delegation of the punitive action by the Above to lesser, demonic beings, who then carry out the former's will. Strauss explains:

> If many men are killed in battle, they say, "He himself, the Ogla [Above], gave away their heads; the heads were "given away" to spirits and demons, who were then able to kill the people because the Ogla had placed them in their power. If, against all expectations, a side is defeated in battle, the people say, "can't you see that he himself, the Above, made openings (i.e., openings for evil powers of magic, the spirits, etc.) which led to their defeat"?²⁶

The observation is capital: it indicates that the cosmic polity does not consist merely of a series of independent metahuman powers but a more or less integrated hierarchy, involving the coordinated action of specialized spirits exercising the functions and potencies delegated to them from the supreme divine source. It is as if the New Guinean's own order of clans and big-men were encompassed in a cosmos that prefigured a bureaucratic state.

Where the powers of divinity such as mana are differentiated from divine beings, they may enter into social circulation, opening possibilities of its appropriation by gifted or privileged humans to their political advantage. A capital demonstration of the way a distinctive mana-power is referred through the cosmic hierarchy of spirit beings to human beneficiaries is provided in Raymond Firth's detailed accounts of kava rites in Tikopia.²⁷ By these rites, the mana that represented the divinities' *arota* (*aloha*) for the people descended from the "great gods" (*atua lasi, tupua*) through a series of notable ancestors to the chiefs and ritual elders of the four Tikopia clans. Thus empowered, the chiefs became the source of the people's welfare, with evident advantages for their own political standing.

The "spiritual bureaucracy" in these social roles thus brings the life-giving mana to the ruling chiefs. But then, in putting it to work for the benefit of the people, the chiefs thus assume the role and powers of the god. Such hubris, I claim, is the essence of human polities in an enchanted universe.

HUBRIS AND HEROES

The basic idea of an elite, especially of an hereditary elite, is in tribal society a religious idea . . . [W]henever elites exist in tribal society they are believed to possess special and supernatural powers . . . Even if elites had arisen because of notable achievements as warriors or hunters, their superior position would not have been stabilized without the religious idea of the concentration of supernatural power among a few.[28]

Many peoples acquire political power by heroic acts of hubris: that is, through the appropriation by and for humans of the life-giving and death-dealing authority of the metahuman powers. In effect, humans would usurp the gods by one or another of a great array of cultural means: as of ritual means ranging from coercion to propitiation, of relationships varying from compact to common descent, of modes of identity from personification to incarnation, of sociopolitical forms from shamanism to divine kingship. In the actual practice of the societies concerned, spiritual power is the essential premise of political power, the condition of its possibility, notwithstanding that by our own common social theory, the spiritual is a symbolic reflex or functional afterthought of the political. In the many societies here at issue, however, the political and the spiritual are structurally inseparable: they coexist in a radical synthesis.

Like the shamans whose powers are those of the familiar spirits they control or who possess them. "Even among the relatively egalitarian Eskimo," writes Irving Goldman, "the shaman is the elementary model of aristocracy."[29] Goldman's appraisal is true enough of the human society: it is relatively egalitarian, being small in scale, shifting in personnel, and structured mainly by interpersonal kinship ties. But on a cosmic scale, the Inuit were already ruled by personages with authority akin to royalty, notably the powerful goddess Sedna, who not only controlled the basic marine sources of subsistence but could also command the deities of weather and fertility, not to mention the demonic forces of illness and death.[30]

Note the implications for theories of sacred kingship. Frazer made much of the ability of divine kings to control nature. Placed in the full spectrum of the ethnographic record, this is no big deal. The Inuit shamans do it, in a society where otherwise, "an *inuk* [individual] should never push himself ahead of others, or show the slightest ambition to control people."[31] Similarly, the Dinka are one of the peoples featured in the well-known volume *Tribes Without Rulers*; but they are not without their priestly Masters of the Fishing Spear, who were the attractive focus of local communities so long as they continued to "bring about what the people wanted."[32] What the people wanted were things such as the fish in the rivers that had been taken away by another spirit, or they wanted rain, or victory in war. What allowed the Masters of the Fishing Spear to bring these things was the power of the clan or subclan god, whom they bodily incarnated. Referring to the regeneration of an important community by a certain priestly subclan, Lienhardt relates that their powers were sought for the fertility of animals and people, for restoring the sick, making people live to a very old age, blessing the crops, keeping the peace, settling disputes, and more. Yes, this is Africa, a continent of kings. Do the Dinka, then, represent their influence—or their possibility?

A plausible argument can be made on structural grounds that it is as possible such powers were developed indigenously as it is likely they were imported historically from some royal regime. The members of descent-based societies, especially the leaders of descent groups, are by their own nature instantiations of founding ancestors who were primordial creators or transformers, or who received vital powers from such godly sources in so-called mythical times. Not only Dinka, but Australian Aboriginals, New Guinea Highlanders, Kwakiutl, and other peoples mentioned here and known elsewhere, come under that description. In many of these societies, the original vital powers conferred on the founding ancestors devolve on their living descendants in rituals that reenact the original transmission from the primal divine sources. This notably happens in annual ceremonies involving visitations of the ancestors or ancestral gods, such as the Winter Ceremonial of the Kwakiutl, the Milamala of the Trobriands, the Makahiki of the Hawaiians, and the like.[33] As is remarked of Aboriginal peoples in the central and western deserts of Australia, the initiated elders and the medicine men or shamans are the closest to the dreamtime and the ancestors, and not only personify them in ceremony but implement their powers, as of fertility and rain. Elkin once met an Ungarinyin man of northern Kimberley, a certain Yaobeda, who was an incarnation of the ancestral hero associated with rain.[34] Lonimel wrote that such men were in the habit of speaking of the dreamtime heroes (*wondjina*) in the first person: "When I came in primeval times, and left my image behind in the stone."³⁵ The painted images or shadows of the ancestors were annually renewed by ritual elders personifying them, while accompanying the repainting with formulas such as, "I am now going to refresh and invigorate myself so that there will be rain."³⁶ A man who as divinity incarnate is able to bring rain and fertility to his people could be an African king but could also be an Australian Aboriginal elder. There are men of such power too in tribes without rulers.

But then humans generally are spiritual beings, even as spirits are essentially human.³⁷ Although the current interest in animism tends to highlight the latter, the person qualities of spirits, it is critical for the human appropriation of spiritual powers that the two are ontological congeners. Indeed, people have the same composition as animic beings, consisting of an invisible, indwelling soul or mind animating a physical body. Too often anthropologists have supposed that the invisibility of spirit persons means that they exist in another "world" or another "reality," but if so, humans also inhabit it. Like the Bentian Dayak, for example, whose soul "is essentially spirit-like, an unseen agency endowed with consciousness . . . as such it is perceived as an invisible counterpart of the person it animates."³⁸ In interesting ways too, humans, like spirits, are metaphysical beings endowed with metaphysical life powers: notably powers of speech, which move others independently of physical contact, and so organize a cultural existence that is not mechanically tethered to sensory stimuli. Speech is impelled by breath, which is life force; accordingly, of locutionary effects, one might even say that humans have mana-like powers themselves. In any event, they have these inner qualities of consciousness, thought, intentionality, and general symbolic capacities by means of which, in conception while awake and dream experience while asleep, they enter into relations with the metahuman sources of human welfare. The mind/soul is the minimum necessary condition of the hubris by which humans harness these powers to their own existence.³⁹

THE COSMIC PRODUCTION OF POWER

Normal social science has long supposed that the alleged spiritual basis of politics is but an ideological rationale of its secular achievement by victorious warriors, cunning shamans, successful hunters, entrepreneurial big-men, and the like. Power is actually established by some pragmatic hold on people; that it came by divine election is a palatable afterthought that makes it acceptable to those subordinated by it. Even Bishop Codrington, in his classic text on mana, clearly with Melanesian big-men in mind, seems to conceive it as an after-the-fact validation, if not obfuscation, of power that was actually political or social in nature:

> Thus all conspicuous success is a proof that a man has *mana*; his influence depends on the impression made on the people's mind that he has it; he becomes a chief by virtue of it. Hence a man's power, though political or social in character, is his *mana* . . . If a man's pigs multiply and his gardens are productive, it is not because he is industrious and looks after his property, but because of the stones full of *mana* for pigs and yams that he possesses.[40]

Still, the good bishop's argument is not altogether persuasive, if only because it is circular: mana is the conclusion alleged of earthly or profane success because it is the presupposition thereof. What is missing from Codrington's account is the spiritual prelude to big-man politics. As a matter of cultural practice, the acquisition of spirit powers is the necessary *means* of political authority, not just its post factum justification. Seeking the aid and potencies of the metahuman powers that be is what the aspiring Melanesian big-man does before the fact in order to make his stratagems of wealth accumulation and distribution successful. If material success is the sign of metahuman powers, it is because, in practice, it is the consequence thereof. Consider the young Kwaio man, Maenaa'adi, of whom Roger Keesing relates that he is learning genealogies, ancestral lore, and magical powers, thereby "acquiring not only an intellectual command of his culture, but powerful instruments in pursuing secular activities as a feast-giver and leader as well." it is no surprise, Keesing notes, that Maenaa'adi "has begun to be a formidable political presence in his neighborhood cluster of descent groups."[41] Keesing observes more generally that:

> . . . in the connection between the command of magic and lore, a presumed special and close relationship with an ancestor (who conveys powers of prosperity and destruction), and worldly power and success is very close. One might want to say that the sacred, ancestral powers are a mystification of real, political ones; but in a world where ancestors are everyday participants in, and controlling forces of life, this conveys political insights only at a great cost to subjective realities.[42]

Perhaps it goes without saying that these "subjective realities" are experiential as far as Kwaio are concerned. It also becomes clear that the post-factum allegations of the big-man's mana power are not just mystifications of his worldly successes but affirmations of the support he merited from the spiritual sources of wealth.

Writing of Hagen people in an instructive article on New Guinea political leaders, Andrew Strathern says that, prior to Christian influence, big-men had "a multitude of sacred and magical appurtenances which played an important part, from the people's own perspective, in giving them the very access to wealth on which their power rested."[43] Here, sacrifice, preferably of pigs, was, so to speak, the dominant mode of political and economic production. As Hermann Strauss put it, sacrifice was the source of power; of begetting; of achieving health, vitality, and peace. "Agriculture, trade, the economy, the various cults—in short all important practices—are centered on the offering of sacrifices."[44] Big-men depended especially on sacrifices to deceased kin as well as to the "great spirits" (*kôr ou*) of the periodic cults for the "miracles" of accumulation and distribution of shell valuables and pork that spread their names abroad and made their standing at home. Pig sacrifices were likewise preliminary to the large-scale distribution of wealth called Moka for which the region is well known.[45]

THE GODS IN CHIEFLY BODIES—OR HIERARCHY AS UNITY

By the powers of associated spirits, the Hagen big-man is able to organize periodic festivals of prosperity on an intertribal scale—thus bringing renown to his own people as well as himself. An occasional Kantorowiczian effect is the big-men's two bodies: as when, in public debates on matters of warfare and alliance, he refers to his tribe's doings in the first person singular. Something like, "when the fighting came, I allied with so-and-so people."[46] For the moment, at least, the big-man is at once himself, a person in his own right, and the tribal body politic.

Kwakiutl chiefs may likewise speak of their lineage (*numaym*) or tribal affairs in the first-person singular. Accordingly, they have also been described as dual beings: "The chiefs are the links with the mythical world, the original source of supernatural powers . . . As the reincarnation of the ancestors they alone have a double existence as persons and as spirit beings."[47] The inheritance of ancestral names by a chief has "the religious significance of a spiritual transformation. The ancestral being leaves one human carrier to be reincarnated in another."[48] The ancestors are customarily recycled from grandparent to grandchild. In this way, the founding ancestor, together with the powers (*nawalak*) and treasures (*tlogwe*) he received from the original divine source, are transmitted through all time. The chief is thus an "eternal individual"—one of the immortals himself.[49] And insofar as he also embodies his lineage or tribe, he is three in one—or perhaps even many more, as he includes all his ancestral predecessors.

As a matter of exalted descent, the incarnation of ancestral being in the chief puts him in the relation of the categorical or encompassing One to the Many of his lineage (*numaym*) or tribe. The effect is to reproduce within human society the hierarchical order of the cosmos as presided over by supreme deities: the two being linked by the descent of ruling chiefs from the primordial gods or animals, or by the contract of the original ancestor with the latter. Thus transmitting sacred being and potencies, descent is a kind of institutionalized hubris.[50] Thus, the person of the founding ancestor is distributed primarily to his privileged successor and secondarily to the members of the group. *Le tribu, c'est moi.*

A Kwakiutl chiefly line attempts to aggressively magnify its divine powers (*nawalak*) and the ceremonial and material benefits they entail by capturing the privileges of other chiefs in war and marriage:

> In the religious sense, the chiefs are the assemblers, the concentrators, and managers of supernatural powers. The first ancestor began the task and each generation repeats it ... The salmon, a Winter Ceremonial Song says, come ashore for the *nawalak* of the house ... The human chiefs go out into alien realms and deal with alien beings to assemble *nawalak* and to concentrate it in the ceremonial house. When they have become centers of *nawalak* the salmon come to them. The power to draw salmon to one's house is equated with the power to draw people. The power to attract salmon derives from *nawalak* and demonstrates its possession. Some supernatural beings in the oceanic world originally gave *nawalak* to humans ... In exchanges of *nawalak* and in the collection of treasures that promote the increase of life and property, the human being is the actively energetic agent. He is the primary intruder into other worlds—though not the only one—the primary collector, and ultimately the central unifier or perhaps the only reunifier of the universe of life.[51]

This is a good example of the present argument: the chief plays the part of the god and becomes the origin of benefits and dangers of which humans as such are incapable.

"In olden times," a man of the Cakaudrove Confederacy in Fiji told A. M. Hocart, "it was The Lord of the Reef [paramount of the ruling diarchy] who was believed in; he was by way of a human god [*kalou tamata*]."[52] On this point of theology, Hocart got the better of Bishop Codrington, who disputed a Fijian chief's claim of "I am a god"—probably *Koi au na kalou*, "I am the god"—on grounds that it referred to a future posthumous status—a contention Hocart found "strained" and "impossible." Fijian sentences of the kind are definitely present; hence the chief in question "was a *kalou*, a god" as he spoke, and "this was no conceited boast but current belief."[53] Like Codrington, the early Methodist missionaries in Fiji had taken such chiefly claims as an ontological scandal: for all that the Methodists worshipped a god in human form themselves, they could not credit the Fijian version. "The great and good difference observed by Christians between approaching man and god," opined Rev. John Hunt, "seems not to be known by this people."[54] Rev. Joseph Waterhouse was equally incredulous: "The great chiefs would sometimes say, 'I am a god,' and they believed it too."[55] But then, like the Vedic kings, the Fijian paramount chief or tribal king could be many gods. Naming the deities of the various clan temples in the ruling town of Tokatoka, the chief told Hocart, "all these are my names."[56]

Indeed, the tribal kings of the great lands of Fiji—such as the Roko Tui Bau, the sacerdotal king of the powerful Bau Confederacy—normally inhabited the temple of the supreme god the day long and into the night, much occupied in drinking the kava initially offered to the latter. And every morning, in so consuming the offering, the king re-created the society, making the ordinary existence of the people possible. The kava was presented at sunrise on behalf of the chieftains of the land—most of them from autochthonous clans (*I taukei*), in contrast to the rulers, who like the supreme gods, were of foreign derivation and, in the case of the deities, not human in origin. Until the king consumed the offering, however, human society was suspended. Total silence and immobility had been imposed on the capital town by the call of the chiefly herald at daybreak. It was now original time, the time of the god. The people were confined to their houses. There, no talk was allowed, nor the crying of children, the barking of dogs, or the crowing of cocks. No work should be done outdoors or in, no gardening or fishing. Gathered in the main temple, priests, heralds, and other chieftains now had the kava prepared, whereupon it was ceremonially offered to the great gods of the land and chiefly ancestors, accompanied by prayers for prosperity and victory over the enemies of the kingdom. An early American trader described the oblation as "a very long yarn regarding the favor of the spirits so that they may have a good yam season, that their enemies may die, that many [European] ships may visit their coasts & get cast away that they may have the whites property and more good natured wishes to the same effect."[57] Having been offered to the gods, the kava was then consumed by the sacred chief, who thus effectively replaced them. (Among other descriptions, Hocart spoke of the chief as the *locum tenens* of the god.) Immediately the king drank, thus accepting the offering, a herald's cry resounded through the town, picked up and amplified in every quarter. The people were released to resume their normal occupations. At the same time, the chieftains in the temple were served kava in order of rank, upon which they continued to sit round the kava bowl, their discussions of affairs of state, punctuated by further rounds of kava, going on for some time. The society was thus reproduced hierarchically in its political order as well as collectively in its mundane occupations—by means of a certain hubris: "The Fijians had invisible gods, sometimes present in the priest or an animal; they preferred a god always present, one they could see and speak to and the chief was such a god. This was the true reason for the chief's existence: he receives the offering of his people, and in consequence they prosper."[58] There has been a lot of discussion about whether to label Fijian and similar polities chiefdoms or states, and their rulers chiefs or kings. I vacillate a bit in the previous discussion but on the whole, I prefer Audrey Richards's hybrid designation (for East Africa) of "tribal kings." That said, we are here on the verge of well-known African kings and the Frazerian descriptions of their assuming the god's part to the extent of the control of nature. Like the Shilluk, Alur, or Lovedu rulers, they at least rained if they did not govern.

AN ENDING

The main thesis is evident. The enchanted cosmology is the source of the human polity. As subordinate components of the complex cosmic regimes of metapersonal powers ruling their existence, human societies have always known forms of governance on the order of kingship and the state—governance in some ways more coercive than they devised for themselves. Even the most egalitarian peoples have deep experience of hierarchical orders whose dominant powers, some of the character of gods, are the agents of their weal and woe. They themselves are not the authors of what makes the plants and animals on which they subsist grow or flourish, nor of the processes of their own propagation and decline, of their illnesses and health, of happy and unhappy accidents, of the rain and shine that determine their prosperity, of the properties of the materials on which they fashion their livelihood—human finitude is their predicament, and dependence on external agencies of human life is the consequence.

I speculate that these agencies have anthropopsychic characters—consciousness, intentionality and will, communicative abilities—and often anthropomorphic forms by the necessity of humans to negotiate some beneficial appropriation of their life-giving and death-dealing potencies. Humanity becomes the ground of cosmic being and intersubjectivity the relationship with the cosmic powers, with a view singular toward humanizing and socializing these potencies in peoples' own interests—if you will, by a politics of hubris. It is critical that individual humans are themselves spiritual beings, endowed with an invisible soul/mind capable of extrabodily feats of mobility, communication, propitiation, shape changing, commanding, seducing, and otherwise interacting with the similarly constituted cosmic powers. One can agree with Tylor that this is a minimum condition of religion, although not just because it is dreamed. It is also the minimum condition of the politics of hubris by which the persons who, by one means or another, acquire life and death powers from their metahuman sources and become persons of authority in human society.

I have by no means tried to document the great variety of these human authorities or their means of securing the metahuman powers on which their authority depends—let alone attempted a comparative study of their characteristics.[59] As Viveiros de Castro put it in a not too different context, "I must stress that there is not a hint of comparison in the present endeavor; there is only generalization."[60] Well maybe a hint in the limited catalogue of personages who in one way or another gain human power by their privileged access to cosmic power: shamans, initiated elders, masked ritual performers, garden magicians of aristocratic status, powerful warriors, prophets, big-men, sorcerers, some priests, many chiefs, numerous kings, and more. Their hubristic appropriation of spirit beings and/or potencies may be episodic, limited to ritual enactments, or it may be a permanent condition of their status, as of certain chiefs, prophets, and kings. The mode of appropriation of spirit powers may consist in personification, incarnation, possession, descent, or other forms of embodiment; or where divine power is hypostatized as a transferable force—*mana, semengat, manitou,* and so on—it may be captured and manifested by persons of charismatic qualities, or again it may be gained by negotiation and compact, by sacrifice and deference, or defiance and aggression. All of this—which is practically everything relevant—is not here studied in the mode of compare and contrast but rather in the mode of what the politics of the enchanted universe is, essentially, the nature of it.

The mobilization of the metapersonal powers that be—by whatever means, from dreams and spells to priestly rituals and incarnate divinity—is the necessary precedent of political action. The political and the metapersonal are structurally inseparable: they are compounded in human action; indeed, gods are the infrastructure of the political praxis. So for all the prevailing social science of divinity as superstructure, as a representation cum mystification of the polity, the morphological effects are often reciprocal rather than one-sided: kings have the attributes of gods, as do gods of kings. "As usual," Hocart wrote, "the human organization reflects the divine, and vice versa, since the two are one."[61] If anything, the kings have more divine aspects than the gods have earthly ones. Although they are radically conjoined, the relationship is asymmetrical: the king defers to the god and not the other way around because he rules by divine powers. "He is expected to carry about in society the same functions which God exercises in the universe."[62] The king, in his hubris, would rule by the referred divine powers of vitality, mortality, and prosperity—which humans do not make.

CODA

Inasmuch as hubris is at issue, I will end with some of the scholarly variety by commenting on a revelatory discussion just recently penned by Alan Strathern on the world-historical ontological break between "immanentism" and "transcendentalism."[63] The break developed out of the speculative philosophies and especially the world religions spawned by the Axial Age of the first millennium BCE from original centers in Palestine, Greece, Northern India, and (arguably) China. All the world before that and around that—the world at issue in this chapter—was by contrast an Age of Immanence. Until the universal religions exiled divinity to an "other world," the gods, ancestors, animistic beings, and other such spirit persons were immanent in human existence as the decisive participating and potentiating agents of social action. For the greater part of human history and the greater number of human societies, the people's existence as culturally constituted has been heteronomous, subject to the governance of metahuman forces of life and livelihood. One could speak of a "determination by the religious basis"—until religion went from an imminent infrastructure to a transcendent superstructure.

To the extent that transcendentalism has penetrated given societies—which is variable and probably never complete, as Strathern demonstrates—it entails a revolution in cultural order, creating the conditions for the erosion of immanent regime. In these regimes, metaperson beings and forces comprised an all-round substrate of social action, structurally compounded with the human means of livelihood, reproduction, social order, and political authority as the prerequisite condition of their realization and efficacy. By contrast to the vital agency of immanent metapersons, the transcendental revolution depersonalized the earthly human habitat so that people, by their own informed action, became culturally self-determining—more or less. Referring to the ancient Hebrews, Henri Frankfort spoke of an "austere transcendentalism" that comes close to an ideal-typical description.[64] "The absolute transcendence of God," he wrote, "is the foundation of Hebrew religious thought." For all that God is the first and final cause of existence, He is "unqualified, ineffable, transcending every phenomenon."

Devoid of divinity, the human world could now be reorganized on a new ontological basis that realized the transcendental divide in a suite of classic binary oppositions: as between spiritual and material, culture and nature, natural and supernatural, subject and object. If these binaries only truly came into their own in the modern world following the Enlightenment, transcendentalism already contained within it their possibility. In the well-known effect, the cultural order is divided into semiautonomous domains of economy, society, polity, and religion, externally related to one another mimetically, metaphorically, and functionally. In the immanentist ethnographies, the metapersonal regime had been indissolubly bound to human life practice as the condition of its efficacy; integrally connected, that is, like an element in a chemical molecule or a bound morpheme in a natural language. Freed of such bonds, religion in a transcendental formation becomes a manipulable matter of "belief," debatable and contestable, and always potentially ideological—whether for or against the powers that be. Add in the well-known individual and soteriological orientation of the world religions, notably the Christian one—Max Weber, your table is ready.

NOTES

Editors' note: This chapter has been edited to about half the length of the draft discussed at the conference. This entailed greatly reducing the range and depth of ethnographic illustration that Sahlins provided in order to preserve the main lines of the argument. We understand that Sahlins enlarged considerably on the theme of this paper in his forthcoming *The New Science of the Enchanted Universe* (Princeton, NJ: University Press, 2022).

1. David Graeber and Marshall Sahlins, *On Kings* (Chicago: HAU, 2017).
2. Thorkild Jakobsen, "Mesopotamia: The Cosmos As State," in *The Intellectual Adventure of Ancient Man: An Essay on Speculative Thought in the Ancient Near East*, eds. H. Frankfort et al. (Chicago: University of Chicago Press, [1946] 1977), 125–84.
3. Jakobsen, "Mesopotamia," 139.
4. Hereafter I refer to these beings—gods, ancestors, demons, anima of the creatures and features of nature, and so on—alternately as "metapersons" or "metahumans." As explained in "The Original Political Society," because of their person-character, I prefer such terms to *spirits*. However, because it is less awkward, in many contexts, I will continue to use the usual *spirit* or *spiritual* in reference to metapersons of various kinds, although always with implied quotation marks.
5. In some ways the present argument is a broad extension of Carl Schmitt's well-known thesis that the significant concepts of the modern state are "secularized theological concepts;" see Carl Schmitt, *Political Theology: Four Chapters on the Concept of Sovereignty* (Chicago: University of Chicago Press, [1922] 2005), 36; but see also Graeber and Sahlins, *On Kings*, 23ff. Also in this vein is Carl Becker,

The Heavenly City of the Eighteenth-Century Philosophers (New Haven, CT: Yale University Press, 1932).

6. Georg F. Vicedom and Herbert Tischner, *The Mbowamb: The Culture of the Mount Hagen Tribes in East Central New Guinea*, 3 vols. (Xerox manuscript, Canberra, Australian National University, 1943–48), 759.
7. Reo Fortune, *Sorcerers of Dobu: The Social Anthropology of the Dobu Islanders of the Western Pacific* (New York: Dutton, 1965), 24.
8. Simon Harrison, *Stealing People's Names: History and Politics in a Sepik River Cosmology* (Cambridge: Cambridge University Press, 1990), 63, 68.
9. Compare R. Godfrey Lienhardt, *Divinity and Experience: The Religion of the Dinka* (Oxford: Clarendon, 1961), 139, on all births as gifts from God.
10. Bronislaw Malinowski, *Magic, Science and Religion and Other Essays* (Boston: Beacon, 1948).
11. Mark S. Mosko, *Ways of Baloma: Rethinking Magic and Kinship from the Trobriands* (Chicago: HAU, 2017); see also Philippe Descola, *In the Society of Nature: A Native Ecology in Amazonia* (Cambridge: Cambridge University Press, 1996).
12. A wide range of examples follows in the original essay: Dobu Islanders, Trobriand-Islanders, the Achuar people of the upper Amazon, the Betian Dayak of Borneo, the central Intuit Igliuk, the West African Tallensi, the Thonga of southern Africa, the Katu people of highland Vietnam, and Aboriginal Australians.
13. Vicedom and Tiscchner, *The Mbowamb*, 680–681.
14. As it is put for a New Guinea people in the Telefolmin Highlands, "the normal principle of Feranmin religion" is that "men defend society through the ability to control or embody the forces which lie beyond it." Robert Brumbaugh, "The Rainbow Serpent in the Upper Sepik," *Anthropos* 82 (1987): 31.
15. The Western Ojibwa or Salteaux, as described by Alfred Irving Hallowell, "Some Empirical Aspects of Northern Salteaux Religion," *American Anthropologist* 36 (1934): 391, offer a pertinent example.
16. Marcel Mauss, "Essai sur le don: Forme et raison del'échanage dans les sociétés archaïques," in Marcel Mauss, *Sociologie et anthropologie*, 3rd ed. (Paris: Presses Universitaires de France, 1966), 167–68.
17. Frank Speck, *Naskapi: The Savage Hunters of the Labrador Peninsula* (Norman: University of Nebraska Press, 1977), 120.
18. I take this argument as consistent with the way Carlos Fausto describes spirit ownership in an instructive study of the phenomenon among Amazonian peoples. "I propose imagining the Amerindian world," he writes, "as a world of owners and owned as a model of the magnified person." Carlos Fausto, "Too Many Owners: Mastery and Ownership in Amazonia," in *Animism in Rainforest and Tundra: Personhood, Animals, Plants, and Things in Contemporary Amazonia and Siberia*, eds. Brightman et al. (New York: Berghahn, 2012), 31.
19. E. E. Evans-Pritchard, *Nuer Religion* (Oxford: Clarendon, 1956), 52.
20. Wyatt MacGaffey, *Religion and Society in Central Africa* (Chicago: University of Chicago Press, 1986), 160.
21. Hallowell, "Some Empirical Aspects," 390–91.
22. Irving Goldman, *The Mouth of Heaven: An Introduction to Kwakiutl Religious Thought* (New York: Wiley, 1975), 186, 197–8. Brackets are my own.

23. Lienhardt, *Divinity and Experience*, 56.
24. Mosko, *Ways of Baloma*, 135 et passim.
25. Herman Strauss, *The Mi-Culture of the Mount Hagen People, Papua-New Guinea* (Pittsburgh, PA: University of Pittsburgh Press, [1962] 1990), 110–17.
26. Strauss, *The Mi-Culture of the Mount Hagen People*, 38–9.
27. Especially in Raymond Firth, *The Work of the Gods in Tikopia* (London: Athlone Press, 1967a), and *Tikopia Ritual and Belief* (London: Allen & Unwin, 1967b).
28. Goldman, *The Mouth of Heaven*, 5.
29. Goldman, *The Mouth of Heaven*, 207.
30. I have written of the Inuit cosmic polity elsewhere: Marshall Sahlins, "The Original Political Society," in Graeber and Sahlins, *On Kings*, 23–64; and see Knud Rasmussen, *Intellectual Culture of the Iglulik. Report of the Fifth Thule Expedition, 1921–1922*, Vol VII (Copenhagen: Gvkkendalske Boghandel, 1939); Franz Boas, *The Central Eskimo* (Washington, DC: Government Printing Office, 1888). Speaking of an analogous disproportion between the egalitarian structure of an Amazonian people and the hierarchical order of their cosmology, Viveiros de Castro writes: "Societies such as the Arawaté reveal how utterly trivial any attempts are to establish functional consistencies or formal correspondences between morphology and cosmology or between institution and representation." Eduardo Viveiros de Castro, *From the Enemy's Point of View: Humanity and Divinity in Amazonia* (Chicago: University of Chicago Press, 1992), 2–3.
31. Jarich G Oosten, *The Theoretical Structure of the Religion of the Netsilik and Iglulik* (Groningen: Rijksuniversiteit de Groningen, 1976), 16.
32. John Middleton, *Tribes Without Rulers; Studies in African Segmentary Systems* (London: Routledge & Kegan Paul, 1958).
33. On the transmission of ancestral power in the initiation rites—and rites of adulthood—of the Walbiri youth, see Nancy Munn, "The Transformation of Subjects into Objects in Wlabiti Pitjantjara Myth," in *Religion in Aboriginal Australia: An Anthology*, eds. Max Charlesworth et al. (St. Lucia: University of Queensland Press, 1984), 57–82; Nancy Munn, *Walbiri Iconography: Graphic Representation and Cultural Symbolism in Central Australian Society* (Chicago: University of Chicago Press, 1986).
34. A. P. Elkin, "Mystic Experience: Essential Qualifications for Men of High Degree," in *Religion in Aboriginal Australia: An Anthology*, eds. Max Charlesworth et al. (St. Lucia: University of Queensland Press, 1984), 45.
35. Andreas Lommel, *The Unambal: An Aboriginal Tribe of North West Australia* (Carnavon Gorge: Takanaka Nowan Kas, 1997), 18.
36. Lommel, *The Unambal*, 18; see also. A. P. Elkin, "Rock-Paintings of North-West Australia," *Oceania* 1 (1930): 257–79.
37. See also Oosten, *Religion of the Netsilik and Iglulik*, 29.
38. Kenneth Sillander, "Relatedness and Alterity in Bentian Human-Spirit Relations," in *Animism in Southeast Asia: Persistence, Transformation and Renewal*, ed. Kaj Århem and Guido Sprenger (London: Routledge, 2016), 165.
39. On Naskapi hunters, see Speck, *Naskapi*.
40. R. H. Codrington, *The Melanesians: Studies in Their Anthropology and Folklore* (New York: Dover, [1881] 1972), 119–20.

41. Roger Keesing, *Kwaio Religion: The Living and the Dead in a Solomon Islands Society* (New York: Columbia University Press 1982), 206.
42. Keesing, *Kwaio Religion*, 206.
43. Andrew Strathern, "Great-Men, Leaders, Big-Men: The Link of Ritual Power," *Journal de la Société des Océanistes* 97 (1993): 147.
44. Strauss, *The Mi-culture of the Mount Hagen People*, 4.
45. Strauss, *The Mi-culture of the Mount Hagen People*, 256–57.
46. Alan Rumsey, "The Personification of Social Totalities," *Journal of Pacific Studies* 23 (1999): 48–70.
47. Goldman *The Mouth of Heaven*, 52.
48. Goldman, *The Mouth of Heaven*, 26.
49. Stanley Walens, *Feasting with Cannibals: An Essay on Kwakiutl Cosmology* (Princeton, NJ: Princeton University Press, 1981), 79.
50. Note that descent itself is a spiritual rather than a biological process because a metaperson third—a god, lineage or clan ancestor, totemic ancestor, and so on—is responsible for the reproductive effect of the sexual act, even as what is transmitted to the embryo are metaphysical properties of the paternal and maternal line.
51. Goldman *The Mouth of Heaven*, 198.
52. Arthur M. Hocart, *The Northern States of Fiji* (London: Royal Anthropological Institute of Great Britain and Ireland, 1952), 93.
53. Arthur M. Hocart, "Chieftainship and the Sister's Son in the Pacific," *American Anthropologist* 17 (1915): 637–38.
54. Rev. John Hunt, *Fiji Journals of John Hunt*, 1 Jan. 1839–29 July 1848, Wesleyan Methodist Missionary Society Collection (London: School of Oriental and African Studies, Box 5b), Journal 1, September 1840.
55. Rev. Joseph Waterhouse, *The King and People of Fiji* (London: Wesleyan Conference Office, 1866), 402.
56. Arthur M. Hocart, *Kings and Councilors* (Chicago: University of Chicago Press, 1970), 88.
57. Joseph Warren Osborn, "Journal of a Voyage in the Ship *Emerald* owned by Stephen C. Phillips... in the years 1833, 1834,1835, and 1836." Pacific Manuscript Bureau 223, (Original in Peabody Museum, Salem, MA), 25 March 1835.
58. Hocart, *Kings and Councillors*, 138.
59. *Editors' note:* The author's approach here certainly counts as comparative in the sense discussed in our introduction.
60. Eduardo Viveiros de Castro, *Cosmological Perspectivism in Amazonia and Elsewhere* (Manchester: HAU Network of Ethnographic Theory, 2012), 64.
61. Hocart, *Kings and Councilors*, 105.
62. Hocart, *Kings and Councilors*, 85.
63. Alan Strathern, *Unearthly Powers. Religious and Political Change in World History* (Cambridge: Cambridge University Press, 2019).
64. Henri Frankfort, *Kingship and the Gods: A Study of Ancient Near Eastern Religion as the Integration of Society and Nature* (Phoenix, AZ: Oriental Institute of the University of Phoenix, 1978), 343.

3

Immanence in the Andes (1000–1700 CE)

Divine Kingship, Stranger-Kingship, and Diarchy

PETER GOSE

This chapter discusses the Andes as a case of "pure" immanence that, unlike the other regions this volume covers, did not develop an indigenous transcendentalism.[1] It will explore Andean political-religious life as it existed during the Late Intermediate period (1000–1400 CE), a period of sustained conflict among hierarchically organized regional polities that ultimately generated the Inca conquest state (1400–1532 CE), which in turn gave way to the Habsburg period of indirect Spanish colonial rule (1532–1700 CE) that relied on the regional indigenous elites whom the Incas had previously subordinated. During this span of seven centuries, the *ayllu*, a territorialized descent group under the direction of a sacralized ruler with a privileged relation to the founding ancestor, was the basic unit of Andean society, out of which the Inca Empire arose and into which it collapsed. These scalable divine kingships clearly aspired to mediate basic life processes and had nearly all of the immanentist features that Strathern identifies.[2] Rather than present them as a mere instantiation of a type, however, the goal here will be to explore their internal dynamics, which establish (among other things) the immanent worldly foundations from which transcendentalism can emerge.

Transcendentalism has a polemical relation to immanence[3] and often distorts it. Most of what we know about Andean *ayllus* comes from colonial "extirpation of idolatry" documents that describe them from inquisitorial Catholicism's hostile transcendentalist perspective and so require careful symptomatic reading when these documents are used as sources.[4] Transcendentalism similarly taints our contemporary descriptive language: to establish the concept of divine kingship, Frazer had to speak of priestly kings and propose an original nondifferentiation of temporal and spiritual domains.[5] What defined the king as such were not secular duties but his identification with the realm and its crops, his mediation of collective access to life, the supreme good in these regimes. Inevitably, this mediation had a strong ritual (and to that extent, "priestly") component but not one separable from the polity's personification. Indeed, Hocart argued that the state's administrative function was a slow outgrowth of a more primordial ritual responsibility, often embodied in a king who "reigns, but does not govern," leaving most practical decision making to decentralized civic or tribal processes.[6] Even secularized administrative states, Hocart held, never entirely overcame their origins in ritual. Hocart challenges transcendentalism by showing how its distinctions between sacred and secular emerge incrementally out of undivided immanence, not a sudden revolutionary sundering. Here, I continue that argument by outlining an immanent but nonteleological progression from divine kingship through stranger-kingship, to diarchy and finally transcendentalism, each as a potential point of departure for the next, subject to the active realization or suppression of immanent possibilities in their actual development. The goal is not only to reaffirm Hocart's immanentist demystification of transcendentalism but also to pose immanence dynamically and articulate it through relevant anthropological concepts.

Divine kingship, with its fundamental emphasis on securing life through undifferentiated political-religious means, lies at the core of immanence as an in-worldly order.[7] Basically a ritual association for the common good, its relation to centralized political power is variable, including many cases where the latter is entirely absent and others (like the Incas) where it is demonstrably derived from ritual. Among divine kingship's ubiquitous and defining features are the priestly nature of the king, his identification with the realm, and his responsibility for the success of the crops and promotion of life within it: a burden for which he might pay with his life in times of dearth or when his own vitality diminishes.[8] This tension between the divine king as deity on the one hand and scapegoat or sacrificial offering on the other was undoubtedly conditioned by the development of institutional state power around him but ultimately intrinsic to his role as representative of and mediator for the realm. While we can treat divine kingship as a type or even a structure, it is more basically a strategy for securing the conditions for life, an answer to a question. That the answer involves elevating a person into a being above and beyond the human condition to mediate with extrahuman forces suggests a view of life as exogenous to human society. Thus, the divine king may drift immanently into the stranger-king.

First identified by Dumézil, the stranger-king was later elaborated conceptually by Sahlins to emphasize the disjuncture between king and people or state and civil society.⁹ This disjuncture is initially one of origins, such that the people are indigenous and the king foreign, thus enabling him to mediate with the outside for influxes of life and fertility as in divine kingship. However, the contrast carries over into social morality because the king breaks with impunity prohibitions against murder, incest, and so on, that the people are expected to uphold. Here we see the emerging dark side of divine kingship, where the king is no longer the people's scapegoat but a usurping transgressive power that stands above them, often (but not always) as the state. The people's challenge therefore becomes how to incorporate and domesticate this alien power without extinguishing its productivity. Marriage to indigenous women is the most frequent strategy but also common is the representation of the foreigner as orphan, whose aggressive demands for care and preternatural growth destine him to rule. Both variants significantly feminize indigenous people, but also render them senior to the intrusive stranger-king in emergent kinship relations. Out of such a process (that both conserve and integrate foreign-indigenous distinctions), diarchy emerges immanently from stranger-kingship.

Diarchy is a worldwide pattern that distinguishes an active, junior, and intrusive sovereign often identified with war and thunder from a passive, senior, and indigenous sovereign often identified with agriculture and the sun. These correspond, respectively, to the heroic and cosmological modes of immanent sacralized kingship articulated by our editors. Both are sacred and reign simultaneously, but the nature of their differentiation predisposes the junior partner to usurp whatever executive power may have developed, and the senior partner to retreat into priestly activities, such that the two can easily be mistaken for king and priest. Diarchy always stops short of any transcendental distinction between the temporal and the spiritual, however, because it retains a complementarity between diarchic functions that transcendentalism necessarily severs. That split begins with the priestly critique of kings that secularizes and morally denounces power but culminates in a more thoroughgoing rejection of the world itself. This radicalization derives practically from literacy and commodity exchange, whose "real abstraction"¹⁰ (of meaning from time, space, and matter, of exchange-value from use-value) generates transcendental sensibilities and betrays their social provenance. Thus, full-blown transcendentalism registers priests' and merchants' will to autonomy and refusal to submit to the king, who subsequently struggles to recuperate their innovations hegemonically. Such developments presuppose but exceed diarchy so that a real continuity from it into transcendentalism can occur, beyond the endless category mistakes that arise from describing immanent realities with transcendental concepts. Diarchy is therefore key to an immanentist critique of transcendentalism. It is the prior basis from which transcendentalism can emerge from immanence and into which it may then backslide. It does not abolish the difference between them but qualifies and situates their contrast, helping us identify what is actually at stake in their differentiation.[11]

In expounding the Andean case below, this chapter will chart a specific version of this immanent drift from divine—through stranger-kingship to diarchy. However, it will also identify the factors that limited diarchy in the Andes and with it, any internal impulse toward a transcendentalist order. The point of this conceptual discussion, then, is not to provide an abstract or transcendental model but rather to highlight broader dynamics that emergent real interests may promote or block. Identifying these points of contention should greatly aid comparative discussion. For expository purposes, I break the three-part immanent progression just outlined into two pairs, divine kingship/stranger-kingship and stranger-kingship/diarchy, each as a section below.

DIVINE KINGSHIP/STRANGER-KINGSHIP IN THE ANDES

Ayllus were localized orders founded around exemplary ancestors who invariably came from afar. The most comprehensive accounts describe these ancestors arising in cohorts from either the Pacific Ocean or Lake Titicaca, from whence they journeyed through a series of *paqarinas* or dawning points before arriving at the localities they were to settle. Typically, this sequence of dawning points proceeded through regionally important lakes, then to mountains, and finally to localized caves, springs, rock outcroppings, or trees. This transition from aquatic to terrestrial is significant, as we will see below. These journeys were subterranean for ancestors arising from the Pacific and aerial for those who arose from Lake Titicaca. Dawning points occurred where those journeys touched the earth's surface. There, ancestral cohorts rested before dispersing in ever-smaller groupings toward their divergent destinations, until they arrived singly, in male-female pairs, or father-son groupings, either from the bowels of the earth or by lightning strike. Upon arrival, they built settlements and agricultural infrastructure or conquered other groups already in the area, thus establishing a patrimony for the localized descent groups they established. After completing their colonizing missions, accounts often mention their spontaneous petrification, an act that marked their metahumanity, not ordinary mortality.[12]

In addition, founding ancestors often left behind mortal bodies that were mummified and that presided over mortuary caves or towers in which the mummies of their *ayllu* descendants accumulated. These founding ancestors were the reference points for calculating rank and the transmission of political office within the *ayllu* so that a succession of elder-rulers (*kurakas*) ostensibly descended from them. But this descent was established less on any genealogical grounds than by presiding over the mummification and mortuary rites of one's predecessor[13] and continuing to offer sacrifice in an active cult. Because descent was fundamentally performative, it gave great political significance to the fulfillment of key priestly duties, which no *kuraka* could neglect or delegate beyond a certain point,[14] and which frequently occasioned significant intrigue. Ancestor worship and filial piety did not provide a missing moral legitimation (as in transcendental regimes) for the outcome of sordid political power struggles but instead expressed them directly because their entire point was to tap into the founders' animating power. Thus, Andean divine kingship might distinguish military prowess from ritual observance, but it did not fundamentally oppose them because both aspired to the same immanentist ends. A successful ruler had to shift fluidly between these modalities and prevent their delegation from hardening into permanent occupational specializations from which he was removed. Andean statecraft thus required a proliferation of surrogates for the ruler, most commonly statues, which he could dispatch to perform various duties in far-flung places while continuing to animate them all in oracular mode as extensions of himself, very much on an ancestral model.[15]

Ancestors remained secluded from their descendants throughout most of the year, stored in mortuary facilities associated with the final dawning points on their journeys. While close to their living descendants on the territories they colonized, these mortuary facilities also pointed to the ancestors' remote origins and the foreignness of their power, which extended to that of the living *kuraka*, who remained somewhat secluded from *ayllu* commoners by prohibitions that could include touching, direct conversation, eye contact, and even public visibility. More powerful *kurakas* also avoided contact with the earth by sitting on a throne and being carried in a litter,[16] as if such contact would establish new dawning points in the manner of the founding ancestors on their journeys of colonization. Here we see that, although the power of ancestors and the rulers descended from them was decidedly immanentist, it nonetheless operated at some remove from ordinary mortals and the life-worlds they inhabited. There was a certain tension between the immanence of this power and its derivation from afar, which distinguished sources or foci of animating power from the world they animated. Andean divine kingship was not a decentered animism but a hierarchical circulation of life that metapersons enacted. To arise as such, these agents had first to be consolidated against their background life-world, and only then could they return to it as an animating force. Andean immanence was thus imminent and not fully present. Rather, it consisted of a pulse involving withdrawal and return in alternation.

This pulse appeared most obviously in annual cycle rituals. Their number and timing varied from one place to another, but minimally and universally included festivities around planting (*poqoymita*) and harvest (*karwaymita*), during which the *ayllu* brought its living and mummified members together for a multiday occasion, called the *vecochina*, in a ceremonial plaza in front of its mortuary cave or tower. Prior to these celebrations, the living had to abstain from sex, corn beer, chile, and salt for five days; confess all transgressions to *ayllu* ministers; and undergo purificatory bathing. These prohibitions involved no elaborated priestly morality or transcendentalist notions of purity and pollution. Rather, they addressed *ayllu* unity and set an appropriate equilibrium of wetness and dryness in living bodies prior to receiving the ancestors' animating power across the osmotic frontier between the living and the dead. The celebrations proper began by recounting the founding ancestors' journeys, then moved to many days of festive drinking, sacrifices, oracular communication, and even dancing with the mummified dead. Perhaps the most intimate care the living offered their mummified dead was to change their clothes and repair any damage to their flesh with copper appendages. Once these festivities ended, the living returned the mummified dead to their mortuary caves or towers until the next such celebration.[17] Thus, intense festive contact between the *ayllu*'s living and dead contrasted with their quotidian separation. It generated an animating charge that drove agrarian production and sexual reproduction within the *ayllu*. As with the founding ancestors' and living rulers' journeys, however, these points of contact with the earth and its life had to be limited and strategic in order to be manageable. The immanence of ancestral power did not mean it was equally present in all things and at all times. It necessarily withdrew and advanced in phases and through ritual interventions.

These seasonal festivals also served as mortuary observances for the *ayllu*'s recently dead, integrating them into the ancestral community. Like established ancestors, they received food and libations during these festivities to meet their ongoing corporeal needs, including a journey to the afterlife. Living relatives danced through the night around the ceremonial plaza and entrance to the mortuary caves with the bodies of the recently dead on their backs in an observance called *paqarikuq* or *paqarikuspa*, meaning "vigil," but also *paqarina*, meaning "ancestral origin point."[18] This is exactly what mortuary caves and towers were, but one that marked the beginning of their journey to the abode of the dead or *upaymarka*, which was located in their ancestors' remote places of origin.[19] Thus *ayllu* dead passed through the same sequence of *paqarinas* as their founding ancestors, but in reverse, starting from the localities their ancestors colonized and ending at their point of departure.[20] The *vecochina* appears to have marked the arrival of the recently dead in the *upaymarka* and submerged their individual biographies in the *ayllu*'s collective seasonal rhythms,[21] essentially an alternation between wet and dry.

Death divided the person into separate components that were spatially distributed. On the one hand, there was the mummified body dried and hardened ideally to the point of imperishability[22] and retained in the locality. On the other, there was a more fluid aspect lost to the body and its locality to remote aquatic ancestral origin points. The Cajatambo idolatry corpus designates these entities as *kamaqnin* and *upani*, respectively.[23] A *kamaqnin* derived from the *kamaq* or ancestral animator. In the first instance, it was that ancestor's statue or mummified body but also designated the transfer of a soul-like entity to the hearts of its decendants via an internal replication.[24] Thus, descendants were "infused" (*kamasqa*) by the ancestor. The Quechua verb *kamachiy* expressed this process. On strictly analytical grounds, it meant "to cause to exist" but in actual usage "to command."[25] Both meanings converged in an immanentist ontological order that inseparably linked animation to political rule. In death, the *kamaqnin*'s power persisted as a localizing or fixing influence manifest in the accumulation of mummified bodies in the mortuary cave over which it presided. Extirpation of idolatry documents frequently mention the mummified dead's thirst,[26] and all dealings with them required offerings of corn beer. Thus, their preservation implied a loss of water and vitality embodied in another aspect of the person that did not remain under the *kamaqnin*'s command.

The *upani*, which meant "shadow" or "deaf-mute being,"[27] was a much weaker shade than the *kamaqnin* but nonetheless eluded its localizing control on death. In contrast to the *kamaqnin*'s fixity, it journeyed to the abode of the dead (*upaymarka*) generally located in distant, large bodies of water.[28] Thus, the *upani* was affiliated to the moist part of the person lost at death. This moisture was not merely lost to the dead person but also to the locality of his or her *ayllu* and to that extent was a geographical issue. The *upani*'s journey to the *upaymarka* enacted in reverse the founding ancestors' journey from their remote points of origin in the Pacific or Lake Titicaca, which were not only the maximal *paqarinas* of the Andean cosmos but also the ultimate collecting points for the watery aspect of the dead.[29] Thus, ancestral colonization and the *upani*'s postmortem return to their ancestors' origin points defined a cycle based on the differentiation of dry, local *paqarinas* from distant wet ones, which drove the redistribution of life between them. Petrified or mummified ancestral bodies lost water to the distant centers from which they originated but also commanded its return in a cycle where animation and political control were endlessly lost and regained.[30]

To summarize, a *kamaqnin* contrasted with an *upani* in several ways. While the former was an exemplary and powerful ancestor who remained in the locality it colonized, an *upani* was a weak and insignificant shadow that drifted away. The *kamaqnin* was a repository and replicator of group life, whereas the *upani* was a remnant of an individual life lost to the group and its locality. A *kamaqnin* stayed dry and hard aboveground, whereas an *upani* journeyed underground through the earth's aquatic interior. Finally, a *kamaqnin* never really died but continued to speak through oracular media and was deemed mute (*upa*) or done (*atisqa*) if it could not, signaling the end of its ancestral career.[31] By contrast, the deceased *upani* was categorically mute.

These distinctions (which at death became separations) were primarily material in nature and to that extent were immanent, not transcendental. Death withdrew and recycled water from desiccated bodies, allowing its redistribution across the landscape and enabling the Andean circulatory cosmos.[32] Geographical separation between the dry and wet poles of ancestral *paqarina* itineraries ensured that vital circulation was not tightly confined to humans in any reincarnation cycle but instead suffused the land itself and was shared with other beings that lived on it, including plants and animals. This circulation's driving force, however, was the founding ancestors whose original journeys established the pathways by which life moved and whose dry, imperishable bodies drew lost vitality back across the landscape to animate the local life-worlds over which they presided. Their remote origins and local fixity defined these animating circuits. Thus, the very dryness of founding ancestral mummies established not just a partitive contrast with aquatic life lost to the periphery but also a means of summoning it across what I call the osmotic frontier in a bidirectional flow. In times of drought, for example, people paraded desiccated mummies across the landscape to petition rainfall.[33] An alternative title for ancestral mummies was *mallki*, a term that also designated "seed," "young plant ready for transplanting," "sapling," and "fruit tree."[34] These entities all awaited the arrival of water to renew life and, to varying degrees, could draw it in. Mummification was thus comparable to the conservation of seeds by drying, and interment was comparable to planting.[35] Aquatic life and the forms it vitalized were sufficiently interdependent that the very dryness of seedlike mummies allowed them to affect distant sources of water, attracting them back toward the localities that were also continuously losing animating liquids. As with other such systems, Andean immanence was not fully monistic or a flat, unmediated presence but more an anticipated arrival of vitality circulating across spatial frontiers.[36]

STRANGER-KINGSHIP AND DIARCHY

Thus far, we have considered Andean divine kingship/stranger-kingship as a relatively unified matter, fundamentally concerned with the loss of life to and attraction of life from distant points of origin. We will return to reaffirm this view, but let us now turn to the duality of the local and the distant implicit in stranger-kingship, which was also basic to moiety distinction within Andean *ayllus* during our time period. Throughout the Andes, moiety divisions between an "upper" (*hanan*) and a "lower" (*hurin*) group were ubiquitous and typically defined the former as intrusive conquerors who originated from Lake Titicaca and the latter as conquered indigenous people who originated from the Pacific.[37] These distinctions tended to be recursive within Andean sociopolitical organization such that upper and lower divisions could be found anywhere from the minimal level of a hamlet up to the maximal level of the polity itself, in classic segmentary fashion. At each level, the upper group outranked and encompassed the lower group such that its leader represented the unity of the two groups to the next ascending level, which at the top of the polity's internal hierarchy became the outside.[38] Thus, Andean moiety distinctions were an outgrowth of stranger-kingship, in which mediation with the external became the dominant principle of internal organization.

The most detailed accounts of how these dualities operated are in the Cajatambo idolatry corpus and the Huarochirí manuscript, both from the central Peruvian highlands.[39] Here, the conquering "upper" group was called *llakwash*, worshiped lightening, and practiced pastoralism, whereas the indigenous "lower" group was called *wari*, worshiped the sun, and practiced agriculture.[40] The Huarochirí account vividly describes the arrival of these intrusive conquerors; the battle of their ancestor Pariaqaqa to displace the indigenous ancestor Wallallo Karwincho as the animator of the land; the intruders' control over water as decisive in subjugating the native agriculturalists; and the relations of intermarriage, reciprocal ancestor worship, and economic interdependence that followed.[41] Of note is that, while the intrusive pastoralists were militarily dominant, they were represented as poor and needy, whereas the indigenous agriculturalists were depicted as economically prosperous. The result was that the latter had to intermarry and share their maize-growing land with the former: interdependence, not ethnic cleansing. Indigenous ancestors who made the area's agricultural infrastructure still received veneration for their ongoing stewardship of the crops, but the intrusive pastoralists' lightening deity was recognized as the distributor of rainfall and thus held the preeminent position in local relations of ritual complementarity. Once again, the stranger-king pattern emerges, not only in the pastoralists foreign origins but also in their mediation with the outside for the inward flow of life, now specifically as water.[42]

These substantive associations of upper and lower moieties correspond quite remarkably to those Hocart outlined for junior and senior diarchs, where the former occupy the active seat of power and are associated with thunder, and the latter are more passive and associated with law, regularity, and the sun.[43] They also conform to the distinction between heroic and cosmological modes of immanentist sovereignty from this volume's introduction. Diarchy integrates those distinctions and renders them complementary and processual, providing a certain basis from which the secular-sacred dichotomy of authority associated with transcendentalism may spring. In what follows, therefore, I will try to unpack the subtleties, dynamics, and contradictions of Andean diarchy, showing how they remain within an immanent framework despite creating openings for transcendence.

Hierarchical complementarity was the normative relation between upper and lower moieties but the dominant position within that hierarchy was contestable and never entirely stable. Moieties retained enough autonomy and competitive symmetry that their complementary integration was not the only dynamic in play. Ritual battles at key points in the agricultural cycle were one occasion where they could pit forces against each other, sometimes with the "upper" group's triumph as a predetermined outcome but always hinting at the possibility of a real competition. Should the latter break out and the "lower" group prevail, the result would be a *pachakuti*, or cataclysmic overturning of the dominance relations between upper and lower divisions and the establishment of a new animating order. At least two Inca crises of rule (Pachakuti Inca's defeat of the Chanka and the Waskar-Atawallpa war of succession) featured an aspirant to power recruiting hitherto dormant "lower" forces to overcome a rival and establish a new dispensation.[44] Thus, previously vanquished powers could return to defeat their conquerors in an open-ended succession of animating regimes. This possibility mitigated against their transformation into the fully domesticated complement of the upper group's political power, that is, into something like disempowered spiritual authority.

Sometimes upper and lower moieties appear to have pursued separate alliances to outside forces as part of their internal rivalry. For example, Medinaceli argues that during the Spanish "conquest," Paullu and Manqho Inca effectively served as diarchs, pursuing policies of collaboration with and resistance to the Spaniards, respectively.[45] Although she does not map these diarchs onto lower and upper divisions, such associations would be entirely in keeping with their respective political stances. A related case was that of the Wanka, a powerful ethnic polity that allied with the Spaniards against the Incas during the "conquest," presumably with the objective of winning back a greater degree of autonomy. So firm was this stance that the Wankas became the most academically recognized Andean ally of the Spaniards in defeating the Incas, although several other Andean polities were equally committed to that cause. It is a surprise, therefore, to find that on Wanka territory, military preparations linked to the Manqho Inca resistance were detected in 1564 and 1565 during the Taki Onqoy anti-Spanish movement,[46] despite the fact that the Wankas continued to be ruled by the collaborationist Apoalaya clan. Another faction of the same polity apparently pursued an opposed political strategy. The advantage of such contradictory stances for a group is that they could always be sure of having one faction come out on the winning side of any larger conflict. By the same token, however, they would always be conflicted over internal supremacy and external loyalties. Because Andean diarchy and moiety divisions were already locked into that competitive dynamic by definition, it follows that their internal rivalry would occasionally spill over into contradictory diplomatic mediations with outside powers.

Of particular interest in this regard are details from "Inca history" that bear on the relation between Upper and Lower Cuzco in the imperial capital. Following the broader Andean pattern, the Inca ruling elite claimed moiety affiliation with Upper Cuzco[47] and left Lower Cuzco to the descendants of the local indigenous people they conquered and those of mixed unions. Along the same lines, the sun and its priesthood were located in Lower Cuzco, even though these priests appear to have been recruited primarily or exclusively from the Inca elite in Upper Cuzco.[48] Thus, an opposition within the Inca elite between the ruler (*sapa Inca*) and the priesthood, particularly the high priest or oracular medium of the Sun (*willaq umu*), superimposed itself on the basic moiety division between conquerors and indigenous people. What interactions and effects resulted?

One tendency was toward complementarity, in which the roles of ruler and priest became differentiated but interlocking halves of an encompassing whole on the model of Andean moieties. For example, Molina underlines the seniority relations involved by describing the Inca sovereign as the "Sun's son" (*indi churi*) and the high priest as the "Sun's servant" (*indivianan*).[49] By acting in place of the Sun, the high priest simultaneously claimed seniority and ceded the active seat of power to the sovereign. Indeed, the *willaq umu*'s principal duty was to act as kingmaker: the final, oracular voice of the Sun in ratifying succession to high office.[50] This role often extended into offering tutelage for young sovereigns without sufficient experience to govern properly.[51] Using such observations, some commentators argue not only that the Incas had a developed diarchy but that it began to approximate a sacred/secular split typical of transcendentalism.[52]

A countertendency was toward overlap or nondifferentiation between the supreme Inca and the high priest of the Sun. For example, the Inca sovereign performed important priestly functions in many imperial rituals, during which he left his governing duties.[53] In this scenario, the high priest was a stand-in who acted on behalf of the Inca, who could reclaim at will the priestly powers he delegated. Thus, when Huayna Capac took office, his first reported deed was to remove the high priest and act as such himself, inspecting all the shrines, oracles, and their estates.[54] Other sovereigns similarly intruded on the role of the *willaq umu*.[55] Even when relations with the *willaq umu* were cooperative, the Inca sovereign would still join or replace him in his priestly duties, particularly during oracular consultations of the Sun. Conversely, the *willaq umu* could assume the duties of the Inca sovereign, as happened during the rebellion of Manqho Inca, when he played an important military role.[56] On these and other grounds, one can challenge the idea that the Inca sovereign and *willaq umu* had a fixed, hierarchical, and complementary division of labor along junior and senior lines.[57] While they certainly joined most Andean peoples in distinguishing upstart militarist modes of power from their established priestly counterparts through moiety system and related forms of ritual practice, cosmology, and narrative,[58] the Incas failed to consolidate these distinctions into stable offices with specific and limited duties. Arguably this made them a more authentic diarchy than polities that did. Rather, the original impulse of divine kingship toward the unified deployment of military and priestly power prevailed. In short, no entrenched distinction between secular political power and transcendental religious authority arose under the Incas: the sovereign not only outranked the high priest in general but also specifically within the priestly domain. Dumont's analysis of South Asia[59] cannot be extended to the Andean case because complementarity never replaced delegation there as the basis of the king-priest relation. The complementarity that did exist in Andean moiety relations thus failed to recast the Inca king-priest relation when the two were superimposed.

The competitive, symmetric aspect of Andean moiety relations was probably the main countervailing force behind the formation of a clear, complementary, and hierarchical division of labor between Inca rulers. Molina states that the high priest was the ruler's "second person"[60] in much the same way that the representative of any lower moiety would be in relation to his counterpart in an upper moiety. As such, his relation to the Inca ruler featured the same mixture of subordination and rivalry that all "lower" authorities had with their "upper" counterparts. According to Cieza, the *willaq umu*'s influence competed with that of the Inca.⁶¹ Indeed, Valera treats the *willaq umu* as formerly having been more powerful than the Inca sovereign, a situation that was only reversed during the reign of Topa Inca.⁶² Using additional sources, Zuidema argues that this reversal enacted the basic categorical assumptions of Andean moiety systems, which posit the defeat by young or intrusive forces of a previously dominant power that becomes priestly, quietist, and associated with indigenous people,⁶³ in short, the basic stranger-king scenario. While this normative reading is undoubtedly correct as far as it goes, it nonetheless presupposes the possibility of struggle and contention, a more symmetric moment in which moieties' hierarchical coding hangs in the balance and is vulnerable to inversion.

During the time period under discussion here, such instability was the rule, not the exception. The Late Intermediate Period out of which Inca imperialism arose was an epoch of petty conquests in which neighboring groups imposed themselves upon each other, a reality registered in the invader/indigenous coding of local moiety systems. While the Inca expansion nominally imposed an overarching order on this panorama, the death of each Inca sovereign nonetheless opened the door to provincial secessionist rebellions and wars of succession among the Inca elite. The Spanish invasion, at least in the short run, only exacerbated this chronic political instability and expanded the possibilities for maneuver. These considerations should caution against an overly "structural" reading of the asymmetric duality of Andean moieties and their hierarchical logic, which attempted to contain political realities that were far more fluid. This logic was aspirational, performative and never precluded the possibility of challenge and reversal from below. If successful, challengers could themselves be assimilated into the same framework as the new dominant ("upper") entity in an endless succession of ex post facto revisions. Thus, some have preferred to treat Andean moieties diachronically as a developmental progression whereby political regimes arise and run their course into senility rather than as a static synchronic order.⁶⁴

All of this is consistent with divine kingship's fundamental premise that sovereignty is subject to violent, reinvigorating renewal. Despite their very real flirtations with diarchy as hierarchical complementarity, Andean polities constantly returned to this disruptive point of departure. Complementarity developed in provincial moiety systems to the point of distinguishing junior intrusive militarists from senior indigenous priests who remained interdependent within a single ancestral framework in which the former dominated. Conquests established new ancestral patrimonies for priestly regulation, which in turn posited a larger cosmos available for imperial control. The Inca imperial project embodied exactly this dynamic: instead of producing two divergent social logics, it strove to perfect divine kingship's basic identification of political sovereignty with the totality and fertility of the land. In realizing this unitary agenda of political and cosmological control, the highest administrative levels of their massive conquest state largely suspended the recursive dualisms of Andean moiety organization to reveal a maximalist divine kingship. Securing a single regime of animating power, whatever its internal hierarchy and multiplicity, was a broadly shared Andean goal that the Incas sought to realize. In so doing, they showed that diarchic tendencies were perfectly compatible with political-cosmological immanence and implied no necessary transition toward transcendentalism.

The Andean material covered here thwarts any teleological expectation that the continuum of divine kingship into stranger-kingship and diarchy discussed at the outset should necessarily lead to transcendentalism. Although Andean diarchy produced something formally comparable to the king-priest distinction of transcendental regimes, the dynamics of that relation turn out to be fundamentally different. Instead of generating two supposedly separate realms defined by opposed values, the worldly versus the transcendental, the Andean case used this distinction to outline divine kingship's progression from vigorous beginnings to senile demise. Each of these states amounted to a different point of view with divergent interests and concerns that might complement or compete with each other but never escaped divine kingship's defining preoccupation with the circulation of life and thus in-worldly immanence. Similarly, a realm of the beyond existed in the ancient Andes, but it was a vast pool of aquatic life at the world's edge, not a spiritual domain entirely outside it.[65] As long as in-worldly power addressed that periphery and attempted to mediate with or control it, the result was an immanentist regime. The first conclusion is therefore that the distinction between immanence and transcendence survives even the mapping of a possible transformational continuum between them. Morphological opportunities for transcendentalism existed but were not realized.

To account for this road not taken is to show how Andean divine kingship imposed its logic on the entire social field and prevented the emergence of subversive practices and actors within it. As a form of hegemony, all divine kinghips directly addresses the primary class relations of an agrarian society by mediating peasant livelihood concerns through sovereign power so that rulers and ruled can find a common cause. The Incas elaborated on this template by linking war to agriculture when the sovereign initiated the agricultural year by breaking ground to the accompaniment of martial songs[66] and undertook imperialist expansion to assert agrarian control over water lost to an aquatic periphery. Priests played an important role within this hegemonic process, sometimes as the sovereign's delegates and others as a distinct occupational group, but their activities never became detached from it to claim a moral monopoly or initiate an alternative transcendentalist social logic. To do so, they would have to draw on social groups and practices that could be detached from divine kinghip's immanentist logic. Comparative work on the Axial Age suggests that merchants were a likely social source of this development because the "real abstraction" of commodity exchange favored transcendental thinking.[67] Therefore, it is significant that the Incas actively suppressed commodity exchange and attempted to subsume it into their tributary system,[68] which they presented as part of a cosmic circulation of life in classic immanentist fashion. That Andean people outside the Inca milieu practiced commodity exchange suggests this Inca policy was deliberate, strategic, and about control. A final impediment to transcendentalism in the Andes was the minimal development of displacement in knotted cord (*khipu*) literacies, whose primary function was the ritualized public accounting of *ayllu* tributary obligations.[69] While some still-undecoded narrative functions also existed, the *khipus'* deployment in contextually disembedded discourse, another key transcendentalist precondition, was limited relative to other literary technologies. In a remarkably thorough immanentist hegemony, then, Andean divine kingship contained most existing social practices but suppressed or incorporated those that might have mounted a transcendentalist challenge.

Perhaps trying to explain why transcendentalism did not emerge endogenously in the Andes is a fool's errand that only perpetuates its false claims to universality and death grip on our descriptive language. By showing that Andean immanentism had its own dynamics that correspond to concepts of divine kingship, stranger-kingship, and diarchy, this chapter has argued, however, that it was not the crude idolatry, empiricism, or metaphysics of presence that transcendentalism disparagingly perceives it to be. Andean immanentism accepted the partiality of human experience, the limits of local political horizons, trafficked in many of the same existential mysteries as transcendentalism, and promoted cosmological elaboration to at least the same degree. In so doing, it produced some formal outlines that resembled those of transcendentalism but retained an alternative social grounding and logic. By highlighting the contingency and hegemonic struggle between the two modes of religiosity, this chapter has argued that transcendentalism has an immanentist basis, but one that failed to materialize endogenously in the Andes.

NOTES

1. Of course, Spanish colonialism did bring an ambiguously transcendental version of Christianity to the area in 1532, one that was still too immanent for the protestant critique. Spanish Catholicism transferred the charge of idolatry that it experienced itself in Europe to its Andean subjects on the colonial periphery, as is evident in nearly all the primary sources on Andean politico-religious practices. Out of this dynamic, a wonderfully inventive Andean Christianity nonetheless emerged, one that is frequently dismissed as such because of its resolutely immanent character. See, among many other studies, Thomas Abercrombie, *Pathways of Memory and Power: Ethnography and History among an Andean People* (Madison: University of Wisconsin Press, 1998); Peter Gose, *Deathly Waters and Hungry Mountains: Agrarian Ritual and Class Formation in an Andean Town* (Toronto: University of Toronto Press, 1994); Peter Gose, *Invaders as Ancestors: On the Intercultural Making and Unmaking of Spanish Colonialism in the Andes* (Toronto: University of Toronto Press, 2008); Olivia Harris, "The Dead and the Devils among the Bolivian Laymi," in *Death and the Regeneration of Life*, eds. M. Bloch and J. Parry (Cambridge: Cambridge University Press, 1982), 45–73; Tristan Platt, "The Andean Soldiers of Christ: Confraternity Organization, the Mass of the Sun and Regenerative Warfare in Rural Potosí (18th–20th Centuries)," *Journal de la Société des Américanistes* 73 (1987): 139–92; Michael Sallnow, *Pilgrims of the Andes* (Washington, DC: Smithsonian Institution Press, 1989).
2. Alan Strathern, *Unearthly Powers: Religious and Political Change in World History* (Cambridge: Cambridge University Press, 2019), 27–46.
3. Srathern, *Unearthly Powers*, 61–63, 68, 242.
4. Pierre Duviols, *La lutte contre les religions autochtones dans le Pérou coloniale (L'extirpation de l'idolatrie entre 1532 et 1660)* (Lima: Institut Français d'Etudes Andines, 1971); Gose, *Invaders as Ancestors*.
5. James G. Frazer, *The Golden Bough: A Study in Magic and Religion*, 3rd ed., 12 vols. (London: MacMillan, 1911–1915), 1: 44–51, 2: 139.
6. Arthur M. Hocart, *Kings and Councillors* (Chicago: University of Chicago Press, 1970), 30–40, 128–55, 135.
7. Frazer, *The Golden Bough*, 1: 420; Hocart, *Kings and Councillors*, 81.
8. Frazer, *The Golden Bough*, 1: chapter 1.
9. Marshall Sahlins, *Islands of History* (Chicago: University of Chicago Press, 1985), chapter 3; David Graeber and Marshall Sahlins, *On Kings* (Chicago: HAU, 2017), chapter 1.
10. Alfred Sohn-Rethel, *Intellectual and Manual Labour: A Critique of Epistemology* (London: MacMillan, 1978).
11. Hocart, *Kings and Councillors*, chapter 12.
12. Pierre Duviols, "Un symbolisme Andin du double: La lithomorphose de l'ancêtre," *Actes du XLIIe Congrès International des Américanistes* IV (1978): 359–64.
13. Juan de Betanzos, *Suma y naración de los Incas* (Madrid: Ediciones Atlas, 1551 [1987]), 207–209, 285–6.

14. José Luis Martínez Cereceda, *Autoridades en los Andes, los atributos del señor* (Lima: Pontificia Universidad Católica del Perú, 1995), 39–43.
15. Peter Gose, "Oracles, Mummies, and Political Representation in the Inka State," *Ethnohistory* 43, no. 1 (1996): 1–33.
16. Martínez Cereceda, *Autoridades*, 91–101.
17. See Pierre Duviols, *Cultura Andina y represión: Procesos y visitas de idolatrías y hechicerías, siglo XVII* (Cuzco: Centro de Estudios Rurales Andinos «Bartolomé de las Casas», 1986), 86–87, 93, 179–80, 188, 195, 281, for the best primary sources on the *vecochina*. For commentary and analysis, see Mary Eileen Doyle, *The Ancestor Cult and Burial Ritual in Seventeenth and Eighteenth Century Central Peru* (Ann Arbor: University of Michigan Dissertation Services, 1988); Kenneth Mills, *An Evil Lost to View? An Investigation of Post-Evangelization Andean Religion in Mid-Colonial Peru* (Liverpool: Institute of Latin American Studies, 1994); and Gose, *Invaders as Ancestors*.
18. Duviols, *Cultura Andina*, 8–10, 13, 16, 19, 25–28, 64–65, 72, 77–79, 81.
19. See Hernando de Santillán," *Relación del origen, descendencia, politica y gobierno de los Incas*" in *Historia de los Incas y relación de su gobierno*, Colección de Libros y documentos referentes a la historia del Perú, vol. 9, ed. H. Urteaga (Lima: Imprenta y Libreria Sanmarti, 1553 [1927]), 33; Pedro de Cieza de León, *La crónica del Perú*, Parts 1 and 2, in *Obras completas*, vol. 1 (Madrid: Consejo Superior de Investigaciones Cientificas, Instituto Gonzalo Fernández de Oviedo 1553 [1984]), 122; Felipe Guaman Poma de Ayala, *Nueva corónica y buen gobierno* (Paris: Université de Paris, 1615 [1936]), 70; José de Arriaga, "Extirpación de la idolatría en el Perú," in *Biblioteca de Autores Españoles*, vol. 209 (Madrid: Ediciones Atlas, 1621 [1968]), 202, 216; and Duviols, *Cultura Andina*, 150, 171, 200, 227, 268–9.
20. Doyle, *The Ancestor Cult*, 241; Peter Gose, "Segmentary State Formation and the Ritual Control of Water under the Incas," *Comparative Studies in Society and History* 35, no. 3 (1993): 480–514.
21. Doyle, *The Ancestor Cult*, 232–3, 240–3, 257.
22. Frank Salomon, "'The Beautiful Grandparents': Andean Ancestor Shrines and Mortuary Ritual as Seen through Colonial Records," in *Tombs for the Living: Andean Mortuary Practices*, ed. Tom D. Dillehay (Washington DC: Dumbarton Oaks Research Library and Collection, 1995), 328.
23. Pierre Duviols, "Camaquen, Upani: Un Concept Animiste des Anciens Péruviens," in *Estudios Americanistas*, vol. 1, eds. R. Hartmann and U. Oberam (Bonn: Collectanea Instituti Anthropos, vol. 20, 1978), 132–44.
24. Duviols, *Cultura Andina*, 67, 143–44.
25. Gerald Taylor, "*Camay, Camac* et *Camasca* dans le Manuscrit Quechua de Huarochirí," *Journal de la Société des Américanistes* LXIII (1974–6): 236.
26. Duviols, *Cultura Andina*, 198, 217, 230.
27. Duviols, "Camaquen, Upani," 143–44; Gerald Taylor, "Supay," *Amerindia* 5 (1980): 51–55.
28. Duviols, "Camaquen, Upani," 136; Taylor, "Supay," 58.
29. Duviols, *Cultura Andina*, 150, 171, 200, 227, 268–69.

30. Jorge Polo de Ondegardo, *De los errores y supersticiones de los indios, sacadas del tratado y averiguación que hizo el Licenciado Polo*, in *Informaciones acerca de la Religión y Gobierno de los Incas*, vol. 1 (Lima: Imprenta y Libreria Sanmarti, 1554 [1916]), 10. Peter Gose, "Segmentary State Formation and the Ritual Control of Water Under the Incas," *Comparative Studies in Society and History* 35, no. 3 (1993): 480–514.
31. Duviols, *Cultura Andina*, 180; Cristóbal de Albornoz, "Instrucción para descubrir todas las guacas del Piru y sus camayos y haziendas," *Journal de la Société des Américanistes* LVI, no. 1 (1967): 18, 37.
32. Peter Gose, "The Andean Circulatory Cosmos," in *The Andean World*, eds. L. Seligmann and K. Fine-Dare (London: Routledge, 2019), 105–27.
33. Polo de Ondegardo, *De los errores errores y supersticiones*, 10.
34. Domingo de Santo Tomás, *Lexicon o vocabulario de la lengua general del Peru* (Lima: Universidad Nacional Mayor de San Marcos, 1560 [1951]), 314; Diego González Holguín, *Vocabulario de la lengua general de todo el Perú llamado lengua Qqichua o del Inca* (Lima: Imprenta Santa María, 1608 [1952]), 224.
35. Frank Salomon and Jorge Urioste, *The Huarochirí Manuscript* (Austin: University of Texas Press, 1991), 43; Luis Valcárcel, "La Religión Incaica," in *Historia del Perú*, vol. 3 (Lima: Mejía Baca, 1980), 81.
36. Strathern, *Unearthly Powers*, 31–3.
37. Pierre Duviols, "Huari y Llacuaz: Agricultores y Pastores. Un Dualismo Prehispánico de Oposición y Complementariedad," *Revista del museo nacional* 39, 153–91.
38. Juan de Matienzo, *Gobierno del Perú* (Lima: Institut Français d'Etudes Andines, 1567 [1967]), 20–21.
39. Duviols, *Cultura andina*; Salomon and Urioste, *The Huarochirí Manuscript*.
40. Duviols, "Huari y Llacuaz."
41. Salomon and Urioste, *The Huarochirí Manuscript*.
42. Gose, "Segmentary State Formation."
43. Hocart, *Kings and Councillors*, 161–6. An alternative but equally applicable definition of diarchy that distinguishes the young, vigorous, militarist, and foreign from the old, luxurious, priestly, and indigenous can be found in Marshal Sahlins, *Islands of History* (Chicago: University of Chicago Press, 1985), 90.
44. Gose, *Invaders as Ancestors*, 62–63.
45. Ximena Medinaceli, "Paullu y Manco ¿Una diarquía Inca en tiempos de Conquista?," *Boletín del Instituto Francés de Estudios Andinos* 36, no. 2 (2007), 241–58.
46. Gose, *Invaders as Ancestors*, 84.
47. José de Acosta, *Historia natural y moral de las Indias* (Madrid: Historia 16, 1590 [1987]), 420.
48. Betanzos, *Suma y Naración*, 291; Pedro Pizarro, *Relación del descubrimiento y conquista de los reinos del Perú* (Lima: Pontificia Universidad Católica del Perú, 1571 [1978]), 91.
49. Molina, *Relación*, 74, 76.
50. Sarmiento, *Historia*, 174, 205, 250–1, 265–6, 268.
51. Betanzos, *Suma y Naración*, 291–2; Sarmiento, *Historia*, 253.
52. R. Tom Zuidema, *The Ceque System of Cuzco* (Leiden: Brill, 1964), 110, 126–8, 245–6; Pierre Duviols, "La dinastía de los Incas: ¿Monarquia o diarquia? Argumentos

heurísticos a favor de una tesis estructuralista," *Journal de la Société des Américanistes* LXVI (1979): 67–83; Pierre Duviols "Algunas reflexiones acerca de las tesis de la estructura dual del poder incaico," *Histórica* IV, no. 2 (1980): 183–96; Franklin Pease, *Los ultimos Incas del Cuzco* (Lima: P. L. Villanueva, 1981), chapter 1; María Rostworowski de Diez Canseco, *Estructuras andinas del poder* (Lima: I.E.P, 1983), chapter 5.

53. Betanzos, *Suma y naración*, 51–52, 149–50, 181–2; Cieza, *La crónica del Perú*, 2, chapter 7.
54. Betanzos, *Suma y naración*, 182–3; Pedro Sarmiento de Gamboa, *Historia de los Incas* (Buenos Aires: Biblioteca Emecé, 1572 [1942]), 238.
55. Sarmiento, *Historia*, 191–2.
56. Betanzos, *Suma y naración*, 292–4, 299; Sarmiento, *Historia*, 253.
57. Peter Gose, "The Past Is a Lower Moiety: Diarchy, History, and Divine Kingship in the Inka Empire," *History and Anthropology* 9, no. 4 (1996): 383–414.
58. Isabel Yaya, *The Two Faces of Inca History: Dualism in the Narratives and Cosmology of Ancient Cuzco* (Leiden: Brill, 2012), chapter 2.
59. Louis Dumont, *Homo Hierarchicus* (Chicago: University of Chicago Press, 1970).
60. Cristóbal de Molina (el almagrista), *Relación de muchas cosas acaescidas en el Perú* in *Biblioteca de Autores Españoles*, vol. 209 (Madrid: Ediciones Atlas, 1553 [1968]), 75–76.
61. Cieza, *La Crónica del Perú*, 2, chapter 30.
62. Blas Valera, *Relación de las costumbres antiguas de los naturales del Pirú*, in *Biblioteca de Autores Españoles*, vol. 209 (Madrid: Ediciones Atlas, 1590 [1968]), 161.
63. Zuidema, *The Ceque System*, 111–3, 156, 161.
64. Gose, "The Past," 402–3; Yaya, *Two Faces*, 88–9.
65. Gose, "Segmentary State Formation."
66. Molina, *Relación*, 82–3.
67. Richard Seaford, *Money and the Early Greek Mind: Homer, Philosophy, Tragedy* (Cambridge: Cambridge University Press, 2004); David Graeber, *Debt: The First 5000 Years* (Brooklyn: Melville House, 2011).
68. For a good recent summary of debate on this subject, see Kenneth Hirth and Joanne Pillsbury, "Redistribution and Markets in Andean South America," *Current Anthropology* 54, no. 5 (2013): 642–47.
69. Frank Salomon, *The Cord Keepers: Khipus and Cultural Life in a Peruvian Village* (Durham, NC: Duke University Press, 2004).

4

Gods and Kings in Ancient Mesopotamia

NICOLE BRISCH

Historically, the monarchy is a remarkably ubiquitous form of government, also in ancient Mesopotamia, although one should strongly emphasize that kingship was never the only form of governance. In fact, kings often needed to rely on local councils and governors for stability and economic exploitation of the territories that they had conquered. Throughout Mesopotamian history, kingship, just as other spheres of society, was never dissociated from religion, and hence it is important to situate kingship within religious systems, as far as they can be reconstructed. Marshall Sahlins called for "something like a Copernican revolution in the sciences of society and culture" and recommended that particularly immanentist religious beliefs should be included (and taken seriously) in anthropological studies.[1] The term *metaperson*, which refers to deities and other supernatural beings that were perceived as a real presence in the immanentist worldview, can be seen as an expression of this mindset.[2] As such, the idea that metapersons were perceived as a real presence, comparable in their reality to persons encountered in the here and now, could be seen as a characteristic of immanentist religions.[3] Whether or not one wishes to adopt Sahlins's terminology, it is nonetheless important for modern scholars of ancient Mesopotamia to understand that religious beliefs in antiquity, also in connection to royal power, should not be dismissed out of hand as mere "propaganda," "politics," or sly royal manipulation. As I hope to illustrate below, however, the nature of writing in ancient Mesopotamia makes it difficult to draw firm conclusions on the thoughts that lay behind the textual traditions, that is, to determine whether the thought concepts and religious discourse can be seen as immanentist or transcendentalist. Much depends on interpretation of the ancient record by modern scholars.

Mesopotamian kingship and religion, the two topics that are at the heart of this investigation, are both exceedingly complex, largely because of the nature of the written data from ancient Mesopotamia, which often record and describe rather than explain. For example, at any given time, the Mesopotamian pantheon consisted of thousands of deities or metapersons. Some of these are only attested in a single textual record, and thus very little can be known about them. At the other end of the spectrum are the most important deities, who appear in thousands of texts throughout the millennia. The mythological texts from ancient Mesopotamia give testimony to the shifting hierarchies within the pantheon; the rise and fall of deities; and, most significantly, the syncretisms or mergers of deities, when several gods or goddesses became merged into one deity. This deity may have been addressed under one name or under several names, reflecting some of the earlier gods that had been absorbed. Localized aspects of religious beliefs are also of exceeding importance: certain rituals and mythologies may show very different manifestations depending on local traditions, and it is well known that at any given point, the Mesopotamian textual record, in particular the mythologies, reflected different, sometimes even contradictory traditions.[4]

Ancient Mesopotamian kingship, on the other hand, has been in the focus of scholarship since the inception of Assyriology, yet scholars writing on kingship tended to focus on the commonalities and traditions rather than the breaks or idiosyncrasies. This particular attention on kingship as a topic of research is probably due to the nature of the written sources, at least in part, because writing belonged mostly to elite circles of Mesopotamian societies. Because at least some of this written documentation can be assigned to circles close to the king, it is likely that the importance and power of kingship may have been exaggerated to a certain extent, at least in the early periods of Mesopotamian history, when royal power was fragile and often in tension with other forms of (local) government, although this may also differ from period to period.[5] This fragility was also recognized by the Mesopotamians themselves: a Sumerian literary composition, whose modern title is *The Lamentation over the Destruction of Sumer and Ur*, presents a poetic rendering of the chaos and disorder that followed the fall of the Third Dynasty of Ur around 2000 BCE.[6] The poetic rendering of the fall of Ur likely dates a couple of hundred years after the actual fall, at least this is when the first manuscripts appear. The well-known passage reads:[7]

> The command of the gods An and Enlil cannot be overturned.
> The city of Ur was given kingship, but it was not given an eternal reign.

> From the olden days, from when the country was founded, until the time when the population grew,
> Who has ever seen a reign of kingship being (always) foremost?

The passage also illustrates that the Mesopotamians saw the gods as those that determine the beginning and end of a dynasty's reign; it is the gods' agency that is pulling the strings behind the curtains, so to speak.

PRELIMINARIES ON KINGSHIP IN MESOPOTAMIA

Kingship underwent profound changes throughout Mesopotamian history. For this reason, it is problematic to make general statements about Mesopotamian kingship that are applicable to the roughly three thousand years of written history. While some continuities have been observed, royal self-representation changed considerably, also depending on the ideological needs of the time. The following account is mainly based on the written sources, yet here it is important to distinguish between sources that were composed long after the events they describe took place and sources that can be dated directly to a king's reign. Thus, royal inscriptions, that is, shorter or longer texts that were inscribed upon architectural features, statues, or votive gifts, date in almost all cases to the reign of the king that is mentioned in them. In fact, it is likely (and known from some cases) that kings approved the contents of royal inscriptions before these were placed onto the objects. Strictly speaking, only royal inscriptions and economic texts offer information about kings that can be dated with any degree of reliability, while literary texts may have been written centuries after the events that they describe, and therefore they have to be carefully evaluated on a case-by-case basis. In addition, the claims that kings made in royal inscriptions are sometimes not historically accurate, and therefore a reconstruction of historical events that relies exclusively on texts that kings issued themselves is questionable at best.

We can identify the beginnings of kingship sometime in the third millennium BCE, with the first rulers of city-states in the southern part of Mesopotamia. In time, these rulers sought to expand their area of influence, leading to military clashes. The earliest of these border conflicts, the Lagash-Umma border conflict (ca. 2600 BCE) was framed in religious terms: the border between the city states of Lagash and Umma was drawn by the gods themselves, but, according to the inscriptions of the king of Lagash, it was the ruler of Umma who disrespected these borders. It was then the god Ningirsu, patron deity of Lagash, who ordered the king to destroy Umma. The Lagash inscriptions frequently depict the gods as the agents in the conflict.[8]

Kings almost always claimed proximity to the divine in their royal inscriptions, as can be seen from the royal inscription of E'annatum, an Early Dynastic IIIb (ca. 2500–2350 BCE) ruler of the city-state of Lagash. The following inscription was written on a baked brick that was used to construct a wall:

> E'annatum, the ruler of Lagash,
> Who was given strength[9] by the god Enlil,
> Who was nursed with the righteous milk by the goddess Ninhursag,
> Who was given a name by the god Ningirsu,
> Who was chosen in the heart by the goddess Nanshe,
> Son of Akurgal, ruler of Lagash,
> Who conquered the land of Elam,
> Who conquered the city of URUxA,
> Who conquered the city of Umma,
> Who conquered the city of Ur:
> At that time
> He built a cistern of baked bricks for the god Ningirsu in the wide courtyard [of his temple],
> His god [= E'annatum's personal god] is the god Shul-utul!
> At that time
> The god Ningirsu loved E'annatum.[10]

The divine gifts are what sets the ruler apart from the remaining population, yet in this instance the king himself is not marked in writing as a god himself. It is only with the first larger-scale territorial expansions during the Old Akkadian dynasty (ca. 2350–2150 BCE) and the Third Dynasty of Ur (ca. 2112–2004 BCE) that we can observe the first instances of divinized kings, that is, kings that were declared gods. Naram-Sin of Agade (r. ca. 2254–2218 BCE) was the first king in Mesopotamia who was divinized while a living ruler. The event is memorialized in an inscription on a fragmentary statue. The text reads:

> Naram-Sin, the strong one, king of Agade: when the four regions [of the world][11] together rebelled against him, through the love that the goddess Ishtar showed him, he was victorious in nine battles in one year and he captured the kings who had risen against him. Because he had protected the foundations of his city during danger, [the people of] his city petitioned with the goddess Ishtar in Eanna [= Uruk] with the god Enlil in Nippur, with the god Dagan in Tuttul,

with the goddess Ninhursag in Kesh, with the god Ea in Eridu, with the god Sin in Ur, with the god Shamash in Sippar, with the god Nergal in Kutha him [= Naram-Sin] as the god of their city of Agade and they built in the middle of Agade his temple.[12]

The goddess Ishtar mentioned in this inscription is the goddess of war; Naram-Sin greatly expanded worship of her during his reign. His divinization is clearly connected to his successful defeat of rebellions against his rule. Even though the request here is formulated as coming from the people of the city of Agade, it is only the gods that can bestow divinity onto the king. Subsequently he also carried the title "the god of Agade" in some inscriptions. Whether there ever existed a temple for Naram-Sin's worship is unclear because the city of Agade has not been located yet. Thus, the divinization here is directly connected to the king's military prowess, with support from the gods, and stands clearly in the heroic mode as outlined in chapter 1. Yet the rebellions against Akkadian overlordship indicate that not everyone accepted the status quo of this new form of kingship with imperial aspirations. The Akkadian territorial state collapsed a couple of decades after Naram-Sin and was followed by a period of political fragmentation. The next territorial state was created by the Third Dynasty of Ur (also referred to as Ur III) some 200 years after the collapse of Akkad.

Shulgi of Ur (r. 2092–2045 BCE) presented his divinity in different ways. In Shulgi's case, it is not always clear whether the numerous praise poems about the king actually stem from his reign or were composed in later times to memorialize the king's fame. Shulgi was probably divinized during the twenty-second year of his reign, perhaps in response to a state crisis that had been caused by the death of his father and predecessor on the throne of Ur, Ur-Namma (r. 2110–2093 BCE). When Shulgi was deified, scribes began using the semantic classifier for divinity when writing his name. Most of his royal inscriptions are rather brief and only use the standard title "(Divine) Shulgi, the strong man, king of Ur, king of the lands of Sumer and Akkad." A single exception is one inscription on a brick that refers to him as:

> Divine Shulgi, the god of his land, the strong one, king of Ur, king of the four regions [of the world], when he destroyed the lands of Kimash and Hurtu, he excavated a ditch and built a mound.[13]

Shulgi's superhuman capabilities are perhaps alluded to in the year name for the seventh year of his reign: "The year in which the king made a round-trip from Ur to Nippur." This event, which predates his divinization, became the topic of

Shulgi hymn A, one of but a few of Shulgi's praise poems that is actually attested from the Ur III period itself.[14] This particular praise poem describes in vivid language the heroic qualities of the king, whose superhuman strength allowed him to run like a "donkey," so that he was able to celebrate important religious festivals in these two cities, roughly 200 km apart, on the same day. The first nineteen lines of the Old Babylonian version of this praise poem read:[15]

> I am king! I am a warrior from the womb [=from before I was born]!
> I am Shulgi! Since I was born, I am a strong/mighty man!
> I am a lion with terrifying eyes, born from a snake-dragon!
> I am king of [all] the four regions of the world![16]
> I am the herdsman and the shepherd of the black-headed people![17]
> I am the trusted/respected one among all the lands.
> I am the son born by the goddess Ninsumun!
> I am the one who was chosen in the womb by the god An!
> I am the one whose destiny was determined by the god Enlil!
> I am Shulgi, beloved by the goddess Ninlil!
> I am the one who was cared for by the goddess Nintur!
> I am the one who was given wisdom by the god Enki!
> I am the strong king of the god Nanna!
> I am the *menacing*[18] lion of the god Utu!
> I am the one who was chosen by the goddess Inanna for his handsomeness!
> I am an onager (?) suited for the road!
> I am a horse whose tail flies on the road![19]
> I am the donkey of the god Shakkan, who loves to run!
> I am the wise scribe of the goddess Nidaba![20]

In addition to all the gifts that the gods bestowed upon him, his physical and mental capacities were exceptional. Shulgi underlined his divinity by creating a divine genealogy: the goddess Ninsumun was his mother and through this he became the brother of Gilgamesh. The references to deities and the divine genealogy place the king in much closer proximity to the gods than previous kings, perhaps with the exception of the Akkadian rulers.

Economic texts as well as archaeological data also offer evidence on temples that were built in Shulgi's worship and priestly offices that were dedicated to his worship.[21] Overt divinization of kings, such as writing their names with the semantic classifier for divinities while they were still alive, referring to them as living gods, building temples and installing priests and priestesses for their worship, cannot be found in the record anymore after the fall of the Third Dynasty of Ur, although offerings were still made to dead kings or to the images of kings.[22] Instead, literary texts and rituals depict the king's proximity to the gods; kings in some cases borrowed divine epithets in their inscriptions, yet to my knowledge there existed not a single temple for the worship of a living king after the fall of the Third Dynasty of Ur. This underlines the fuzzy nature of royal divinization in ancient Mesopotamia: kings that were not actually deified—that is, strictly treated as gods per se—were still divinized according to the definition outlined in chapter 1.

After the fall of Ur, a linguistic and cultural split took place.[23] The Akkadian language split into two dialects: Assyrian, which was spoken in northern Mesopotamia, and Babylonian, spoken in southern Mesopotamia. Significant differences in the conceptualization of kingship in Assyria and Babylonia can be observed. Babylonian kingship, at least initially, maintained the traditions of the Third Dynasty of Ur and the kings of Agade, while Assyrian kingship moved into a different direction yet also included elements from the dynasty of Agade, which continued to function as a paradigm of kingship in Mesopotamia. There is not enough space here to go into the details of religious, socioeconomic, and cultural differences between Assyria and Babylonia; yet a few general comments may be in order. The Assyrian pantheon was headed by the god Assur, who was probably originally the divinized city of Assur. There is no mythology about Assur, and originally no family relationship with other deities were established for him.[24] In Assyrian royal self-presentation, it was always the god Assur who was the king of Assyria, that is, the land of Assur, and the earthly king was his steward. This ideology finds its clearest expression in a quote from Ashurbanipal's coronation hymn: "The god Assur is king—indeed the god Assur is king! Ashurbanipal is the [representative] of the god Assur, the creation of his hands."[25] During the second and early first millennium BCE the city of Assur was both the religious and political capital of Assyria; it was only in the ninth century (apart from a single failed attempt in the thirteenth century BCE) when kings began separating the political from the religious capital (the successive political capitals of Assyria were Nimrud, Khorsabad, and Nineveh).

Babylonia, or southern Mesopotamia, was overall more fragmented, politically and religiously. In the third and early second millennia, city-states were the predominant polities in southern Mesopotamia, interrupted by brief attempts at territorial states. Although the first religious center of Babylonia was the city of Nippur, whose patron deity was the god Enlil, the head of the Babylonian pantheon during the third and second millennia, Nippur was never the seat of a royal dynasty. The Sumerian Kingslist, which cannot be deemed historically accurate by any reasonable means, listed a number of dynasties, all located in southern

Mesopotamian cities, and stated that kingship went from one city to the next. This changed with Hammurabi of Babylon (r. 1792–1750 BCE), who broke away from this pattern of royal legitimation and created different traditions, tracing his dynasty back to the "kings who lived in tents." Dynasties in the third and early second millennium BCE were closely tied to the cities, in which they had their power bases; a dynasty could, but did not have to, consist of members of the same family. The Assyrian royal family, by contrast, may have been one of the longest unbroken dynasties, with kings coming from the same family for more than seven centuries, offering an unbroken line from the fourteenth to the seventh centuries BCE.[26]

In the third and early second millennia BCE, Enlil was the head of the Babylonian pantheon. Although Hammurabi attempted to elevate Marduk to the highest position instead of Enlil, this did not succeed until many centuries later, perhaps toward the end of the second millennium BCE.[27] The so-called Babylonian Epic of Creation (*Enuma Elish*), perhaps composed in the twelfth century BCE, is a mythological underpinning of Marduk's elevation to primary god of Mesopotamia and firmly establishes Babylon as the new axis mundi.[28] Thus, Babylon became the new religious center, but Nippur continued as a place where religious traditions were maintained. Borsippa, home of the god Nabu, became the second most important city after Babylon in the first millennium, but other cities, such as Uruk and Ur, also continued as important religious centers next to Babylon and Borsippa. Babylon had been the political capital of the Old Babylonian dynasty under Hammurabi and under the Kassites (a people not native to Babylonia who became kings during the Middle Babylonian period); it remained an important place of resistance against Assyrian domination and finally became the capital of the Neo-Babylonian empire. In spite of historical changes, Babylonian kings were never the "steward" of their gods; they referred to themselves as kings (Akkadian: *šarru*) and paid tribute to the gods. Yet according to their royal inscriptions, their main duty was to maintain regular offerings for the gods; to build their temples; and to invoke their favors through celebrating important religious festivals, such as the Akitu or New Year's festivals.

RITUALS AND KINGSHIP

Mesopotamian deities were embodied in statues that had to be washed, fed, and clothed on a regular basis. The gods received between two to four meals per day. Most of the time, temples were in charge of organizing the meals for the gods, but during times of strong centralization, kings were also involved in managing these meals. These food offerings may indicate further differences between Babylonia and Assyria.

Nicholas Postgate proposed that worship of the god Assur in the form of food offerings that were donated to the temple of the god Assur in the city of Assur translated into a geopolitical reality: those provinces and cities of the Assyrian state that contributed to food offerings for Assur held the designation "the land of the god Assur" (in Akkadian *māt Assur*).[29] Stefan Maul has also shown the importance of these food offerings for creating community in Assyria.[30] Those provinces that were conquered by Assyria but did not contribute to the food offerings for the Assur temple were said to bear the "yoke of Assur" (in Akkadian *nīri Assur*). These offerings represented a considerable economic expense, in particular for those who had fallen on hard economic times.[31]

By contrast, Babylonia remained religiously multicentered until the very end of Babylonian culture, although Babylon, the city whose patron deity was the god Marduk, was both a political and a religious capital. Even within Babylonia, and in spite of Babylon's primacy, other cities remained important: for example, the Akitu festival of the spring, the famous Babylonian New Year's festival, was not only celebrated in Babylon (although this was the most important place of celebration) but also, for example, in Uruk.[32]

All of this indicates that Babylonia was more religiously decentralized than Assyria: the first head of the pantheon, Enlil, resided in the religious center of Nippur; he was later replaced by Marduk, who resided in Babylon; beginning in the first half of the first millennium BCE, the god Nabu in Borsippa became a co-regent of Marduk and gained more and more in popularity. While Assyria had one religious center and one head of the pantheon, the Babylonian pantheon acknowledged more than one head, and even if a deity or a city lost in importance, the worship of the most important deities did not end, perhaps until the Hellenistic period and after. There is textual evidence, although it is rare, that the god Anu, the sky god who belonged to the oldest stratum of the Mesopotamian pantheon, continued to receive food offerings in his city of Uruk until at least the third century BCE. Perhaps the religious decentralization is a remnant of the times in which city-states, their patron deities, and the local pantheons were the most characteristic polities in southern Mesopotamia.

There are indications that Babylonia was often considered culturally superior to Assyria, even by the Assyrians themselves.[33] Assyrian kings frequently exploited Babylonian scholarship and accumulated knowledge, but also religious worship is telling in this context: there is thus far very little evidence for Assyrian gods, including the god Assur, having been worshipped in Babylonia, but there is considerable evidence that Babylonian gods, including Marduk, were worshipped in Assyria.[34]

Differences between Assyria and Babylonia can also be observed in how the New Year's festivals were celebrated. The Babylonian Akitu festival of the spring is by the far the best known and has been discussed time and again.[35] These festivals stand as classic examples of the rites of cosmic kingship. Although there is evidence for Akitu festivals and similar festivities having been celebrated already in the third millennium BCE, most of our textual evidence for the festivities dates to the first millennium. Both the gods and the king were required to participate in the Akitu festival; otherwise the festival did not take place.[36] In some cases, political instability prevented the images of the gods from traveling. For example, on some occasions, the god Nabu was unable to travel from Borsippa to Babylon, or Marduk could not leave his temple to travel to the Akitu house, which was located outside the city perimeters. Although Akitu festivals were celebrated in many cities in Babylonia, it is not clear if the king was able to participate in all of these festivals in person.[37] The most important Akitu festival took place in Babylon. The Babylonian festival consisted of private and public parts. The rituals took place in Marduk's temple in Babylon and in the Akitu house. The gods gathered in the Akitu house, and several rituals took place in front of the Marduk statue; a priest had to recite the "Babylonian Epic of Creation" (*Enuma Elish*[38]), the mythological elevation of Marduk as head of the pantheon. Afterward, the king had to surrender the insignia of kingship, the priest pulled the king by ear to make him kneel before Marduk, and the king had to utter his so-called negative confession ("I did not sin against Babylon, . . ."). This was followed by the priest slapping the king's face twice: if the king cried, it was a good omen for the coming year; if he did not cry, it was a negative prediction. The king's ritual humiliation took place in private and was followed by his performing rituals in front of the assembled gods, who had come to Babylon from all over Babylonia. Finally, the assembly of the gods determined the king's fate for the coming year and thus renewed his reign for another year.

A much less well known second Akitu celebration took place in the autumn. The texts have only recently been edited and analyzed.[39] For the second Akitu celebration, the king also had to surrender his royal insignia and was subsequently imprisoned for one night in a reed hut outside the city perimeters. He emerged from the reed hut the following morning, was blessed, and was given back his insignia.

The Assyrian New Year's festival of the spring differed from the Babylonian one in significant ways. While there is some scant evidence that the New

Year's festival was celebrated in the city of Assur before the reign of Sennacherib (r. 704–681 BCE), it was only with Sennacherib's attempt to transfer the Babylonian New Year's festival to the city of Assur that an Akitu house was built outside the city, just like in Babylon,[40] and most of our information about the festivities comes from the Neo-Assyrian period.[41] There is not enough room here to go into detail about the celebrations in Assur, which remained the most important city for the Assyrian kings and the place where they were buried. In contrast to the Babylonian festival, which required the participation of a priest to mediate between Marduk and the king, the Assyrian king interacted directly with the god Assur during the festivities, even wearing Assur's crown, which itself was also divinized, and the king paraded around with it, perhaps even in public. A ritual humiliation of the king, as described for the two Babylonian Akitu festivals, is not mentioned in the texts on the Assyrian Akitu festival. All of these factors together show again significant differences in the religious and ideological underpinnings and conceptualizations of kingship in Assyria and Babylonia.

ROYAL ACCOUNTABILITY, THE UNLUCKY KING, AND IMMANENTISM

In a volume debating the Axial Age transformations, Hayim Tadmor proposed that some compositions may hint at a growing awareness of royal accountability in the course of the first millennium BCE. He discussed, among others, a text called "The Sin of Sargon," in which Sargon II of Assyria was held accountable for having brought misfortune over Assyria.[42] Tadmor focused particularly on the role of scholars, in his words the *literati*, who acted as advisers to the king. Since the appearance of his article in 1986, many new texts have been published that offer a much more detailed picture of the role of the king's advisers. As already described by Tadmor, the royal advisers fell into two groups: the magnates and scholars (the latter are Tadmor's *literati*). The magnates were men from elite families, some of whom were castrates so that they could not endanger the Assyrian royal line of succession. But princes were also among the magnates, apparently so that they could become trained in the governance of the empire through firsthand experience.[43] The second group of advisers consisted of scholars; in contrast to the magnates, the scholars depended on the king for their livelihood. Their relationship to the king can best be described as that of patronage.[44] Their expertise was in divination, that is, the observation and interpretation of ominous signs, which revealed the will of the gods, to aid the king in governing. With the publication of new materials, our understanding of divination as an ancient science has matured, and images of "mad kings" who relied on superstitious advice from quacks have been abandoned.[45] It has been particularly the publication of the letter correspondence between kings and scholars, as well as the reports and queries that the Neo-Assyrian kings placed to the gods, that have led to a new evaluation of the role of scholars at the Assyrian court. The divination experts fall into several categories: those that observed the sky and the earth and those that observed the innards of sacrificial animals. The king did not just rely on the advice of a single expert but instead relied on reports by different experts who made observations independently of each other.[46] They sent their reports and their often divergent interpretations to the king independently of each other. It was up to the king to choose how to act on the basis of the advice that was given to him by the scholars and the magnates.[47] The experts that observed the innards of sacrificial animals, most often sheep, worked in groups and may also have been used as an independent fail-safe for other types of divination.

However, neither the magnates nor the scholars were always faithful servants of their king. We know of at least one major conspiracy of scholars under Esarhaddon of Assyria (r. 680–669 BCE).[48] The conspirators sought to bring one of the magnates on the throne of Assyria, but the conspiracy was discovered, leading likely to the execution of many of the magnates. There was also an incident under Sennacherib, Esarhaddon's father, in which scholars had colluded against the king to avoid informing him of negative omens.[49] This must have represented a major threat to the king because negative portends could be averted using the substitute king ritual. In this ritual, a substitute king was put on the throne of Assyria in order to draw the negative prediction onto his person, while the actual king went into hiding, where he could be protected. While the king was in hiding, he was addressed by his courtiers as the "farmer." Meanwhile, the substitute king was paraded around the country and fulfilled all of the royal duties. After 100 days had passed, the substitute king was removed from the throne and probably killed so that the Assyrian king could resume his position. Thus, the conspiracy not to tell Sennacherib about negative portends was a serious one, yet it is unclear whether the scholars did not fully inform the king because they were afraid of him or because they actively wanted to harm him.

How Assyrian kings used divination has to be situated therefore in a historical context. Tadmor mentioned the composition with the modern title "The Sin of Sargon" in his deliberations on royal accountability. The main protagonists of this composition are Sargon II of Assyria (r. 721–705 BCE) and his son Sennacherib. Sargon II had died an ignoble death on the battlefield while he was on a military campaign. In fact, it was even impossible to retrieve his body. In ancient Mesopotamia, this amounted to a calamity for kingship because it showed that the gods had withdrawn their favor not only from the king but also from the entire country that he governed. It is probably for this reason that his son Sennacherib, who followed him on the throne, disavowed his father and hardly ever mentioned him. He even abandoned the newly built capital at Khorsabad (Dur-Sharruken) and moved the capital to Niniveh. Sennacherib's Babylonian "problem" is well known; he constantly dealt with uprisings in Babylonia and led several military expeditions to Babylonia. When he finally had had enough, he claimed to have fully destroyed Babylon and to have taken the image of the god Marduk with him to Assyria. Sennacherib also found an infamous death, which was even recounted in the Bible: he was murdered by one of his own sons, who was unhappy about not having been chosen as crown prince.[50] Sennacherib's designated heir to the throne, Esarhaddon, thus came into an extremely difficult situation upon his father's death. He first had to fight his brother, who had illegitimately claimed the throne of Assyria, until he acceded the throne two months after his father's murder. Next, he also had to deal with the Babylonian problem. Esarhaddon spent enormous sums on rebuilding Babylon, but it was not until his son Ashurbanipal succeeded him on the throne that Marduk was finally returned to his home city. Thus, the story of "The Sin of Sargon," which was probably composed in the reign of Esarhaddon, has to be read against this background. The text is written in the first person and recounts how Sennacherib was worried about the death of his father and decided to ask the haruspices[51] what his father's sin may have been. He divided them into several groups to work on the answer independently of each other. The question posed to the gods was whether Sargon had honored the gods of Babylonia too much and neglected the gods of Assyria. In fact, Sargon had been known for his "Babylonia-friendly" politics, he even went to Babylon to celebrate the New Year's festival there as an acknowledgment of Babylonian traditions. Sennacherib, of course, did the opposite. To explain Sennacherib's bad luck of having been murdered by his own son, the text lays the blame for Sennacherib's failure with the Assyrian scribes, who prevented the king from making a statue of Marduk. This is interpreted as the reason for Sennacherib's murder. The text finishes with admonishing future kings to pay attention to both the gods of Assyria and of Babylonia.

It is difficult to interpret texts like "The Sin of Sargon" and other such compositions that depicted kings as fallible and out of favor of the gods. The editors of the text already connected it to the composition of the Cuthean Legend, and there are, in fact, other literary compositions depicting kings in a negative light going back to the third millennium BCE, both in Sumerian and in Akkadian.[52]

Both the Curse of Agade and the Cuthean Legend were in fact tales about Naram-Sin of Agade (see above). In the Curse of Agade, Naram-Sin is depicted as a weak ruler, who was abandoned by Enlil, the head of the pantheon. The king had attempted to build a temple for Enlil in Nippur, yet the gods withheld the proper omen from him that would have allowed him to finish building the temple. In the end, Naram-Sin becomes angry and destroys the temple, and this sacrilege spells the fall of the dynasty of Agade. Some manuscripts of this composition can be dated to the Ur III period (2112–2004 BCE), yet the majority of texts date to the Old Babylonian period (ca. 2004–1591 BCE). The Cuthean Legend is also about Naram-Sin: the composition is attested in different versions from the beginning of the second to the middle of the first millennium BCE.[53] Written in the first-person singular, the tale is about Naram-Sin deliberately ignoring the will of the gods that was communicated to him through divination. The results are devastating military defeats and the reputation of the king's reign as a failure.

Assyriologists have interpreted such texts in different ways. "The Sin of Sargon" has been read as a propaganda piece justifying Esarhaddon's enormous expenses in rebuilding Babylon to make up for his father's mistreatment of Babylonian gods: "On closer examination, however, it becomes evident that the real purpose of the author [that is, of "The Sin of Sargon"] was much more concrete: *to give Esarhaddon a useful pretext to ignore inconvenient domestic criticism, and a means for legitimizing practically any political action he decided to take.*"[54] Michalowski has interpreted other such compositions about "unlucky rulers" in light of historical narratives that contemplate the unpredictable nature of divine will and the dangers for kings who rely too much on military achievements alone,[55] while Pongratz-Leisten interprets texts such as the Cuthean Legend or the Babylonian Epic of Gilgamesh as important messages that were addressed to future kings who were meant to learn from the past.[56]

Tadmor located "that elusive embryo of 'Axial-Age' notions of the accountability of rulers" in ancient Mesopotamia in two compositions: the Hellenistic text describing the Babylonian New Year's festival, and a composition called the *Fürstenspiegel* or *Advice to a Prince*.[57] However, such an interpretation is far from clear. The well-known ritual humiliation of the Babylonian king during the Babylonian New Year's festivals, in both the spring and autumn, has been interpreted as a rite of passage, a renewal of kingship. And, as Claus Ambos has pointed out, Babylon had been plundered several times in its history, and Marduk's statue had been abducted several times.[58] The ritual humiliation and the king's affirmation therefore may be seen as a historical reflex. And, as mentioned earlier, the ritual humiliation is absent from the Assyrian New Year's festival. The composition variously referred to as *Fürstenspiegel* or *Advice to a Prince* is a text from the scholarly milieu that is only rarely attested and commonly counted among the body of wisdom literature.[59] It lists undue behavior by kings that will elicit negative reactions from the gods. The first line reads: "If a king does not heed justice, his people will be thrown into chaos, and his land will be devastated."[60]

Other compositions that have been counted among the body of wisdom literature push the boundaries of what is acceptable religiously even further, for example, the "Dialogue of Pessimism," a text that is reminiscent of the book of Ecclesiastes.[61] This dialogue between a master and his servant weighs arguments and counterarguments of various aspects of life, such as driving to the palace, banquets, hunts, marriage, love, rebellions, and sacrifice, and seems to debate the futility of life and good deeds. The following example concerns the positive and negative aspects of worshipping the gods:

> Slave, listen to me!—Here I am, master, here I am!
> —Quick, fetch me water for my hands, and give it to me:
> I want to sacrifice to my god.—Sacrifice, master, sacrifice!
> The man who sacrifices to his god is satisfied at heart:
> He accumulates benefit after benefit!
> —O well, slave, I do not want to sacrifice to my god!
> —Do not sacrifice, master, do not sacrifice!
> You will teach your god to run after you like a dog,
> Whether he asks of you (to perform) the rites, or (whether he asks you) "Do you not consult your god?" or (whether he asks of you) anything else.[62]

This unique composition is not easy to interpret. It's almost certainly a composition of the first millennium BCE. Assyriologists have interpreted it either as a serious work showing the beginnings of transcendentalism in Mesopotamia or alternatively as a work of satire. There is no doubt that there are satirical aspects in the composition, yet one can hardly deny that the irreverence displayed in the text can be referred to as skepticism, although the dialogue form remains a format that was often used for the purpose of entertainment and parody in ancient Mesopotamia.[63] Bottéro, who explicitly discussed the "Dialogue of Pessimism" in the context of transcendence, concluded that in ancient Mesopotamia, the idea of transcendence "seems to have been, so to speak, in an embryonic state."[64]

Rather than framing works of literature about unlucky rulers within a context of Axial Age transformations and the idea of transcendence, one could equally interpret these compositions as attempts by scholarly elites to explain historical misfortune in retrospect in an attempt to gain a better understanding of how to avoid such calamities in the future. Esarhaddon's ascension to the throne of Assyria was accompanied by a difficult heritage: both his grandfather Sargon and his father Sennacherib had met violent deaths, while he himself was afflicted by severe illnesses.[65] In the Mesopotamian worldview, illness and misfortune were caused by demons, witchcraft, or angry gods; if a king was ill or met an unfortunate death, it therefore signified that he had lost divine benevolence. To counteract misfortune and illness, incantations and rituals had to be performed. A person could inadvertently offend a god to make him or her angry, and so divination experts were needed to determine the cause of the illness or misfortunate, and then exorcists and other medical experts could perform the appropriate incantations and treatments.

In Esarhaddon's inscriptions, the destruction of Babylon is often phrased as the will of Marduk, who had abandoned his own city, yet in "The Sin of Sargon," it was the Assyrian scribes who prevented Sennacherib from honoring Babylonian gods. Within the Mesopotamian context, it seems more likely to interpret works that discuss royal misfortune as contemplations on the difficulty of humans to understand and interpret divine will, in other words, within the parameters of immanentism as laid out by Alan Strathern, perhaps with a few exceptions.[66] It was really the gods who determined a king's and a country's fate, yet their will remained elusive, in spite of the most advanced scientific techniques.[67]

CONCLUDING REMARKS

This whirlwind tour through some religious aspects of Mesopotamian kingship can only be superficial by necessity. Many complex topics could only be mentioned briefly or not at all. I hope to have illustrated that, throughout Mesopotamian history, divine will remained foremost among the driving forces of history and of kingship, and religion remained polytheistic, as the Seleucid ritual texts from Uruk and Babylon show.[68] The textual sources from ancient Mesopotamia offer an abundance of information, yet the mode of writing is ambiguous for modern historical interpretations. While it is important, as discussed in the beginning of this contribution, to take ancient religiosity seriously, our sources only rarely allow us to grasp fully the thoughts that lay behind the textual corpus. Our texts inform us how kings represented themselves, yet it is unclear how their contemporaries, including scholars, elites, and nonelites, perceived these kings. There are many tales about the *Nachleben* of Mesopotamian kings from other ancient sources, yet these sources have their own biases.[69] The instances of rebellions and conspiracies clearly show that not everyone was convinced of a king's divine right to rule, while the correspondence of scholars shows that it was not always clear how to interpret the will of the gods, who were seen as the main actors in world history. While kings and people were able to act, to a certain extent, within these parameters, for example, by worshipping the gods and celebrating the most important festivals, divine will remained elusive.

NOTES

I would like to express my gratitude to A. Azfar Moin and Alan Strathern for the opportunity to participate in this stimulating conference and the resulting volume. I am also very grateful for their feedback on an earlier draft of this chapter.

1. Marshall Sahlins, "The Original Political Society," in *On Kings*, ed. David Graeber and Marshall Sahlins (Chicago: HAU, 2017), 57.
2. The term *metapersons* was coined by Marshall Sahlins to express the agency and motivations that "supernatural beings" have. See Alan Strathern, *Unearthly Powers: Religious and Political Change in World History* (Cambridge: Cambridge University Press, 2019), 4 and n. 6, et passim; see also David Graeber and Marshall Sahlins, *On Kings* (Chicago: HAU, 2017) and chapter 2 in this volume by Sahlins.
3. Strathern, *Unearthly Powers*, 4. Strathern discusses in depth the characteristics of immanentist and transcendentalist religions in world history. While many of the criteria proposed there can be applied to ancient Mesopotamian religion, some may require clarification. For example, according to Strathern, *Unearthly Powers*, 35, the afterlife in immanentist religions is relatively undifferentiated and insignificant. In ancient Mesopotamia, there are stories about the afterlife, for example, the Sumerian tale of Gilgamesh, Enkidu, and the Netherworld, which was translated into Akkadian as the twelfth tablet of the Babylonian Epic of Gilgamesh, or the myth of Inanna's/Ishtar's Descent to the netherworld. The Mesopotamian notions show that the netherworld (literally, the "land of no return") was imagined as a rather bleak place where the dead eat dust and were in that sense distinct and separated from the world of the living; however, it did not hold promises of a better existence in the manner of transcendentalist religions. Another facet of immanentist religions (Strathern, *Unearthly Powers*, 60) is that the inner self is not the focus of religious life as it is in transcendentalist traditions. In ancient Mesopotamia, we can observe a development toward the end of the second and early first millennium, in which the personal god or goddess of a person takes on greater importance. While the gods are still seen as the masters of history, the ones who determine all the destinies, much of wisdom literature debates the justice or injustice of divine will. One sign of something like transcendentalism occurs with the way that the wisdom literature explicitly puzzles over the ethics and inscrutability of divine agency. For example, works such as "Let me

praise the Lord of Wisdom," an intricate composition that has often been compared to the biblical Book of Job, debate exactly this question: if a person has not committed any missteps, why is she or he being punished by bad luck and illness? The reason given relates to the inability of humanity to understand divine will. A question that can be asked here is: how then are these Mesopotamian discourses different from the biblical world? The most obvious difference is, of course, monotheism and the idea of salvation.

4. One only needs to consult the many different creation stories that circulated in ancient Mesopotamia. See Wilfred G. Lambert, *Babylonian Creation Myths: Mesopotamian Civilizations*, vol. 16 (Winona Lake, IN: Eisenbrauns, 2013).
5. Norman Yoffee and Andrea Seri, "Negotiating Fragility in Ancient Mesopotamia: Arenas of Contestation and Institutions of Resistance," in *The Evolution of Fragility: Setting the Terms*, ed. Norman Yoffee (Cambridge: McDonald Institute for Archaeological Research, 2019), 183–96. Here ancient Mesopotamia differs from Egypt, see chapter 5 in this volume by Assmann.
6. Piotr Michalowski, *The Lamentation over the Destruction of Sumer and Ur*: *Mesopotamian Civilizations*, 1 (Winona Lake, IN: Eisenbrauns, 1989).
7. Lines 365–68 of the literary work with the modern title: *Lamentation over the Destruction of Sumer and Ur*; translation after Michalowski, *Lamentation*, 59.
8. See Jerrold S. Cooper, *Reconstructing History from Ancient Inscriptions: The Lagash-Umma Border Conflict*. Sources from the Ancient Near East, vol. 2, fasc. 1 (Malibu, CA: Undena, 1983).
9. The Sumerian word for "strength" (*a2*) also has a connotation of power and influence.
10. The inscription can be found in Douglas Frayne, *Pre-Sargonic Period (2700–2350 BC)*. The Royal Inscriptions of Mesopotamia. Early Periods, 1 (Toronto: University of Toronto Press, 2008), 156–58, text E.1.9.3.9. E'annatum's title in the inscription is the Sumerian word *ensi2*, which is often translated as "ruler," "governor," or the like. In the Early Dynastic period, it was one of several titles that described the word *ruler* or *king*. See Gianni Marchesi, "Toward a Chronology of Early Dynastic Rulers in Mesopotamia," in *History and Philology*, ed. W. Sallaberger and I. Schrakamp (Turnhout, Belgium: Brepols, 2015), 139.
11. This expression means "the entire known world at the time."
12. For the most recent translation, see Benjamin R. Foster, *The Age of Agade: Inventing Empire in Ancient Mesopotamia* (London: Routledge, 2016), 318–19. Foster's translation diverges from previous interpretations; he argues that the people of Agade requested that Naram-Sin be the god of the city of Agade together with all the other deities mentioned in the text. See Foster, *The Age of Agade*, 27 n. 39. However, this interpretation seems rather doubtful, and the passage remains difficult.
13. Douglas Frayne, *Ur III Period (2112–2004 BC): Royal Inscriptions of Mesopotamia*, vol. 3/2 (Toronto: University of Toronto Press, 1997), 140–41, E.3/2.1.2.33.
14. Gonzalo Rubio, "On the Orthography of the Sumerian Literary Texts from the Ur III Period," *Acta Sumerologica* 22 (2000): 203–225. It remains unclear whether the numerous other praise poems for Shulgi were actually composed during the king's reign or whether they may have been posthumous glorifications of the king.
15. This passage is unfortunately not preserved on the Ur III manuscript.

16. Literally, "the four corners of the world," that is, the cardinal directions. This phrase refers to a claim to rule over the entire world.
17. The phrase "black-headed people" is the indigenous term for the native population of southern Mesopotamia, that is, the Sumerians.
18. Literally, "open-mouthed." I interpret this to refer to a gesture of intimidation or power.
19. I interpret this as a metaphor of speed: the horse is running so fast that its tail extends long behind him.
20. These are lines 1–19 of Shulgi hymn A. For editions, see Jeremy A. Black, G. Cunningham, Jarle Ebeling, Esther Flückiger-Hawker, Eleanor Robson, Jonathan Taylor, and Gabor Zólyomi, *The Electronic Text Corpus of Sumerian Literature* (http://etcsl.orinst.ox.ac.uk/), Oxford 1998–2006; and Ludek Vacín, "Šulgi of Ur: Life, Deeds, Ideology and Legacy of a Mesopotamian Ruler as Reflected Primarily in Literary Texts," PhD diss. (School of Oriental and African Studies, The University of London, 2011).
21. Nicole Brisch, "The Priestess and the King: The Divine Kingship of Šū-Sîn of Ur," *Journal of the American Oriental Society* 126 (2006): 161–76; Clemens Reichel, "The King Is Dead, Long Live the King: The Last Days of the Šū-Sîn Cult at Ešnunna," in *Religion and Power: Divine Kingship in the Ancient World and Beyond*, ed. N. Brisch, Oriental Institute Seminars, 4 (Chicago: Oriental Institute, 2008), 133–55.
22. It is not always possible to determine whether such offerings were made to images of living or dead kings, or both.
23. It is likely that some differences between northern and southern Mesopotamia existed before this linguistic split, but the textual attestations are uneven, and for this reason, a coherent picture cannot be drawn with any degree of certainty.
24. This only changed very late, when family relations were created for the god Assur.
25. Alasdair Livingstone, *Court Poetry and Literary Miscellanea*: *State Archives of Assyria*, 3 (Helsinki: Helsinki University Press, 1989), 26.
26. Karen Radner, "The Trials of Esarhaddon: The conspiracy of 670 BC," in *Assur und sein Umland: Im Andenken an die ersten Ausgräber von Assur*, ed. P. Miglus and J. Mª., Cordóba, Isimu, vol. 6 (Madrid: Universidad Autónoma de Madrid, 2003), 165–84.
27. Walter Sommerfeld, *Der Aufstieg Marduks in der babylonischen Religion des zweiten Jahrtausends v.Chr*. Alter Orient und Altes Testament, 213 (Kevelaer: Butzen & Bercker, 1982); Walter Sommerfeld, "Marduk. A. Philologisch I. In Mesopotamien." *Reallexikon der Assyriologie*, vol. 7 (Berlin: DeGruyter, 1987–1990), 360–70; Jonathan S. Tenney, "The Elevation of Marduk Revisited: Festivals and Sacrifices at Nippur during the High Kassite Period," *Journal of Cuneiform Studies* 68 (2016): 153–80.
28. See Lambert, *Babylonian Creation Myths*.
29. See J. Nicholas Postgate, "The Land of Assur and the Yoke of Assur," *World Archaeology* 23 (1992): 247–63.
30. Stefan M. Maul, "*Den Gott Ernähren*. Überlegungen zum regelmäßigen Opfer in altorientalischen Tempeln," in *Transformations in Sacrificial Practices. From Antiquity to Modern Times*, ed. E. Stavrianopoulou et al. (Berlin: LIT Verlag, 2008), 75–86; Stefan M. Maul, "Die tägliche Speisung des Assur (*ginā'u*) und deren

politische Bedeutung," in *Time and History in the Ancient Near East: Proceedings of the 56th Rencontre Assyriologique Internationale, Barcelona, July 26–30, 2010*, ed. L. Feliu et al. (Winona Lake, IN: Eisenbrauns, 2013), 561–74.

31. Jan-Gerrit Dercksen, "The Silver of the Gods: On Old Assyrian *ikribū*," *Archivum Anatolicum* 3 (1992): 75–100.

32. Claus Ambos, *Der König im Gefängnis und das Neujahrsfest im Herbst. Mechanismen der Legitimation des babylonischen Herrschers im 1. Jahrtausend v.Chr. und ihre Geschichte* (Dresden: ISLET Verlag, 2013), with further references.

33. Peter Machinist, "On Self-Consciousness in Mesopotamia," in *The Origins of Diversity of Axial Age Civilizations*, ed. S. N. Eisenstadt (Albany: State University of New York Press, 1986), 184–91; Grant Frame, "Babylon: Assyria's Problem, Assyria's Prize," *Journal of the Canadian Society for Mesopotamian Studies* 3 (2008): 21–31; Eckart Frahm, "Assyria and the South: Babylonia," in *A Companion to Assyria*, ed. E. Frahm. (Hoboken, NJ: Wiley, 2017), 286–98.

34. John A. Brinkman, *Prelude to Empire. Babylonian Society and Politics, 747–626 B.C*, Occasional Publications of the Babylonian Fund, 7 (Philadelphia: University Museum, 1984), 19–27; Grant Frame, "The God Assur in Babylonia," in *Assyria 1995: Proceedings of the 10th Anniversary Symposium of the Neo-Assyrian Text Corpus Project, Helsinki September 11–15, 1995*, ed. S. Parpola and R. M. Whiting (Helsinki: The Neo-Assyrian Text Corpus Project, 1997), 55–64; Frahm, "Assyria and the South."

35. See, for example, Jeremy A. Black, "The New Year's Ceremonies in Ancient Babylon: 'Taking Bēl by the Hand' and a Cultic Picnic," *Religion* 11 (1981): 39–59; Amelie Kuhrt, "Usurpation, Conquest and Ceremonial: From Babylon to Persia," in *Rituals of Royalty: Power and Ceremonial in Traditional Societies*, ed. D. Cannadine and S. Price (Cambridge: Cambridge University Press, 1987), 20–55; Annette Zgoll, "Königslauf und Götterrat. Struktur und Deutung des babylonischen Neujahrsfestes," in *Festtraditionen in Israel und im Alten Orient*, ed. E. Blum and R. Lux. Veröffentlichungen der Wissenschaftlichen Gesellschaft für Theologie, 28 (Gütersloh: Gütersloher Verlagshaus, 2006), 11–80; Ambos, *Der König im Gefängnis*.

36. The Chronicles, for example, reported that the New Year's festival could not take place while the statue of Marduk was kept prisoner in Assur (Ambos, *Der König im Gefängnis*, 24 with further references). The festival also did not take place while Nabonidus (r. 556–539 BCE) spent ten years in exile in the Southern Arabian oasis of Teima. See Ambos, *Der König im Gefängnis*, 25.

37. Ambos, *Der König im Gefängnis*, 22.

38. Lambert, *Babylonian Creation Myths*.

39. Ambos, *Der König im Gefängnis*.

40. Govert van Driel, *The Cult of Assur* (Assen, The Netherlands: Van Gorcum, 1969), 163.

41. Brigitte Menzel, *Assyrische Tempel, Band 1, Untersuchungen zu Kult, Administration und Personal*, Studia Pohl: Series Maior, vol. 10/1 (Rome: Biblical Institute Press, 1981), 55–57; Stefan M. Maul, "Die Frühjahrsfeierlichkeiten in Aššur," in *Wisdom, Gods and Literature: Studies in Assyriology in Honour of W. G. Lambert*, ed. A. R. George and I. L. Finkel (Winona Lake, IN: Eisenbrauns, 2000), 389–420.

42. For the original text, see Hayim Tadmor, Benno Landsberger, and Simo Parpola, "The Sin of Sargon and Sennacherib's Last Will," *State Archives of Assyria Bulletin* 3 (1989): 3–51. See also Hayim Tadmor, "Monarchy and the Elite in Assyria and Babylonia: The Question of Royal Accountability," in *The Origins and Diversity of Axial Age Civilizations*, ed. S. N. Eisenstadt (Albany: State University of New York Press, 1986), 203–224.
43. The princes obviously did not have to undergo castration.
44. Eleanor Robson, "Empirical Scholarship in the Neo-Assyrian Court," in *The Empirical Dimension of Ancient Near Eastern Studies*, ed. G. Selz (Vienna: LIT Verlag, 2011), 603–29; Eleanor Robson, *Ancient Knowledge Networks: A Social Geography of Cuneiform Knowledge in First-Millennium Assyria and Babylonia* (London: UCL, 2019).
45. See, for example, Eleanor Robson, *Mathematics in Ancient Iraq: A Social History* (Princeton, NJ: Princeton University Press, 2008); Francesca Rochberg, "The History of Science and Ancient Mesopotamia," *Journal of Ancient Near Eastern History* 1 (2014): 37–60.
46. Robson, "Empirical Scholarship," 609–611.
47. Karen Radner, "Royal Decision-Making: Kings, Magnates, and Scholars," in *The Oxford Handbook of Cuneiform Cultures*, ed. K. Radner and E. Robson (Oxford: Oxford University Press, 2011), 358–79.
48. Eckart Frahm, "Hochverrat in Assur," in *Assur Forschungen. Arbeiten aus der Forschungsstelle "Edition literarischer Keilschrifttexte aus Assur" der Heidelberger Akademie der Wissenschaften*, ed. S. M. Maul and N. Heeßel (Wiesbaden: Harrassowitz Verlag, 2010), 89–139; Radner, "The Trials of Esarhaddon."
49. Radner, "Royal Decision-Making," 368; Robson, *Ancient Knowledge Networks*, 77–78.
50. The Assyrian king could choose one of his male relatives as his successor; it did not necessarily have to be the eldest son. See Radner, "The Trials of Esarhaddon," 166.
51. Divination experts who examine the entrails of sheep.
52. Other such compositions depicting kings in a negative light existed. See Nicole Brisch, "Changing Images of Kingship in Sumerian Literature," in *The Oxford Handbook of Cuneiform Culture*, ed. K. Radner and E. Robson (Oxford: Oxford University Press, 2011), 715–17.
53. Joan Goodnick Westenholz, *Legends of the Kings of Agade. The Texts: Mesopotamian Civilizations*, vol. 7 (Winona Lake, IN: Eisenbrauns, 1997), 263–368.
54. Italics original. Tadmor, Landsberger, and Parpola, "The Sin of Sargon," 47.
55. Piotr Michalowski, "Early Mesopotamia," in *The Oxford History of Historical Writing*, vol. 1, ed. A. Feldherr and G. Hardy (Oxford: Oxford University Press, 2011), 5–28.
56. Beate Pongratz-Leisten, *Religion and Ideology in Assyria*, Studies in Ancient Near Eastern Records, vol. 6 (Berlin: DeGruyter, 2015), 277.
57. Hayim Tadmor, "Monarchy and the Elite," 217–18.
58. Ambos, *Der König im Gefängnis*, 136.
59. Wilfred G. Lambert, *Babylonian Wisdom Literature* (Oxford: Clarendon, 1960), 110–15.
60. Lambert, *Babylonian Wisdom Literature*, 113.

61. Lambert, *Babylonian Wisdom Literature*, 139–49. Jean Bottéro, "The Dialogue of Pessimism and Transcendence," in J. Bottéro, *Mesopotamia: Writing, Reasoning, and the Gods* (Chicago: University of Chicago Press, 1992), 251–67.
62. Translation after Bottéro, "The Dialogue of Pessimism," 255.
63. Enrique Jimenez, *The Babylonian Disputation Poems. With Editions of the* Series of the Poplar, Palm and Vine, *the* Series of the Spider, *and the* Story of the Poor, Forlorn Wren. Culture and History of the Ancient Near East, vol. 87 (Leiden: Brill, 2017).
64. Bottéro, "The Dialogue of Pessimism," 267.
65. Radner, "The Trials of Esarhaddon," 169.
66. A coexistence of immanentist and transcendentalist features of sacred kingship can also be observed in ancient Greece. See chapter 6 in this volume by Mitchell.
67. One should remember that cuneiform texts remained in a particular mode of expression; in the course of the first millennium, Akkadian was slowly replaced by Aramaic as a spoken language. Because Aramaic was written on papyri and other perishable materials, they did not preserve in the climate of Western Asia, and thus we are missing a large part of the written record. On the basis of the cuneiform written record, it is impossible to know what a Mesopotamian king really may have believed or what scholars advising the king really thought of kingship and divine will.
68. Marc J. H. Linssen, *The Cults of Uruk and Babylon: The Temple Ritual Texts as Evidence for Hellenistic Cult Practices*, Cuneiform Monographs, 25 (Leiden: Brill, 2004).
69. Ronald H. Sack, *Images of Nebuchadnezzar: The Emergence of a Legend. Second Revised and Expanded Edition* (Selinsgrove, PA: Susquehanna University Press, 2004); Isaac Kalimi and Seth Richardson, eds., *Sennacherib at the Gates of Jerusalem. Story, History and Historiography*, Culture and History of the Ancient Near East, vol. 71 (Leiden: Brill, 2014).

5

Pharaonic Kingship and Its Biblical Deconstruction

JAN ASSMANN

The thesis of the following paper is that the biblical, especially Deuteronomist, conception of rule and state was directed particularly against the ancient oriental system of sacred kingship in its most extreme and paradigmatically immanentist form, that is pharaonic kingship.[1]

Ancient Egypt was the first big state in human history. Thus, it had to be created without the possibility of following or rejecting any preexisting models and traditions.[2] In Egypt, the transition from a situation of rival chiefdoms to the foundation of the unified state took place with surprising swiftness, in the course of one or two centuries, and led to a veritable explosion of imagery and symbolic representation.[3] In sharp contrast to the archaeological evidence that bespeaks a peaceful process of economic and cultural spread and standardization, the images tell a story of violent conquest, subjugation. and annexation of the north by the south. On the famous palette of king Narmer,[4] the most typical icon of pharaonic power makes its first appearance: the pictogram of Pharaoh smiting his enemies.[5]

There must have been some conflict accompanying the emergence of the state, and the swift transition from prehistoric chiefdoms to history and state resulted, as far as political imagination is concerned, in a very fundamental dualism of south and north. Egypt is called "the two lands," and even the modern Hebrew name of Egypt, Mitzrayim, retains in its dual form (*-ayim*) the ancient Egyptian idea of duality. Pharaoh wears two crowns and two royal titles, one for Upper (*njswt*) and one for Lower Egypt (*bjtj*). We would be much mistaken, however, if we took this symbolism as expressive of any real duality. There never reigned in pharaonic history a *biti* in the north alongside a *njswt* in the south. If the kingdom split in several kingdoms in times of trouble, both or

PHARAONIC KINGSHIP AND ITS BIBLICAL DECONSTRUCTION   95

FIGURE 5.1 Palette of Narmer, (a) obverse and (b) reverse.

Source: ART181255 and ART112995, Werner Forman / Art Resource, NY

all kinglets used the title *njswt bjtj* (*insibia*), calling themselves "lord of the two lands." The dominating concept of kingship was the overcoming and unification of a foregoing duality.

The earliest royal title is Horus. It is the name of a god, the lord of Hierakonpolis, the prehistoric capital where the process of unification started. The king is the living avatar of this deity, the god of his city. Horus is a falcon, thus associated with the sky on the one hand, and with a predatory, aggressive character of swift violence on the other. The name means "the far one," derived from a verb *hrj* ("to be far") written with the sign for "heaven" or "sky" because the sky is the paradigmatically far element.

The earliest representation of Horus dating from the time of unification shows him as a falcon in a boat sailing over the sky and represented by a pair of wings, hovering above another falcon sitting on the palace façade, the *serekh*, that encloses the name of the king, "Serpent."[6] While the lower falcon functions as

FIGURE 5.2 Ivory comb of King Uadj or Djet.

Source: Public Domain

FIGURE 5.3 Senwosret III Sed Festival relief, Egypt, twelfth dynasty, 1994–1781 BCE, Madamud.

Source: ART592481, © Bildarchiv Foto Marburg / Art Resource, NY

the royal title and represents the king, the upper falcon can only refer to the sun. The whole is a remarkable visualization of the Egyptian idea of kingship as the terrestrial representation of solar power and cosmogonic energy. Horus-the-far-one expresses distance not only in the spatial but also in the social sense, meaning superiority, or lordship, and this is the obvious meaning of the name as a royal title.

An iconic representation of Horus as a sun god shows him as a sun disk with wings. This icon became, from a certain time (third dynasty, around 2750) onward, the official heraldic emblem or coat of arms of pharaonic Egypt. It was later taken over by Assyria and Persia and might have inspired other ornithomorphic imperial emblems such as the eagles and double eagles of Rome and its successors in Germany, Austria, Russia, and the United States. This icon does not refer to a god but to the idea of pharaonic kingship and may thus be recognized as a very early, original, and powerful example of political imagination.

At the time, when Horus was chosen as a royal title, this god was presumably worshipped as the highest god of the Egyptian pantheon, both as a god of the sun and as a god of the state. In all stages of Egyptian history, the roles of sun god and of state god went together and were always played by the highest god of Egypt. Thus, it is the name of the highest god that served as a title for the king, who was thereby identified with this god as his terrestrial incarnation or avatar. The king is not only a god but also the highest god incarnate.[7]

At a somewhat later stage, the original concept of incarnation is complemented by the concept of sonship. Pharaoh continues to wear the title of Horus but assumes in addition the title of "son of Re" (the sun god), which becomes even more important. This corresponds to a "constellational" concept of divinity that becomes dominant during the Old Kingdom. The divine descent of the Pharaoh is represented in a myth that must date back to the time of the great pyramids, in which the idea of pharaonic kingship finds its most grandiose expression, the time around the middle of the third millennium.[8]

The first allusion to this myth occurs in a papyrus dating from only around 1600 BCE, but the story refers to the transition from the fourth to the fifth dynasties that happened 800 years earlier.[9] Pictorial representations of the myth may date back to the same time but are only preserved from the fifteenth century on. The first occurrence appears in the funerary temple of King Hatshepsut (king, not queen, because she ruled as king and not as a king's wife) and is attested in varying versions until Roman times.

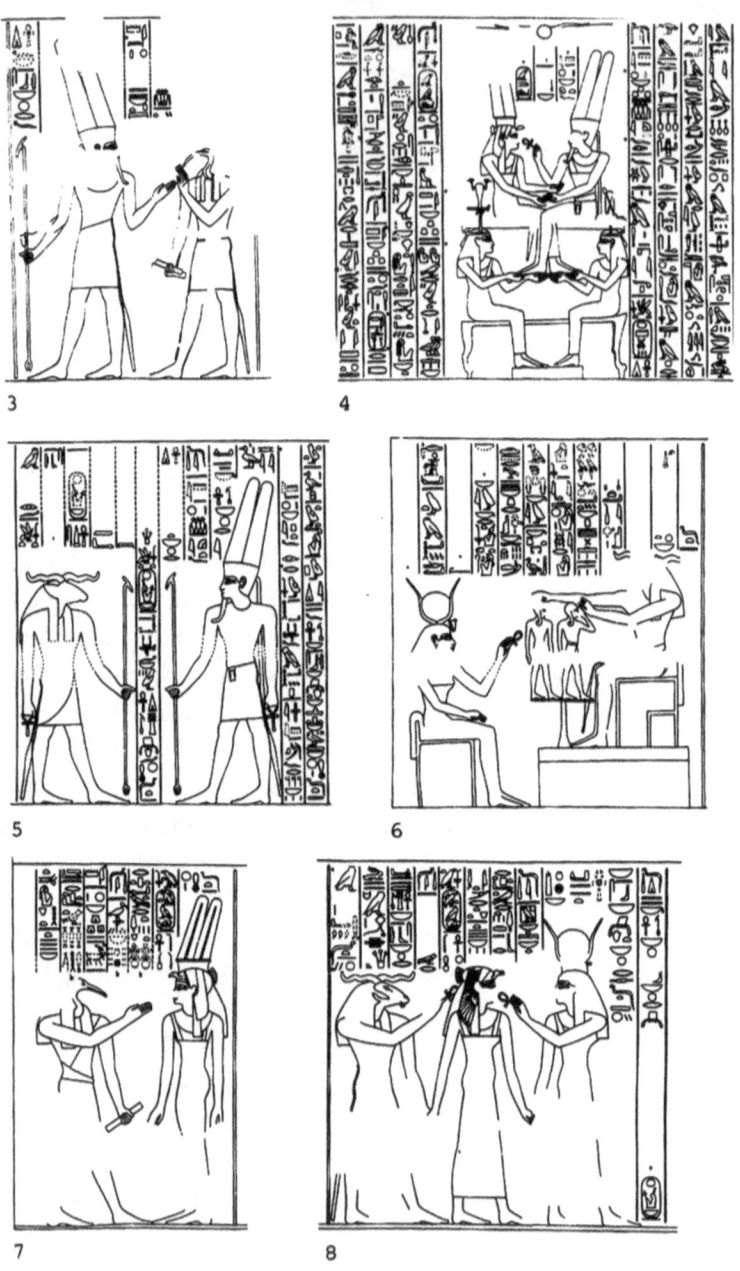

FIGURE 5.4 Divine birth of pharaoh (*Die Geburt des Gottkönigs*), scenes 1–12. From Jan Assmann et al., *Funktionen und Leistungen des Mythos* (Vandenhoeck & Ruprecht, 1982), between pp. 15 and 16.

Source: Reprinted with permission from Peeters, Leuven, Belgium and from Jan Assmann

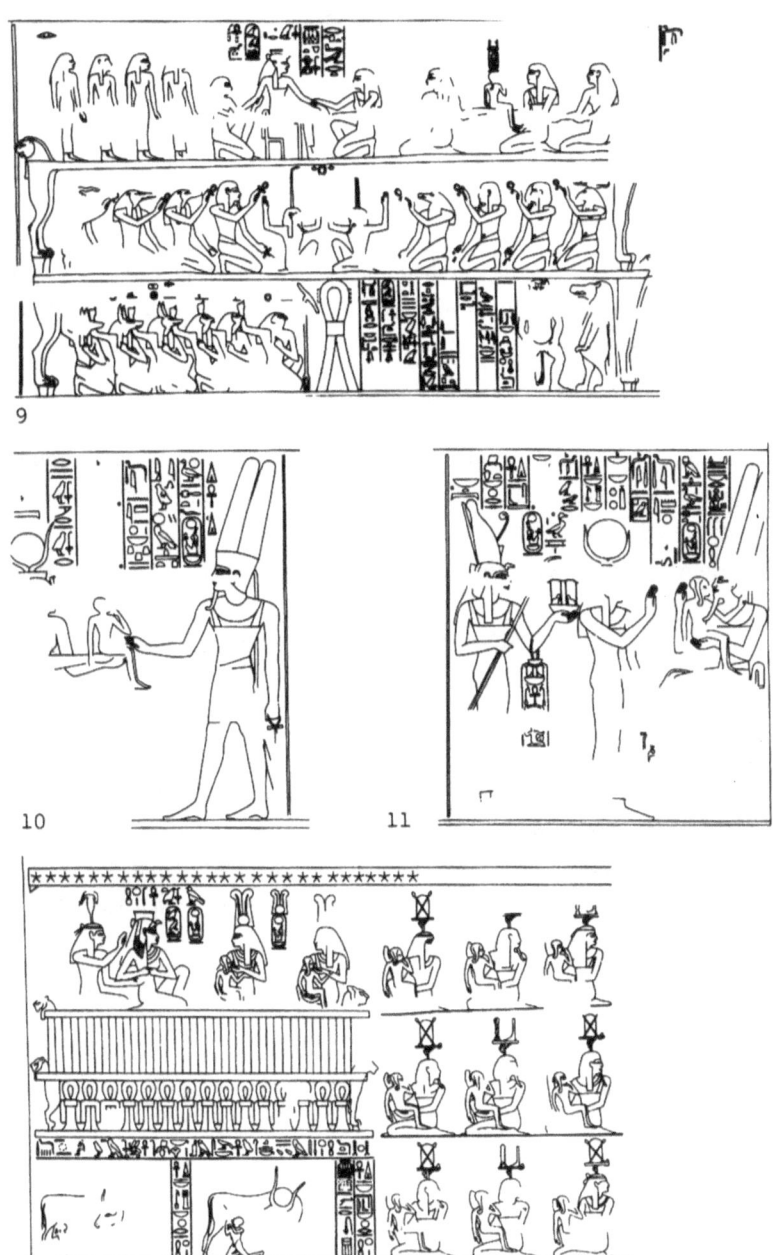

FIGURE 5.4 *Continued*

The myth is divided into a cycle of seventeen scenes, of which I am going to describe the first nine.

1. The highest god, sun god and state god, who is now Amun-Re, decides to beget a son on earth who will become king and serve the gods with temples, altars, and sacrifices, and declares his decision before the assembly of the gods.[10]
2. Amun consults the god Thot, the Hermes of the Egyptians, about a mortal woman who has raised his interest. He learns from Thot that this is the young queen of Egypt.
3. Amun is led by Thot to the queen.
4. Amun approaches the queen in the shape of her husband, the reigning king, but reveals to her his true identity.[11] The *hieros gamos* is very decently adumbrated. Amun forms the name of the future child from words exchanged between the two lovers.
5. Amun commissions the god Chnum to form the child after the image of his royal father.
6. Chnum forms the child and his "Ka" on his potter's wheel. The goddess Heqet animates the child with the sign of life.
7. Thot announces to the queen her future motherhood, addressing her with a series of strange titles.
8. The pregnant queen is led by Khnum and Heqet to the bed where she is to give birth to the divine child.
9. Several deities assist the queen who is giving birth to the child. The birth is shown in a very strange view that combines plan view and side view. This is obviously a somewhat mistaken rendering of an OK model, when this convention was in general use.

The following scenes show the recognition of the newborn child by his father Amun as his own, the breastfeeding of the child, his circumcision, purification, and final presentation to the same divine assembly in fulfilment of the former decision.

In its representation in Egyptian temples, this myth forms part of the coronation ritual. The idea is that the future king enters this divine genealogy in the course of the ritual of coronation. It is a kind of fictive rebirth and biography that is now bestowed on the king. We are dealing with a transformation, an apotheosis by coronation. The king assumes divinity together with the insignia of kingship, the crowns, sceptres, and robes. And we must not forget that all this refers only to the office and role with which the king is here invested. In all periods of Egyptian history, the Egyptians were able to distinguish between the divine office and its mortal tenant.

A frequently attested text of canonical status explains the position and task of the king on earth. Like the scenes of the divine conception and birth, this text is for the first time attested in the temple of Hatshepsut (around 1470 BCE) but is doubtlessly much older. The first stanzas describe the cosmological knowledge of the king as one initiated into the mysteries of the solar course. The last stanza begins with a more general statement:

> Re has placed the king
> on the earth of the living
> for ever and ever
> satisfying the gods, judging mankind,
> creating Ma'at, annihilating isfet.
> The king gives divine offerings to the gods
> and funerary offerings to the blessed dead.[12]

The task of the king consists in creating *Ma'at*, meaning justice, truth, order, and social harmony, and dispelling its contrary, *isfet*, thus injustice, lawlessness, lies, disorder, and disharmony.[13] He achieves this in both directions, upward, toward the gods and the dead, by means of the sacrificial cult, and downward, toward humankind, by administering justice. This is explained in other texts as rescuing the weak and poor from the strong and rich. Its main goal is not to punish the criminal but to reestablish social harmony. The main task of the Egyptian state was to establish harmony: on earth by enforcing justice, which means to rescue the suppressed, and in the cosmos by integrating society into nature, that is, into the cosmic processes of the solar circuit, the inundation, and the agricultural cycles.[14] Creating Ma'at means to establish community between state and society; humankind and the divine world; and, above all, between the living and the dead. Ma'at is the quintessential connective principle, the personification of what transforms a set of items such as people, gods, kings, spirits, and the dead into a community. Without Ma'at, there is no community, and without kingship, no Ma'at. Ma'at—this is the weak point of the Egyptian conception—depends on the state. There is a rich pessimistic literature describing and bewailing a world from which Ma'at has disappeared because the state has collapsed.[15] The aim of this literature is, of course, to teach the importance of kingship. As the world depends on the sun from which all life flows, thus humankind depends on the king, who establishes justice on earth.

Ma'at is a political concept because it answers the very political question, What keeps people together and transforms them into a community? Carl Schmitt would have answered this question by pointing to the distinction between friend and foe. The Egyptian model may be read this way. We have seen the canonical pictogram of Pharaoh smiting his enemies that runs through all periods of Egyptian history and constructs the Egyptian world in rather violent terms: Egypt against an external world of foes that must be subdued. Inside Egypt reigns Ma'at as the principle of harmony and solidarity, toward the outer world reigns violence in the service of annihilating isfet. It is easy to interpret Ma'at as the will of Pharaoh and doing Ma'at as submission to his will and regime. In its proper and classical interpretation, however, Ma'at is neither the will of Pharaoh nor of God but the abstract and independent principle of order, truth, and justice that emanates from the sun in the form of light, dispelling darkness, and that the king has to translate into the human conditions on earth in the form of enforcing justice and dispelling injustice. Therefore, Pharaoh is not absolute: he is responsible to a higher authority; he is just the son and junior partner in the task of maintaining the world.[16]

ISRAEL: PROPHETIC OPPOSITION AND DEUTERONOMISTIC REVOLUTION

In the second part of this chapter, I would like to confront this account of ancient Egyptian political imagination with its very opposite: the world of ancient Israel and its pronounced rejection of images. This confrontation highlights the political meaning of biblical iconoclasm. In the ancient world, political power tends, as we have seen, to occupy the realm of its control with iconic and symbolic representations. This may have applied also to the period of monarchy in ancient Israel, from the times of Saul, David, and Solomon down to the fall of Jerusalem, a fact that may be gathered from the numerous prophetic invectives against idolatry.[17] We must not confuse the Mosaic Law as it is codified in the second through the fifth books of Moses, which for us has become the core of biblical monotheism, with what prevailed as mainstream religion in Israel during the kingdom. The iconoclastic and monolatrous movement of the Torah was a matter of opposition born by the prophetic tradition from Amos and Hosea down to Jeremiah and Ezekiel and by a literate elite that finally asserted itself under king Josiah and gave rise to the first iconoclastic cleansing of official religion and the redaction of canonical scripture centered around Deuteronomy, containing a quite revolutionary conception of state and religion. This innovation on the political-theological plane did not lead to an iconic turn but to its contrary, a ban on images.

The prohibition of images occurs at the most prominent place within the Bible: as the first or second commandment of the Decalogue[18], together with a commentary that refers unequivocally to the political sphere:

> You shall not make for yourself a carved image, or any likeness of anything that is in heaven above, or that is in the earth beneath, or that is in the water under the earth. You shall not bow down to them or serve them, for I the LORD your God am a jealous God, visiting the iniquity of the fathers on the children to the third and the fourth generation of those who hate me, but showing steadfast love to thousands of those who love me and keep my commandments.

God resents the making of images as an act of defection and apostasy. The distinction between friend and foe, those who love and those who hate God and His Law, has a predominantly political meaning. Carl Schmitt even saw in this distinction the hallmark of the political in general. This may be going too far, but nobody will deny that the principle of association and dissociation has a fundamentally political significance. If God makes the question of images a criterion of friend or foe, belonging or exclusion, he gives it a political meaning. Whoever wants to belong to the community of God's friends must abstain from any image making and image worshipping. This story is not only about the foundation of a new form of religion but also of a new form of polity built on a treaty or covenant between God and the children of Israel. This is made clear by the whole body of legislation that follows the Decalogue as well as by the story of Exodus that forms its frame. It is highly significant that this concept of divine leadership precludes the making of images. The idea of the covenant implies a conception of direct theocracy. In the same way as the idea of direct democracy, the idea of direct theocracy precludes any mediating institutions of representation. The will of God chooses Moses as interpreter, and Moses will be followed in this function by a line of prophets down to the times of Artaxerxes, but he bans from his covenant all representations because he wants to reign directly and not by representation.

The political sense of the prohibition of images is made clear at the very beginning, during the reception of the covenant at Mount Sinai, by the scene of the golden calf, which functions as a kind of primal scene of idolatry. Moses climbed on top of Mount Sinai and stayed there for 40 days.

> When the people saw that Moses delayed to come down from the mountain, the people gathered themselves together to Aaron and said to him, "Up, make us

gods who shall go before us. As for this Moses, the man who brought us up out of the land of Egypt, we do not know what has become of him."

So Aaron said to them, "Take off the rings of gold that are in the ears of your wives, your sons, and your daughters, and bring them to me."

So all the people took off the rings of gold that were in their ears and brought them to Aaron.

And he received the gold from their hand and fashioned it with a graving tool and made a golden calf. And they said, "These are your gods, O Israel, who brought you up out of the land of Egypt!"[19]

The people did not want to defect to other gods but to replace the vanished Moses, whom they believed dead, with a representation, an image. They wanted the calf for a leader to take over what Moses had done for them, to go ahead, represent God, and intimidate any possible enemies. Moses acted for them as a representative of God; now they needed another form of mediation and fell back on Egyptian idolatry.

Representation and mediation were the principal functions of the king in the ancient world. Covenantal law aimed at destroying any forms of mediation, to radically eclipse the figure of sacred kingship, and to establish an immediate link between God and the people.

Instead of images, the king is instructed to make a copy of the text of the Torah and to learn it by heart so that his royal activities become nothing but a fulfilment of scripture.[20] This is the exact counterimage of the usual dynamics of political and iconic display of power. Where the power is handed over to an invisible God, the images must disappear and give way to scripture. We may call this a scriptural and aniconic turn and may recognize in it the same interrelatedness of politics and image making as in Egypt, only in an inverse key. The ban on images amounts to an eclipse of the king as a representative of God and a mediator between God and humankind.

The Deuteronomistic concept of the covenant or treaty—*berît* in Hebrew—that JHWH established between himself and the children of Israel has a primarily political meaning. The term *berît* occurs, however, already a century earlier with the prophet Hosea, but couched in bridal and filial metaphors and without any political connotations. Hosea is the first one to conceive of monotheism as a matter of fidelity, truthfulness, or loyalty. Like Amos, Hosea reproaches Israel for its sins, but in his eyes, these sins do not consist primarily in injustice and oppression but in "whoredom" with alien gods. I collate here several of Hosea's most striking invectives against Israel's infidelity:

They sacrifice upon the tops of the mountains, and burn incense upon the hills, under oaks and poplars and elms, because the shadow thereof is good: therefore your daughters shall commit whoredom, and your spouses shall commit adultery. I will not punish your daughters when they commit whoredom, nor your spouses when they commit adultery: for [the men] themselves consort with whores, and they sacrifice with harlots: therefore the people that doth not understand shall come to ruin.[21]

I found Israel like grapes in the wilderness; I saw your fathers as the firstripe in the fig tree at her first time: but they went to *ba'al pe'ōr*, and separated themselves unto that shame; and their abominations were according as they loved.[22]

A different image used by Hosea for the special bond between YHWH and his people is that of a father-son relationship: "When Israel was a child, then I loved him, and called my son out of Egypt. But the more they were called, the more they went away from me: they sacrificed unto Baalim, and burned incense to graven images."[23] About a century after Hosea, the original version of Deuteronomy was presented in Jerusalem as an accidental finding during restoration work in the temple and identified as a book dating from the time of Moses. This legend has a kernel of truth because it refers to the truly "Mosaic" spirit in which it is written. Deuteronomy codifies the covenant in the form of a formal treaty of alliance, thereby giving it the status of an institution recognized under international law. The covenant is now no longer metaphorical but the real thing.

The authors of Deuteronomy borrowed the model of a political contract from Assyria. The loyalty oath that in 672 BCE King Essarhaddon had his subjects and vassals swear to his designated successor, Ashurbanipal, makes its influence felt right down to the wording of the biblical text. One of those vassals must have been King Manasseh of Judah, so it may be assumed that a copy of the succession treaty and oath was stored in the royal archive in Jerusalem.[24] When applying this Assyrian template to the covenant between YHWH and the people, the biblical authors adopted and adapted it in two ways. First, God does not make this treaty with the king, in his capacity as the people's representative before the gods, but directly with the people themselves; second, the loyalty clauses are not between the people and the king, in his capacity as the gods' representative before the people, but between the people and God. In a startling innovation, the king's position as representative and intermediary is thus bypassed. Through the "transference"[25] of the king-god relationship and the king-people relationship to the relationship between God and his people, Assyrian state ideology is converted into Israelite covenant theology. The fact that God makes his covenant with the people as a whole rather than through the intercession of royalty, priesthood, or some other representative authority becomes the basis for a new; specific; emphatic; and, to some extent, "democratic" conception of the people. The people—not Moses, not the seventy elders, not Aaron, not the Levites—assume the role of a sovereign partner in the covenant. This direct access to God is what lends the biblical concept its democratic force.

In Egypt, the Pharaoh was regarded as the son of the supreme deity and given the title, son of Ra.[26] The Jerusalem monarchy also adopted the model of the king's divine sonship from Egypt. "Thou art my son; this day have I begotten thee," God tells the king in Psalms 2:7.[27] God chooses the king to be his son, a transformation that takes place the instant he is crowned. In Psalm 89:27, God pledges: "I will make him my firstborn, higher than the kings of the earth."

The image of Israel's divine sonship is firmly anchored in the Exodus myth. Unlike the bridal metaphor, which, with the prophets Hosea, Jeremiah, and Ezekiel, always has tragic connotations and looks backward to the adulterous violation of the covenant, the image of sonship in Exodus has positive connotations and looks forward to Israel's election and the fulfillment of God's promises: "Thus saith YHWH, Israel is my son, even my firstborn. And I say unto thee: let my son go, that he may serve me. And if thou refuse to let him go, behold, I will slay thy son, even thy firstborn."[28] Rather than looking back in anger at the broken covenant, the image of sonship here looks forward in hope to the liberation of Israel, soon to be exacted by the death of the Egyptian firstborn, and to the covenant, which will make the children of Israel God's chosen people and hence his adopted son.[29]

Whereas the sonship is transferred from the king to the people, the function of legislator is transferred from the king to God. On the famous Louvre-stela of Hammurabi, we see the king presenting his law code in a gesture of recitation to Shamash, the sun god and god of justice. According to the biblical concept, Moses receives the law from God. Bereft of his prerogatives of sonship and legislation, there is nothing peculiar left to the king. This is what Deuteronomy has to say concerning the role of the king:

> If, having reached the country given by Yahweh your God and having taken possession of it and, while living there, you think, "I should like to appoint a king to rule me"—like all the surrounding nations, the king whom you appoint to rule you must be chosen by Yahweh your God; the appointment of a king must be made from your own brothers; on no account must you appoint as king some foreigner who is not a brother of yours.

He must not, however, acquire more and more horses, or send the people back to Egypt with a view to increasing his cavalry, since Yahweh has told you, "You must never go back that way again." Nor must he keep on acquiring more and more wives, for that could lead his heart astray. Nor must he acquire vast quantities of silver and gold.

Once seated on his royal throne, and for his own use, he must write a copy of this Law on a scroll, at the dictation of the levitical priests. It must never leave him, and he must read it every day of his life and learn to fear Yahweh his God by keeping all the words of this Law and observing these rules, so that he will not think himself superior to his brothers, and not deviate from these commandments either to right or to left. So doing, long will he occupy his throne, he and his sons, in Israel.[30]

This is no longer the idea of kingship as represented in a paradigmatic way by King David. The king is no longer chosen by God, who says to him "Thou art my Son; this day have I begotten thee,"[31] or with regard to him—"I will be his father and he will be my son" and "Also I will make him my firstborn, higher than the kings of the earth."[32] Instead, the king is appointed by the people if they like and is seen as a danger rather than a blessing that must be restricted in his display of power as much as possible. The original idea of kingship is deferred into the future and turned into as a figure of messianic expectation. The new religion as worked out by the exilic prophets and the deported literary elite emerged in a situation of total loss: of kingship, state, temple, and territory and enabled Judaea to do without external stabilizers. Law, statehood, temple, and priesthood were created at Mount Sinai, in the desert, and in a radically extraterritorial situation. This new concept of religion no longer depends on state, kingship, and territory; it can be realized wherever Jews live and follow the law of the covenant. In this differentiation and emancipation of religion from state and territory lies the secret of the survival of Judaism and Jewry as the only nation of antiquity over two millennia of diaspora and persecution, whereas ancient Egypt and all other states and cultures of antiquity succumbed to the assault of Christianity and Islam.

NOTES

1. Like any other political entity, ancient Egypt was an "imagined community" in the sense of Benedict Anderson's *Imagined Communities: Reflections on the Origin and Spread of Nationalism* (New York: Verso, 1990). The Egyptian idea of governance

and social coherence was the achievement of political imagination. The term *imagination* is related to *image*, and I would like to start by looking at the images through which the ancient Egyptian political imagination found its most important and normative expression.
2. As a political organization, Mesopotamia is as old as Egypt, perhaps even older; it did not, however, constitute a big territorial state in the way Egypt did. It took the form of small city-states in a network of competitive and cooperative relations.
3. For the emergence of statehood in archaic societies, see Norman Yoffee, *Myths of the Archaic State: Evolution of the Earliest Cities, States, and Civilizations* (Cambridge: Cambridge University Press, 2005). For ancient Egypt, see Michael A. Hoffman, *Egypt Before the Pharaohs: The Prehistoric Foundations of Egyptian Civilization* (London: Routledge and Kegan Paul, 1980); see also Jan Assmann, *The Mind of Egypt: History and Meaning in the Time of the Pharaohs* (Cambridge, MA: Harvard University Press, 2003), chapter 1. What is perhaps most astonishing about the symbolic representations accompanying the emergence of the first Egyptian state around 3000 BCE is the fact that they seem to give a picture of the historical processes that is totally different from what may be culled from the results of archaeology. Judging from the archaeological evidence, one would reconstruct the process of unification as a peaceful process of economic and cultural spread "and" standardization. Naqada, a place near Dendera in Upper Egypt that gave the prehistoric and transitional period in Egypt its name, seems to have been the center of mass production of pottery and other commodities that spread in the course of a very short time, one or two centuries, all over Egypt, parallel to the extension of political power.
4. In this early stage of political imagination, symbolic representation had not yet formed its proper genres and made still use of prehistoric types such as slate palettes, mace heads, knives, and so on.
5. The editors would like to thank John Baines for his help with identifying and discussing some of the images discussed and presented in this essay.
6. R. Engelbach, "An Alleged Winged Sun-Disk of the First Dynasty," *ZÄS, 65 (1930)*: 115 f. pl., VIII.
7. In earliest times, when the god Horus was worshipped as a sun god, he formed a constellation with the sky in the form of the goddess Hathor, whose name signifies "the house of Horus." The king entered the same kind of relationship on earth with the land of Egypt. The land was to the king what the heaven was to the sun. With respect to the king, the goddess Hathor symbolized the land of Egypt. Hathor was the goddess of love and beauty (and in later times identified with Aphrodite and Venus), and she was worshipped as the lady of Dendara near Nagada, which was the very cradle of Pharaonic culture. Horus, on the other hand, was the lord of Hierakonpolis, which was the center of the victorious chiefdom. In later times, Dendera and Edfu were connected by a very important feast whose celebration lasted several weeks, when Hathor of Dendera visited Horus of Edfu in the form of a naval procession in order to perform a sacred marriage. One could thus presume that the relationship of king and land was also symbolized as a *hieros gamos* by means of which the king is wedded to the land, so to speak. This corresponds also to the Mesopotamian type of sacred kingship where the king

performs the *hieros gamos* with Inanna or Ishtar, the equivalent of Hathor as the goddess of love and beauty.

8. See Hellmutt Brunner, *Studien zur Überlieferung eines altägyptischen Mythos* (Wiesbaden: Harrassowitz Verlag, 1964); Jan Assmann, *Ägyptische Geheimnisse* (Munich: Wilhlem Fink Verlag, 2004), chapter 3.

9. Papyrus Westcar, as transcribed in *The Story of King Kheops and the Magicians*, ed. A. M. Blackman (London: J.V., 1988); Verena M. Lepper, *Untersuchungen zu pWestcar: Eine philologische und literaturwissenschaftliche (Neu-) analyse* (Wiesbaden: Harrassowitz Verlag, 2008).

10. This description follows the earlier version of the scene in the temple of Deir el Bahari (Hastshepsut).

11. In this, the Egyptian myth parallels the myth of Amphitryon that tells how Zeus fell in love with Alkmene, the Theban queen, and approaches her in the shape of her husband, who is engaged in a military campaign. Amun's motive is not love, however, but the wish to intervene in human history to create a new king that would prove more pious and faithful to the gods.

12. Jan Assmann, *Der König als Sonnenpriester: ein kosmographischer Begleittext zur kultischen Sonnenhymnik in thebanischen Tempeln und Gräbern* (Glückstadt: Verlag J. J. Augustin, 1970).

13. Jan Assmann, *Ma'at: Gerechtigkeit und Unsterblichkeit im alten Ägypten* (Munich: C. H. Beck, 1992).

14. These are the main functions already of the tribal chief, constituting his aspects as "rainmaker" and "lawgiver." In Egypt, there is no need for rain, and the rainmaker function is transformed into assisting the sun in its course, the Nile in its rising and falling and nature in its cycles of sowing and harvesting; these are the main functions of the cult. See also Henri Frankfort, *Kingship and the Gods: A Study of Ancient Near Eastern Religion as the Integration of Society and Nature* (Phoenix, AZ: Oriental Institute of the University of Phoenix, 1978).

15. F. Junge, "Die Welt der Klagen," in *Fragen an die altägyptische Literatur (Studien zum Gedenken an Eberhard Otto)*, ed. Jan Assmann, Erika Feucht, and Reinhard Grieshammer (Wiesbaden: Reichert Verlag, 1977); Aleida Assmann "Gewalt und das kulturelle Unbewusste. Eine Archaologie des Abendmahls," in *Aufgeklärte Apokalyptik: Religion, Gewalt und Frieden im Zeitalter der Globalisierung*, ed. Wolfgang Palaver, Andreas Exenberger, and Dietmar Regensburger (Innsbruck: Innsbruck University Press, 2007), 253–68.

16. It is tempting to reconstruct the relationship between sun and king, Ma'at, state, and humankind in terms of immanence and transcendence. The uncontested divinity of the king is a classical phenomenon of immanence, but the distinction between the divine office and the humanity of its tenant is one of transcendence and immanence. The indistinction between truth, justice, and order in the concept of Ma'at may be interpreted as immanentism, but Ma'at is certainly an ideal and transcends the immanent, the given.

17. Biblical archaeology, however, has yielded very little evidence of political imagery in ancient Israel. See Othman Keel and Christoph Uehlinger, *Göttinnen, Götter und Gottessymbole* (Freiburg: Herder, 1992), 298–321

18. The Decalogue occurs twice in the Bible, in Exodus and in Deuteronomy. In Deuteronomy, the prohibition of images belongs to the first commandment, the prohibition of worshiping other gods forming its commentary, "You shall not have other gods besides me (i.e.) you shall not make for yourself any graven image." In Exodus, the prohibition of images forms a commandment of its own. In the Jewish tradition, the prohibitions of worshiping other gods and of making images form together the second commandment, the opening self-presentation "I am YHWH your God" being counted as the first.
19. Exodus 32, 1–4.
20. Deuteronomy 17. See note 29.
21. Hosea 4:13–14.
22. Hosea 9:10.
23. Hosea 11:1–2.
24. Hans Ulrich Steymans, "Die Literarische und historische Bedeutung der Thronfolgeregelung Asarhaddons," in *Die Deuteronomistischen Geschichtswerke*, ed. Jan Christoph Gertz et al. (Berlin: De Gruyter, 2006), 331–349; Eckart Otto, *Das Gesetz des Mose* (Darmstadt: Wissenschaftliche Buchgesellschaft, 2007), 119.
25. On this concept, see Jan Assmann, *Herrschaft und Heil: politische Theologie in Altägypten, Israel und Europa* (Munich: Hanser, 2004), 63–71.
26. Mia Rikala, "Sacred Marriage in the New Kingdom of Ancient Egypt: Circumstantial Evidence for a Ritual Interpretation," in *Sacred Marriages*, ed. M. Nissinen and R. Uro (University Park: Pennsylvania University State Press, 2008), 115–44. In religious ceremonies, Pharaoh played the role of son to all the gods and goddesses in the Egyptian pantheon, his putative mothers and fathers.
27. In their commentary on the Psalms, Friedholm Hartenstein and Bernd Janowski place Psalm 2 in the "late Persian or early Hellenistic period," seeing verses 7–9 as an older relic integrated into this late psalm. Friedhelm Hartenstein and Bernd Jankowski, *Psalmen: Biblischer Kommentar (XV/1)* (Neukirchen-Vluyn: Neukirchener, 2012), 76–77).
28. Exodus 4:22–23.
29. In Jeremiah 31:9, too, God looks ahead to the new covenant by calling Israel/Ephraim his firstborn: "For I am a father to Israel, and Ephraim is my firstborn."
30. Deuteronomy 17:14–20.
31. Psalm 2:7.
32. 2 Samuel 7:14 and Psalm 89:27.

6

King, Divinity, and Law in Ancient Greece

LYNETTE MITCHELL

Т
he principle of the rule of law has often been important in the organization of western societies, from antiquity to the modern world, although not always in the same ways at all times, or with the same trajectories in all places.[1] It is a second-order principle and in this sense is "transcendent" because it arises out of a critique of the state, of what is considered to be the "natural order of things,"[2] and it is an external measure against which the behaviors of societies and their membership are judged, both in the particular and also on the general level. So law acts as a measure of what is just and morally right not only on a first order (a law-by-law) basis but also as an exterior and abstract force to which everyone has access as a power of constraint within society, and particularly the constraint of mortal rulers. The idea that rulers were no longer the embodiment of cosmic order but became constrained by law was a significant achievement of the Axial Age breakthrough.[3]

In the Greek world, the rule of law came to have a central place in both practical politics and political philosophy. Even if it is anachronistic to talk about the rule of law as such as early as the eighth century BCE and the Homeric world, one can sense the glimmerings of what would become its later significance when in epic the Cyclopes, who did not recognize law, were regarded as living outside society. In the *Odyssey* Odysseus tells the story of his travels to the land of the one-eyed monsters:

> Then we sailed on further grieving in our hearts,
> And we came to the land of the Cyclopes, arrogant and lawless ...
> For them there are neither market squares for the making of decisions
>   nor divine ordinances (*themistes*) ...

> But each makes his own ordinances (*themisteuei*) for his children and
> wives, and they do not pay any heed to each other.[4]

In the world of epic, law (the *themistes*) was immanentist in the sense that it was of the moment. It had a divine origin because it came from Zeus. Laws were not written down; were not canonized; and were interpreted principally through omens, portents, oracles, and a divinely inspired wisdom about the world.[5] The accessing of the interpretation of divine law is what the Homeric Cyclopes were unable to achieve so that they were separated from both the world of men and the world of gods and were not even able to live with each other. It is imagined, because they have no way to access law, that they are completely outside community.

The isolation from community of the Cyclopes makes it more pointed that written laws first appeared in the seventh century, particularly as a statement of community. The purpose of the earliest extant example of written law (the so-called Dreros law) was to constrain public officials (on which, see discussion below), although laws were still seen as divinely authorized and, on some level, through the just ordering of society, an expression of divine will.[6]

At the end of the fifth and beginning of the fourth centuries BCE, some intellectuals embarked on a secularizing rejection of the divine origins and nature of law, exploring its human and natural bases instead.[7] By the fourth century *nomos* was the word normally used for "law" and primarily the laws of a community, as opposed to *physis*, which was "nature." Some authors liked to play with this apparent contrast. For example, Thucydides, the historian writing at the end of the fifth century and the early fourth century, made the link between *nomos* and *physis* that justified the rights of the strong over the weak, when he has the Athenians say (in relation to their right to empire): "it is a general and necessary law (*nomos*) of nature to rule whatever one can. This is not a law we made ourselves, nor were we the first to act upon it when it was made. We found it already in existence, and we shall leave it to exist forever among those who come after us."[8]

It is in this context that Plato has Callias, in his *Gorgias* quote Pindar's poem, which began "*Nomos* is king (*basileus*) of all, of mortals and immortals" (fr. 169). There has been considerable discussion about what Pindar, writing in the first part of the fifth century, meant by *nomos* here.[9] Regardless of what Pindar intended, Plato's Callicles interprets the poem to mean that it is a natural law (*nomos*) that the possessions of the weak should be transferred to the strong. Plato's Callicles also quotes the next few lines of the poem, which explicitly emphasize the violence of this *nomos*. It is particularly pointed that this ruling *nomos* (as interpreted by Plato) is immanentist and "heroic," but it is so in a deliberately challenging way, just as Thucydides also wants to draw out and challenge the violence of the imperial "necessary law of nature" by which the Athenians claim the right to kill all the male citizens of the island of Melos and to sell the women and children into slavery.

Nevertheless, the understanding that the rule of law, encompassing all, was "of Zeus" persisted, even if the understanding of the nature of god had changed since the formation of Homeric epic. As the fourth century progressed, so did the understanding of law. The extent to which this notion of the law as a "transcendent" principle can be assimilated to "transcendentalism" as an ideal type of religiosity outlined by the authors of the introductory chapter is open to debate.[10] In general, it remained closely connected to immanentist understandings of the divine, although the exact nature of that relationship was not closely pinned down.[11] Indeed, despite the fact that, as Sally Humphreys observes, religious authority was weak,[12] the very permeability and flexibility of religious understanding gave it strength so that traditional ideas of the divine largely withstood and survived the transcendentalist tendencies emerging in philosophical circles. There were written laws that could be put on public display,[13] but no law books. There was no priestly authority outside the traditional roles, which remained pervasive in its reliance on omens to understand divine will. In the Greek context, the search for purity, at least in terms of the pursuit for "excellence" (*aretē*), as often observed, was a question for the philosophers, but even then, there was little consensus about what precisely *aretē* should encompass.

It is particularly significant that when law "rules" it is largely through the immanentist mode. Abstract law may "rule" in place of any other kind of mortal agent, but its authority still comes from the divinely ordered cosmos. So law may be transcendent in some senses, and it may also be transcendentalist in some ways because even rulers must be subject to it. As has often been recognized, it is the Greek political philosophers of the fourth century BCE (predominantly Plato and Aristotle, but also—although less frequently discussed—Xenophon) who question the relationship between kingship and law and between kingship and divinity. However, the idea of "law," like *aretē*, remains by and large an abstract virtue that is often only hazily (and inconsistently) understood in its relation either to the community or to the divine.

The matter becomes more complicated when we introduce real-life (rather than abstract or idealized) kingship into the analysis. It is often asserted that the *polis* as a "republican" political formation was the predominant form of political organization in the Greek world.[14] That assumption underpins much Axial Age scholarship so that Eisenstadt, for example, claims that the effect of the

Axial Age breakthrough in Greece was different from elsewhere because it had a different conception of accountability, which was to the community,[15] and it also underpins the analysis of Sally Humphreys, a cultural historian of ancient Greece who engages with the Axial Age.[16] However, scholarship about legitimate kingship and the Greek world (and its apparently negative counterpart, tyranny) has moved on in recent years, and it has become increasingly clear that the *polis* encompassed a variety of legitimate regime types and that the elaborated taxonomies of Greek constitutional forms by the intellectuals of the late fifth and fourth centuries are often overly schematic.

As we will see, in the Greek world, kingship, where it existed, remained essentially charismatic and heroic. While one-man rule was often ultimately rejected by these theorists, that was not because one-man rule was theoretically an impossibility or that it was not a real feature of the Greek political landscape. For Plato, the Philosopher King was desirable but, because of the natural pessimism in Greek thought, actually unachievable (Plato says that even a city constituted by the rule of the best will be shaken and disturbed "since for everything that has come into being there is ruin")[17] and so must be replaced by the rule of law. Aristotle also could contemplate the possibilities of one-man rule (as we will see below). For him, however, as for Plato, even these theoretical rulers were charismatic rulers (in the manner of real-life rulers). Yet for Aristotle too, law must rule because a living man could not achieve the perfection of *aretē* that law could.

Even if it attained a kind of transcendent status, however, law was difficult to conceive without its embodiment in at least a kind of kingship. This led to a paradox. On the one hand, akin to transcendentalist religion, it acted as the abstract judge of even kings (for Aristotle, this is implied in his claim that no man, because of his very nature, could always rule completely rationally), on the other hand, law was still understood in essentially charismatic terms. For this reason, when Alexander the Great arrived on the scene, it was possible for him, at the height of his own perfection as a charismatic king, not only to become a living god but also to take to himself the authority of law.

In the rest of this chapter, we will focus on the two strands of thinking around kingship and law in the Greek world that ran in tandem, one immantentist and one transcendent, which at different points spoke to each other and were in tension with each other, in the period from the Early Iron Age to the early Hellenistic periods, roughly the period from the eleventh to the fourth centuries BCE. We will begin in the next section by considering traditional kingship, which remained immanentist in character. The third section will look at the strand of transcendent thinking that began to emerge in the archaic period and had a different understanding of the relationship between god, king, and law: law was still of god (although the notion of god also came under discussion), but in this newly understood cosmic order, law ruled and legitimate kings were subject to it. Even when there was second-order transcendent thinking, however, there was never really a breakthrough into transcendentalism, with a complete restructuring of the relationship between god, king, and law. That is, in the Greek world, there was no righteous kingship, strictly conceived, although in a broader sense we find hints of it in the philosophical speculation of Plato. These ideas, derived from an understanding of Plato in the Roman period by the Middle and Neo-Platonists, came to be developed into something more recognizably transcendentalist and was later adopted and adapted in Islamic traditions. In the second half of the fourth century BCE, however, immanentist thinking was given a new surge with the kings who were also gods: in the final section we will turn to the age of Alexander, which marked another major shift in the relationship between kings and gods and between kings and law. Although Alexander may have been more tentative in his assertions of the relationship between rule and law at the beginning of his reign, by the mid-320s BCE, he not only seems to have declared himself divine but also seems to have insisted that, if not exactly the embodiment of law, then he was the embodiment of the power who authorized law.

TRADITIONAL AND IMMANENTIST KINGSHIP: GOD, KING, AND LAW

In the twelfth century BCE, the Mycenean palace societies of the Greek Bronze Age collapsed. In their wake, a new political order emerged, which we can mostly see in a series of "snapshots." In the first instance, these reemerging communities were small and unstable, mostly of 100 people or less, which tended to emerge and then disappear fairly rapidly. The community of Nichoria in the western Peloponnese was one of the longest-lived and at its height still numbered about forty families (about two hundred people). These Early Iron Age communities, although small and impoverished, appear to have been hierarchical in their structure, as is evident from the archaeological record, and a number of them had what has been called by Mazarakis Ainian "rulers' houses," which were not only houses where the ruler lived but also centers of cult for the community and include evidence of ritual dining.[18] At Nichoria, such a house has been identified and seems to have been the center of the community for about two hundred years. These buildings had a central hearth and an apse at one end, and they seem in many ways to prefigure archaic temples. The ruler of the community appears also to have had some kind of metahuman status (as Graeber and Sahlins have put it),[19] at least mediating between the mortal community and the divine.

From the eighth century, we find communities becoming more stable, becoming increasingly prosperous, and experiencing dramatic growth in population size and density. These factors combined brought new challenges, however, not least of which was competition among the burgeoning elite that were resolved in a variety of ways. In some communities one man dominated the rest as ruler, either through force or by election, although in others an accommodation was found—even if a tense one—for variations on power sharing among the elite, such as is suggested in Homeric epic in the description of the many *basileis* ("rulers") of Ithaca after the departure of Odysseus,[20] or rule in Phaeacia, where there were twelve *basileis* in council but Alcinous ruled as the thirteenth.[21]

Traditionally, ruling in Greek communities was charismatic and so on this level was also "heroic," in the sense that ruling was achieved through *aretē*, excellence: in warfare, through victories in the games, and in city foundations.[22] Even in the Early Iron Age there is evidence from pottery of elite pursuits,[23] and the so-called (and possibly misnamed) "Heroön" at Lefkandi on Euboea dating to the tenth century contains, alongside a high prestige warrior burial and the inhumation of a woman bedecked in gold jewelry, a burial of four horses, which perhaps suggests chariot racing.[24] In the eighth century, writing suddenly reappeared in the middle of what had obviously been a lively oral tradition,[25] and the earliest written texts, at least in part, reflect an immanentist cosmological structure in which Zeus became king of the gods because of his victory over the Titans.[26] Historical rulers in the immanentist mode also pursued charismatic strategies in order to legitimize their kingship. Victory in war was important for justifying one's right to rule, but also, with the development of games, especially the stephanitic circuit (or "crown games": Olympic, Pythian [Delphi], Nemean, and Isthmian) in the sixth century, rulers were able to make a display of their wealth and power on a panhellenic stage, and the foundation (or refoundation) of cities was also seen as a heroic activity.[27]

The heroic nature of ruling was emphasized through its connection to hero-cult. It was traditional for panhellenic victors and city founders to receive heroic-cult (whether or not they were also rulers) as a reflection of their metahuman status. But such heroic activities could also lead to ruling. Pittacus, for example, was elected ruler of Mytilene partly on the basis of his victory in a Homeric/heroic *monomachia* (one-on-one battle) over an Olympic victor (so he bettered the best) and seems to have received cultic honors on his death.[28] Miltiades of Athens was asked to become ruler of the Dolonci after his success in the games and was given cultic honors as a refounder of their city.[29] Battus I of Cyrene was also not only the first ruler but also founder of the city of Cyrene in Libya[30] and was given heroic honors on his death at his tomb in the city square.[31] In this sense, these rulers were divinized, although hero-cult did not make rulers divine (unlike later ruler-cult).[32] Hero-cult was generally achieved on death, although by the fifth century, it became increasingly possible for men to be given hero-cult during their lifetimes. It was chthonic and local rather than Olympian, however, and brought the immortality not of divinity but of eternal remembrance through cult and festivals.[33]

As well as being "heroic," Greek rulership also had a cosmic and priestly element. It is notable that the Early Iron Age rulers seem to have also been the chief religious officials for their communities, but later rulers also had or acquired priestly roles. The Deinomenid ruling family of Sicily (a family of brothers who ruled in eastern Sicily in the first half of the fifth century BCE) were the hereditary priests of the main cult of Demeter and Persephone on Sicily,[34] although their rule was based primarily on their victories in war and at the panhellenic festivals. In more traditional kingships, however, the role of the king as sacrificer and reader of portents was essential and was based on his descent from ancient heroes, especially the mythical Heracles, who achieved apotheosis (not just hero-cult) because of his deeds. At Macedon, Briant argues that if the role of the *basileus* could be reduced to one function, it would be that of "chief priest," and it is notable that after the death of Alexander the Great, his older half-brother Philip Arrhidaeus—who was thought mentally unfit to rule—accompanied the army on campaigns so that he could make the necessary sacrifices.[35] The kings of Sparta were also defined by their descent from Heracles,[36] which allowed them to undertake the sacrifices; they were also given hero-cult on death.[37]

These archaic and classical rulers ultimately received their authority to rule from Zeus. Hesiod, writing in the eighth or seventh century, says that as king on Olympus, mortal rulers were also "from Zeus."[38] Zeus gave *basileis* the scepter and the *themistes*,[39] and an important role of the ruler was to settle disputes.[40] Hesiod says:

> Calliope, she who is the chiefest of them all [the Muses], . . . attends on worshipful *basileis*: whomever of god-nourished *basileis* the daughters of great Zeus honour and behold at his birth, they pour sweet dew upon his tongue, and from his lips flow gracious words. All the people look towards him while he settles *themistes* with straight judgements *(itheiaisi dikaisi)*: and he, speaking surely, would soon make wise end even of a great quarrel; for this reason are there *basileis* wise in heart, because when the people are being misguided in

their assembly, they set right the matter again with ease, persuading them with gentle words. And when he passes through a gathering, they greet him as a god with gentle reverence, and he is conspicuous amongst the assembled: such is the holy gift of the Muses to men.[41]

The early rulers also promoted their legitimacy to rule through personal charisma. Gelon of Syracuse won an Olympic victory in the four-horse chariot race (the quadriga) in 488[42] and, already a renowned military commander, won an important battle against the Carthaginians in 480 at Himera.[43] For this victory he was acclaimed, according to Diodorus, as benefactor (*euergetēs*); savior (*sōtēr*), at least in terms of being their "rescuer" from physical danger; and *basileus* (king).[44] When he died, he was buried on the estate of his wife, Demarate, and awarded hero-cult, a sign of his "immortal remembrance."[45]

The epinician praise poetry of Pindar for the last rulers of the Battiad dynasty in Cyrene and the Deinomenid rulers of Sicily also presents us with a very traditional view of kingship, so that Kathryn Morgan has said that, while we should look to epic for the beginnings of the discussion of good and bad kingship, epinician poetry presents us with the model of the virtuous king.[46] For example, Pindar says that Hieron (ruler of Syracuse), in an ode celebrating his Olympic victory in 476 BCE, wields a *themisteion skaptron*, a scepter of lawfulness,[47] and in the ode celebrating his victory at Delphi in 470, recommends that he guides the people with a just rudder (*dikaios pēdalios*);[48] connects Hieron as *basileus* with good order and the "divinely built freedom of Hyllus [one of the sons of Heracles];" and says that, as leader (*agētēr anēr*), he instructs his son that by apportioning honors to the people he might turn them to harmonious quiet (*symphōnos hēsuchia*).[49]

Pindar also connects Hieron with Zeus, especially in the first *Pythian* (470 BCE), where Pindar invokes Zeus with his thunderbolt and "sleeping" eagle as ruler of the volcanic mountain of Aetna, the newly founded city of Aetna, and the victory at which the foundation itself was announced:

> Grant, O Zeus, grant that I may please you,
> you who rule that mountain, the brow of a
> fruitful land whose neighbouring city that bears
> its name was honoured by its illustrious founder,
> when at the racecourse of the Pythian festival
> the herald proclaimed it
> in announcing Hieron's splendid victory
> with the chariot.[50]

Indeed, Hieron himself makes the connection with his rule and the rule of Zeus. One of the Aetnaean coin issues used the iconography of an explicitly Olympian Zeus with his eagle on the scepter together with the quadriga driven by Athena and accompanied by Nike (the goddess of victory),[51] which was issued at the same time as the founding of Aetna was announced at the games at Delphi. Hieron (who must in some sense have orchestrated this coincidence of epinician and coinage)[52] wanted to present himself as a divinized ruler whose authority derived from Zeus (and was closely associated with Zeus), like the *basileis* of Homeric epic. Diodorus says that Hieron founded Aetna so that he might receive hero-cult, which he did on his death.[53]

TOWARD TRANSCENDENTALISM? GOD, LAW, AND KINGS

As noted above, the eighth century saw the reintroduction of writing in the Greek world, which had been lost with the collapse of the Bronze Age Mycenean civilization. However, these eighth-century literary works had clearly existed for a number of centuries previously as oral traditions. As a result, when they came to be produced as written texts, they operated on different levels. On one level, as we have seen, they seem to portray an immanentist cosmos where human kingship normatively reflects and flows seamlessly from the divine, and mortal kings deliver in unruptured continuity the divine will as mortal law. On another level, however, these very same texts also present a rather different and far more critical view of the relationship between mortal kings and their divine counterparts. Some parts of this early literary production are self-consciously antiheroic. The seventh-century poet Archilochus, for example, makes jokes about losing his shield in battle.[54]

However, even texts that present an immanentist worldview can simultaneously present a critique of rulership. Hesiod's *Works and Days*, in particular, delivers a bitter attack on the bribe-devouring *basileis*, who have made judgment in favor of Hesiod's brother, Perses, and deprived Hesiod of his inheritance:

> You *basileis*, mark well this punishment you also, for the deathless gods are near among men and mark all those who oppress their fellows with crooked judgements (*skolais dikais*), and do not pay heed to the anger of the gods. For upon the bounteous earth Zeus has thrice ten thousand spirits, watchers of mortal men, and these keep watch on judgements and deeds of wrong as they roam, clothed in mist all over the earth. And there is virgin Justice (*Dike*), the daughter of Zeus, who is honoured and reverenced among the gods who dwell

on Olympus, and whoever hurts her with lying slander, she sits beside her father Zeus the son of Cronus, and tells him of men's wicked heart, until the people pay for the mad folly of their *basileis* who, evilly minded, pervert judgement and give sentence crookedly. Keep watch against this, you *basileis*, and make straight your judgements, you who devour bribes; put crooked judgements altogether from your thoughts.[55]

From passages like this one, it is clear how pressured early archaic society had become by the behavior of rulers and how little trust there was in their judgments. Justice (*Dike*) as the daughter of Zeus had a role in advising Zeus, while the role of the *basileis* in delivering divine judgments is questioned, although the law-giving authority is still the mortal king. There is a kind of "proto-transendentalism" implied here: it is justice that should constrain mortal rulers.

In fact, the growing need to control the behavior of the elite is evidenced by the first known written law, which dates to the seventh century, from Dreros on Crete:

> May God be kind (?). The *polis* has thus decided; when a man has been *kosmos*, the same man shall not be *kosmos* again for ten years. If he does act as *kosmos*, whatever judgements he gives, he shall owe double, and he shall lose his rights to office, as long as he lives, and whatever he does as *kosmos* shall be nothing. The swearers shall be the *kosmos* and the *damioi*, and twenty of the *polis*.[56]

This law, laid down by the *polis*, that is, the city, appears to be an attempt to control the office of the highest magistrate in the city, the *kosmos*, and to prevent the officeholder from seizing sole rule. That such magistracies were liable to be used as a route to sole ruling is evident from other cities that resisted autocracies, such as Athens, where the role of the *archon*, the chief magistrate, likewise could prove difficult to wrest from a determined officeholder. In the early sixth century, after years of civil disruption in which the annual office of *archon* was twice suspended, a certain Damasias, who had been elected to the office, held it for two years and two months until he was driven out by force.[57]

In the law from Dreros, it is "the *polis*" that enacts the law, and Gagarin argues that this seems to mark a stage in the development of communal self-awareness at Dreros, where the political community wanted to assert itself,[58] although it is notable that the law is authorized by Zeus. However, written laws of this early period were not systematic and were not all directed at settling social and political unrest,[59] although the fact that they were written was significant. As Gagarin says: "Over the course of the archaic period . . . the new technology of writing allowed Greek law to develop from a preliterate, oral process, relying on traditional communal norms, to a more formal institution supported and defined by a body of written legislation regulating both substance and procedure."[60] As Solon, the early sixth-century Athenian lawgiver appointed as chief magistrate with full powers in 594 BCE to deal with the current crisis, says in his poetry (he was lawgiver and poet):

> I did these things by my power,
> joining strength and justice,
> and I carried it through as I promised.
> I wrote laws (*thesmous . . . egrapsa*) the same for the bad and the good,
> fitting straight justice to each.[61]

Writing, then, played an important part in the move toward the transcendent breakthrough, although it was not the whole reason for it. However, as McGlew has shown, it was important for the autonomy of the law that the fiction could be maintained that law was eternal and divine but that its nature was still essentially human and rational.[62]

More generally, the early archaic period saw a movement toward constitutionalism, which itself partly arose out of the early wave of Greek city foundations across the Mediterranean. Nevertheless, not all Greek cities had specifically written law. Apart from the Great Rhetra, it seems that the Spartans had no early written law,[63] although they did have laws that, it was said, Lycurgus, the seventh-century Spartan lawgiver, obtained from the oracle at Delphi.[64] Nevertheless, "the law" as embodied in the Great Rhetra, which formalized the relationship between the different power-sharing bodies at Sparta (the council of elders, the kings, and the assembly),[65] does seem to have existed as a written text. In the original Rhetra ("Law"), it seems that the assembly was privileged, although a later rider to the decree enacted by the two kings gave final power to the *gerousia* (the council of elders) and the *archegetai* (the two kings—Sparta had a diarchy rather than a monarchy) to overrule the assembly if it was deemed they had made crooked judgments.[66] To these bodies were later added the ephorate (at least by the middle of the sixth century), a small board of annually elected magistrates, who by the fifth century had the most power at Sparta. According to Aristotle, the ephors had responsibility for "great judgements" "on their own discretion" (*autognōmenes*)—although it would be better, Aristotle says, if they had made their judgments according to written law because the ephors were only ordinary men (*hoi tuchontes*).[67] However, the Great Rhetra, in formalizing the Spartan constitution, served also to constrain the powers of the kings. By the classical period, the Spartan kings were able to act autonomously only when they were on campaign,[68] and even then they were required to obey the commands of the ephors, which was considered law.[69]

By the sixth century, transcendent ideas were on the rise across the Greek world as part of the wave of rationalist and critical thinking about the natural world and its relation to the cosmos that was emerging largely out of Asia Minor. These new ideas changed the relationship between gods and men and between kings and gods, and the nature of the gods themselves.[70] Xenophanes, a poet as well as a political thinker from the city of Colophon at the end of the sixth century, is the first known of the early philosophers to challenge the traditional anthropomorphic views about the gods.[71] Heraclitus of Ephesus, who may have been influenced (even if not directly) by Xenophanes,[72] was said to have renounced his claim to kingship in favor of his brother[73] and claimed that it is law informed by a divine but abstract ideal of justice that holds a city together:

> It is necessary for those who speak with sense to use all their strength for the common cause of all, just as even a city is strengthened by law (*nomos*). For all human laws (*pantes hoi anthropeioi nomoi*) are nourished by one law, the divine law (*theios*); for it rules as much as it wishes, is sufficient for all, and is superior.[74]

Toward the end of the sixth century, it became a standard trope, especially in the literature associated with or coming out of Athens, that law should rule and that kings ruled under law, even if the nature of that law (divine law or human law) was also being questioned.[75] Any ruler who did not accepts the constraints of law was branded a tyrant. Herodotus, in particular, the historian of the Persian Wars (born in Halicarnassus but probably writing primarily for an Athenian democratic audience in the 420s BCE), developed the contrast between the tyrannical king (who ruled outside law) and the democratic state,[76] and the same idea plays out in other literature of the period. Euripides, in his play *Suppliants* (also produced in the 420s), has Theseus, mythical king of Athens, say:

> There is nothing worse for a city than a tyrant.
> In the first place where there are not common laws (*koinoi nomoi*),
> but one man rules and law
> resides in his own person, there is no longer equality (*ison*).
> But where the laws are written down, the man who is weak
> and the one who is wealthy have equal access to justice (*diken isen echein*) . . .
> and the small man with right on his side defeats the great man.[77]

In the late fifth century and early fourth century, ideas about rulership took another turn, and (rather surprisingly) a positive theory of kingship emerged in democratic Athens.[78] It is striking that even in the political imagination, legitimate rulers (even if ruling under law) had to be charismatic and heroic. For example, in Herodotus, when the case is made for positive kingship (rather than tyranny), it is rule of the "best" man, who rules through, and as a result of, ancestral law (*patrioi nomoi*).[79] Likewise, in the fourth century, Xenophon, Plato, and Aristotle also play with the idea of ideal rulers, who are essentially divinized and heroic in character.

Xenophon, for instance (writing probably in the mid fourth century), in his *Cyropaedia* (the *Education of Cyrus*, a pseudohistorical work about the sixth-century Cyrus the Great of Persia), attempts to reinvigorate the idea of legitimate rulership (apart from tyranny) by means of its charismatic character and suggests that the good and legitimate ruler achieves the willing obedience of his subjects through his superior *aretē* in all things. Willing obedience was the central pillar of Cyrus' success and security as a ruler.[80] It is based on the good ruler, who is wiser (*phronimōteron*—in the sense of having greater learning: 1.6.23), stronger, and braver than anyone else[81] and better able to endure hardship.[82] Xenophon tells us elsewhere (in reference to another Persian, a contemporary of Xenophon's, Cyrus the Younger, in whose Greek mercenary army—the Army of the Ten Thousand—Xenophon fought) that it is the proof of a ruler's excellence, his *aretē*, when his subjects obey him willingly and that it was the younger Cyrus' eagerness to exert himself and work hard that made him a good man.[83]

Yet the relationship between the ruler and law was not uncomplicated. In the *Cyropaedia*, Cyrus (the Elder) is trained in written law, as was his father.[84] Nevertheless, Xenophon says that Cyrus justified his right to rule because he was "particularly adorned among men with *aretē*," and that, while he understood the importance of written law, he thought the good ruler was "seeing law" for his subjects "because he was in a position to make an assessment, see the wrong-doer, and punish them."[85] What Xenophon means by "seeing law" is not entirely clear, but Aristotle later seems to echo the thought when he says that "Law provides rulers with an education fit for purpose, and then sets them to judge and manage the rest with a mindset which is most just. Further, it permits them to correct whatever seems, in their experience, to be better than the established laws."[86]

However, Aristotle rejects the rule of an earthly ruler in favor of civic law. This is in part brought out through his analysis of the *Pambasileus* (King of all; Absolute King), who, he says, in order to justify his rule, must have incomparable *aretē*. In his discussion of the *Pambasileus*, Aristotle does not clearly define "incomparable *aretē*," although in the *Nicomachean Ethics*, he says that *aretē* encompasses Homeric ideas of military skill and courage but also other qualities, such as temperance and endurance, and that superabundant *aretē* in particular is a human quality aimed at achieving, through actions and choices, happiness and the good life, which by practice becomes habit.[87] In the *Politics*, however, the *Pambasileus* is like a god among men.[88] As a result, he cannot be subject to law, for men of this kind are law, and if there were to be any man of such exceptional *aretē*, Aristotle argues, it would not be possible for him to be ruled because that would be like ruling Zeus.[89]

Nevertheless, Aristotle finally rejects the idea that this man rather than law should rule because a man always has passion that corrupts him, whereas law is reason without desire.[90] For Aristotle, the rule of law is the rule of god and reason,[91] and law, which is divinized to some extent, is fundamental because laws are needed to restrain the natural impulses of men so that they can live in community with each other and to provide a framework for the good man to live his life well.[92]

Plato, on the other hand, Aristotle's teacher, had a different soteriological vision. As has been noticed, it is Plato who comes closest of the Greek philosophers to transcendentalism, in whose philosophy the purpose of life is the search for "justice." Throughout his dialogues, he turns to the acquisition of *aretē* by individuals through education for creating the best society,[93] although for Plato (like Aristotle) *aretē* is generally defined in terms of moral virtues rather than the more strictly martial sense of epic.[94] While, as Annas has shown, even in the *Republic*, the law is fundamental for the creation of the ideal city and for education, especially of the rulers,[95] the best society is achieved through the search for justice, which does not bring about individual happiness itself so much as create a situation where those who are just are also happy.[96] In the *Republic* the Philosopher King, who is a "lover of wisdom,"[97] is so aligned with divinity and orderliness that he will make himself as divine and orderly as is humanly possible[98] because only divine kingship would be able to interpret the divine (or natural) law of the cosmos; then, like a painter and craftsman, through his constitution, he makes the characters of men pleasing to god.[99]

In Plato's *Laws*, on the other hand, god and law are central, but Plato had become disheartened with the possibility of the Philosopher King,[100] who cannot bring salvation because any man would become hubristic and unjust (this sentiment echoes Herodotus, who says that no ruler, even the best man, ruling alone, would be uncorrupted).[101] As is often noted, the *Laws* begins by asking whether the laws are from god or from man, and the Athenian stranger says emphatically that they are from god,[102] a point reinforced throughout the *Laws* but especially in Book 4. These laws encompass unwritten laws (*agrapha nomima*), ancestral laws (*patrioi nomoi*), and written laws—even those laws still to be written.[103] Nevertheless, these laws are necessary for achieving "*aretē* as a whole (*pasa aretē*),"[104] so that it is now the city and its laws (rather than the Philosopher King) that bears the responsibility for creating just citizens. In fact, Plato insists that even rulers must be subject to the laws: "for in whatever state law is master (*despotēs*) of the rulers, and the rulers are slaves of the law," then (the Athenian stranger says), "I see that the gods give salvation (*sōtēria*) to cities and as many good things as there are."[105] So the route to virtue (and happiness) for Plato, in his divinely inspired philosophical cosmos, is god-inspired law for the city.[106]

ALEXANDER THE GREAT: KING AS GOD AND LAW

It is against the philosophical background of Xenophon, Plato, and Aristotle (or in the middle of the philosophical maelstrom that they created) that we also need to understand Alexander the Great, who became the ruler in Macedon in 336 BCE on the death of his father, Philip II. Alexander was probably tutored by Aristotle, at least for a short time, in his youth, so he was almost certainly aware of this philosophical theorizing of kingship. Nevertheless, in practical terms, he seems to have assumed the parts of kingship theory that suited his own ambitions.

If we can believe Plutarch (writing in the second century CE), Alexander seems to have taken seriously his alleged descent from Achilles (from his mother) and Heracles (through the Argead clan of his father[107]), and modeled himself on the heroes of epic.[108] If our sources can be believed (which admittedly are generally very late), he saw himself in competition with these mythological predecessors, especially Heracles (who was said to have achieved apotheosis on death because of his achievements) and the god Dionysus.

His rule was charismatic, like that of his predecessors in Macedon, a claim that could be made principally on account of military success—his father Philip II had been almost continuously at war throughout his reign, and Alexander himself was already an accomplished warrior when, at the age of eighteen, his father put him charge of the prestigious left wing of the cavalry at the battle of Chaeronea in 338 BCE.[109] This was a decisive victory and gave Philip control of Greece, as a result of which he created a Greek league for an attack on Asia (an ambition that had excited the Greek imagination since the Persian wars at the beginning of the fifth century).[110] However, in 336 BCE, having put together plans for a campaign in Asia, Philip was assassinated at the wedding of his daughter Cleopatra.

Alexander became king of the Macedonians (probably by acclamation of the army), although he had a half-brother Arrhidaeus, who, for reasons that are obscure (he was said to be incapacitated), was not considered able to rule.

In 334, after putting down rebellions in Greece and to the north against the Illyrians, Alexander undertook the campaign against Asia his father had planned, although whether his father's ambitions were the same as Alexander's are unclear. Alexander, a brilliant military tactician, had unprecedented success against the Persian armies, first at the river Granicus in 334 BCE, then (after success in Asia Minor) another major victory against the Persian king, Darius III, at Issus (in which Alexander took the Persian baggage train, including the Persian royal family) in 333 BCE. He then moved down the coast of the Levant, taking by siege Tyre and Gaza, and undertook a detour to Egypt, which had been under Persian control on and off since the sixth century BCE but which relinquished itself willingly into his hands. In 331 BCE, he faced another battle against Darius at the strategic site of Gaugamela in Mesopotamia (near the important river crossing at Arbela). The Persian army again was defeated, and the king fled. Alexander meanwhile made his way south to Babylon, Susa, Persepolis and Pasargadae (all major Persian centers—Pasargadae was where the tomb of Cyrus the Great, founder of the Persian Empire, was located), before pursuing Darius to Ecbatana (modern Hamadan), and then into Hyrcania. Darius was betrayed by members of the inner court, however, and left on the road to die. Alexander declared himself Lord of Asia.

It seems probable that Alexander now had "world conquest" in his sights (such was the limited understanding of geography at the time that this was thought possible),[111] and Alexander then continued to Bactria (capturing, torturing, and killing Darius' assassin, as Darius' "legitimate successor") and then through Sogdia into the Hindu Kush. On this route he was undefeated in battle, even by the formidable forces of the Indian Porus and his elephants. At the river Hyphasis, however, our sources tell us that Alexander's soldiers rebelled and refused to carry on further east. Alexander and his land army then returned to Babylon (almost disastrously by way of the Gedrosian desert); he died at Babylon from uncertain causes in 323 BCE.

At some point during his reign Alexander seems to have assumed the status of a living god, although it is uncertain at what point this was fully realized. There is no doubt that Alexander lived the life of a charismatic and heroic ruler, having been undefeated in battle. Hero-cult for rulers, as we have seen, was well established, but the claim for Olympian status was different. Alexander was not the first Greek to claim full divinity: this was said to be Lysander, who was the Spartan commander who engineered the Spartan victory over Athens in 404 but who died in 396 BCE,[112] and Dion of Syracuse in the 350s also seems to have been given honors as a living god.[113] There are also suggestions that Philip II of Macedon, Alexander's father, may also have been tempted by ideas of his own divinity. After his victory over the Greeks at Chaeronea in 338 BCE, he built the Philippeium, a building in the sanctuary at Olympia that included statues of the royal family, and just before he was assassinated in 336 BCE at his daughter's wedding, part of the ceremonial included a procession of statues of the gods—and of Philip as the "thirteenth" [Olympian] god.[114]

Nevertheless, it was a significant step for Alexander to assume his own divinity as an Olympian god and on equal standing with Zeus. During his visit to Egypt in 332 BCE, Alexander visited the sanctuary of Zeus Ammon at Siwah in Libya. The ancient accounts vary considerably about what happened at the sanctuary, but it does seem possible that he was at least declared by the priests to be the "son of Zeus Ammon," whatever the full implications of that may have been.[115] Recently discovered inscriptional evidence from Egypt proves that he acquired the titulary "son of Ammon" probably when he became pharaoh of Egypt (this was part of the normal titulary for Egyptian pharaohs and was part of the indication of the divinity they acquired on succession).[116] However, the significance for Alexander is less certain. Does this just mean that he was taking on the normal pharaonic titulary, or was this the moment when there was a shift in his thinking and he came to understand himself not just as a hero but as a man who had become a god, and an Olympian god at that?

Certainly by 326 or shortly after, he seems to have been linking himself directly with Zeus. The so-called Porus medallion, a silver coin now in the British Museum from an unknown mint, depicts a small figure on horseback fighting an elephant on the obverse (see figure 6.1a), and on the reverse what is in all likelihood meant to be the same figure now holding a thunderbolt (in Greek iconography it is normally only Zeus who carries the thunderbolt; see figure 6.1b). This coin is usually interpreted as representing Alexander's victory over Porus and his elephants at the Hydaspes River in the Indus in 326 BCE. Yet as further evidence of his ambitions, in 324 he seems to have sent an edict to the Greek cities requiring that they worship him as a god: evidence from Athens suggests that a statue was erected for him there as *aniketos theos*, "unconquered god."[117]

He also seems to have seen himself increasingly as the authorizer of law, although it is unclear whether this sprang from his rulership, which had become increasingly absolute, or his divinity. When Philip, Alexander's father, had defeated the Greek armies at Chaeronea in 338, he made a settlement with the Greeks (the so-called League of Corinth) that had a constitutional framework drawing on Greek diplomatic precedents. The constitution of the league seems

FIGURE 6.1 The Porus Medallion, after ca. 326 BCE. Silver coin. Weight 42.200 grams. Representation of Alexander the Great after his victory over Porus.

Source: Reprinted with permission the Trustees of the British Museum

to have included a number of clauses to protect the Greek cities from each other and possible incursions from league members (Philip was very careful to call himself "leader" of the league rather than ruler or king). Key among these were clauses that prevented interference with the constitutions of the member states and forbade the forced return of political exiles and dissidents to the Greek cities.[118] However, in 334 BCE, in a decree from the Greek island of Chios, Alexander commanded the Chians to reconstitute their city as a democracy; to redraft the laws, which had then to be approved by him; and to take back the exiles.[119] While there are some questions about the relationship of the island states to the League of Corinth, Alexander in this decree is being strongly interventionist,[120] but even more he becomes the authority that authorizes civic law.

That Alexander came to the point of explicitly overturning the constitution of the League of Corinth is made clear by that fact that, in 324, Alexander issued a decree (the Exiles Decree) requiring the Greek cities to accept any exiles back into their citizen bodies, with the threat of Macedonian reprisals if they did not.[121] While Alexander was not claiming he was "above law" (although some accused him of acting tyrannically[122]), he observes law as the chief arbiter and interpreter of what *is* law, as absolute king and presumably as god incarnate.[123] In assuming this position, he goes beyond even the immanentist world of the

Homeric heroes, who are not gods; he is making very particular claims about his metahuman status—he has completely surpassed the human state and achieved (before death) his apotheosis to Olympus.

Rather than thinking about a transition from immanentist thinking to transcendent thinking or even transcendentalism in relation to kingship, we can see that in the Greek experience these strands of thought existed in parallel. In trying to establish "traditional" claims for kingship, Greek rulers emphasized the ways that they were upholding Homeric virtues and replicating Homeric patterns of charismatic and heroic rulership. In the earlier periods, this kind of rule often led to cultic honors, which were local and chthonic, and normally achieved on death. In the fourth century, Alexander's kingship was rather different as he seems to have come to view himself as an Olympian god (indeed even on a par with Zeus). On the other hand, there was another strand of thinking that was increasingly critical, rational, and transcendent in character, and took a different view on kingship, where a king could only rule legitimately if he himself ruled under law. If he did not place himself under law or ruled outside law, then he would be a tyrant.

The issue of tyranny was something that rulers came to feel very defensive about. Dionysius I of Syracuse, who at the end of the fifth century seems to have tried to model his own rule in some ways on that of the Persian kings, also wrote a poem (he was also a prize-winning dramatist at Athens) in which he declares that "tyranny is the mother of injustice."[124] Xenophon's *Cyropaedia* tries to demonstrate that not all autocratic rule is illegitimate rule, especially if the ruler is able to capture the willing obedience of his subjects. It is also probable that Alexander was more careful in the earlier part of his reign to present himself as a "lawful" king, although that claim inevitably became more strained, especially after he murdered and had assassinated various key members of the inner court.

Thinking on kingship, however, still understood kingship under law as essentially charismatic: Greek rulers needed to show that they were born to be heroic kings (they claimed descent from heroes, even if this was retrospective) and then spent the rest of their careers proving it. Cyrus in the *Cyropaedia* is king because, through a combination of his innate qualities and education, he has greater excellence than anyone else (e.g., 8.1.21), just as Plato's Philosopher King or Aristotle's *Pambasileus* also had an abundance of *aretē*. For the most part, thinking on kingship only reached toward transcendentalism, and then for the most part only in the context of abstract thinking on ideal kingship. Once Alexander and his successors declared themselves living gods, the question of how to rule in relation to law was repositioned, and the lines were redrawn. In 291 or 290 BCE, Demetrius Poliorcetes (the "Beseiger") was received in Athens with hymns and libations for a god incarnate;[125] however, afraid of his displeasure, the Athenians also voted that whatsoever King Demetrius should ordain, this should be held righteous toward the gods and just toward men.[126]

That did not mean, however, that there was not resistance to these god-kings. The Athenians may have given Alexander his statue of the "unconquered god," but that was only after debate in the assembly. Apparently, when the Spartans were asked to acknowledge Alexander's divinity, they replied, "If Alexander wishes to be a god, let him be a god."[127]

Through deity, however, Alexander and his successors solved the problem of kings ruling under law: as gods, they were law. As Aristotle had argued, if there was a man of such exceptional *aretē*, he could not be subject to law, for men of this kind are law, and it would not be possible for him to be ruled because that would be like ruling Zeus, especially if that man also dared to hold Zeus' thunderbolt.

NOTES

1. B. Z. Tamanaha, *On the Rule of Law: History, Politics, Theory* (Cambridge: Cambridge University Press, 2004), provides an interesting summary of the development of the different strands of the idea of the rule of law from antiquity to modern Western liberal democracy.
2. See A. Momigliano, *Alien Wisdom: The Limits of Hellenization* (Cambridge: Cambridge University Press, 1975), 8–9; S. C. Humphreys, "'Transcendence' and Intellectual Roles: The Ancient Greek Case," *Daedalus* 104 (1975): 91–118.
3. S. N. Eisenstadt, "The Axial Age: The Emergence of Transcendental Visions and the Rise of the Clerics," *European Journal of Sociology* 23 (1982): 303.
4. Homer, *Odyssey* 9.105–15.
5. See J. L. Ready, "Omens and Messages in the *Iliad* and *Odyssey*: A Study in Transmission," in *Between Orality and Literacy: Communication and Adaption in Antiquity*, ed. R. Scodel (Leiden: Brill, 2014), 29–55. The Greeks considered the earliest oracle to be at the sanctuary of Zeus at Dodona in northwest Greece (Herodotus 2.52.2).
6. There is still significant debate about the extent to which laws were codified at this early date. See K.-J. Hölkeskamp, "Written Law in Archaic Greece," *Proceedings of the Cambridge Philological Society* 38 (1992): 87–117; K.-J. Hölkeskamp (1992), "Arbitrators, Lawgivers, and the 'Codification of Law' in Archaic Greece," *Mètis* 7 (1992): 49–81. See also R. Osborne, "Law and Laws: How Do We Join Up the Dots?" in *The Development of the Polis in Archaic Greece*, ed. L. G. Mitchell and P. J. Rhodes (London: Routledge, 1997), 74–82.

7. Some Athenian intellectuals asserted that laws were simply human convention, just as the gods themselves were convenient mortal inventions, for example, Critias? Fragment 19 (*Sisyphus*) with M. Wright, *The Lost Plays of Greek Tragedy: Volume 1: Neglected Authors* (London: Bloomsbury, 2016), 56–58. In fact, it was often argued, nature, *physis*, had preeminence over *nomos*: see, for example, W. K. C. Guthrie, *The Sophists* (Cambridge: Cambridge University Press, 1971), chapter 4. Antiphon's treatise *On Truth* (late fifth or early fourth century) understands law as a human construct whereas *nature* carries a greater compulsion for men to act justly: "A man ... can best conduct himself in harmony with justice, if when in the company of witnesses he upholds the laws, and when alone without witnesses he upholds the edicts of nature. For the edicts of the laws are imposed artificially, but those of nature are compulsory" (Antiphon, in G. J. Pendrick, *Antiphon the Sophist: The Fragments* (Cambridge: Cambridge University Press, 2002), fragment 44(a) I.12–27).
8. Thucydides 5.105.2.
9. Plato, *Gorgias* 484a–c. See M. Ostwald, "Pindar, *Nomos*, and Heracles (Pindar, Frg 169 [Snell2]+POxy. No. 2450 Frg. 1)," *Harvard Studies in Classical Philology* 69 (1965): 109–38.
10. See chapter 1; see also Alan Strathern, *Unearthly Powers: Religious and Political Change in World History* (Cambridge: Cambridge University Press, 2019), 21–22.
11. Sophocles' *Antigone* (440s BC) plays out the tension between the universal law of the gods that the dead should always be properly buried and the civic law, which prohibited the burial of her brother, Polyneices.
12. S. C. Humphreys, "Dynamics of the Greek Breakthrough: The Dialogue Between Philosophy and Religion," in *The Origins and Diversity of Axial Age Civilizations*, ed. S. N. Eisenstadt (Albany: State University of New York, 1986), 93.
13. At Athens, Solon's laws were published on the *axones/kyrbeis* in the marketplace from the sixth century BCE, but there are questions about levels of literacy and the degree to which they were actually canonical. See R. Thomas, *Oral Tradition and Written Record in Classical Athens* (Cambridge: Cambridge University Press, 1989), 34–93. One of the real problems for Athenian written law until the reforms of the early fourth century was that it was generally based on decreesof the assembly with no proper administration or archive, and so was quite random, disorganized and often contradictory. See, for example, M. Carnevero, "*Nomothesia* in Classical Athens: What Sources Should We Believe?," *Classical Quarterly* 63 (2013): 139–60.
14. See J.-H. Gehrke, "States," in *A Companion to Archaic Greece*, ed. K. A. Raaflaub and H. van Wees (Malden, MA: Blackwell, 2009), 394–410.
15. Eisenstadt, "The Axial Age," 303.
16. Humphreys, "'Transcendence' and Intellectual Roles"; Humphreys, "Dynamics of the Greek Breakthrough."
17. The idea that all things must decline is deeply rooted in Greek thought. See Hesiod, *Works and Days*, 109–201 (on the so-called ages of man from the race of gold, which descended to the race of iron); Thucydides 2.64.3: "it is also natural for all things to decline." For parenthetical quote, see Plato, *Republic*, 545d–546a.
18. A. Mazarakis Ainian, *From Rulers' Dwellings to Temples: Architecture, Religion and Society in Early Iron Age Greece (1100–700 BC)* (Jonsered: Paul Åströms förlag, 1997).

19. D. Graeber and M. Sahlins, *On Kingship* (Chicago: HAU, 2017).
20. For example, Homer, *Odyssey* 1.389–98.
21. Homer, *Odyssey* 8.390–91.
22. See L. G. Mitchell, *The Heroic Rulers of Archaic and Classical Greece* (London: Bloomsbury, 2013), 57–90.
23. J. P. Crielaard, "*Basileis* at Sea: Elites and External Contact in the Euboean Gulf Region from the End of the Bronze Age to the Beginning of the Iron Age," in *Ancient Greece: From the Mycenean Palaces to the Age of Homer*, ed. S. Deger-Jalkotzy and I. S. Lemos (Edinburgh: Edinburgh University Press, 2006), 271–97.
24. The name Heroön may be a misnomer because there is no evidence of cult (although the question has been asked about what cult would look like at this date). However, whether the building was ever a ruler's house or whether it was built as the tomb of the warrior remains unclear. M. R. Popham, P. G. Calligas, and L. Hugh Sackett, *Lefkandi II: The Protogeometric Building at Toumba: Part 2, The Excavation, Architecture and Finds* (Athens: British School at Athens, 1993).
25. One of the earliest pieces of extant evidence for writing in Greek is a vase from an eighth-century Greek burial at Pithecusae in southern Italy. The cup (so-called Nestor's cup) has inscribed on it what appears to be a joking reference to Nestor's golden cup from the *Iliad* 11.632–67.
26. Hesiod, *Theogony* 881–86. See also Hesiod, *Works and Days*, 668.
27. See especially Mitchell, *The Heroic Rulers*, 73–78.
28. See Mitchell, *The Heroic Rulers*, 65.
29. Herodotus 6.35–36, 38.
30. R. Meiggs and D. Lewis, *Greek Historical Inscriptions to the End of the Fifth Century*, rev. ed. (Oxford: Oxford University Press, 1988), no. 5.
31. Pindar, *Pythian* 5.86–95.
32. On ruler-cult, see especially S. Price, *Rituals and Power: The Roman Imperial Cult in Asia Minor* (Cambridge: Cambridge University Press, 1984), 23–40.
33. On hero-cult in the Greek world, see K. Buraselis et al., "Einleitung: Terminologische Vorklärung," s.v. "Heroiserung und Apotheose," in *ThesCRA*, vol. 2, ed. K. Buraselis et al. (Los Angeles: J. Paul Getty Museum, 2004), 126–29.
34. Herodotus 7.153.2–154.1. See also Diodorus 5.2.3. The Deinomend family had been among the original Greek settlers of Sicily and founded the cult of Demeter and Persephone: Lindian Chronicle, *Brill's New Jacoby* 532 fragment 3.28, scholia for Pindar, *Pythian* 2.27b, both with T. J. Dunbabin, *The Western Greeks: The History of Sicily and South Italy from the Foundation of the Greek Colonies to 480 B.C.* (Oxford: Oxford University Press, 1948), 64n6.
35. P. Briant, *Antigone le Borgne. Les débuts de sa carrière et les problèmes de l'assemblée macédonienne* (Paris: Les Belles Lettres, 1973), 326–27n2.
36. Herodotus 8.114.2; Xenophon, *Lacedaimonion Politeia* 15.2.
37. Mitchell, *The Heroic Rulers*, 138–39.
38. Hesiod, *Theogony* 96.
39. For example, Homer, *Iliad* 9.96–99.
40. M. Gagarin, *Early Greek Law* (Berkeley: University of California Press, 1986), 19–50.

41. Hesiod, *Works and Days* 79–93. Adapted from the translation by H. G. Evelyn-White *Hesiod, the Homeric Hymns and Homerica* (Cambridge, MA: Harvard University Press, 1977).
42. Pausanias 6.9.4. See also *Inschriften von Olympia*, ed. W. Dittenberger and K. Purgold (Berlin: Asher and Co., 1896) 143. M. Scott, *Delphi and Olympia: The Spatial Politics of Panhellenism in the Archaic and Classical Periods* (Cambridge: Cambridge University Press, 2010), 176 ("One of the most impressive [of the athletic victory statues at Olympia] was the tyrant Gelon, who dedicated the sanctuary's second life-size chariot group following his victory in 488 BC.")
43. Diodorus 13.94.5.
44. Diodorus 11.26.6. On the face of it, these titles may appear anachronistic, but as titles of praise, they do appear in Pindar, so they may well be genuine. See Mitchell, *The Heroic Rulers*, 85, note 68.
45. Diodorus 11.38.4–5, and Diodorus 11.38.6; cf. 14.63.3.
46. K. Morgan, *Pindar and the Construction of Syracusan Monarchy in the Fifth Century BC* (Oxford: Oxford University Press, 2015), 2–3.
47. Pindar, *Olympian* 1.12.
48. Pindar, *Pythian* 1.186.
49. Pindar, *Pythian* 1.60–65, and *Pythian* 1.69–70.
50. Pindar, *Pythian*, 1.29–33. Translated by W. H. Race, *Pindar: Olympian Odes, Pythian Odes* (Cambridge MA: Harvard University Press/Heinemann, 1997).
51. K. Rutter, *Greek Coinages of Southern Italy and Sicily* (London: Spink, 1997), 127–29.
52. See C. Dougherty, *The Poetics of Colonization. From City to Text in Archaic Greece* (New York: Oxford University Press, 1983), 83–102.
53. Diodorus, 11.49.2.
54. Archilochus in M. West, ed., *Iambi et Elegi Graeci*, 2nd edition (Oxford: Oxford University Press, 1989-92), fragment 5.
55. Hesiod, *Works and Days* 248–64. Adapted from the translation of H. G. Evelyn-White, *Hesiod, the Homeric Hymns and Homerica* (Cambridge MA: Harvard University Press/Heinemann, 1977).
56. R. Meiggs and D. Lewis, *Greek Historical Inscriptions to the End of the Fifth Century*, revised ed. (Oxford: Oxford University Press, 1988), no. 2. The *kosmos* must be the principal official for the city.
57. *Athenaion Politeia* = *Constitution of the Athenians* 13.1–2.
58. M. Gagarin, *Writing Greek Law* (Cambridge: Cambridge University Press, 2008), 78–79.
59. See note 5 above.
60. Gagarin, *Writing Greek Law*, 92.
61. Solon in M. West, ed., *Iambi et Elegi Graeci*, 2nd ed. (Oxford: Oxford University Press, 1989-92), fragment 36.15–20.
62. J. F. McGlew, *Tyranny and Political Culture in Ancient Greece* (Ithaca, NY: Cornell University Press, 1993), 107–8.
63. Plutarch, *Lycurgus* 13.1. See D.M. MacDowell, *Spartan Law* (Edinburgh: Edinburgh University Press, 1986), 3–5.

64. Herodotus 1.65.2–4; Xenophon, *Constitution of the Lacedaemonians* 8.5. Nevertheless, not all laws in our sources said to be "laws of Lycurgus" were enacted by Lycurgus, but a large part of the Spartan constitution, especially as it was known in the classical period, was retrospectively attributed to him. See, for example, M. Flower, "The Invention of Tradition in Classical and Hellenistic Sparta," in *Sparta: Beyond the Mirage*, ed. A. Powell and S. Hodkinson (London: Classical Press of Wales, 2002), 191–217.

65. The text preserved in Plutarch is problematic, but there is general agreement (supported by a fragment of Tyrtaeus: fragment4 *IE* West) that in the original law, the *demos* (the people) had the ultimate power of decision making. Z. Papakonstantinou, *Lawmaking and Adjudication in Archaic Greece* (London: Bloomsbury, 2008), 58, 162, n. 32.

66. Plutarch, *Life of Lycurgus* 6.1–2, and 6.7–8. Papakonstantinou, *Lawmaking and Adjudication*, 58–59.

67. Aristotle, *Politics* 2.1270b27–31.

68. See Thucydides 8.5.3.

69. Even Agesilaus, a fourth-century Spartan king who managed to assert his will beyond that achieved by normal Spartan kings and who in some ways can be seen as a precursor to Alexander the Great, abandoned his successful campaign in Asia in 394 BCE and returned home when summoned by the ephors because he thought he was constrained by law (Xenophon *Hellenica.* 4.2.1–4; *Agesilaus* 1.36). In the *Agesilaus*, Xenophon says that Agesilaus chose not to be the greatest man in Asia but to rule at home according to the laws and to be ruled in respect of them (2.16).

70. See, for example, Humphreys, " 'Transcendence' and Intellectual Roles."

71. J. H. Lesher, *Xenophanes of Colophon: Fragments—A Text and Translation with a Commentary* (Toronto: University of Toronto Press, 1992), 80–118.

72. C. H. Kahn, *The Art and Thought of Heraclitus: An edition of the Fragments with Translation and Commentary* (Cambridge: Cambridge University Press, 1979), 1–24.

73. Diogenes Laertius 9.1.6.

74. H. Diels and W. Kranz, *Die Fragmente der Vorsokratiker*, 6th ed., in 3 vols (Berlin: Weidmann, 1951-1952), B 22 fragment 114.

75. A debate seems to have emerged in the mid-fifth century about the relative importance of the mortal and divine laws, as seen most clearly in Aeschylus' *Eumenides* of 458 BCE (which affirms the right of mortals to judge divine law) and Sophocles' play *Antigone* of the 440s (where the laws of the city—as formulated by the king, Creon—are brought up sharply against the "natural" laws of the gods).

76. See Herodotus 3.80.

77. Euripides, *Suppliants* 429–38.

78. L. G. Mitchell, "Political Thinking on Kingship in Democratic Athens," *Polis* (2019): 442–65. See also W. D. Desmond, *Philosopher-Kings of Antiquity* (London: Continuum, 2011), 19–43; and M. Schofield, *Plato* (Oxford: Oxford University Press, 2006), 22.

79. Herodotus 3.82.2, 5.

80. *Cyropaedia* 1.1.3; cf. Xenophon, *Oeonomicus* 21.12.

81. Xenophon, *Cyropaedia* 1.6.22–6, 3.1.20: "If people think others are better than themselves, they will generally obey them willingly without compulsion." See also 4.1.19, 22–24, 2.11.

82. Xenophon, *Cyropaedia* 1.6.20-5. See also. *Agesilaus* 4.3, 10.2.
83. Xenophon, *Oeonomicus* 4.19 and 4.25. See also *Cyropaedia* 8.1.39.
84. Xenophon, *Cyropaedia* 1.3.16–18; see also 1.2.3, 6–7.
85. Xenophon, *Cyropaedia* 8.1.21–22.
86. Aristotle, *Politics* 3.1287a25-8.
87. Aristotle, *Nicomachean Ethics*, 1.1103a2–7, 2.1103a14–1103b25, 2.1106b36–1107a2, 6.1144a1–22, 6.1144b1–7.1145a27, 7.10.1178a9–1179a32. R. Kraut, "Aristotle's Ethics," in *The Stanford Encyclopedia of Philosophy*, ed. E. N. Zalta, Summer 2018 Edition, https://plato.stanford.edu/archives/sum2018/entries/aristotle-ethics/.
88. Aristotle, *Politics* 3.1284a9-11; see also *Nicomachean Ethics* 7.1145a27–9.
89. Aristotle, *Politics* 3.1284a11–14, 3.1284b25-34; see also 3.1288a15–29.
90. Aristotle, *Politics* 3.1287a8–32 with 3.1284a3–22, 3.1284b25–34, 3.1286a18–20, 33–5. W. R. Newell, "Superlative Virtue: The Problem of Monarchy in Aristotle's *Politics*," in *Essays on the Foundation of Aristotelian Political Science*, ed. C. Lord and D. O'Connor (Berkeley: University of California Press, 1991), 191–211.
91. Aristotle, *Politics* 3.1287a28–30.
92. Aristotle, *Politics* 7.1326a29-31, and *Nicomachean Ethics* 9.1180a14-18. See also T. H. Lindsay, "The 'God-like Man' Versus the 'Best Laws': Politics and Religion in Aristotle's *Politics*," *Review of Politics* 53 (1991), 488–509.
93. For example, Plato, *Republic* 492a.
94. See Desmond, *Philosopher–Kings of Antiquity*, 19–43. See also M. Schofield, *Plato* (Oxford: Oxford University Press, 2006), 37.
95. J. Annas, *Virtue and Law in Plato and Beyond* (Oxford: Oxford University Press, 2017), 10–31; but compare to Cohen, who argues that Plato rejects the rule of law: D. Cohen, *Law, Violence and Community in Classical Athens* (Cambridge: Cambridge University Press, 1995), 43.
96. E. Brown, "Plato's Ethics and Politics in *The Republic*," *The Stanford Encyclopedia of Philosophy*, ed. Edward N. Zalta (ed.), 2017 https://plato.stanford.edu/archives/fall2017/entries/plato-ethics-politics.
97. For example, Plato, *Republic* 500c.
98. Plato, *Republic* 500c–e; note especially c–d.
99. Plato, *Republic*, 501a–b, 502b. Schofield notes, "By this point the philosopher has turned into a figure of sacral authority: a divine incarnation, a law-giving prophet like Moses": M. Schofield, *Plato: Political Philosophy* (Oxford: Oxford University Press, 2006), 161–63 (quotation from 162). See also Desmond, *Philosopher–Kings of Antiquity*, 27–28. See also *Theaetetus* 175b-176b: to become like God is 'just and holy with intelligence' (176b), an idea picked up and developed by later Platonists, such as Plutarch and Plotinus, in the Roman period.
100. Plato, *Laws* 875a–b; see also 712a, 713e.
101. Desmond, *Philosopher–Kings of Antiquity*, 30–31. For Herodotus, see 3.80.3.
102. Plato, *Laws* 624a.
103. Plato, *Laws* 793a–c.
104. Plato, *Laws* 630e.
105. Plato, *Laws* 715e.
106. For example, Plato, *Laws* 718b.

107. See also Herodotus 5.22 with 8.138.2.
108. For example, Plutarch, *Life of Alexander* 2.1, 8.2.
109. Diodorus 16.86.1, 3.
110. See L. Mitchell, *Panhellenism and the War Against the Barbarian in Archaic and Classical Greece* (Swansea: Classical Press of Wales, 2007).
111. See K. Geus, "Space and Geography," in *A Companion to the Hellenistic World*, ed. A. Erskine (Malden, MA: Blackwell, 2003), 232–45. Some have argued, however, that Alexander did not intend to do more than take the Persian Empire and had no thoughts of further conquest; most recently T. Howe and S. Müller, "Mission Accomplished: Alexander at the Hyphasis," *Ancient History Bulletin* 26 (2012): 21–38.
112. Douris of Samos, *Brill's New Jacoby* 76 fragment 71.
113. See Chr. Habicht, *Divine Honors for Mortal Men in Greek Cities: The Early Cases*, trans. J. N. Dillon (Ann Arbor: Michigan University Press, 2017), 1–3, 5–6.
114. On the Philippeium, see especially E. D. Carney, *Women and Monarchy in Macedonia* (Norman: University of Oklahoma Press, 2000), 212–15.
115. This seems to be the implication of both Arrian's and Diodorus' account of Alexander's visit to Siwah (Arrian, *Anabasis*, 3.3.–4; Diodorus, 17.49.2–51.4). Plutarch also knows this version of the story but undercuts it by saying that it was a slip of the tongue; he claims that Alexander was only addressed by the oracle as "my son" (*o paidion*) rather than as "son of Zeus" (*o pai dios*) (*Alexander* 27).
116. F. Bosch-Puche, "The Egyptian Royal Titulary of Alexander the Great, I: Horus, Two Ladies, Golden Horus, and Throne Names," *The Journal of Egyptian Archaeology* 99 (2013): 131–54; F. Bosch-Puche, "The Egyptian Royal Titulary of Alexander the Great, II: Personal Name, Empty Cartouches, Final Remarks, and Appendix," *The Journal of Egyptian Archaeology* 100 (2014): 89–109.
117. Hyperides, *Demosthenes* 32.
118. Pseudo-Demosthenes 17.10, 16.
119. P.J. Rhodes and R. Osborne, *Greek Historical Inscriptions, 404–323 BC* (Oxford: Oxford University Press, 2003), no. 84.
120. Rhodes and Osborne, *Greek Historical Inscriptions 404–323*, 418–23.
121. Diodorus 18.8.3–5.
122. Pseudo-Demosthenes 17.4.
123. L. Mitchell, "Alexander the Great: Divinity, and the Rule of Law," in *Every Inch a King: Comparative Studies in Ancient and Medieval Kingship*, ed. L. Mitchell and C. Melville (Leiden: Brill, 2013), 91–107.
124. Dionysius, *Tragicorum Graecorum Fragmenta*, ed. R. Kannicht, B. Snell and S. Radt, in 5 vols. (Göttingen: Vandenhoeck & Ruprecht, 1971–2004), 1.76 fragment 4.
125. Demochares, *Brill's New Jacoby* 75 fragment 9. See A. Chaniotis, "The Ithyphallic Hymn for Demetrios Poliorketes and Hellenistic Religious Mentality," in *More Than Gods and Less Than Men: Studies on Royal Cult and Imperial Worship*, ed. P. P. Iossif, A. S. Chankowski, and C. C. Lorber (Leuven: Peeters, 2011), 157–95.
126. Plutarch, *Life of Demetrius* 24.3–4.
127. Aelian, *Varia Historia* 2.19.

7

Humanizing the Divine and Divinizing the Human in Early China

Comparative Reflections on Ritual, Sacrifice, and Sovereignty

MICHAEL PUETT

This chapter will explore the workings of ritual orders in regard to sovereignty, as well as the attempts to unmask such orders from a transcendental perspective—both in antiquity and in more recent scholarship. I will begin by sketching out the comparative categories that have been developed for these issues. I will then bring material from China into the discussion to see how our categories may be enhanced.

SACRIFICE AND REJECTIONS OF SACRIFICE

For much of human history, rituals of sovereignty were focused predominantly on the practice of sacrifice. Before turning to these rituals, however, it may be helpful to turn first to the recurrent attempts to unmask these rituals and, in many cases, reject sacrifice altogether. Such attempts have appeared throughout world history. But in Eurasian history, the move has been institutionalized at particular moments.

The first of these moments occurred in the first millennium BCE. This was a distinctive period in Eurasian history. The agricultural regions of Eurasia had been dominated for some two millennia by a Bronze Age aristocracy. Over the course of the first millennium BCE, these Bronze Age kingdoms collapsed. Because this was a pan-Eurasian phenomenon, the reasons for the collapse are, not surprisingly, pan-Eurasian as well. The spread of iron technology throughout Eurasia made available for use a naturally occurring substance that could be mass-produced for agricultural implements as well as weapons. The mass production of agricultural implements led to a tremendous population growth, while the mass production of iron weapons, together with the growing population, encouraged the emergence of mass infantry armies. The latter in turn encouraged the growth of various forms of centralized states to build, arm, and train such mass infantry armies. The result was the gradual (and sometimes not so gradual) collapse of the Bronze Age kingdoms across the agricultural areas of Eurasia as well as a collapse of the institutionalized forms of rituals supported by these kingdoms.

Throughout these areas, the collapse also led to the emergence of new religious movements calling for even more radical transformations. Many were opposed to the emerging mass infantry states and formed alternate religious communities. This is the period that has come to be known as the Axial Age—roughly the fifth through second centuries BCE.[1] Some of the most famous examples of these movements include the Orphics, Pythagoreans, Platonic Academy, and Aristotelean Lyceum in Greece; the Jains and Buddhists in India; and the Mohists, the followers of Confucius, and the followers of Laozi in China.

Meanwhile, centralized states based on mass infantry armies continued to grow, and by the last few centuries of the common era, the agricultural areas of Eurasia had become dominated by a limited number of empires—the Roman empire in the western end of Eurasia, the Han in the eastern end, and the Mauryan in South Asia. In reaction to the success of these empires, a series of salvationist religions began breaking out in the first centuries of the common era. Many of these involved a radicalization of the earlier religious movements of the Axial Age. Among these include Christianity and (later) Islam in the western end of Eurasia, Mahayana Buddhism in South and later East Asia, and the Celestial Masters (the beginning of the Daoist religion) as well as the Great Peace movement in China.

The movements in both of these periods—the Axial Age movements of the first millennium BCE and the salvationist religions of late antiquity—involved some common claims that we will explore below. Alan Strathern has proposed a general terminology to mark this distinction in religious orientations: immanentist versus transcendentalist.[2] *Immanentist* refers to the dominant forms of religious practice throughout much of the world, and *transcendentalist*, as the name implies, refers to those movements—institutionalized strongly in the Axial Age and the subsequent salvationist religions—that appeal to transcendental sources of truth. But one generalization that holds with few (and telling) exceptions is that almost all of these movements rejected sacrifice and worked to unmask earlier sacrificial ritual according to transcendental claims. No longer would the world depend on ritual relations with a wide range of divine powers.

With these general themes in mind, let us turn to the different ways these tendencies became manifest in different areas of Eurasia, as well as the historical ways these differences played out. As we will see, in some areas of Eurasia, the salvationist religions gained state support, thus leading ultimately to the eradication of sacrifice as well as the forms of sovereignty based on the practice, whereas elsewhere we see the emergence of hybrid regimes. These different permutations had tremendous historical implications.

COMPARATIVE FORMS OF SOVEREIGNTY

Let us begin with the world of sacrifice—the immanentist practices, as Strathern has called them. And let us do so by turning to the work of Georges Dumézil. Although Dumézil's main concern was with reconstructing Indo-European mythology, he occasionally pointed to moments when the issues he was discovering had larger comparative significance. One of these issues was the set of rituals concerning the installation of a king. Dumézil pointed out that the rituals he was discovering concerning the installation of rulers in Rome, Persia, and India had clear analogues from a larger anthropological perspective with those seen in Polynesia and Africa.[3]

Inspired by Dumézil, Marshall Sahlins has since undertaken such a comparison of these installation rituals, with a particular focus on the Fiji Islands.[4] Sahlins follows Dumézil in analyzing the ways in which different social groups are placed in the installation rituals and the ways in which the monarch is presented as ultimately encompassing them all—noting throughout the parallels with Rome, India, and Persia. In an endnote, Sahlins remarks in passing on the parallels historically between this ritual sequence and historical sequences in antiquity and modern Europe: "And should we not notice the longer historical duration in which monarchy is superseded by republic, to be replaced in turn by a totalitarian imperialism—or even the repetition of the cycle in modern European history?"[5]

For Sahlins, paralleling both the ritual complex explored by Dumézil as well as this larger historical pattern are myths of the origins of the state, myths that often revolve around what Sahlins has termed a "stranger-king": a transgressive, usually foreign figure who breaks into the world of the indigenous populace, introducing violence into a previously peaceful world. In many of these narratives, the populace then kills the stranger and domesticates his transgressions. The result is a hierarchical social order that partakes of both the initial, peaceful population and the transgressive introducer of violence.[6]

In Dumézil's terminology, that hierarchical social order consists of the populace below (the third function); the military, now defined as a particular function (the second function); and the priests of the indigenous gods (the first function). But in Sahlins's reformulation, such a hierarchical structure is just one possible outcome of the dynamic described. On top is a kingship that partakes of both of the initial founding principles and thus encompasses the entire social order. This can result in a diarchic kingship in which the one ruler represents the more warrior-like transgressive figure, and the other ruler represents the claims of gravitas associated with the priests. It can also result in a kingship in which both claims exist simultaneously, with the ruler partaking of each at particular moments. And the degree to which a given royal lineage traces itself back to a founder in the form of a stranger-king or in the form of a domesticated sacerdotal ruler has tremendous implications for the nature of the claimed sovereignty.[7]

Two of the mythic founders of Rome that Dumézil discusses fit this larger pattern as well: Romulus, who is associated with violence (*celeritas*), and Numa, who is associated with sacerdotal status (*gravitas*).[8] Sahlins builds on this point, analyzing the narratives from Livy, Plutarch, and Dionysius of Helicarnassus that discuss the war between the followers of the militaristic Romulus and the peaceful Sabines. The Roman state is then presented as a result of this war, with a resulting tension between violence and fertility.[9]

Strathern has discussed this distinction as well and proposed a more broadly comparative terminology of heroic kingship and cosmic kingship. Heroic forms of rulership would involve the more active portions, while cosmic forms would involve the sacerdotal portions.[10] Such a broader terminology allows for the inclusion of more examples than those that fit into a framework specifically derived from—as we shall see—a particular type of ritual order.

Let us say a bit more about that ritual order and the forms of sovereignty found therein.

VITALITY AND VIOLENCE

The variations we have touched on so far derive from Indo-European and Polynesian materials. In both cases, we see a world of vitality, understood as the generative processes of the land and the indigenous inhabitants who oversee it, and on the other hand, an introduction of violence that shatters this world of vitality. The transgressive dimensions of the founding figure are then symbolically sacrificed, as he is remade by and remakes the domestic order. The result is a new hierarchical social order that links the vitality of the land with the militaristic violence of the outsider, overseen by a sovereign that encompasses both.

Ritual in both cultural areas demonstrates the logic clearly. Sacrifice in both Indo-European and Polynesian societies was often a ritual instantiation of this violent appropriation of vitality for the sake of humanity—a ritual equivalent of the transgressive stranger-king breaking into the world of nature and appropriating its fruits for himself. The world prior to sacrifice would often be posited as continuous, with everything interrelated and often derived from a common ancestor. The goal of sacrifice was to break humanity from this continuity and thus allow humanity to appropriate some of the vitality of that continuity for itself. For many Polynesian cosmologies, for example, everything prior to sacrifice was claimed to be linked in genealogical lines of continuity.[11] Humans would then break from this continuity, achieving both autonomy for humanity as well as the ability to appropriate the natural world for human consumption.[12]

Or, to return to the Indo-European world, a clear example is Vernant's famous reading of the myth of Prometheus as given by Hesiod. According to Hesiod, sacrifice recapitulates the transgressions of Prometheus, transgressions that won for humanity autonomy from the gods, but at the cost of a life of deprivation and ultimately death. Sacrifice recapitulates this as both an act of submission to the gods and a ruse of stealing at least some vitality from them.[13]

Many of the dominant strains of sacrificial theory come out of the study of rituals along these lines. As many scholars have argued, what allows this double act to occur in sacrifice are processes of identification. I will use Maurice Bloch here as an example. The sacrificer first identifies with the victim—representing, for Bloch, the purely vital element of the cosmos. The symbolic death of the victim then represents the death of vitality, with the sacrificer identifying with the divine powers. In the resulting feast, the sacrificer returns to the world of humanity but now, empowered by the divine, as a full consumer of the world of vitality.[14]

In short, from myths of the origin of the state to myths of the origin of sacrifice, a very similar dialectic recurs. The original world is one of continuity, with humans living in an undifferentiated state and in harmony with the divine and natural worlds. A transgression—an act of violence—breaks this continuity. The resulting order is one in which humanity has gained both a limited autonomy from that continuity and an ability to appropriate the vitality of that former continuity for its own uses.

This is the same ritual logic that, as seen above, Sahlins has noted in sovereign installation rituals in Fiji and Hawaii: the ruler, in his transgressive persona, would be symbolically sacrificed so that he could then be reborn in his sacerdotal form. This ritual interplay of transgressive and sacerdotal roles could be appropriated in historical practice, as both Sahlins and Valeri note across Polynesia.[15] Sovereignty is thus both transgressive and sacerdotal, both heroic and cosmic, and hence the variants that play out in various forms across the Indo-European and Polynesian worlds.

TRANSCENDENTAL SOVEREIGNTY

Sovereignty as conceptualized—and in many places in Eurasia put into practice—from the point of view of Axial Age movements and the subsequent salvationist religious movements involved a radical reformulation of these ideas. In many cases, the claim was made that a higher, transcendental order existed, and the goal was to accord with that order. Many of the movements explicitly rejected the practice of sacrifice. Adherents were called on to have faith that the world is coherent, organized according to normative principles, and in many cases even governed by a moral divinity. The entire basis of sacrificial activity, and the social world constructed through that activity, was rejected.

These ideas came to the fore in the Axial Age movements of the fourth and third centuries BCE and were radicalized in the subsequent salvationist religious movements of the first few centuries of the common era. The salvationist religions of Mediterranean late antiquity provide a clear example of the latter. In Christianity, and later in Islam, the world was seen as having been created by a benevolent deity who also revealed scriptures on how to live properly within this world. The world itself was coherent and moral, and its creator of that world provided the guidelines for proper behavior. Sacrifice was explicitly rejected, and in its place was put the importance of faith in the precepts of the creator deity.[16]

While such transcendentalist movements involved rejections of earlier immanentist cosmologies, they often built on key elements of those cosmologies. As Strathern notes, transcendentalist claims tend to fall back into the immanentist practice. Thus, the specific forms of ritual and sacrifice that are prevalent in various places have a tendency to continue in different forms, even after the transcendentalist eradications have been attempted.[17]

To give an obvious example: in Christianity, the transgression that breaks the earlier unity is read, via earlier Jewish sources, as a fall from grace, requiring the intercession of a salvationist figure (in this case, the son of the transcendent deity) to offer redemption. Instead of the transgressive figure being sacrificed, it is the salvationist redeemer who sacrifices himself to erase the transgression. Christianity is thus an antisacrifice movement, but it is so because it reverses the earlier sacrificial rituals and places them into a transcendental framework: instead of humans sacrificing transgression to the gods, the transcendent God sacrifices his own son to cleanse human transgression.

Sovereignty was altered through such transcendental frameworks as well. As Strathern and Azfar Moin have argued, transcendental frameworks call for a righteous kingship. The distinction between active and sacerdotal sovereignty continues, but the distinction is no longer between heroic and cosmic forms of sovereignty; rather, it is between zealous kingship (actively converting the faithless) and doctrinal kingship (following the precepts of the higher deity).[18] A clear example in later European history would be the dialectic between kings and popes.

RITUAL AND THE DYNASTIC CYCLE IN CHINA

Let us now finally turn to China, where one finds different permutations on many of these themes. Here too, we will begin with the immanentist practices and then turn to the transcendental ones.

The Bronze Age kingdoms in the north China plain came to be known as the Three Dynasties—the Xia, the Shang, and the Zhou. Materials from the latter part of the Shang Dynasty and the subsequent Zhou Dynasty allow us to reconstruct at least parts of the sacrificial system. The world was dominated by a series of spirits and governed by a higher deity—Di for the Shang, Heaven for the Zhou. The spirits required constant sacrifices. The offerings to them included humans, animals, grains, and wine. The sacrifices were given to appease a very clearly volatile and unpredictable set of spirits.

The Shang divinatory record reveals a clear hierarchy in the divine pantheon. Recently deceased ancestors tended to be actively involved with the living, and these ancestors were often highly capricious. A number of divinations involve attempts to see if the illness of a member of the royal family, for example, was in fact a curse by one of the recently deceased ancestors. If it was believed to be a curse, divinations would then be given to determine what sacrifices might appease the ancestor. Sometimes the sacrifices would work; sometimes they would not. The sense was clearly that the spirits were more powerful than the rituals that were being used to control them.

The more distant ancestors tended to be even more powerful yet also increasingly removed from the living. They too were capricious, but not in the sense of attacking the living. They were capricious rather in the sense of being indifferent. If the recently deceased were actively involved—and often in a dangerous way—with the living, the distant ancestors tended to be removed and uninterested. By the same token, the recently deceased ancestors were far more responsive to human ritual. In the divination record are examples of a hosting (*bin*) ritual, in which the living would host the recently deceased, who would in turn then be called on to host the next generation above—ultimately all the way to the founding ancestors and the high deity Di.

The implications of such a sacrificial system become clear in the subsequent Zhou Dynasty, from which we have far more evidence. In the eleventh century BCE, the Zhou overthrew the Shang and founded a new dynasty. The Zhou recognized Heaven as the highest divinity. The ruler's title was the Son of Heaven. This was a ritual title: he was not seen literally as a descendent of Heaven but rather as ritually Heaven's supporter on earth.

The founders of the Zhou Dynasty were kings Wen and Wu. In subsequent sacrifices, Wen and Wu were seen as residing with the high deity Heaven. As subsequent generations came to the throne, that also meant Wen and Wu, and thus access to Heaven, were farther and farther away. This resulted in an inherent decline in the dynasty: as the generations passed, the founders and Heaven became more distant and more removed.[19]

The political theory of the Zhou replicated these ritual workings. The Shang were seen as a dynasty that had superseded the Xia, just as the Zhou had superseded the Shang. In each case, the dynasty would begin with a great founder, and then the dynasty would gradually decline until a new dynasty would be started. History consisted of an endless cycle of rising and falling dynasties.

In their public statements, the Zhou further read this cycle in terms of virtue—the first introduction of an ethical calculus to the workings of the relationship between humans and the divine in China. The dynastic founders were of high virtue and thus received the support of Heaven. The ensuing decline of the dynasty was the result of a decline in this virtue. The dynastic cycle was thus read as a Mandate of Heaven, with Heaven granting the Mandate to virtuous rulers and withdrawing it from the unvirtuous.

Heroic and cosmic forms of kingship were built into this cycle as well. The heroic ruler would be the one who defeated the former dynasty in battle, while the cosmic ruler would be the one who either preceded or succeeded the heroic founder. With the Zhou, the cosmic ruler was Wen, who received the Mandate of Heaven, and the heroic was his son Wu, who then conquered the Shang in battle.

Although these proclamations of a moral Heaven would later play a significant role in Chinese political theory, the proclamations should be thought of for the Zhou as—to use a term to which I will return below—ritual statements. Within the ritual, Heaven is a moral entity, and humans are moral beings. Outside the ritual, Heaven is a capricious deity requiring recurrent sacrifice. The Chinese Bronze Age very much fits Strathern's definition of immanentist: constant sacrifices were required to work with a highly capricious set of divine powers.

THE AXIAL AGE

What sorts of transcendental movements emerged in opposition to such forms of sacrificial practice and attendant sovereignties? In the fourth century BCE, a charismatic figure named Mozi emerged. He started a movement based on the claim that the world was coherent and rationally structured. It was created by a perfectly moral deity for the sake of humanity, and that deity—Heaven—ruled it according to a clear system of rewards for the good and punishments for the bad. Heaven also ruled over a pantheon of ghosts, who were themselves purely moral, working to reward good behavior and punish bad behavior among the living. Sacrifices were acceptable, not to transform the ghosts into beneficent spirits or ancestors but rather to inculcate the proper feelings of reverence for the divine and the proper belief in their existence. The divine powers—Heaven itself and the ghosts underneath—were purely beneficent and did not need to be transformed through sacrifices. The move here consists of taking the Zhou ritual statements concerning the Mandate of Heaven, reading them as statements of fact, and then generalizing them to read Heaven as a moral creator deity. The result is a complete rejection of the notion of capricious spirits and the attendant sacrificial system.[20]

Also in the fourth century BCE a series of self-divinization movements emerged. These too were antisacrifice movements: instead of trying to influence spirits through divination and sacrifice, humans were called on to undertake self-cultivation practices that would allow them to become spirits directly. The movements made explicit claims that the cosmos was continuous and generated from a single source—variously called the One, the Way, or the Great One. This source was more primordial than and more powerful than the divinities (Heaven, ghosts, and spirits) who were the objects of sacrifice. The self-cultivation techniques would allow humans not only to become spirits but also to move closer to the Great One—thus gaining powers over those divinities that humans otherwise had to resort to sacrifice to influence.[21]

However, one of the distinctive aspects of China is that yet another of these Axial Age movements—those traditions that trace themselves to Confucius—developed its practice out of a rereading of, yet active support for, the earlier ritual traditions. Instead of asserting the importance of believing in a coherent, stable order created by a beneficent deity or demiurge, and instead of rejecting sacrifice in particular and the rituals of working with divinities more generally, the traditions coming out of Confucius, on the contrary, built directly on the claim that the world was governed by capricious deities and fully embraced the earlier ritual traditions developed to work with such capricious deities. Unlike so many Axial Age movements across Eurasia, these traditions continued to emphasize the importance of ritual in general and sacrifice in particular.

The ethical imperative seen in so many Axial Age traditions thus came to be focused not on a rejection of sacrifice but rather on a rereading and reorientation of the practice. This reinterpretation involved a rejection of the claim that the sacrifices should be undertaken in a transactional way—to give offerings to the spirits in order to get benefits in return. On the contrary, the goal should be the ethical transformation of the participants through the ritual process. The outcome of such ritual work would be that humans would learn to live harmoniously with each other and in relationship to the divine powers.

The primary focus is on the ethical transformation of the *human* participants. The degree to which the divine powers themselves are actually transformed by the rituals is often unclear. It was hoped that they would be transformed and develop ethical dispositions toward humanity, but that is not a given: the spirits often continue to be capricious. However, humans should strive to be ethical regardless. And, in direct opposition to the Mohists, Confucians strongly opposed the claim that ethical action on the part of humans would necessarily result in divine reward. The goal is for humans to act as ethically as possible, even if the divine powers continue to act capriciously. Because the focus was on the ethical transformation of the participants, the earlier rituals were also altered, and particular aspects of the sacrifices were dropped altogether. For example, human sacrifice was strictly rejected.

Given the later prominence that this movement would come to have on forms of sovereignty in subsequent centuries of Chinese history, it will be worth discussing the arguments of this movement in more depth. The focus on ritual would mean that the movement developed one of the most sophisticated bodies of ritual theory in world literature—a body of theory that, as we will see, adds some interesting permutations to the theories of ritual and sacrifice that have become dominant in Euro-American approaches.

RITUALS OF DOMESTICATION

Confucian ritual theory involved a rereading of Bronze Age sacrifices. Many of these texts on ritual theory were written during the fourth through second centuries BCE. They were then collected during the second century BCE into a work called the *Book of Rites*, which would become the most influential work on ritual theory in China.

We begin with narratives concerning the emergence of the state and the emergence of sacrifice. Of particular note is the world presented as existing prior to the creation of sacrifices and the state. There was certainly vitality in that world, but not the vitality of a continuous, generative order. On the contrary, the world was, from the point of view of humanity, one of discontinuity—of discrete things interacting poorly and often violently. For humanity, this meant a world of being eaten by wild animals, freezing to death in the winter, and starving for lack of food. The turning point was not the disruptive introduction of violence—the stranger-king, a transgressive act—into this continuous world of vitality. The turning point was rather the introduction of human domestication. Through domestication, we are told, a world of discontinuous things was transformed into a world of continuity.[22] Once plants and animals were domesticated, the otherwise seemingly random and often extremely dangerous shifts of weather and temperature became part of a larger, integrated system: the shifts were termed "seasons," and, far from being dangerous, they became a key aspect of the forces that allowed the domesticated crops to grow. Continuity and coherence were products of domestication. And once the world was properly domesticated, humanity was at the center, with the rest of the cosmos hierarchically defined around humanity.

Rituals were introduced as part of this same domestication and with the same goal: to domesticate the world by transforming the dangerous interactions that usually dominated relationships—in this case, human and divine relationships—into a proper series of hierarchical ones in which humans could flourish. Here, too, the domestication would result in humanity—and particularly the ruler—being at the center. More explicitly, the human and divine worlds would be connected through chains of patrilineal relationships. Humans would be organized into lineages; deceased humans—ghosts—would be transformed (at least in terms of human dispositions toward them) into ancestors of these lineages; the ruler would become the father and mother of the people, linking the myriad lineages through himself; and the ruler would also become the Son of Heaven. Through sacrifice, the ruler would connect the human and divine realms and forge it into a single patrilineal lineage, from Heaven to himself as Son of Heaven, and then through his children, the myriad lineages.

These rituals would allow the human participants to train their dispositions, with the populace treating the ruler as their father and mother, and the ruler treating the populace as his children. If the divine powers participate (always a question), they too would develop these same dispositions, with Heaven treating the ruler as his son and the deceased supporting living humans as their descendants. The goal of the rituals was thus to link a discontinuous series of figures into lines of continuity, with sacrifice domesticating the human and (perhaps) divine worlds just as agriculture domesticates the natural world. But in the case of ritual, the result would be a moral world: by performing the sacrifices in which these genealogies are ritually constructed, the participants would develop the proper dispositions of how to act ethically toward everyone else.

But the ethical transformation is never complete, and so the negative emotions and desires that usually underlie human relations with each other and with the divine always return. Hence the need to continue undertaking the rituals again and again.

The focus of this theorization was the hosting ritual. In these rituals, the living would serve as a host to the deceased. Within the ritual space, the living would become descendants, serving their ancestors, and the deceased would become ancestors, supporting their descendants. In the center, the ruler would serve Heaven, becoming the Son of Heaven to Heaven, who would support the ruler as his descendant.

Substitutions were integral to the ritual, but the ritual substitutions focused not on identifications with the victim but rather on substitutions and role reversals between the participants.[23] In ancestral sacrifices, for example, the grandson would play the role of his deceased grandfather, and the father would play the role of the son to his own son. The substitutions would help inculcate into each the proper dispositions of these different roles within a patrilineal system.

Here, the theories open up interesting lines of comparison with the understandings of sacrifice that have become dominant in Euro-American theory. As we have seen, the dominant understandings of sacrifice take the victim of sacrifice as a substitute for the sacrificer in his disordered state. The focus of the theorization, in other words, is on rituals of expiation. Is it possible that the prevalence of sacrifices of expiation in our theories comes from reading these practices through Christian frames? As we noted, Christianity involved taking particular themes of sacrifice and reversing them. But such a move required focusing on particular aspects of the sacrificial practice that could then be reversed—in this case, taking the symbolic sacrifice of the transgressor and reversing it so that the higher God's son sacrifices himself to expiate the transgressions of humanity. Could it be that the predominance of expiation in our theories of sacrifice comes from a secularization of this Christian emphasis?

Sacrifices of expiation were performed throughout the world, most certainly including China. But these are not the focus of the body of ritual theory that is picked up in the texts pulled together in the *Book of Rites*. On the contrary, the *Book of Rites*, as we have seen, is focused primarily on theorizations of hosting rituals. In the lengthy discussions in the *Book of Rites*, it is telling that there is not a single discussion of the victim as a substitute for the sacrificer. The substitutions are focused on the substitutions of the participants in a hosting ritual.

The work of the sacrifice is thus not to expiate the transgressions (or, in the Christian term, sin) of the sacrificer. It is rather the ethical work that comes from the play of role substitutions. The result, when successful, would be the construction of a world in which the entire human, natural, and divine elements would be connected into a cosmic patriline. Genealogical continuity, in other words, is the constructed product of sacrifice, rather than, as we saw in the models of Indo-European and Austronesian materials developed by Sahlins and Bloch, the world that preexisted sacrifice.

In a related theme, the overall framework is not one of a continuity that is being restored, at a higher level, by sacrificing and then incorporating the transgressive introduction of discontinuity. On the contrary, the concern is that the world consists of things—humans, ghosts, and so on—that are interacting poorly. The problem is one of discontinuity. And the work of sacrifice involves creating the continuity—a continuity that will then incorporate all of these different elements, pulled together into a continuity that then incorporates all of these elements and within a hopefully productive set of relations.

Are we dealing, then with a radical distinction between Indo-European and Polynesian worldviews, based on beliefs in a fundamental continuity that is broken by a transgression that needs to be expiated and incorporated, and a Chinese worldview based on beliefs in a fundamental discontinuity? On the contrary, it is more likely that we are dealing here with different theorizations. As we have seen, the Christian rejection of sacrifice also involved a transcendental rereading of earlier expiation sacrifices. And recent theorizations of sacrifice have often been based on a secularized version of these same practices.

But we have in China one of the most complex indigenous theorizations of ritual and sacrifice that we possess. Utilizing these theories as theories—utilizing them to explore sacrificial rituals around the world—may yield insights that we have missed by utilizing so exclusively theories coming from secularized Christian readings. Just as using these largely secularized Christian readings has proven to be highly insightful for specific aspects of sacrificial practice in early

Indo-European and Austronesian societies, so would it likely be productive to utilize theories that arose in China to explore sacrificial practices around the world—including for Indo-European and Austronesian materials that may have otherwise missed our attention. The ultimate goal should be to work toward a more generalized theory of sacrifice, as opposed to the more restrictive views that we have been working with, derived from Christian readings of particular earlier Mediterranean practices.[24]

We develop the point by way of an example mentioned above. Interpreting ancient Greek sacrifice according to the generalized theory of sacrifice proposed by figures like Bloch requires reading the offerings of the sacrifice as being a substitute for the transgressive aspects of the sacrificer. But such a substitution is never mentioned in Hesiod's reading of Prometheus—nor is it clear that Hesiod's reading of Prometheus should be so strongly privileged in interpretations of Greek sacrifice anyway.[25] Reading Greek sacrifice through other lenses—say, from theories that arose in China—may open up a number of insights that the expiatory reading coming through a secularized Christianity may have missed.

EMPIRE

The Warring States period in China came to an end in 221 BCE, when the state of Qin defeated the other kingdoms and created the first empire in Chinese history. The new ruler immediately sought to distance himself from the forms of sovereignty that had been dominant in the Three Dynasties. As noted above, the ritual system from the Bronze Age ensured that each generation would become further removed from the founders, thus creating a self-perceived decline in the dynastic system. The ruler of the first empire tried to break this ritual system. His goal was to destroy the past and create a completely new order. That new order would be a never-ending empire—a dynasty that would never die. To accomplish this, the ruler tried to become a god himself. He declared himself the first "August Thearch" ("Emperor") and associated himself with the Great One—a deity more primordial and more powerful than Heaven or the various ghosts and spirits. The First August Thearch (usually translated as "First Emperor") also sought immortality to avoid becoming a ghost and becoming part of the (endlessly declining) sacrificial systems. His successors would not become further removed from him because he would still be there, continuing to rule over them, and he would also continue to exercise direct control over his successors. He would destroy the past, supersede the sacrificial system, and create an enduring empire. It was, in many ways, the first major millenarian movement in Chinese history, although begun not by a transcendent deity but rather by a divinized sovereign.

The effort failed. The Qin fell soon thereafter. The subsequent Han Empire, however, attempted to resurrect many of these efforts. The rulers maintained the Qin title of August Thearch and in the second century of the common era, Han Wudi re-created much of the ritual of the Qin First Emperor. Using Strathern's terminology, the First Emperor was the heroic divinized sovereign and Han Wudi the cosmic sovereign, working to consolidate the innovations of the first Thearch.

But this would be the height of the imperial system with a divinized ruler. The empire began to decline over the subsequent century. By the end of the first century BCE, the rulers abandoned the divinization claims of the Qin and early Han rulers and turned to a claimed reconstruction of the Bronze Age sacrificial system. The five classics purportedly compiled and edited by Confucius became the primary texts for the education of the elite. One of these classics was the *Book of Rites*, the body of ritual theory mentioned above. The ruler once again took the title of Son of Heaven, once again undertook sacrifices to Heaven and Earth and his ancestors, and once again defined himself as a human within a dynastic cycle. The Han was simply a dynastic follower of the Zhou rather than an empire breaking from the past. The Bronze Age sacrificial system, as reread through Confucius, was fully embraced, as was a rejection of self-divinization movements.

MILLENARIAN MOVEMENTS

In the second century of the common era, a series of millenarian movements emerged in opposition to the imperial court. The movements explicitly made claim to the self-divinization practices that had been rejected by the court, but they did so under calls for faith in a benevolent creator deity rather than a divinized ruler—a merging, in other words, of Mohist visions along with the self-divinization movements. They also accordingly called for a complete rejection of sacrificial practice.

One of these millenarian movements, the Movement of Great Peace, led a revolt against the Han Empire. Although the revolt was put down, the Han was greatly weakened and fell soon thereafter. Another, called the Celestial Masters, broke from the Han and formed an autonomous community in the southwest.

All later Daoist movements would trace themselves back to the Celestial Masters. I will focus here on the Celestial Masters as a telling example of these millenarian movements.

The Celestial Masters began in 142, when the Way took human form as the god Laozi to give revelations to humanity.[26] The cosmos, as the revelations made clear, had been created by the Way. But Laozi was not only a creator deity. Laozi was also a moral deity, ruling over a hierarchical pantheon of deities who rewarded the good and punished the bad. The overall cosmology is thus directly reminiscent of the Mohists: a benevolent creator deity has formed a just cosmos that flawlessly rewards moral conduct. In addition, the populace was called on to have faith and to believe that the high deity and the spirits below were beneficent and rewarding the good. Sacrifice was also rendered irrelevant because the spirits are already benevolent.

But sacrifice for the Celestial Masters was more than just irrelevant. In order for the cosmos to be healthy, Laozi needed spirits to be generated. According to the revelations of the Way, spirits can only be generated through the cultivation of energies within bodily forms. Indeed, the Way had created human bodies for precisely this purpose: to produce spirits. Humans were thus called on to generate spirits—the very things that sacrifices were trying to do as well by transforming ghosts. But humans had failed to listen to these revelations and had instead started undertaking this work through sacrifices—practices that actually only fed and thus empowered ghosts. The result was that the world was being overrun with ghosts, and the entire cosmos was in danger of collapsing. The further revelations from Laozi included calls on practitioners to begin nourishing spirits within their bodies again. Those who did so would become divinized and become the seed people for the cosmos to come.[27]

In other words, instead of humans using sacrifices to transform ghosts into spirits, humans needed to use their own bodies to cultivate spirits. This involved appropriating the same techniques practiced by the self-divinization movements beginning in the fourth century BCE. Only now the self-divinization movements were not being undertaken by humans to empower themselves but were rather being undertaken at the behest of a creator deity to help the cosmos. And the result of the self-divinization would not be autonomy from the social world but rather promotion within a divinely guided bureaucracy.

As with Christianity, the Celestial Masters opposed sacrifice, but they also appropriated the sacrificial logic—in this case, the forming of spirits. Also like Christianity, the Celestial Masters reversed the orientation: the practices (whether sacrifice itself or self-divinization) were not undertaken by humans to empower themselves vis-à-vis the divine but rather were directed from a beneficent high deity to redeem the world.

In short, the Celestial Masters developed an extraordinary synthesis of the Mohists and the self-divinization movements. The cosmos is monistic, does not therefore require sacrifice, and involves humans at their best cultivating themselves to become divine and generate spirits. And yet the Way is also read as a deity along the lines of the Mohists—a deity who has created a perfectly moral cosmos and who rewards the good, that is, those who properly follow the dictates of the high deity.

RITUALS OF SOVEREIGNTY

The types of sovereignty that would be endlessly appropriated and played on in later Chinese history are already becoming clear. The dominant public position was of the ruler as distinctly human but ritually occupying the position of Son of Heaven. That ruler would offer sacrifices to Heaven, Earth, and his ancestors, and oversee the sacrifices to the pantheon of spirits. He would rule within a dynasty that would maintain its control based on its claim of governing with virtue. When the dynasty failed to rule with virtue, it would be overthrown and another dynasty would take its place. Each dynasty would claim to be simply continuing the dynastic cycles that had begun in the Bronze Age. The fact that the ruler was now overseeing a grand imperial bureaucracy was not a problem to the framework: this was simply one more thing that the Son of Heaven needed to incorporate and oversee.

The contrast with much of the rest of Eurasia is striking. Unlike the kingdoms that converted to Christianity, Islam, or Buddhism, in which sacrifice was strictly forbidden, sovereignty in China continued to be predicated on the importance of sacrifice, with the sovereign as the primary sacrificer, making offerings to Heaven and Earth.

Very much like these antisacrifice sovereignties, however, the Son of Heaven would claim his rule to be based on ethical criteria. This was a form of doctrinal kingship, even though in this case the precepts being followed were those refined by a human sage, Confucius, instead of revealed by a divine power.

At the same time, however, rulers would also keep the title of August Thearch, thereby making implicit calls to the divinization legacy of the Qin and early Han. They would also patronize the Daoist lineages that traced themselves back to the revelations of Laozi in 142, and, with the Daoist priests, undertake esoteric and nonsacrificial rituals. They would thus connect themselves to the divinization practices last seen at the imperial level in the Qin and early Han dynasties, but they would be interpreted through the lens of the transcendentalist framework of the Celestial Masters. Emperor Huizong of the Song Dynasty (1082–1135) is a clear example of someone who strongly played up these divinization sides.[28]

Millenarian movements would also continue to emerge throughout Chinese history, with calls for faith in a salvationist, beneficent creator deity and for a rejection of sacrifice.[29] Such movements would rarely become dominant, but several played key roles in bringing down dynasties.

HISTORICAL DYNAMICS

As noted above, Sahlins links the historical sequence of republic, monarchy, and empire to rituals of sovereignty. He sees the sequence more specifically as the result of a dynamic in which a transgressive stranger-king breaks into an otherwise peaceful indigenous population. That dynamism then plays out historically. It can certainly result in a rigid, static hierarchy—the relatively static tripartite structure, emphasized by Dumézil, of three functions governed by a sovereign. But it can also result in radically transgressive figures—an Alexander, a Napoleon. For a Sahlins, this would be one of the many ways that the mythic structure could be built out in historic time.

In the very different set of political rituals in China, a similar dynamic is at play. A monarchical dynastic cycle comes to be seen as the norm, but with millenarian movements emerging repeatedly to challenge the order. The most historically significant millenarian movement was led by Mao, who also explicitly compared himself to the First Emperor and declared that he was destroying the past and creating a completely new order. His perceived failure opened the way for a later Xi Jinping to style himself implicitly as a Han Wudi, consolidating the First Emperor's creation into a new institutional order.

Myths and rituals of sovereignty need not result in static hierarchies. They instead open a constant array of permutations in the practice of sovereignty, with an endless interplay between the active and sacerdotal forms.

TRANSCENDENTAL UNMASKINGS

Transcendental critiques of rituals and myths, and sacrifice in particular, are found throughout the world. As we have seen, they became particularly pronounced in Eurasia in the religious movements of the first millennium BCE and the salvationist movements of late antiquity. A recurrent tendency in these transcendental critiques is to unmask the rituals as doing something other than participants are being led to think the rituals accomplish.

One of the key moves made in these unmaskings is to deny the world of ritual substitutions and read the activities in the ritual literally. We have seen how, for millenarian movements in China, making offerings to ghosts did not entail transforming them into spirits or ancestors; it simply meant one was feeding them and thus empowering them.

Once the unmasking occurs, it is revealed that the sacrifice is really serving to reify and mystify existing social hierarchies, to justify the existence of sacrificial experts who are really charlatans, to justify a priestly class that supports a particular elite social structure, to convince a naive populace that they can control things like sickness and weather, and so on.

A great deal of Euro-American social theory in the twentieth and twenty-first centuries operates in this mode as well, with the social scientist unmasking the beliefs instantiated through ritual and demonstrating them to be nothing other than products of human activity. In looking back at early Indo-European sacrifice, for example, Bruce Lincoln argues that they should be unmasked for what they are: attempts at "ideological legitimation for an exploitative and oppressive—and exceedingly stable—social hierarchy."[30] For Lincoln, unmasking these rituals as simply attempts to legitimize hierarchies would allow humans to see the world as contingent. The more we can see rituals as simply legitimation, the more we can reject rituals and allow humans to make their own history.

In Lincoln's case, the unmasking is being done for humanistic reasons—ultimately from a Marxist perspective. For transcendental movements like Christianity and the Celestial Masters, it is being done for theistic reasons—following the guidelines of a divine power who sees through human rituals. But the former is simply a secularized version of the latter. In both cases, the transcendental unmasking involves rejecting the world of ritual as a human construction.

Indeed, as Strathern has argued, transcendental traditions have an inherent tendency toward disenchantment.[31] There is nothing uniquely modern about such disenchantment. And one of the reasons for such disenchantment is precisely that a recurrent move in these transcendental traditions lies in unmasking earlier ritual orders. The modern social scientist unmasking traditional ritual orders is simply a variation of earlier transcendental movements doing the same.

Here again we see an interesting variant from China. The same transcendental unmaskings can certainly be seen among the Mohists and Celestial Masters. But the nature of the sacrificial rituals, and the fact that these traditions were picked up in the Axial Age by the followers of Confucius, had a dramatic effect on what would become one of the most important branches of Chinese social and political theory. One finds in China more specifically an entire body of critical theory developing out of concerns with ritual. The goal was not to unmask ritual but rather to emphasize the social constructionism of ritual—to make it as overt and thus as hopefully efficacious as possible.

As we have seen, much of this ritual theory in China emerges out of a problematic of discontinuity, of a concern with discrete things that interact poorly and thus need to be domesticated to construct better forms of interaction. Ritual then becomes an inherent part of achieving a moral world. In the sacrifices in question, that work of ritual construction and domestication is made as overt as possible. Here is an obvious example: at various times in Japanese history, the imperial line was claimed to be genealogically descended from Amaterasu. An unmasking would seek to show that this was simply a claim being made to legitimate a given power structure. But, in the case of imperial China, there was never a claim that the Son of Heaven was actually descended from Heaven. This was presented as simply a ritual title, which the ruler could hold only as long as he lived up to the moral qualities required of the title. One does not need to unmask the fact that the Son of Heaven was not really the descendant of Heaven or that he was not really the father and mother of the people: these were explicitly presented as ritual constructions. They do not operate by trying to socialize practitioners into believing in a certain type of order; on the contrary, the efficacy assumes that ritual is creating a domesticated order that will, if it is successful, lead to a greater flourishing of humanity.

The critiques that emerge out of this tradition thus take the form of questioning particular social constructions and advocating others instead rather than unmasking ritual itself. Indeed, the closest moments toward an unmasking that one finds in Confucian texts are when an author criticized practitioners for thinking that ritual is about affecting the spirits rather than about affecting humanity. For example, Xunzi, a third-century BCE thinker, criticized practitioners of sacrifices and divinations who thought that the rituals were about affecting divine powers. But his point is not that sacrifice and divination should be unmasked and therefore no longer performed; his concern was to ensure that the rituals were being undertaken for the right reasons—to train properly the dispositions of the practitioners.[32] The second-order claim concerning ritual, in other words, was not to see through it and reject it but rather to reinterpret it as being about social construction.

Much of Chinese political theory focuses much less on the questions of when and how the state should be allowed to intervene in society and instead revolves much more around the types of worlds the state should construct—how the state

HUMANIZING THE DIVINE AND DIVINIZING THE HUMAN | 157

should guide humans into certain patterns of behavior rather than others. In short, alongside the transcendental unmaskings, critical theory can also emerge out of these ethicized rereadings of ritual traditions.

So let us now recast our larger models, but this time informed by the Chinese material. In the world of sacrificial practice—the world Strathern has termed immanentist—phenomena were seen as governed by a series of ghosts, spirits, and demons who operated out of their own interests, sometimes with concern for humans but often mixed with combinations of anger, jealousy, and hostility. The world was thus, from the humans' point of view, fundamentally capricious. The goal was to use practices like sacrifice to coerce these divine powers into supportive relationships with humans. To the degree to which these sacrifices were efficacious, and because, if they were, the resulting order would be relatively temporary and based on a (limited) human attempt to construct the world in a certain way, the sacrifices had to be undertaken endlessly.

Much of the focus of this ritual work came down to questions such as: why were the relationships between humans and divine powers so potentially fraught? What type of divine-human relationship should be called for in the rituals? Answers to these questions could involve a seemingly endless series of possibilities. Here, we summarize just the two approaches mentioned in this essay.

One possibility is to see the existing world of capricious spirits as the result of a human transgression that broke an earlier harmony—the transgressions of Prometheus, the introduction of a stranger-king, in other words, an earlier continuity broken by the introduction of discontinuity. The result was that humans gained their autonomy from the gods but at the cost of being in a constant agon with them. Sacrifice was thus seen as endlessly recapitulating this movement of both appeasing the divine powers while still maintaining the autonomy of humanity, both expiating the transgression against the gods while reasserting it at the same time. Sovereignty would then be portrayed as creating a higher continuity, incorporating the transgressions while relinking humanity with the divine world. Sovereign power would thus play on both of these modes—a heroic (transgressive) mode and a cosmic (sacerdotal) mode.

Another possibility is to see the existing world of capricious spirits as simply a given—the natural state of the world. Human activity is then aimed at domesticating the world so that humans could flourish. In this view, humans were constructing a world in which everything would be domesticated and reorganized around humanity. An earlier discontinuity is broken by the ritual creation of continuity. Sovereign power building on such rituals would emphasize the rise and fall of successful attempts to build such ritual orders of harmony—a rise and fall, with active and heroic and cosmic modes built into a dynastic cycle.

Although these ritual claims have been laid out with Indo-European and Polynesian materials, on the one hand, and Chinese materials, on the other, this is largely the result of the theoretical models that have developed in Europe and China, with each picking up on particular rituals in these immanentist traditions. As we have noted, expiation rituals became the paradigmatic form of sacrifice for theoretical models based on the continuity approach, and hosting rituals became the paradigmatic sacrifice for theoretical models based on the discontinuity approach.

And where did these theoretical models come from? The Axial Age movements that started in the mid-first millennium BCE, and the salvationist religions in the first few centuries of the common era involved reactions to these sacrificial traditions. They also involved second-order claims, with attempts to unmask or explicate the earlier sacrificial traditions. These second-order claims involved theorizations of various sorts of the immanentist sacrifices.

By far, the most common move among the Axial Age movements and the salvationist religions in the first few centuries was an outright rejection of sacrifice based on transcendental claims. Such a move involved assertions that the cosmos was—prior to the involvement of humans—coherent, structured, and organized according to moral principles. As such, humans needed to align their behavior with this coherent world. This often entailed positing the existence of a benevolent creator deity (God in Christianity, Allah in Islam, Heaven for the Mohists, Laozi for the Celestial Masters) or a divine power more primordial than the usual spirits of sacrifice (Brahma, Taiyi). These creator deities and primordial figures did not accept sacrifices and usually opposed sacrifices to the lesser spirits. They instead required faith on the part of the practitioners that they represented a higher truth of an inherent unity and coherence of the cosmos.

Because this coherence preceded human activity, the highest goal of humanity was to accord with it. This also entailed a rejection of earlier systems of ritual—particularly sacrifice. Thus, the movements tended to call for a rejection of sacrifice altogether as well as a radical rethinking of earlier systems of ritual. Proper behavior, on the contrary, meant following the moral imperatives of the creator deity.

Another move involved self-divinization claims that would allow the practitioner to reject sacrifice and ultimately gain the powers of the spirits directly. This too would often involve the claim that there were higher patterns in the cosmos with which the divinized humans would be able to accord. But yet another move was to place self-cultivation within the rituals themselves. Here, sacrificial rituals were supported, but they were reinterpreted into a moral framework.

Many of the theoretical bodies of literature that we possess on sacrifice and ritual were developed in these Axial Age movements and salvationist religions. In one genealogy we have been tracing, the unmasking seen in transcendentalist movements has resulted, in secularized forms, in much of the theory that has become dominant in the Euro-American tradition. In another genealogy, we have traced the emergence of a body of ritual and political theory in China not based on these same unmasking moves. This latter body of theory, I would argue, has much to inform our larger generalized understandings.

This chapter has involved unpacking a number of layers in the deep history of humanity, with openings toward a wide-ranging series of comparative implications for our understandings of sovereignty and critiques of sovereignty. Building on the work of Dumézil, Sahlins, and Strathern, we have seen paradigmatic forms of sovereignty that emerged out of a set of sacrificial rituals and myths on the origin of human society and the state, and we have noted the particular permutations of these rituals that became dominant in China. We also noted the permutations that developed as well during the emergence of transcendentalist movements midway through the first millennium BCE and again in the second century CE.

In this chapter, I have focused in particular on the ritual practices, the body of theory arising out of these ritual practices, and the rejections of these ritual practices in early China. I have noted how the ritual theories seen as developing from Confucius became one of the most powerful Axial Age positions in China and later became one of the dominant political frameworks in China as well. As a result, transcendentalist movements in China became important, but often in the form of critiques of the dominant political order. This has had major ramifications for the types of sovereignty that have played out in China as well as for the forms that political theory has taken.

One of the interesting aspects of comparative studies is to find societies facing comparable problems and tensions, to trace the debates and struggles that emerged out of these tensions, and to explore the historical implications of the different ways these struggles played out. In the case at hand, we have explored the tensions between sacrifice and transcendental rejections or rethinkings of sacrifice in key moments of Eurasian history. The ways these tensions played out in different parts of Eurasia has had profound implications for the historical dynamics of sovereignty.

NOTES

1. The term *Axial Age* was coined by Karl Jaspers in his *The Origin and Goal of History*, trans. Michael Bullock (New Haven, CT: Yale University Press, 1953). The most powerful discussions of these issues from even larger comparative points of view are those of David Graeber, *Debt: The First 5,000 Years* (Brooklyn: Melville House, 2011), and Alan Strathern, *Unearthly Powers: Religious and Political Change in World History* (Cambridge: Cambridge University Press, 2019).
2. Strathern, *Unearthly Powers*.
3. Georges Dumézil, *L'héritage indo-européen à Rome* (Paris: Gallimard, 1949), 41–42.
4. Marshall Sahlins, *Islands of History* (Chicago: University of Chicago Press, 1985), 73–103.
5. Sahlins, *Islands of History*, 92n12.
6. Sahlins, *Islands of History*, 73–103.
7. For an example of the former, see Alan Strathern, "The Vijaya Origin Myth of Sri Lanka and the Strangeness of Kingship," *Past & Present* 203 (2009): 3–28.
8. Georges Dumézil, *Mitra-Varuna: An Essay on Two Indo-European Representations of Sovereignty* (New York: Zone, 1988), 47–55.
9. Sahlins, *Islands of History*, 84–91.
10. Strathern, *Unearthly Powers*, 164–95.
11. Claude Lévi-Strauss, *The Savage Mind* (Chicago: University of Chicago Press, 1966), 233; Michael W. Scott, *Severed Snake: Matrilineages, Making Place, and a Melanesian Christianity in the Southeast Solomons* (Durham, NC: Carolina Academic, 2007).
12. On Hawaii, for example, see Valerio Valeri, *Kingship and Sacrifice: Ritual and Society in Ancient Hawaii* (Chicago: University of Chicago Press, 1985).
13. Jean-Pierre Vernant, "At Man's Table: Hesiod's Foundation Myth of Sacrifice," in *The Cuisine of Sacrifice Among the Greeks*, ed. Marcel Detienne and Jean-Pierre Vernant, tran. Paula Wissing (Chicago: University of Chicago Press, 1989), 21–86.
14. Maurice Bloch, *Prey Into Hunter: The Politics of Religious Experience* (Cambridge: University of Cambridge Press, 1992).
15. Sahlins, *Islands of History*, 73–103; Valerio Valeri, "Diarchy and History in Hawaii and Tonga," in *Culture and History in the Pacific*, ed. Jukka Siikala (Helsinki: Finnish Anthropological Society, 1990), 45–79.
16. Guy Stroumsa, *The End of Sacrifice: Religious Transformations of Late Antiquity* (Chicago: University of Chicago Press, 2009); Guy Stroumsa, *The Making of the Abrahamic Religions in Late Antiquity* (Oxford: Oxford University Press, 2015).
17. Strathern, *Unearthly Powers*, 204–218.
18. See chapter 1. See also Strathern, *Unearthly Powers*, 195–204.
19. Michael Puett, *To Become a God: Cosmology, Sacrifice, and Self-Divinization in Early China* (Cambridge, MA: Harvard University Asia Center, 2002), 31–79. For an excellent comparative discussion of these issues, see David Graeber and Marshall Sahlins, *On Kings* (Chicago: HAU, 2017), 428–433.
20. Puett, *To Become a God*, 101–103.
21. Puett, *To Become a God*, 145–200.

22. Michael Puett, "Ritualization as Domestication: Ritual Theory from Classical China," *Ritual Dynamics and the Science of Ritual, Volume I: Grammars and Morphologies of Ritual Practices in Asia*, ed. Axel Michaels, Anand Mishra, Lucia Dolce, Gil Raz, and Katja Triplett (Wiesbaden: Harrassowitz Verlag, 2010), 365–376.
23. Michael Puett, "The Offering of Food and the Creation of Order: The Practice of Sacrifice in Early China," in *Of Tripod and Palate: Food, Politics, and Religion in Traditional China*, ed. Roel Sterckx (New York: Palgrave MacMillan, 2005), 75–95.
24. As Michael Scott has argued, ritual practices based on discontinuity are underdiscussed and undertheorized in the anthropological literature. See Scott, *Severed Snake*. Stanley Tambiah has made a similar point in his discussion of the Trobriands in "On Flying Witches and Flying Canoes: The Coding of Male and Female Values," in *Culture, Thought, and Social Action: An Anthropological Perspective* (Cambridge, MA: Harvard University Press. 1985), 287–315.
25. The prominence that Hesiod's account has been given in explications of ancient Greek sacrifice has been criticized by several recent scholars. See in particular F. S. Naiden, *Smoke Signals for the Gods: Ancient Greek Sacrifice from the Archaic Through Roman Periods* (Oxford: Oxford University Press, 2015); C. A. Faraone and F. S. Naiden (eds.), *Greek and Roman Animal Sacrifice: Ancient Victims, Modern Observers* (Cambridge: Cambridge University Press, 2012); and S. Hitch and I. Rutherford (eds.), *Animal Sacrifice in the Ancient Greek World* (Cambridge: Cambridge University Press, 2015).
26. Terry F. Kleeman, *Celestial Masters: History and Ritual in Early Daoist Communities* (Cambridge, MA: Harvard University Asia Center, 2016); Michael Puett, "Forming Spirits for the Way: The Cosmology of the *Xiang'er* Commentary to the *Laozi*," *Journal of Chinese Religions* 32 (2004): 1–27.
27. Michael Puett, "Ghosts, Gods, and the Coming Apocalypse: Empire and Religion in Early China and Ancient Rome," in *State Power in Ancient China and Rome*, ed. Walter Scheidel (Oxford: Oxford University Press, 2015), 230–259.
28. Peter K. Bol, "Emperors Can Claim Antiquity Too: Emperorship and Autocracy Under the New Policies" in *Emperor Huizong and Late Northern Song China: The Politics of Culture and the Culture of Politics*, ed. Patricia Buckley Ebrey and Maggie Bickford (Cambridge, MA: Harvard University Asia Center, 2006), 171–205.
29. David Ownby, "Chinese Millenarian Traditions: The Formative Age," *American Historical Review* 104, no. 5 (1999): 1513–30.
30. Bruce Lincoln, *Myth, Cosmos, and Society: Indo-European Themes of Creation and Destruction* (Cambridge, MA: Harvard University Press, 1986), 169.
31. Strathern, *Unearthly Powers*, 199–204.
32. *Xunzi*, "Tianlun," Sibu beiyao edition (Shanghai: Zhonghua Shuju, 1936).

8

Caliphal Sovereignty or the Immanence of Transcendence

AZIZ AL-AZMEH

The anthropological orientation informing this volume and the conference on which it is based, as sketched in chapter 1, broadens the thematic and comparative horizons normally associated with the historical study of kingship. It affirms that the histories of kingship, in its various manifestations, need to be attuned analytically to that which is generically anthropological in kingship. Appreciative mention of works such as A. M. Hocart's *Kingship* were, until recently, expected to be met with perplexity, perhaps with amusement. That one may be permitted to speak of that which is generic in kingship, and to think of Constantinople and Baghdad in terms that can also accommodate New Guinea and Baffin Island, opens vistas otherwise foreclosed by disciplinary introversion. This chapter shall discuss conceptual and historical issues arising from kingship anthropologically considered and shall use Islamic material for purposes of analysis and of general conceptualization.

Like Marshall Sahlins's gods, whom he classifies as metapersons,[1] concepts are partible and must be partible in order to make sense of complexity. I will take this as a point of departure for outlining elements for the interpretation of a specific historical constellation of kingship. This constellation is late antique kingship in the eastern Mediterranean–West Asian continuum, as represented principally by the Caliphate. The Caliphate and its Byzantine parallel, sibling and rival, both presided over polities with imperial and ecumenical vocations, and they invite comparison on several counts. An interpretation of this specific constellation of kingship will be offered here in terms of specific redactions of the notion of sovereignty, in a register that associates kingship with divinity in a variety of ways, with varying degrees of diffidence, affirmation, distance, differentiation, and intensity.

The offices of Caliph and Basileus are generically associated in the sense that they accord with a broader concept of sovereignty, as they both pertain to the class of phenomena described by this concept and belong to the concept's range of reference. In this type of approach, specific instances of sovereignty figure as variants within a class that describes a range of variants within the historical phenomenon kingship of which no one instance is sui generis. This is what I would count as meaningful comparativism: a Hegelian move, arguably, in which an individual case is treated as a particular instance of a general phenomenon. This is different to a very common practice of comparison, which takes the sheer plurality of individual cases as its point of departure.

Such an outlook facilitates meaningful comment on some of the central preoccupations arising from the first chapter to this volume: sovereignty, immanentism, transcendentalism.[2] The Caliphate is often considered to be a loftily transcendent office defined by legal formality, demystifying by definition. This chapter is designed in part to demystify this notion and to describe the workings of the Caliphate's id without necessarily denying the relevance of its superego. In the final analysis, I wish to restore the immanent and, indeed, the savage to the Caliphate and, by extension, other forms of transcendentalist kingship.[3] That immanentism is the default mode of religiosity cannot be emphasized enough, nor can the continuum connecting immanentism to transcendentalism.[4] Implication of the sacred in the sovereign is a running theme below, as is the implication of the immanent in the transcendent, which will be conceived by the analogy with a gliding movement along a musical scale. Let it be noted that, throughout this chapter, the immanentism of sovereignty will not be confined to meaning a fetishism of power[5] or the treatment of the sovereign as a metaperson. It refers to an elemental, kinetic energy stored in and transmitted by a sovereign, an energy that will be described as sacral insofar as it is uncanny and sublime, and as it is set apart, however visceral its workings.

It is being argued here that an untamed royal id is recalcitrant and persists throughout all manifestations of transcendence. From this perspective, this chapter seeks to recover the Caliphate for history, adding to narrated events in the history of the Caliphate the generic anthropological fulness of sovereign kingship, a character commonly obscured by focus on doctrine and theology. In this respect, this chapter intends to show that the anthropological sensitivity of A. Azfar Moin's work on the Muslim polities of the Safavids and Mughals illuminates the classical Caliphate in equal measure to that which applies for the early modern period.[6]

The very complex phenomenon of the classical Caliphate is still discussed commonly in terms of legalism in mainstream scholarship, which adopts uncritically a truncated version of the self-image, sociopolitical ambitions, and normative frameworks of the more pietistic elements among the Muslim priesthood, generally known as the ulama.[7] It is undeniable that the classical Abbasid Caliphate did have a transcendentalist description, as guardianship of an order regulated by a legal regime that, like the Caliphate itself, has divine sanction and is of divine origin. But this is only one description of the Caliphate, relevant to some registers of discourse and context but not to others, and with an interesting relation to complex historical realities. There is scant historical justification to hold that the nomocratic register was either the central cultural and political description of the Caliphate or that it was the overriding modus operandi of this office. Nor might one legitimately assume that transcendentalist descriptions of the Caliphal office were a barrier to the natural workings of sovereignty—not least because the numinous element in sovereignty, as in divinity, is only ambivalently transcendent. This chapter wishes to argue, as the savage is brought back in, that conceptual confinement, bounded by transcendentalist constraints, is itself almost invariably aligned to nonpropositional sets of practices that convey the sublimity of the office by plastic means into which immanentism is decanted—ritual and ceremonial—and which a transcendentalist register would disallow.

The classical Caliphate is an excellent instance of this. But none of these considerations imply a devaluation of the propositional, ethical, and legal history of this office. What is intended rather is to direct attention to the Caliphate's history in the overall economy of enunciations on kingship and sovereignty, discursive or otherwise, all duly conjugated with practice and the conceptual implications of practice.[8] The two types of kingship are often instantiated by one sovereign person. One type conveys kinetic immanence; the other manifests sacral and pious righteousness in lofty registers. The two are complicit and complementary, connected by an osmotic membrane signaled by historical practice. Their alignment takes place, as shall be indicated more concretely below, by a play of associations, by a glissando, a gliding movement along a scale between intervals of pitch, a sweep between the one register and the other, between the divinely sovereign and the merely regal, the transcendent and the immanent, both participating in the common property of sublime sovereignty, which constitutes the scale of this glissando. As I argue this point, I hope that the classical Caliphate will be naturalized into a broader context of sovereignty; there is little about the Caliphate that is sui generis conceptually insofar as it is a variant of sovereignty. Its legalistic expression is an adjacent technical register.

A somatic quality adheres to the immanence of the sublime and is in practice communicated to the register of transcendence as well. It is memorably suggested by Edmund Burke. He defines the sublime in terms of visceral constituent sentiments: "Whatever is fitted in any sort to excite the ideas of pain, and danger, that is to say, whatever is in any sort terrible, or is conversant about terrible objects, or operates in a manner analogous to terror, is a source of the sublime." The sublime is thereby always and quite simply "some modification of power," and more precisely "whatever is qualified to cause terror."[9] The conjoint nature of the visceral and the lofty, of the immanent and the transcendent within the transcendent, is fundamental to the analysis of the sublime, and of the glorious sovereign, even when ostentatiously pious.

This consideration will again refer back the glissando: the sovereign air is a majestic alternance of suggestion, implication, and affirmation. This alternance, contingent upon circumstances, is between the utterable and the unutterable: between that which is doctrinally admissible in a transcendentalist setting in terms of ethics, jurisprudence, or indeed theology, and what is inadmissible on prevailing criteria and therefore unsayable. This is a movement of the "as if," on which there is concord between the pragmatic epistemology of Hans Vaihinger a century ago and contemporary cognitive psychology. This shadow play intensifies the effect of vexation, and consequently of fascination and of sublimity. It is also an instance of doing things with words. When Eusebius throughout his *Tricennial Orations* used the title *Basileus* to refer both to Constantine and to Christ,[10] the ambiguity and the double nature of the referent was part of the rhetorical occasion, and by no means the least important part; the same would apply to the designation of Khomeini as *Imam*, a title reserved in principle by Twelver Shi'ites for the Messiah. The figure of the *Basileus* is partible, and the glissando governing the movement of alternance and gliding between registers involves implications of parity, which were doctrinally inadmissible and therefore unutterable propositionally.

The move across intervals of register connecting sovereigns with divinity takes place by a variety of means, some but not all of which apply to Constantine: ambiguity, analogy declared or undeclared, figuration, mimesis, iconicity, apostolate, emanation, and descent, depending on the discursive, rhetorical, and ceremonial register.[11] In plastic form, the relationship between the two terms of *emperor* and *deity*, in principle incommensurable, is expressed in allegory, which is the visual counterpart of literary allegory in the medium of time that is called typology: a relation of reenactment by figuration, prefiguration, instantiation, and fulfillment. This related Constantine to both Augustus and Christ, and involved also David, Melchizedek, and other types played in other histories as well, which, among other things, involved royal *christomimesis/imitatio Christi*, which by implication agglutinates sovereign and deity, as they were agglutinated in the title Christ the King[12]

I do not wish to discuss issues relating to claims made for the so-called Axial Age invoked by the editors of this book, except to say that the relation between immanentism and transcendentalism in that hypothetical evolutionary leap would have been not so much a transition in which one superseded or displaced the other as much as a superaddition, including superaddition of the sort that has been referred to as "loss of innocence":[13] forms of self-vigilance and invigilation of others. These two modes of perceptual and organizing principles of religious experience, if the transition be admitted, have since been compounded with each other related by coevolution (mutualism, parasitism, predation, competition), and by deevolutionary eddies.[14] They also correspond conceptually to two forms of sovereignty. Transcendentalism's historical incidence as a form of kingship has been fitful and has more generally been salient, in a practical sense, to historically restricted domains. A broader distribution of religious goods of the transcendentalist kind relating to government pertained more generally to post-Reformation redevelopments in the religious as the political fields,[15] and to the seemingly irreversible redefinition of the central forms of political authority globally during the period 1750–1918.[16]

It would be appropriate to round off the foregoing discussion by pausing briefly to observe a heightened form of transcendentalism before the argument of this chapter is continued. Modern transcendentalism might be seen to be avowed by Reformed Christianity across its spectrum. Remarkable are the connections and analogies between forms of Reformation Christianity and Muslim Reform of the late nineteenth century as generically related phenomena in the history of religion, to which reform Judaism belongs equally. Compelling is the perception of kinship between more radical Muslim Reform and Calvinist government, and that between Jihadism and Anabaptism.[17] The abstract legalism of al-Qaeda, the Taliban, and Daesh (otherwise known as Islamic State of Iraq and Syria [ISIS]) add acute edges to this series of developments. Here, the point of reference is an entirely disembodied conception of the legal order, *shari'a*, as the sole social order that is imperative, legitimate, and right.

The transcendent abstraction of the legal order is the consequence of a situation where sovereignty is, in principle, reserved for God impartibly, all claims to the contrary being idolatrous.[18] Sovereignty resides in an instance that is generally imperceptible except for its broader signals, and for practical purposes absent, perhaps a more radical redaction of the arrangement whereby transcendentalist sovereigns are secluded.[19] What the first chapter to this volume calls "extreme forms of righteous kingship" might well, as the authors suggest, see their specific agency and personal charisma recessed by forms of confinement, with impersonal imperatives being the operative agents of government and of order. But one might argue that this abstraction of tangible presence does not apply across the board and that it rarely accounts for the natural history of the exercise of sovereignty, for absent power manifests itself in palpable effects.

One might also argue that this is comparable to the confinement of the sovereign Ottoman Sultan behind the walls of Topkapı palace, radiating terror. But even these particularly austere settings cannot evade immanentist moorings: witness, for instance, Mulla Omar, leader of the Taliban, who in 2001 placed upon his own shoulders a length of cloth, supposedly the mantle of Muhammad the Prophet, thereby conducting to his own physical person the immanence no less than the transcendence imparted by Muhammad's inherence in his relic. Certainly, the terror that radiated from Topkapı was not entirely a matter of sentiment but was signaled by public Sultanic actions outside palace walls and news of happenings inside. Not dissimilarly, and for all his outward, almost self-effacing austerity, the Caliph of Daesh manifested his sovereignty and that of the whole system of the Islamic State by inscribing it on individual bodies, with personal appearance and conduct minutely regulated, and, of course, by the exhibitionistic political theater of slaughter and its marks on the flesh, sacrifice to the body politic offered ceremonially.

A THERAPEUTIC CALIPHATE?

Moin shows with wonderful detail relating to the Timurids, Mughals, and Safavids that what are today taken for the orthodox, nomocratic forms of political conduct and self-representation of and by Muslim sovereigns were in fact more contingent and therefore in themselves more in need of explanation. Moin's gunpowder sovereign royalty poured itself into the "mythic molds of the hero, the saint, and the messiah."[20] Timur was Lord of the Conjunction[21]—the Grand Conjunction of Jupiter and Saturn that, according to Arabic astrological lore, occurred at intervals of 960 years, along with differently positioned conjunctions of less consequence (the last incidence was on December 21, 2020). This association with cosmic regularity gave the conqueror very special historical consequence, an almost natural-scientific inevitability related also to judicial astrology and letter magic that associate major epochal changes with the Grand Conjunction. Subsequent Timurids, and Safavids with greater ease at their inception, according to Moin's study, came to acquire strongly accented mystical as well as eschatological attributes, elaborated in terms of sufi conceptions, of mastery over things exoteric and esoteric and the receipt of divine effulgence.

The supposedly legalistic Caliphate, according to this story, thereby gave way to a cult of saints, later amalgamated with millenarian, saintly kingship among the Timurids and Safavids. So also did Ottomans acquire thaumaturgical attributes, with an equal measure of notions of divine election, as a recent study of Süleyman the Magnificent shows in detail and with broad contextualization.[22] But it is important to note that the history of the Timurid, Safavid, and Ottoman developments are not histories entirely *internal* to what one might think of as specifically Muslim kingship, although interpretations drift in this direction frequently. They cannot be understood in terms of what some might take for a specifically and homogeneously Muslim culture.[23] Instead, these developments of kingship need to be conceived regionally and ethnologically: in terms of Indic Devaraja ideas and *dharma/danda*, and whatever traces of Zoroastrianism or Shamanism might have retained regionally, brought by Uzbek, Turkomen, and Ghuzz peoples who came to found these three states. The nomocratic element here should not be neglected because it persisted and indeed thrived alongside the mystical. To this one would need add the *shariʿa/siyāsa* dyad, the one referring to authority wielded in terms of normative religion, the latter to authority exercised at the discretion of the ruler, arising from the precedents of Muslim sovereigns.[24] One might find analogues in other histories that would invite comparison. *Dharma/danda* would come to mind readily from Mauryan and other Indic historical experiences.

Commenting on the issue of shariʿist and mystical representations of sovereignty, Alan Strathern noted the manifestly enduring immanentism of Muslim kingship and inquired about the absence of a transcendentalist pushback, a lack which, he maintained, required explanation, given the bypassing of "normative Islam" in the mystical turns discussed here.[25] One might wonder if it might not rather be the expectation of such pushbacks, and their sparse occurrence, that would have required explanation. There had certainly always been adverse bookish comment by pietists critical of the hallucinatory and hubristic attributes applied to Muslim sovereigns and to their practices and actions as well, including using the royal title, which some thought should be reserved for God, *malik* ("king") being one Qurʾanic attribute for God. That the rigorist and pietist Wahhabi kings of Saudi Arabia never considered this to be a problem is a significant indicator of historical practice. What needs to be noted is that the expectation of a pushback is premised on an assumption that the master template of Muslim kingship was to be defined in nomocratic terms. It is very commonly assumed that the nomocratic conception of the Caliphate was the standard and preeminent form of representation, typified by the Abbasids, to which other forms conformed or departed, in all cases being the standard against which other forms are to be measured.

In this perspective of doctrinal determinism, the legal definition of the Caliphate as a communal legal obligation is often taken for a pervasive "cultural grammar," one that was "deeply embedded," "potent," "deeply ingrained," a collective "need," and a "desire."[26] Inexplicably, the legal institutes of the Caliphate, which were developed cohesively only in the eleventh century, are commonly thought to be coeval with the office itself, which emerged three centuries previously. It is not noted often enough that such topoi have no historical justification and might better be considered as a standard mode of ulamaic self-representation, foregrounding their claim for the centrality of their roles and functions, and for the hegemonic character of their pietistic culture. Such topoi also accede to the view of rigorist ulamaic sections that the ulama were always, as a corporate body, autonomous with respect to the ruling instance.[27]

And indeed, recent work on the Muslim gunpowder empires is premised narratively on the presumption that the eschatological and mystical conceptions of sovereignty that came to predominate in the early modern period were novel and that they were responses to the traumatic eradication of the ostensibly nomocratic Abbasids by the Mongol sack of Baghdad in 1258, an effort of collective therapy—who the suffering subject was, and who it was that administered the therapy, are not altogether clear. Correlatively, a mystical conception of the sovereign office is regarded as a substitute, a compensation with heightened pathos, for a regime hitherto, so it is assumed, defined in the language of jurisprudence.[28] Prior to that, it is often maintained, the Abbasids had become a lifeless relic from the latter half of the ninth century, surrounded by ulamaic brooding. It is true that the Abbasid Caliphate had been tamed politically, first by its own military commanders in the age of military anarchy in the mid-ninth century, followed by the takeover of Baghdad by the Buyids, a clan of Iranian condottieri, in 945, and by the Saljuq Turks a century later. However, the dynasty persisted and was certainly far more than a "holy relic," securing a connection between the Buyids and sacred sovereignty.[29]

The common assertion reviewed here is that, of the Caliphate, only an ineffectual symbolic aspect persisted soon after its beginning, making it a vacuous office awaiting the greater destitution inflicted in 1258, after which the early modern Muslim gunpowder empires stepped in with Sufism and millenarianism.

This emergent view in scholarship seems to obscure a number of important matters. For a proper historical appreciation, attention would need to be paid to the various means deployed by the Caliphs to preserve their prerogatives and independence even in the darkest hours of the Buyids, using all the tricks of a weaker party with higher social and symbolic, indeed religious, capital. The reigns of some impressively capable Caliphs need to be considered, especially al-Qadir (r. 991–1031). One might think of the often precarious position of the Basileus in Greece and Balkans, and in the Byzantine Commonwealth broader still, of ebb and flow of power relations between the Basileus in Constantinople and Bulgarian, Serb, and Ottoman princes, and indeed of the restored Basileus after the Frankish sack of and rule over Constantinople between 1204 and 1261.

The revived Caliphate after the mid-eleventh century, especially under the vigorous al-Mustadi' (r. 1170–1180) and al-Nasir (r. 1180–1225), became again important and independent players, albeit over much reduced territory. Both Caliphs magnified their authority with symbolic, iconic, and religious authority and attributes of sovereignty. Al-Nasir's connection with and patronage of Sufism was connected less with the futuwwa *Männerbunde* of Baghdad as "a spiritual organ"[30] than with rather more prosaic concerns, these being at the time a crucial element in the operation and management of city politics,[31] much like the concern of the Basileus with circus factions in Constantinople. Earlier, for all the control over the Caliphs and their finances by some Buyids, no serious attempt was ever made to usurp or abolish the imperial office. Use by some Buyids of the ancient title *Shahanshah* ("King of Kings") was made in conjunction with Abbasid polity, the sovereignty of whose Caliphs was continually, from the ratification of Buyid authority to appearing on the ultimate emblem of sovereignty, on Buyid coins that named the Caliph, with the Shahanshah on the obverse.[32] It might be recalled that no shogun tried to usurp the office of Tennō in Japan between 1185 and 1868. This would seem to hold despite the audacious moves of the shogun Ashikaga Yoshimitsu (1358–1408) to achieve sovereign dominance. His definition of himself in terms analogous to Buddhist notions of kingship rendered irrelevant any act of usurpation because the terms he used for himself were hedged, in a play of glissando, by what was arguably a transcendentalization using Buddhist analogues to certain imperial titles to which the shogun was not entitled in principle.

The sack of Baghdad by Hulagu's Mongol army in 1258 has been construed in current scholarship as a trauma for "all segments of Islamicate societies."[33] Poetical locutions have been used liberally to convey the pathos of this supposedly traumatic condition, with the saint stepping in to fill the "cosmological vacuum" left by a Caliphate now defunct,[34] now become an "echoing void."[35] The one study that has been devoted entirely to memorializing the consequences of 1258 shares the assumption of nomocracy as a primary point of political identification for Muslims, taken for a community of enthusiasts uniform in essence and sensibility, given interminably to doleful lamentation over an office that, in actual historical fact, would have been familiar to only few. This plaintive motif is transposed into a political leitmotif for subsequent centuries. It inflates in far greater measure and with far less plausibility what is claimed to have occurred following the abolition of the Ottoman Caliphate in 1924.

The driving force in the argument reviewed here is the indivisible mandate of Muslim law, and the study cited here shares the assumption of Muslim homogeneity that presumes Caliphal legalism to have been the central, the predominant, and the hegemonic notion of political office, generating a collective and persistent Muslim desire for restoration after 1258. The historical record does indeed preserve Jeremiads, many formally tailored according to standard poetical conventions using standard, formulaic sentiments. But these need to be placed in time and space severally, each allocated a relative place and weight in the moral economy and in the culture and politics of each of these times, places, milieus, sentimental regimes, and literary and elegiac conventions. This would have been more interesting than piling up citations with little interpretative context, thereby suggesting a collective pathological grief disorder.[36]

PRETERNATURAL SOVEREIGNTY

The historical plausibility of claims for a sequence of loss and compensation apart, the fact is that ideas of mystical kingship were as old as the ostensibly stolid Caliphate and that the classical Caliphate itself was not an office in which the legal moment was either foundational or primary. It was in all cases an act of power. One might note that thaumaturgic Muslim sovereigns, alive to the magic of numerology, judicial astrology, mysticism, and millenarianism, were not confined to the early modern "Balkans to Bengal belt." Nor were the more explicitly thaumaturgic redactions of Muslim kingship late, flowery placebos for the real thing or responses to a trauma of bereavement. It might be recalled that Ibn Tumart, founder of the twelfth-century Almohad empire in North Africa and Spain, was a *Mahdi* ("Messiah"). One might bring up a specific and highly influential, even hegemonic type of esoteric Sufism transmitted by the Murcia-born Ibn ʿArabi (d. in Damascus in 1240), who was to become in effect the patron saint of the Ottoman dynasty,[37] with a whole complement of astrological and numerological lore.[38]

This type of visionary political Sufism was first formulated explicitly in Cordoba, Almeria, and Seville in the tenth and eleventh centuries. In its militant version, it fed directly into a series of messianic and Sufi anti-Almohad rebellions. These included the short-lived principality set up by Ibn Qasi in Mértola in Algarve, lasting until 1151—Ibn Qasi staged eschatological tableaux around himself, and he was reputedly able to perform wonders.[39] One might recall in this connection that Ibn Khaldun's lengthy and precious account of numerology, gematria, the Grand Conjunction, and related matters rests on North African and Spanish material anterior to the Timurids.[40] Ibn Khaldun relates in his autobiography an account of his audiences with Timur, encamped outside the walls of Damascus in 1400 prior to his sack of the city. He delights in telling the reader how he flattered the conqueror so copiously and elegantly and how he spoke to him of both the conqueror's predicted coming and the Lord of the Conjunction. In the course of this conversation, Ibn Khaldun tells his reader, he attributed his knowledge of this prognostication, and of calendrical calculations coinciding with the advent of Timur, to astrologers and Sufis in the Maghreb, some of whom he knew and mentioned by name.[41]

Directly relevant to this argument also is the splendid Fatimid Caliphate, first in what is today Tunisia and later based in Egypt (909–1171), who were at one time a serious threat to the Abbasids. The dynasty propounded an esoteric, Imamist-Caliphal eschatology as a primary motif, inscribed within an elaborate cyclical theology of history, in which the imams and the Imam-Caliphs, infallible and impeccable during their epiphany, preexisted the world in spectral form. The office of the Imam-Caliph was a primary constituent in a cosmic chain of being, with parallel mythical and philosophical registers of stations in which ranks of Intellects correspond to angelical beings. The Imam-Caliph corresponded to the active cosmic principle, this being the First (and demiurgical) Intelligence in the order of emanation, subordinate in station only to the otiose God. He occupies the supreme station in a descending order of human stations that runs parallel to the stages of initiation into Ismaili esotericism. As in all neo-Platonic schemes, lower rungs of the Chain of Being were so many ranks in a downward movement of intensifying privation, running parallel to the upward movement of amplifying ontological plenitude.[42]

To the above need to be added some observations on the founding moments of the Caliphal office and to weigh this against the claims made for its nomocratic foundations so the matter might become clearer from both points, the beginning and early modern developments. It is perhaps not often enough noted that the Qur'an was and still is largely more Beatific Audition than a book of instruction; it was more an epiphany than a lecture. The text's acoustic materiality betokens logolatry, performance that transmitted little information,[43] containing what William Robertson Smith called "procedural" as distinct from "declarative" knowledge, corresponding to what Harvey Whitehouse called "spontaneous exegetical reflection" associated with his imagistic religiosity.[44]

Toynbee was one of a few to have been unimpressed by the cliché of Qur'anic origins for a whole range of historical phenomena, affirming justifiably that it was "stony ground" for legal and institutional developments.[45] If a norm for public authority were to be had from it, this would be rather featurelessly theocratic: a form of rule resting on command and on obedience to God and His Apostle. Qur'anic commands and prohibitions relating to aspects of public life, and these were sometimes contradictory, were made by the direct authority of God and His Apostle in the form of arbitrary decrees. The Qur'an contained no legal discourse or deliberation as such, and there existed in Muhammad's time no judicial institution, no ordinances of law, no legal argumentation or reasoning, and certainly no legally defined mediation between political fiat and society. These were later, second-order discourses upon the Qur'an. It might well be noted here also that, in theological terms, the Qur'an is acutely monotheistic in its later portions but was monolatrous and henotheistic at other points.[46]

As for commonly accepted assumptions about the Muhammadan paradigm of rule, there is no reason to share the common view that there was in the Paleo-Muslim period a tension between his royal and his prophetic personae.[47] His manner of leadership was very much in line with fairly basic Arab practices of kingship, with all its prerogatives, including the discretionary delimitation of sacred and of grazing ground, receipt of tribute, first choice among war captives, a canopy of red leather, the prerogative of ultimate arbitration, and so forth. Muhammad presided over a cultic association aligned with a specific territorial and military alliance, initially monolatrous, later monotheistic, in the traditional Arab polytheistic manner; this is what Paleo-Islam in fact was, emblematized by a cult for a novel preeminent deity, Allah. Muhammad had prophetic functions, as a Seer and a Warner to his own people, the Quraysh of Mecca, before he addressed a wider audience as God's Apostle.

The Umayyads constructed an imperial religion from Damascus, centered first around the persons of the Caliphs, as commanders and rulers, and as Allah's direct legatees, an office which the Umayyads gradually allowed to come into competition with the emergent cult of Muhammad, which they themselves patronized and promoted. Muhammad was God's Apostle, and the Umayyads were his legatees as Vicars of God's Apostle (*Khalifat Rasul Allah*) as well as God's direct Vicars (*Khalifat Allah*)—Muhammad's own alleged mantle was worn ceremonially later by Abbasid Caliphs; other relics emerged later, including his alleged standard that turned up in a Damascus bazaar at the time of the Ottoman conquest and was hoisted by the Ottomans at the battle of Mohács in Hungary in 1526, to be copied later by Daesh. The Umayyads were also Muhammad's kin, he who was to become the prime culture hero of their Arab polity,[48] much like Aeneas and Romulus to the Romans and Nyikang to the Shilluk. With reference to etiological heroes and founders, Strathern takes up in a broad sweep Sahlin's discussion of the stranger-king motif and, building on his own discussion of the strangeness of kingship in the Vijaya origin myth of Sri Lanka, speaks of symbolism of transgression and of royal "flirtation with the liminal," of royal indulgence in excess, maintaining that what was involved was a logic that, if pushed, would locate kings "somehow outside society as well as at its very center." Muhammad, because his biography is patterned in the received grand narrative, might be described as a stranger among his own people, suffering ostracism, adversity, and intense enmity before he returns to capture the town of his birth. To this might be added doubts cast about his paternity and descent, ascribed to his contemporaries.[49]

As for Umayyad entitlement to Caliphal sovereignty, various members of the dynasty and their protagonists invoked a number of elements in various permutations, much of which was expressed in panegyric poetry but also in the imperial architectural style of 'Abd al-Malik (r. 685–705) and his son al-Walid (r. 705–715), in numismatics and in private iconography.[50] As mentioned already, they claimed that they had been mandated by God directly, being God's Caliphs (vicars or legatees), a claim that was to continue through Abbasid times, amplified by elaborate and at times almost hallucinatory ceremonial.[51] Like many other sovereigns, they reigned and ruled quite explicitly by right of conquest, as did Constantine before them. They were the legatees to world dominion, inheritors of the Romans, the Persians, and other powers with claims or titles to ecumenical dominion. This includes the previous period of world dominion by Himyarites of Yemen, genealogically converted into Arabs and worked into legendary history writing at the Umayyad court. Locally, they were not only Muhammad's kin but were also the elect among Quraysh, Muhammad's people, and in turn God's elect among the Arab Mudar, their election attested by conquest with God's help.

The Umayyads were moving to elaborate forms of transcendentalism and second-order religion: moving Paleo-Islam from being the cultic association of a ruling caste to an imperial religion along familiar lines, a move commensurate with a shift of the Arabs from a warrior caste with genealogical, cultural, and geographical proximities to becoming an imperial ruling class duly dispersed and stratified. They thereby transposed their origins using the figure of Muhammad as etiological founder, to a past recent yet construed in part in terms of mythical molds, and came gradually to conceive the Qur'an as a second-order prooftext, occupying an abstract point of central reference in a large-scale polity.[52] Muhammad also became a legal oracle gradually, and a behavioral exemplar, material for later Muhammadomimetic outlooks and behaviors.

This transcendentalizing supplement was to develop and to continue and persist throughout the various redactions of Muslim kingship. By the twelfth century, a body of nomocratic redactions that formalized the office as a legislative and executive office was formulated in systematic form, based on Abbasid monarchical precedent as well as on arguments from Muslim jurisprudence. Other attributes, prerogatives, and natures of the Caliphate, anthropological, political, and ethical, remained very much in circulation and were neither obscured nor overcome by legal discourse.[53]

The nomocratic construal never stood alone, nor was it the exclusive or always the predominant mode of conceiving power. There was no such thing as "juristic imperative of High Islam,"[54] whatever this may be thought to mean. Such grandiose claims tend to convey a disproportionate image of a sovereign office beholden to legalism, when in historical fact the Caliph was surrounded by competing conceptions of the social, political, and cultural order, in which legalism was one component conception of the sovereign office, often in combination with others. The legalistic commonplace rests less on historical justification than on the adoption of the more pietistic 'ulama's normative claims, pietistic ulama who, it must be said, were themselves not infrequently and in the course of their careers complicit with the immanentist representations of the Caliphate and who held offices dispensed by the Caliphate as it lived up to its nature.

The immanentism of Caliphal—and often of sultanic power—did continue earlier trends, in varying measures and in different times and places, according to a set of morphological features that will now be sketched. It is not entirely vicarious that the Umayyads had themselves construed as Time, Destiny, and Fate (*al-dahr*), a concept that had been pointedly engaged with hostility in Paleo-Islamic times as monotheism was coming to predominate, with doctrinal (and later theological) success but not much practical consequence.[55] One might flash back to an earlier, momentous move made by Muhammad, to observe an interesting case in point to the taming of nature herself by sovereignty. With the support of a Qur'anic pronouncement, Muhammad decreed that the long-standing Arab system of calendrical lunisolar intercalation be abolished in favor of the lunar calendar exclusively, which later became the Hijra calendar. Time had come full circle, he said, and its recommencement coincided with Muhammad's conquest of his city of birth. An abstract instance of command commanded time with Muhammad's dominion and came to replace a calendrical arrangement negotiated annually, which had for a long time aligned the calendar of devotions (including pilgrimage rites) with the seasonal rhythms of transhumance and of markets. Muhammad's move to govern social time severed the connection between variant local and federal devotions and the political alliances correlative with them. The natural rhythms of social time embedded in the rhythm of the seasons were subordinated to an abstract instance of sovereignty commanding cyclical, natural time, and moving from a social temporality immanent in social relations and their rhythms, to a transcendent instance of calendrical reckoning.[56]

Caliphs and other sovereigns continued for a long time to be considered under the aspect of natural inevitability, quite apart from the ineluctability of time and fate that has been encountered. The great pagan Arab poet al-Nabigha al-Dhubyani (d. ca. 600) had, according to Arab literary lore, once given his patron al-Nu'man, King of Hira in southern Iraq, cause to take offense. He put to flight and, from a safe distance, petitioned his patron in a celebrated apologetic and panegyric ode in which he said: "You are like the night, engulfing me/even though I imagined myself at a vast distance from you." Similarly, addressing the Umayyad Caliph Abd al-Malik's ferocious viceroy in the east, Al-Hajjaj b. Yusuf (d. 714), the celebrated satirical poet al-Farazdaq (d. 728–730) chanted: "If the wind were to carry me and you pursued me/I would be as someone trapped by wind's lots."[57]

SELF-REFERENTIAL SOVEREIGNTY

The Umayyad's identification with time and fate, not unlike the Muhammadan command over calendrical cycles, are acts of pure sovereignty. There is a decided arbitrariness to them; they appear as acts of abstract energy and of self-referential potency. Self-referentiality is crucial to the definition of ultimate sovereignty and characterizes the two cognates, divinity and kingship. It was crucial to the solipsistic self-definition of the Israelites' Iron Age deity, who declared: "see now that I, I am He," and indeed to Allah as Paleo-Islam moved toward monotheism from monolatry, when the theonym of Allah came to comprehend exclusively and indivisibly the very concept of divinity, the one divine person becoming polyonymous rather than several, as previous gods had been.[58] This is a pure act of doing things with words and a perfect charter for enchanted and enchanting absolutism that, like Fate, or Muhammad's lunar calendar decree, possesses "extreme forms of agency."[59]

So also with sovereigns. The irreducibility of the sublime instance of pure command had been a common property of both divinity and the king, long before the emergence of monotheism. To the irreducibility of the instance of power and command, which lie at the heart of conceptualizing states of exception and of decisionism, is another feature of this package: states of exception, which include instances of foundation, appear generally to be arbitrary. The point of sovereign majesty, according to Jean Bodin, is the giving of law without the consent of subjects.[60]

This matter might be considered with reference to the notion of arbitrariness as used not only in linguistics but also as an analytical category in the sociology of education and culture, where it acts as a defining, self-referential, and irreducible premise.[61] This might be seen as the cognitive homologue of political decisionism, or the political moment in culture and cognition. In this sense, sovereignty might well be seen by extension as "the ability to carry out arbitrary violence with impunity," impunity assuming lack of reciprocity. Royal subjects are equal in that they are all equally nonroyal; that this makes them potential victims as well may be hyperbolic, but it is not inconsistent with the premise of sovereignty.[62] So regarded, sovereignty can be described as an elementary form of human sensibility, a perceptual grid, an "immediate datum of consciousness,"[63] a figure of representation implicit in the conception of order, vaguely reminiscent of a Dumézilian ideological "function" (in the context of the three functions: sacrality, war, and labor). Removal of reciprocity is inherent to the structure in terms of which sovereignty is defined therefore, but not necessarily to the concrete functioning of this structure.

All this is conveyed by signals of recognition, by emblems. A sovereign, according to Bodin, is recognizable by attributes, by marks not shared by subjects: the sovereign would not be sovereign if such attributes were to be shared.[64] Exclusiveness applies to royal insignia, splendid buildings, cabinets of curiosities and particular types of clothes: dyed with porphyry for the East Roman emperor; red slippers for the emperor, the Pope, and the Abbasid Caliph; yellow cloaks for some later Umayyads; or the magnificent wardrobe of Elizabeth I or Louis XIV. A nonking who would be king can, conversely, be uncovered by special somatic marks: thus, in early modern Russia, the identification of impostors pretending to be divinely ordained tsars.[65]

Exclusiveness is also indicated by the receipt, possession, and giving of rare, curious, and especially precious objects, including ones with magical powers.[66] One would need also to mention here the possession, and the giving, of women: polygyny is a Darwinian differential reproductive strategy with sociopolitical effect. Extravagant polygyny is often associated with royalty, as a form of "autocratic sexual mass consumption" conveying strength, abundance, and fertility, like the possession of unique objects. This was practiced all across Asia and involved huge numbers in a variety of ways. In this perspective, Christian monogamy (and the accumulation of mistresses and bastards) was anomalous and would require explanation.[67] Closely related to this is a marriage pattern that placed sovereigns above social reciprocity: it was not only the Abbasid Caliphs, from the second half of the ninth century, who preferred anisogamy, marriage to women of slave origin. The Ottomans did likewise after having settled, first, on xenogamous marriages with Byzantine and Balkan princesses and then, from the time of Bayezid II (r. 1481–1516), tended hypogamously to give their own daughters in marriage to the upper ranks of office holders, formerly slaves of the palace.[68]

It has been suggested above that gods and kings are related by a glissando, a continuous gradation of tonality, through a shared common quality—sublime sovereignty in this case. The Leviathan, "to speak . . . reverently" is indeed the "Mortall God, to which we [the commonwealth] owe under the Immortal God, our peace and Defence."[69] Reverently or irreverently, the "as if" gloss is effective. The immanence of the Leviathan, the "Mortall God" with his body politic, can with the substance of "our peace and Defence," and with the godly nomination, glide over to play the latter register, that of "Immortal God," the ultimate point of sovereignty under which it, the "Mortall God," is subsumed as a lower register of the same line, that of divinity parsed as sovereignty, and of sovereignty parsed gingerly and analogically as divinity.

If sovereigns should be beyond reciprocity in principle, they need to be, like God, beyond ordinary judgment. The issue of kingship, of the "Mortall God" regulating the commonwealth beyond moral charters, was raised long ago by Hocart. The deity might be the fount of good and righteous conduct, but in His elementary form, as preserved in Yahweh and the Qur'anic Allah, He is in himself amoral, being beyond morality, as He exudes arbitrary, pure energy—like acts of fate, the Umayyad Caliph Abd al-Malik's panegyrist al-Akhtal (d. 710) said to his patron, there could be no shame in anything the Caliph did.[70]

Yet shame brings up social embodiment, because, abstraction notwithstanding, the practical exercise of sovereignty finds frequent expression in terms of dispensations and obligations, and generally entails displaying tokens of exchange. This might mitigate arbitrariness and suggest transcendentalist royalty. This hegemonic mitigation of arbitrariness is also played in the "as if" mode as it begets consent to be ruled, which is most suggestively defined by Maurice Godelier as "the portion of power added by the dominated to that which the dominant directly exercise over them."[71] Such dispensations and obligations, by which political transcendentalism is constituted, are mediated by bodies of propositions generally called doctrines, maxims, rules, or indeed legal provisions. These are often vaguely conceived and given broad generic labels like *dharma/dhamma, shariʿa, themis*, or *maʾat*. These propositions are also mediated and guarded by specific social estates: a clerisy, generically understood, like the *ʿulama*, the church or the *sangha*, although the independence of these estates can be overstated when represented as "radically independent."[72] But this mitigation of arbitrariness is more often than not counterweighted by the "as if" character of kingship under such conditions: one accepted doctrine stated explicitly in propositional form but acted both practically and affectively as if the sovereign properties of irreducibility, indivisibility, arbitrariness, and impunity trumped the logos of righteousness. Guardians of transcendentalism often staged and wrote royal sovereign actions.

The congeniality to the immanent nature of kingship by transcendentalism's institutional guardians has been more common than is often thought and more regular. Immanence possessed domains of expression evident to all, figural and somatic: in sequences of visual, kinetic, auditory practices, what we call ritual. This is the material counterpart and equivalent of the rhetoric of kingship, and one might be reminded that a rhetorical utterance is one that cannot be expressed nonrhetorically.[73] Both rhetoric and ritual slide from one pitch to another along a glissando, bring together sovereign and deity by manners of identification and equivalence, expressed as degrees of identification and mimesis. At one extremity, full identity in an ontological sense can be expressed in epiphany or apotheosis, both sublimated expressions of transmogrification.[74] Correspondence can be expressed by filiation, however conceived: Pharaohs, Christ the Son and Pantocrator, Christ the King, with the emperor as his icon.

At the other end of the spectrum, we find a variety of mimetic strategies, expressed in the figures of the apostolate (Muhammad), of priesthood broadly conceived (the Byzantine emperor had a lowly priestly status, which nevertheless gave him access to the altar behind the *ikonostasis*), dispensation (Muhammad again and Messianic figures like Thomas Müntzer or Shiʿite imams), appointment (Caliphs), preexistence (Christ, Shiʿite imams), and other tropes of representation. All of these seem to be redactions of a primal disposition to typological representation, holding the one to be the figure of the other, under the signature of sovereignty. Involved are magical forms of transmission. Such is the anointment of medieval European sovereigns with holy oil brought down by the Virgin herself or by the Holy Spirit, itself an all-purpose, tangibly kinetic extension of the deity. Such is also the somatic sign of prophecy impressed upon Muhammad's back, or the in vitro anointment of the Byzantine Porhyrogennetoi, emperors born into the purple.

SOVEREIGNTY, NATURE, AND CULTURE

We can now gather the threads laid out in the foregoing sections and weave them around elements constitutive of Late Antique and Caliphal sovereignty, the two connected both genetically and generically. It is not only that the late Roman lawmaker emperors, Theodosius II (r. 408–450) and Justinian (r. 527–565), basing themselves on older legal traditions expressed under the Severans by Ulpian of Tyre (d. 223 or 228), wrote themselves outside and beyond the norms of legality, or the assertion that the emperor be *nomos empsychos/lex animata*. There is in parallel a relationship of figuration that relates the emperor, the Autocrator, to Christ the Pantocrator; the emperor acquires *dynamis* from the Holy Spirit, pure kinetic energy. He participates together with Christ in the common terms of majesty and energy, this participation played as a glissando. There is a wholesale transfer of names and attributes between sovereigns and Christ. Both are referred to by the same terms; both have the epithet Basileus, like Zeus, as indicated already—Eusebius' *Tricennial Orations* before Constantine play fundamentally on this association. Figuration and indirection step in when the sacrality of the sovereign—as distinct from the function of sovereignty—is inexpressible because of transcendentalist dogmatic restrictions on the mortal person.

Resort is made to ritual expressions, epithets, and somatic movements with a force deriving from the illocutionary energy possessed by ritual language as its propositional force is depleted. Such is the case of a Byzantine emperor in the aspect of a Christomimetic figure, formalized and frozen in iconography, ceremony, metaphor, and etiquette. These all inhabit a world of magical contiguity in which the emperor is, in functional terms, an icon of the divinity: as can be inferred from the practice of churchgoers, an image becomes an icon functionally by sympathetic magic which transmits presence and the energy of presence.[75]

Figuration and participation in essence with varying degrees of intensity along the glissando are expressed very well in royalist typology. This is ubiquitous in monotheistic kingship, and is the locus of the theology of history. Constantine was the figure of Christ (and of Augustus), and a second David. Later emperors were second Constantines. Pope Pius II wrote to Mehmet the Conqueror in 1461 promising that he would recognize him as a new Constantine and a new Stephen and that he would recognize his control of Greece and the East and over Pannonia if only he would accept baptism.[76] Typologies, allegorical apparitions in the medium of time, were everywhere among Christian and Muslim monarchs. Similarly, Constantinople was the Second Rome, and Moscow the Third.[77] For their part, Abbasid Caliphs presided over court ceremonies dressed in black, reputedly the color favored by Muhammad, their insignia being Muhammad's mantle and stave, with the original Qur'an of Uthman before them.[78] Dressing his envoys, officials, and judges in black made them iconic representatives of his person. Similarly, just as the Basileus was in certain ways, as discussed here, infused with the substance of Christ, so also was the icon of the Basileus, sent to the provinces, infused with his real presence, in a manner conceptually parallel to that in which the real presence of Christ's flesh and blood were present in the Eucharist.

This rhetorical participation, and the mutual implication of sacral and sovereign substances, is displayed by the Caliphate in a variety of pure forms. The statement by Franz Cumont that, by the turn of the fourth century, under the emperors Galerius, Diocletian, and Constantine, ancient Caesarism was about to be transformed into a sort of Caliphate,[79] not only expressed old-fashioned views of late Rome's incremental orientalization, then commonly held. It also bears a crucial conceptual and historical truth expressive of both historical continuity and generic affinity between late Caesarism and the Caliphate, conveying the idea that the Caliphate was a consummate form of Late Antique kingship. Muhammad did indeed beget "a race of sacred kings in the guise of the Caliphs."[80]

The juristic theory of the Caliphate much in evidence today among Islamists and scholars alike is the product of special circumstances in eleventh-century Baghdad, while that other discursive expression of Caliphal transcendentalism, expressed in the philosophical-ethical and gnomological prescriptions of kingship, was constantly circulated at court in a fairly standard traditional mode. These sententious disquisitions stressed the golden mean; temperance; the maintenance of justice; and the importance of self-control, self-restraint, and self-improvement, with generally concordant reference to Muhammad, Ali, Aristotle, Alexander, and Persian kings and sages. Otherwise, the topic of kingship in Arabic letters was a matter for belles lettres (including popular literature and, crucially, poetry), histories (including Caliphal biographies), epistolary and advice literature, official documents, coins, and certain philosophical and theological works—no less than the nonpropositional representations of royalty in ceremony, architecture, courtly etiquette, and heraldry.[81]

But the Caliphate, like kingship altogether in Arabic letters, derived its energy from participation both in the divine mandate and the elemental, immanent capillary energies of executing its mandate. Arabic discourse on kingship, including the Caliphate—and I am considering the Caliphal office here as an historical specification within the broader concept of sovereignty, with its nomocratic description a further technical specification in terms of jurisprudence—rests almost invariably upon a pessimistic anthropology, to be understood less as a genetic model than a morphological description. Social order is brittle given that humans are, by their nature, violent, greedy, and unjust, and the genesis of human sociality is the foundational political act of a force, kingship, *sultan*.[82] This restrains humans and constrains them into an unnatural condition of orderly association that we call culture and civilization, their natural condition being nasty, brutish, and short.

The unstated assumption is that the sovereign, of whom the Caliph is a specific instance, is the demiurge of sociality, the sovereign being the force of nature that ensures the maintenance of the cultural order by resort to instruments of nature herself. This the sovereign does by the vigilant and continuous conservation and maintenance of a condition that is, by nature, unnatural and precarious because humanity is congenitally recidivist. 'Abd al-Hamid ibn Yahya al-Katib (d. 750), Secretary to the last Umayyad Caliph and a canonical figure for classical Arabic stylistics, stated in an epistle to the crown prince that the disposition to evil "inheres in humans as fire inheres in a flint-stone."[83] The sovereign is the condition of order, including order arising from legal restraint and regulation.

In this scheme of things, *shari'a* is an instrument of discipline and for the maintenance of good order. Muslim jurisprudence proposed that legal causality is distinct from natural causality, although the two can meet at various points concerning human interest comprehended by the purposes of law. It also recognized that many prescriptions are without evident cause and are arbitrary: such as the number of daily prayers, or their precise order of procedure. When an explanation was proffered for such arbitrariness, it was that arbitrary requirements were requisite instruments for training in obedience.[84] The maintenance of *shari'a* is a political function in a manner similar to the Sanskritic *danda/dharma* combine, the rod protecting the law—the Arabic word for politics, *siyasa*, applies equally to the management of humans and to the husbandry of animals. The Caliph is the untamable tamer, the savage domesticator, continuously deploying primal violence, or the threat of primal violence, to contain and correct chaos at every horizon, rather in the mood of the *Enuma Elish*. His element is pure immanence.

This much is well articulated propositionally in Arabic letters of various genres. In addition, sovereign sacrality materialized in practices of abjection and propitiation analogous to those offered to the deity, and in metaphors that evoke the deity, these last generally are also very present in panegyric poetry. One conservative Muslim theologian, with no time for playing down the scale of glissando, went in headlong and sought to demonstrate the unicity of God by analogy with the indivisibility of royal sovereignty. The standard proverb had it that a scabbard cannot hold two swords: analogies with the figures of indivisibility, arbitrariness, impunity, and irreducibility are foundational here.

Hubris and impunity are primary. Caliphal hubris and impunity express themselves in the Caliphs' (and any sovereign's) famous unpredictability, disloyalty, inconstancy, unaccountability, caprice, covetousness, narcissistic amorality, much like the character of the monotheistic deity. Subjects, however elevated, are defined by pliant subjection and are undifferentiated when viewed from the full plenitude of the apex. Such natural characteristics of kingship were expressed by a specific Arabic term, *taghayyur*, inconstancy, referring to the unpredictability and violent shifts in favor and disfavor, of elevation and exclusion, of life and death. The first Umayyad Caliph Muʿawiya (r. 661–680), once a young secretary to Muhammad, is supposed to have said that the sovereign had the ire of a lad and the covetousness of a lion.

Manuals of conduct written for courtiers are catalogs of stories of misfortune and enjoin cunning, hedging, prudence, and sycophancy lest the sovereign have a change of heart: sovereigns are by nature capricious and inconstant, two natural attributes of savage sovereignty insofar as it is unbridled energy. The assumption is that a sovereign needs to be managed so that his natural tendency to devastate those around him and those in his service is stemmed because the courtier is entrapped without hope of escape in courtly life, whose primary modality is instability and unpredictability, perpetually on the edge of ruin and worse for oneself and one's family and associates.

A sovereign is beyond social reciprocity with regard to human sentiment as well, even the natural sentiment of paternity—distance is a prime characteristic of the sovereign, expressed in spatial terms very elaborately and perhaps best expressed in the fact that the Abbasid Caliphs were very rarely seen outside their palaces, from which they radiated a terribly majesty. The institution of *hijaba*, of regulating access to the sovereign, was highly elaborate. Caliphs and sultans may not have been described as holy, but the sentiment of hallowed majesty is conveyed by relations of physical distance and by rituals and other manifestations of abjection by their subjects. This was one function of *hijaba*, which might be interpreted functionally as the management of precisely the glissando of unstated sacrality, acting between the savagery of power and the vagaries of politics, mediating society and the space of dread, discipline, and trepidation that is the sovereign presence.[85]

All these characteristics are present in and constitutive of ceremonial, to which manifestations of distance and splendor are fundamental, working toward a hallucinatory enhancement of sovereign hubris. Many ornaments come into play to signal majesty, like the fly-whisk and parasol of East and South Asian sovereigns, or the scepter and globe of European kings. Unaccountable and exemplary violence is yet another embellishment and token of sovereignty: to us negative ornaments of power, accumulating sometimes macabre capital. The Caliphal palace in Baghdad kept a cabinet of severed heads, with labels attached for identification. The supposedly transcendentalist Caliph is not only transcendent with respect to a scalar hierarchy he oversees but pulsates with immanent materiality. Caliphal Mohammadomimesis by the Abbasids was itself almost entirely physical, staged as visual typology: it consisted of sitting in his audience chamber dressed entirely in black except for the red slippers, black being the emblematic color of Abbasid vestments and of all Caliphal officers (the Fatimids preferred white). Officials in black in the provinces can be interpreted as icons of Caliphal presence, like the imperial icon and likeness of the East Roman emperor. The legal theory of the Caliphate ran parallel to this but did not trump it.

As with Eusebius on Constantine, the Caliphate is attuned to the glissando, back and forth between the utterable and the unutterable, the admissible and the inadmissible, officiated by the play of rhetorical suggestion, with the savagery of nature transposed to other media by metaphor and by nonlinguistic enunciations. A repertoire of dogmatic statements concerning public authority certainly existed, conceived as *siyasa shar'iya*, shar'ist, or nomocratic politics. But this was not so much pushback against the savage Caliphate as much as advice for mitigation, not unlike sententious moralism of ancient vintage in the form of philosophical ethics or wisdom literature, enjoining the sovereign to adhere to the provisions of reason and of Muslim jurisprudence. The classical legal theory of the Caliphate gave the Caliph very considerable leeway for judgment and discretion in this very regard. The classical jurist al-Mawardi (d. 1058), whose name is synonymous with the juristic theory of the Caliphate, presented the Caliph with a body of sometimes contradictory Abbasid and other precedents, and with a repertoire of more strictly juristic rulings, and asked him to exercise his discretion, even on the consumption of alcohol. The transcendent rested on the assertion of immanence, the immanence of sovereign discretion.[86] It also rested on the politics of the day: Al-Mawardi legislated for a Caliphate emboldened to ambition by the demise of the Buyids.

Some ulama did object to some prerogatives of the Caliphate and attempted, as advisers and not as antagonists, to domesticate sovereignty, most concertedly after the fall of the Caliphate and after the ulama became duly constituted professionally as a self-perpetuating estate. But it must be stressed that they acted generally as advisers, not as competitors or alternative sources of authority, even after the emergence of the doctrine that the ulama were the legatees of prophecy—once the Caliphate had been relegated to the past. There was no doctrine of rebellion in Muslim jurisprudence apart from doctrines generated among ephemeral or marginal groups. Muslim jurisprudence recognized only one legal category of dissidence or resistance, and this was the crime of sedition (*hiraba*). It was very widely held that an eternity of injustice is preferable to a night without a sovereign.

In this regard, it is indeed often easier to see common dynamics across Christianity, Islam, and Buddhism than to generalize about structural differences between them relative to sovereigns and clerisies. The Christian church is a truer instance of the proposition that "Clerisies and Rulers Steal Each Other's Clothes and Plunder Each Other's Realms,"[87] and the symbiosis between ulama and Caliphs and sultans was less antagonistic than between kings and bishops or popes in Europe, and the division indeed neater.

In all these respects, we find Caliphs virtually removed from the order of humanity (but not of mortality) and placed at a remove in the world of *mirabilia*—not so much for containment but for license. This marvelous quality is reflected in the tonalities and vocabularies with which Caliphs are described, vocabularies and tonalities shared by accounts of *mirabilia* and imaginary lands, and by descriptions of monuments such as the pyramids and the ruins of Palmyra, supposedly built by the Djinn. It is unsurprising that Caliphal and royal antics should provide substance for the *Thousand and One Nights*, which opens with a sovereign who, before Scheherazade tricked him serially, 1001 times, thought little of intending to deflower a virgin every night, then have her put to death. The control exercised on him and by him when, 1001 nights after the start of the story, he married his storyteller and gave up his wicked habit, was neither ethical nor religious. There is no suggestion of contrition or of scruples gained, no evocation of justice; no transcendentalist dispositions were involved. What was involved was self-indulgence, enchantment by the stream of stories that had him ensnared. The question is, With the savage never having departed, which is it that domesticated the other, immanence or transcendence?

NOTES

1. David Graeber and Marshall Sahlins, *On Kings* (Chicago: HAU, 2017), 3.
2. This immanentist/transcendentalist distinction has now been elaborated in detail: Alan Strathern, *Unearthly Powers: Religion and Political Change in World History* (Cambridge: Cambridge University Press, 2019), chapter 1, passim. This bears conjunctive comparison with concepts developed by Harvey Whitehouse, "Modes of Religiosity: Towards a Cognitive Explanation of the Sociopolitical Dynamics of Religion," *Method and Theory in the Study of Religion* 14 (2002): 293–315.

3. I would also join the late Robert Bellah in pleading for a renewed proper consideration of the work of Lucien Lévi-Bruhl, beyond the fog of polemical tropes: Robert Bellah, "What Is Axial about the Axial Age?," *Archives Européens de Sociologie* 46 (2005): 79, note 25. The following earlier foray is suggestive: Howard Eilberg-Schwartz, *The Savage in Judaism: An Anthropology of Israelite Religion and Ancient Judaism* (Bloomington: University of Indiana Press, 1990).
4. Strathern, *Unearthly Powers*, 5, 204–17.
5. The concept of fetishism, for certain reasons no longer very familiar, is far from being exhausted or defunct. See Roy Ellen, "Fetishism," *Man*, New Series, 23 (1988): 213–35.
6. A. Azfar Moin, *The Millennial Sovereign: Sacred Kingship and Sainthood in Islam (1400–1700)* (New York: Columbia University Press, 2012).
7. For a critical discussion of the normal commonplaces of the history of the Caliphate as a political form, and of the history of ideas associated with it, see Aziz Al-Azmeh, "God's Caravan: Topoi and Schemata in the History of Muslim Political Thought," in *Mirror for the Muslim Prince: Islam and the Theory of Statecraft*, ed. Mehrzad Boroujerdi (Syracuse, NY: Syracuse University Press, 2013), 326–97.
8. Aziz Al-Azmeh, *Muslim Kingship: Power and the Sacred in Muslim, Christian and Pagan Polities* (London: I. B. Tauris, 2001), 122–43, 155–63; and the comment of Alan Strathern, "Drawing the Veil of Sovereignty: Early Modern Islamic Empires and Understanding Sacred Kingship," *History and Theory* 53 (2014): 83, note 8.
9. Edmund Burke, *A Philosophical Enquiry into the Sublime and the Beautiful* (London: Penguin Books, 2004), 107.
10. Harold A. Drake, *In Praise of Constantine: A Historical Study and New Translation of Eusebius' Tricennial Orations* (Berkeley: University of California Press, 1976).
11. Al-Azmeh, *Muslim Kingship*, 18–19.
12. Al-Azmeh, *Muslim Kingship*, 41–48. See the detailed analysis of Gilbert Dagron, *Emperor and Priest: The Imperial Office in Byzantium*, trans. Jean Birrell (Cambridge: Cambridge University Press, 2003), especially part 2.
13. The term is that of Alan Strathern, "Transcendental Intransigence: Why Rulers Rejected Monotheism in Early Modern Southeast Asia and Beyond," *Comparative Studies in Society and History* 49 (2007): 364. See also Strathern, *Unearthly Powers*, 19–28. This is averred in many ways by other proponents of the Axial Age idea; see, for instance, Bellah, "What Is Axial about the Axial Age?," 83–85.
14. Whitehouse, "Modes of Religiosity," 310–12.
15. In some ways, this is continued today by a transcendentalizing moralism marking post–Cold War liberal regimes, all premised on degrees of disenchantment. See the discussion of Richard Jenkins, "Disenchantment, Enchantment and Re-enchantment: Max Weber at the Millennium," *Max Weber Studies* 1 (2000): 11–32.
16. Jeroen Duindam, *Dynasties: A Global History, 1300–1800* (Cambridge: Cambridge University Press, 2016), 185.
17. This issue has not had its proper share of research and analysis. See Reinhard Schulze, "Islam und Judentum im Angesicht der Protestantisierung der Religionen im 19 Jahrhundert," in *Judaism, Christianity and Islam in the Course of History:*

Exchange and Conflicts, eds. Lothar Gall and Dietmar Willoweit (Munich: Oldenburg, 2010), 139–164; Aziz Al-Azmeh, "Al-Iṣlāḥiyūn al-nahḍawīyūn wa fikrat al-iṣlāḥ." *Al-Mustaqbal al-'Arabī* 455 (2017): 75–99.

18. This with the notion of *hakimiyya*, crucial to radical Islamism. The literature is vast, and the reader might conveniently consult Stephane Lacroix, "Ḥākimiyya," in *Encyclopaedia of Islam*, 3rd ed., ed. Kate Fleet et al., accessed February 2020, http://dx.doi.org/10.1163/1573-3912_ei3_COM_30217. See chapter 13.

19. On various techniques for screening sovereigns away, see Duindam, *Dynasties*, 187–8.

20. Moin, *The Millennial Sovereign*, 54.

21. Moin, *The Millennial Sovereign*, 23–55. Moin holds this to be a "millennial" title, inexplicably, for it bears a primarily cyclical burden with no necessary eschatological interpretation. For astrology and political astrology, see Stephen P. Blake, *Time in Early Modern Islam* (Cambridge: Cambridge University Press, 2013), 141–47 and chapter 5, passim.

22. Hüseyin Yılmaz, *Caliphate Redefined: The Mystical Turn in Ottoman Political Thought* (Princeton, NJ: Princeton University Press, 2018).

23. For a discussion of the broader but conceptually homologous issue of East and West, and for the argument that East-West typologies and clichés tend to reflect modern political ideologies more than history, and the related proposition that before the sea change that occurred in the eighteenth and nineteenth centuries a far greater equivalence characterized the environments of rulers, see Duindam, *Dynasties*, 298–9 and "Conclusion," passim.

24. The idea that the spheres of religion and of the secular are indistinguishable "in Islam" is resilient and is often taken for common sense. See the recent cataloguing of another pair of ubiquitous terms relative to this same classification of spheres: Rushain Abbasi, "Did Pre-Modern Muslims Distinguish the Religious and the Secular? The *Dīn-Dunyā* Binary in Medieval Islamic Thought," *Journal of Islamic Studies* 31 (2020): 185–225.

25. Strathern, "Drawing the Veil of Sovereignty," 86, 89.

26. Mona Hassan, *Longing for the Lost Caliphate: A Transregional History* (Princeton, NJ: Princeton University Press, 2016), 17, 14.

27. Al-Azmeh, *Muslim Kingship*, "'ulama" at Index; Al-Azmeh, "God's Caravan," 362–8, 374–5.

28. Yılmaz, *Caliphate Redefined*, 1, asserting also, counterfactually, that the classical Caliphate was a "moral paradigm" that sought the rule of the most perfect (*al-afḍal*) and, again counterfactually, that Muslim jurists "in consensus" ruled that the Caliphate ended with Ali (Yılmaz, *Caliphate Redefined*, 8–10, 282).

29. See Azfar Moin, "Sovereign Violence: Temple Destruction in India and Shrine Desecration in Iran and Central Asia," *Comparative Studies in Society and History* 57 (2015): 473–4.

30. Yılmaz, *Caliphate Redefined*, 278.

31. On this phenomenon in broader perspectives, see the foundational study of Claude Cahen, "Mouvements populaires et autonomisme urbain dans l'Asie Musulmane du Moyen Age," *Arabica*, V (1958): 225–50, VI (1959): 225–56, 223–65.

32. Eric J. Hanne, *Putting the Caliph in His Place: Power, Authority and the Late Abbasid Caliphate* (Madison, NJ, Fairleigh Dickson University Press, 2007); Angelika Hartmann, *Al-Nāṣir li-Dīn Allāh (1180–1225): Politik, Religion, Kultur in der späten ʿAbbāsidenzeit* (Berlin: Walter de Gruyter, 1975).
33. Yılmaz, *Caliphate Redefined*, 1.
34. Azfar Moin, "The Politics of Saint Shrines in the Persianate Empires," in *The Persianate World: Rethinking a Shared Sphere*, ed. Abbas Amanat and Assef Ashraf (Leiden: Brill, 2018), 113.
35. Hassan, *Longing for the Lost Caliphate*, 14.
36. Hassan, *Longing for the Lost Caliphate*, 14. This very well researched book proceeds with a rather uncritical reading of the sources, confined in large measure to juristic self-construal. Literary motifs, political courtesies, and hyperbole are taken quite literally. Abbasid ceremonial in Cairo after 1258 is taken literally, for an expression of political realities of the time (chapter 2). Not until the very end (at 258–60) is there any evident concern with mapping and measuring social and political incidence and the extent of the literature of elegy and lamentation. For the rest, one has the impression that the author was describing an historical pathology, an unremitting brooding, the remedy for which would be, according to this diagnosis, the restoration of Caliphal nomocracy. This cliché is very common among Islamists and Euro-American students of Islamic history.
37. Yılmaz, *Caliphate Redefined*, 18.
38. See the overview of Mercedes García-Arenal, *Messianism and Puritanical Reform: Mahdīs of the Muslim West* (Leiden: Brill, 2006).
39. Al-Azmeh, *Muslim Kingship*, 197–202, and references there. This phenomenon is little studied.
40. Ibn Khaldūn, *Al-Muqaddima*, ed. ʿAbd al-Salām Shaddādī, 3 vols. (Casablanca, Bayt Dār al-Funūn wa'l-ʿUlūm wa'l-Ādāb, 2005), 1:179–86, 2:149–68, 3:119–63; M. Redjala, "Un texte inédit de la *Muqaddima*," *Arabica*, 22 (1975): 320–23.
41. Ibn Khaldūn, *Riḥlat Ibn Khaldūn*, ed. Muḥammad b. Tāwīt al-Ṭanjī (Abu Dhabi: Dār Al-Suwaidī, 2003): 406–7. For the English translation of Ibn Khaldun's account of his meeting with Tamerlane, see Ibn Khaldūn, *Ibn Khaldun and Tamerlane*, trans. with commentary by Walter J. Fischel (Berkeley: University of California Press, 1952), 35–36.
42. Al-Azmeh, *Muslim Kingship*, 193–7. For the Chain of Being, see Aziz Al-Azmeh, *Arabic Thought and Islamic Societies* (New York: Routledge Library Editions, 2014), 2–9. There is a large bibliography, and the reader can always turn for reliable orientation to Farhad Daftary, *The Isma'ilis: Their History and Doctrines* (Cambridge: Cambridge University Press, 1990), passim. See also Mohammad Ali Amir-Moezzi, *The Divine Guide in Early Shi'sim*, trans. David Streight (Albany: New York University Press, 1994); and *L'ésoterisme shi'ite, ses raciness et ses prolongements*, eds. Mohammad Ali Amir-Moezzi et al. (Turnhout: Brepols, 2017). See also chapter 9.
43. Roy A. Rappaport, "Liturgies and Lies," *Internationales Jahrbuch für Wissens- und Religionssoziologie = International Yearbook for Sociology of Knowledge and Religion* (Berlin, Springer Verlag, 1976), 86–89.

44. William Robertson Smith, *Lectures on the Religion of the Semites* (London: Adam and Charles Black, 1894), 20; Whitehouse, "Modes of Religiosity," 305–6; Harvey Whitehouse, "Implicit and Explicit Knowledge in the Domain of Ritual," in *Current Approaches in the Cognitive Study of Religion*, ed. Veikko Antonnen and Ilka Pyysiäinen (London: Continuum, 2002), 133.
45. Arnold Toynbee, *A Study of History* (Oxford: Oxford University Press, 1951), 2:53.
46. Aziz Al-Azmeh, *The Emergence of Islam in Late Antiquity. God and His People* (Cambridge, Cambridge University Press, 2014), 306–15.
47. For a consideration of some medieval discussions, see Samuela Pagani, "Roi ou serviteur? La tentation de choix d'un modèle," *Archives des Sciences Sociales des Religions* 178 (2017): 43–68.
48. Al-Azmeh, *The Emergence of Islam*, 517–520, and chapter 6, passim; Al-Azmeh, *The Arabs and Islam in Late Antiquity* (Berlin: Gerlach, 2014), 68–9.
49. See Strathern, "Drawing the Veil of Sovereignty," 85; Graeber and Sahlins, *On Kings*, chapter 4; Al-Azmeh, *The Emergence of Islam*, 376.
50. On the imperial style and numismatic projection, see Al-Azmeh, *The Emergence of Islam*, 504–10; Finbarr Barry Flood, *The Great Mosque of Damascus* (Leiden: Brill, 2001), 182–221; Stefan Heidemann, "The Evolving Representation of the Early Islamic Empire and Its Religion on Coin Imagery," *The Qurʾān in Context*, ed. Angelika Neuwirth, Nicolai Sinai, and Michael Marx (Leiden: Brill, 2010), 149–95. On private expression in its broader context, see Garth Fowden, *Quṣayr ʿAmra: Art and the Umayyad Elite in Late Antique Syria* (Berkeley: University of California Press, 2004), chapters 4, 5, and 6.
51. Al-Azmeh, *Muslim Kingship*, 74–7, 203–5; Al-Azmeh, *The Emergence of Islam*, 508–14. See also Susanne Stetkevych, "Al-Akhtal and the Court of ʿAbd al-Malik: The *Qasida* and the Construction of Umayyad Authority," in *Christians and Others in the Umayyad State*, ed. Antoine Borrut and Fred M. Donner (Chicago: The Oriental Institute, 2016), 129–155. Thus, to claim (Yılmaz, *Caliphate Redefined*, 18, 108–9, 196–9) the title of *khalifat Allah*, used by the Ottomans under Süleyman, superseded the more pietistic *khalifat Rasul Allah*, Vicar/Caliph of God's Apostle of the Abbasids, and drawing conclusions regarding the supposed compensation for traumatic loss rests on fragile foundations. Both titles were used throughout.
52. Al-Azmeh, *The Emergence of Islam*, 516–18.
53. Al-Azmeh, *Muslim Kingship*, 101–112, 163–88.
54. Yılmaz, *Caliphate Redefined*, 17.
55. Al-Azmeh, *The Emergence of Islam*, 511–13; 512, note 102; 371–2.
56. Al-Azmeh, *The Emergence of Islam*, 332–3.
57. Beatrice Gruendler, ed. and trans., *The Life and Times of Abū Tammām by Abū Bakr Muḥammad Ibn Yaḥyā l-Ṣūlī* (New York: New York University Press, 2015), §§13.1, 13.3.
58. Deut. 32.39 in *The Five Books of Moses*, trans. Robert Alter (New York: Norton, 2008); Al-Azmeh, *The Emergence of Islam*, 306–26, 368–9.
59. Robert A. Yelle, *Sovereignty and the Sacred* (Chicago: University of Chicago Press, 2019), 19.

60. Jean Bodin, *On Sovereignty*, ed. Julian H. Franklin (Cambridge: Cambridge University Press, 1992), 23.
61. Pierre Bourdieu and Jean-Claude Passeron, *Reproduction in Education, Society and Culture*, trans. Richard Nice (London: Sage, 1977), chapters 1 and 4. See also the discussion of Yelle, *Sovereignty and the Sacred*, 20–22.
62. Graeber and Sahlins, *On Kings*, 66. It is difficult incidentally to adopt this view and yet wash one's hands of its direly reactionary political consequences, after the fashion of Georges Bataille and others, as Graeber seems to hope (Graeber and Sahlins, *On Kings*, 73 n. 5). See also Yelle, *Sovereignty and the Sacred*, 11–12. Compare the consideration of sovereignty in the most stimulating work of Thomas Blom Hansen and Finn Stepputat, "Sovereignty Revisited," *Annual Review of Anthropology* 35 (2006): 295–315, doi:10.1146/annurev.anthro.35.081705.123317.
63. Roger Caillois, *L'Homme et le sacrée*, 3rd. ed. (Paris: Gallimard, 1950), 18. For further conceptual and historical elaboration, see Aziz Al-Azmeh, "Monotheistic Monarchy," in *The Times of History*, ed. Aziz Al-Azmeh (New York: Central European University Press, 2007), 267–89.
64. Bodin, *On Sovereignty*, 46–7.
65. Boris A. Uspenskij, "Tsar and Pretender: Samozvancestvo or Royal Imposture in Russia as a Cultural-Historical Phenomenon," in B. A. Uspenskij and Victor Zhivov, *"Tsar and Pretender" and Other Essays in Russian Cultural Semiotics*, ed. Marcus Levitt (Boston: Academic Studies, 2012), 113–52.
66. For the Caliphate, see Ibn al-Zubayr, *The Book of Gifts and Rarities*, trans. Ghada Hajjawi al-Qaddumi (Cambridge, MA: Harvard University Press, 1996). For recent considerations, see Zoltán Biedermann, Anna Gerritsen, and Giorgio Riella (eds.), *Global Gifts: The Material Culture of Diplomacy in Early Modern Eurasia* (Cambridge: Cambridge University Press, 2018).
67. Duindam, *Dynasties*, 108–22. On mistresses and bastards, see Duindam, *Dynasties*, 122–7.
68. Al-Azmeh, *Muslim Kingship*, 134; Gürlu Necipoğlu, *Architecture, Ceremonial and Power: The Topkapı Palace in the Fifteenth and Sixteenth Centuries* (Cambridge, MA: MIT Press, 1991), 161; Duindam, *Dynasties*, 110–12.
69. Thomas Hobbes, *Leviathan*, ed. Richard Tuck (Cambridge: Cambridge University Press, 1996), 120.
70. Gruendler, *The Life and Times of Abū Tammām*, §13.6.
71. Maurice Godelier, *The Mental and the Material*, trans. (London: Verso, 2011), 13.
72. Strathern, "Transcendental Intransigence," 363.
73. See Yuri M. Lotman, *Universe of the Mind. A Semiotic Theory of Culture*, trans. Ann Shukman (London: I. B. Tauris, 1990), 57, 141–3.
74. In this connection, see the analysis of the Nicene Christology in terms of a magical substructure in Al-Azmeh, *The Emergence of Islam*, 85–6.
75. Al-Azmeh, *The Emergence of Islam*, 79–99, and works referred to there. See especially Per Beskow, *Rex Gloriae: The Kingship of Christ in the Early Church* (Stockholm: Almqvist & Wiksell, 1962); and Martin Wallraff, "Viele Metaphern—viele Götter? Beobachtungen zum Monotheismus in der Spätantike," in *Metaphorik und Christologie*, ed. Jörg Frei, Jan Rohls, and Ruben Zimmermann (Berlin: Walter de Gruyter, 2013), 151–66.

76. Enea Silvio Piccolomini (Pape Pie II), *Lettre à Mahomet II*, trans. Anne Duprat (Paris: Editions Payot et Rivages, 2002), 131 ff., 156. It is not certain that this letter was ever sent or whether it was more than an instrument to aid the pope's negotiation with his royal interlocutors in Europe and his bid to organize a crusade.
77. Al-Azmeh, *Muslim Kingship*, 17–34; Al-Azmeh, *The Emergence of Islam*, 98–99; 99, note 334; and references made there.
78. Al-Azmeh, *Muslim Kingship*, 136–8, 143–4. See Hilāl al-Ṣābī, *Rusūm Dār al-Khilāfa (The Rules and Regulations of the ʿAbbāsid Court)*, trans. Elie A. Salem (Beirut: American University of Beirut, 1977), 73–74; see pages 64–68 for a description of a major investiture ceremony.
79. Franz Cumont, *The Oriental Religions in Roman Paganism* (New York: Dover Publications, 1956 [1911]), 141; carried over by Oswald Spengler, *The Decline of the West*, 2 vols. (New York: Alfred A. Knopf, 1932), 1:72, 405. See Aziz Al-Azmeh, *The Emergence of Islam*, 94–96, 98–99.
80. Strathern, *Unearthly Powers*, 143.
81. Unless otherwise indicated, this discussion draws on Al-Azmeh, *Muslim Kingship*, passim.
82. *Sultan* is the generic term used for sovereigns. It is employed as a title for a royal or princely office, and it is often generically applied to Caliphs in works of history. The word means, literally, "power," and the best cognate in a European language would be the generic use of *prince*, or indeed, more literally, *podestá*, although this last was not as elevated a title.
83. Al-Azmeh, 78. There has been some work published since, especially for the history of ideas on politics, somewhat wanting in conceptualization. For elements of ceremonial and court, see *Crisis and Continuity at the Abbasid Court*, ed. Maaike van Berkel. (Leiden: Brill, 2013). See also Nadia Maria El Cheikh, "The Institutionalization of 'Abbasid Ceremonial," in *Diverging Paths? The Shapes of Power and Institutions in Medieval Christendom and Islam*, ed. John Hudson and Ana Rodriguez (Leiden: Brill, 2014), 351–70. See also Jenny Oesterle, *Kalifat und Königtum: Herrschaftsrepräsentation der Fatimiden, Ottonen und frühen Salier an religiösen Hochfesten* (Darmstadt: Wissenschaftliche Buchgesellschaft, 2009). For recent broad comparisons, somewhat concerned with civilisational comparisons, see Almut Höfert, *Kaisertum und Kalifat: Der Imperiale Monotheismus in Früh- und Hochmittelalter* (Frankfurt: Campus, 2015).
84. See Aziz Al-Azmeh, "Chronophagous Discourse," in *The Times of History*, ed. Aziz Al-Azmeh (New York: Central European University Press, 2007): 139–164.
85. Muḥammad Ḥayyān al-Sammān, *Fī Tadbīr al-qadāsa: Adab al-Dukhūl ʿalā al-Sulṭān fī al-Turāth al-ʿArabī al-Islāmī* (Doha: Arab Centre for Research, 2018), chapters 3 and 4, page 27. Chapters 5 and 6 in this book also discuss the way in which Chamberlains regulating access to the sovereign were able to seize effective and often formal power in certain Muslim polities, especially in Spain and North Africa. See Duindam, *Dynasties*, 202.
86. Al-Azmeh, *Muslim Kingship*, 163–88.
87. Strathern, *Unearthly Powers*, 143–44.

9
Neoplatonic Kingship in the Islamic World

Akbar's Millennial History

JOS GOMMANS AND SAID REZA HUSEINI

Any king who learns wisdom and persists in his consecration of the Light of Lights, as we said before, will be given the Great Royal Light (kiyān kharra) *and the luminous light* (farra). *Divine light will bestow upon him the robe of Royal Authority and of majesty. He will become the natural ruler of the world. He will receive aid from the lofty realm of heavens. Whatever he says will be heard in the Heavens. His dream and his personal inspirations will reach perfection.*

—Shihab al-Din Suhrawardi[1]

In AH 990/1582–1583 CE, just one year before the occurrence of the great Saturn-Jupiter conjunction (*qirān*), the Mughal emperor Akbar (r. 1556–1605) commissioned a group of scholars to write a new history of the world. This *Tarikh-i Alfi*, or "History of the Millennium," was to commemorate the first Islamic millennium that would soon come to a close.[2] Looking at the result, the reader is faced with a mélange of often well-known histories from a wide range of sources, which were not merely copied and pasted together but reorganized and reinterpreted to produce a new Mughalized metatext. Although this massive, three-part book of almost 6,000 (printed) pages is extremely revealing of Akbar's effort to build a new universal empire, the work was soon overshadowed by the much more polished chronicle of Akbar's reign, the *Akbar Nama*.[3] In this chapter, we highlight this unique chronicle in the context of two wider developments, first and diachronically, the making of a Neoplatonic kingship tradition in the aftermath of the Mongol conquests during the long thirteenth century; second and synchronically, the occurrence of a near global renaissance of Neoplatonic thought during the long sixteenth century.

The *Tarikh-i Alfi* was a truly remarkable intellectual project, a universal history written by an international team of some of the most avant-garde thinkers of their time. As its millennial title indicates, it was in fact a project of post-Islam. In a radical move, by declaring the end of the Islamic millennium, it skipped over the Prophet Muhammad to announce the coming of Akbar as saviour with a new covenant of universal peace (*ṣulḥ-i kull*). This Neoplatonist reconceptualization of Islamic history stressed the king's extraordinary new *ratio* and criticized the old Prophetic religion for introducing religious difference and violence—what Jan Assmann calls the "Mosaic Distinction." Looking for a universal, more inclusive alternative, it replaced the Arab prophetic model with that of the Mongol royal model. For this reason, it redeployed traditional Neoplatonic elements of immanentist, divinized kingship based on the transmigration of the soul and the worship of the sun. To put it in terms of global history, the *Tarikh-i Alfi* turns Akbar into a Neoplatonic messianic philosopher-king. As such, Akbar follows in the footsteps of like-minded rulers such as the Roman emperor Julian the Apostate (r. 361–363), the Abbasid Caliph al-Ma'mun (r. 813–833), or the Ottoman sultan Mehmet II the Conqueror (r. 1444–1446; 1451–1481). But more directly relevant for the case of the Mughals was the example set by their Mongol ancestors and the way the Mughals achieved spiritual concord with their peers in Europe, such as Rudolph II of Habsburg (r. 1576–1612) and James I Stuart of England (r. 1603–1625).[4]

Interpreting this Akbar "the Apostate" as a Neoplatonic ruler, however, begs the question, what is actually meant by the term *Neoplatonism*? Hence, the first part of the chapter discusses three long-term interconnected Neoplatonic spheres of the *Tarikh-i Alfi* by zooming in from its global to its Islamic, to its specific Akbari context. The second half engages with three important Neoplatonic aspects of the chronicle itself.

1. NEOPLATONISM IN TIME AND SPACE

Neoplatonism remains a rather elusive label used in a myriad of different fields—primarily in philosophy, history, and art history—covering almost two millennia of global history. For the present purpose, when using the term Neoplatonism, we do *not* suggest a specific school of philosophical thinking that goes back to the

Hellenistic philosopher Plotinus (204–270 CE) and his followers, who thrived in particular in the eastern parts of the late Roman Empire. Instead, we take Neoplatonism more broadly as a metadiscourse that, as a result of its fluid, layered hierarchical structure, was able to absorb, appropriate, and harmonize creatively the various other philosophical and religious traditions that it encountered. Despite its breadth, this metadiscourse can be identified by four philosophical-cosmological features: idealism, monism, emanationism, and the human potential for divinization.[5]

First, Neoplatonists assume that mindful Consciousness (*nous*, Intellect) is, in an important sense, ontologically prior to the physical realm, which is itself taken as being the ultimate reality. Neoplatonists agree with Plato (against Aristotle) that the objects of mindful Consciousness (abstract concepts) are also ontologically prior. And so Neoplatonism inevitably turned out to be an idealist type of philosophy. Second, Neoplatonists assume that reality, in all its cognitive and physical manifestations, depended on a highest principle of conscience that is unitary and singular. Neoplatonic philosophy is a strict form of principle-monism, which strives to understand everything on the basis of a single cause that they consider divine and indiscriminately referred to as "the First," "the One," or "the Good."

From this follows the third Neoplatonist assumption, emanationism: that the universe was created in a great Chain of Being, that reality emanates from the First in coherent stages so that one stage functions as the creative principle of the next, and that every activity in the world is in some sense double because it possesses both an inner and an outer aspect. Neoplatonists insist that there is nothing on the lower ontological levels within the chains of causality that is not somehow prefigured on the corresponding higher levels. In general, no property emerges unless it is already, in some way, preformed and preexistent in its cause. This thinking in terms of top-down emanation—often compared to light radiating out from the sun—creates various levels of being. Hence the derivative outer activity of the first principle, Consciousness (*nous*) becomes a second "hypostasis." In turn, inner active life of Consciousness produces further outer effect, the Soul or *psychê*. In the same way—whether or not with the help of a Demiurge or divine craftsman—Soul facilitates the manifestation of form in matter. Further distinctions are drawn between the hypostases to articulate the transitions from one level of being to another. As a result, every aspect of the natural world, even the meanest piece of inorganic and apparently useless matter, has an eternal and divine moment. From this, it follows that human existence is a striking representation of the cosmos as a whole, a microcosm in which all levels of being (Unity, Consciousness, Soul, Nature, Matter) are combined into one organic individual.

This leads to the fourth, moral Neoplatonic assumption, which is targeted at individual deification through a sincere and arduous effort of the mind to return to the One and forever abrogate any concerns for the body.

In the sixteenth century, this extensively employed Neoplatonism, not as a specific philosophical school but as a well-established cosmological framework, facilitated the incorporation of various Sunni, Shia, Sufi, Millenarian, Hindu, and other philosophical and religious traditions that constituted Akbar's new imperial ideology. It is not so much the outcome but the process of assimilation itself that strikes us as thoroughly Neoplatonic and that reminds us so much of similar imperial projects, indeed going back to the late Roman emperor Julian. By using the term *Neoplatonic kingship*, we will be able to detect a type of kingship that has been forgotten today but in the premodern era is easily recognizable as a global spectacle that cuts across civilizational and religious boundaries. As such, we hope this will stimulate further comparative and connective research that engages with the political legacy of the Greek philosopher Plato, one in which the rightful monarch is the divinized philosopher-king who acts as the sole intermediary between the world of material existence and the world of higher (Platonic) Forms in different layers of being.

In the first systematic study of Neoplatonic political philosophy, Dominic O'Meara argues against the still conventional idea that Neoplatonism failed to find a valid relation between its metaphysical and its practical philosophy. For O'Meara, the first step on the king's path to divinization involves the cultivation of the political virtues described by Plato in his *Republic*: wisdom, courage, moderation, and justice. These political virtues, although not godlike, mirror the divine. All this is mediated by the enlightened philosopher-king whose soul has been emancipated from preoccupation with the body to bring him nearer to the perfection of divine life. In the words of the tenth-century Neoplatonist Al-Farabi, this divinized king "has reached a high degree of human happiness or felicity, a proximity to the life of the transcendent Agent Intellect which we can compare to the 'assimilation to the divine' sought by the Neoplatonic philosopher."[6]

In all its different avatars, Neoplatonic kingship is thoroughly monist and as such goes beyond any specific religious denomination and is, in fact, perfectly able to incorporate any of them.[7] It is also thoroughly personal because it is only the king who, through divinization, becomes the *lex animata*, "the living law," thereby overruling the authority of a hierocracy consisting of prophets, jurists, theologians, and ritualists. More important than correctly adhering to any transcendent or scriptural law was devotion to the philosopher-king, who had revealed himself through both mysticism (Sufism) and occult sciences.

Such kings equipped themselves with ancient, universal wisdom of a *philosophia perennis* to counter the doctrinal criticism of jurists and keepers of sacred law derived from just one monotheist truth. In such situations, kings became indistinguishable from thaumaturges, saints, and messiahs—metapersons, to use the vocabulary of Marshall Sahlins. Their authority was not determined by truth or dogma but by divine grace, often demonstrated by heroic deeds, mostly on the battlefield. The all-encompassing, monist characteristic of Neoplatonism especially suited those miraculously victorious "world conquerors" who stood in need of a universal ideology for vast imperial realms with subject populations of immense religious diversity.

The Neoplatonic Moment

Neoplatonic authority has appealed to rulers at all times and in both the Western and the Eastern parts of the post-Hellenistic ecumene that shared this Platonic legacy; however, it became particularly fashionable during a global Renaissance that characterized at least the European and Islamic worlds from about 1450 to 1650. During this Renaissance, kings attempted to emancipate themselves from the clutches of the religious establishments, whether it was through the Reformation in Europe or through other forms of religious renewal in the Islamic world. In Europe, though, it seems that political Neoplatonism remained a sporadic and rather marginal phenomenon, more written and thought about than acted upon. At about 1200 CE, medieval Europe had already started to lose interest in Plato in favor of Aristotle. The European revival of Neoplatonism was primarily instigated from the outside following the arrival of Greek scholars in the wake of the Byzantine sage Georgios Gemistos Pletho (c. 1355–1454) whose Neoplatonism was shaped in his tripartite engagement with Byzantium, the Ottoman Empire, and Italy.[8] From Quattrocento Italy a revived Neoplatonic-Hermetic worldview spread across the European courts but gradually succumbed under the unitary "inquisitorial chauvinism" of increasingly disenchanted and confessional states.[9] A nonpolitical version of Neoplatonism was allowed to live on as esoteric knowledge and even flourish in the arts.[10]

In the Islamic world, this sixteenth-century Neoplatonic revival was nothing really new but actually another wave in a three-century-long dynamic that started with the pagan Mongols and their warband, which unleashed not only a new type of kingship but also a revolution in philosophical thought, with Neoplatonism providing the cosmological substratum. In fact, by embracing

Neoplatonism, the so successful meritocratic openness of the nomadic warband could actually be maintained under more settled conditions.[11] Hence, we would like to argue that Neoplatonism proved particularly attractive in postnomadic situations of transition, at the initial stage of state formation when a mobile warband had to be reorganized into a settled state, one that needed to incorporate the highly diverse elements of the conquered realm.

Notions of kingship in such situations of recent conquest tended to be extremely open and eclectic. Hence, these conquering kings began to stress the mystical and occult interpretation of their charisma. Instead of a chauvinistic scriptural-dogmatic dispensation, they tended to embrace various kinds of monist ideologies that enabled them to impose unity over the religious diversity of the peoples in their new territories. This situation is particularly relevant for areas where the so-called Arid Zone created sharp but porous *inner* frontiers between nomadic and settled societies from the Middle East to Central Asia. Under these conditions, postnomadic empires never became entirely settled, and kingship always remained in a state of transition.[12] Indeed, this particular frontier context of Asia's Arid Zone proved to be a much more fertile ground for an all-inclusive monist political theology encapsulated in Neoplatonism than Europe with its much more rooted, sedentary kingdoms. Since the beginning of the second millennium, Europe lacked postnomadic state formation as well as direct interaction with "pagan" religions such as Zoroastrianism, Buddhism, Hinduism, and Mongol shamanism. Thus far, it has not been recognized that postnomadism was a key factor in the long-term survival of immanentist sacred kingship, making Neoplatonism such a phenomenal success story in the Islamic world.

To translate this Neoplatonic moment into the wider scheme of things, as proposed by Alan Strathern and A. Azfar Moin, the nomadic conquests of Central Asian warbands during the long thirteenth century replaced the "transcendentalist righteous kingship" of the Islamic *ancien regimes* across Asia with the immanentist "heroic kingship" of the conquerors.[13] After a conquest, however, with some routinization of power, the more active immanence of the first heroic conquerors gave way to a more static immanence of postnomadic rulers, who then fashioned themselves as cosmic kings. The political philosophy that suited this transition from heroic to cosmic kingship, at least in the Islamic world, was indeed the eclectic monism of a Neoplatonic brand. The repetitive nature of nomadic conquest continuously undermined a tendency from these more immanentist forms of kingship toward a more transcendentalist, righteous kind of kingship. Hence, in the frontier regions surrounding the Arid Zone, at least until the eighteenth century, there was never a fixed transcendent static order imposed by a scripture-based clergy that, in Strathern and Moin's words, "could promote a codified form of 'knowledge as indispensable 'truth.'" In other words, although Neoplatonism created a bridge between "heroic" and "cosmic kingship," it also prevented a permanent transition toward the "righteous" or "zealous kingship," propagated and guarded by the jurists of Islam, the keepers of scriptural truth. Although Neoplatonism thus fundamentally operated as a profound means by which immanentism, especially divinized kingship, was validated, we should not forget that it also has a transcendentalist dimension. Plato himself is the closest the Greek world comes to transcendentalism in his depiction of an ethicized absolute higher reality and why the philosopher-king is not just superhumanly powerful in the form of a heroic king but is also a model of perfection in terms of virtue. It is exactly this dual nature of Neoplatonism that makes it so useful as a bridge for postnomadic regimes.

Neoplatonism in the East: From Mongols to Mughals

Although nomadic conquest remained a prominent phenomenon until the nineteenth century, the most critical phase of nomadic conquest and the establishment of postnomadic empires has been the long thirteenth century, when the Mongol conquest of western Asia destroyed the caliphal-sultanic jurisprudential model that had become standard in Islamic societies. Under the Caliphate, Plato's philosophy—mostly in Aristotelian guise but in Neoplatonic interpretation—had persisted in fits and starts. Although Plato's political legacy can be found in the universalizing policies of the Abbasids and the Fatimids, whether or not supported by the Neoplatonic ideas of primarily Isma'ili philosophers, it was the Mongol invasions that really triggered a renewed interest in Neoplatonic political thought, first, via the Sufism of the Arab Andalusian scholar Ibn 'Arabi (1165–1240) and, second, via the Illuminationism of the Persian polymath Shihab al-Din Suhrawardi (1155–1191).

Although the relationship between the two is rather complex, the engagement of Sufism with Neoplatonism definitively generated major changes in the history of Islamic political thought. Like other mystically oriented authors of Al-Andalus, Ibn 'Arabi was profoundly influenced by eastern Isma'ili Neoplatonism through the Epistles of the Brethren of Purity. At the same time, Ibn 'Arabi tended to deintellectualize Neoplatonic notions. With many Sufi thinkers, he shared a somewhat condescending attitude toward the intellect (*'aql*) as a means for obtaining truth.[14] More important, however, is that both Sufism and Neoplatonism criticized the literal following of scripture (*taqlīd*) and instead supported a more direct experience (*kashf*) of inner, higher truth. Ibn 'Arabi had promoted an alternative method of reading scripture (*taḥqīq*) in order to unveil various aspects of divinity immanent across all the levels of the cosmos. By this technique, one could even achieve the status of the *insān-i kāmil*, "the perfect human being," who uniquely mediates God's creation and represents the entire universe as a human microcosm.[15] Not surprisingly, Ibn 'Arabi's monist ideas had an immediate appeal to the Mongols. According to one of their fiercest critics, the fourteenth-century judge Ibn Taymiyya, Ibn 'Arabi served them well because the Mongols revered "many things such as idols, human beings, animals and stars."[16]

More intellectualist Neoplatonic was Suhrawardi's philosophy of Illumination, *Hikmat al-Ishraq*, literally "wisdom of the rising of the sun." A highly complicated elaboration of the metaphor of light and vision as offered in Plato's *Republic* V–VIII using logic, epistemology, and cosmology, Suhrawardi presented Illuminationism as the culmination of pre-Socratic wisdom, which originated in the Egyptian sage Hermes, "the father of wisdom" (*wālid al-ḥukamā'*), and over millennia absorbed the learned and divinely revealed accomplishments of philosophers, saints, prophets, and kings. In short, Illuminationism offered the most direct path to the attainment of enlightened wisdom. While it made divine inspiration accessible to everyone, it especially opened up a path for the divinization of kings, especially those marked by the radiating royal or divine light (*kharra-yi kiyāni* or *farra-yi izadi*). Bestowed with such divine majesty, the king could achieve the sacred status of saints and prophets.[17]

Far more explicitly than Ibn 'Arabi, Suhrawardi had incorporated pre-Islamic Iranian and Hellenistic aspects of cosmos worship into his philosophical system. For instance, according to Susan Maneck, although Ishraqi cosmology is based on emanations, Suhrawardi personalized those emanations by identifying them with Zoroastrian angels or deities. Besides this hierarchical order of angels, Suhrawardi held that there existed a nonhierarchical order corresponding to Platonic archetypes, to which Suhrawardi assigned the names of the Amshaspands—the Avestan archangels of the realm of light—which he associated with separate powers or attributes of God.[18]

As suggested already, Illuminationism became particularly popular in the thirteenth century, especially after the Mongol conquests ushered in a new political era. Ishraqi thinking was eagerly sought because of its potential use in formulating a sophisticated, all-embracing ideology of Mongol rule, lending it scientific and proven authority.[19] Like Sufism, Suhrawardi's Neoplatonic synthesis was all the more attractive because it kept the Islamic scriptural and legal establishment in the conquered regions at a distance. As in the case of their

Neoplatonic colleagues of the European Renaissance, the Muslim followers of Suhrawardi cultivated a reputation of unpredictable noncompliant recalcitrance, if not outright revolt, against the religious establishment. Although acknowledging the prophethood of Muhammad and the authority of the Qur'an, Ishraqis also promoted the authority of other, equally esteemed sages going back to Hermes, passing on the light along various branches to include ancient Persian sages, Old Testament figures, and even the Indian Brahmins. Suhrawardi's Illuminationism thus became the basis of a new mode of sacred Muslim kingship, catalyzed by the needs of neo-Muslim conquerors, especially the Mongols.[20]

Both Sufism and Illuminationism became a political force in the wake of the Ilkhanid conquest of Iran. Exploiting the settled wealth of Iran from their capitals in the rich meadows of Azerbaijan, the Ilkhanids found themselves in gradual transition from a nomadic warband to a settled dynasty. As new postnomadic rulers, they required an inclusive political ideology that was to reach out to Islam but without becoming bound to the establishment of Islamic jurists. With this in mind, the Ilkhanids sponsored the construction of the impressive academic complexes of Maragha and Tabriz with massive research libraries stocked by the rich Caliphal and Isma'ili collections of Baghdad and Alamut. Under the direction of polymaths-*cum*-administrators like Nasir al-Din Tusi (1201–1274) and Rashid al-Din (1247–1318), there emerged a highly cosmopolitan scientific-philosophical spirit that stimulated the study of Islamic, Greek, Chinese, Indic, and pre-Islamic Persian thought, with a certain predilection for the most universal of disciplines like mathematics, astrology, and the occult sciences. These Mongol seats of learning generated an open intellectual milieu in which hybrid strands of thought, which had previously been suppressed as heretical and dangerous, could flourish.[21]

Due to his Isma'ili background, Tusi himself had a fairly relaxed relationship with the Sharia, which for him contained both exoteric and esoteric aspects.[22] Among his very wide-ranging oeuvre, his work on political morals (*akhlāq*) has been most influential and enduring. *Akhlāq* offers a mixture of Greek, Persian, and Islamic political traditions that was to inspire so many forthcoming generations of postnomadic Turco-Mongolian rulers, including the Indian Mughals.[23] An even greater harmonizer was Rashid al-Din, who was deeply inspired by the Qur'anic verse 4:128 that stresses the importance of reconciliation (*wa-l-ṣulḥu khayrun*). Although Rashid al-Din is best known for his impressively inclusive world history—the *Jami' al-Tawarikh* (Compendium of Histories), not surprisingly a major source for our own *Tarikh-i Alfi*—his assimilative mindset shows even more in his neglected theological work in which he aimed to create harmony (*muwāfaqah, ṣulḥ*) between the apparently contradictory doctrines of ancient and modern, Islamic and non-Islamic scholars.[24] In this highly cosmopolitan context, in which scholars-*cum*-administrators were seeking ways to assimilate different worldviews, the works of Neoplatonic thinkers like Suhrawardi, Fakhr al-Din Razi, but also the work-in-progress of Tusi's star-pupil Qutb al-Din Shirazi, provided a perfect philosophical toolbox to overcome diversity and to fabricate an all-encompassing new ideology of cosmic rule in a world without end.

Very much claiming this Ilkhanid legacy, the fifteenth-century Timurids developed this new Neoplatonic dispensation into even more occult and performative forms with an increasing focus on saintly shrines. Even more so than under the Ilkhanids, sultans and Sufi saints competed fiercely with one another in laying claim to sacred power: sultans becoming saint-kings; Sufis becoming sultans. This Timurid version of "Millennial Sovereignty" was now indelibly stamped with the four signatures of Neoplatonism: idealism, monism, emanationism, and the tendency of the individual self toward divinization.[25] It attained hegemonic status throughout the postnomadic Persianate world, and most emphatically so along its Indian frontiers: the various sultanates of the Deccan and the Mughal Empire.

Although the Neoplatonic craze that filled the sixteenth-century Indo-Islamic courts was a result of the spread of monist ideals that had earlier taken post-Mongol Iran by storm, it became fueled by these courts' increasing interaction with Indic philosophy.[26] As in Europe, where translations of the Neoplatonic Hermetic texts had helped to engender a Neoplatonic renaissance if not *the* Renaissance, at these Indo-Islamic courts, the translations of Sanskrit works, especially from India's rich monist tradition, engendered another trend, one similar to the Renaissance, that, even more so than in Europe, strengthened the immanentist, cosmic characteristics of kingship.[27] Here we should not forget, of course, that Neoplatonism had, from its inception, always been orientalist avant la lettre and as such was possibly inspired by Indic monist thought.[28] As a consequence, by the early 1600s, we find a lengthy monist continuum, one that even crosses the Hindu-Muslim divide and connects the courts of Akbar (r. 1556–1605) in the north to that of Ibrahim Adil Shah II (r. 1580–1627) of Bijapur in the middle, down to Venkata II (r. 1585–1614) of Vijayanagara in the south of the subcontinent. It may perhaps be stretched even further, across the Bay of Bengal, to include the courts of Iskandar Muda (r. 1607–1636) in Aceh and Sultan Agung (r. 1613–1645) in Mataram (Java).[29] Perhaps the island of Buton, with its so-called *Martabat Tujuh* constitution, based on the seven grades of being, provides the most eastward, "Utopian" case of this Neoplatonic continuum.[30] Anyway, it seems that these courts developed an imperial ideology based on various branches of Neoplatonic political thought. Safavid Iran was the least monist of them because Neoplatonism had to make compromises with doctrinal Shi'ism. In India, however, inspired by the Vedanta revival, Neoplatonism could continue its earlier millenarian, mystical spirit.

This was the backdrop to what is arguably the most successful example of Neoplatonic kingship in world history: Akbar's cosmic kingship. The *Tarikh-i Alfi* then is not just another chronicle but rather a millennial world history that culminates in the rise of the divinized Neoplatonic philosopher-king who, as Lord of the Age and Renewer of the Second Millennium (*mujaddid-i alf-i thānī*), directs the way to a new cosmic era.[31]

Neoplatonic Authorship

The *Tarikh-i Alfi* was commissioned after Akbar revealed himself as a millennial being, a saintly and messianic figure above the constraints of Islamic or any other revealed law. To compose a history of the thousand years that culminated in this miraculous unveiling of the cosmic king, the emperor assembled a team of international Neoplatonists. A central figure in the project was Abul Fazl, Akbar's chief adviser and hagiographer, a scion of a prominent family Indian Muslim scholars who openly promoted the teachings of Ibn 'Arabi and Suhrawardi. The original committee of authors comprised seven members. There were four scholars from Safavid Iran: Naqib Khan (d. after 1610), Shah Fath Allah Shirazi (d. 1587), Hakim Humam (d. 1595), and Hakim Ali Gilani (d. 1619). From Herat, there was Nizam al-Din Ahmad Haravi (d. 1594), whose family had been loyal supporters of the earlier Timurid rulers. The other two were Indian-born Muslims: Abd al-Qadir Bada'uni (d. 1615) and Haji Ibrahim Sarhindi (d. 1584). Apart from these seven, Abul Fazl was to coordinate the project, and he wrote the (now lost) introduction and epilogue to the book.

Although at first sight the background of the authors seems quite diverse, they were all polymaths who were knowledgeable in a wide array of fields, including theology, philosophy, mathematics, medicine, and metaphysics and the occult sciences. Most of them occupied practical administrative positions and participated in the religious discussions that were organized by the emperor. At least six of them—Naqib Khan, Bada'uni, Abul Fazl, Nizam al-Din, Mulla Ahmad, and Jafar Beg—were experienced historians, and the first was the grandson of the celebrated Safavid historian Mir Yahya (1481–1555) and the son of Akbar's tutor Mir Abd al-Latif Qazvini. He is described by Jerome Xavier, the Jesuit missionary at Akbar's court, as one "whose office is to read histories."³² But Hakim Ali, for example, was not a historian and was primarily known as a medical scholar and an expert on Ibn Sina.³³ He was also Akbar's physician. At least four of them—Naqib Khan, Fath Allah, Bada'uni, and Sarhindi—had been involved in Akbar's Sanskrit translation project, which started as early as the mid-1570s and included an extensive collection of data that would also characterize the *Alfi* project.

If we look at the group as a whole, most of the authors seem one way or another to have been connected to the wider Neoplatonic philosophical tradition, including Ibn 'Arabi. At least three of them can be linked more specifically to the Ishraqi school through the important figure of Shaykh Mubarak Nagori (d. 1592), who was not only the father of Abul Fazl but also the venerated teacher of at least two other authors, Naqib Khan and Bada'uni.³⁴ However, the author with the most impressive Illuminationist credentials was Fath Allah Shirazi, who came from Iran via the Deccan to the Mughal court, where he was officially praised as "the Learned of the Age, the Plato of all times."³⁵ He had studied philosophy with the influential Mir Ghiyath al-Din Dashtaki, the chief religious functionary (*ṣadr*) of Safavid Iran who was dismissed because of his Neoplatonic disdain for Islamic law. What his teacher Dashtaki was unable to accomplish under the Safavids, however, Fath Allah managed to achieve under the Mughals. The Mughal poet laureate, Faizi, wrote thus of Akbar's sadness at the death of Fath Allah, his "Plato":

> The world-emperor's eyes were full of tears at his death.
> Alexander shed tears of grief when Plato left the world.³⁶

As a typical Ishraqi scholar, Fath Allah's training was not only in philosophy and theology but also involved much more practical disciplines, which—apart from astrology, mathematics, and the occult sciences—also included statecraft. When Fath Allah moved from the Deccan to the Mughal court, he helped rationalize imperial revenue collection, partly by confiscating the *waqf* properties of North Indian ulama. In line with these fiscal reforms, he also facilitated the collection of revenues by devising a new calendar that would replace the Islamic lunar one with a solar *ilāhī* (divine) calendar, which, in keeping with Illuminationist Neoplatonism, introduced old Persian months and festivals.³⁷

Looking beyond the immediate Ishraqi circle, at least one author of the *Tarikh-i Alfi*, Hakim Humam, was associated with the so-called Nuqtavis, another important Neoplatonic movement of post-Islam from Iran that had partial success in Safavid Iran but bloomed in Mughal India. The Nuqtavi were followers of Mahmud Pasikhani (d. 1427), who had taught that the universe was created through emanations from a "point" (*nuqṭa*).³⁸ The Nuqṭavis had strong millennial expectations. They predicted that the conjunction of Saturn and Jupiter (*qirān*), which would happen in 990/1582–1583, would mark the end of the Arab era and the beginning of a Persian period and the coming of the Mahdi.³⁹ Although for the Nuqṭavis the Mahdi was Pasikhani, through the transmigration of the soul, their millennial expectations could easily be transferred to someone else who was willing to embrace their ideas. Indeed, it was Akbar who invited various Iranian Nuqṭavi refugees who were being persecuted by the Safavid emperor. One of these refugees was Sharif Amuli, who declared that Akbar had all qualities to be the Mahdi because his name in the Abjad numeral system was equivalent to 990. Indeed, the *Tarikh-i Alfi* confirms that it can only be Akbar who will be the Renewer of the Second Millennium (*mujaddid-i hazāra-yi duyyum*) if only because the dots in Akbar's name are equal to justice (*'adl*) and the messiah (*mahdī*).⁴⁰

The millennial frenzy of the Nuqṭavis linked well with the millennial expectations of the sons and disciples of Shaykh Mubarak, who was considered a Mahdavi, that is, a follower of Sayyid Muhammad of Jaunpur (d. 1505), who had declared himself to be the Mahdi. The Shaykh's sons, Abul Fazl and Faizi were prominent Mahdavis but may also have corresponded with the neo-Zoroastrian Azar Kayvan (1533–1618), another Illuminationist author from Shiraz that had attempted to construct a millennial ideology of cosmic and solar kingship for the Safavids along Islamic-Zoroastrian and astrological lines.⁴¹ Overall, the amalgam of millennialist-Neoplatonist movements—Ishraqi, Nuqṭavi, Azari, and Mahdavi—provided the main ingredients of Akbar's imperial ideology as set out in the two major postmillennial chronicles of his reign, the *Tarikh-i Alfi* and the *Akbar Nama*. These works were produced in collaboration by a learned circle of cutting-edge Neoplatonic polymaths who combined knowledge of the religious and the secular, science, and philosophy, the theoretical and the practical, the seen and the unseen. Their main objective was to construct an imperial world history that would suit the one and only philosopher-king, Akbar, the Renewer of the Second Millennium.⁴²

2. A NEOPLATONIC PROJECT OF WORLD HISTORY

The *Tarikh-i Alfi* is a Neoplatonic Mughal world history designed to cover the events of the previous millennium. Unlike the majority of such Islamic histories, the *Tarikh-i Alfi* starts not from creation nor the prophet's birth but, in a radical fashion, from the latter's death (*raḥla*), which occurred ten years after his migration to Medina in 622 CE, the conventional start of the Islamic Era. The *Tarikh-i Alfi* was designed to be superior in scope and content to all other historical works that had been compiled previously and was to include the histories of all Muslim rulers along with an analysis of their rise and fall.[43] Organized in three parts, it emphasized the role of the Mongols in the history of Islam. The first part deals with events from the death of the prophet to Chinggis Khan, the second continues the chronological narrative to cover the Mongol conquest and its aftermath, and the third begins with the reign of the Ilkhanid ruler Ghazan Khan (r. 1295–1304) and ends with events related to the beginning of Akbar's rule and the consolidation of the Mughal Empire.[44]

Overall, the book seems to be conceived as the first part of a wider Neoplatonic global history that rather heretically starts with the death of the prophet and with Akbar as its apotheosis. It reads like a Neoplatonic Old Testament, one that paves the way for the coming of the saviour who will be described in more detail in the Mughal New Testament, the *Akbar Nama*.[45] As ever, the latter states it loud and clear: "Be this ancient world new through him; may his star shed rays of light like the sun."[46] Indeed, the *Akbar Nama* was launched in the year AH 1000/1591–1592 CE, the start of the new millennium.[47]

Universal Peace and the King's Ratio

If the previous millennial order had been for prophetic Islam, the new millennium was an era of universal peace (*ṣulḥ-i kull*). While Mughal universal peace is often thought of today as a South Asian version of the values of the Enlightenment—secularism, rationalism, and tolerance—it makes more sense to view it as a form of late Illuminationism in which scriptural-doctrinal prophethood was replaced by embodied-cosmic kingship. Far from offering a Weberian style disenchantment, the *Tarikh-i Alfi* actually uses an occult-Pythagorean version of Neoplatonism to prove Akbar's divinized status.[48]

It begins with the observation that the number 12 should be used as a sacred number because the Islamic *shahada* has twelve letters, a calendar has twelve months, and a day has twelve hours. Referring to the foundational Timurid historian Sharaf al-Din Ali Yazdi, it mentions that the ruler whose name has twelve letters will have an eternal rule. But because Akbar's name does not meet this condition, the *Tarikh-i Alfi* combines Akbar's name with that of Humayun and then removes the letters that recur to conveniently arrive at the number 12.

And see what happens as a sign from the unseen (*ghayb*): reversing them creates a new message that reads "his lordship is great" (*pirāya-yi buzurg-i u 'aẓīm ast*).⁴⁹ Indeed, like the later *Akbar Nama*, the *Tarikh-i Alfi* can but confirm Akbar's special talent for the occult sciences. As he combines material power (*padishāh-i ṣuwarī*) with spiritual authority (*salṭanat-i ma'nawī*), he spends all his time thinking about the kingdom, engaging in meditation and strenuous types of praying (*riyāḍāt wa 'ibadāt-i shāqqa*). One example of Akbar's magical power is the *Tarikh*'s remarkable story about the war against the Afghans, when Akbar refused to kill the captured and injured leader Himu. Why kill him twice, the story goes, because Akbar had already killed him when he was a boy and had subsequently painted a figure with a dismantled body called Himu.⁵⁰

In the midst of such magical exercises, the *Tarikh-i Alfi* declares that Akbar was a man of reason ('*aql*). Indeed, in the *Akbar Nama*, Abul Fazl highlights Akbar's intellectual capacity by mentioning his "perfect reason" ('*aql-i kāmil*) and "sound intellect" ('*aql-i salīm*).⁵¹ The *Tarikh-i Alfi* also stresses that Akbar's aim was to produce a true narrative that is based on human capacity and not on legends. Abul Fazl also refers to miracles as fraudulent events that were meant to confuse and mislead ignorant people.⁵² As such, the authors were instructed that if they were not sure about a narrative or did not have access to accurate information, then that narrative or information should not be included.⁵³ But, despite all its sobriety, the book makes an exception for the position of the Mahdi, who possesses the science of divination ('*ilm-i jafr*). By declaring Akbar to be the promised Mahdi, the *Tarikh-i Alfi* clearly implies that Akbar had access to these sciences, which means the Mughal emperor was not an ordinary person but a true philosopher-king who possessed both perfect logic as well as the perfect intellect to perceive the divine plan.⁵⁴ Thus, Akbar's horoscope drawn by Fath Allah showed that happiness upon happiness would come from the unseen world ('*ālam-i ghayb*) and that only Akbar's brilliant mind would be able to fathom the depth of the unknown.⁵⁵ Whereas on the outside (*ẓāhir*) Akbar displayed the splendour (*farr*) of the mythical Iranian kings Jamshid and Faridun, his interior was bestowed with the wisdom of Socrates and the perspicacity of Plato. In other words, "his eye and heart were with the origin of emanation," which, so close to the reference to Plato, reads like Abul Fazl's description of the One.⁵⁶

But what about Akbar's belief in Islam? Here, we have to rely on the secret chronicle of Bada'uni, who was a senior courtier of Akbar but had become extremely disgruntled, yet continued to work for the emperor.⁵⁷ Bada'uni records that, under the influence of Abul Fazl, Abul Fath Gilani, and the court jester Birbal, Akbar completely lost his belief in the Islamic revelation (*waḥy*), the prophet's ascension to heaven (*mi'rāj*), the resurrection (*ma'ād*), and other miracles (*muʿjizāt*) because these contradicted plain reason.⁵⁸ He also mentions that Akbar even lost his belief in the prophet, his companions, and the Hadith because of his understanding of history.⁵⁹ This understanding was shaped by the Neoplatonist frame of the *Tarikh-i Alfi*.

The *Tarikh-i Alfi* makes a striking observation about prophets and kings. It notes that, although prophets are sent to distinguish between right (*ḥaq*) and false (*bāṭil*), their tendency is to divide people on the basis of the religion that they teach. It dismisses religious leaders who misuse religion to exploit the ignorance of the people and to create sectarian conflicts for their own benefits.⁶⁰ This argument, which comes close to Assmann's "Mosaic Distinction," is attributed to unnamed Sufis—most likely Nuqtavis—who believed that the last millennium had been the "Period of the Prophets" (*daur-i nabuwwat*), an era of disunity and disagreement. By contrast, the *Tarikh-i Alfi* presents Akbar as a unifier of the new millennium. The emperor not only accepted and respected the diversity of creatures (*tawḥid wa jamʿ*) but also the oneness of the creator. He believed that everyone has true faith, and each individual has his own way to understand the divine; as such, there is no reason to sow divisions between people because of their faith. The *Tarikh-i Alfi* then continues by stating that the Period of the Prophets had ended to make way for the Period of Unity, one in which all creeds and traditions would be united.⁶¹ Unlike the divisive approach of the prophets (*ʿayn al-kithrat wa al-tafraqa*), Akbar as king understands the world as it was created and sees all creatures through the divine eye (*naẓar-i ḥaq*). His approach is inclusive and accepts everything as it is (*mashrab-i wilāyat*). He believes that unity is in diversity (*ʿayn al-waḥdat wa al-jamʿ*), thus paving the way for Akbar's imperial ideology of universal peace.⁶²

The Mongol Legacy of Universal Peace

Although the *Tarikh-i Alfi* gives full credit to Akbar's new covenant of universal peace, it also makes the point that religious tolerance was part of the Mongol heritage going back to Chinggis Khan, who is staged as an alternative source of legitimacy to that of the prophet and scripture of Islam. Based on earlier Mongol chronicles such as Rashid al-Din's already mentioned *Jamiʿ al-Tawarikh* and Juvayni's *Tarikh-i Jahangusha*, the *Tarikh-i Alfi* reiterates that Chinggis Khan did not discriminate against people because of their religion; instead, he was simply doing God's will by not being a follower (*muqallid, tābiʿ*) of any specific religion.⁶³ It mentions that almost all Mongol rulers believed in the equality of religions and that they allowed the people to perform their religious rituals freely. Indeed, the *Tarikh-i Alfi* draws a parallel between Akbar and Chinggis Khan by referring to a discussion between Chinggis and qadi Ashraf of Bukhara. According to our *Tarikh*, the Mongol khan believed in one God and actually agreed that the Prophet Muhammad preached some good teachings. Then follows a revealing and significant episode in which Chinggis Khan compared himself with the prophet and said that he had also sent messengers (*īlchīyān*) to the people of all regions. Chinggis further disagreed with qadi Ashraf on the issue of the mandatory pilgrimage to Mecca by saying, "the whole world is the house of God and there are ways to God everywhere."[64] As a result of this dialogue, qadi Ashraf declared Chinggis Khan to be a Muslim ruler, but some other mullahs denied it because Chinggis Khan disagreed about the hajj. The author of this part of the *Tarikh-i Alfi* may have been aware of the fact that Akbar—like most Muslim rulers of Iran, Central Asia, and India—had not gone on the hajj.

In highlighting the divinized roles of kings, the *Tarikh-i Alfi* gives much space to Mongol rulers in general. For example, in a short introduction to the reign of the Ilkhanid ruler Ghazan Khan (r. 1295–1304), the text discusses the traditional Persian-Islamic idea that God chooses a person and elevates him as king to perform His will. It is God who selects the one who has the right capacity, and his essence (*dhāt*) will be filled with honesty and absolute good. The message seems to be that God does not randomly select a king but only the most capable one—a rather elegant rationalization of the well-known Mongol meritocracy.[65] In providing a list of ideal rulers, as well as Ali, the *Tarikh-i Alfi* mentions Chinggis Khan, Ögedei, Möngke, Kaidu, Kubilai, and Timur because of their inclusive and tolerant policies. It reserves a special place, though, for Zayn al-Abidin, the cosmopolitan sultan of Kashmir (r. 1418–1470). He is presented as a lover of science, music, and nature, and as a polyglot who translated Indian books on astrology and medicine. He revived the Hindu rituals that were banned by his predecessor Sultan Sikandar (r. 1389–1413) and returned religious authority to the Brahmins. He also banned killing cows and hunting and allowed those Hindus who were forced to accept Islam to reconvert.[66] All these kings provided a model of royal tolerance that Akbar followed.

To further underscore the religious tolerance of the Mongols, the *Tarikh-i Alfi* gives the examples of Ögedei Khan and Möngke, son and grandson of Chinggis Khan, respectively. Of the latter, it is said that he kept scribes and secretaries from each group of people in his court. If the Khan needed to address these people, he would be able to address them in their own tongue.[67] The work also contrasts Mongol policy with that of the Persians and other rulers and advises all kings of the world to follow this good tradition (*rasm-i pasandīda*).[68] Further elaborating on Möngke, the chronicle recounts how he ordered that his day of coronation should be commemorated as a special day. He ordered that no one should fight each other, animals should not be killed, plants and trees should not be cut down, and flowing water should not be polluted. People must prepare their food with meat they already had at home. Then, here, the *Tarikh-i Alfi* takes the opportunity to compare Akbar—now mentioned as a caliph—directly with Möngke by saying that the latter's order covered just one day, whereas Akbar managed to ban animal killing for several days of the year.[69] With examples like this, the *Tarikh-i Alfi* clearly suggests that Akbar's policy of universal peace had Mongol antecedents.

As far as the unity of the principle is concerned, the Mongols again provide the model. Chinggis Khan is cited saying that the state's stability is in the unity of the ruling class and their absolute obedience (*iṭāʿat-i muṭlaq*).[70] The state cannot survive without laws (*yasāq*), discipline (*naẓm*), honesty (*pākī*), caution (*iḥtiyāṭ*), awareness (*ḥazm*), and skilled and knowledgeable people to run the administration.[71] In a surprisingly analytical description that reminds one of Ibn Khaldun's famous circular theory of nomadic state formation, the *Tarikh-i Alfi* elaborates on the history of the Mongols before and after Chinggis Khan and relates how the Mongols' worldview, traditions, and lifestyle gradually changed after they settled in the cities of China and Iran, as the Mongol Ilkhans became Persianized and the Mongol Yuan becoming Sinified.[72]

Perhaps it is precisely this context of early settlement after conquest that made rulers like Ghazan and Möngke such appealing models for Akbar, who experienced the same after the initial conquests of his father and grandfather. In any case, the chronicle shows how nomadic life in the deserts of Mongolia were the ideal stage for heroic achievements in ongoing wars, whereas the postnomadic life in the grand palaces of Iran and China limited the space for such activity. Instead, palace life led the Mongols in new directions: conversion, construction, learning about their subjects, hunting and playing, discussion with scholars, and becoming ideal rulers to their new subjects and changing their image from pagan-barbarian heroes to civilized rulers. Thus, these later generations led lives of great pleasure and, when pleasure prevails, forgot how their ancestors built the empire.[73] However, it was not only palace life that threatened to undermine the new state; the postnomadic Mongols were also facing Muslim and non-Muslim religious leaders who had their own understanding of kingship, one that was significantly different from that of the Mongols.[74]

From the above, it is evident the *Tarikh-i Alfi* builds on the Mongol chronicles to offer an almost Ibn Khaldunian cycle of state formation, including the idea of degeneration under more settled conditions after a conquest. We use the word *almost* because the *Tarikh-i Alfi* also finds the religious establishment to blame for this. In addition, it is not Ibn Khaldun's tribal cohesion or ʿaṣabiyya, but the law, as issued by the Great Khan, that realizes the strength of the nomads. By contrast, in an astonishingly perceptive historical analysis, the *Tarikh-i Alfi* states that the formation of the Mongol Empire was actually the result of a collaboration between *different* groups of people (*ba barakt-i ittiḥād wa dust-i bā yakdigar*) under one strong leadership (*yak kas*).[75] What really held them together were the commands (*yasāq*) and laws (*qawānīn*) that derived from the wisdom of Chinggis Khan. If not enforced, the empire would be lost (*padishāhī mutazalzil wa munqaṭiʿ gardad*).[76]

Overall, we may conclude that the *Tarikh-i Alfi* constructs an Akbari universal peace that builds on the Mongol model. The ancient Persian kings; the Arab caliphs, including Ali; and even Akbar's direct Timurid ancestors play only a secondary role. Although the Mongols may have provided the model, the light that enlightens Akbar is the light of Illuminationism: it is direct and the result of Akbar's personal intuition, something that does not require the interference of any historical precursor. The Chinggis legacy and this reverence for light converge in one of the illustrations of the *Chinggis Nama*, another chronicle commissioned by Akbar, where we see Chinggis Khan sitting on a hill praying to the source of all light: the sun, *not* as God but as His image.[77]

The Sun and the Soul

To facilitate the building of a universal empire for a population that remained majority Hindu, the *Tarikh-i Alfi* provided Akbar with a comprehensive framework of inclusion. Here we would like to discuss two examples of the Indic religious experience that the *Tarikh-i Alfi* attempted to incorporate in its universal metanarrative: worship of the sun and transmigration of the soul. As has been demonstrated by Carl Ernst in what may be Faizi's work on Krishna and yoga, the *Tarikh-i Alfi* also interpreted these phenomena very much in terms of a generalized form of Illuminationist philosophy. In so doing, it "naturalized and familiarized these 'Hindu' themes along lines familiar to Muslim intellectuals."[78] Of course, it is worth knowing that Akbar himself was both an avid sun worshipper and also believed in the return of the soul because both contributed to the legitimacy of his universal imperial ideology and, at the same time, helped to build a bridge with the Indic religious traditions in his empire.

The argument of the *Tarikh-i Alfi* in favor of sun worship starts by implicitly endorsing the pre-Islamic and Indic practice of sun worship. Even before the Islamic Era, the term that is used for the sun is *Great Luminous Being* (*nayyir-i aʿzam*), which is the same as used later by the Mughals.[79] The main source on Indic sun worship is the twelfth-century Persian historian Muhammad al-Shahristani's *Kitab al-Milal wa al-Nihal* (The book of sects and creeds), which offers an extensive, nonpolemical overview of the world's religions.[80] In summarizing Shahristani, the *Tarikh* writes that the Hindus stand before the sun, prostrate, and recite a prayer called "the secondary praising" (*tasbīḥ-i thanāʾī*), which is either directed toward the sun as the first light (*nūr-i awwal*) or, if there is a higher and brighter light than the sun, toward the creator of the sun. In both cases, the devotee comes closer to the light through purification of body and soul.[81]

Later in the story, the *Tarikh-i Alfi* adds another sun prayer, from the *Taskhir al-Kawakib* (The possession of stars), which is attributed to the famous ninth-century astrologer Abu Mashar al-Balkhi (d. 886). Abu Mashar himself was already deeply influenced by Indic notions of cyclical time and bequeathed the idea to both the Islamic and Christian worlds via the science of astrology. With a Persian translation of his Arabic prayer, the *Tarikh* gives a long description of the sun ritual, which should be performed during sunrise while the worshipper wears a royal dress that is gold in color. He should hold a golden firebox with particular material related to the sun. The materials should contain saffron and should be mixed with cow's milk. It cites a prayer that gives almost all specific epithets of God to the sun. In other words, it replaces God with the sun. At the end, it asks the sun for prosperity and completes the ritual with prostration to the sun.[82]

Although the *Tarikh-i Alfi* reproduces Abu Mashar's passages on the veneration of the sun, the language that is used recalls the Illuminationist idea of light as the origin of creation. It calls the sun "the pure light" (*nūr-i khāliṣ*), "the perfect shining" (*ḍauʾ-i tamām*) and "the origin of all" (*aṣal-i hama*). The life of all stars and planets depends on the sun and light connects them to the sun. Suhrawardi himself had also composed prayers in Arabic addressed to the great Heavenly Sun, Hurakhsh, but also referred to again as *al-nayyir al-aʿzam*, the sun being the heavenly counterpart of a king on earth. In the words of Hossein Ziai, just as Hurakhsh shines in the heavens, so does the light of kings (*kiyān kharra*) shine on earth. Both the sun and the king have manifest luminous qualities, which is why they are obeyed by their subjects.[83] All this neatly fits Akbar's own ideas about sun worship. Akbar followed Suhrawardi's idea that the sun was not God but just His image, His light. Hence the worship of the sun was actually the worship of God's light. Abul Fazl's brother Faizi compared the sun to the Kaʿba and the Qibla. But to understand the sun, one should see it through the eyes of Akbar. Each of his eyes is an astrolabe; the sun itself is Akbar's educator; and, in turn, Akbar himself is the educator of the world.[84]

Intersecting with the treatise on sun worship, the *Tarikh-i Alfi* also discusses the transmigration of the soul from pre-Islamic, Indic, and Muslim points of view. The *Tarikh-i Alfi* and Bada'uni's *Muntakhab al-Tawarikh* (The selection of histories) provide the two main sources for Akbar's understanding of *tanāsukh*—the Persian term for the transmigration of the soul, also called metempsychosis. According to Bada'uni, Akbar revealed to Azam Khan in 1582 that he was "absolutely convinced and satisfied on the issue of metempsychosis."[85] This is the very same year that the *Alfi* project was launched, so we should not be surprised that *tanāsukh* attracts much attention within it. The *Tarikh-i Alfi*'s discussion on *tanāsukh* was the first major attempt to harmonize Indic and Islamic Neoplatonist ideals of reincarnation of the soul.[86] Following the Illuminationist philosopher Qutb al-Din Shirazi, it stressed that Hermes, Agathasimon, Pythagoras, Socrates, and Plato supported it, as did other philosophers of Greece, Iran, Babylon, and India; even Aristotle seems to have agreed with it.[87] Later, the Indian sages Buzasf (Buddha) and Barjamis (Burjumaniyun) are added to the list. In addition, an attempt is made to create a full Illuminationist consensus about the issue, bringing together the works of Qutb al-Din, Davani, and Dashtaki, which are then concluded by the great master himself, Suhrawardi. In short, as used in the *Tarikh-i Alfi*, Neoplatonism had again proven its mettle as an irresistible force of assimilation.

All this raises the important question, however: how did the sun and the soul contribute to the legitimacy of Akbar's universal rule? Our provisional answer to this question is provided by the work of Suhrawardi's contemporary and fellow Neoplatonist, Fakhr al-Din Razi. We have noticed him already as a major scholarly authority at the Ilkhanid academies. Like Suhrawardi, it seems that Razi's understudied occult work experienced something of a revival in Mughal India at the turn of the Islamic millennium.[88] Mughal interest in Razi was raised by the way he used the Hermetic tradition to link knowledge of the celestial realm—the sun, the planets, and the stars—to knowledge of God and the achievement of gnosis. To harmonize his court with the celestial sphere, Akbar's father, Humayun, had designed the so-called Carpet of Mirth on which "each group was ordered to sit in accordance with one of the seven planets," Humayun himself sitting in the "golden sphere, similar to the sun in lustre, light and pureness."[89] Far from being a Mughal invention, the complexity of this celestial carpet derived directly from Razi, who in his turn followed Hermetic ideas of heliocentrism.[90]

Whatever the complexities of Neoplatonic astral thinking, to be in tune with the celestial sphere could occur only when the soul rose beyond the confines of the body. Hence, purification of the soul and separation of the body is one of the goals of astrological practice. In Hermetic terms, the ultimate goal of self-purification and the seeking of knowledge was the rebirth of the human soul not in the body but free from that corporeal prison in order to attain gnosis and ascent to the celestial realm. In the words of Nora Jacobsen Ben Hammed:

> Razi views the celestial beings as mediators between human beings, whose souls are of the same genus as the angels, and God. God's light, perfection, and knowledge flow through these entities to the prophets and the rest of humanity. It is the greatest goal of the human being to perfect his or her soul and to join the lowest ranks of these celestial kin.[91]

For an "intellectual person" (*ʿāqil*), such an ascent to the celestial level—also called the universal intellect (*ʿaql-i kull*)—results in prophethood.[92] In this way, ratio, sun, and soul become closely connected as the prime deliverers of the perfect prophet-*cum*-king. Hence, it seems that, through the Neoplatonic interpretation of both sun worship and metempsychosis, the *Tarikh-i Alfi* created an autonomous source of legitimation for its great intellectual patron's universal rule.[93]

The general influence of Neoplatonism in the history of Western and Islamic philosophy is well known. What is much less acknowledged, however, is the way in which Neoplatonism, in all its various avatars, became one of the ideological mainstays of sacred kingship in the Islamic world after the Mongol conquests. Since the thirteenth century, the monist, hierarchically layered nature of Neoplatonist thought provided ambitious postnomadic kings with a powerful framework to accommodate a diversity of religious and philosophical traditions. The result was a remarkably successful Neoplatonic version of cosmic kingship that thrived in particular along the arid frontiers of the Islamic world ruled by Turco-Mongolian conquerors in need of a new, autonomous universal ideology to encompass their vast empires. During the long sixteenth century, driven by the intensified links between Iran, Central Asia, and India, there emerged a continuum of Islamic royal courts that immersed themselves in Neoplatonic thought. To its west, this continuum suddenly linked rather well with the new Neoplatonic mood at the courts of Europe, generating an even more extensive, global Neoplatonic Renaissance. To its east, along its Indian frontiers, the cultural cauldron of the Mughal and Deccan courts amalgamated Indic monist traditions with a mixture of philosophical, mystical, and occult Islamic traditions, giving rise to new works of literature and imagination that sought religious inclusion on an ever more global scale. The *Tarikh-i Alfi* is a brilliant case in point.

NOTES

We are grateful to the following colleagues for their comments on earlier drafts: Bert van den Berg, Gabrielle van den Berg, Ebba Koch, Richard van Leeuwen and Hans van Santen. It also profited tremendously from the comments of the editors of this volume.

1. Cited from *Partawnama* ("Epistle of Emanation") in Hossein Ziai, "Source and Nature of Authority: A Study of Suhrawardi's Illuminationist Political Doctrine," in *The Political Aspects of Islamic Philosophy*, ed. Charles Butterworth (Cambridge, MA: Harvard University Press, 1992), 329.
2. Qadi Ahmad Thattavi and Asaf Khan Qazvini, *Tarikh-i Alfi: Tarikh-i Hazar Sala-yi Islam*, ed. Ghulam Reza Tabatabai Majd, 8 vols. (Tehran: Intisharat-i 'Ilmi wa Farhangi, 1382/2002).
3. *Tarikh-i Alfi* was partially published for the first time by Sayed Ali Al-i Davoud, who considered only the last part of the book: Sayed Ali Al-i Davoud, *Tarikh-i Alfi: Tarikh-i Iran wa Kishvarha-yi Hamsaya dar Salha-yi AH 850–984* (*Tarikh-i Alfi*: History of Iran and the Neighbouring Countries from AH 850–984) (Tehran: Intisharat-i Fikr-i Ruz, 1377/1999), based on three manuscripts preserved in Astan-i Quds Library in Mashhad and the library of Tehran University. Majd published the text in eight volumes without describing the manuscripts that he used or any kind of text criticism, introduction to the text, or reference to Al-i Davoud's work.
4. The only other work that—albeit in passing—interprets Akbar as a Neoplatonic ruler is Ebba Koch, "The Intellectual and Artistic Climate of Akbar's Court," in *The Adventures of Hamza: Painting and Storytelling in Mughal India*, ed. John Seyller (Washington: Freer Gallery of Art and Arthur M. Sackler Gallery, 2002), 22. For a discussion of this Neoplatonic Renaissance in a global context, see Jos Gommans, "The Neoplatonic Renaissance from the Thames to the Ganges," in *India after World History: Literature, Comparison, and Approaches to Globalization*, ed. Neilesh Bose (Leiden: Leiden University Press, 2022).
5. Christian Wildberg, "Neoplatonism," in *The Stanford Encyclopedia of Philosophy*, ed. Edward N. Zalta (Summer 2019 edition), https://plato.stanford.edu/archives/sum2019/entries/neoplatonism, accessed September 11, 2020.
6. Dominic J. O'Meara, *Platonopolis: Platonic Political Philosophy in Late Antiquity* (Oxford: Oxford University Press, 2003).

7. Perhaps a better term for monism would be henoism, that is, belief in a number of deities, but also in something greater than those deities, some greater cosmic order or consciousness. For us, both terms refer to a pluralistic theology wherein different deities are viewed to be of a unitary, equivalent divine essence.
8. Maria Mavroudi, "Pletho as Subversive and His Reception in the Islamic World," in *Power and Subversion in Byzantium*, ed. Dimeter Angelov and Michael Saxby (Farnham, Surrey: Ashgate, 2013), 177–203. See also Alison Brown, "Platonism in Fifteenth-Century Florence and Its Contribution to Early Modern Political Thought," *Journal of Modern History* 58 (1986): 383–413. It was Pletho in particular who reintroduced the Neoplatonic legacy to Italy and inspired the well-known translation movement under Marsilio Ficino (1433–1499). Hence, as usual in such earlier globalizing moments, Neoplatonism demonstrated its force to assimilate familiar strands of thought, in this case Hermetic and Kabbalah traditions to have a substantial, albeit short-term impact on European Renaissance courts, in particular under the Medici, the Habsburgs, and the early Stuarts. Since the seminal but also controversial work of Frances Yates, the European developments lack an overall historical survey, but see Vaughan Hart, *Art and Magic in the Court of the Stuarts* (London: Routledge, 1994), and more recently, Anthony F. D'Elia, *Pagan Virtue in a Christian World: Sigismondo Malatesta and the Italian Renaissance* (Cambridge, MA: Harvard University Press, 2016).
9. Matthew Melvin-Koushki contrasts this early modern Latin "inquisitorial chauvinism" with the Persianate "radical ecumenism" driven by "a brand of occult-scientific imperialism." See Matthew Melvin-Koushki, "How to Rule the World: Occult-Scientific Manuals of the Early Modern Persian Cosmopolis," *Journal of Persianate Studies* 11 (2018): 140–54. See also Wouter J. Hanegraaf, *Esotericism and the Academy: Rejected Knowledge in Western Culture* (Cambridge: Cambridge University Press, 2012).
10. For some surprising, artistic Neoplatonic commensurabilities, see Jos Gommans, *The Unseen World: The Netherlands and India from 1550* (Amsterdam: Rijksmuseum/Nijmegen: VanTilt, 2018). A thought-provoking Platonic reading of Islamic art is offered by Wendy M. K. Shaw, *What Is "Islamic" Art? Between Religion and Perception* (Cambridge: Cambridge University Press, 2019).
11. It is also in the specific context of the empire building and globalization in that century that we find the most ambitious attempts by rulers to epistemologically order their ever-expanding universe in universal histories and encyclopedias. As an example of the latter, Qazvini's *'Aja'ib al-Makhluqat* (The Wonders of Creation) has a deeply Neoplatonic view on creation in which visible things also have invisible, Platonic forms and thus each wonder is a sign pointing to the oneness of its creator; see Persis Berlekamp, *Wonder, Image, and Cosmos in Medieval Islam* (New Haven, CT: Yale University Press, 2011), and Stefano Carboni, *The Wonders of Creation and the Singularities of Painting* (Edinburgh: Edinburgh University Press, 2015).
12. Jos Gommans, *The Indian Frontier: Horse and Warband in the Making of Empires* (London: Routledge, 2018), 229–331.
13. See also Alan Strathern, *Unearthly Power: Religious and Political Change in World History* (Cambridge: Cambridge University Press, 2019).

14. Michael Ebstein, *Mysticism and Philosophy in Al-Andalus: Ibn Masarra, Ibn al-ʿArabī and the Ismāʿīlī Tradition* (Leiden: Brill, 2014); Godefroid de Callataÿ, "Brethren of Purity," in *Encyclopaedia of Islam, THREE*, ed. Kate Fleet et al., http://dx.doi.org.ezproxy.leidenuniv.nl:2048/10.1163/1573-3912_ei3_COM_25372, accessed March 12, 2021.
15. Ilker Evrim Binbaş, *Intellectual Networks in Timurid Iran: Sharaf al-Din ʿAlī Yazdī and the Islamicate Republic of Letters* (Cambridge: Cambridge University Press, 2016), 99–103, 150, 258.
16. See A. Azfar Moin, "Millennial Sovereignty and the Mughal Dynasty," in *Oxford Handbook of the Mughal World*, ed. Richard Eaton and Ramya Sreenivasan (Oxford: Oxford University Press, forthcoming).
17. Although Ishraqi philosophy has been studied extensively by Henry Corbin and Hossein Nasr, this and the next section builds primarily on some of the more recent summaries provided by Ziai, "Source and Nature of Authority," 304–344; John Walbridge, *The Wisdom of the Mystic East: Suhrawardī and Platonic Orientalism* (Albany: State University of New York Press, 2001); Roxanne Marcotte, "Suhrawardi," *The Stanford Encyclopedia of Philosophy*, ed. Edward N. Zalta (Summer 2019 edition), https://plato.stanford.edu/archives/sum2019/entries/suhrawardi, accessed January 9, 2020; and Hossein Ziai, "Illuminationism," *Encyclopædia Iranica*, vol. 3:, Fasc. 6, 670-2, and Vol. XIII, Fasc. 1, 1–2, http://www.iranicaonline.org/articles/kadimi-zoroastrian-sect, accessed January 9, 2020. See also Ian Richard Netton, who sees Ishraqi as a mixture of Platonic, post-Aristotelian, and Neoplatonic ideas. In our view, it is this mixture itself that makes it Neoplatonic. Ian Richard Netton, "Suhrawardī's Heir: The Ishrāqī Philosophy of Mīr Dāmād," in *The Heritage of Sufism*, vol. 3: *Late Classical Persianate Sufism (1501–1750)*, ed. Leonard Lewisohn and David Morgan (Oxford: One World, 1999), 232.
18. Susan Stiles Maneck, *The Death of Ahriman: Culture, Identity and Theological Change among the Parsis of India* (Bombay: K. R. Bed Oriental Institute, 1997), 49–70.
19. Ziai, "Illuminationism," 670–2. In a more elaborate discussion, Ziai also points out that some of Suhrawardi's work had been commissioned by the Seljuk rulers Ala al-Din Kay-Qubad, Sulaiman Shah, and Malik Imad al-Din; see Ziai, "Source and Nature of Authority," 322.
20. Jonathan Brack, "Theologies of Auspicious Kingship: The Islamization of Chinggisid Sacral Kingship in the Islamic World," *Comparative Studies in Society and History* 60 (2018): 1143–71.
21. Stefan Kamola, *Making Mongol History: Rashid al-Din and the Jamiʿ al-Tawarikh* (Edinburgh: Edinburgh University Press, 2019), 63–78, 92–115.
22. George E. Lane, "Ṭusi, Naṣir-al-Din," *Encyclopaedia Iranica*, http://www.iranicaonline.org/articles/tusi-nasir-al-din-bio, accessed April 19, 2018.
23. Muzaffar Alam, *The Languages of Political Islam: India, 1200–1800* (Chicago: University of Chicago Press, 2004).
24. Robert Wisnovsky, "On the Emergence of Maragha Avicennism," *Oriens* 46 (2018): 270–1. For Rashid al-Din's theological work, see also Dorothea Krawulsky, *The Mongol Īlkhāns and the Vizier Rashīd al-Dīn* (Frankfurt: Peter Lang, 2011), and Josef van Ess, *Der Wesir und seine Gelehrten* (Wiesbaden: Abhandlungen für die Kunde des Morgenlandes XLV/4, 1981).

25. A. Azfar Moin, *The Millennial Sovereign: Sacred Kingship and Sainthood in Islam* (New York: Columbia University Press, 2012); A. Azfar Moin "The Politics of Saint Shrines in the Persianate Empires," in *The Persianate World: Rethinking a Shared Sphere*, ed. Abbas Amanat and Assef Ashraf (Leiden: Brill, 2018), 105–24. For the rise of the occult sciences, see Matthew Melvin-Koushki, in particular his "Powers of One: The Mathematicalization of the Occult Sciences in High-Persianate Tradition," *Intellectual History of the Islamicate World* 5 (2017): 127–99; Melvin-Koushki, "How to Rule the World," 140–54, and Matthew Melvin-Koushki, "Early Modern Islamicate Empire: New Forms of Religiopolitical Legitimacy" in *The Wiley Blackwell History of Islam*, ed. Armando Salvatore and Roberto Tottoli (Chichester: Wiley, 2018), 353–75. It should be stressed that the adding of the label *Neoplatonism* to these developments is ours.

26. The history of how Illuminationism developed across Iran and Central Asia, spreading to South and North India is a complex one. Recent studies include Marco Di Branco, "The 'Perfect King' and his Philosophers: Politics, Religion and Graeco-Arabic Philosophy in Safavid Iran: The Case of the Utūlūǧiyā," *Studia Graeco-Arabica* 4 (2014): 191–218; Ali Anooshahr, "Shirazi Scholars and the Political Culture of Sixteenth-Century Indo-Persian World," *The Indian Economic and Social History Review* 51, no. 3 (2014): 331–52; Carl W. Ernst, *Refractions of Islam in India: Situating Sufism and Yoga* (New Delhi: Sage, 2016), 406–407; Emma J. Flatt, *The Courts of the Deccan Sultanates: Living Well in the Persian Cosmopolis* (Cambridge: Cambridge University Press, 2019).

27. Audrey Truschke, *Culture of Encounters: Sanskrit at the Mughal Court* (New York: Columbia University Press, 2016). For the comparison with the European Renaissance, see also Ebba Koch, "Being like Jesus and Mary: The Influence of the Jesuit Missions on Symbolic Representations of the Mughal Emperors Revisited," in *Transcultural Imaginations of the Sacred*, ed. Margit Kern and Klaus Krüger (Munich: Fink Verlag, 2018), 197–230.

28. Walbridge, *The Wisdom of the Mystic East*, 13–17. Unfortunately, the search for such horizontal philosophical linkages is looked down upon in modern academia and has caused scholars to ignore the earliest Indian connections of Neoplatonism. See, however, some of the suggestive comparative work of Thomas McEvilley, *The Shape of Ancient Thought: Comparative Studies in Greek and Indian Philosophies* (New York: Allworth Press, 2002), and the inspiring volume edited by Richard Seaford, *Universe and Inner Self in Early Indian and Early Greek Thought* (Edinburgh: Edinburgh University Press, 2016). For a recent discussion of the Greco-Indian linkages, see Joachim Lacrosse, "Plotin, Porphyre et l'Inde: Un ré-examen," *Le Philosophoire* 41 (2014): 87–104.

29. For a provisional discussion of the South Indian part of this continuum, see Jos Gommans, "Cosmopolitanism and Imagination in Nayaka South India: Decoding the Brooklyn *Kalamkari*," *Archives of Asian Art* 70, no. 1 (2020): 1–21. In the Indonesia archipelago, Neoplatonic notions were primarily spread through a network of pantheist Shattari Sufis, which, via the work of Shams al-Din Sumatrani—the main religious figure under Iskandar Muda of Aceh (r. 1607–1636)—was connected to the Indian subcontinent, in particular to Muhammad ibn Fazl-Allah al-Burhanpuri. This Indonesian branch of Neoplatonism was at that time already criticized as being

"Vedantic." See Denys Lombard, *Le sultanat d'Atjéh au temps d'Iskandar Muda, 1607–1636* (Paris: École Française d'Extrême-Orient, 1967), 163.

30. J. W. Schoorl, "Power, Ideology, and Change in the Early State of Buton," in *State and Trade in the Indonesian Archipelago*, ed. G. J. Schutte (Leiden: KITLV, 1994), 17–57.

31. During sixteenth- and seventeenth-century Mughal rule, at least twelve other world histories were written. Most of these followed more or less the existing model that had started with Balʿami (*Tarikhnama*) and Gardizi (*Zain al-Akhbar*) and continued gradually to incorporate the eastern Islamic world after the Mongol invasions with the chronicles of Juzjani (*Tabaqat-i Nasiri*), Rashid al-Din (*Jamiʿ al-Tawarikh*), Mustaufi (*Tarikh-i Guzida*), and Mirkhwand (*Rauzat al-Safa*). Apart from the *Tarikh-i Alfi*, Akbar commissioned another world history, the *Rauzat al-Tahirin*, written by Tahir Muhammad Sabzavari (1602–1607). Like the *Tarikh-i Alfi*, all these chronicles were compilations that built on the most important earlier works available to the Mughal historians. For an excellent survey of these works, see Stephan Conermann, *Historiographie als Sinnstiftung: Indo-persische Geschichtsschreibung während der Mogulzeit (932–1118/1516–1707)* (Wiesbaden: Reichert Verlag, 2002), 364–82.

32. Cited in Muzaffar Alam and Sanjay Subrahmanyam, "Frank Disputations: Catholics and Muslims at the Court of Jahangir (1608–11)," *Indian Economic and Social History Review* 46, no. 4 (2009): 482. Of Naqib Khan, it was said that his historical knowledge was unequaled and that he had learned the seven volumes of Mirkhwand's world history *Rauzat al-Safa* by heart. See Shah Nawaz Khan, *Maʾathir al-Umara*, ed. Maulawi Abdur Rahim and Mirza Ashraf Ali, 3 vols. (Calcutta: Bibliotheca Indica 112, 1888–91), 3: 812–17.

33. Antonio Monserrate, *The Commentary of Father Monserrate, S.J., on his Journey to the Court of Akbar*, trans. J. S. Hoyland, anno. S. N. Banerjee (London: Oxford University Press, 1922), 420; Nur al-Din Muhammad Jahangir, *Tuzuk-i Jahangiri*, ed. Muhammad Hashim (Tehran: Bunyadi-i Farhang-i Iran, 1980), 88.

34. Saiyid Athar Abbas Rizvi. *Religious and Intellectual History of the Muslims in Akbar's Reign with Special Reference to Abuʾl Fazl, 1556–1605* (New Delhi: Munshiram Manoharlal, 1975), 80; Azra Nizami, "Social-Religious Outlook of Abul Fazl," *Medieval India, A Miscellany* 2 (London: Asia, 1972), 48.

35. In Persian: ʿallāmat al-zamāni aflāṭūn al-ʿawāmi. See Abul Fazl, *The History of Akbar*, ed. and trans. Wheeler M. M. Thackston, 6 vols. (Cambridge, MA: Harvard University Press—Murty Classical Library of India, 2017), 3: 30.

36. In Persian: *Shahanshāh-i jahān rā dar wafātash dīda pur nam shud / Sikandar ashk-i ḥasrat rīkht ki Aflāṭūn zi ʿālam shud*. Cited in Shah Nawaz Khan, *Maʾathir al-Umara*, I, 100–105.

37. S. A. Husain, "Hakeem Ali Gilani: A Commentator of Canon of Avicenna," *Bulletin of the Indian Institute for the History of Medicine* 27 (1997): 47. Amanat, "Persian Nuqṭawīs and the Shaping of the Doctrine of 'Universal Conciliation' (ṣulḥ-i kull) in Mughal India," in *Unity in Diversity: Mysticism and Construction of Religious Authority in Islam*, ed. Orkhan Mir-Kasimov (Leiden: Brill, 2014), 371). Although not an Ishraqi himself, Mulla Ahmad had been at the Bijapur court with Fath Allah and they remained friends in Agra.

38. More broadly, this worldview was an extension of the Neopythagorean ideas of his teacher Fazl Allah Astarabadi (d. 1394), founder of the Hurufi (*lettrist*) movement. See Amanat, "Persian Nuqṭawīs," 374; Shahbaz Bashir, "Between Mysticism and Messianism: The Life and Thought of Muhammad Nurbakhsh (d. 1464)," PhD diss. (Yale University, 1998), 54.
39. Abd al-Qadir Bada'uni, *Muntakhab al-Tawarikh*, ed. W. N. Lees and Munshi Ahmad Ali, 2 vols. (Calcutta: Asiatic Society of Bengal, 1865), 2: 312; Amanat, "Persian Nuqtawīs," 378–81.
40. Thattavi and Qazvini, *Tarikh-i Alfi*, 1, 241–3.
41. Daniel Sheffield, "The Language of Heaven in Safavid Iran: Speech and Cosmology in the Thought of Azar Kayvān and His Followers," in *There's No Tapping Around Philology*, ed. Alireza Korangy and Daniel Sheffield (Wiesbaden: Otto Harrassowitz Verlag), 161–83.
42. Melvin-Koushki, "Early Modern Islamicate Empire," 368. At least two authors, Bada'uni and Sarhindi, remained extremely critical of the whole project, but, as A. Azfar Moin has shown, even Bada'uni, who is generally viewed as a stern orthodox jurist, showed a great deal of interest in the occult sciences. See A. Azfar Moin, "Challenging the Mughal Emperor: The Islamic Millennium according to ʿAbd al-Qadir Badayuni," in *Islam in South Asia in Practice*, ed. Barbara Metcalf (Princeton, NJ: Princeton University Press, 2009), 375–90.
43. Bada'uni, *Muntakhab al-Tawarikh*, 2, 318–19.
44. In Majd's printed edition, the first part is from pages 27 to 3526 and covers volumes 1–4/5. The second part is from pages 3526 to 4244 and covers volumes 4/5–7. The third part is from pages 4244 to 5929 and covers volumes 7–8. The beginning of the second part is marked by a short introduction by Mulla Ahmad regarding the title of the book and Akbar's order about the book. Similarly, the beginning of the third part is marked with an introduction written by Jafar Beg that mentions that Mulla Ahmad wrote two parts before his death and Akbar's order to him to complete the book. See Thattavi and Qazvini, *Tarikh-i Alfi*, 1, 3527; 7, 4244.
45. This Christian comparison was originally suggested in the early twentieth century by F. W. Buckler, "Firdausī's Shāhnāma and the *Genealogia Regni Dei*," *Journal of the American Oriental Society*, Suppl. 1 (1935): 1–21.
46. Abul-Fazl, *The History of Akbar*, 1, 27.
47. It is important to note that none of the surviving manuscripts of *Tarikh-i Alfi* we consulted include events later than 984/1576.
48. For a more secular, "modern" reading of the *Tarikh-i Alfi*, see Ali Anooshahr, "Dialogism and Territoriality in a Mughal History of the Islamic Millennium," *Journal of the Economic and Social History of the Orient* 55 (2012): 220–54. For a more in-depth discussion on Neoplatonism in the making of *ṣulḥ-i kull*, see Jos Gommans and Said Reza Huseini, "Neoplatonism and the Pax Mongolica in the Making of *Ṣulḥ-i Kull*: A View from Akbar's Millennial History," *Modern Asian History* (forthcoming).
49. Thattavi and Qazvini, *Tarikh-i Alfi*, 1, 406–407; M. A. Alvi and A. Rahman, *Shah Fathullah Shirazi: A Sixteenth Century Indian Scientist* (New Delhi: National Institute of Sciences of India, 1968), 10–11.

50. Thattavi and Qazvini, *Tarikh-i Alfi*, 8, 5738–9.
51. Abul-Fazl, *The History of Akbar*, 1, 22–23; 27; 1, 122–3.
52. Abul Fazl, *Ai'n-i Akbari*, ed. H. Blochmann, 3 vols. (Calcutta: Asiatic Society of Bengal, 1872), 3: 182–8; Bada'uni, *Muntakhab al-Tawarikh*, 2, 211; Rizvi, *Religious and Intellectual History of the Muslims*, 385.
53. Thattavi and Qazvini, *Tarikh-i Alfi*, 8, 5375, 5617.
54. Thattavi and Qazvini, *Tarikh-i Alfi*, 1, 273.
55. Abul-Fazl, *The History of Akbar*, 1, 126–7.
56. In Persian *mabda'-i fayyāḍ*. See Abul-Fazl, *The History of Akbar*, 1, 23–25.
57. In his alienation and rivalry from Abul Fazl, he wrote a scurrilous account that paints the emperor as an apostate and anti-Christ. Nevertheless, much of Bada'uni's criticisms can be corroborated by Jesuit reports as well as by statements in the imperial chronicles. See Moin, "Challenging the Mughal Emperor."
58. Bada'uni, *Muntakhab al-Tawarikh*, 2, 211.
59. Bada'uni, *Muntakhab al-Tawarikh*, 2, 211.
60. Thattavi and Qazvini, *Tarikh-i Alfi*, 5, 3295, 3403–3508; Thattavi and Qazvini, *Tarikh-i Alfi*, 7, 4244.
61. Thattavi and Qazvini, *Tarikh-i Alfi*, 1, 242–3.
62. Thattavi and Qazvini, *Tarikh-i Alfi*, 1, 242.
63. Thattavi and Qazvini, *Tarikh-i Alfi*, 6, 3744.
64. Thattavi and Qazvini, *Tarikh-i Alfi*, 6, 3722. These words attributed to Chinggis Khan are not mentioned in any chronicles from the Mongol period.
65. Thattavi and Qazvini, *Tarikh-i Alfi*, 7, 4261.
66. Thattavi and Qazvini, *Tarikh-i Alfi*, 8, 5376–82.
67. Thattavi and Qazvini, *Tarikh-i Alfi*, 6, 3914.
68. Thattavi and Qazvini, *Tarikh-i Alfi*, 6, 3914.
69. Thattavi and Qazvini, *Tarikh-i Alfi*, 6, 3902–3903.
70. Thattavi and Qazvini, *Tarikh-i Alfi*, 5, 3649. Later, the *Tarikh-i Alfi* again stresses the extreme obeisance of the Mongols to their kings. See Thattavi and Qazvini, *Tarikh-i Alfi*, 6, 3891.
71. Thattavi and Qazvini, *Tarikh-i Alfi*, 5, 3749. See also Thattavi and Qazvini, *Tarikh-i Alfi*, 6, 3748, which likewise stresses the meritocratic principles of Chinggisid rule.
72. *Tarikh-i Alfi* mentions that, in the middle of the month of Muharram, Ghazan Khan and his generals changed the old Chinggisid garment and wore the turban like the Muslims (*muntaṣaf-i Muḥarram, Ghāzān Khān libās-i ghadīm-i Changīz Khānī rā taghīr dāda ba tarīq-i Musalmānān ba ittifāq-i jamī'-i 'umarā dastār bast*); Thattavi and Qazvini, *Tarikh-i Alfi*, 7, 4290. It also gives detailed information on Kubilai's palaces and the Chinese traditions in them. Thattavi and Qazvini, *Tarikh-i Alfi*, 6, 4166–72.
73. Thattavi and Qazvini, *Tarikh-i Alfi*, 6, 3751. The Persian text reads as follows: *ba'd az mā urūq-i mā qabāha-yi zar dūkhta bipūshand wa ni'mat hā-yi charb wa shīrīn bikhurand wa bar asbān-i nīkū bar nishīnand wa khātūnān-i khūbruy dar bar kashand nagūyand ki īnhā rā padarān wa aqāyān-i mā jam' kardah-and wa ān ruz-i buzug ra farāmūsh kūnand*.
74. Thattavi and Qazvini, *Tarikh-i Alfi*, 7, 4144–6. The example is Sultan Ahmad Teguder; his reign witnessed opposition from Mongols who saw the Muslim high officials as their rivals.

75. Thattavi and Qazvini, *Tarikh-i Alfi*, 6, 3742, 3747.
76. Thattavi and Qazvini, *Tarikh-i Alfi*, 6, 3748–9. Quite tellingly, on another occasion the *Tarikh* uses Juvayni but omits his comment on the similarity between the *yasāq* and Islamic law; see Thattavi and Qazvini, *Tarikh-i Alfi*, 6, 3742. This focus on the Yasa comes fairly close to the analysis of the contemporary Ottoman historian Mustafa Ali, except that the latter left at least some room for the revealed law of Islam. See Cornell Fleischer, "Royal Authority, Dynastic Cyclism and 'Ibn Khaldunism' in Sixteenth-Century Ottoman Letters," *Journal of Asian and African Studies* 18 (1983): 198–220.
77. Naindeep Chann, "In the Shadow of the Khan," in *Empires and Diversity: On the Crossroads of Archaeology, Anthropology, and History*, ed. Gregory E. Areshian (Los Angeles: Cotzen Institute of Archaeology Press, 2013), 241. For this miniature, see https://www.akg-images.com/archive/-2UMDHUR9T8Y7.html.
78. Ernst, *Refractions of Islam in India*, 370–1.
79. Thattavi and Qazvini, *Tarikh-i Alfi*, 1, 253.
80. Thattavi and Qazvini, *Tarikh-i Alfi*, 1, 380–1.
81. Thattavi and Qazvini, *Tarikh-i Alfi*, 1, 253, 381.
82. Thattavi and Qazvini, *Tarikh-i Alfi*, 1, 381–2.
83. Ziai, "Source and Nature of Authority," 320. See also Moin, *The Millennial Sovereign*, 209.
84. For discussions, see Moin, *The Millennial Sovereign*, 219–24, and Gerard Grobbel, *Der Dichter Faiḍī und die Religion Akbars* (Berlin: Klaus Schwarz Verlag, 2001), 51–67.
85. Bada'uni, *Muntakhab al-Tawarikh*, 2, 300.
86. It "contains some of the earliest and most detailed attempts by the Mughal court at harmonizing the Hindu notions of reincarnation with Islamic thought, particularly of the branch promoted at the Shiraz School through the commentaries of Suhrawardi." See Ali Anooshahr, "Shirazi Scholars," 347–9.
87. Thattavi and Qazvini, *Tarikh-i Alfi*, 1, 378–81; Qutb al-Din Shirazi, *Sharh-i Hikmat al-Ishraq*, ed. Mahdi Muhaqqiq and Abd Allah Nurani (Tehran: Anjuman-i Asar wa Mafakhir-i Farhangi, 1383/2004).
88. The Paris Bibliothèque Nationale de France and the Rampur Raza Library have copies of late sixteenth-century and early seventeenth-century Persian translations of Razi's *Al-Sirr al-Maktum* (The Hidden Secret), at least one of which was composed for Akbar: Živa Vesel, "The Persian Translation of Fakhr al-Din Rāzī's al Sirr al Maktūm ('The Occult Secret') for Iltutmish," in *Confluence of Cultures: French Contributions to Indo-Persian Studies*, ed. Françoise 'Nalini' Delvoye (Delhi: Manohar, 1994), 14–22.
89. Eva Orthmann, "Court Culture and Cosmology in the Mughal Empire: Humayūn and the Foundations of the Dīn-i Ilāhī," in *Court Cultures in the Muslim World: Seventh to Nineteenth Centuries*, ed. Albrecht Fuess and Jan-Peter Hartung (London: Routledge, 2011), 203–204. The citations about the Carpet of Mirth (*basāṭ-i nishāṭ*) come from the *Qanun-i Humayuni* written by Humayun's contemporary Khwandamir.
90. Razi's work that mentions exactly the same celestial sphere as the Carpet of Mirth is *Maṭālib al-ʿāliya*. See Nora Jacobsen Ben Hammed, "Knowledge and Felicity of the Soul in Fakhr al-Dīn al-Rāzī," PhD diss. (University of Chicago, 2018), 220.

91. Jacobsen Ben Hammed, "Knowledge and Felicity of the Soul," 242–3. This entire section on Razi is based on this work.
92. Here, we use the fairly conventional wording of Ibn Sina. See Jacobsen Ben Hammed, "Knowledge and Felicity of the Soul," 81. It indicates that much of the Neoplatonic hierarchy was already part of mainstream Islamic metaphysics, which was not the case for the role that the occult sciences could play in achieving gnosis. Although the latter became increasingly popular in post-Mongol courts, in theological and philosophical circles, it remained controversial.
93. Of course, this metaphysics of sun and light is not only Ishraqi but can also be associated with the Neoplatonization of the Light of Muhammad at a much earlier stage. See the recent survey of Khalil Andani, "Metaphysics of Muhammad: The Nur Muhammad from Imam Jaʿfar al-Sadiq (d.148/765) to Nasir al-Din al-Tusi (d.672/1274)," *Journal of Sufi Studies* 8 (2019): 99–175.

10

Hobbes the Egyptian

The Return to Pharaoh, or the Ancient Roots of Secular Politics

ROBERT A. YELLE

PART ONE: AN EXODUS FROM SACRED KINGSHIP?

Why are we speaking now, or again, about sacred kingship? Why did David Graeber and Marshall Sahlins choose, as the cover image for their book *On Kings* (2017), to redeploy the frontispiece from Thomas Hobbes's *Leviathan* (1651) by superimposing the figure of this "Mortal God" over an Eskimo village? Was this an implicit claim that issues of sovereignty addressed by Hobbes at the threshold of modernity—the indivisibility and absolute nature of sovereign power; the need for its representation in one figure; and the aesthetic, indeed sacral, dimensions of authority that ground the legitimacy of rulership—are perennial and are not a product of the vicissitudes of one particular tradition? Indeed, Graeber and Sahlins claim, "Even when kings are deposed, the legal and political framework of monarchy tends to live on, . . . the power once held by kings still exists, just now displaced onto an entity called 'the people,'"[1] and that "even when kings are gone . . . they are likely to linger in ghostly form, precisely as . . . a unifying principle."[2] Conversely, "the state" may be a "fetish" that "never existed at all."[3] In the conclusion to the final chapter, Graeber poses the question, "What does all this have to say about our situation in the present?"[4] The main reason he gives is that the principle of sovereignty as a form of "ultimately arbitrary power" inherited from kings remains with us.[5] The reader is left with the distinct impression that sacred kingship, in one form or another, is inescapable; that democracy may be nothing more than a ripple on a pond or a footnote to kingship.

This is a conclusion that might have appealed to Hobbes, who, while advocating a novel theory of the social contract, was also one of the strongest exponents of absolutism and of a unitary sovereign, if not of monarchy per se. Yet the legacy of sacred kingship in our ostensibly "secular age"[6] poses a riddle for our understanding of secularization as an historical process, which usually has been defined as the separation between politics and religion[7] and, in the case of Hobbes, as the foreclosure of any political theology that would reintroduce a threat, based on claims of religious truth, to the modern secular state, whose lineaments he helped to draw.[8] The fact that he did so by collapsing the ecclesiastical power into the civil (in a move that, while sometimes identified with Erastianism, was, as we shall see, far more radical) signals that modernity in fact has pursued two opposed paths to secularism. On the one hand, there is the relatively benign formula of a separation between church and state, for example, as articulated by John Locke, who in this regard rejected Hobbes's solution to the problem of religion.[9] On the other hand, there is Jean-Jacques Rousseau's argument, following Hobbes, for a "civil religion" that, by reuniting the "two heads of the eagle," that is, of religion and politics, would not only avoid the challenge of an independent religious authority but also provide an apparently crucial supplement to the legitimacy of the state.[10]

Formulas such as "sacred kingship," "political theology," and "civil religion" all have in common that they unite the two categories of politics and religion, and thereby appear from a contemporary perspective as potential challenges to any definition of secularism that regards the separation between these two categories as both possible and desirable.[11] Meanwhile, such formulas also present a thorny epistemological puzzle because they imply the inadequacy of our contemporary language to describe the past or other cultures in which "religion" and "politics" did or do not denote distinct domains of culture and society. For example, as the German Egyptologist Jan Assmann has demonstrated in a series of brilliant and provocative writings over the past few decades,[12] in ancient Egypt under the condition of "cosmotheism," religion and politics were inextricably linked, in the form of the pharaoh as god-king. Only the monotheism and iconoclasm of the "Mosaic Distinction," as represented by the Exodus out of Egypt, ended this condition by inventing a new form of religion, which Assmann calls "secondary" or "counter-religion," that was separate from politics.

Assmann's argument, which is restated in his contribution to this volume, represents a version of an historical thesis that is articulated also by Alan Strathern and A. Azfar Moin in this volume's first chapter:[13] namely, that the universal status quo ante in large-scale human societies with complex sociopolitical orders was a form of sacred kingship and that the Axial Age witnessed the rise of a new form of relation between religion and politics that disturbed this older settlement. Strathern and Moin label this the shift from immanentism to transcendentalism: from the idea that divine beings inhabit our world and embody political authority directly to the inauguration of a divide between religion and politics in which religion has separated itself enough both to reflect critically on and perhaps to offer escape from the conditions of immanentism. The independent authority of religion may be embodied in such institutional forms as a distinct class of priests, a church, and a canon of scripture. Yet it requires first a break with the existing immanent order. In Judaism, this break was represented by the Exodus from Egypt.

As Assmann has noted, the idea of a separation between religion and politics was codified in the Christian theological doctrine of the Two Kingdoms or Two Swords of pope and emperor.[14] This doctrine had roots in the New Testament and developed with the institutionalization of power in the Roman Catholic Church and papacy. Drawing on pagan Roman ideas of a separation of powers, Pope Gelasius I in 494 CE juxtaposed the "sacred authority" (*auctoritas sacrata*) of the priesthood (*sacerdotium*) to the "royal power" (*regalis potestas*) of the crown (*regnum*).[15] Precisely because this represented a certain claim to worldly power on the part of the papacy, however, the Two Kingdoms doctrine established something more like a parallelism or parity rather than a clear separation between religion and politics. Although possibly as old as the Axial Age, this division of authority was most characteristic of the Middle Ages. The division of authority into what the anthropologist Rodney Needham called "dual sovereignty" is typical of many traditional societies, in particular of complex societies after the Axial Age.[16] This brief sketch already raises serious problems for any attempt to define secularism as the separation of religion from politics, because a form of such separation predated our secular age.[17]

The early modern period witnessed a profound interrogation and destabilization of the traditional Christian balance of power as represented by the Two Kingdoms doctrine. In the aftermath of the wars of religion and with the rise of the modern nation-state, the political domain often, in the name of a unitary sovereignty, reabsorbed the powers that had long been granted to the Roman Catholic Church. The church universal became a state church, subordinate to the sovereign nation-state, which reigned supreme on a particular territory. In some cases and over time, religion was privatized completely, which involved a more or less thorough loss of its coercive power. The state emerged triumphant, having asserted a monopoly over the exercise of violence. The separationist doctrine, for example as advocated by Locke, retained the Two Kingdoms doctrine in a vestigial form, mainly in order to make room for individual freedom of conscience and religious toleration.

Hobbes's solution to the problem of the entanglement of religion with politics was more radical than Locke's. In the middle of the English civil war and on the threshold of secularism and Enlightenment, Hobbes attempted to untie the Gordian knot that connected religion to politics by demonstrating that it was, in fact, a single, continuous strand, one that led directly back: *not to religion, but to politics*. Confronting the dangers of religious dissent in his own time—an age in which Roman Catholics, Puritans, and others had fomented revolt against the English crown—Hobbes worked methodically to restore the original unity of religion and politics by collapsing the former into the latter. He deliberately set out to undo the division of the Two Kingdoms defended by Gelasius. Hobbes did not argue merely that the English crown should rule the Church of England, although his argument was consonant with the 1534 Act of Supremacy. Instead, he implied that *religion had never been anything other than a misrecognized form of politics*, reaching all the way back to the original religious revolt against political authority, namely, the Exodus depicted in the Hebrew Bible. Carl Schmitt already noted Leo Strauss's view "that Hobbes regarded Jews as the originators of the revolutionary state-destroying distinction between religion and politics."[18] Assmann himself astutely observed that any attempt to reunite politics with religion represents symbolically the desire to return to Egypt, which is "the secret desire of many conservative thinkers, who see in the unity of rule [*Herrschaft*] and salvation [*Heil*] the foundations of political order."[19]

The sign of this radical conclusion is the frontispiece of Hobbes's book, where the image of the Leviathan appears, looming over the countryside. I will argue that Hobbes drew on an existing tradition that identified the Leviathan or dragon in the Hebrew Bible with the Egyptian Pharaoh who oppressed the Hebrews. As Michael Walzer has shown, a strong tradition in 1630s and 1640s England invoked the Exodus story to justify political revolution.[20] By choosing as his sovereign emblem the Leviathan, a mythical sea monster already identified with Pharaoh—and with the devil—Hobbes implicitly sought to reverse the Exodus and, with this, the possibility of a revolutionary politics carried out in the name of religion. Because this conclusion was blasphemous, he could not declare it openly but rather intimated it with a symbol designed to provoke his opponents.

Hobbes's understanding of the relationship between religion and politics suggests a new perspective on the theoretical categories deployed in the present volume. Hobbes regarded religion as nothing other than a disguise for politics. This explains his systematic reduction of religious categories to political and, more broadly, material ones. Hobbes held that the starting point of sacred kingship was politics rather than religion.[21] There are profound convergences between Hobbes's and Assmann's interpretations of the Hebrew Bible. They diverge, however, on an essential point. According to Hobbes, the "religion" invented during the Exodus was not a new form of religion but rather good old-fashioned politics under a new and false name. Rather than calling this a "counter-religion" as Assmann does, we should, if we follow Hobbes's argument, call it a "counter-sovereignty" expressed in the form of a revolutionary or prophetic politics.[22] Hobbes implicitly advocated a rejection of transcendentalism and an embrace of immanentism, of a certain sort. This was signaled by his designation of Leviathan as a "Mortal God."[23] Hobbes's metaphorical return to Egypt represented a kind of reversal of the Axial Age: a reversion to sacred kingship and to the (re)union of religion with politics, or possibly to an exit from religion altogether. This did not lead, however, to a reenchantment of the world such as was arguably characteristic of pre-Axial traditions. Hobbes's Leviathan, and the state that it headed, was a giant machine, a mechanism constructed by human artifice. Its magic lay either in the attraction of what Michael Taussig called "state fetishism"[24] or in the absolute powers that it held and exercised. Hobbes's legacy is ambivalent because it has led to the consolidation of authority in the state and, under the rubric of civil religion, occasionally to a form of totalitarianism. Although Hobbes's solution to the problem of political religion may be the most logically rigorous one, it remains vulnerable to certain objections, above all those emanating from a concern for justice, as expressed through a prophetic politics, which was precisely one of the most important consequences of the rise of transcendentalism. While drawing out the consequences of Hobbes's total collapse of religion into politics, I also point to its dangers. To the extent that it fulfills the need for justice, a prophetic politics cannot be excluded from the state and represents our own memory of the Exodus.

To draw out the significance of Hobbes's reversal of the Exodus, it will be useful first to outline what the latter represented according to Assmann. The extent of Assmann's publications and the complexity of his arguments regarding the Mosaic Distinction defy any simple summary. My space is limited, and my intention in raising his thesis is primarily to contrast it with that of Hobbes. Assmann has argued that the application of our contemporary categories of religion and politics to ancient Egypt represents an anachronism because in that culture, and indeed throughout the ancient Near East before the arrival of the Mosaic Distinction, the ruler, such as pharaoh, was regarded as a god incarnate, and politics was therefore a part of religion. Under these conditions, which Assmann labels cosmotheism, deity was immanent in the world and was represented in the form of cult images as well as in the person of the ruler. The Exodus from Egypt enacted a radical break with this older system. Assmann described this break as the invention of a counterreligion in opposition to the original system of cosmotheism or immanentist theopolitics. In a series of monographs and essays, he has framed a cumulative argument, which is both innovative and provocative, that the Mosaic Distinction was marked, inter alia, by iconoclasm, intolerance, and alphabetic writing, each of which contributed to a disembedding from the status quo in Egypt and could therefore be said to mark an Axial breakthrough. According to Assmann, we live in the aftermath of this breakthrough, which has been transmitted to the inheritors of biblical traditions through a form of cultural memory or mnemohistory.

In one of the earliest presentations of his argument, Assmann states, "The further one goes back in time, the more difficult it is to distinguish between religious and political institutions."[25] In ancient Egypt, for example, this distinction made little sense: "One could just as well name the Egyptian state a church . . . [o]ur concepts of 'state' and 'church' are equally unsuitable in relation to Egypt."[26] Assmann argues that "religion" in something like our sense was "invented" (*erfunden*) in ancient Israel but that this was a secondary religion that opposed itself to the primary religion of idolatry, typified by Egyptian zoolatry. In opposition to Schmitt's argument that contemporary political concepts are secularized (i.e., translated and disguised) Christian theological concepts, Assmann argues that the Hebrew Bible "theologized" politics.[27] The Hebrews redeployed, for religious purposes, originally political institutions, such as the idea of the covenant (*berith*) as a suzerainty contract or agreement of submission to a king.[28] The ideas of God's wrath and love were linked to this political covenant.[29] This shows again the theologization of politics because "[r]ighteous wrath, which is incensed by injustice, is absolutely the political affect per se (*schlechthin*)."[30]

Why was this shift undertaken? Assmann points to the manner in which the pharaoh was a "living law" (*nomos empsychos*), whose word was writ.[31] Conversely, the Deuteronomic legislation represented a critique of such ideas of absolute rule[32] and introduced the idea that the sovereign should be subordinate to the law. This was achieved by making the law divine, as well as by fixing it in writing:

> [T]he radical new thought arose, to make God himself the lawgiver . . . The novelty and defining characteristic of secondary religion is the law-giving God . . . The all-decisive step of Israel consists, in transposing justice from the social and political into the theological sphere and subordinating it to the immediate will of God.[33]

This step, which was unprecedented in the ancient Near East, had the effect of removing such absolute authority from pharaoh or any other mortal ruler who acted as a despot: "The image of despotism comes from the idea of a compulsory unity [*Zwangseinheit*] of rule [*Herrschaft*] and salvation [*Heil*], thus from the model of Caesaropapism."[34] As Assmann immediately acknowledges, such a formulation as applied to pharaoh would be anachronistic because it implies the (re)unification of what has not yet been separated, namely, politics and religion. Only after the Exodus does it make sense to speak of such a separation: the Jewish theocracy prepares the way for the (previously described) Christian idea of Two Kingdoms, in which "the kingdom of God constitutes the otherworldly [*überweltliche*] counterpart to the worldly kingdom of Rome."[35] Indeed, fundamentally, "Israel stands in opposition [to Egypt] for the separation of rule and salvation, either in the theocratic sense, which admits human rulership only in a subordinated form, or in the dualistic sense, which reaches its peak in the doctrine of the Two Kingdoms."[36] Assmann's subsequent books, especially *Moses the Egyptian* and *The Price of Monotheism*, develop these arguments further, defining ancient Israelite monotheism as a counterreligion that distinguished between true and false religion. Assmann focuses on the attack against idolatry as crucial to the Mosaic Distinction, which introduced a new form of religion, one characterized by iconoclasm and a new conception of divinity. However, Assmann continues to argue that "the political meaning . . . of the Mosaic distinction lies in the separation of politics and religion."[37]

To my knowledge, Assmann offers no specific account of secularization; his focus is squarely on the Axial Age and the ancient Near East. Both cosmotheism and the Mosaic Distinction supposedly continue, sedimented in the cultural memory of European traditions. Assmann's account will serve as context for the discussion of Hobbes that follows. The great English political philosopher was one of the strongest critics of religion, or at least of an independent church, and as such a founder of what we call secularism. Hobbes's argument for a (re)unification of religion with politics was directly opposed to the Mosaic Distinction, as Assmann defined this.

PART TWO: HOBBES'S REDUCTION OF RELIGION TO POLITICS

Hobbes's doctrine regarding the relation between church and state is generally identified with Erastianism, or the idea that there should be a state church governed by the sovereign of the realm. This was a position named after the Heidelberg professor Thomas Erastus (1524–1583). Because Hobbes was writing during a time of civil war in which the parties were divided on religious grounds, he aimed to remove the possibility of political dissent and rebellion on the basis of an independent claim to religious authority. It has by now been recognized increasingly that Hobbes's Erastianism was more radical than what is normally understood by this term because he advocated for the complete control of all religious matters, down to the interpretation of scripture, by the king.[38] One obvious precedent for Hobbes's argument was Henry VIII's Act of Supremacy in 1534. Complicating our understanding of what Hobbes meant is that he tried to remain just this side of Protestant orthodoxy. This was not only in order to avoid a charge of blasphemy or heresy. His stance was also consistent with his philosophical conviction that authority in religious matters resided with the English sovereign. What I offer below is a reading of Hobbes that is esoteric, in keeping with the conviction that a number of his most important conclusions were implied yet not explicitly stated because of their incendiary nature at the time.

Hobbes regarded religion as a projection from or mystification of politics. In chapter 29 of *Leviathan*, he condemns religion as a form of "ghostly authority," which creates a division of sovereignty within a kingdom.[39] Hobbes states that "a kingdom divided . . . cannot stand," echoing a line uttered by Jesus in a case of demonic possession,[40] and implying that those who follow the authority of the church may themselves be possessed. In chapter 39, following William Tyndale's translation of *ekklesia* as "congregation"[41]—a translation that undermined the idea of a universal church—Hobbes argues that "a Church . . . is the same thing with a civil commonwealth . . . Temporal and spiritual government are but two words brought into the world to make men see double and mistake their true sovereign."[42] In chapter 47, he calls the papacy "the ghost of the Roman Empire."[43] With such arguments, Hobbes attempted to overturn the ancient doctrine that there are Two Kingdoms.

He does this from the beginning of his book. Opening the book and gazing upon its famous frontispiece, one sees the symbols of the state on the left, those of the church on the right. The castle is opposite a church, the crown opposite a bishop's mitre. Above all of these symbols, and uniting them, is the giant figure of the Leviathan, the "Mortal God" who straddles the land, striking fear into its inhabitants and thus bringing peace. The Leviathan holds both royal sword and ecclesiastical scepter, representing graphically the union of the temporal and spiritual powers. This image, which consists of many small bodies, representing individual citizens, combined into one huge body, matched Hobbes's insistence that sovereignty is indivisible and that a people can represent themselves as such only in the figure of the one who rules them. This *e pluribus unum* aspect of the image has been traced to the medieval idea of the *corpus mysticum* of the church, which served in turn as the basis for the legal fictions of both the body politic and the business corporation.[44] This represented a distinctively Christian version of a broader anthropological phenomenon: Arthur Maurice Hocart noted that sacred kings or chiefs are often spoken of in the plural, or they use the first-person singular to describe the achievements of the tribe as a collective.[45]

Encountering later in the work Hobbes's argument that religion is nothing other than a mystification of politics, the reader is led to a different, more radical interpretation of the frontispiece; that is, the religious images on the right of the page are just distorted and inverted versions of the political images on the left. The movement from left to right, in the normal direction of reading, is from truth into metaphor, from light into darkness. There is a parallel in the division of the book into two parts, the first dealing with natural reason and political philosophy, and the second with scripture and eventually the "kingdom of darkness." At first sight, it appears that Hobbes's attacks against religion are directed against the papacy and the Puritans, or those who would claim an independent authority and right of rebellion on religious grounds. As noted already, he does not overtly dispute the truth of Christian revelation.

Whereas Hobbes stood at the threshold of modernity and dedicated himself to laying the foundations of what we think of as the secular nation-state, he did so while looking backward at the history of the biblical tradition. Like many in seventeenth-century England, he contributed to the genre of Christian Hebraism, a sustained meditation on the religious roots of European culture that was inspired by the Protestant focus on scripture and that reinterpreted the past for the political purposes of the present.[46] Hobbes did not shrink from commenting on the political dimensions of the Sinai covenant, which introduced the kingdom of God and which he claims was merely a polity in which, uniquely, God served as the king through various regents such as Moses.[47] This lasted until the institution of the monarchy under Saul. The Exodus, like Jesus's mission, was a movement aimed at instituting a new polity led by God or His lieutenant.[48]

Although Hobbes took pains not to call into question the authority of the Bible, and often echoed the orthodox Protestant theology of his day, on occasion his interpretations of scripture were radically unorthodox or even heretical. For all its lucidity of exposition, the *Leviathan* is an esoteric text; it is often necessary to read between the lines in order to understand Hobbes's full meaning. Perhaps his most blasphemous act was the choice of the name of the biblical Leviathan, a sea monster with diabolical connotations, for the title of his book, and as the name for the "Mortal God" depicted on its frontispiece. I will suggest that the Leviathan was intended, among other meanings, as a representation of the biblical Pharaoh, the enemy of the Hebrews. This interpretation is consonant with what I shall argue is both the most radical and the most probable interpretation of Hobbes's view of the Exodus and of the relation between religion and politics: namely, that religion was merely politics under another name and that the Exodus was a political revolution against a rightful ruler, a revolution that never should have taken place.

PART THREE: HOBBES'S LEVIATHAN AS PHARAOH

The frontispiece of Hobbes's *Leviathan* has been the subject of intense study and speculation since the work's publication.[49] Recent scholarship, particularly that of Noel Malcolm, has made progress in elucidating further meanings symbolized in this, perhaps the most famous image of modern political thought.[50] Malcolm attempted to answer "the most basic question that arises in connection with Hobbes's use of this term [i.e., Leviathan]. . . : why did he select, for the thing he valued most highly in human existence, a name which was so freighted with negative implications—a name likely to conjure up, in the minds of many of his readers, at best a monster and at worst the Devil himself?"[51] As Schmitt noted, both Leviathan and Behemoth "became symbols of the heathen world powers that were hostile to Jews, a designation that can be applied to the Babylonian, Assyrian, Egyptian, and other pagan realms."[52] Indeed, it is partly on these grounds that scholars, including Malcolm, have long puzzled at Hobbes's choice of such a sinister image. Malcolm's proposed solution to this problem is that, within certain exegetical traditions, the Leviathan had acquired more positive connotations. Scholars, including the seventeenth-century Parisian Capuchin Jacques Boulduc, interpreted the Hebrew word, *livyatan*, to mean a "joining together" or association, perhaps because of the monster's closely joined scales and its entourage of lesser fish.[53] This made the Leviathan an especially appropriate name for the composite image on Hobbes's frontispiece. Malcolm argues that Boulduc "left far behind any association with the Devil—even an indirect one, via the Egyptian Pharaoh"[54] and made Leviathan something of an "honorific term."[55]

Malcolm's argument is erudite and illuminating.[56] However, I will differ with his premise: it was precisely the traditional identification of Leviathan with Pharaoh that Hobbes intended to invoke as a provocation against his opponents, including the dissenters who composed the Geneva Bible. Like its counterpart and enemy, the land giant Behemoth,[57] the Leviathan is sometimes called by a plural Hebrew word, making this an especially apt name for a composite creature.[58] *Livyatan* is not itself grammatically plural. However, this is only one of several terms used in the Hebrew Bible for the sea monster. Another is *rahab*, and another is *tannin*—a word often translated as "whale," "serpent," "dragon," or "sea monster," although its original meaning was likely "crocodile"–which appears in several places in its plural form, namely, as *tanninim*. One place where the term *tanninim* is used is in Psalm 74, a hymn composed during the Babylonian exile that mourns the desolation experienced by the oppressed Israelites and cries out for God's justice and vengeance. This psalm, which seems tailormade to express the conditions of the English civil war, contains echoes of older Canaanite mythology, according to which Yahweh was a dragon slayer. Following are the relevant verses from the Geneva Bible translation:

> 13. Thou didst divide the sea by thy strength: thou brakest the heads of the dragons [*tanninim*] in the waters.
> 14. Thou brakest the heads of leviathan [*livyatan*] in pieces, and gavest him to be meat to the people inhabiting the wilderness.

Verse 14 relates to a tradition according to which the Israelites will feast upon the flesh of the Leviathan at the end of days.[59] Following Calvin's commentary on this psalm, the Geneva Bible glosses "dragons" (*tanninim*) as "Pharaoh's army," while Leviathan itself is explained as a reference to "Pharaoh." This is a conceit, of course; the two references are simply different names for the same creature, an example of the phenomenon of parallelism common in the Hebrew Bible and particularly the Psalms. In making this distinction, Calvin was evidently attempting to preserve the plural sense of *tanninim*; the Geneva Bible follows him in translating the plural literally, as in "the heads of the dragons," unlike the Vulgate, which used the singular, *caput draconum*. Malcolm does not note this plural form, or more precisely synonym, of "leviathan." Neither, apparently, did Boulduc.[60]

Yet Hobbes could easily have been aware of this plural usage from either the Geneva Bible or other commonly available English texts. The Westminster Assembly's *Annotations upon All the Books of the Old and New Testament*, published in 1645 and 1651, repeated the identification of Leviathan in Psalm 74 with Pharaoh and Pharaoh's army. The same text identified the "great whales" (*tanninim*) created by God in Genesis 1:21 with the Leviathan, "which name in the Originall is a compound of two words, *Lavah* which is *to couple*, and *Thannin* a Serpent, or Dragon; because by his bignesse he seems not one single creature, but a coupling of divers together; or because his scales are closed, or straitly compacted together."[61] Note that this particular (false) etymology of leviathan actually makes this word a derivative of *tannin*. The *Annotations*, a Calvinist text contemporary with *Leviathan*, may have served as a conduit for Hobbes's knowledge of the exegetical tradition represented by Boulduc and excavated by Malcolm. One reason for the (erroneous) interpretation of *livyatan* as a collective noun was evidently to harmonize this with the use of the plural *tanninim* in Genesis 1:21, Psalm 74:13, and other texts. These same Calvinist sources reinforced the identification of the Leviathan with Pharaoh.[62] Malcolm notes that Psalm 74's "references to dividing the sea, and breaking the heads of the dragons and leviathan, connected it with ... the passage of the Israelites through the Red Sea and the destruction of their pursuers, Pharaoh and his army. In ... other passages the term 'dragon' [*tannin*] was used, explicitly or implicitly, to refer to Pharaoh."[63] This poses a serious problem for Malcolm's argument that Hobbes had "moved far beyond" the obvious negative connotations of the name Leviathan.[64]

The problem is removed if we simply accept that this identification of the Leviathan with Pharaoh was precisely what Hobbes intended. Hobbes was concerned mainly to eliminate the threat of religious dissent that would lead to revolution against the king. The Geneva Bible was authored by religious dissidents, English Puritans who removed to Geneva during Queen Mary's persecution of Protestants in England. In *Behemoth*, his history of the English civil war, Hobbes pointed specifically to the role that these dissidents had played in encouraging private religious opinions that led to the dissolution of the monarchy.[65] Thomas Fulton has shown that the Geneva translators imported their own political as well as theological opinions into the text, perhaps most strikingly by using the word *tyrant* more than one hundred times, as opposed to zero times in the Authorized Version superintended by King James in 1611.[66] By choosing the Leviathan as the emblem for his sovereign—which was tantamount to a demand for submission to Pharaoh, if not the devil himself—Hobbes meant to provoke his staunchest opponents among the Puritans who, as Walzer showed, invoked the Exodus story as a basis for dissent against the English crown. Hobbes aimed to rehabilitate the title of pharaoh as a title of honor and, at the same time, to discredit the English Calvinists and their Hebrew forebears, both of whom had used religion as grounds for rebelling against their rightful ruler. By deliberately selecting the Leviathan, alias Pharaoh, as his "Mortal God," Hobbes was signaling his conviction that the Exodus was an illegitimate rebellion against a rightful king. Because this was a truly blasphemous position, he could not state it openly. Indeed, Hobbes never cited Psalm 74, although it is one of only a handful of places in the Bible in which the term leviathan appears,[67] and he could not have been unaware of this text and of the association of Leviathan with Pharaoh that was based on the harmonization of this text with other biblical passages.

For Hobbes, the interpretation of *livyatan/tanninim* as a collective noun or plural form was too good an opportunity to pass up. This usage appeared to coincide with the then-current idea of the body politic as a corporation consisting of many individual members.[68] There was another likely reason. Hobbes may have believed that such plural forms, as applied to gods and kings, were honorifics, polite forms of address suitable for a sovereign. As previously noted, Malcolm correctly surmised that Hobbes regarded the name Leviathan as an honorific. We can identify specific sources for this idea, including John Selden's *Titles of Honor*, one of the few contemporary works cited in *Leviathan*.[69] One of the great antiquarians, lawyers, and Christian Hebraists of his age, Selden proposed in this work a euhemerist theory of religion. The first gods supposedly were kings, who were idolized after their death.[70] The identification of gods with kings was reinforced by the fact that such sovereigns were addressed by similar titles. Such singular beings were often addressed as if they were plural,[71] a practice Selden evidenced also in the case of the Hebrew Bible, which referred to the true God as, inter alia, *Elohim*.[72] Similar practices of addressing sacred kings have been noted by Hocart, who took such uses of the plural literally.[73] Most scholars would interpret these uses of the plural either as metaphors for the greatness of majesty or as versions of the taboo on naming a superior directly, an explanation advanced already by Selden.[74] Selden did not discuss the name Leviathan in this work; however, he did explain that "Pharao" simply meant a "king."[75] When Hobbes selected the image of the Leviathan from the Hebrew Bible to depict his "Mortal God," he appears to have been drawing on the idea of royalty and divinity as plural, at least in name. This idea coincided perfectly with his argument that a body politic was a corporate form that required personation by a sovereign.[76] This underscores the radical, indeed blasphemous, implications of Hobbes's formulation. He regarded such corporate entities as (necessary) legal fictions,[77] and he presumably held the same opinion of the biblical *Elohim*. In fact, the plural does not necessarily carry any honorific meaning in biblical Hebrew. Certain uses of the plural are demonic, denoting formlessness and chaos, such as that of the primal waters (*mayim*).[78] Whereas *elohim* may have been an honorific, *behemoth* and *livyatan/tanninim* carried negative connotations, while still signaling, through the use of the plural, the power and size of these mythical creatures. Beyond the bare use of the plural, there was no suggestion that any of these entities was corporate.[79]

The repetition in Psalm 74 of the phrase, "the heads [*roshei*] of the dragons... the heads [*roshei*] of leviathan," converged with the familiar image of the king as the head of the body politic, suggesting the appropriateness of the Leviathan as an image or emblem of sovereign power. That this metaphorical head had been severed at the same time that Charles I's literal head had been detached from his natural body in January 1649, just a few years prior to the publication of *Leviathan*, would likely also have been in Hobbes's mind. Putting the head back on the Leviathan was Hobbes's first order of business. But this was tantamount, in the eyes of Parliament's supporters, to a demand for submission to Pharaoh. And by making this demand, Hobbes was effectively calling for a reversal of the Exodus, the original political revolution that had disturbed the organic unity of church and state.

PART FOUR: THE EXODUS AS A DEMOCRATIC REVOLUTION

To say any of this explicitly was quite impossible in the mid-seventeenth century. Although the identification of Leviathan as Pharaoh was well established, Hobbes did not invoke it directly. He maintained a level of plausible deniability regarding his truly heretical opinions. Through dissimulation, Hobbes was able to achieve several objectives at once: (1) avoid a charge of blasphemy or heresy; (2) conform to his own philosophical argument that, in order to avoid political dissent on religious grounds, the sovereign's interpretation of scripture and of prophecy must be accepted; and (3) quarantine the danger of a revolutionary theopolitics to the historical cases in the Bible.

The uniqueness of the cases of Moses and of Jesus was not in the nature of the polity that each established, but rather by virtue of whom they represented, or in whose name they served, as God's lieutenant.[80] Hobbes admits such cases but quarantines them already in chapter 18, §3:

> And whereas some men have pretended for their disobedience to their sovereign a new covenant, made (not with men, but) with God, this also is unjust; for there is no covenant with God but by mediation of somebody that representeth God's person, which none hath done but God's lieutenant, who hath the sovereignty under God. But this pretence of covenant with God is so evident a lie, even in the pretenders' own consciences, that it is not only an act of an unjust, but also of a vile and unmanly disposition.

Apart from this sole exception, Hobbes disallows any revolution based on a claim of divine revelation or religious inspiration. Meanwhile, as was argued in part two of this chapter, he collapses religion, as a form of "ghostly authority," back into politics, effectively returning us to the unity of religion with politics that obtained just prior to the Mosaic revolution. Hobbes argues that, during the kingdom of God, when Moses acted as God's lieutenant, the civil and ecclesiastical powers were joined.[81] However, the union of these two powers was not unique to the Jewish theocracy but is a general requirement that follows from the indivisibility of sovereignty, as Hobbes affirms throughout *Leviathan*, from its title page onward. What was unique to the Jewish theocracy was instead only that the true God ruled as king. Just as God had once been a king, all kings should be treated like gods. Should that not have applied to Pharaoh as well? The implication is that the Exodus was a revolution and, as such, almost certainly illegal.

Indeed, the most straightforward reading of the Exodus is that it tells the story of a political revolution and the birth of a new nation or people. Some of Assmann's key insights regarding the Exodus reinforce this as the story of an antimonarchical or protodemocratic movement that sought to subordinate sovereignty to the law. Therefore, it would be better to regard the Exodus as a movement for "counter-sovereignty." Moses conveys to Pharaoh the demand that the Hebrews be allowed to journey into the wilderness for three days in order to make a sacrifice to their God.[82] This is already a revolutionary demand because sacrifice is the seal of a covenant, which is an agreement of political submission, in this case to a deity other than Pharaoh. When Pharaoh naturally refuses the demand, the Ten Plagues descend upon Egypt. Of course, the tradition understands these as miraculous signs of God's awesome power and of the truth of the Mosaic Distinction. Yet plagues—like famines and bloodshed, which are also represented among the Ten Plagues—may also be signs of a state of exception or of insurrection. Partly this derives from the ability of a literal pestilence to cause a breakdown in polity, as happened during the first year of the Peloponnesian War, when Athens was reduced by plague to a condition of *anomias* or lawlessness.[83] As the translator of Thucydides, Hobbes was well aware of the linkage between plague and insurrection, and he appears to have worked this symbolism into the frontispiece of the Leviathan, where the figures of plague doctors roam the city under the condition of civil war.[84]

Assmann introduced the idea of mnemohistory, or the dissemination and preservation of cultural narratives regarding both Egypt and Israel. The Egyptian version of the Exodus, which constitutes a counternarrative to the biblical story, describes this as a revolt of lepers led by a character named Osarsiph who is identified with Moses. Assmann argues ingeniously that this version conflated the Exodus of the Hebrews with an earlier episode of iconoclasm carried out by the fourteenth-century pharaoh Akhenaten.[85] While his argument is compelling, Assmann may place too much emphasis on the characteristic of iconoclasm shared by these two revolts. The more obvious link between the biblical and

Egyptian versions of the story, in any case, is the association between plagues and revolutions rather than the memory of iconoclasm.

Another mnemohistorical clue identifies the Exodus as a slave revolt. According to the biblical story, Pharaoh's sins are those of enslaving the people and of not permitting them a holiday for the purpose of worshiping their God. In his history of the Egyptians, Herodotus relates that similar bad deeds were attributed to the pharaohs who built the Great Pyramids: "They said that Egypt until the time of King Rhampsinitus was altogether well-governed and prospered greatly, but that Kheops, who was the next king, brought the people to utter misery. For first he closed all the temples, so that no one could sacrifice there; and next, he compelled all the Egyptians to work for him."[86] His successor Khephren was no better. Forced labor and the repression of religion in this case were the hallmarks of tyranny. We may detect a parallel in the (earlier) Exodus account, where it is the Hebrews who are forced to work and not allowed to worship as they choose. As Assmann and others have noted, the same Hebrew word, *avodah*, denoted both "servitude" to Pharaoh and "service" or worship of Yahweh.[87] The Hebrew term for idolatry, *avodah zarah*, translates literally as "strange service," that is, service to foreign gods. There was originally no distinction made between political and religious service.

All of these events may therefore be redescribed in straightforward political terms. Indeed, Hobbes interprets even the main innovations of the Mosaic Distinction—namely, monotheism and iconoclasm—in strictly political terms. He describes the purpose of the First and Second Commandments already at the end of the second part of *Leviathan*, where his argument is based mainly on reason rather than on revelation; and he adopts the fairly orthodox position that the Ten Commandments consisted largely or entirely of natural law, although republished, in the mode of revelation, as divine positive law.[88] The First and Second Commandments were a matter of simple loyalty to the sovereign, the principle of one god-king at a time:

> Th[e] desire of change [of rule] is like the breach of the first of God's commandments; for there God says *Non habebis Deos alienos*, Thou shalt not have the Gods of other nations, and in another place, concerning *kings*, that they are *Gods*. . . . For that sovereign cannot be imagined to love his people as he ought that is not jealous of them, but suffers them by the flattery of popular men to be seduced from their loyalty, . . . which may fitly be compared to the violation of the second of the ten commandments.[89]

In chapter 42, Hobbes describes the First Table of the Commandments as containing the "law of sovereignty," and explains the Second Commandment as a prohibition against the people "choos[ing] to themselves, neither in heaven, nor in earth, any representative of their own fancying."⁹⁰ This account of the Commandments as a simple corollary of sovereignty might explain monotheism sufficiently. However, the Second Commandment expressly forbids the making of images. Hobbes's account is less than satisfactory as an explanation of this prohibition. This appears to be another case of Hobbes glossing over inconvenient details in scripture. More in line with traditional models of sacred kingship, Hobbes believed that sovereignty must be represented or personated,⁹¹ and that this was the function also of idols,⁹² presumably including his "Mortal God," the Leviathan. Even the true God had to be represented by Moses.⁹³ Because Hobbes appears to have regarded euhemerism or idolatry, in the form of ruler worship, as the original or default mode of religion, and perhaps even as universal, we cannot look to him for an adequate account of biblical iconoclasm.⁹⁴

Here Assmann offers some further insights. Noting that the covenant (*berith*) tradition in the Hebrew Bible was modeled on ancient Near Eastern suzerainty contracts, Assmann suggests a political interpretation of the First and Second Commandments that resembles Hobbes's earlier interpretation.⁹⁵ Assmann adds, however, that iconoclasm, like direct democracy, precludes any mediating institutions of representation, especially those associated with kingship.⁹⁶ The prohibition on representing the divine coordinated with the rejection of sacred kingship, of the type exemplified by Pharaoh. Assmann emphasizes the democratic nature of this revolution. This insight converges with Norman Gottwald's quite different argument for the nature of Yahwistic monotheism as a revolution against elites in Canaan.⁹⁷ There are many traces in the Hebrew Bible that speak in favor of the interpretation of this as the biography of a social justice movement. We can describe this movement, with some caveats, as protodemocratic and egalitarian.⁹⁸ It was also antimonarchical, as evidenced by its negative depiction of kings such as Saul, David, and Solomon once these appear in ancient Israel. The institution of human kingship for the Israelites is depicted as a reversion to idolatry, as Moshe Halbertal and Stephen Holmes have argued.⁹⁹

Assmann states that the pharaoh was a living law (*nomos empsychos*, alias *lex animata*, *lex loquens*), meaning that his word stood for law or rather that he was above the law. This was a form of absolute sovereignty revived in Europe in the High Middle Ages and again by Hobbes and Schmitt. Assmann notes further that one consequence of the Mosaic Distinction was to make law itself divine and to fix it in written form, which had the effect of taking such absolute, lawbreaking (and -making) sovereignty out of the hands of any worldly king.¹⁰⁰ The writing or engraving, first of the Decalogue and then of subsequent laws, was merely a corollary of the fixing of the law in order to render it unchangeable and not subject to the arbitrary whims of the next ruler. The Second Commandment can be interpreted as a prohibition against identifying sovereignty with some concrete, visible form, as a rejection of the idea that absolute power should be embodied by some immanent figure, such as Pharaoh, understood as a living law. In other words, the prohibition against idolatry deepened the antimonarchical tendency.

EXEUNT OMNES, BUT AN EXIT TO WHERE EXACTLY?

My objective in this chapter has been twofold: (1) to understand better the relationship between religion and politics implied by contemporary scholarly discussions of sacred kingship and political theology, and (2) to historicize this relationship by introducing the category of the secular as a specific transformation of this relationship. To reach both parts of this objective, I fabricated a dialogue on the meaning of the Exodus between Assmann and one of the architects of secularism, namely, Hobbes. Both of these thinkers agree on the fundamentally political nature of this movement, which constituted a revolution against sacred kingship if not against monarchy altogether. Where they appear to part company is in the further conclusions to be drawn from this insight. Assmann, as we have seen, argues that the Mosaic Distinction inaugurated a new chapter in human history by instituting a break or divide between religion and politics and inventing a new form of religion—a secondary or counterreligion—that was exclusivist, iconoclastic, and intolerant. Because his focus remains on the initial contrast between Egypt and the Exodus, he does not offer an explicit account of secularism but presents these two contrasted modes of being as perennially available options that persist in a tense amalgam in our cultural memory.

For Hobbes, religion is an illusion, a sort of double vision or a childish belief in ghosts. Properly recognized, religion is nothing other than a form of power politics. Hobbes sought to reverse the Two Kingdoms doctrine that had been accepted in Christianity for a thousand years or more, throughout the Middle Ages. He labeled the religion of the English clergy a "ghostly authority" that competed with that of the authentic sovereign and he thereby identified religion as the *Doppelgänger* of politics, an uncanny twin of worldly power, that disturbed the soul in a manner akin to demonic possession. But the demon could be exorcized. Hobbes performed a genealogical reduction of biblical traditions that relied on the nascent anthropology of religion available in his day. Contemporary anthropology has identified much more evidence that the division of labor and authority between religion and politics may be cross-cultural, a form of "dual sovereignty."[101] This evidence calls into question also the special role that Assmann has assigned to the Mosaic Distinction in inventing religion.

From one perspective, Hobbes was trying to reunite religion with politics and to return to a form of sacred kingship—a wish fulfilled, perhaps, by the Restoration of Charles II in 1660. In a more fundamental sense, however, Hobbes was fighting to reverse the entire series of revolutions that opened the Axial Age and inaugurated the birth of transcendentalism. This did not mean a return to magical immanentism. Hobbes's universe was a disenchanted mechanism from which prophecy and miracles had largely been excluded.[102] This disenchantment continued apace with additional revolutions. Following Charles II's massive deployment of the Royal Touch, the last English monarch to perform the Touch was Queen Anne in 1714. French kings continued to do so more or less until the French Revolution in 1789, with a last attempt to restore the practice by Charles X in 1825. Although the Age of Absolutism ended, together with those miracles that Schmitt recognized as its chief signs, the idea that plenary sovereignty must be possessed by some individual remains within our republican systems, in institutions such as the pardon power and the theory of the unitary executive, and possibly also in what Taussig called "state fetishism."[103]

Hobbes's bid to bring back both sacred kingship and a form of idolatry, as represented by the image of Leviathan, anticipated the contemporary scholarly focus on sacred kingship as the oldest political institution, or perhaps as a necessary supplement for state authority, in the mode of Rousseau's civil religion. Hobbes argued that the indivisibility of sovereignty requires the (re)union of religion with politics, not only to avoid the threat of revolution based on the claim of revelation but also because the legitimacy of the sovereign requires both personation, in the form of the body politic, and the absorption of all "ghostly authority" into this same body. The apparent breakdown of consensus regarding the adequacy of secular institutions to command authority and the concomitant rise of postsecular thought, as exemplified by the revival of sacred kingship as a topic of serious discourse, suggests that Hobbes's bid may have failed or at least that we are still struggling with a version of the same problem.

Hobbes's attempted solution to the problem of religion was logically rigorous because it enabled him to explain religion in terms of a consistently materialist conceptual vocabulary that collapsed church into state. This avoided the duplicity, the doubling of the body politic, represented by the Two Kingdoms doctrine. The virtues of Hobbes's approach were also its sins because his embrace of Pharaoh was a rejection of the Exodus, of the revolutionary idea of a separate place from which to look back on and criticize the land that one has left.

Hobbes's metaphorical return to Egypt, which Assmann correctly diagnosed as the secret desire of conservative thinkers, was an attempt to exclude a prophetic or messianic politics that could lead to rebellion and dissension. However, if we regard the choice not as one between religion and politics but as one between revolution and tyranny, we may be closer to understanding what is at stake.

NOTES

For their suggestions for revision, I would like to thank the editors of this volume, the anonymous reviewers for the press, and the following colleagues who were generous enough to comment on earlier drafts of this chapter: Milinda Banerjee, Ronald Beiner, Agata Bielik-Robson, Arthur Bradley (who suggested the chapter title), Jeffrey Collins, Montserrat Herrero, Bruce Rosenstock, Jonathan Sheehan, Richard Sherwin, Devin Singh, and Winnifred Fallers Sullivan. Special thanks to Natalie Cobo, who helped me to access some of Jacques Boulduc's discussions of the Leviathan in the Hebrew Bible. Wenzel Braunfels compiled the bibliography.

1. Marshall Sahlins and David Graeber, *On Kings* (Chicago: HAU, 2017), 1.
2. Graeber and Sahlins, *On Kings*, 12.
3. Graeber and Sahlins, *On Kings*, 21–22.
4. Graeber and Sahlins, *On Kings*, 462.
5. Graeber and Sahlins, *On Kings*, 464.
6. The allusion is, of course, to Charles Taylor, *A Secular Age* (Cambridge, MA: Harvard University Press, 2007).
7. For an approach that evaluates this separation as itself dependent on contingent developments internal to European discourses, including theological ones, see Robert A. Yelle, " 'By Fire and Sword': Early English Critiques of Islam and Judaism as 'Impostures' or Political and 'Unfree' Religions," *Patterns of Prejudice* 53 (2020): 91–108.
8. On Hobbes's rejection of political theology, see, for example, Mark Lilla, *The Stillborn God: Religion, Politics, and the Modern West* (New York: Vintage, 2007), 75–93.
9. John Locke, *Letter on Toleration* (1689), defines *church* and *commonwealth* in terms of a strict division of labor and states, "There is no such thing under the Gospel as a Christian commonwealth." Both claims appear designed to reverse Hobbes's definition of *church* as a commonwealth or polity in chapter 39 of *Leviathan*, http://www.let.rug.nl/usa/documents/1651-1700/john-locke-letter-concerning-toleration-1689.php, accessed March 10, 2021.
10. Jean-Jacques Rousseau, "Civil Religion," in *The Social Contract*, ed. Donald A. Cress, *The Basic Political Writings*, 2nd ed. (Indianapolis: Hackett, 2011), 243–51. Rousseau's reference to the two-headed eagle is ambiguous. It could have been to the "double eagles of Rome and its successors," including the Holy Roman Empire, noted in Jan Assmann's contribution to this volume, which also speculates that the Roman case might have been inspired by the even earlier Egyptian winged sun disk.

11. For a recognition and critical assessment of this challenge, see Hans Blumenberg, *The Legitimacy of the Modern Age*, trans. Robert M. Wallace (Cambridge, MA: MIT Press, 1983), Part 1, "Secularization: Critique of a Category of Historical Wrong," 3–121, especially 89–102, which focuses on Carl Schmitt's formula of "political theology" and attempts to refute the challenge posed to the "legitimacy" and independence of modern thought by such formulas.
12. The number of publications across which Assmann has elaborated his argument in different versions is fairly large. For purposes of this chapter, I have confined myself to a close reading of the following texts: Jan Assmann, *Politische Theologie zwischen Ägypen und Israel*, ed. Heinrich Meier, 4th ed. (Munich: Carl Friedrich von Siemens Stiftung, 2017 [1992]); Jan Assmann, *Moses the Egyptian: The Memory of Egypt in Western Monotheism* (Cambridge, MA: Harvard University Press, 1997); Jan Assmann, *The Price of Monotheism*, trans. Robert Savage (Stanford, CA: Stanford University Press, 2010); Jan Assmann, *From Akhenaten to Moses: Ancient Egypt and Religious Change* (Cairo: American University in Cairo, 2014); Jan Assmann, *The Invention of Religion: Faith and Covenant in the Book of Exodus*, trans. Robert Savage (Princeton, NJ: Princeton University Press, 2018).
13. See also Alan Strathern, *Unearthly Powers: Religious and Political Change in World History* (Cambridge: Cambridge University Press, 2019), especially 27–80 (on the distinction between immanentism and transcendentalism).
14. Assmann, *Politische Theologie*, 75, 111.
15. Gelasius I, *Duo sunt*, trans. J. H. Robinson. https://sourcebooks.fordham.edu/source/gelasius1.asp, accessed October 27, 2021. For an analysis of the structural relationship between religion and politics in terms of the dynamic between *auctoritas* and *potestas*, see Ivan Strenski, *Why Politics Can't Be Freed from Religion* (Malden, MA: Wiley-Blackwell, 2010).
16. Rodney Needham, "Dual Sovereignty," *Reconnaissances* (Toronto: University of Toronto Press, 1980), 63–105.
17. For a critique of separationist definitions of secularism, see Robert A. Yelle, "Was Aśoka Really a Secularist Avant-la-Lettre? Ancient Indian Pluralism and Toleration in Historical Perspective," *Modern Asian Studies* (in press).
18. Carl Schmitt, *The Leviathan in the State Theory of Thomas Hobbes: Meaning and Failure of a Political Symbol*, trans. George Schwab (Chicago: University of Chicago Press, 2008), 10.
19. Assmann, *Politische Theologie*, 110; see also 105, ascribing this move already to Constantine.
20. Michael Walzer, *Exodus and Revolution* (New York: Basic Books, 1985).
21. This is in direct opposition to Sahlins's and Graeber's provocative argument, following Arthur Maurice Hocart, that religion or cosmology preexisted government and that gods preceded kings. Graeber and Sahlins, *On Kings*, 23–24. As we shall see, Hobbes most likely embraced a form of euhemerism, the idea that the first gods were dead kings worshiped in the form of statues.
22. For this term, *counter-sovereignty*, I draw on Sigrid Weigel, who has used it in reference to martyrdom.
23. Hobbes refers to the Leviathan as a "Mortal God" at Thomas Hobbes, *Leviathan*, chapter 17, §13. All citations to *Leviathan* are to the edition by Edwin Curley (Indianapolis: Hackett, 1994 [1651]).

24. Michael Taussig, "Maleficium: State Fetishism," in *The Nervous System* (New York: Routledge, 1992), 111–40. Taussig refers to Hobbes's Leviathan on the first page of the chapter.
25. Assmann, *Politische Theologie*, 23–24. All translations from German are my own unless otherwise stated.
26. Assmann, *Politische Theologie*, 60.
27. Assmann, *Politische Theologie*, 36.
28. Assmann, *Politische Theologie*, 81.
29. Assmann, *Politische Theologie*, 82ff.
30. Assmann, *Politische Theologie*, 93.
31. Assmann, *Politische Theologie*, 41.
32. Assmann, *Politische Theologie*, 41.
33. Assmann, *Politische Theologie*, 64–65.
34. Assmann, *Politische Theologie*, 42.
35. Assmann, *Politische Theologie*, 75.
36. Assmann, *Politische Theologie*, 111.
37. Assmann, *The Price of Monotheism*, 48. Compare, more recently, Assmann, *The Invention of Religion*, xv: "the Book of Exodus is . . . about the establishment of a completely new type of religion, or even 'religion' as such."
38. See, for example, Devin Stauffer, *Hobbes's Kingdom of Light: A Study of the Foundations of Modern Political Philosophy* (Chicago: University of Chicago Press, 2018), 261–3; Johan Olsthoorn, "The Theocratic Leviathan: Hobbes's Arguments for the Identity of Church and State," in *Hobbes on Politics and Religion*, ed. Laurens van Apeldoorn and Robin Douglass (Oxford: Oxford University Press, 2018), 10–28.
39. Hobbes, *Leviathan*, chapter 29, §15.
40. Jesus uses this line in all of the synoptic gospels, for example, at Matthew 12:25–26.
41. Hobbes, *Leviathan*, chapter 39, §2. Thomas Fulton, "Toward a New Cultural History of the Geneva Bible," *Journal of Medieval and Early Modern Studies* 47, no. 3 (2017): 493, notes that the 1560 Geneva Bible replaced the 1557 edition's *congregation* (borrowed from Tyndale) with the "safer word" *church*.
42. Hobbes, *Leviathan*, chapter 39, §5. See also chapter 33, §24.
43. Hobbes, *Leviathan*, chapter 47.
44. Frederic William Maitland, "The Crown as Corporation," in *Selected Essays*, ed. H. D. Hazeltine, G. Lapsley, and P. H. Winfield (Cambridge: Cambridge University Press, 1936), 104–27 at 108 (mentioning Hobbes). This was one of the sources for Ernst Kantorowicz, *The King's Two Bodies: A Study in Medieval Political Theology* (Princeton, NJ: Princeton University Press, 1957), which never mentions Hobbes, however, nor goes past Shakespeare. Hobbes could have been familiar with this idea from any number of sources, for example, the popular Edmund Plowden's *Reports*, which were originally published in 1571. See A. P. Martinich, *The Two Gods of Leviathan: Thomas Hobbes on Religion and Politics* (Cambridge: Cambridge University Press, 1992), 364, citing Kantorowicz, *The King's Two Bodies*, 13, 15, citing Plowden. See note 76 below for more information.
45. Arthur M. Hocart, *Kingship* (Oxford: Oxford University Press, 1927), 131.

46. See, for example, Eric Nelson, *The Hebrew Republic: Jewish Sources and the Transformation of European Political Thought* (Cambridge, MA: Harvard University Press, 2010), 24–26 (discussing Hobbes).
47. Hobbes, *Leviathan*, chapter 40. On Hobbes's idea of the "kingdom of God," see Stauffer, *Hobbes's Kingdom of Light*, 133–37, 148–58.
48. Hobbes, *Leviathan*, chapter 40–41; see also chapter 33, §20.
49. See, for example, in addition to the works cited below, Horst Bredekamp, *Thomas Hobbes Der Leviathan: Das Urbild des modernen Staates und seine Gegenbilder, 1651–2001*, 4th ed. (Berlin: Akademie Verlag, 2012); Timothy Beal, *Religion and Its Monsters* (New York: Routledge, 2002), 25–28, 30–33, 94–100; Noel Malcolm, "The Title Page of *Leviathan*, Seem in a Curious Perspective," in *Aspects of Hobbes* (Oxford: Clarendon Press, 2002), 200–33; Philip Manow, Friedbert W. Rüb, and Dagmar Simon (eds.), *Die Bilder des Leviathan: Eine Deutungsgeschichte* (Baden-Baden: Nomos, 2012).
50. Noel Malcolm, "The Name and Nature of Leviathan: Political Symbolism and Biblical Exegesis," *Intellectual History Review* 17 (2007): 21–39.
51. Malcolm, "Name and Nature," 23.
52. Schmitt, *The Leviathan*, 8.
53. Malcolm, "Name and Nature," developing John M. Steadman, "Leviathan and Renaissance Etymology," *Journal of the History of Ideas* 28 (1967): 575–6. See also Samuel I. Mintz, "Leviathan as Metaphor," *Hobbes Studies* 2 (1989): 3–9, at 5; Patricia Springborg, "Hobbes and Schmitt on the Name and Nature of Leviathan Revisited," *Critical Review of International Social and Political Philosophy* 12 (2010): 297–315, at 301.
54. Malcolm, "Name and Nature," 34.
55. Malcolm, "Name and Nature," 35.
56. I agree with Springborg's conclusion, in "Hobbes and Schmitt," 308, that "Malcolm's 'Name and Nature of Leviathan' (2007) is an invitation to further scholarship, so as better to see how the pieces of the puzzle fit together." My interpretation is offered in this spirit.
57. Patricia Springborg, "Hobbes's Biblical Beasts: Leviathan and Behemoth," *Political Theory* 23, no. 2 (1995): 353–75, at 358, 360, discusses the use of the plural for Behemoth. This reinforces the parallelism between Behemoth and Leviathan. See Springborg, "Hobbes and Schmitt," 301.
58. Agata Bielik-Robson has told me (personal communication) that such usages of the Hebrew plural are a form of the "diabolical plural" that connote chaos, formlessness, and evil, such as that of the primal waters (*mayim*) associated with the Leviathan. See also Schmitt, *The Leviathan*, 8: "According to . . . Jewish-cabbalistic interpretations, the Leviathan represents 'the cattle upon a thousand hills' (Psalm 50:10), namely, the heathens." Bielik-Robson has also told me that the Hebrew word for Egypt, *mitzrayim*, meaning "straits" or "narrows," carries similar associations. Compare Jan Assmann's explanation of this word, in his chapter for this volume, as a literal translation of the indigenous understanding of Egypt as dual, a combination of northern/upper and southern/lower regions, as reflected in the pharaoh's dual crown. In any case, other Hebrew plurals, such as *Elohim*, carried positive connotations.

59. Schmitt, *The Leviathan*, 9.
60. Natalie Cobo, personal communication.
61. John Downame, *Annotations upon All the Books of the Old and New Testament* (London, 1645). Steadman already noted this gloss; see Steadman, "Leviathan and Renaissance Etymology," 576.
62. See also Springborg, "Hobbes and Schmitt," 305, noting Calvin's identification of the dragon as Pharaoh in his commentary on Isaiah.
63. Malcolm, "Name and Nature," 26. The "other passages" are Ezekiel 29:3, 32:2; Isaiah 51:9–10.
64. Springborg, "Hobbes and Schmitt," 306, expresses similar reservations on this point.
65. Fulton, "Toward a New Cultural History."
66. Fulton, "Toward a New Cultural History," 499.
67. Fulton, "Toward a New Cultural History," 24.
68. Malcolm, "Name and Nature," 35. As noted above, Hobbes's use of the metaphor of the body politic as a corporation was pointed out by F. W. Maitland.
69. Selden, *Titles of Honor* (London, 1614). Revised editions appeared in 1631 and 1672. Hobbes, *Leviathan*, chapter 10, §52, cites the work without specifying which edition he used. Malcolm, "Name and Nature," 38, notes that Selden was familiar with Boulduc's commentary on Job and posits this as one possible source of Boulduc's influence on Hobbes. Selden himself is a much more direct source for the idea of plural Hebrew terms as honorifics. However, the name Leviathan is not interpreted this way by Selden.
70. Selden, *Titles of Honor*, 9, 12–13.
71. Selden, *Titles of Honor*, 62, 114.
72. Selden, *Titles of Honor*, 115.
73. Hocart, *Kingship*, 131: "In seeking for origins it is always a safe rule to take expressions, and indeed beliefs generally, in a literal sense ... superiors were originally addressed as many because they were conceived to be many, or as a third person because a third person was supposed to be actually present."
74. See Selden, *Titles of Honor*, 50–51, on the prohibition against pronouncing the Tetragrammaton, and the substitution of Adonai. See also Selden, *Titles of Honor*, 3rd ed.(London, 1672), 87.
75. Selden, *Titles of Honor*, 74.
76. Kantorowicz, *The King's Two Bodies*, 407, quotes Plowden's *Reports* on the use of the Royal "We": "And the reason is because *the King is a Body politic*, and when an act says 'the king,' or says 'we,' it is always spoken in the person of him as King, and *in his Dignity royal*, and therefore it *includes all those who enjoy his function*" (emphases original). As noted above, Plowden was an early modern representative of the common idea of the body politic as a corporation.
77. Hobbes, *Leviathan*, chapter 16.
78. See note 58 above.
79. Some later Christian theologians, looking for prophecies of the Gospel in the Hebrew Bible, took Elohim as evidence for the Holy Trinity. See Selden, *Titles of Honor*, 115.

80. Hobbes, *Leviathan*, chapter 16, §12; chapters 40–41. Ronald Beiner has pointed out to me that Hobbes declared Moses and those who sat in his seat after him as legitimate. Indeed, this was part of Hobbes's argument, sometimes against counterevidence, that the Hebrew Bible endorsed his model of a unitary sovereign. For this and other reasons, my reading of Hobbes must represent an esoteric, Straussian reading. In my view, the evidence that Hobbes's Leviathan was a coded reference to Pharaoh outweighs Hobbes's dissimulations of orthodoxy. This places me, of course, directly at odds with A. P. Martinich, *The Two Gods of Leviathan*, 367, who states: "I do not detect any skepticism or cynicism toward religion in this frontispiece. If Hobbes had some secret message he wished to convey in *Leviathan*, he should have given some indication of it here." In fact, he did.
81. Hobbes, *Leviathan*, chapter 40, §9. This argument required Hobbes either to ignore or to explain away occurrences of dual or shared sovereignty in the Hebrew Bible, such as the division of labor between Moses and Aaron; the council of elders who assisted Moses during the Exodus; and the conflicted relationship between Samuel and Saul, types of the priest-prophet and king, respectively.
82. Exodus 3:18.
83. Thucydides, *The Peloponnesian War*, trans. Richard Crawley (New York: Dutton, 1910), book 2, chapter 7 (§2.53). In his translation of this passage, Hobbes rendered *anomias* with "licentiousness."
84. See, for example, Giorgio Agamben, *Stasis*, in *The Omnibus Homo Sacer* (Stanford, CA: Stanford University Press, 2017), 247–92, at 279, discussing Francesca Falk's and Horst Bredekamp's interpretations of this detail.
85. See especially Assmann, *Moses the Egyptian*, chapter 2.
86. Herodotus, *Histories*, book 2, ed. A. D. Godley (Cambridge, MA: Harvard University Press, 1920), §124.
87. Assmann, *The Invention of Religion*, 3.
88. See also Hobbes, *Leviathan*, chapter 42, §37, which interprets the Decalogue in similarly rationalist terms and which states that some of the Ten Commandments, including all of the Second Table, were "laws of nature."
89. Hobbes, *Leviathan*, chapter 30, §§7–8.
90. Hobbes, *Leviathan*, chapter 42, §37.
91. Hobbes, *Leviathan*, chapter 16.
92. Hobbes, *Leviathan*, chapter 16, §11.
93. Hobbes, *Leviathan*, chapter 16, §12.
94. Assmann, *The Price of Monotheism*, 28, notes that the Wisdom of Solomon traces idolatry "to two historical sources: the cult of the dead and that of the ruler," echoing Hobbes's and Selden's euhemerism.
95. See also Assmann, *From Akhenaten to Moses*, 49, interpreting the First Commandment and God's covenant with Israel in terms very similar to Hobbes.
96. See Jan Assmann, chapter 5 in this volume.
97. Norman Gottwald, *The Tribes of Yahweh: A Sociology of the Religion of Liberated Israel, 1250–1050 BCE* (New York: Maryknoll, 1979). See also chapter 1 in this volume, in which Strathern and Moin point out that "none of the transcendentalist religions began as cults of state but rather as movements outside major imperial centers." If we

apply this to ancient Israelite religion and accept that this evolved in Canaan, this requires rejecting the historical nature of the Exodus account.

98. Jon Levenson, "Exodus and Liberation," *Horizons in Biblical Theology* 13 (1991): 134–74. However, Levenson has noted a number of difficulties with certain modern-day readings of the Exodus in terms that assimilate this anachronistically to modern notions of democracy and egalitarianism. Among other caveats, the Hebrews had slaves. One may speculate that it was precisely the inability to move immediately beyond the inherited model of monarchy to some notion of direct democracy that led to the device that Assmann terms "direct theocracy," or the invention of the biblical God.

99. 1 Samuel 8. See especially v. 8. Moshe Halbertal and Stephen Holmes, *The Beginning of Politics: Power in the Biblical Book of Samuel* (Princeton, NJ: Princeton University Press, 2017), 9–10.

100. Assmann, *Politische Theologie*, 41.

101. See note 16.

102. For references and discussion, see Robert A. Yelle, " 'An Age of Miracles': Disenchantment as a Secularized Theological Narrative," in *Narratives of Disenchantment and Secularization: Critiquing Max Weber's Idea of Modernity*, ed. Robert A. Yelle and Lorenz Trein, 129–48. London: Bloomsbury, 2020.

103. Taussig, "Maleficium."

11
Ancient Apostasy, Modern Drama

Henrik Ibsen's Emperor and Galilean

NICOLE JERR

On the face of it, Henrik Ibsen, the so-called father of modern drama, registers as a highly unlikely—even suspect—resource for the exploration of sacred kingship in world history. After all, Ibsen secured his title precisely by drafting plays highlighting late nineteenth-century bourgeois characters. His pioneering social realism in works such as *A Doll House*, *The Wild Duck*, and *Hedda Gabler*—to name just a few—ensured a legitimate place on the stage in serious drama for ordinary individuals held captive and stifled by domesticity and conventional morality.

And yet, in 1873, at the precise midpoint of what turned out to be a fifty-year-long writing career, Ibsen produced *Emperor and Galilean*, a sprawling, ponderous, epic drama about the fourth-century Roman emperor Julian. In fits and spurts over the course of nearly a decade, Ibsen researched Julian and his remarkable, if thwarted, attempt to revive the worship of pagan gods and curb the spread of newly sanctioned Christianity. "The historical theme I have chosen," Ibsen explained, "also has a closer connection with the currents of our own age than one might at first think. This I regard as an essential demand to be made of any modern treatment of material so remote, if it is, as a work of literature, to be able to rouse any interest."[1] Ibsen makes no attempt to specify the relevance he ascribes to the "currents" of his own contemporary world, but the play's treatment of Julian and the tensions he gives expression to over the course of the play suggest something more nuanced than a simple desire to reject Christianity.[2]

Ibsen's Julian articulates concerns about the political-theological entanglements attendant to the concept of sovereignty. Again and again, Julian puzzles over the conundrum of the biblical injunction to "Render unto Caesar, the things which are Caesar's ... and unto God the things that are God's." Julian's apostasy from Christianity, in Ibsen's telling, fuses with his decision to embrace his chance to take the throne. Julian's conception of sovereignty ultimately demands limitless scope, and he endeavors to be understood as divine himself, not merely divinely appointed as emperor. As I will explore in this chapter, *Emperor and Galilean* provides rich material not only for exploring the historical Julian and the particular fourth-century crossroads of immanence and transcendence at which he finds himself but also for understanding late nineteenth-century existentialist preoccupations with self-sovereignty and the freedom and self-narration such sovereignty implies. I will also argue that explorations of sovereignty continue to structure Ibsen's later prose dramas, revealing Ibsen's participation in a modern shift—messy and incomplete—away from a conception of sovereignty in strictly political terms and toward an understanding of the significance of sovereignty in personal, individual terms.

JULIAN IN HISTORY

Any study of Emperor Julian is necessarily a study of how his story has been recorded and received. Julian reigned for less than two years (361–363), but his efforts to return to polytheistic cult practices and stem the growth of Christianity has sustained polarized historical and imaginative interest in him over the centuries. Although sympathetic accounts circulated in late antiquity, ecclesiastical narratives dominated through the Middle Ages, rendering Julian an evil enemy for what they characterized as his aggressive persecution of Christian believers. Sentiment shifted notably during subsequent historical periods, with an increased focus on Julian as a statesman and rational thinker. Praised for his self-possession and reason by eighteenth-century luminaries such as Diderot and Voltaire, Julian likewise secured a favorable position in Edward Gibbon's *History of the Decline and Fall of the Roman Empire*.

More recent scholarship, sensitive to the rhetorical contexts of the accounts that make up the archive, paints a picture of a judicious if cunning Julian, averse to illegality. Along these lines, H. C. Teitler provides strong evidence that Julian rejected violence and neither ordered nor promoted any kind of general persecution of Christians.[3] To be sure, his court reforms might have disproportionately affected Christian subjects because they had been favored for court positions under his predecessors, but his reforms were designed as austerity measures in keeping with his ascetic temperament and its rejection of material luxury and bureaucracy. Julian's contempt for Christianity and its adherents, whom he referred to as "Galileans," is indisputable. But as G. W. Bowersock points out, Julian "preferred subtler means" to open persecution, with edicts, for example, meant to restrict Christians from teaching.[4]

Ibsen's 1873 ten-act double-drama, *Emperor and Galilean* stands out in the reception of Julian because this play refuses to characterize the emperor in the absolute either/or terms of previous accounts: he is neither, strictly speaking, a diabolical villain nor a rational hero.[5] Instead, Ibsen chronicles an earnest human struggle to understand spiritual and philosophical concepts that prove frustratingly elusive. The sheer length of the work—clocking in at well over eight hours if performed unabridged—allows Ibsen to develop a character who waffles and converts, who exults and despairs, and who inspires admiration and pity. Ibsen's Julian ultimately articulates a vision of what he terms "the Third Empire"—an empire that does not mark a simple retrogression to pantheistic cult practices with Christianity under erasure but rather a synthesis of the immanentist and transcendentalist values each offers. Even after his apostasy, which Ibsen portrays as an agonizing decision, Julian recognizes the appeal of Christian hope and love, and he longs to transfer these virtues to those who sacrifice to Apollo and Dionysus. In his treatment of Julian, Ibsen emerges as a creative mind sensitive to the pressures, temptations, and influences of both immantentist and transcendentalist worldviews, especially as they bear on the concept of sovereignty.

EMPEROR AND GALILIEAN IN IBSEN'S OEUVRE

Much to the consternation and puzzlement of many of Ibsen's literary critics, the playwright often referred to *Emperor and Galilean* as his most important work.[6] Although the play is seldom discussed and even more rarely performed, such pronouncements on Ibsen's part have contributed to the efforts scholars have made to understand a perplexing play that bears little immediate resemblance in either content or form to the work for which he is best known. To be sure, the vast landscape of the Roman Empire is worlds away from the nineteenth-century parlors in which Ibsen set his subsequent dramas. Ibsen's "regard for [*Emperor and Galilean*] may be pardoned," offers one scholar in a grudging tone often adopted in discussions of the play, "since perhaps more protracted and fatiguing labour went to its composition than to any other and it embodied the result of more abstract and philosophical ratiocination."[7]

It has become a commonplace to understand the significance of *Emperor and Galilean* as Ibsen's final break with historical subject matter before turning his attention to contemporary contexts.[8] Narve Fulsås and Tore Rem, however, have recently found evidence showing that Ibsen entertained the idea of writing plays based on other historical material in the years after completing his epic drama, rendering that explanation invalid.[9] In several instances, scholars have taken bolder positions, finding in *Emperor and Galilean* a key to Ibsen's later work[10] or the beginning traces of his modernism.[11]

For my part, I am similarly motivated to make sense of the relationship between *Emperor and Galilean* and the rest of Ibsen's oeuvre, and I recognize that such bridge construction is a delicate task. The larger context within which I situate Ibsen's work concerns sovereign figures in modern drama. The story I trace runs at an oblique angle to the usual story theater historians have told, not only about Ibsen but also about the modern drama he ushered in. The usual story, of course, is that modern drama has done away with—for good—kings and queens on stage. As I noted above, Ibsen's social realism trained a spotlight on ordinary, bourgeois characters, and modern dramatists after him followed suit. This was a groundbreaking move because serious drama, from antiquity forward, was understood to be the special aesthetic preserve of sovereign figures or those from the nobility. To have tragic stature, traditionally, one had to be royal, not common. Ordinary individuals were eligible for comedy, and later melodrama, but tragedy was off-limits. These aesthetic "rules" for drama reached their height during the neoclassical period, but the French Revolution, with its spectacular replacement of absolute sovereignty with popular sovereignty, carried profound consequences for aesthetics in its political wake.

Ibsen's impressive body of work, spanning fully half a century, demonstrates in microcosm the trajectory of theater history—the common individuals of his last twelve prose plays upstage, so to speak, the mostly royal and noble characters who populate the dramas of the first half of his career. Within this basic scheme of forward progression, *Emperor and Galilean* marks Ibsen's final departure from incorporating sovereign figures into his dramas. But just as this play did not turn out to signal an absolute break with his interest in historical material, neither does it herald an absolute break with his interest in sovereign figures. Although their point is specifically about Ibsen's continued interest in historical material, Fulsås and Rem show that both assumptions are wrong. Not only does a newly discovered letter indicate that Ibsen was drafting a play set in medieval Norwegian history,[12] but another letter written just a few weeks earlier provides corroborating evidence that his intended subject was almost certainly a sovereign figure. Ibsen requested "good Norwegian translations" of several texts: *The King's Mirror*, the *Sagas of the Kings*, and of a work that Ibsen believed was "ascribed to King Sverre and is in some way connected with *The King's Mirror*—and this is all I know about it."[13] Apt words—"this is all I know about it"—for they extend to whatever project Ibsen had in mind. It is unclear whether Ibsen's friend was able to send these texts to the dramatist, uncertain whether Ibsen studied them, and a complete mystery whether the playwright drafted any material based on their themes and stories. Yet I think it is worth holding on to the fact that just over a year after the publication of *Emperor and Galilean*, Ibsen was evidently still intrigued by questions of sovereignty.

The current volume is considering different modes and situations in which the shift to transcendentalism is unable to completely blot out or override the underpinnings of immanentism, as well as the way in which the shift to popular sovereignty failed to destroy the lingering resonance of kingship. *Emperor and Galilean* recapitulates both shifts. I am suggesting that, in the aesthetic shifts toward modern drama, Ibsen did not lose sight of the value of sovereign figures in drama but rather found a way to incorporate them. Not only are his subsequent, "ordinary" characters preoccupied with many of the same concerns as their sovereign predecessors, but two of Ibsen's late dramas—*The Master Builder* (1892) and *John Gabriel Borkman* (1896)—blatantly appropriate the language and imagery of sovereignty.[14] At the conclusion of this chapter, I will briefly gesture toward the analogous ways in which the thematic preoccupations related to sovereignty that Ibsen develops in *Emperor and Galilean* resurface in his penultimate play, *John Gabriel Borkman*, suggesting a new way to understand why Ibsen considered his epic drama on Emperor Julian his most important work.

AESTHETIC PRIORITIES: REALISM (SORT OF) AND HISTORY (SORT OF)

Ibsen breaks *Emperor and Galilean* into two parts, each containing five acts. Part One, "Caesar's Apostasy," covers the years 351–361 and relates Julian's keen interest in philosophy and learning, his military successes in Gaul, and his gradual break with Christianity. Part Two, "The Emperor Julian," covers the brief period of Julian's reign (December 361–June 363) during which Julian attempts to rid the imperial court of extravagant holdovers from the previous regime, undertakes to revive worship of Apollo and Dionysus, grows increasingly frustrated with Galilean insubordination, and hazards a military campaign against Persia. To all appearances, the play seems to be a straightforward biography, innocuous and traditional enough. Perhaps the only hint of Ibsen's personal ambitions for the work is its designation, unique within his oeuvre: "a world-historic drama." Ibsen chose an ancient emperor for his subject matter, yet his plans for the play included a significant—and counterintuitive—artistic risk and challenge: *Emperor and Galilean* is the first play Ibsen wrote in which "realism" took on aesthetic value for him.[15]

To be sure, Ibsen's initial foray into realism does not correspond to gritty social realism. His effort was not guided by a desire to move away from protagonists of elevated position in order to celebrate the common individual; rather, two simple but significant maneuvers indicate his strategy: he forgoes idealization of the sovereign, and he is emphatic about the use of prose. In fact, Ibsen links these strategies, outlining in a letter his intentions to "cast [the play] in a form as realistic as possible; it was the illusion of reality I wanted to produce . . . If I had used verse, I would have run counter to my own intentions and to the task I had set myself." Ibsen goes on to explain that "the form of the language must be adapted to the degree of idealization that is given to the account. My new play [*Emperor and Galilean*] is no tragedy in the old style; what I wanted to portray was people, and it was precisely for that reason that I did not allow them to speak with 'the tongues of angels.' "[16]

If it is "no tragedy in the old style," it is also not depicting sovereignty in the old style. On my reading, Ibsen's choice of prose is related to a desire to display the concept of sovereignty under siege and embattled. Ibsen conspicuously haunts Julian's world with the twin threats of flattery and skepticism. Whether depicting the imperial court, conversations between brothers and childhood friends, philosophers with their students, lamenting women, tortured insubordinates, or soldiers on the march, nearly every scene in this epic drama is performed within the world of the play with a consciousness of a triple audience: those in their immediate presence; those in political power who may learn of what they say and do; and, crucially, the ever-watchful eye of whichever god or gods hold sway at that particular moment. Within the opening scene, Ibsen establishes the anxiety Julian will inherit, revealing an Emperor Constantius terrified not only of court intrigue and political betrayal but even more so of spiritual discovery. Just as he proceeds to enter the church for the Easter vigil, Ibsen's Constantius "braces himself" for the challenge awaiting him. The emperor stammers to his young nephew: "That I—I—must enter in before the sight of the Lord! Oh pray for me, Julian. They will offer me the consecrated wine. I can see it! It sparkles like a serpent's eyes in the golden chalice . . . [*Screams.*]"[17] In the world Ibsen depicts, the Christian faith antagonizes even the emperor who authorizes and upholds it.

Although Julian occupies a stage located at the convergence of major epochs and his actions seek to change the course and texture of the world, his struggles are intensely personal, a point to which I will return in my analysis to follow. Self-doubt colors Julian's experience, not only in Part One, where Julian has not yet arrived on the throne but also, more surprisingly, in Part Two, where there is no question about his political title. The problem, of course, is that his sovereignty is challenged by the Galileans. Specifically, Ibsen brings into focus a critical tension within the concept of sovereignty: between sovereignty within or over the earthly, material, and temporal world, on the one hand; and sovereignty within or over the spiritual, inscrutable, and infinite world, on the other. The scope and effect of Julian's sovereignty turn out to have unbearable limitations. Unbearable, because for Julian limited sovereignty is tantamount to negated sovereignty. "The Galilean is alive" Julian concedes, "however thoroughly the Jews and the Romans imagined they had killed him. He is alive in men's rebellious minds; he is alive in their defiance and scorn of all visible power."[18] Julian recognizes that the contempt the Galileans have toward his sovereignty is more than an emotional attitude or religious stance; it represents active opposition. When reminded that his two predecessors, Constantine and Constantius, were each able to come to peaceable terms with the Galilean, Julian laments, "Yes, if only I could be as easily satisfied as they were. But do you call that ruling the world? Constantine extended the boundaries of his dominions. But didn't he narrowly restrict the boundaries of the spirit and will? You overestimate the man when you call him 'the great.' Not to mention my predecessor; he was more slave than Emperor, and the name alone is not enough for me."[19] Ibsen's Julian resists the theatrical position in which he finds himself. He does not want to play the role of emperor unless that role comes with genuine power over both the earthly and spiritual realm. As Ibsen relates it, Julian's political power and sense of personal purpose are constantly in question. To bring this back to Ibsen's choice of writing in prose, verse might have gestured toward neat resolutions that Ibsen sought to avoid. In prose, then, Ibsen presents what is arguably the very form of his realism: the story of an individual grappling with what it means to be sovereign; the story of an individual who questions—among other things—whether such a thing as being sovereign is possible with a divine sovereign checking every move.

Alongside his commitment to being "realistic" in his portrayal of Julian, Ibsen's discussions of *Emperor and Galilean* indicate a complementary dedication to grounding his account in history. In a letter describing the play, Ibsen claims that he "kept strictly to history," but in fact the work reveals a playwright making dramatically expedient choices to convey a coherent story; in a variety of instances, characters, events, and locations are combined or rearranged to fit his dramatic purposes.[20] Such decisions to elide distinctions or reorganize chronology seem par for the course when translating history to theater. What Ibsen seems to have meant when he said he kept "strictly to history" has more to do with the way he kept (for the most part) to his sources on Julian. He consulted many sources over the course of nearly a decade, but drafts and notes reveal that two principal sources dominate the play: Ammianus Marcellinus, a fourth-century pagan historian and admirer of Julian, provided much of the material Ibsen includes in Part One, whereas Albert de Broglie, a nineteenth-century historian hostile to Julian, supplied crucial accounts found in Part Two.[21]

This combination and ordering of sources might suggest that in the end, Ibsen favored the account constructed by church historians, a triumphalist narrative that interprets Julian as God's instrument for strengthening Christianity, allowing Christians to show their willingness to suffer and die for their faith. I am arguing, however, that Ibsen used these different sources side-by-side as one way to demonstrate an ongoing, reciprocal set of tensions at work between immanentist and transcendentalist orientations. Rather than taking up the cause of one versus the other, Ibsen explored their interrelations. As he put it to Georg Brandes, "I look at the characters, at the intersecting plans, at the *history*, and do not concern myself with the 'moral' of it all."[22] To be sure, scholarship on late antiquity reveals that the shift toward monotheism and transcendentalism was far from a clean, absolute break with the immanentist practices of polytheism. The historical Julian materially contributes to our understanding of this friction, but not merely because he opposed Christianity and sought to reestablish the worship of pagan gods. Far more intriguing are the ways in which Julian's efforts lay bare the dependence of early Christian discourse on Greek pagan culture and, conversely, the influence of Christianity on the paganism Julian sought to establish.

A few key historical examples will serve to set the stage for what I am claiming caught the attention of Ibsen fifteen hundred years later. On the one hand, Julian responded to the rise of Christianity with an attempt to restrict Christian access to the younger generations. His edict on education, issued in June 362, forbade Christians from teaching the pagan Greek classics. The idea was that Christians should not teach works of grammar, rhetoric, and philosophy that they did not themselves understand or promote as truth. Julian's policy exposed the porous line of distinction Christians were using in rejecting Hellenistic paganism but holding on to Hellenistic intellectual culture.[23] According to Bowersock, Julian's educational ban "was a decision of diabolical cunning, the kind of decision that only a former Christian could have made. He knew that the great Christian intellectuals of his own day and before had been steeped in Greek culture and loved it."[24] On the other hand, Julian responded to the growing popularity of Christianity by incorporating some of its appeal into the paganism he was reviving. That is, Julian did not promote a purely conservative return to traditional rites and practices; instead, he attempted to introduce a new kind of paganism. He noticed, for example, that the practice of philanthropy toward strangers stood behind Christianity's widespread success, so he sought to replicate it within the pagan community by ordering the establishment of guesthouses in the cities and charitable distributions for the poor.[25]

While it was unsurprising that Julian's paganism emphasized ritual and sacrifice, less welcome was his insistence on the ascetic lifestyle he himself embraced. It is difficult not to see hints of Julian's Christian upbringing in the demands on pagan priests to avoid pleasures and luxuries and to immerse themselves in philosophical study. Indeed, it is difficult not to see the influence of a transcendentalist outlook where self-denial and self-sacrifice are endured in the belief that such behavior will be rewarded in the afterlife.[26] Perhaps most interesting in this context are Julian's monotheistic impulses even within the framework of the polytheistic paganism he practiced. As Teitler notices, in Julian's own *Hymn to King Helios*, he points out that several gods—Zeus, Hades, Helios, Serapis— were merely "different names for one godhead."[27] Although Julian's cult practices did not deny the existence of other deities, traces of what Jan Assmann refers to as the "Mosaic Distinction"—the monotheistic absolutism that, in positing the one true religion, renders all other religions false and pernicious—manifest themselves in Julian's categorization of Christianity as an "atheism," the "stain" of which he enjoined the Romans to remove in his concluding lines of the *Hymn to the Mother of the Gods*.[28]

With realism and historical accuracy undergirding Ibsen's stated aesthetic priorities, it would be an exaggeration to suggest that Ibsen understood the aims of his play in terms of immanence and transcendence. To be sure, Ibsen never uses such vocabulary, nor does he detail any political or theological positions motivating his interest in Julian's story. Yet Ibsen's sensitivity to the push and pull between immanentism and transcendentalism plainly emerges when we consider not only what Ibsen emphasizes in his portrayal of Julian's struggle to understand his role in history and the scope of his sovereignty but especially when we notice Ibsen's significant departures from historical accounts—departures, to be clear, that take the form of dramatic additions to Julian's story. I will address these interrelated elements of Ibsen's undertaking in the following sections.

SOVEREIGN CONVERSION

Emperor and Galilean: the conjunction links the two figures as though a couple, but within Ibsen's play they are fierce opponents. What is at stake in this duel? How does the ruler of the Roman Empire come to feel he must fight with a long-dead Jewish upstart from a provincial corner that could hardly be considered a military threat? As Ibsen recounts it, Julian arrives at this battle position through a series of highly personal attempts to understand his own significance. Ibsen goes to great lengths to present Julian's story as an angst-ridden struggle, not only with the Christian faith but equally with the sovereignty available to him.

Despite the fact that Ibsen left more drafts and notes on *Emperor and Galilean* than any other of his plays, he never explicitly accounts for his interest in Julian or the fourth-century world he inhabits. Instead, Ibsen emphasizes his own personal connection to the struggles he imagines for Julian. "What I am putting into this book is a part of my own inner life," he asserted while working on *Emperor and Galilean*, "what I describe are things I have myself experienced in different forms."[29] As with so many of Ibsen's pronouncements about his work, one wishes for much greater specificity to guide a critical interpretation. Just what of Ibsen's "inner life" does he suppose corresponds to Julian's? What are these "different forms" of experience that have analogs to Julian's life? Obviously, Ibsen's personal life had none of the high political stakes of Julian's experience. And yet, given the "inner life" Ibsen provides Julian, the playwright appears to have made a productive connection between Julian's struggle to come to terms with being sovereign and that of the playwright's struggle as a modern individual in the late nineteenth century.[30] Put another way, Ibsen projects certain modern existential preoccupations onto his fourth-century emperor protagonist, effectively creating a link between sovereignty in the political sphere and sovereignty in the personal sphere.

Although Ibsen's Julian ultimately fights for absolute authority, he did not always seek such sovereign status nor was he always against the Christian faith. On the contrary, Julian initially shuns the throne and is on the side of Christianity, two crucial factors that later serve to add to his spleen. Had Ibsen only wanted to record a pagan emperor's attempt to overturn Christianity, he could have dispensed with Part One of his epic drama. Instead, "Caesar's Apostasy," which traces Julian's double reversal away from Christianity and toward sovereignty, foregrounds Ibsen's insistence that Julian's "inner life" constitutes the crux of the drama.[31] Spiritual and philosophical considerations dominate the mood and action of the play. As the drama opens, Julian's personal predilection for philosophical study over and above political power immediately distinguishes him from the rest of Constantius' imperial court. Julian feels his calling is to uphold the truth of Christianity, following after the philosopher Libanius in order to better understand and debate the pagans. Ibsen shows the young prince coming to bitter realizations about the hypocrisy of those claiming to be Christian and the elusiveness of Christian truth. Ibsen's Julian does not simply trade in Christianity for pagan philosophy, however, but finds himself disappointed with both. He complains of having "that horrible feeling of nausea you get on a ship becalmed, tossing backwards and forwards between life, scripture, pagan wisdom and beauty." He insists that there must be "a revelation of something new" because "the old beauty is no longer beautiful, and the new truth is no longer true."[32] Julian's desire for something beyond these two categories contributes to his readiness to explore mystery cult practices. Eventually, Julian's spiritual journey leads him to change the terms of his battle: Life versus The Lie.[33] Julian's hunger for life in the temporal world persuades him that Christianity has distorted truth by standing as a wall, obstructing individual freedom and desire. Ibsen locates Julian's proto-Nietzschean struggle precisely at the intersection between the immanentist focus on the present world and the transcendentalist focus on the afterlife.[34] "My whole youth has been a perpetual dread of the Emperor and Christ," Julian explains in an impassioned outburst.

> Oh, he is terrible, this mysterious ... this merciless god-man! Wherever I wanted to go, he loomed up large and forbidding in my path, adamant and pitiless in his demands ... When my soul curled up inside me, consumed with a piercing hatred for the murder of my family, the commandment said: "'Love thine enemy!" When my spirit, bemused by beauty, thirsted for the traditions and images of the lost world of the Greeks, I was paralysed by the Christian command: "Seek only the one thing needful!" ... "Die unto this life, and live in the life beyond!" All human emotions have been forbidden since that day the seer of Galilee began to rule the world. With him, to live is to die ... We are told to *will* against our own will![35]

Julian's repeated insistence on his personal "freedom" to act or "will" as an individual emerges as perhaps the most pronounced of the existential concerns Ibsen confers upon his protagonist. Julian's emphasis on freedom appears in the play, first, in a rejection of sovereign power and, later, in a rejection of Christianity. When Constantius names Gallus, Julian's brother, as the emperor-elect, Julian is not the least envious but relieved, even overjoyed, exclaiming, "I am free, free, free!"[36] Julian will echo this incantation of freedom in the pivotal scene where he consults with spirits conjured by the mystic Maximus and yet again when Julian decisively breaks his covenant with Christianity.[37]

As earnest as Julian is about freedom and life in the sentient realm, ironies abound in his efforts to distance himself from Christianity, not only because Christianity continues to have a hold on Ibsen's apostate but principally because of Julian's simultaneous attempt to claim sovereignty. For one, Julian makes the error of attempting to impose freedom on his subjects, ultimately devolving into plain tyranny. For another, his increasingly ascetic lifestyle in tandem with his obsessions with the spiritual world and his historical legacy belie the joy he anticipated in choosing freedom within the earthly world. Ibsen exposes these contradictions of Julian's character, but the drama goes to great lengths to avoid judging him. Julian unravels, not simply as some insatiably power-thirsty emperor but as an individual wrestling with the philosophical complexities of sovereignty: his ruling strategies are bids to test and define sovereignty as such. Although Ibsen shows Julian to be reluctant to the point of terror at the prospect of being sovereign, once he claims the throne, he will brook no dissent, least of all by a spiritual rival. Julian looks past the Galileans who are his political subjects to the source of their strength and declares Jesus "the greatest rebel who has ever lived . . . he murders every Caesar and every Augustus alike."[38]

Within this opposition toward Christian believers who withhold their full obedience to the emperor, Ibsen reveals a tension between the unabashed theatricality of immanentist practices and the ostensible antitheatricality of transcendentalist values. Beyond those seeking favor in his court, Julian fails to rouse genuine interest in restoring worship of the ancient gods, and the emptiness of his endeavor is not lost on him. After a crowd "looks on in dumb amazement" as Julian leads a festive procession dressed as the god Dionysus, Julian comes away disgusted. "Was there any beauty in that?" he asks, "Ugh, this foul debauchery!"[39] In contrast, Julian acknowledges that the readiness with which the Christians are tortured and martyred would find no parallel in followers of Socrates, Plato, or Diogenes.[40] Recognizing the complete sway Jesus has over the *wills and minds* of his followers, Julian comes up against the boundaries of his earthly political sovereignty, which can only reign over the *actions* of his subjects.[41] Julian finds this galling because wills and minds are capable of authentic belief and loyalty, whereas actions may be only outward displays. At his core, Julian yearns for something else that falls within the province of wills and minds: love. Ibsen's Julian wants to believe he is loved not only by people (which seems to him to be out of reach) but more importantly by historical forces. He wants to believe, paradoxically, both that he has chosen and willed himself to be a significant figure on the world stage but also that he has been destined for that greatness.

DRAMATIC INVENTIONS

If Ibsen more or less keeps to history in terms of the main outline of Julian's biography, his priorities for telling Julian's story come more clearly into focus when we examine how he colors and shades these events. With palpable existential anxieties tormenting him, Julian worries about the choices he is making and the narrative he is crafting for himself. As Julian charts his world-historical course, Ibsen supplies his protagonist with personal omens to guide and reassure him. From the beginning of the play through to its end, Ibsen casts Julian above all as a seeker of signs, peppering the play with dreams, oracles, prophecies, and visions. Indeed, Ibsen's hand is nowhere more apparent than in the special portents he creates (and withholds) for Julian as he determines what his calling is and how he will heed it. It is significant that Ibsen borrows these signs from both immanentist and transcendentalist traditions, further revealing the extent to which the tension between these traditions animates the play.

As noted earlier, Ibsen introduces Julian as someone whose Christian devotion generates a pronounced lack of interest in assuming the throne. Emperor Constantius is worried about the Persian War, but Julian wants to wage a spiritual war against pagan philosophy. "The Lord God has called to me with a loud voice," Julian asserts, "Like Daniel, I will go confidently and joyfully into the lion's den."[42] Aligning Julian with a prominent hero from the Hebrew Bible makes sense in this context where Julian plans to join a group of philosophy students in order to understand their "pseudo-wisdom" and argue with them. Curiously, Ibsen's development of the Julian-as-Daniel theme goes no further than this single mention. Instead, Julian's personal touchstone, particularly within Part One of the play but also at a significant moment in Part Two, turns out to be a different heroic character: Achilles.

Although Ibsen does not invent Julian's association with Achilles, he changes its frame of reference. When Julian is linked with Achilles by his fourth-century contemporaries (most notably Ammianus Marcellinus, whom Ibsen relied upon as a key source, but also Julian himself in a speech), the reference invokes the dynamic between Achilles and Agamemnon to explain the mounting tension between Julian and the Emperor Constantius.[43] Ibsen deflects attention from the political situation, however, and keeps his protagonist within a realm of spiritual decisions and actions. With repeated references to his mother's dream in which she was "giving birth to Achilles," Ibsen's Julian seizes on the notion that he is refraining from battle where he is most needed.[44] When the pagan philosopher Libanius refers to the young prince as "an Achilles of the spirit," Julian eagerly embraces this as proof that he is an actor not only on an earthly stage but, more urgently, on a metaphysical stage. Consonant with the historical evidence of Christian latitude toward the study and incorporation of Hellenic myth and rhetoric, Ibsen's Julian displays no sense of incongruity for assuming the role of a Greek mythological hero in the context of a Christian purge of pagan thought. Ibsen's drama integrates the push and pull between immanentist and transcendentalist traditions in the tensions and even inconsistencies at work in Julian's character.

Even after Julian has led a successful military campaign in Gaul and is next in line to succeed Constantius, he still longs to sequester himself in order to study and write, not rule. But Julian recognizes the reality: his very existence poses a political threat to those in power; he would never be left in peace to "pursue wisdom" in solitude.[45] In another play, this might be enough of an inducement to embrace the opportunity to seize the throne. In Ibsen's characterization of Julian, political expediency is insufficient motivation. Indeed, he is unwilling to actively pursue "the purple" until he interprets the—conflicting—signs in a way that suggests it uniquely falls to him to be sovereign. When the mystic Maximus arranges a symposium with the spirits, Julian is confronted with the suggestion that he shares a lineage with Cain and Judas, two antiheroes of the Judeo-Christian tradition. Rejecting the idea that he acts "under the wrath of necessity," Julian proclaims his freedom but simultaneously clings to an omen that promises him "the pure woman" as a sign that "the divine will" has singled him out for world-historical significance.[46] He believes his wife Helena is this pure woman, and her delirious deathbed confession of her infidelity with a Christian priest brings Julian to his culminating crisis at the center of Ibsen's epic drama.

The plot points are less interesting than the interplay of immanentist and transcendentalist dispositions. Paradoxically, the acute disappointment of an immanentist ideal of purity forces Julian to take stock of the spiritual and political landscape and ultimately to break with Christianity and seize the throne. Ibsen stages the final act of Part One in a vault in the catacombs, where Julian seeks omens for how to proceed. In the church above, mourners celebrate Helena's ascent to heaven. Julian bristles with the irony. Meanwhile, Julian's soldiers are anxious to declare him emperor and fight Constantius on his behalf, but Julian is reluctant and fearful of making a decision that would displease God. He expresses his envy of those whose "gods are far away; they hinder no one; they are no burden; they leave a man plenty of scope for action. Oh, happy Greeks, with their sense of freedom!"[47] Ibsen's mise en scène highlights the contest between pagan cult practices and Christian liturgical praise, ending in a draw: the hymn singing in the church above makes it impossible for Maximus to discern any clear signs in the catacombs below. As a result, the mystic gives Julian nineteenth-century existentialist advice: "Go forward blindly... Take your fate into your own hands."[48] The apostasy is Julian's desire, Julian's will.

As one of the most persistent allusions within the world of the play, Ibsen's choice to figure Julian as Achilles demonstrates the dramatist's attention to the fluid exchange between immanentist and transcendentalist traditions. In deciding to be sovereign while in the catacombs, Julian links himself once more with Achilles the warrior.[49] The context has shifted because Julian's goal is no longer to "purify the world" of pagan abominations in the name of Christianity but the opposite. "They spend their lives in morbid brooding, stifling every stirring of ambition," Julian observes of those professing the Christian faith. The transcendentalist outlook means that "the sun shines for them, and they do not see it; the earth offers them its abundance, and they do not desire it; their only desire is to renounce and suffer, so that they may die."[50] In this iteration of Julian's understanding of himself, his equation with Achilles is particularly apt. Without contradiction or irony, Julian borrows from the archetypal image of heroism and the exercise of sheer untrammeled will in leading his insurgency against transcendentalism.

By the end of *Emperor and Galilean*, Julian comes to understand his role as Achilles in yet another light. He no longer fights on behalf of Christianity, but he also passes through the stage of fighting against Christianity. Maximus reminds Julian of his affinity with Achilles to encourage the emperor to believe in his world-historical significance. "Fortune has borne you," he suggests, "on mighty wings through a tumultuous and dangerous life."[51] Aiming to extinguish the spread of Christianity in order to reestablish worship of the ancient gods is to miss the opportunity to participate in something greater: the creation of something altogether new. "You wanted to make the youth into a child again," Maximus chides Julian. "The empire of the flesh has been swallowed up by the empire of the spirit. But the empire of the spirit is not the final stage, any more than the youth is. You wanted to prevent the youth from growing... to prevent him from becoming a man."[52] In a move that sets Ibsen's account of Julian apart from other philosophical and literary interpretations, the emperor seeks to reconcile the pagan and the Christian, the earthly and the spiritual, into his vision of what he calls the Third Empire:[53] "the empire of the great mystery, the empire which shall be founded on the tree of knowledge and the tree of the cross together."[54] For Julian, the Third Empire will appear when he consolidates sovereignty, becoming "the god of the earth and the Emperor of the spirit in *one*."[55]

MODERN CURRENTS

Speaking in 1887 about "the age we now stand in," Ibsen asserted that "something new is in the process of being born . . . I believe that the ideals of our age, by suffering eclipse, show a trend towards what I have intimated in my drama *Emperor and Galilean* by the term 'the Third Empire.' "[56] Ibsen's nineteenth century witnessed the ideological protest against the Judeo-Christian tradition emerging anew, succinctly captured by Nietzsche's pronouncement that "God is dead." Within the parallel battle between transcendentalist and immanentist priorities, Ibsen's drama explores a significant concern related to sovereignty. For all of his heady talk of ruling heaven and earth, Ibsen's Julian is all too human and, what is more, he has distinctly modern anxieties. He wants to be a free, self-determining subject with a keen focus on the here and now, but these desires are at odds with his Christian upbringing, with its emphasis on self-denial and the afterlife. In other words, Julian is seeking an immanentist mode of existence, but he is haunted by underlying emotional and psychological features of transcendentalism. In his book, *The Persistence of Subjectivity*, Robert Pippin examines the modern difficulty of *leading* a life "wherein one's deeds and practices are and are experienced as one's own, due to one, not fated."[57] Ibsen locates his Julian precisely at this modern crossroads, replete with mixed signals. The imperative to "Choose!" intersects with the question, "Do not all the signs and omens point with an unerring finger to you?"[58]

The modern subject feels called on to "lead a life, take up the reins, as it were," but as Pippin makes clear, "this is something at which 'modernism' discovers, *we can fail* (oddly, especially when we try very hard to do it)."[59] Although the ostensible historical context in Ibsen's play is the fourth century, Julian expresses modern frustrations. Indeed, Ibsen's insistence on the contemporary relevance of *Emperor and Galilean*—its "connection with the currents of our own age"—finds its most compelling expression here, in what Ibsen seems to diagnose as the anxieties symptomatic of an attempt to move beyond the Judeo-Christian worldview.[60] For Julian, to *lead* a life coincides with political sovereignty over the Roman Empire, but his overwhelming desire is for a personal, individual sovereignty over his life and the narrative he is crafting for himself. Despite the occult nature of some of the signs Julian consults, and despite the "world-historical" nature of the lens through which he sees himself, there is at base an attempt to determine what his unique role or mission in life might be (a pursuit that links him with Ibsen's later "ordinary" characters). Julian wants to bring about a new, changed world, one that takes pleasure in itself, and the divine signs seem to indicate that it fits his hands to do this. But Julian never forgets it was he himself who has read them this way. Indeed, once Julian determines *for himself* in his first act of individual sovereignty that the *conflicting* signs mark him elect as the creator and ruler of a new empire, his increasing intolerance of Christianity must be understood as a mounting fear that he was wrong *about himself* and what he was meant to do because he has been unable to do it.

Toward the conclusion of the play, when Julian is in despair over putting his army into an untenable military position, he considers suicide. "Do you think if I were to vanish from the earth without trace, and my body were never found, and no one discovered what had become of me," Julian asks Maximus, "do you think a legend would grow that Hermes had come to me and had carried me off, and that the gods had admitted me into their company?"[61] Here is a narrative he can live with, so to speak, as opposed to the narrative that seems to be emerging: that it is he "who succumbed and [the Galilean] who conquered," that, as the Galileans have taunted him, he is merely a tool in God's hand, forced to be a rod of correction to the ultimate glory of the Christian God.[62] This contemplative moment is a late addition to Ibsen's drafts of *Emperor and Galilean*, indicating the dramatist's sense that the ending of his play needed to register as forcefully as possible Julian's desire for crafting his story. Maximus's response to Julian is optimistic, and I take it to be Ibsen's optimism: "The time is near when men shall not need to die in order to live as gods on earth."[63]

As noted earlier, Ibsen claimed that he put parts of his "own inner life" into *Emperor and Galilean*, things he had "experienced in different forms."[64] He provides a hint of what he means by this in a speech he gave to Norwegian students in 1874, just a year after the publication of his play. Referring to "something I have lived through," Ibsen recounts a scene when Julian describes a dream.[65] In the dream, Julian succeeds in expunging the memory of Jesus from earth, only to discover the futility of his victory because he sees Jesus in another world leading a processional with a cross on his back. The point of the dream for Julian goes beyond the impossibility of vanquishing his enemy; he recognizes just what would elude his grasp even if he managed to triumph. Earthly sovereigns, Julian speculates, are remembered "with cold astonishment . . . while the other one, the Galilean, the carpenter's son, reigns as the king of love in the warm believing hearts of men."[66] Driving Julian's despondency at this moment is his acute awareness of the limitations of an immanentist mode of seeking power and success. He may scorn the transcendentalist virtue of self-sacrifice, but there is no alternative access to love: Julian can command respect and obedience as the sovereign ruler; he cannot command love.

Ibsen seems to have discerned that he was onto something of decisive importance because the high cost of sovereignty that excludes warmth and human love turns out to be an abiding insight. Two decades later, in his penultimate play, Ibsen returns to an exploration of sovereignty, but his characters are taken from contemporary everyday life, not from the history books. Political sovereignty is no longer an aesthetic prerequisite for the protagonist. In *John Gabriel Borkman* Ibsen gives the stage to a former banker who has lost the financial and social "empire" he had ruthlessly established, actively choosing wealth and success over love. In a scene of raw emotional reckoning, Ella tells Borkman that "an icy blast" blows from the "kingdom" with which he is obsessed, whereas he might have had love because "up here, in the light of day, there throbbed a warm and living human heart. Beating for you."[67] Like Julian, Borkman's ambitions leave him with strictly nothing on an interpersonal level.

In terms of its basic form and content, the 1896 contemporary play stands in stark contrast to the epic, lofty grandeur of *Emperor and Galilean*. And yet in *John Gabriel Borkman*, Ibsen foregrounds, in an explicitly modern setting, the tensions he explored in the drama he considered his most important work. Borkman has served a prison term, but during the time of the play he lives in a prison of another kind. Banished by his wife to the top floor of a borrowed home (she occupies the first floor), Borkman continues to fantasize about a triumphant restitution and professional reinstatement. Ibsen demonstrates, however, that his sense of exile is self-imposed. Borkman cannot bear to face the outside world except in a sovereign role, and when this is out of reach, he imagines himself as a martyr. His hopes for a restored reputation take on the quality of a faith in the afterlife. In this way, *John Gabriel Borkman* reveals the ongoing tensions between immanentist and transcendentalist modes of existence. Ibsen also exposes the political-theological heritage haunting the concept of sovereignty. If Julian was tormented by an unrelenting battle with a divine sovereign, Borkman similarly understands himself to be in competition with God. Borkman does not name God outright as an adversary, but when he has climbed high up the mountain, he surveys all below as belonging to *his* "infinite" and "inexhaustible" kingdom. "And now it lies there," he laments, "defenceless, leaderless, exposed to thieving and plundering and attack." In this scene, Ibsen includes profound echoes with Julian's apostasy in the catacombs. Borkman eventually enunciates his blasphemy because in striving after "the kingdom . . . and the power . . . and the glory," he has rejected Ella and her love.[68] Similarly, Julian exalts, "Free, free! Mine is the kingdom!" while the choir in the church above incants their prayer to God, "Thine is the kingdom, and the power, and the glory."[69]

Ibsen's first dramatic undertaking motivated by realism provided the playwright with the opportunity to develop a realism that explores and gives voice to an internal struggle over what it means to be sovereign, what it means to lead a life. As Ibsen represented Julian's historical situation at the intersection of immanentism and transcendentalism, he found expression for the modern desire to preside freely over one's life and choices, recognizing a concurrent wistfulness for the assurances a transcendentalist worldview would provide. "The play treats of the struggle between two irreconcilable powers in the history of the world," Ibsen said of *Emperor and Galilean*, adding, "a struggle that will always repeat itself."[70] Neither Julian nor Borkman find their way to the "empire" they each want to establish, where their individual sovereignty coexists with human love. Ibsen suggests the struggle for this empire continues.

NOTES

1. Ibsen, Letter to Edmund Gosse, October 14, 1872, quoted in Henrik Ibsen, *The Oxford Ibsen: Emperor and Galilean*, ed. James McFarlane (London: Oxford University Press, 1963), 4: 603.
2. Critical interpretations of the play often presume Ibsen was drawn to Julian as a defector from Christianity. Some understand the play as the "tragedy" of "falling away" from Christianity "into emptiness." See, for example, Paulus Svendsen, "Emperor and Galilean," in *Ibsen, A Collection of Critical Essays*, ed. Rolf Fjelde (Englewood Cliffs, NJ: Prentice-Hall, 1965), 80–90.
3. H. C. Teitler, *The Last Pagan Emperor: Julian the Apostate and the War Against Christianity* (Oxford: Oxford University Press, 2017).
4. G. W. Bowersock, *Julian the Apostate* (Cambridge, MA: Harvard University Press, 1978), 83.
5. For a concise account of the reception of Julian by philosophers, historians, and writers from antiquity through the twentieth century, see Robert Browning, *The Emperor Julian* (Berkeley: University of California Press, 1976), 219–35. Browning dismisses Ibsen's play as "both bad history and bad theatre."
6. See, for example, Gunhild Hoem, "Emperor and Galilean: The Problem Child of Literary Scholars," in *Proceedings: IX International Ibsen Conference, Bergen 5–10 June 2000*, ed. Pål Bjørby and Asbjørn Aarseth (Øvre Ervik, Norway: Alvheim & Eide Akademisk Forlag, 2001), 309–14.
7. Brian W. Downs, *Ibsen: The Intellectual Background* (Cambridge: Cambridge University Press, 1948), 151.
8. See Bjørn Hemmer, "Ibsen and Historical Drama," in *The Cambridge Companion to Ibsen*, ed. James McFarlane (Cambridge: Cambridge University Press, 1994), 12–27.
9. Narve Fulsås and Tore Rem, *Ibsen, Scandinavia, and the Making of a World Drama* (Cambridge: Cambridge University Press, 2018), 70.
10. Notable here is the work of Brian Johnston, who understood Ibsen's project through a Hegelian lens. See Brian Johnston, *To the Third Empire: Ibsen's Early Drama* (Minneapolis: University of Minnesota Press, 1980).

11. See, for example, Toril Moi, *Henrik Ibsen and the Birth of Modernism: Art, Theater, Philosophy* (Oxford: Oxford University Press, 2006). Moi devotes a central chapter of her book to *Emperor and Galilean*.
12. Ibsen, Letter to D. C. Danielssen, February 26, 1875, Bergen Museum, referenced in Fulsås and Rem, *Ibsen, Scandinavia, and the Making of a World Drama*, 70.
13. Ibsen, Letter to Ludvig Daae, February 4, 1875, in *Letters of Henrik Ibsen*, trans. John Nilsen Laurvik and Mary Morison (New York: Fox, Duffield, 1905), 281–2. *The King's Mirror* and the *Sagas of the Kings* were Old Norse texts.
14. Ibsen plays a crucial role in my current book project on the strange persistence of sovereign figures in modern drama. In addition to *Emperor and Galilean*, Ibsen's 1863 play, *The Pretenders*, concerning a thirteenth-century fight for the Norwegian throne, also serves as an early source of Ibsen's interests in the sovereign themes I argue he develops in his late plays.
15. See Moi, *Henrik Ibsen and the Birth of Modernism*, 188–222. Moi establishes this play as Ibsen's crucial but imperfect turn to realism and the everyday. According to Moi, Ibsen's efforts in this play manage to hit on nearly all the core features of what come to be recognized as his realist concerns in the second half of his career.
16. Ibsen, Letter to Edmund Gosse, January 15, 1874, quoted in Ibsen, *The Oxford Ibsen*, 4: 606.
17. Ibsen, *The Oxford Ibsen*, 4: 205.
18. Ibsen, *The Oxford Ibsen*, 4: 400.
19. Ibsen, *The Oxford Ibsen*, 4: 400.
20. Ibsen, Letter to Edmund Gosse, February 20, 1873, quoted in Ibsen, *The Oxford Ibsen*, 4: 604.
21. For an overview of Ibsen's sources and the extent of his fidelity with history, see Graham Orton, Appendix II: Sections 3 and 4, in Ibsen, *The Oxford Ibsen*, 4: 597–603.
22. Ibsen, Letter to Georg Brandes, September 24, 1871, quoted in Ibsen, *The Oxford Ibsen*, 4: 603. Emphasis in the original.
23. See Bowersock, *Julian the Apostate*, 83–84; Teitler, *The Last Pagan Emperor*, 66.
24. G. W. Bowersock, *Hellenism in Late Antiquity* (Ann Arbor: University of Michigan Press, 1990), 11–12. Bowersock points to the outraged reaction of Gregory of Nazianzus (Invective against Julian 1) to demonstrate how Julian's edict hit its mark.
25. See Teitler, *The Last Pagan Emperor*, 28; Bowersock, *Julian the Apostate*, 87. As Bowersock notes, these efforts were tailored to "wrest from the Galileans the credit they had earned from good works."
26. See Bowersock's chapter "The Puritanical Pagan," in *Julian the Apostate*, 79–93; and Teitler, *The Last Pagan Emperor*, 28.
27. Teitler, *The Last Pagan Emperor*, 27.
28. Julian, *Hymn to the Mother of the Gods*, March 362, quoted in Bowersock, *Julian the Apostate*, 83. See Jan Assmann, *The Price of Monotheism*, trans. Robert Savage (Stanford, CA: Stanford University Press, 2010).
29. Ibsen, Letter to Edmund Gosse, October 14, 1872, quoted in Ibsen, *The Oxford Ibsen*, 4: 603.

30. For further comments in which Ibsen links his personal experience to the experience he writes for Julian, see his Letter to Edmund Gosse, February 20, 1873 ("There is much self-anatomy in this book"); and his letter to Ludvig Daae, February 23, 1873 ("There is to be found in the character of Julian . . . more personal inner experience than I care to admit to the public"). Both letters quoted in Ibsen, *The Oxford Ibsen*, 4: 604.
31. Ibsen yokes the idea of apostasy with taking the throne early and explicitly when Julian swears to his brother Gallus that he has no imperial ambitions. "If this head of mine were to be anointed, would that not be apostasy . . . a mortal sin? Would the Lord's holy oil not burn me like molten lead?" Ibsen, *The Oxford Ibsen* 4: 224.
32. Ibsen, *The Oxford Ibsen*, 4: 244.
33. Ibsen, *The Oxford Ibsen*, 4: 313.
34. The ideas Ibsen's work explores share many affinities with Nietzsche's philosophy, and although the two were contemporaries, there is scant evidence that either figure directly influenced the other. See Thomas F. Van Laan, "Ibsen and Nietzsche," *Scandinavian Studies* 78, no. 3 (2006): 255–302.
35. Ibsen, *The Oxford Ibsen*, 4: 309.
36. Ibsen, *The Oxford Ibsen*, 4: 228.
37. Ibsen, *The Oxford Ibsen*, 4: 263, 316.
38. Ibsen, *The Oxford Ibsen*, 4: 399–400.
39. Ibsen, *The Oxford Ibsen*, 4: 341.
40. Ibsen, *The Oxford Ibsen*, 4: 438.
41. Ibsen, *The Oxford Ibsen*, 4: 409.
42. Ibsen, *The Oxford Ibsen*, 4: 227.
43. See Timothy D. Barnes, "The New Achilles," in *Ammianus Marcellinus and the Representation of Historical Reality* (Ithaca, NY: Cornell University Press, 1998), 143–65.
44. Ibsen, *The Oxford Ibsen*, 4: 209, 217, 229, 311, 314, 412.
45. Ibsen, *The Oxford Ibsen*, 4: 305.
46. Ibsen, *The Oxford Ibsen*, 4: 254, 259.
47. Ibsen, *The Oxford Ibsen*, 4: 305.
48. Ibsen, *The Oxford Ibsen*, 4: 308.
49. Ibsen, *The Oxford Ibsen*, 4: 311, 314.
50. Ibsen, *The Oxford Ibsen*, 4: 311.
51. Ibsen, *The Oxford Ibsen*, 4: 412.
52. Ibsen, *The Oxford Ibsen*, 4: 401.
53. Not only does Ibsen's "Third Empire" mark a departure in terms of the reception and portrayal of Emperor Julian, but it also marks an important shift within the history of theater and its relations to sovereign figures. Early modern drama during the age of absolutism primarily put forward sovereign figures in the transcendentalist mode (i.e., Shakespeare's Richard II, Henry IV, Henry V). Christopher Marlowe's *Tamburlaine the Great* is interesting in this regard for a depiction of Tamburlaine that seems to advocate a return to an immanentist model of sovereign will. See A. Azfar Moin, "Akbar's 'Jesus' and Marlowe's 'Tamburlaine': Strange Parallels of Early Modern Sacredness," *Fragments: Interdisciplinary Approaches to the Study of*

Ancient and Medieval Pasts 3 (2013–2014): 1–21. In this way, we can see early modern dramatists taking an either/or approach to immanentist versus transcendentalist models of kingship. Perhaps for Marlowe, the only (or clearest) way to contest a transcendentalist model of kingship was to put forward Tamburlaine, with his godlike will. What makes Ibsen "modern" in this context is his attempt to move beyond these distinct categories. As the quoted passages indicate, Ibsen goes to great lengths in *Emperor and Galilean* to show that looking backward (to either immanentism or transcendentalism) is the wrong, misguided move. Ibsen wants a new, third way that acknowledges both.

54. Ibsen, *The Oxford Ibsen*, 4: 259.
55. Ibsen, *The Oxford Ibsen*, 4: 432.
56. Ibsen, Speech at a banquet in Stockholm, September 24, 1887, quoted in Ibsen, *The Oxford Ibsen*, 4: 608.
57. Robert Pippin, *The Persistence of Subjectivity: On the Kantian Aftermath* (Cambridge: Cambridge University Press, 2005), 10.
58. Ibsen, *The Oxford Ibsen*, 4: 313, 412.
59. Pippin, *The Persistence of Subjectivity*, 21.
60. Ibsen, Letter to Edmund Gosse, October 14, 1872, quoted in Ibsen, *The Oxford Ibsen*, 4: 603.
61. Ibsen, *The Oxford Ibsen*, 4: 445.
62. Ibsen, *The Oxford Ibsen*, 4: 418, 447.
63. Ibsen, *The Oxford Ibsen*, 4: 445.
64. Ibsen, Letter to Edmund Gosse, October 14, 1872, quoted in Ibsen, *The Oxford Ibsen*, 4: 603.
65. Ibsen, Speech to the Norwegian Students, Christiania, September 10, 1874, *Ibsen: Letters and Speeches*, ed. Evert Sprinchorn (New York: Hill and Wang, 1964), 149–52.
66. Ibsen, *The Oxford Ibsen*, 4: 446. In his speech to the students, Ibsen translates this into an author's fear of being "remembered by clear and cool heads with respectful appreciation, while his opponents live on, rich in the love of warm, living hearts." See Ibsen, Letter to Edmund Gosse, October 14, 1872, quoted in Ibsen, *The Oxford Ibsen*, 4: 603. Unfortunately, reducing it to professional rivalry shortchanges the insight at the core of Julian's realization.
67. Henrik Ibsen, *The Oxford Ibsen: John Gabriel Borkman*, vol. 8, ed. James McFarlane (London: Oxford University Press, 1977), 231.
68. Ibsen, *The Oxford Ibsen*, 8: 231.
69. Ibsen, *The Oxford Ibsen*, 4: 316.
70. Ibsen, Letter to Ludvig Daae, February 23, 1873, in *Ibsen: Letters and Speeches*, 135.

12

The Last Hindu King

How Nepal Desanctified Its Monarchy

DAVID N. GELLNER

> *The history of the Shah Dynasty is intertwined with the history of Nepal. The singular credit for the unification of Nepal and bringing together the diverse religio-ethnic and cultural groups under one banner also goes to the kings of the Shah dynasty. It would, therefore, not be incorrect to surmise that the Institution of Monarchy in Nepal is an integral part of her history and ethos . . . The constitution of the Kingdom of Nepal 1990 regards His Majesty as the "symbol of Nepalese nationality and unity of the Nepalese people," while, at the same time, reposing on him the responsibility of preserving and protecting the Constitution "by keeping in view the best interests and welfare of the people of Nepal." His Majesty has, ever since his accession, made it clear that he intends to fulfill his responsibilities to the best of his abilities in the paramount interest of the Nepal and the Nepalese people.*
>
> —"Overview of the History of the Shah Dynasty" (November 2003), official website of the royal court of Nepal, www.nepalmonarchy.gov.np (accessed August 7, 2005; no longer available)

Hindu kingship and Hindu society present a conundrum for Weberian and Axial Age theories. Is Hinduism merely a highly sophisticated development of the pre-Axial world, an exemplar of what Alan Strathern calls immanentism, innocent of soteriology and transcendence? That was the conclusion of Robert Levy in his magnum opus

Mesocosm, an 829-page portrait of the city of Bhaktapur in Nepal.¹ For Levy, drawing on Fustel de Coulanges, as well as on Robert Redfield and Milton Singer, Bhaktapur, with its social complexity and profusion of festivals and rituals, was an archaic city in the specific sense that its culture was an outgrowth of its rural hinterland and not in tension with it. Yet, as Levy was aware, South Asia knew Axial Age religions in the form of Buddhism, Jainism, and other renouncer movements, and there are and have been plenty of soteriological paths within Hinduism as well. So perhaps it would be more apt to say that Hinduism "absorbed" and tamed the lessons of transcendence, maintaining a predominantly this-worldly or immanentist worldview. That, at any rate, would seem to have been Max Weber's view, as well as Louis Dumont's, and Strathern also seems to have considerable sympathy with this way of viewing Hinduism.²

The developed theory of Hindu kingship blends both ends of the spectrum implied by Strathern's ideal-typical distinction between divinized and righteous kings.³ As will be described in this chapter, the rituals of Hindu kingship imply divinization, the identification of the king with many gods but particularly with Vishnu (latterly in his avatar as Rama). At the same time, however, the king's duty is to uphold dharma. Indeed *dharma-raja* means "righteous king," and kings were supposed to support, and be fundamental for, both social and transcendent morality. The monotheistic and Abrahamic religions, insisting on an absolute cleavage between God and his creation, including (and perhaps especially) humankind, have arguably been more likely to insist on righteous kingship at the expense of divinized kingship.⁴ By contrast, in Asia, including in a Buddhist context, one can be both divinized and righteous. It was perhaps the particular genius of Hinduism to fuse both kinds of kingship into a single model.

The Kathmandu Valley has long been recognized as a kind of time machine, where the cultural conditions of medieval India—Tantric Hinduism, the survival of Sanskrit-based Buddhism, minimal influence of Islam—can still be observed. Colonel Kirkpatrick, who visited the valley briefly in 1793, described it as having "nearly as many temples as houses, and as many idols as inhabitants."⁵ Sylvain Lévi, the great French Sanskritist and historian (no relation of the American anthropologist Robert Levy) spent two months in the Kathmandu Valley in 1898 and wrote its history in three volumes. In a much-cited phrase, Lévi said that Nepal (by which he meant the Kathmandu Valley) was "India in the making" (*le Népal, c'est l'Inde qui se fait*).⁶ Lévi's history of Nepal drew on vernacular chronicles that portrayed Nepal's kings as (1) bringers of justice and social order and (2) mediators between gods and humans, and, in particular, as the key sacrificer responsible for introducing or reintroducing important local cults.⁷

In line with Lévi's view of it as the home of archaism, Nepal made a point of labeling itself, from 1962 until 2007, long after India had adopted a secular constitution, as "the world's only Hindu kingdom."[8] The constitution of 1990 defined the country as "a Hindu and Constitutional Monarchical Kingdom." Both the 1962 and 1990 constitutions specified that the king must be "a descendent of the Great King Prithvi Narayan Shah and an adherent of Aryan culture and the Hindu religion."[9] Everything changed with the Interim Constitution, adopted in January 2007 following the end of the ten-year Maoist insurgency/civil war and the removal of King Gyanendra from power. This Interim Constitution stipulated that all the properties of King Birendra and Queen Aishwarya and their families were to be held in trust for the nation, as well as all property "acquired by King Gyanendra in the capacity of King." Furthermore, "[n]o power to rule the country shall be vested in the King . . . the Constituent Assembly shall decide by simple majority at its first meeting about whether or not to continue the monarchy in existence." By December 2007 the matter had been decided and, following the Third Amendment, the Interim Constitution specified that "Nepal shall be a federal democratic republican state," reiterating that the king should have no power and specifying that "[t]he Prime Minister shall conduct all the functions of the head of the state until the republic is implemented."[10] In the new constitution, promulgated in 2015, there is no mention of the words *king*, *monarch*, or *Hinduism*. Nepal is defined as "an independent, indivisible, sovereign, secular, inclusive, democratic, socialism-oriented, federal democratic republican state."[11]

The idea of kingship had been pervasive and fundamental to local ideas of a well-run polity as recently as 1990. The constitution makers of that year "took for granted the essentially political idea of the inner unity of the Nepali State and nation historically grounded in the institution of the Shah monarchy . . . [these were] the ontological and ideational foundations of the Nepali State . . ."[12] By 2007, however, just seventeen years later, abolishing the monarchy seemed both natural and necessary. Having taken that decision, how did Nepal manage to convert itself from the world's last Hindu monarchy, where the king served as the symbol of national unity and was the chief sacrificer to the gods, into a federal republic in which the former monarch is simply "Mr. Shah"?

Removing the king from public life in Nepal turned out, in practice, to be far from simple or straightforward. How and when should the president take on ceremonial roles formerly filled by the king? How can the ex-king be prevented from reasserting his place in the imagination of the nation? And what remains of the idea of kingship when a supposedly secular president attends public rituals in his place? In a society that remains far from secularized, to what extent do representatives of political authority need religious legitimation? Thanks to the detailed work of several Nepal specialists, it is possible to answer some of these questions.[13]

CLASSIC THEORIES OF HINDU KINGSHIP

In Hindu law texts, kings were thought to be necessary because human beings had lost the ability to follow their duties instinctively. A society without a king was therefore subject to the "law of the fishes," that is, a lawless state of predatory nature, analogous to Hobbes's war of all against all.[14] Insofar as a king embodies *ksatra* ("royal power"), he is independent and can do what he likes, although he should make use of a body of wise and qualified counselors.[15] At the same time, the king's *dharma*, or "religious duty," obliges him to protect his subjects.[16] Protecting his subjects has four aspects: recalling people to their duties, enforcing penances on sinners, repressing criminals, and arbitrating disputes.[17] In fulfilling his royal function, the king has two rights: to tax and to punish. But the right to tax depends on no contract; the king must protect all his subjects, whether they can afford to pay taxes or not, and he has a right to taxes, whether he succeeds in protecting his subjects or not. If he fails to do so, the sanction is not the subjects' withdrawal of taxes but the consequences he must face in a future life for not fulfilling his duty. The king's right to punish provides him with "an unlimited power on the temporal plane ... the king is the sole judge of the means to be employed to accomplish his mission."[18] No matter how he behaves (and regardless of whether he is responsible for the deaths of his immediate family) a king remains pure. He (and unlike the other members of his caste) also outranks his priestly Brahmins.[19] In the words of the Laws of Manu, "Even a boy king should not be treated with disrespect ... for this is a great deity standing there in the form of a man."[20] Sheldon Pollock has stressed the importance of the Sanskrit language to the imagination and construction of kingship in South Asia: "When the king's grammar is correct, the king's politics are correct, and his rule will be as just as his words. The king who did not command the language of the gods could command the polity no better than a drunkard."[21] At a later period, this was generalized from Sanskrit to a command of all locally prestigious languages. Kings—including kings in Nepal—did indeed claim to be poets and did compose (or had attributed to them) verses and dance dramas in which they themselves performed.[22]

One of the best-known, but most misleading, articles on Hindu kingship is that by Louis Dumont.[23] Dumont argued that Hindu kingship had undergone an early form of secularization with the specialization of Brahmins in the sacred function. In other words, kings had lost some of their original sacred aura. Dumont was describing the king-priest relationship at a very archaic period, 2,000 years ago, before the rise of Hindu monotheism and before the rise of Tantra and the goddess cults.[24] Clifford Geertz's famous depiction of nineteenth-century Balinese kingship as a "theatre state," in which elaborate royal ritual was not a prop to shore up power but was rather the whole point of holding power, described a system that was very close to medieval Hinduism.[25] However, Geertz was seriously misled by Dumont's description of a secularized Hindu king into believing that Southeast Asian kingship was fundamentally different from the classic Indian model. In fact, Balinese Hinduism and the place of the king within it, as described by Geertz, is the descendant of the same medieval Tantric and Puranic Hinduism, with the same highly divinized form of kingship, that is found in Nepal.

Tantras were new forms of scripture, emerging first, around 4–500 CE, in Hinduism, but subsequently becoming equally influential within Buddhism. They emphasized elaborate and esoteric rituals, combined with mysticism, and were aimed at the individual practitioner. They promised worldly powers and, unlike earlier Indian soteriological paths, they did not posit a radical opposition between such magical powers and the attainment of salvation. Medieval Hindu kingship came to find its primary legitimation precisely in Tantrism and the cult of the goddess.[26] "Tantra is a form of religion in which worldly, temporal goals and theology are perfectly integrated. It advocates the worship of power for the attainment of power."[27] With the rise of Tantric goddess worship, Hindu kings, to the extent that they had ever been secularized, became resacralized, so to speak. Their power was seen to depend on their relationship to the local goddess, identified with the earth, and with whom the king enters into a form of marriage. The king himself incarnates all the gods, especially Vishnu (in Nepal, Indra and Bhairava were also important). Pollock argues that "the unifying principle of the entire [*Ramayana*]," the most influential epic in South and Southeast Asia, is the king's possession of divine power both to protect and to punish.[28] The identification of Hindu kings with Vishnu, combined with their worship of the goddess Durga for regal power, goes back at least as far as the Gupta Empire (fourth to the sixth centuries CE). At that time, the prime identification seems to have been with the Varaha (boar) avatar, as representative of the earth.[29] On the basis of the architectural and inscriptional evidence, Pollock argues that the identification of the king with Rama became significant only from the twelfth century.[30]

In his study of Tamil temple myths, David Shulman remarks that the king's role as the foremost ritualist of the kingdom "tends to expand metaphorically to the point where he subsumes all others."³¹ He points to similarities with Geertz's theater kings, but sees the king less as "an impassive, immobile icon" and more of "a shadowy escapist torn by inner contradictions, a self-transforming actor charged with safeguarding the equally elusive, internally divided dharmic order."³² Mythically the king is compared to death, and he inevitably accumulates sin. Shulman quotes Arjuna's realist political philosophy from the Mahabharata:

> No one can attain great glory without striking at others' vitals, or without doing terrible deeds, without killing like a fisherman. Only a killer has fame on earth, and wealth, and offspring... People worship those gods who are killers... Only a few men sacrifice to those who are impartial toward all creatures, the restrained pacified deities intent on tranquillity. I see no being which lives in the world without violence. Creatures exist at one another's expense; the stronger consume the weaker... see *dharma* for what it is!³³

There are plenty of Nepali proverbs that reflect the same realist attitude, for example, *janne sarkar, najanne tarwar*, which means, approximately, "When they want to know you, it is the (legitimate) government, when they don't, it is a sword." In other words, beware of royal power because it can turn hostile and lethal at any moment.³⁴

NEPALESE KINGSHIP IN THE MALLA (1280–1768) AND SHAH (1769–1951) PERIODS

Before 1769, what is today the nation-state of Nepal, strung out west to east along the Himalayas, consisted of a series of small kingdoms. The name Nepal referred only to the Kathmandu Valley. Following the fall of the Khasa Empire (eleventh to the fourteenth centuries) in the west of Nepal, in the Karnali river basin, there were "twenty-two kingdoms" and in the midwest, in the Gandaki river basin, the "twenty-four kingdoms."³⁵ In the fertile Kathmandu Valley were the three Malla kingdoms of Kathmandu, Patan/Lalitpur, and Bhaktapur. In the east, rather than kingdoms there were tribal confederacies.³⁶ Kings tended to worship forms of the goddess Durga to obtain the power to defeat their enemies. In the hills there was a simple caste system, with Brahmins, known as Bahuns, who provided the priests, astrologers, and recordkeepers, at the top, and the various Untouchable artisan castes (drummers/tailors, blacksmiths, and cobblers) at the bottom. Tribal groups, with traditions of transhumant shepherding and military service, principally (in the west) the Magars and Gurungs, slotted into the middle of the hierarchy. Marie Lecomte-Tilouine has emphasized how this caste-based division of labor was also adapted to warfare: "Warfare was therefore the only activity which brought the whole society together around its sovereign, each participating according to specialism and rank, in a common project."[37]

The Kathmandu Valley was different from the rest of the Himalayan foothills because it was flatter and more fertile. It therefore controlled the trade between India and Tibet. More complex social forms and more elaborate religious traditions could flourish here to a degree that was impossible elsewhere.[38] The three kingdoms of the valley fought against each other, allying sometimes one way, sometimes another, in trying to control the valuable trade routes to the north. There was a constant round of festivals in which key roles were the coveted privilege of particular caste segments and lineages. The annual calendar of public festivals and rituals comprised what Levy called a "civic ballet."[39] The king's presence, either in person or symbolized by a sword, was crucial. Newar settlements that today lack an actual palace building still nonetheless often have a central point that is recognized as "the palace," as the pivot for big festivals.[40] During the ten days of the "Kartik dances" in Patan, the king himself played the role of Narasimha, the man-lion avatar of Vishnu, who "kills" the demon Hiranyakashipu, played by a man from the Chitrakar (or painter) caste.[41]

As Gérard Toffin shows in his beguiling study of the Indra Jatra festival, these annual festivals were (and to a considerable extent still are) multisided and multisited performances in which the public were both participants and spectators. These dance drama festivals were key to the reproduction of urban space as sacred space.[42] At the same time as being the star performer in the "civic ballet," the king was also the lead ritualist and had more ritual specialists serving him than anyone else.[43] He was also involved in more powerful cults than anyone else: Bhairava (as the fierce, powerful, and territorial version of Shiva); serpent gods (Nagas); and above all the secret goddess Taleju, whose mantra was passed on, on his death bed, to his successor.[44] He lived in a palace at the center of the city and therefore at the center of a three-dimensional mandala, surrounded by temples to the highest gods (forms of Shiva and Vishnu), with the goddess herself (Taleju, Durga, Duimaji) housed inside his palace.[45] In the highly Buddhist city of Patan, the king was also identified with Loknath/Avalokitesvara/Karunamaya, the patron divinity of the city.[46]

This world of complex, sometimes agonistic, ritual and ritualized interstate warfare continued from the late fifteenth until the second half of the eighteenth century. At the time when the British East India Company was expanding its power in the Gangetic plains, an ambitious young king appeared in the small hilltop fortress of Gorkha, about forty miles west of the Kathmandu Valley. Prithvi Narayan Shah (1723–1775) embarked on a lifelong campaign of conquest.[47] His great-great-grandfather, the lawgiver Ram Shah of Gorkha, had already claimed to be a partial incarnation of Vishnu (and that his queen was a partial incarnation of the goddess Laksmi).[48] Prithvi Narayan succeeded, after many attempts and frequent setbacks, in conquering the Kathmandu Valley in 1768–1769. He marched into the city of Kathmandu during the Dasain festival of 1768, when many of those who might have resisted him were drunk and bloated by feasting. He went directly to the special temple-residence of the living goddess, Kumari, opposite the royal palace at the center of the city, and received her blessing (*tika*) in place of the last Newar king, Jaya Prakash.[49] Legends describe Gorakhnath, the patron saint of Gorkha, as the disciple of Matsyendranath (the Hindu identity of the Buddhist bodhisattva Lokesvara-Karunamaya), the most popular deity of the cities of Kathmandu and Patan. This mythic guru-disciple link thus serves to legitimate the Gorkha-derived rule of Prithvi Narayan and his descendants over the kingdoms of Kathmandu and Patan.[50]

Prithvi Narayan's dynasty ruled Nepal between 1768 and 2006. Between 1846 and 1951, the Shah kings were forced into what Strathern refers to as the "ritualization trap" with the consequent creation of "diarchy," or dual sovereignty.[51] The kings were reduced to a symbol of rule, confined to their palace and kept under close watch, while all actual decisions were made by their Rana prime ministers. Jang Bahadur Rana, the first of these prime ministers, had himself conferred the title of "maharaja" or "great king" of Lamjung and Kaski districts. He raised his family from Khas to Thakuri status, changed their surname from Kunwar to the royal "Rana," and married his daughter to the crown prince, and thereafter the Ranas systematically intermarried with the royal family.[52] Many royal marriages ended up being with cousins (something that was forbidden to the wider Bahun and Chhetri castes).[53] The king remained superior, entitled the prefix *shri-* five times, whereas the prime minister was only thrice "shri."[54] Right up to the end of the monarchy, there was a conflation in popular speech between the government and the monarch (and also the Rana prime minister during the Rana period): all were equally referred to as *sarkar*.[55]

Confined to his palace during the Rana period, the king was necessarily a distant and godlike figure. As Anne T. Mocko points out, the position of the Shah kings during the Rana period demonstrates that kings did not need to be involved in the practical business of ruling in order to be kings:

> The Nepali monarchy was not indissolubly bound up with the technical administration of the government: it rather had a performative value that far exceeded—even floated free of—the king's practical involvement in politics.

The king's role in the daily running of government offices or legislation was inconsistent over time, and apparently entirely negotiable. What was not inconsistent and not negotiable was the performance of his unique status as king, primarily in the context of formal religious rituals.[56]

And yet the Rana prime ministers were also kings, just one step below the king:

> The Rana Prime Minister enjoyed all the powers of rule associated with kingship: the power of life and death, the power to declare war, conclude peace and negotiate treaties, the power to appoint and dismiss all civil and military officials, and the power to make and repeal laws. He also enjoyed many of the symbols of kingship: he went in procession on an elephant, he was protected by a ritual umbrella on state occasions and he sat on a throne. As did the King, the Prime Minister wore a jewel-encrusted crown to which was attached the plumage of a bird of paradise.[57]

Against these authors, who have emphasized the divinized nature of both king and prime minister in the Rana period, Simon Cubelic and Rajan Khatiwoda have entered a note of caution. For all that the Rana regime was in practice a patrimonial state, Jang Bahadur's Muluki Ain law code of 1854 introduced a vision of the state that placed even the monarch and the prime minister under the law. It expressly envisaged that they could be removed if they acted against the interests of the state.[58] They therefore provide support for the argument of Mahesh Chandra Regmi and J. Whelpton that, at least by the nineteenth century, the state or *dhungo* (literally "stone") was regarded as independent of those who occupied its offices and that the latter could be held to account for failing to fulfil their duties.[59]

So was the king a god? Toffin affirms that, unlike the kings of Southeast Asia or Sumeria, the Malla king, in Nepal, was not a god.[60] However, he was closer to the gods than other people.[61] In a hierarchical polytropy, everyone incarnates some god or gods to some degree, and the boundary between gods or spirits and humans is far less stark than in Abrahamic religions.[62] Bert van den Hoek argued, against Toffin, that the king was between being a god and a person: in "a kind of excluded middle, . . . it is the king occupying the throne and acting accordingly who embodies divinity and extends his relationships into the realm of the divine."[63] Performing kingship is like a sacrifice, and the king's key power is to be the lead sacrificer of the country. Mocko emphasizes that the title of her book, *Demoting Vishnu*, is tongue in cheek and that no Nepalis she met ever thought that the king *was* Vishnu; indeed, they found her title funny.[64] And yet, as we will see in the next section, the identification of the monarch with Vishnu continued to be asserted by means of ritual throughout the Panchayat period.

THE MONARCHY AFTER 1951

Because the king had been kept a prisoner by the Ranas for more than a century, the fall of the Ranas in 1951 enabled the king to return to power as the bringer of democracy and the champion of antiautocratic forces. King Tribhuvan (1906–1955) might possibly have permitted Nepal to evolve toward parliamentary democracy, but his son King Mahendra (1920–1972) had other ideas. He permitted parliamentary elections in 1959, but under a constitution that left emergency powers in his hands. Not much more than a year after the elections, he threw B. P. Koirala, the Congress prime minister, into jail and instituted a nonparty, guided democracy, known as the Panchayat system, which was, it was argued, "more suited to the soil" of Nepal.[65]

The thirty years of the Panchayat regime, 1960 to 1990, were the period when the foundations of Nepal's modernization were laid. At the start of it, literacy was 5 percent and average life expectancy was thirty-five years; by the end, the figures were 40 percent and fifty-four (today the figures are 64 percent and seventy).[66] Schools and hospitals spread throughout the country, and roads were built. As in Thailand and nearby Bhutan, the king legitimated his position as both the symbol of the unity of the country and the bringer of democracy and development. Members of the royal family were patrons of major government foundations. They led the army. They invested in big hotels and led the setting up of national parks. The king's and queen's portraits were ubiquitous, included in every school textbook. Sayings of the king were painted on huge signboards at the major crossroads of the capital, and statues of the monarchs of the past were set up in towns across the country. Prithvi Narayan Shah was designated "the Great" and his birthday around January 11 every year was used to celebrate the unity and unification of the country.[67] This was followed shortly after, on January 29, by Martyr's Day, memorializing the four martyrs for democracy hung by Juddha Shamsher in 1941. These holidays of civic patriotism were rounded out by Democracy Day on February 19, Constitution Day on December 16, and the king's birthday on December 29. These were secular holidays celebrating a civic nationalism that was fused with the religious and cultural nationalism in which the king was ritually created and recreated as divinely blessed.

Axel Michaels argues that the classic Hindu view was still to be found in Nepal, at least up to the coronation of King Birendra in 1975:

> In traditional Sanskrit literature . . . the king was not only the preserver of public order and the chief warrior, he was also considered as a creator, a savior, and the first and foremost sacrificer, as the protector and embodiment of the Dharma,

as god. Coronation was deification and—at least in the Nepalese monarchy—that is still the case. A Raja is a Deva (god); worship of him is Puja (divine service). The king does not produce the Dharma, he implements it; he *is* the Dharma. The king is beyond good and evil, unblemished, undying. Therefore, he has all divine characteristics, and at his death, it is not the 'king' who dies, but only the earthly king.[68]

The divinizing purpose of the coronation ritual (*rajyabhiseka* or "royal lustration/initiation") as carried out for King Birendra in 1975 was clear.[69] A statue of Vishnu was set up and worshipped; the manner of its worship mimicked the "earth bath" (*mrttikasnana*) that the king received the following day. The ritual transformed the king into a "walking Vishnu."[70] The earth for the bath was taken from sixteen different places in the kingdom, meaning that the king was identified with his territory "as a sort of cosmic *purusa*" ("primeval man"), while also "becoming the lord and husband of the Earth, as is typical for Puranic mythology."[71]

The king was finally made king by being sprinkled with waters of all the oceans by representatives of the four *varnas*, that is, the whole representing the totality of the king's subjects. In the coronations of kings Mahendra and Birendra, a courtier from what was then called a "hill tribal," and today would be called a Janajati, background was selected to play the role of the fourth, Shudra, or servile, category. This was controversial. An army colonel, one Dhan Bahadur Gurung, was selected for this "honour" in 1956. Despite being offered promotion to general and a huge tract of land in the Tarai, he refused, for which brave act the Gurung community, many years later, proposed making a statue of him.

Practicing Hindus of the older generation were brought up to revere the king as a religious figure. During daily personal worship, offerings have to be made to ancestors, gurus, and to the king; and when consuming one's daily rice, a small amount has to be offered to each before eating. A kingdom without a king was thought to be like a household without a head—a recipe for chaos. The king therefore was believed to be the guardian of the nation in a very literal sense, and he was often said to be "like our father." The main criteria for serving the king as a state functionary were loyalty and reliability.

Whether or not ordinary Nepalis viewed the king as divine, they certainly saw him as symbolizing the kingdom in a significant way. His and the country's welfare were supposed to be intimately connected to the correct performance of ritual for and worship of the country's many gods. Every Nepali knows the story, related above, of how Prithvi Narayan Shah finally conquered Kathmandu in 1768 and received a legitimating *tika* from the virgin goddess Kumari. There are numerous stories of disasters occurring during the festivals of the gods, which presage political problems for the king or prime minister of the day.[72]

THE DECLINE OF THE MONARCHY: 1990, 2001, AND BEYOND

As in much of the rest of the world, 1990 marked a major watershed for Nepal. Following street demonstrations (in which forty-one died), led by a joint front of Congress activists and communists, the Panchayat regime fell. A new constitution was introduced the same year, and a new era of openness and parliamentary constitutional democracy commenced. In 1996, however, the Maoists launched their "People's War." Within about five years, they controlled large swathes of the countryside in the western hills.[73]

At the beginning of June 2001, Nepal dominated the front pages of the world's press for a week, thanks to the gunning down of ten members of the royal family, including King Birendra and Queen Aishwarya. It looked initially like a classic palace power grab, violence within the royal family, as happened many times in the nineteenth century. Many Nepalis still believe that this is what happened. But in the end, it was more Columbine—younger generation revenge and resentment supercharged by the availability of high-velocity weapons—than a repetition of the Kot massacre in which Jang Bahadur Rana had seized power in 1845, as claimed by the Maoists.[74] The rumors and half-truths that surrounded the palace massacre undoubtedly harmed the legitimacy of the monarchy as an institution, a change in the political climate that King Gyanendra, who came to power following the royal massacre, seems to have been incapable of comprehending.[75]

In reporting the massacre, many Western journalists seized on the factoid that the king was an incarnation of Vishnu and repeated it ad nauseam in their reports. In an interview with *Time* magazine in January 2004, Gyanendra was asked directly if he was a living god. He replied, "On the living-god thing, let me interpret it this way: we were given the personification of Vishnu, and Vishnu is the preserver of all things. And I'm glad that my role—the role I have to play—has been spelled out like that."[76] Baburam Bhattarai, chief ideologue of the Maoists, responded to Gyanendra's interview within five days with an article in the *Kathmandu Post*:

> We in the revolutionary democratic camp are particularly thankful to the King for vindicating our long-standing view that he is no constitutional monarch but a thinly veiled autocrat. This is amply proved by his open threat to the political parties repeatedly in the interview and his subtle claim to be above the constitution and a "living-god." It is good that the cat is finally out of the bag.[77]

As repeated foreign policy decisions demonstrated, Gyanendra misread the international situation, offending even India, with disastrous consequences.[78] He drove the political parties into the arms of the Maoist rebels and they combined, with tacit Indian support, to remove him from power in 2006.

Once the king was gone, the question arose of who should fill the king's traditional roles in the key national rituals. The issue was not only about replacing the king but also about how and in what sense Nepal should be a secular country. What form of secularism should Nepal adopt? There simply was no full discussion about the issue, nor was a referendum on the question ever seriously contemplated by politicians, even though some came to think that such a significant question of identity ought to be put to the people in this way.[79]

Mocko, in her important study of the removal of the king from public life, distinguishes two classes of ritual: consecration rituals, by which princes are turned into kings, and reinforcement rituals, by which kings are reconstituted as kings through key public ritual events throughout the year.[80] Gyanendra never succeeded in having a full coronation (*rajyabhiseka*), as his elder brother did. All he did was "ascend the throne" or go through "enthronement" (*gaddi arohan*).[81] Gyanendra went on tour to different parts of the country in preparation for his coronation, but the time was never right and he was removed from power before he could be consecrated. In all principal public rituals, in the immediate aftermath of the removal of the king, he was replaced (as envisaged in the Interim Constitution) by the new prime minister, Girija Koirala (the younger brother of the first elected prime minister, whom Gyanendra's father had thrown in jail). This led to a perception that no one had ever been as powerful as Girija because he was both prime minister and head of state. From July 2008, the first president, Dr Ram Baran Yadav, took over these ritual roles.

As Astrid Zotter has emphasized, replacing one ruler by another in public rituals follows an old script for conquest, in which the new king simply adopts the gods of the old regime and makes himself into their premier worshipper.[82] But presidents are not the same as kings. They cannot be a sacred actor in the same sense that a king is; in presiding over, or being a chief guest at, a ritual, they are simply a witness that tradition is being maintained. Zotter shows how Newar intellectuals writing in Nepal Bhasa disagree on how to interpret the three-way relationship between local traditions (including the local people who perpetuate them), god, and state.[83] In the wider newspaper-reading public, there was considerable questioning about just how secular Nepal was. Why did the president attend Hindu, Hindu-Buddhist, or Buddhist rituals but not

Christian or Muslim ones? What if a Christian or a Muslim or a Dalit was elected president?[84]

As case studies of her "reinforcement rituals," Mocko discusses three key public rituals that the king customarily participated in: (1) appearing at the Bhoto Jatra (the showing of the sacred vest during the Matsyendranath festival), (2) receiving the blessing of the Kumari or "Living Goddess," and (3) giving blessings on the main day of the Dasain festival. The last year in which King Gyanendra attended the Bhoto Jatra was 2006. By then his position was already seriously attenuated, but he was still king. The Maoists held a rally on the very same day on the route from the palace to Jawalakhel in Patan where the Bhoto Jatra takes place. It is highly likely that the Maoist rally was organized precisely in order to intimidate the royal procession. There were multiple uncertainties, but in the end, the Maoist rally was mostly peaceful, and Gyanendra arrived at the Jatra, even if late, and received blessings, made offerings, and showed himself as the key ritual actor in the Bhoto Jatra. By the following year, the government had decided that the king should not attend and that the prime minister should go instead. Despite his physical frailty, Girija Prasad Koirala attended, marched through the crowd, and took the place of the king.[85]

The second major ritual described by Mocko is that of receiving the blessing of the girl-goddess Kumari. Like the Matsyendranath festival, of which the Bhoto Jatra is a part, the cult of the goddess Kumari links the ruler of the nation-state of Nepal to the deep culture of the Kathmandu Valley and its indigenous people, the Newars. The mythological power of the Kumari's blessing (recapitulating, as it does, her forebear's blessing of Prithvi Narayan Shah) made it, in Mocko's words, "the single event most foundational to the annual ritual reproduction of the monarchy."[86] This very centrality also meant that the palace did everything it could to resist the new government's attempts to exclude the king. While the Indra Jatra festival itself is ancient (an index of the Kathmandu Valley's archaic culture), the role of the Kumari Jatra within it, as noted above, is a late addition, going back only to the eighteenth century. It was only with considerable effort that representatives of the government were able in 2007 to persuade the local organizing committee not to invite Gyanendra to open the Kumari Jatra and to invite the prime minister instead.[87] When the time came for the key ritual of receiving the *tika* blessing from the Kumari, Gyanendra achieved a partial victory by turning up without seeking Home Ministry permission. The government managed to ensure that the prime minister went first, but they could not stop the king going, supposedly as a private citizen, very late that same evening. The government issued a strong reprimand to Gyanendra's private secretary shortly afterward.[88]

THE CENTRALITY OF THE DASAIN FESTIVAL

Mocko's third main example of a reinforcement ritual is the king's blessings at Dasain. The Ranas developed and encouraged the Dasain festival (Durga Puja, known as Dassera in north India) throughout the territory ruled by them.[89] It became the preeminent ritual of patriliny, of local power, and of kingship, as well as male power over females.[90] The Ranas continued from pre-Rana times the annual *pajani* ceremony, in which their top civil servants had to appear before them and be reappointed by being presented with a turban. If anyone was sent away without a turban, it was a very public humiliation. During the Panchayat times, high-ranking civil servants were expected to parade at Dasain in national dress, demonstrating their support for the regime and the government. Taeko Uesugi describes how Dasain was observed in the British Gurkhas as a kind of duty or social religion, even by those who are Buddhists and even by their British, culturally Christian officers. One Gurkha major told her:

> Dasain, being a celebration of victory, has a special significance for the Gurkhas. At the same time, being a martial race, we have special devotion to pray to Durga Devi for provision of strength, courage, good will, and victory over the evil powers of the world. To the Gurkhas, the goddess Durga Devi plays a vital role in our lives. We pray to her for victory and protection against our enemies.[91]

Today, and for as long as people remember, Dasain has been the biggest public holiday in Nepal. It is the one festival for which Nepalis everywhere try to be at home. Everyone is supposed to receive a blessing (*tika*) in the form of vermilion, curd, and rice grains affixed to the forehead on the tenth day of the month, the climax of the festival, from their household head, from the elders of their lineage, and ideally from the king himself. Even Muslims participate.[92] There have been campaigns by Janajati ethnic activists to boycott Dasain, but most Janajatis still observe it as a social, if not a religious, event.[93]

According to Mocko, the lines of the general public queueing up to receive Dasain *tika* from King Birendra grew longer and longer throughout the 1990s, to such an extent that the king spent much of the following week with his arm bound up in athletic tape.[94] Dasain was also the preeminent time when the king's close relationship to the army, and his dual role as both commander-in-chief and chief ritualist, seamlessly combining tradition and modernity, was most on display, with public army parades and Hindu rituals happening side by side.[95] Each regiment also performed its own Dasain ritual, with officers sacrificing animals with their own hands, and one of them dipping his hands in the blood of the animal and making handprints on the regiment's flag.[96]

In 2006, the Dasain rituals went ahead more or less as usual, but few politicians went to receive *tika* from the king. The prime minister, Girija Koirala, pointedly absented himself from Kathmandu and spent Dasain in his hometown of Biratnagar. A year later it was clear that Gyanendra had to be removed from public Dasain rituals. While the government was committed to continuing all traditional rituals, it was faced with the problem of determining which of them were private, Shah family rituals over which Gyanendra could continue to preside and which were state rituals, from which he must be barred.[97] The prime minister's office was put in the position of having to decide on the spot where the prime minister had to be included; Mocko details some of the mix-ups that resulted in 2007.[98] The key point was that the prime minister should take the place of the king in public ceremonies. From 2008, the president has stood in. The president now provides *tika* blessings to members of the government on the morning of the tenth day of Dasain and to the general public in the afternoon. Meanwhile, in parallel, Gyanendra opens the doors of his private home to anyone who wants to receive *tika* from him, as many of those who had links to the palace in the past still wish to do.[99]

Mocko points out, "It was fundamental to the process of unmaking the monarchy that the interim government scrupulously upheld reinforcement rituals while excluding the king from their performance."[100] Once that argument had been won and the king had been clearly excluded from power, the president's office could quietly start dropping some of the more obscure rituals from the president's annual calendar. And in fact, it is certain that this process has happened before. There are many local Newar rituals in different parts of the Kathmandu Valley where the king is symbolically present, represented by a sword, or represented by a local dignitary, where the king may well have been present in person at some point in the distant past. Having a representative of the state present enhances the prestige of the event, but it also means dealing with politicians, with all the ambiguities and problems that brings with it.[101]

THE POWER OF (EMPTY) SPACE

The old palace of Kathmandu, Hanuman Dhoka, is where the key Dasain rituals are held. The sacrifices of male buffaloes are held nearby in the Kot or fort as well as in the Mulchowk or "main courtyard" of the old palace. Immediately opposite is the Kumarighar, the official residence of the main royal Kumari. Already in the late nineteenth century, the Ranas moved the Shah king away from the sacred center in the heart of the old city and into a modern palace in Narayan Hiti. In the 1960s, King Mahendra demolished the old Narayan Hiti palace and built a new one that was meant to embody and express his project of modernizing the nation under the leadership of the monarch. The ways in which the different rooms were named and laid out in relation to each other was an expression of Panchayat-period nationalism.[102]

With the fall of the monarchy and its replacement by a federal republic, it became essential to displace the king and to mark the monarchy definitively as part of history, as no longer relevant to the present or future of the country. It was not enough to remove the king's and queen's portraits from government offices, to remove the king's image from the country's currency, and to rewrite the national anthem so that it was no longer a paean to monarchy.[103] Turning the main royal residence at the heart of the capital city into a museum was a powerful way to do this. As Bryony R. Whitmarsh, the ethnographer and historian of the palace, puts it: "the opening of the Palace Museum does more than mark the transition of Nepal from a monarchy to a republic; it creates and curates public narratives in the city through a re-articulation of the past."[104]

Most of the existing palace staff were kept on as museum employees. The decision to proceed quickly to the opening of the museum was taken at the highest level in January 2009. The new staff members were given two days' training in how to talk to the public and how to explain the historical significance of what people would see.[105] The Narayanhiti Palace Museum has never, like other museums supported by government funding, come under the Department of Archaeology; it has always been the responsibility of one or another ministry, currently the Ministry of Culture, Tourism, and Civil Aviation. Currently, there is a five-member management board, with representatives of other ministries as well.

While the politicians wanted the general public to receive the message that monarchy was definitively in the past, there was no guarantee that this was happening—especially with former palace staff acting as guides. In fact, staff members fairly rapidly ceased giving guided tours, partly because they were made very uncomfortable by visitors' questions about the royal massacre.[106] Rabi Thapa wrote in *Nepali Times*, "Bereft of royals, Narayanhiti Palace is simply a junkshop of mediocre art."[107] Many Nepalis, overcome with emotion at visiting the empty palace and site of the royal massacre, wrote in the visitors' book comments such as "We need monarchy."

In response to this situation, under the Maoist government of 2008–2009, Bhattarai, the finance minister, allocated R50 million for a republican memorial. Many reported to Whitmarsh that this was "Bhattarai's pet project."[108] A competition was held—the brief was to reflect Nepal's geographical beauty, its national unity and diversity, the courage and martyrdom of political movements, and the republican system—and a winning design selected. "The *Ganatantra Smarak* and the Narayanhiti Palace Museum were intended together to enable visitors to clearly recognize the monarchical past as a world left behind, that could be discarded for the republican, mass future."[109] It was not until Republic Day in 2019 that it was officially opened, and the public are still not allowed entry. The politics of representation are highly complex, far more than can be conveyed here. The original idea was that access to the Republic Memorial should be via the palace museum, but this needs the agreement of the Nepal Army, which controls the land in between. It seems unlikely that the government will permit free public access to the Republic Memorial without going via the museum because it could then be used rather easily for contestation or protest.

The Republic Memorial was meant to inspire quiet reflection on the sacrifices that have created the new republican nation. It is supposed to be experienced as the logical and historical culmination of a visit to the palace, which in turn was intended to be read as a relic of an unmourned and unrecoverable feudal past. As we have seen, however, it is impossible to impose such readings on the visiting public. Calls of *raja ao, desh bachao* ("King [Gyanendra] come and save the country") are still heard sporadically in the public sphere, although not so far from any prominent politicians.

In the aftermath of the 2015 earthquakes, the major symbol of the nation turned out to be—through no conscious design on the part of government or anyone else—the collapsed Dharahara or Bhimsen Tower,[110] a building of almost no artistic or architectural merit but with the signal advantage of being a prominent landmark with no connections to religion, ethnicity, or even the monarchy. I interpret this as evidence that the Nepali public sphere has in fact been secularized and modernized to quite a significant degree. As we have seen, the increasing denials and embarrassment, from the 1980s onward, around claims that the king is supposed to be viewed as a god would seem to indicate the same conclusion.

This chapter has aimed to show what kingship meant to Nepalis and how, without resorting to regicide, they were able to remove it, both practically and symbolically, from the imagination of the nation. I have not attempted to provide a complete explanation for the decline and fall of the Nepalese monarchy. That long and complicated story would involve the whole history of the Maoist insurgency/civil war, including its causes and the way it was handled at all its different stages. Such a history would need to consider the gradual secularization of the Nepalese system of government and legitimation more generally,[111] as well as international factors, and the role of the army and its links to the Indian army and state.[112] It would also have to include mention of the repeated mistakes of ex-king Gyanendra, who seemed determined to follow a policy of "alienate and unite," pushing all his enemies and potential allies, whether internal or external, into combining against him. This was the exact opposite of the "divide and rule" strategy adopted by his father, King Mahendra, on whom he was supposedly modeling himself.[113] As van den Hoek, analyzing the revolution of 1990, presciently observed, "The king must avoid being left with nothing to sacrifice but himself—that is, if he wants to stay in power."[114]

Nepali politicians and bureaucrats evidently had a subtle and intuitive understanding of their own society. They knew that to stop Gyanendra from being a king, it was not enough just to rename the government or to paint out the word *royal* on numerous signboards. Nor was it enough to remove his powers under the constitution and deprive him of the prestige and influence consequent on being commander-in-chief of the army. In order to strip Gyanendra of kingship in the eyes of the people, he had to be prevented, physically, if necessary, from being present at key public rituals while simultaneously maintaining those very rituals. He also had to be removed from the key site, the royal palace, where royal receptions and visits of state were held. The presence of the president in place of the king at major rituals and the conversion of the palace into a museum, where every Nepali citizen could now wander through rooms that had been strictly out of bounds before, were the two key steps in desanctifying the Nepali king. By 2008, for many, perhaps most, Nepalis the king was no longer seriously considered to be in his own person essentially divine; but, just to be sure, he had to be kept away from those key festival moments and the key central space that might confer on him the aura of having a special mediating relationship with the gods.

NOTES

For comments and suggestions that have materially improved earlier versions of this chapter and helped me to avoid some errors, grateful thanks are due to D. P. Martinez, A. A. Moin, A. Strathern, K. Hachhethu, B. Whitmarsh, J. Pfaff-Czarnecka,

A. Zotter, D. Acharya, K. Adhikari, K. Thomas, B. Sarkar, J. Smith, C. Letizia, and J. Whelpton. Any errors that remain are my responsibility.

1. Robert Levy with Kedar Raj Rajopadhyaya, *Mesocosm: Hinduism and the Organization of a Traditional Newar City in Nepal* (Berkeley: University of California Press, 1990). For my analysis of Levy, see D. N. Gellner, "Does Symbolism 'Construct an Urban Mesocosm'? Robert Levy's *Mesocosm* and the Question of Value Consensus in Bhaktapur," *Journal of Hindu Studies* 1, no. 3 (1997): 541–64, and D. N. Gellner, "Civilization as a Key Guiding Idea in South Asia," in *Anthropology and Civilizational Analysis: Eurasian Explorations*, ed. J. P. Arnason and C. Hann (New York: SUNY Press, 2018), 99–119.
2. Max Weber, *The Religion of India: The Sociology of Hinduism and Buddhism*, ed. and trans. H. H. Gerth and D. Martindale (New York: Free Press, 1958); Louis Dumont, *Homo Hierarchicus: The Caste System and Its Implications* (Chicago: University of Chicago Press, 1980), appendix A; Alan Strathern, *Unearthly Powers: Religious and Political Change in World History* (Cambridge: Cambridge University Press, 2019), 204.
3. Strathern, *Unearthly Powers*, 204f, 323.
4. See A. A. Moin, *Millennial Sovereign: Sacred Kingship and Sainthood in Islam* (New York: Columbia University Press, 2012), for examples of how the principle was compromised in practice by Muslim rulers.
5. Colonel Kirkpatrick, *An Account of the Kingdom of Nepal* (Delhi: Manjusri, 1969 [1811]), 150.
6. Sylvain Lévi, *Le Népal: étude historique d'un royaume hindou*, vol. 1 (Paris: Leroux, 1905), I: 28. Lévi's vision underlies both my study of the Newars' Tantric Buddhism, D. N. Gellner, *Monk, Householder, and Tantric Priest: Newar Buddhism and Its Hierarchy of Ritual* (Cambridge: Cambridge University Press, 1992), and Levy's *Mesocosm*.
7. Manik Bajracharya and Axel Michaels, *History of the Kings of Nepal: A Buddhist Chronicle*, vol. 1, (Kathmandu: Social Science Baha and Himal, 2016), x.
8. R. Burghart, *The Conditions of Listening: Essays on Religion, History and Politics in South Asia*, ed. C. J. Fuller and J. Spencer (Delhi: Oxford University Press, 1996), 266ff, shows how the idea, in different formulations, went back to the eighteenth century.
9. Dhungel et al., *Commentary on the Nepalese Constitution* (Kathmandu: DeLF, 1998), 226.
10. United Nations Development Programme (UNDP) bilingual version of July 2010, and Constitutionnet.org.
11. Constitutionnet.org.
12. M. Malagodi, *Constitutional Nationalism and Legal Exclusion: Equality, Identity Politics, and Democracy in Nepal (1990–2007)* (New Delhi: Oxford University Press, 2013), 178.
13. M. Witzel, "The Coronation Rituals of Nepal, with Special Reference to the Coronation of King Birendra," in *Heritage of the Kathmandu Valley*, ed. N. Gutschow and A. Michaels (Sankt Augustin: VGH Wissenschaftsverlag, 1987), 415–67; Gérard Toffin, *Le palais et le temple: La fonction royale dans la vallée du Népal*

(Paris: CNRS, 1993); G. Toffin, *La fête-spectacle: Théatre et rite au Népal* (Paris: Editions de la Maison des Sciences de l'Homme, 2010); Marie Lecomte-Tilouine, "Regicide and Maoist Revolutionary Warfare in Nepal: Modern Incarnations of a Warrior Kingdom," trans. D. N. Gellner, *Anthropology Today* 20.1 (2004): 13–19; Marie Lecomte-Tilouine, "The Transgressive Nature of Kingship in Caste Organization: Monstrous Royal Doubles in Nepal," in *The Character of Kingship*, ed. D. Quigley (Oxford: Berg, 2005), 101–122; Marie Lecomte-Tilouine, *Hindu Kingship, Ethnic Revival, and Maoist Rebellion in Nepal* (Delhi: Oxford University Press, 2009); Marie Lecomte-Tilouine, ed., *Revolution in Nepal: An Anthropological and Historical Approach to the People's War* (Delhi: Oxford University Press, 2013); Marie Lecomte-Tilouine, "The Fictional Kings of Nepal: An Exploration of the Monarch's Pluri-Selfhood," *Cahiers d'Extrême-Asie* 24 (2015): 211–229; B. G. Shrestha, "The Death of Divine Kingship in Nepal: Nepal's Move from Autocratic Monarchy to a Fragile Republican State," in *Contesting the State: The Dynamics of Resistance and Control*, ed. A. Hobart and B. Kapferer (Wantage: Sean Kingston, 2012), 195–223; M. Hutt, "The Last Himalayan Monarchies," in *Globalization in the Himalayas: Belonging and the Politics of the Self*, ed. G. Toffin and J. Pfaff-Czarnecka (New Delhi: Sage, 2014), 419–443; Anne T. Mocko, *Demoting Vishnu: Ritual, Politics, and the Unraveling of Nepal's Hindu Monarchy* (New York: Oxford University Press, 2016); Astrid Zotter, "The Making and Unmaking of Rulers: On Denial of Ritual in Nepal," in *The Ambivalence of Denial: Danger and Appeal of Rituals*, ed. U. Husken and U. Simon (Wiesbaden: Harrassowitz, 2016); Astrid Zotter, "State Rituals in a Secular State? Replacing the Nepalese King in the Pacali Bhairava Sword Procession and Other Rituals," in *Religion, Secularism, and Ethnicity in Contemporary Nepal*, ed. D. N. Gellner, S. Hausner, and C. Letizia (Delhi: Oxford University Press, 2016), 265–301; Astrid Zotter, "Conquering Navarātra: Documents on the Reorganisation of a State Festival," in *Studies in Historical Documents from Nepal and India*, ed. Simon Cubelic, Axel Michaels, and Astrid Zotter (Heidelberg: Heidelberg University Publishing, 2018), 493–531; Astrid Zotter, "Who Kills the Buffalo? Authority and Agency in the Ritual Logistics of the Nepalese Dasaī Festival," in *Nine Nights of Power: Durgā, Dolls and Darbārs*, ed. U. Husken, V. Narayanan, and A. Zotter (Albany: State University of New York Press, 2021), 193–220; Byrony R. Whitmarsh, "Staging Memories at the Narayanhiti Palace Museum, Kathmandu," *Himalaya* 37.1 (2017), article 13, digitalcommons.macalester.edu/himalaya/vol37/iss1/13/; Byrony R. Whitmarsh, "The Narayanhiti Palace Museum: Memory, Power, and National Identity," unpublished PhD diss. (University of London, 2018); Byrony R. Whitmarsh, "*Ganatantra Smarak* (Republic Memorial): The Politics of Memory," *Studies in Nepali History and Society* 24.1 (2019): 171–216.

14. R. Lingat, *The Classical Law of India*, trans. J. D. M. Derrett (Berkeley: University of California Press, 1973), 207.
15. Manu, *The Laws of Manu*, ed. and trans. W. Doniger and B. K. Smith (London: Penguin, 1991), 7.54–56, p. 134.
16. The Mahabharata (13.60.19–20) goes so far as to say that a bad king who fails to protect his subjects should be killed like a diseased dog. I owe this reference and that in the previous note to Diwakar Acharya.

17. Lingat, *The Classical Law*, 211 and 223.
18. Lingat, *The Classical Law*, 214–15.
19. On the complex question of the mutual ranking of kings, Brahmins, and ascetics, see the various contributions by Burghart, *The Conditions of Listening*, Part 1.
20. Manu, *The Laws of Manu*, 128.
21. Sheldon Pollock, *The Language of the Gods in the World of Men: Sanskrit, Culture, and Power in Premodern India* (Berkeley: University of California Press, 2006), 256, glossing the Kashmiri text, the Rajatarangini.
22. On Pratap Malla's famous inscription describing himself as *kavindra*, "king of poets," see B. Bledsoe, "An Advertised Secret: The Goddess Taleju and the King of Kathmandu," in *Tantra in Practice*, ed. D. G. White (Princeton, NJ: Princeton University Press, 2000), 195–205; and Pollock, *The Language of the Gods*, 293–4.
23. Originally appearing in *Contributions to Indian Sociology* in 1962, it was republished as appendix C in the full revised edition of *Homo Hierarchicus*. See L. Dumont, *Homo Hierarchicus: The Caste System and its Implications* (Chicago: The University of Chicago Press, 1980).
24. S. Gupta and R. F. Gombrich, "Kings, Power and the Goddess," *South Asia Research* 6, no. 2 (1986): 123–138.
25. Clifford Geertz, *Negara: The Theatre State in Nineteenth-Century Bali* (Princeton, NJ: Princeton University Press, 1982).
26. For an account of how, in the attempt to appeal to royal patrons during the first millennium of the common era, Buddhism, a religion of renunciation and nonviolence, became permeated by new scriptures that celebrated sexual imagery, antinomianism, magical powers, and the destruction of one's enemies, see R. M. Davidson, *Indian Esoteric Buddhism: A Social History of the Tantric Movement* (New York: Columbia University Press, 2002). See also Strathern, *Unearthly Powers*, 94–95. For my commentary on Davidson's strange omission of Nepal from his history, see D. N. Gellner, "Himalayan Conundrum? A Puzzling Absence in Ronald M. Davidson's *Indian Esoteric Buddhism*," *Journal of the International Association of Buddhist Studies* 27, no. 2 (2004): 411–417.
27. Gupta and Gombrich, "Kings, Power and the Goddess," 125.
28. Sheldon Pollock, "The Divine King in the Indian Epic," *Journal of the American Oriental Society* 104, no. 3 (1984): 527.
29. M. Willis, *The Archaeology of Hindu Ritual: Temples and the Establishment of the Gods* (Cambridge: Cambridge University Press, 2009); B. Sarkar, *Heroic Shaktism: The Cult of Durga in Ancient Indian Kingship* (Oxford: Oxford University Press, 2017).
30. Sheldon Pollock, "Rāmāyaṇa and Political Imagination in India," *Journal of Asian Studies* 52, no. 2 (1993): 261–297.
31. David Dean Shulman, *The King and the Clown in South Indian Myth and Poetry* (Princeton, NJ: Princeton University Press, 1985), 22.
32. Shulman, *The King and the Clown*, 21n62, quoting Geertz, *Negara*, 130.
33. Shulman, *The King and the Clown*, 29, quoting Mahabharata 12.15.10ff.

34. The saying could also be interpreted "When the ruler is knowledgeable, you have a (proper) government; when he is not, it is just a sword." The sword is a key symbol of Hindu rulership. See Lecomte-Tilouine, "The Fictional Kings of Nepal."
35. J. Whelpton, *A History of Nepal* (Cambridge: Cambridge University Press, 2005), 22–25.
36. K. Pradhan, *The Gorkha Conquests: The Process and Consequences of the Unification of Nepal with Particular Reference to Eastern Nepal* (Calcutta: Oxford University Press, 1991), 82.
37. Lecomte-Tilouine, "Regicide and Maoist Revolutionary Warfare," 14.
38. D. N. Gellner, "Civilization as a Key Guiding Idea in South Asia," in *Anthropology and Civilizational Analysis: Eurasian Explorations*, ed. J. P. Arnason and C. Hann (New York: SUNY Press, 2018), 99–119. See M. Slusser, *Nepal Mandala: A Cultural Study of the Kathmandu Valley* (Princeton, NJ: Princeton University Press, 1982), for a comprehensive cultural history of the valley.
39. Levy, *Mesocosm*. See also Toffin, *La fête-spectacle*.
40. See Gérard Toffin, *Société et religion chez les Néwar du Népal* (Paris: Editions du CNRS, 1984), 242, 245.
41. Gérard Toffin, "A Vaishnava Theatrical Performance in Nepal: The "Kāttī-pyākhā" of Lalitpur City," *Asian Theatre Journal* 29, no. 1 (2012): 126–63.
42. Toffin, *La fête-spectacle*.
43. Gellner, *Monk, Householder, and Tantric Priest*, 61–62.
44. Toffin, *Le palais et le temple*; see page 45 for the power of the Taleju mantra.
45. Gellner, *Monk, Householder, and Tantric Priest*, 45–48; K. Pradhan, "Domestic and Cosmic Rituals Among the Hindu Newars of Kathmandu, Nepal," PhD diss. (Delhi School of Economics, 1986), 381; Levy, *Mesocosm*, 176; Toffin, *Le palais et le temple*.
46. Toffin, *Le palais et le temple*, 146; D. N. Gellner, "The Emergence of Conversion in a Hindu-Buddhist Polytropy: The Kathmandu Valley, Nepal c. 1600–1995," *Comparative Studies in Society and History* 47 (2005): 765. Malla-period coins from Patan (but not from the other cities) have "Loknath," or later "Karunamaya," on them. See E. H. Walsh, *The Coinage of Nepal* (Delhi: Indological Book House, 1973), 36, 59.
47. L. Stiller, *The Rise of the House of Gorkha: A Study in the Unification of Nepal, 1768–1816* (Delhi: Manjusri, 1973).
48. T. Riccardi, "The Royal Edicts of King Rama Shah of Gorkha," *Kailash* 5, no. 1 (1977): 55.
49. Anticipating his end, Jaya Prakash had tried to save his throne by expanding the cult of the Kumari, including building the temple house where she lives and starting her annual chariot festival. Evidently, none of these acts were sufficient to win her favor. See T. R. Vaidya, *Jaya Prakash Malla: The Brave Malla King of Kantipur* (New Delhi: Anmol, 1996), 278–9.
50. J. Locke, *Karunamaya: The Cult of Avalokitesvara–Matsyendranath in the Valley of Nepa* (Kathmandu: Sahayogi, 1980), 418ff; Slusser, *Nepal Mandala*, 367ff. For similar stories about other gods of the valley accepting the new dynasty, see Zotter, "The Making and Unmaking of Rulers," 273.
51. Strathern, *Unearthly Powers*, 186ff.

52. A. Sever, *Nepal Under the Ranas* (Sittingbourne: Asia, 1993), 124, 426; J. Whelpton, "The Ancestors of Jang Bahadur Rana: History, Propaganda and Legend," *Contributions to Nepalese Studies* 14, no. 3 (1987): 191.
53. Lecomte-Tilouine, "The Transgressive Nature of Kingship," 114.
54. In the coins of the Malla period, deities are three times "shri" and kings twice. See Walsh, *The Coinage of Nepal*. In the Rana period, the royal priest (*rajguru*) outranked even the king as six times "shri." See Bert van den Hoek, "Does Divinity Protect the King? Ritual and Politics in Nepal" *Contributions to Nepalese Studies* 17, no. 2 (1990): 152.
55. Lecomte-Tilouine, "The Fictional Kings of Nepal," 211.
56. Mocko, *Demoting Vishnu*, 14.
57. Sever, *Nepal Under the Ranas*, 300. Sever points out that the crowns of other members of the Rana family could have only one cand ornament, indicating that they were only "shri" a single time. The use of the bird of paradise feathers in the crown was taken from the Mughals; the Ranas also incorporated European symbols and armorial devices into what remained fundamentally Hindu and Sanskritic legitimating devices. See Sever, *Nepal Under the Ranas*, 301–304.
58. Simon Cubelic and Rajan Khatiwoda, "Nepalese Monarchy in an Age of Codification: Kingship, Patriotism, and Legality in the Law Code of 1854," in *Transnational Histories of the 'Royal Nation'*, ed. M. Banerjee, C. Backerra, and C. Sarti (Cham: Palgrave Macmillan, 2017), 67–86.
59. Mahesh Chandra Regmi, "Preliminary Notes on the Nature of the Gorkhali State and Administration" *Regmi Research Series* 10, no. 11 (1978): 141–71; J. Whelpton, "Political Identity in Nepal: State, Nation, and Community," in *Nationalism and Ethnicity in Nepal*, ed. D. N. Gellner, J. Pfaff-Czarnecka, and J. Whelpton (Kathmandu: Vajra, 2008 [1997]), 42.
60. Toffin, *Le palais et le temple*, 30.
61. Local Buddhist scholar, Hemraj Sakya, writing during the Panchayat period, stressed that the king is the avatar of the five *parameswars*, that is, Brahma, Vishnu, Shiva, Karunamaya, and Indra, and that, in the Samyak festival, "our king, according to Buddhist custom, is to be welcomed as equivalent to a bodhisattva and a god." See Hemraj Sakya, *Samyak Mahadan Guthi* (Kathmandu: Jagatdhar Tuladhar, 1979), 107. In Nepal Bhasa, the language of the Kathmandu Valley, the same honorific auxiliary verb, *bijyaye*, a contraction of "to do victory," is used for priests, kings, and gods.
62. Toffin, *Le palais et le temple*, 32. On polytropy, see M. Carrithers, "On Polytropy: Or the Natural Condition of Spiritual Cosmopolitanism in India: The Digambar Jain Case," *Modern Asian Studies* 34, no. 4 (2000): 831–61; and Gellner, "The Emergence of Conversion." S. Parish, *Moral Knowing in a Hindu Sacred City: An Exploration of Mind, Emotion, and Self* (New York: Columbia University Press, 1994), 85ff, 190ff, explores Bhaktapur Newars' ideas that people are "like a god" and have Narayana (Vishnu) in their heart.
63. Van den Hoek, "Does Divinity Protect the King?," 150, 151–2. For a similar position, see Lecomte-Tilouine, "The Fictional Kings of Nepal." See also Strathern, *Unearthly Powers*, 180.

64. Mocko, *Demoting Vishnu*, 6. In 1991, a survey asked 1,000 Nepalis whether they thought it was true or false that the king was a reincarnation of Vishnu: 42 percent said it was true; 51 percent (mostly those voting for leftist parties) said that it was false. See O. Borre et al, *Nepalese Political Behaviour* (Delhi: Sterling, 1994), 149, 187.
65. Whelpton, *A History of Nepal*; B. L. Joshi, and J. Rose, *Democratic Innovations in Nepal: A Case Study of Political Acculturation* (Berkeley: University of California Press, 1966); R. Shaha, *Essays in the Practice of Government in Nepal* (Delhi: Manohar, 1982); K. Hachhethu and D. N. Gellner, "Nepal: Trajectories of Democracy and Restructuring of the State," in *Routledge Handbook of South Asian Politics*, ed. P. Brass (London: Routledge, 2010), 131–46.
66. Whelpton, *A History of Nepal*, 137. In 1951, literacy was estimated to be 2 percent.
67. The dates of these holidays were fixed according to the Vikram Era and calendar, and therefore did not always fall on the same day according to the Gregorian calendar.
68. A. Michaels, *Hinduism, Past and Present*, trans. B. Harshav (Princeton, NJ: Princeton University Press, 2004), 277; original emphasis.
69. Witzel, "The Coronation Rituals of Nepal."
70. Witzel, "The Coronation Rituals of Nepal," 443. King Tribhuvan's personal Swiss masseuse, Erika Leuchtag, *With a King in the Clouds* (London: Hutchinson, 1958), 58, claims that his body was tattooed "from neck to ankle" with fern, flower, and peacock feather patterns. King Birendra's Harvard tutor describes the "earth bath" ritual and writes: "The vigor and proper functioning of the King-Emperor's limbs and organs were thereby symbolically associated with the smooth functioning of the nation's ecosystem. If foods and liquids flowed through the King-Emperor's digestive tract without disruption, rivers and streams could similarly be expected to flow quietly through the country, bestowing health and prosperity." See F. G. Hutchins, *Democratizing Monarch: A Memoir of Nepal's King Birendra* (Kathmandu: Vajra, 2007), 51.
71. Witzel, "The Coronation Rituals of Nepal," 448. See also Hutt, "The Last Himalayan Monarchies," 425–6.
72. Christoph Emmerich, " 'All the King's Horses and All the King's Men': The 2004 Red Matsyendranāth Incident in Lalitpur," *Indologica Taurinensia* 32 (2006): 27–65. See S. B. Dangol *The Palace in Nepalese Politics, With Special Reference to the Politics of 1951 to 1990* (Kathmandu: Ratna Pustak, 1999, 206–8) on how King Birendra's difficulties in 1980 and 1990 were ascribed to his neglect of the national deity, Pashupati. On the earthquake, see D. N. Gellner, S. Hausner, and C. Letizia (eds.), *Religion, Secularism, and Ethnicity in Contemporary Nepal*, (Delhi: Oxford University Press, 2016), xii.
73. On the Maoist insurgency, see M. Hutt (ed.), *Himalayan 'People's War': Nepal's Maoist Rebellion* (London: Hurst, 2004); Lecomte-Tilouine, *Revolution in Nepal*; J. Pettigrew, *Maoists at the Hearth* (Philadelphia: Pennsylvania University Press, 2013); P. Jha, *Battles of the New Republic: A Contemporary History of Nepal* (London: Hurst, 2014); A. Adhikari, *The Bullet and the Ballot Box: The Story of Nepal's Maoist Revolution* (London: Verso, 2014). For a timeline of the decline of the monarchy, see Shrestha, "The Death of Divine Kingship," 206–7.

74. Baburam Bhattarai, *Monarchy vs Democracy: The Epic Fight in Nepal* (Delhi: Samkaleen Teesari Duniya, 2005), chap. 3; Lecomte-Tilouine, "Regicide and Maoist Revolutionary Warfare," 17–18.
75. M. Hutt and P. Onta (eds.), *Political Change and Public Culture in Post-1990 Nepal* (Cambridge: Cambridge University Press, 2017), chaps. 2 and 3; Adhikari, *The Bullet and the Ballot Box*, 62–64.
76. Bhattarai, *Monarchy vs Democracy*, 101.
77. Bhattarai, *Monarchy vs Democracy*, 101. On the way in which Maoist poets were able to mobilize traditional imagery of Hindu kings as antinomian killers against the regime, see Lecomte-Tilouine, *Hindu Kingship*, and Lecomte-Tilouine, "The Fictional Kings of Nepal."
78. Jha, *Battles of the New Republic*, 95ff; Adhikari, *The Bullet and the Ballot Box*, 177. In its issue of December 4, 2004, *The Economist* labeled Nepal "a failing state."
79. On the secularism issue, see Chiara Letizia's work: "Shaping Secularism in Nepal," *European Bulletin of Himalayan Research* 39 (2011): 66–104; "The Goddess Kumari at the Supreme Court: Divine Kingship and Secularism in Nepal," *FOCAAL— Journal of Global and Historical Anthropology* 67 (2013): 32–46; "Ideas of Secularism in Nepal," in D. N. Gellner, S. Hausner, and C. Letizia (eds.), *Religion, Secularism, and Ethnicity in Contemporary Nepal*, (Delhi: Oxford University Press, 2016), 35–76; "National Gods at the Court: Secularism and the judiciary in Nepal," in *Filing Religion: State, Hinduism, and Courts of Law*, ed. D. Berti, G. Tarabout, and Raphaël Voix (Delhi: Oxford University Press, 2016), 34–68. See also Gellner, *Religion, Secularism, and Ethnicity*; D. N. Gellner and C. Letizia, "Hinduism in the Secular Republic of Nepal," in *The Oxford History of Hinduism: Modern Hinduism*, ed. T. Brekke (Delhi: Oxford University Press, 2019), 275–304; and D. N. Gellner and C. Letizia, "Religion and Secularism in Contemporary Nepal," in *Routledge Handbook of South Asian Religions*, ed. K. Jacobsen (Abingdon: Routledge, 2021), 335–54.
80. Mocko, *Demoting Vishnu*.
81. Mocko, *Demoting Vishnu*, 67–68, 72, stresses the unconvincing nature of the enthronement ritual and the protests in the city, during which police shot three people dead. Subsequent rituals during the extraordinary conditions following the royal massacre also "flopped" and/or were "highly infelicitious."
82. Zotter, "The Making and Unmaking of Rulers"; Astrid Zotter, "State Rituals in a Secular State? Replacing the Nepalese King in the Pacali Bhairava Sword Procession and Other Rituals," in D. N. Gellner, S. Hausner, and C. Letizia (eds.), *Religion, Secularism, and Ethnicity in Contemporary Nepal*, (Delhi: Oxford University Press, 2016), 265–301.
83. Zotter, "The Making and Unmaking of Rulers," 293.
84. Zotter, "The Making and Unmaking of Rulers," 296; Gellner and Letizia, "Hinduism in the Secular Republic of Nepal," 11–13.
85. Mocko, *Demoting Vishnu*, chap. 4.
86. Mocko, *Demoting Vishnu*, 120. Zotter, "The Making and Unmaking of Rulers," 271, calls the story of Prithvi Narayan and the Kumari "one of the foundation myths of modern Nepal." Both M. Allen, *The Cult of Kumari: Virgin Worship in Nepal*

(Kirtipur: INAS, TU, 1975,) and Toffin, *Le palais et le temple*, 231ff, had already indicated the importance of the Kumari for the legitimation of the king.

87. Mocko, *Demoting Vishnu*, 138.
88. Mocko, *Demoting Vishnu*, chap. 5; Zotter, "The Making and Unmaking of Rulers," 282, points out that Gyanendra has adopted the same strategy, of turning up on the key occasion and invoking his right to worship as a private citizen, in other religious sites as well.
89. On Dasain in Nepal, see G. Krauskopff and M. Lecomte-Tilouine (eds.), *Célébrer le pouvoir: Dasai, une fête royale au Népal* (Paris: CNRS, 1996); Levy, *Mesocosm*; J. Pfaff-Czarnecka, "A Battle of Meanings: Commemorating the Goddess Durga's Victory over the Demon Mahisa as a Political Act," *Kailash* 18, no. 3–4 (1996): 57–92; and D. N. Gellner, *The Anthropology of Buddhism and Hinduism: Weberian Themes* (Delhi: Oxford University Press, 2001), 75–7. Astrid Zotter (personal communication) believes that the Shah kings already performed Dasain rituals throughout their realm, but it was the Ranas who imposed on their subjects an obligation to carry out versions of them in their own households as well. See Astrid Zotter, "Conquering Navarātra: Documents on the Reorganisation of a State Festival," in *Studies in Historical Documents from Nepal and India*, ed. S. Cubelic, A. Michaels, and A. Zotter (Heidelberg: Heidelberg University Publishing, 2018), 493–531.
90. On this latter point, and the subtle nuances introduced by what she calls the filiafocal ideology, which involves "worshipping" female relatives, especially daughters, see L. Bennett, *Dangerous Wives and Sacred Sisters: The Social and Symbolic Roles of High-Caste Women in Nepal* (New York: Columbia University Press, 1983 [reissued Himal Books, Kathmandu, 2004]), 141ff.
91. Taeko Uesugi, "Re-examining Transnationalism from Below and Transnationalism from Above: British Gurkhas' Life Strategies and the Brigade of Gurkhas' Employment Policies," in *Nepalis Inside and Outside Nepal: Social Dynamics in Northern South Asia Vol. 1*, ed. H. Ishii, D. N. Gellner, and K. Nawa (Delhi: Manohar, 2007), 396.
92. M. Gaborieau, *Ni Brahmanes, ni Ancêtres: Colporteurs Musulmans de Népal* (Nanterre: Société d'Ethnologie, 1993), 244.
93. On the Dasain boycott, see S. I. Hangen, "Boycotting Dasain: History, Memory, and Ethnic Politics in Nepal," *Studies in Nepali History and Society* 10 (2005): 105–33; S. I. Hangen, *The Rise of Ethnic Politics in Nepal: Democracy in the Margins* (London: Routledge, 2010); on earlier resistance, Pfaff-Czarnecka, "A Battle of Meanings."
94. Mocko, *Demoting Vishnu*, 155.
95. The army recognized its close links to the monarchy with the slogan *raj bhakti hamro shakti* or "loyalty to the king is [the basis of] our power." See I. Adhikari, *Military and Democracy in Nepal* (London: Routledge, 2015), 221.
96. Mocko, *Demoting Vishnu*, 159. On Dasain sacrifices more generally, see Krauskopff and Lecomte-Tilouine, *Célébrer le pouvoir*; and Zotter, "Who Kills the Buffalo." On the enclavement of Newar traditions within the state-sponsored kingly and military events of the festival, see B. van den Hoek, *Caturmāsa: Celebrations of Death in Kathmandu. Nepal* (Kathmandu: Vajra, 2014 [2004]), 119–21.
97. Mocko, *Demoting Vishnu*, 164–5.

98. Mocko, *Demoting Vishnu*, 166–8.
99. Mocko, *Demoting Vishnu*, 178–9.
100. Mocko, *Demoting Vishnu*, 181.
101. Zotter, "The Making and Unmaking of Rulers," 295–6.
102. Thus, the central rooms of the palace were named after the origin districts of the Shah dynasty: Kaski, Lamjung, and Gorkha. Byrony R. Whitmarsh, "The Narayanhiti Palace Museum: Memory, Power, and National Identity," PhD diss. (University of London, 2018), 74, points out that studies, or even mentions, of the palace were omitted from architectural writing or curriculums on modern architecture in Nepal, mainly because of the secrecy and deference surrounding the monarchy at the time.
103. On the anthem, see M. Hutt, "Singing the New Nepal," *Nations and Nationalism* 18, no. 2 (2012): 306–25.
104. Whitmarsh, "Staging Memories," 85.
105. Whitmarsh, "The Narayanhiti Palace Museum," 162.
106. Whitmarsh, "The Narayanhiti Palace Museum," 180.
107. Whitmarsh, "The Narayanhiti Palace Museum," 195.
108. Whitmarsh, "*Ganatantra Smarak*," 180, note 18. This was a considerable hardening of Bhattarai's earlier stance from 2008, when he had suggested that the king could retain "cultural rights" (interpreted to mean the right to preside over rituals) after abdication. See Hutt, "The Last Himalayan Monarchies," 427.
109. Whitmarsh, "*Ganatantra Smarak*," 207.
110. M. Hutt, "Revealing What Is Dear: The Post-Earthquake Iconization of the Dharahara, Kathmandu," *The Journal of Asian Studies* 78, no. 3 (2019): 549–76.
111. Marc Gaborieau, "Les rapports de classe dans l'idéologie officielle du Népal," *Purusartha* 6 (1982): 251–90; Gellner, *Religion, Secularism, and Ethnicity*; Gellner and Letizia, "Hinduism in the Secular Republic of Nepal"; Gellner and Letizia, "Religion and Secularism in Contemporary Nepal."
112. See Adhikari, *Military and Democracy in Nepal*. Rookmangud Katuwal, *My Story* (Kathmandu: Nepalaya, 2016), 392ff, chief of staff of the army, records the pressure he came under in 2007 from senior politicians and others to stage a coup (which he resisted). Adhikari, *The Bullet and the Ballot Box*, 68–71, documents the way in which the army leadership (including Katuwal) was enthusiastic in supporting the king when he suppressed the political parties.
113. See Adhikari, *The Bullet and the Ballot Box*; Jha, *Battles of the New Republic*; Lecomte-Tilouine, *Revolution in Nepal*; and, for a viewpoint sympathetic to the Maoists, see S. Shrestha, "Maoist Defeat in Nepal: The Price of a Missed Opportunity," *Economic and Political Weekly* 49, no. 4 (2014): 13–16.
114. Van den Hoek, "Does Divinity Protect the King?," 154. On Gyanendra's deep unpopularity, see Hutt, "The Last Himalayan Monarchies," 430–3.

13
A Caliphate Beyond Politics

The Sovereignty of ISIS

FAISAL DEVJI

In an English-language video released soon after Daesh, or the Islamic State of Iraq and Syria ([ISIS), or simply the Islamic State, proclaimed its caliphate in 2014, a Chilean convert is shown kicking over and trampling a sign demarcating the border between Iraq and Syria.¹ By its title, "The End of Sykes-Picot," this video refers to the famous and initially secret agreement between Britain and France to carve up the Middle East between them after the Ottoman Empire had been defeated in World War I. Jumping back and forth, across the now invisible line dividing these former Ottoman provinces, the Chilean seems to be announcing the return of a caliphate lost during World War I. Yet we shall see that the political claims made in the video, as well as by the emergence of the Islamic State itself, were everywhere belied by its rhetoric and practices. This prompts me to ask the following question: what if the brutality of ISIS emerged not from its claim to politics but the reverse, by the fact that it was unable or unwilling to assume a political identity?

Speaking directly to the camera, the narrator proceeds to take us on a tour of some captured military base. A number of bound prisoners, soldiers from the Syrian army, are shown inside the facility. The narrator chats amiably with a few of them, each identified by his sectarian identity. We then leave the building with the Chilean, who continues his smiling, TV-presenter's patter in the sport utility vehicle (SUV), out of which he eventually climbs to get a good view of the prison in the distance. And as he burbles on, we see the place blown up with all those inside. Important about this video is its refusal to define anything it depicts in a recognizably political way. Unlike the ostentatiously statelike conventions of terrorist propaganda, such as the militant's communiqué and list of demands or the captive's confession and execution, this video takes the form of a documentary whose presenter finds everything interesting and even amusing, but he never finds any of it the subject of indignation or an occasion to express regret for the "unfortunate necessity" that tends to accompany more traditional terrorist attacks.

Portrayed in the most detached fashion, the events of the video are also treated as if they were quite banal in character and thus lacking in the distinction from everyday life that usually accompanies important political statements. The prisoners are killed without any ceremonial, while neither the narrator nor his car and driver are seen to possess any official status. Having not been ritually invested with the authority that separates the body of the sovereign or his representative from that of a subject, in other words, these members of the Islamic State were not placed in any formally or at least traditionally political relationship with their victims. Even the initial scene, in which the Iraqi-Syrian border is erased, may thus be interpreted as an elimination of the state and also of politics as such. One reason why such a situation might not be so puzzling has to do with the history of political thought in modern Islam, from which antistatist themes ISIS intermittently draws.

Between the seventeenth and twentieth centuries, Muslim populations around the world were absorbed into European empires. Even where their traditional rulers remained in place, the power they wielded was considerably diminished, often depending on the assent and support of colonial overlords. The waning of Muslim traditions of rulership, however, proved a blessing for those who laid claim to a religious authority that had until then been variously subordinated to kings and chieftains, aristocrats and tribal elders.[2] Unable to appropriate Islamic authority for themselves in any significant way, the European empires left the religious leaders who claimed it relatively free as long as they remained loyal subjects. This resulted, all over the world, in a vast expansion of new Islamic movements and practices unconstrained by the old political orders. Modern Islam, in this sense, was a product of what we might call colonial secularism.[3]

Not content with escaping the grasp of princes and potentates, these religious authorities sought to repudiate the entire political vocabulary that had for centuries defined Muslim societies. While the occasional pious monarch was praised, the idea of monarchy itself was now often seen as being irreligious in its hereditary essence and, more important, decadent in its sinful practices, which included the proverbial temptations of wine, women, and song. Indeed, it was the aristocratic culture of the Muslim past that such religious figures most frequently blamed for the colonization of their lands. But once the old language of Muslim politics was thrown out with its rulers, there was nothing to take its place. This meant, in effect, that colonized Muslims had either to adopt suitably modified versions of

European political thought or work up an entirely nonpolitical theory of social order, sometimes even both at the same time.

The primary way in which Muslim religious authorities, from clerics to mystics, traditionalists to reformers, approached the problem of fashioning a new political language was to focus on Islam's legal structure. Whether it was to be superintended by a prince or parliament, left entirely in the hands of jurists, or subject to modification in whole or in part, the law was now meant to define not only Muslim society but what it meant to be Muslim altogether. Such a conception could be entertained in a colonial as well as independent state, a monarchy as much as a republic, but in all cases was marked by a deep suspicion of traditional as much as modern forms of sovereign power. By the first half of the twentieth century, in fact, it had become commonplace for religious Muslims of many persuasions to claim that sovereignty belonged to God alone. Having abandoned the precolonial language of Muslim politics, however, those who made this claim were placed in the ironic position of attributing to God a vision of sovereignty that was purely European in form.[4]

ISLAM AGAINST THE STATE

The implications of reserving sovereignty for God, that is, denying it to men, were forcefully laid out by the lay and often Western-educated intellectuals who founded the Islamist movements of the mid-twentieth century. Dominated by the Pakistani writer-activist Abul Ala Maududi and the Egyptian Sayyid Qutb, these movements were suspicious of both politics and the state.[5] Emerging as they did either under colonial rule or in the sometimes secular but authoritarian nation-states that succeeded it, such movements sought to limit the inroads of modern politics into Muslim societies. The modernity of such a politics, after all, consisted in its autonomy from the sacred law, even when it recognized and honored the latter. And it was this autonomous logic that Muslim thinkers sought to subordinate if not destroy.

Islamists were critical of the modern state, whether manifested in a democracy or dictatorship, because they thought its desire for sovereign power would subordinate the sacred law and its universal ideal of justice to the transient whims of individuals and assemblies. Such forms of human authority could never be truly sovereign, in the sense of possessing that absolute and legitimate power that the legal concept of sovereignty demanded, and could thus only betray it in violence as itself a perversion and indeed limitation of power.

Maududi, for instance, who founded the Jamaat-e-Islami party in India and Pakistan, well understood that the concept of sovereignty, as enunciated by European thinkers such as Thomas Hobbes, implied its displacement of God in a newly autonomous political sphere.[6] Just as God transcended even His own law so, too, did the prince or president of a republic exercise a sovereign power that put him both within and outside it. However mythical its power, in other words, the idea of sovereignty gestured to the autonomy and indeed priority of politics in public life. It is this priority that allows politics to become the most important site of freedom in modern times.

Not only did the law, even if only theoretically, require the sovereign for its founding, it could also, on occasion, be suspended for its own protection, whether by stripping citizens of certain rights or for example, by allowing the U.S. president to press that famous red button and launch a nuclear attack, without consultation, in defense of the country. Maududi thought that such practices of sovereign transcendence, modeled on those of divine power, could never match their theoretical form as absolutely free or self-possessed acts and were doomed to corruption and failure, therefore only leading to violence and despotism. In other words, it was their inability to achieve sovereign power that made men violent. Which is why he, like other Islamists after him, thought to expel sovereignty from human affairs by reserving it for God and make of government only a fulfillment of divine commandments, a kind of management of society in which people were ruled by the sacred law as interpreted by experts outside the state rather than by those in possession of the instruments of power. Unlike the common understanding of political theology, in other words, for which secular states inherit categories like sovereignty from their religious predecessors, Maududi thought just the opposite was true. It was the secular state that he saw as being truly theological in claiming a sovereignty he thought its predecessors could not. And this meant that the religious state was paradoxically more secular than its successors because it was unable to instantiate divine qualities like absolute power on purely theological grounds.

Like other colonized intellectuals, Islamists early in the last century often took their cue from anarchism or bolshevism, with their doctrine about the withering away of the state. Whereas a figure such as Mohandas Gandhi would minimize the state by calling for the self-rule of society in a pluralistic and open-ended way, Maududi, who early in his career was an admirer of the Mahatma, replaced his vision of society consisting of a set of negotiable customs with that of a divinized sacred law that the state might enforce but could never control let alone change—because it was to be interpreted by a class of specialists who were based outside the state in society and who exercised only a supervisory function over government. In more recent times, some have turned to a neoliberal model of social management by the market, with Muslim countries like Malaysia and to some degree Turkey leading the way.[7] In either case, however, Muslim thinkers turned the old orientalist argument about Islam subordinating the state to itself, which could never therefore become secular, into a theory about a separation of powers that prevented the emergence of despotism.

In both anarchist and neoliberal visions of Islam, government was to be reduced to governance, and the state was to be deployed in an active role only in the beginning, to replace man's sovereignty by God's, just as Marxism's "dictatorship of the proletariat" was meant to displace the capitalist state before dissolving it entirely into Lenin's "administration of objects." When Gandhi was asked by one of India's Muslim leaders what he thought of Lenin, his response was to say that he would begin where the Russian ended—with the withering away of the state. The problem with this deeply society-centric and even antipolitical vision was that it could never quite suppress the need or desire for sovereignty, which in Islamist narratives came to be understood as the most cardinal of sins, that of attributing partners to God or indeed claiming divine status for oneself. This was why Maududi and Qutb saw all political forms defined by sovereignty, from absolute monarchy to nationalism, as being fundamentally idolatrous. Refusing as they did to recognize or institutionalize sovereignty, Islamists tended to manifest it in disavowed and so opportunistic forms of violence, thus lending a perverse reality to Maududi's fears. It has never been possible to establish a society on the basis of law alone, one in which sovereign power has been eliminated and, with it, all untrammeled freedom or transcendence, including that of God Himself.

The Islamist refusal to vest sovereignty in the state has arguably led to its ghostly as well as random or uncontrolled appearance across the spectrum of Muslim social, political, and indeed economic life. Let us take Pakistan, the world's first Islamic republic, as an example, because all three versions of the country's constitution are marked by the refusal of sovereignty to its people, president, or legislature.[8] While its initial preamble proclaimed that God's sovereignty was delegated to the people, the final one reserves the category for Him alone and so makes law and politics into nothing more than forms of administration or governance. Yet this refusal to institutionalize sovereignty has in practice meant that it remains unanchored in the Pakistani state and therefore continues to haunt it, most prominently in the form of the coup d'état, whether military, judicial, or indeed presidential. The coup is the purest form of sovereign power, explicit as it is in suspending if not abrogating the law and constitution in order to secure them more strongly after what is invariably meant to be a temporary hiatus. In this sense, it has the theological status of a miracle understood as a suspension of norm or nature. It is akin to the transgressive charisma that premodern kings had wielded in the heroic mode, to use the terms of A. Azfar Moin and Alan Strathern in the first chapter in this volume.

These paradoxical visions of an Islamic state were in vogue until the end of the Cold War, when such ways of thinking about Islam in terms of the ideological state were put at risk with the collapse of the Soviet Union, the decline of its third world clients, and the emergence of a global arena for what came to be called "new social movements." While in some places neoliberal ideas about Islamic governance took the place of older narratives about revolutions and constitutions, in others, a new kind of militancy emerged out of authoritarian or lawless contexts. Of these, the chief one was, of course, al-Qaeda, a global movement that had always refused to adopt the model of a state. As such, its dealings with sovereignty were vested not in territories and institutions but in individuals, and in particular the iconic figure of the suicide bomber who both kills and dies to embody power in all its purity, with nothing left over from the act of violence.[9]

Gandhi, too, had vested sovereignty in the individual, who exhibited it in nonviolent acts like fasting, celibacy, noncooperation, civil disobedience, and finally martyrdom, all forms of sacrifice set against the protection and flourishing of life that legitimized colonial rule. These sacrificial acts were meant, in other words, to negate rather than merely augment the positive and supposedly life-enhancing universality of imperialism, to claim India's freedom by its rejection.[10] Al-Qaeda's sacrificial acts, however, rhetorically addressed themselves to the West's lack of universality, its refusal to extend life and security to those under its power but beyond its domains. This explains al-Qaeda's common refrain: if we can't enjoy life and security, neither will you. As such, militant forms of sacrifice served to universalize the insecurity and death to which the West was seen as consigning its enemies, as if it were the mocking echo of a promise betrayed. And it is to the profoundly nihilistic character of this sacrifice that I now turn.

THE LOGIC OF MIRRORS

Like every other form it takes, the individualization of sovereignty has to be disavowed because it, too, threatens to usurp that which belongs to God alone in an extreme version of the transcendentalist principle that Moin and Strathern describe in their opening chapter. And this might be one reason why al-Qaeda's acts were justified not simply by the sacred law they were meant to uphold but also as the mirror images of Western attacks on Islam. This logic has indeed become gruesomely familiar: we kill your civilians, including women and children, as you do ours. Beyond trying to disclaim responsibility for violence, al-Qaeda's ubiquitous logic of mirroring was important because it deferred and displaced the sovereignty of its own actions onto those of its enemies. Militant actions were seen as being negative in character and so deprived of ontological weight, with any positive identity they happened to possess derived from the deeds of their enemies in a kind of performative contradiction. Only in this indirect way, it seems, were they capable of partaking in a sovereignty that had otherwise to be repudiated. But this, by the same token, entailed the militant's paradoxical experience as well as recognition of intimacy with an enemy from whom he derived his own subjectivity. And indeed, compared to the vocabulary of radical incomprehension that characterizes Western views of al-Qaeda, its members never spoke of their rivals in anything but the most familiar of ways.[11]

Al-Qaeda's deterritorialized arena of operations, however, marked by individualized if indirect forms of sovereignty, was put at risk by the War on Terror. While this war was seen as being unprecedented in its global nature, what it in fact did was to reterritorialize Islamic militancy by attacking Afghanistan and Iraq and thus defining its enemy in conventional ways as rivals for the control of territory. Out of this emerged not only insurgencies of a more or less familiar kind in both countries but also a movement such as the Islamic State, which rejected al-Qaeda's unfixed position in the global arena, founding instead a new state to which it gave the hoary title of a caliphate. While ISIS continued to draw on the repertoire of its predecessors, making use of communiqués and confessions as much as suicide bombers and practices that mirrored those of their enemies, these had all taken on a novel meaning if not lost one altogether.[12]

The American journalist Jim Foley was dressed in an orange jumpsuit and repeatedly waterboarded before his execution in 2014 but for no other reason than to imitate what Americans do with their jihadi suspects. His waterboarding was merely a form of torture that didn't seek to extract any information, while the tracksuit did not have the function of marking him out as a prisoner easily spotted in the event of an attempted escape. This truncated form of mimicry suggests that the Islamic State no longer derived ontological meaning from the West, not least because its great enemy was now internal to Islam, represented by the Shia in particular but many other groups similarly defined in sectarian rather than civilizational terms. The West had become merely a site of global publicity and recruitment for ISIS. This is one reason why al-Qaeda's practice of mimicry was overshadowed by other forms of violence, such as the burning alive of a Jordanian pilot in a cage or the casting of homosexuals from rooftops, which did not apparently invoke the logic of mirroring but was occasionally drawn from the *shari'a*. But, of course, by setting alight the caged Jordanian pilot in 2015, ISIS was staging the death he would have suffered had he remained in his stricken fighter plane, which after all had become nothing more than a burning metal cage.

Yet this punishment no longer represented a form of mimicry or imitation lacking ontological gravity but instead a form of analogical thinking or judgment, perhaps modeled on the classical juridical principle of *qiyas*, or reasoning by analogy. But such reasoning was also typically modern in its detachment from any given school of law or tradition of jurisprudence because it drew on Islamic texts and practices almost at random and without much consideration for their historical and intellectual contexts. Whatever else the legal debates among ISIS authorities indicate, I want to suggest that this freewheeling approach to the law had as its immediate predecessor the nineteenth-century liberal attempts to modernize it. And before this there was the eighteenth-century Wahhabi and what in South Asia is known as the *ghayr muqallid* or antitraditional vision of Islam, which in good Protestant fashion would abandon the received Muslim legal tradition and claim the freedom to return to original sources.[13] Despite disagreeing with the illiberal conclusions of these earlier thinkers, it is interesting to note that Muslim liberals well into the twentieth century acknowledged an intellectual kinship with them.

Unlike the Wahhabi or what in India, Pakistan, and Bangladesh is known as the Ahl-e Hadith movement, however, the Islamic State's legal practice appeared to be far more liberal in its reasoning if not results. By ranging across the jurisprudential tradition without regard to its distinctive schools of thought, ISIS had in effect adopted something like the Anglo-Saxon model of case law—although without the inherited custom on which the latter depends. Its highly original legal decisions became precedents in the making of a new tradition no longer based on the old principles of jurisprudence. Far more than al-Qaeda, then, which at most sought legal justification for its practices from a number of disparate authorities generally beyond its control, the Islamic State produced its own law but was, for this very reason, animated by a concern with disavowing sovereignty when doing so. This concern was manifested in its increasingly fragmented if not desperate recourse to scripture, whose efforts at legitimization went well beyond any juridical tradition, to say nothing of mere propaganda. Its effective adoption of a case law model lacking sovereign status did nothing more than define this legal order in purely social terms so that what exists or is visible becomes identical with what is lawful. It was the absolute dominance of jurisprudence in militant actions that prevented them from becoming political ones.

Politics requires some degree of autonomy and integrity outside or even within the parameters of the law, an arena of action that was given no conceptual ground in the Islamic State. ISIS was obsessed about defining all human relations in legal terms, therefore, because it identified law with a social realm outside which nothing could be allowed to exist. Jan Assmann's essay in this volume calls this kind of phenomenon an extreme example of "total religion," which he argues is a latent potential within biblical monotheism that tends to manifest in times of social disruption.

If al-Qaeda's logic of mirrors was shattered by the Islamic State, which had gone on to elaborate a new and analogically defined vision of legal practice and punishment, the militant's subjectivity was also transformed in similar ways from one movement to the other. For example, suicide bombers ceased to be iconic figures drawing an indirect sovereignty from their enemies but were now workaday martyrs who enjoyed no particular celebrity. The militant subjectivity of al-Qaeda's suicide bombers was largely posthumous, coming into view only in their martyrdom videos, whose virtual immortality was achieved just as their real selves and messier, more complex or contradictory lives came to an end. The subjectivity of ISIS fighters, by contrast, was no longer posthumous in nature and disdained the webcam or reality TV model of al-Qaeda's martyrs. Indeed, they almost entirely discarded the martyrdom video as a form of self-expression. Instead, their elaborately staged spectacles of violence, achieved by the use of multiple camera angles, clever editing, and special effects, created two different kinds of subjects.[14] There was the coherent and uniform virtual self, as produced in the studio and archived on the internet, on the one hand, and on the other, an increasingly fragmented original more and more dependent for meaning on its studio-produced doppelganger. It might even be the case that the making of a virtual militant allowed the original to behave more freely or, as was increasingly common among ISIS fighters, in a less Islamic fashion otherwise.

For al-Qaeda, Islam was represented by the medieval flummery on view in militant forms of dress, speech, and habit, which rehearsed the sovereign gestures of an imagined past in a kind of fancy dress. But there was nothing homogeneous about this sartorial repertoire, with militants both named for their national origins, for example, "Al-Britani," or the Britisher, and dressed in some combination of national costumes generally linked to important sites of contemporary jihad like Afghanistan or Chechnya. This gave them a highly diverse and even multicultural appearance. But such habits were always mixed with other traditions of sovereign action, from the military fatigues of regular and would-be armies to the Kalashnikovs of earlier terrorist movements. ISIS retained much of this repertoire, to which it added objects like the white trainers or running shoes common to American and European gang culture, as popularized in rap music videos, and ninja-style black costumes from Hollywood films, both forms of dress legitimized by its founder Abu Musab al-Zarqawi during the American occupation of Iraq.[15] In other words, the evolution of militant symbolism seems to proceed in two directions simultaneously: on the one hand the conventionally political language of the state or indeed the international order and, on the other, a social rhetoric of popular culture and crime. It is as if some of the rituals of investiture that mark conventional political authority were retained alongside practices that deliberately abjured them.

I would like to suggest that, despite its establishment of a state, although one possessing neither actual nor proclaimed borders, ISIS was still characterized by the old Islamist obsession with society or social order and self-regulation. But then this is not so unlike the neoliberal state of either Muslim or Western vintage. This might be why its claims to sovereignty were so ambiguous, from a largely silent caliph given little or no command and charisma (an example of what Moin and Strathern describe in their chapter in this volume as one trajectory of righteous kingship in which the ruler's agency is eliminated) to violence exercised in ways that did not distinguish between the social and the political, and indeed refused to lend the latter any autonomy. If anything, the Islamic State derived its own indirect and disavowed sovereignty from its Shia enemies, represented as they were by the Islamic Republic of Iran. In the heavily sectarian rather than anti-Western narrative that defined ISIS, therefore, the caliph served as an antithesis to Iran's Supreme Leader, while the *sahaba*, or "companions of the Prophet," were made counterparts to the sinless imams of the Shia. It was only after the Islamic Revolution in Iran that the caliphate, as well as the sacred status of Muhammad's companions, became important parts of Sunni thought after decades of oblivion.[16] Of course, these institutions weren't always anti-Shia, and in the immediate aftermath of Iran's revolution, they often represented little more than a Sunni effort to imitate Shia political thought, and that too among radicals and moderates alike.

Unlike its Sunni peers, the Shia version of Islamism embraces sovereignty and so politics, allowing for the suspension and even abrogation of the sacred law in the name of public interest or welfare (*maslahat*).[17] As a way of defining what the German jurist Carl Schmitt called the sovereign exception, of course, public welfare seems to reverse the conventional relationship between norm and exception, where it is precisely welfare that represents the legal order and its suspension that describes sovereignty as a form of exception. But in the Islamic Republic of Iran, it is naturally the divine law that constitutes the norm, one whose own claims to public welfare are indeed undercut by *maslahat* as a juridical principle that doesn't merely add to or supplement the law but can in fact suspend it. The law is defined here not so much by its functionality or social purpose but by truth, and this is what leaves welfare or the social question outside its normative order as a human rather than a divine decision, one that doesn't make a claim on eternal truth but is instead defined by temporary needs and expediencies. And in this sense, sovereignty in the Islamic Republic may be defined as secular or at least nondivine in nature. This is exactly the reverse of the situation that pertains in ostensibly secular states, whose sovereignty is theologically construed as a divinized exception to the norm of welfare.[18]

The sectarian narrative that defined ISIS had emerged soon after the Iranian revolution in countries like Pakistan and tied the Islamic State to its Shia alter ego, the Islamic Republic, in a parasitical relationship of violent intimacy. After all, the task of Sunni sectarianism is to inveigh against what it considers Iran's attempt to usurp God's sovereignty by associating partners like the imams or supreme leader with it. And yet it can do so only by imitating the very innovations that such sectarianism abhors, with ISIS deploying its own anti-imams and anti–supreme leaders against Shia Iran, which, for a number of reasons having to do with its institutionalization of a clerical establishment and belief in the continuity of divine authority within a line of imams, is the only country to have defined an Islamic politics in fully sovereign terms. Like the mirroring rhetoric of al-Qaeda, this process of negative imitation imbibed a disavowed sovereignty from the world of its enemies but in a way that constantly threatened to collapse one into the other, which may be why the Shia were characterized primarily by their seduction in ISIS narratives.[19]

A SECRET SOVEREIGNTY

If the Islamic State's rhetoric was so consumed by the threat of Shia deception, this is surely because it recognized the latter's seductive power. Traditionally linked to the Shia doctrine of dissimulation or *taqiyya*, which obliged its followers to assume Sunni attitudes when they were in a minority or under threat, this emphasis on secrecy has in the past lent support to an esoteric view of religion and in more recent times has been considered a gesture of courtesy toward dominant social norms. But sectarian polemics have tended to paint it in the colors of hypocrisy, if not treachery, and the idea of deception in ISIS rhetoric has in fact come to represent the most important threat it faces as well as the chief accusation it makes against enemies of all kinds.[20] The Shia might constitute its most depraved form, but deception and the hypocrisy that attended it assumed a more general salience in the demonology of the Islamic State. But why should this be the case?

The Islamic State's fear of all that is concealed and its concomitant desire to render everything transparent suggested, I think, a deep anxiety about the sovereignty it disavowed. The social visibility ISIS demanded was always placed under the name of the law insofar as every one of its actions, however bizarre and repugnant, had to be justified and indeed glorified by invoking scriptural precedent. What remained invisible, therefore, was not only outside or against the law but, by that very fact, something that transcended its purely social realm. Included in this transcendence was, of course, God as the sovereign power who founds the law and exists beyond it, as also the political sovereignty that Islamists have always suspected of usurping His place. If the Islamic State was therefore obsessed with transparency, to the degree of publicizing even its most revolting acts, this had to do not simply with the requirements of propaganda but rather a will to reduce everything to the social or at least its juridical form.

As a form of social rather than political life, the divine law played the role of a second nature, in both the idiomatic and literal sense of that term, for Islamists as much as militants of all kinds. It represented, in other words, not only a reality located firmly outside the state in the hands of experts and the hearts of believers but was also meant to displace pre-Islamic, heretical, profane, and even the merely inherited culture of the Muslim past as society's true or second nature. Culture seen as inherited custom was the dark matter that must be destroyed and substituted by a divine law that, like the ideologies of the Cold War, had to be naturalized to become a new social reality. But if the insistent visibility of this new nature presupposed the evisceration of all inner life, seen as a redoubt for the secret and seductive falsehood best represented by the Shia, it did not, for its part, require the presence of some alternative reality behind the strictures of the law. In tune with the media images that defined him, the militant subject was quite flat or even superficial, with his brutality perhaps meant to destroy rather than build an inner life. The superficiality of the new terrorist subject was manifested in the unprecedented rapidity of militant radicalization, which no longer required the kind of indoctrination that once characterized ideological movements during the Cold War, whose aim was precisely to build a new kind of inner life. But while the destruction of such a life, by its subordination to the avatar or virtual identity of social and digital media, might speed up radicalization, it was also likely to produce remarkably brittle subjects.

Like al-Qaeda's game or mirrors that I described earlier, the Islamic State's legal forms were empty, appearances without a reality lurking somewhere in the background. What they appeared calculated to do was turn the men and women under their sway into nothing more than legal subjects, giving existential reality to the abstract legal person otherwise invoked only when acting as signatory to a contract or made responsible for some duty as much as infraction. By rejecting inner life for outward appearance and depriving the latter of its traditional antonym, that is, reality, the Islamic State's obsession with the law as social visibility transformed militant acts into gestures and rituals. The world of ISIS, as seen through its media-defined spectacles of violence, was therefore one defined by the aesthetic rather than by its cunning deployment as mere propaganda behind which some other reality lurks.

A LIFE ON THE SURFACE

Ignoring the importance of militancy's life on the surface, our accounts of movements like al-Qaeda, and later ISIS, tend to be structured as attempts to plumb their depths. These efforts can be defined historically, as when we trace its militancy to recent or far-off events like the invasion of Iraq or the Ottoman Empire's defeat and dismemberment after World War I. Or they may be described sociologically by looking at the age, class, and social prospects of ISIS supporters. And most commonly, of course, this search for hidden depths is conducted as an inquiry into militant ideology, which in some cases can reach back as far as the founding of Islam. Yet what if it isn't depth but surface that proves the more important factor in understanding the militancy of a group like ISIS?

The unparalleled rapidity of its fighters' radicalization, especially when it emerges out of largely stable personal or social backgrounds, and outside the Middle East, seems to give the lie to sociological narratives about ISIS, as it had for al-Qaeda before, because the followers of neither group appeared to fit any demographic profile except perhaps in terms of age group. But then the same is true for all forms of militant activism. The equally rapid reversion of some among these radicals to nonmilitant forms of belief, the unprecedented number of converts to Islam who are involved, and the ignorance of Muslim tradition and theology among many fighters (illustrated by the two British men who purchased *Islam for Dummies* and *The Koran for Dummies* on Amazon before setting off to fight for the Islamic State in Syria) also appears to cast doubt on accounts relying on the historical and ideological depth of such militancy.

It is possible, of course, to identify any number of personal and particular motives that go into the making of ISIS. But as a globally dispersed movement, it surely possesses its own integrity and can't simply be understood as the sum of such motivations. It might be the movement's very globalization that allows its followers to discard deeper and more located forms of identity to live instead on the screens and surfaces of social media. Becoming shallow, we might say, is a difficult task; only by refusing any kind of anchored subjectivity is the militant given over to his cruelties. Many of these latter, such as the long-abandoned practices of concubinage, slavery, or some of the Islamic State's more peculiar forms of execution, have no modern precedent that goes back much more than a decade even in the history of radical Islam and therefore possess no intellectual or political genealogy.[21]

Now to focus on the surface of militancy is not to suggest that it is superficial. For terms like *surface* and *depth* do not describe some physical reality but permit us to recognize how the brutal rhetoric and practices of the Islamic State, for instance, occur as the detached and impersonal fulfillment of a purely external duty. This is why their propaganda films depart from the impassioned denunciations of earlier terrorists to showcase figures unperturbed and even laughing at the violence they unleash—and from which they appear to be entirely disconnected. ISIS was in fact dominated by a hatred of all historical, sociological, and ideological depth, which, after all, justified its destruction not only of pre-Islamic monuments but also of all "traditional," "heretical" or "infidel" persons, practices, and sites, including mosques and the shrines of Sufi saints.

HYPOCRISY AT BAY

The Muslim radicalism of our day is obsessed with the loss of sincerity in hypocrisy. But why should this "ordinary vice," as the American philosopher Judith Shklar describes it, play a role so important among militants as to represent their chief term of opprobrium for enemies of all kinds?[22] These include Muslims who deny the need for jihad, as well as Europeans and Americans who claim to be acting in the name of freedom or human rights. Such an attitude toward hypocrisy is common, however, and had played an important role among anticolonial activists in the past. Today it can be recognized in the accusation of double standards that has become a mainstay not only of militant reasoning but also that of many others, whether Muslim or not. The double standards of the West in upholding ideals like democracy, then, receive more attention from the critics of hypocrisy than any analysis of the principles it betrays.

It is not the content of the West's principles that is put into question, or even seriously considered in such accusations, but the hypocrisy revealed in their affirmation. And while this position is a natural one for those who would defend the fulfillment of such ideals, it can be found even among those who explicitly reject them. For militants, this sometimes amounts to an oddly pluralistic desire: that the West be true to itself rather than being judged by other principles, as communists, fascists, or fundamentalists had once done. An example of such anarchist criticism is provided by the 9/11 "mastermind" Khalid Sheikh Mohammed's testimony at Guantanamo Bay.[23] Instead of making an argument based on Islamic law as a universally valid set of principles, Mohammed turned his tribunal into a trial of the U.S. justice system by arguing that its officials had betrayed their own ideals. Such an inversion, of course, was not unfamiliar to anticolonial activism in the past, its most famous example being Gandhi's "confession" during his trial for sedition in 1930.

While he certainly believed in the *shari'a*'s universality, Khalid Sheikh Mohammed knew that it offered no common ground for a conversation with his captors, who thus had to be engaged in what I am calling an anarchist way and judged by their own ideals. But this meant that the content of Mohammed's own principles was also not as important as his lack of hypocrisy in living by them. His approach to the sacred law in which these principles were embodied was therefore existential rather than merely social or indeed juridical in character. He demonstrated Islam's truth by having it compete with its rivals, if only to see whose supporters remained faithful to the principles they professed. This competition was about being true to a set of external prescriptions, with Mohammed demanding the sacrifice of an inner life whose very autonomy from the law was taken as a sign of hypocrisy.

This concern with a life on the surface is taken to another level in the Islamic State's obsession with transparency, visibility, and sincerity, which demonstrates a fear of all that is secret, hidden, and profound. Remarkable about the ISIS lexicon of blame is its domination by sins like hypocrisy, dissimulation, and even sorcery, all examples of hiddenness. Such an anxiety about depth was never part of al-Qaeda's project, which had to do with distinguishing the militant's sovereignty from that of his enemy in a global arena where responsibility had become dispersed and universalized. In an address from September 2014, called "Indeed your Lord is ever watchful," the Islamic State's chief propagandist, Shaykh Abu

Muhammad al-Adnani ash-Shami, described his Western enemies in the following way:

> They argue in their favour, falsify the events and realities, fool people and endeavour to mobilise them against the rightful while portraying the people of falsehood with every aspect of rightfulness and power in desperate attempts to falsify at all times the truth and to scare and defeat its followers.[24]

His description of the Shia "heretics" (*rafidah*) deploys the same reasoning. Because of their esoteric forms of religion, especially the doctrine of *taqiyya* or "protective dissimulation," the Shia have traditionally been accused of dissembling in Sunni polemics, but with ISIS they simply represented hypocrisy's purest form and were not otherwise distinguished from the Islamic State's other enemies. Indeed, the language of hypocrisy has become so universalized that it even characterizes the views of anti-Muslim movements in the West, which routinely accuse so-called moderates of doublespeak. Here is al-Adnani ash-Shami's view on Shia hypocrisy in particular:

> O Sunnis of Iraq, it is time for you to learn from the lessons of the past, and that nothing works with the Rafida but the slicing of their throats and the striking of their necks; they pretend to be helpless until they get strong; they hide their hatred, anger and enmity towards the people of the Sunnah, they plot and conspire against them; they show false affection towards them and flatter them as long as the Sunnis are strong, while they try to keep in step with them, compete with them and try their hardest to weaken them when they are equal in power.[25]

Naturally the deception identified in the enemy can also be found in oneself, which is why it might need to be so ferociously externalized. So al-Adnani ash-Shami warns the Islamic State's troops:

> Know that from time to time a trial, purification and selection are necessary since some people, who are not of you, as well as pretenders have entered your ranks and disorder has taken place. A trial is therefore necessary to drive out the dirt and purify the ranks.[26]

How did an apparently minor vice like hypocrisy become the Islamic State's chief object of fear? The hypocrite (*munafiq*) was, of course, an important figure in the Qur'an, serving as the name for those who only pretended to follow Muhammad. But even there—to say nothing about later Muslim texts and societies—he by no means represented Islam's greatest enemy. In Europe's more recent history, however, and for apparently the first time since the early modern hermeneutics of suspicion that was deployed against Iberian *conversos* and *moriscos* after the Reconquista, or by Catholics and Protestants against one another during and after the Reformation, hypocrisy became a significant political category with the French Revolution.[27]

In her book, *On Revolution*, the German-American philosopher Hannah Arendt writes about how men like Robespierre sought to unmask the hidden motives of those he considered France's enemies.[28] This he did to destroy the hypocrisy, now increasingly secretive, on which the old regime's decadent and corrupt society had been founded. In her consideration of hypocrisy's twentieth-century afterlife, Arendt went on to argue that in fascist and communist states, its unmasking took on a teleological character, where the race or class enemy appeared according to the logic of history and had to be unmasked periodically. She suggests that show trials and forced confessions in these states were used by those who held power not simply to dispose of defeated rivals but because such unmasking was required and so legitimized by the laws of history.

Given its rejection of history and ideology, it seems unlikely that the Islamic State's anxiety about hypocrisy and its desire for sincerity can be identified with any of the cases Arendt considered. Instead, its obsession with transparency and will to live entirely on the surface was manifested in ISIS by the requirement that all action be rendered visible as law—itself conceived in an unsystematic and merely arithmetical rather than ideological way. Unlike al-Qaeda, then, which didn't have to justify its acts legally if they were simply mirroring those of an enemy, ISIS had to give all its practices the name of law. This included even those bizarre forms of murder, such as throwing people off buildings, setting them alight, or drowning them, for which it was difficult to find textual or traditional justification.

THE ABSENT SOVEREIGN

By exposing even their most brutal acts to public scrutiny, ISIS not only meant them to inspire fear or attract recruits but also as a consequence to refuse the open secret of sovereign power. In conventional states, this open secret, by which sovereignty is manifested outside the very law it institutes, tends to occur in the routine, if extralegal practices of the police, army, or intelligence services.[29]

The Islamic State lacked the kind of extralegal force that defines sovereignty as a form of transcendence. Its most horrific acts were performed not as an open secret but publicly, and even on film, by agents who murdered with smiles on their faces as if to repudiate the pretended exceptionality of the sovereign act. Even al-Qaeda, in this respect following its terrorist predecessors in different parts of the world, used to accompany its violence with expressions of regret, justifying them as an unfortunate necessity. But the way in which ISIS conducted itself demonstrates that, by subordinating all action to the law, it was unable to behave in a sovereign or transcendent manner. The suicide bomber was no longer its iconic representative.

If ISIS had no sense of political transcendence, it curiously didn't possess one of a religious kind either—apart, that is, from the God its fighters ritually pointed to in a banalization of the transcendental. Its caliph was not endowed with any special power or charisma and indeed was rarely heard from, representing a quite different figure than Osama bin Laden in this respect. Even the apocalyptic visions for which the Islamic State was known appear to have been of a banal and ritualistic kind. Its online magazine, *Dabiq*, named for the Syrian town in which the messiah was meant to appear, was full of the most quotidian and even anodyne stories about the opening of schools or regulation of trade in the marketplace. Here, too, the language of the law triumphed over any belief or practice that would serve as a form of exception to it, with apocalypse providing the only way to imagine sovereignty as a kind of transcendence—but only as one that is yet to come.[30]

If there existed a genuinely apocalyptic element in the Islamic State's rhetoric, it was a parochial one having to do with the caliphate conceived of as Islam's last stand. By announcing the institution's reappearance, something no other Islamic movement had done since its abolition by Turkey in 1924, the Islamic State in the same movement resigned its own room for maneuver as well. Having fallen, therefore, the caliphate should never rise again because all attempts to institute it subsequently would have to inherit, repudiate, or otherwise account for its refounding by ISIS. In this way, the movement seemed to be deliberately claiming Islamic categories in such a way that it instituted them in the form it preferred, and if not, then allowed them to be destroyed forever. The Islamic State may thus represent a point of no return for Muslim militancy in general, which could also explain the sheer brutality of its violence—which it would be difficult for any successor to better.

The apocalypse, in other words, is in some sense peculiar to Islam, with ISIS propagandists drawing on a theme made popular in the early twentieth century, when Muslims were warned that if they didn't remain true to the faith,

God would reject them for their enemies—at that time Europe's colonial powers. As we have seen, such relations with the enemy were politically ambiguous, so this threat was deployed both by those who urged Muslims to draw closer to the West as well as by those who counseled the opposite. Here is how the ISIS spokesman al-Adnani ash-Shami describes this last stand, in the now familiar vocabulary of anxiety about the threat of deception and the corresponding desire (expressed by a quotation from the Qur'an) for truth made visible so that life can be lived on the surface:

> O soldiers of the Islamic State, be prepared for the final crusade. Yes, it will, God willing, be the final one. Thereafter, we will raid them, with God's permission, and they will not raid us. Be ready, as you are, with God's permission up to it. The crusaders have come back with a new campaign. They have come to you so that the dust clears, the fog dissipates and the masks fall, so that the deception of falsehood is exposed and the truth becomes visible, and so that those who were to perish (for their rejecting the faith) might perish upon clear evidence, and those who were to live (i.e., believers) might live upon clear evidence (Sura 8, Spoils of War, 42).[31]

Arendt argued that, in its twentieth-century forms, forced confessions and show trials, the politics of sincerity had sought to unmask hypocrisy in a mechanical way. That is, hypocrites needed to be unmasked in order to fulfill the laws of history, which meant that ideology in communist and fascist states worked as a kind of infernal machine, requiring the periodic revelation of treachery for its justification. Of course, liberal democracies also rely on the periodic occurrence of scandals that serve to correct and so legitimize them. Such revelations, however, are personal in nature and made by the private media, with the secrets exposed those of financial or sexual impropriety. It is this that makes liberal hypocrisy an ordinary vice.

In the case of ISIS, unmasking hypocrisy was no longer crucial because its supporters already knew who these sectarian, religious, and other enemies were and so needed to guard only against their own susceptibility to being deceived by them. By destroying these enemies, then, they were in some sense externalizing and eliminating their own inner selves in an effort to live entirely on the surface—not least in the ability to endure their own violence without any apparent effect. And this required that all their actions be rendered visible in the form of law, even those whose brutality was earlier seen as breaking all legal convention. It is not the laws of history, then, that made ISIS rhetoric into an infernal machine but the attempt to bring all action under the authority of

God's law, by eliminating the hypocrisy that would conceal any extralegal or sovereign desire.

It is as if the militant subject had been reduced to the virtual self in video games like *Assassin's Creed*, itself gesturing toward a medieval Muslim history and, perhaps not accidentally, popular among some of the Islamic State's European and American followers. Like ISIS propaganda, *Assassin's Creed* is also filled with apocalyptic references that gesture to a sovereignty and transcendence yet to come and of whose mystical reality the gamer is only vaguely aware. The video game's virtual player, of course, is placed within a received narrative where all enemies and obstacles are known, and his or her task is to surmount and defeat them by the use of skill alone. More interesting than its virtual reality, however, is the possibility that this militant figure is meant to instantiate a legal subject, hitherto simply an abstraction or mask—a persona, as Arendt would say.[32]

On the one hand, ISIS was dominated by the desire to destroy all religious, institutional, and other forms of mediation between the believer and God as a figure of sovereignty and transcendence, thus, the now familiar gesture used by its fighters, who pointed to the skies as if to justify their acts by direct reference to the deity, or the archaic-looking image of the prophet's seal that was impressed upon the ISIS flag, as if Muhammad himself had validated its followers. But on the other hand, this transcendent power was made to disappear within the law. Eliminating sovereignty in this way, by repeatedly absorbing and making it visible within the law, can even be said to represent the Islamic State's principle of movement—by which the law devours everything, including its own limits and therefore its very possibility.

The fundamentalist vision of *shariʿa*, we might say, was ideological because it rationalized the law as an instrument of social justice. And yet the *shariʿa* bore a largely negative character because it was meant to prevent the exercise either of democratic or dictatorial sovereignty—the power to constitute and abrogate law being reserved for God alone, with only minor details being left for religious specialists to decide upon. In this sense, fundamentalism was antipolitical, despite its project to create an Islamic state, and its engagement with politics was correspondingly opportunistic and therefore violent.

Al-Qaeda dispensed with law as an instrument of ideology and made it a set of prescriptions by which one could live without hypocrisy, in a sacrificial and therefore transparent way. Spectacular acts like suicide bombing were meant to demonstrate the law's truth in their very sincerity, best enunciated in the braggadocio about militants loving death more than their enemies did life. But sacrifice as a form of sovereignty, one that exceeded the law by destroying its subject, remained a negative and even nihilistic act incapable of proposing any kind of alternative order or reality to the West that al-Qaeda's practices tended self-consciously to mirror.

For ISIS, the law continued to exist without ideological rationalization, but its practices had now lost much of their excessive or sacrificial aspect and therefore the possibility of sovereign action as well. Instead, it was concerned with forms of pleasure that were more mundane than heroic, as befits "ordinary" life in a state. From its earliest days, even before it had achieved a state or official name, ISIS had advertised its project as one in which fighters could enjoy not only the rule of *shari'a* but also money, goods, and sex in addition to power. Early advertising for the jihad in Syria was dominated not by the language of sacrifice so much as Instagram images of "conquered" villas and swimming pools for fighters to enjoy. The law here seems to have abandoned its repressive form altogether to make permissible all manner of hitherto outrageous desires, from elaborately imagined executions to sexual slavery. As Moin and Strathern point out in the first chapter to this volume, ideas of righteous kingship have always permitted such contradictions to those who displayed the requisite zeal in the name of truth. But rather than achieving what they call a righteous politics, ISIS, by eliminating almost every vestige of kingship, appeared to have set in place a righteous society instead.

More than forsaking its repressive function, the law had actually become an instrument to compel its subject's enjoyment, as if in a perverse homage to the Western "decadence" against which its leaders routinely inveighed. Here, then, was one place in which the mirror that al-Qaeda held up to the West continued to play its role. But to compel enjoyment is also to destroy its freedom and even, perhaps, its substance. The fantasies of desire played out by men as well as women in ISIS territory, then, became ever-more excessive in order to reclaim their sovereignty, which had nevertheless to be exorcised continuously to end up in the law's embrace. Such pleasures, then, became duties without an existential source, obliging their militant agents to live on the surface of things in a perpetual performance of themselves.

NOTES

1. "Video: Islamic State Media Branch Releases 'The End of Sykes-Picot,'" July 1, 2014, *The Belfast Telegraph*, https://www.belfasttelegraph.co.uk/video-news/video-islamic-state-media-branch-releases-the-end-of-sykes-picot-30397575.html. For a consideration of militant video, see Anne Stenerson, "A History of Jihadi Cinematography," in *Jihadi Culture: The Art and Social Practices of Militant Islamists*, ed.

Thomas Hegghammer (Cambridge: Cambridge University Press, 2017), 108–27. For ISIS in particular, see Charlie Winter, *The Terrorist Image: De-Coding the Islamic State's Photo-Propaganda* (London: Hurst, 2021).

2. Recent scholarship has stressed the conceptual and ritual as much as political autonomy of kingship in premodern Islam. See, for instance, A. Azfar Moin, *The Millennial Sovereign: Sacred Kingship and Sainthood in Islam* (New York: Columbia University Press, 2014); Neguin Yavari, *Advice for the Sultan: Prophetic Voices and Secular Politics in Medieval Islam* (London: Hurst, 2014); Hüseyin Yilmaz, *Caliphate Redefined: The Mystical Turn in Ottoman Political Thought* (Princeton, NJ: Princeton University Press, 2019).

3. One of the earliest places this happened was in the expanding Russian Empire, which started absorbing Muslim territories and populations from as early as the sixteenth century. See, for instance, Danielle Ross, *Tatar Empire: Kazan's Muslims and the Making of Imperial Russia* (Bloomington: Indiana University Press, 2020). Scholarship on Muslim revival in later European empires is legion. For some classic examples from India, which possessed the world's largest Muslim populations, see, Barbara D. Metcalf, *Islamic Revival in British India: Deoband, 1860–1900* (Princeton, NJ: Princeton University Press, 1982); David Lelyveld, *Aligarh's First Generation: Muslim Solidarity in British India* (Princeton, NJ: Princeton University Press, 1978); Usha Sanyal, *Devotional Islam and Politics in British India: Ahmed Riza Khan Barelwi and His Movement, 1870–1920* (New Delhi: Oxford University Press, 1999); Francis Robinson, *The Ulama of Farangi Mahall and Islamic Culture in South Asia* (London: Hurst, 2001).

4. For this, see SherAli Tareen, *Defending Muhammad in Modernity* (Notre Dame: Notre Dame University Press, 2020).

5. For this, see Muhammad Qasim Zaman, "The Sovereignty of God in Modern Islamic Thought," *Journal of the Royal Asiatic Society* 25, no. 3 (2015): 389–418.

6. For Maududi's conception of sovereignty, see Faisal Devji, "Islamism as anti-politics," *Political Theology Blog*, August 2, 2013, http://www.politicaltheology.com/blog/political-theology-and-islamic-studies-symposium-islamism-as-anti-politics/. More generally, see Jan-Peter Hartung, *A System of Life: Maududi and the Ideologisation of Islam* (London: Hurst, 2014).

7. See, for instance, Johan Fischer, *The Halal Frontier: Muslim Consumers in a Globalized Market* (New York: Palgrave Macmillan, 2011). See also Peter Mandaville, "Post-Islamism as Neoliberalism," in *Islam After Liberalism*, ed. Faisal Devji and Zaheer Kazmi (London: Hurst, 2017), 279–96.

8. See, for instance, Fazlur Rahman, "Islam and the Constitutional Problem of Pakistan," *Studia Islamica* 32 (1970): 275–87; Fazlur Rahman, "Islam and the New Constitution of Pakistan," *Journal of Asian and African Studies* 8, no. 3–4 (1973): 190–204.

9. For al-Qaeda's thought and practices, see Faisal Devji, *Landscapes of the Jihad: Militancy, Morality, Modernity* (Ithaca, NY: Cornell University Press, 2005); Faisal Devji, *The Terrorist in Search of Humanity: Militant Islam and Global Politics* (New York: Columbia University Press, 2009).

10. See Faisal Devji, *The Impossible Indian: Gandhi and the Temptation of Violence* (Cambridge, MA: Harvard University Press, 2012).

11. For perhaps the most important work on the historical background and emergence of al-Qaeda, see Thomas Hegghammer, *The Caravan: Abdallah Azzam and the Rise of Global Jihad* (Cambridge: Cambridge University Press, 2020). For Osama bin Laden's thought, see Flagg Miller, *The Audacious Ascetic: What Osama bin Laden's Sound Archive Reveals About Al-Qa'ida* (London: Hurst, 2015).
12. For the shift from al-Qaeda to ISIS, see Mohammad-Mahmoud Ould Mohamedou, *A Theory of ISIS: Political Violence and the Transformation of the Global Order* (London: Pluto, 2018). For a study of the movement's organization and operations, see Ahmed S. Hashim, *The Caliphate at War: The Ideological, Organisational and Military Innovations of Islamic State* (London: Hurst, 2018).
13. See, for example, Ahmad S. Dallal, *Islam Without Europe: Traditions of Reform in Eighteenth-Century Islamic Thought* (Chapel Hill: University of North Carolina Press, 2018).
14. See David B. Cook, "Contemporary Martyrdom: Ideology and Material Culture," in *Jihadi Culture: The Art and Social Practices of Militant Islamists*, ed. Thomas Hegghammer (Cambridge: Cambridge University Press, 2017), 151–70.
15. See Afshon Ostovar, "The Visual Culture of Jihad," in *Jihadi Culture: The Art and Social Practices of Militant Islamists*, ed. Thomas Hegghammer (Cambridge: Cambridge University Press, 2017), 82–107; Aaron Tugendhaft, *The Idols of ISIS: From Assyria to the Internet* (Chicago: University of Chicago Press, 2020).
16. See Simon Wolfgang Fuchs, *In a Pure Muslim Land: Shi'ism Between Pakistan and the Middle East* (Chapel Hill: University of North Carolina Press, 2019).
17. For a classic account, see Chibli Mallat, *The Renewal of Islamic Law: Muhammad Baqer as-Sadr, Najaf and the Shi'i International* (Cambridge: Cambridge University Press, 1993). See also Alexander Nachman, "Outside of the Law: Khomeini's Legacy of Commanding Right and Forbidding Wrong in the Islamic Republic," *Sociology of Islam* 7 (2019): 1–21.
18. For a contemporary account of this situation in the United States, see Paul Kahn, *Political Theology: Four New Chapters on the Concept of Sovereignty* (New York: Columbia University Press, 2012).
19. See the September 2014 address by ISIS spokesman Abu Muhammad al-Adnani ash-Shami, "Indeed, Your Lord Is Ever-Watchful," in *Al-Qaeda 2.0: A Critical Reader*, ed. Baldvin Donald Holbrook and Cerwyn Moore (New York: Oxford University Press, 2017), 154–67. For a collection of ISIS texts and their interpretation, see Haroro J. Ingram, Craig Whiteside, and Charlie Winter, *The ISIS Reader: Milestone Texts of the Islamic State Movement* (London: Hurst, 2020).
20. For a discussion of treason and the internal enemy in premodern religious thought, see Philippe Buc, "Civil War and Religion in Medieval Japan and Medieval Europe: War for the Gods, Emotions at Death and Treason," *Indian Economic and Social History Review* 57, no. 2 (2020): 261–87.
21. For the movement's lack of historical or ideological context and its general inability to be understood in conventional ways, see the views of a highly placed American intelligence official, Anonymous, "The mystery of ISIS," *The New York Review of Books*, August 13, 2015, http://www.nybooks.com/articles/archives/2015/aug/13/mystery-isis/.

22. Judith N. Shklar, *Ordinary Vices* (Cambridge, MA: Belknap, 1985).
23. Unclassified Verbatim Transcript of Combatant Status Review Tribunal Hearing for ISN 10024. I discuss this document in Devji, *The Terrorist in Search of Humanity*, 85–96.
24. Al-Adnani ash-Shami, "Indeed, Your Lord Is Ever-Watchful," 154.
25. Al-Adnani ash-Shami, "Indeed, Your Lord Is Ever-Watchful," 162.
26. Al-Adnani ash-Shami, "Indeed, Your Lord Is Ever-Watchful," 156.
27. For a classic account see Lionel Trilling, *Sincerity and Authenticity* (Cambridge, MA: Harvard University Press, 1973). See also Katherine Bergeron, "Melody and Monotone: Performing Sincerity in Republican France," in *The Rhetoric of Sincerity*, ed. Ernst van Alphen, Mieke Bal, and Carel E. Smith (Stanford, CA: Stanford University Press, 2009), 44–59. For hypocrisy and its opposite, sincerity, during the Counter-Reformation, see Jane Taylor, "'Why Do You Tear Me from Myself?' Torture, Truth and the Arts of the Counter-Reformation," in *The Rhetoric of Sincerity*, ed. Ernst van Alphen, Mieke Bal, and Carel E. Smith (Stanford, CA: Stanford University Press, 2009), 19–43; Frans-Willem Korsten, "The Irreconcilability of Sincerity and Hypocrisy," in *The Rhetoric of Sincerity*, ed. Ernst van Alphen, Mieke Bal, and Carel E. Smith (Stanford, CA: Stanford University Press, 2009), 60–77.
28. Hannah Arendt, *On Revolution* (New York: Penguin, 1977). For another account stressing conspiracy and the fear of secrecy in the French Revolution, see Francois Furet, *Penser la Révolution Française* (Paris: Gallimard, 1978).
29. For this, see Kahn, *Political Theology*.
30. For the apocalyptic themes of contemporary militancy, see Jean-Pierre Filiu, *L'Apocalypse Dans L'Islam* (Paris: Fayard, 2008).
31. Ash-Shami, "Indeed, Your Lord Is Ever-Watchful," 156.
32. Arendt thought that figures like Robespierre and his communist or fascist successors wanted to destroy the persona and expose the inner depths of life to public view, an impossible desire that would end by eliminating its subject. My argument is that ISIS wants to destroy this interiority altogether and reduce the subject to its mask or legal persona.

14
Sacred Kingship

A Synthesis

A. AZFAR MOIN AND ALAN STRATHERN

IMMANENTISM AND THE ORIGINAL ENCHANTMENT OF POLITICS

To understand what kind of thing kingship actually was for most of humanity, we must first look at societies that were stateless and kingless.[1] This is why, following our theoretical framework in chapter 1, the volume begins with Marshall Sahlins's chapter, aptly titled, "Kings Before Kingship." Sahlins expands upon his concept of "the original political society" by examining the cosmological imagination of small-scale communities. He argues that the germ of the state developed when humans living in face-to-face groups, in an effort to flourish, entered into formal relationships with a cosmos suffused with anthropomorphic sentience. Sahlins thus returns us to themes originally deployed by James G. Frazer and Maurice Hocart, and a method of world comparative anthropology, but with the benefit of many generations of professional scholarship and a wealth of new insight.

What Sahlins refers to as "determination by the religious basis" is the assumption, widespread in the ethnographic record, that all life and flourishing comes ultimately from a supernatural origin. As he notes in the coda to his paper, the worldview sustaining the cosmic polity that preceded and shaped earthly politics was essentially that of immanentism. It is precisely a measure of the subsequent transcendentalization and secularization of our imagination that the religious origins of politics are so rarely appreciated. Note, however, that the societies that Sahlins describes did not conceive of religion or politics as autonomous categories. Indeed, his ironic Marxian language entails a critique of legitimation theory, namely, that religion and ceremonial life are simply a way of validating the existing political order[2] or that economic production is the basis for state power and religious cult is a mere mystifying aftereffect. On the contrary, he shows that, in immanentist ontologies, "production" is inconceivable without the intervention of ancestors, spirits, and gods. These metapersons wield the divine powers on which life depends; they form a cosmic hierarchy that governs human affairs and often reaches its apex in a remote and all-powerful encompassing deity.[3] All human political arrangements, then, however flat or steep—whether yielding the shamans of essentially egalitarian groups or the rulers of great empires—are constructed in relation to the preexisting cosmic state. From this perspective, divinized kingship is just one of the many acts of hubris by which individuals distinguish themselves through their capacity to usurp the vital powers of metapersons. Contained within this line of thought is a most striking implication: the powers that such kings wield over the natural, social, cosmic worlds are not commensurate with the extent of their actual political hegemony. Even shamans and the pettiest of chiefs may be credited with such ritual functions.

The production of life, order, and polity in immanentist settings is therefore a matter of constructing and maintaining relationality, what Claude Lévi-Strauss called structure; the tense relations between people and metapersons are just one dimension of this. Peter Gose's chapter helps us see that the immanentist realm is only "monist" in a highly specific sense, which becomes clear when it is contrasted with transcendentalist visions.[4] Considered in its own terms, it is not unitary at all but rather dependent on a whole series of material and spatial polarities—and yet these dualisms must be ceaselessly overcome for society to thrive.[5] Human flourishing originated in the movements between the dry and the wet, the near and the far, the human and the nonhuman. More generally, production in the immanentist universe involves interactions between observable reality and ancestral realms, between profane and sacred activity, pollution and purity, life and death, priests and chiefs, the domestic and the foreign, and—perhaps the foundational principle of them all—between female and male. As Gose puts it, "Andean immanence was thus imminent, not fully present; rather, it consisted of a pulse involving withdrawal and return in alternation." Ritual was the pump that kept these movements of vitality in circulation, and it needed constant work; there was to be no final resting point. Michael Puett makes a similar point about the inherent incapacity of sacrificial ritual in China to achieve any lasting effect.[6] This recalls Sigmund Freud's insistence that obsessive-compulsive acts—or, more politely, ritual behaviors—are the unconscious engine of religious life.

DIVINIZED KINGSHIP: HEROIC AND COSMIC

The theoretical framework in chapter 1 set up divinized kingship as the essential means of sacralizing rulership in immanentist societies. Divinized kingship proceeds by continually blurring the distinction between the humanity of the ruler and the divinity of the gods, an ever-incomplete project that may leave rulers in a state of cultivated ambiguity.[7] The suggestion that divinized kingship may in turn be broken down into heroic and cosmic forms was taken up by all the authors describing societies in which immanentism loomed large.

In Nicole Brisch's chapter on early Mesopotamia, the sheer closeness and kinship of the ruler to the gods is concretely expressed in the inscription on E'annatum (ca. 2500–2350 BCE) of the city-state of Lagash, who was given strength by the god Enlil, nursed by the goddess Ninhursag, named by the god Ningirsu, and chosen in the heart by the goddess Nanshe. Although E'annatum was not treated directly as a god, Naram-Sin of Agade (r. ca. 2254–2218 BCE) was directly declared as such after crushing major rebellions "through the love that the goddess Ishtar showed him." It was the generation of charisma through military victory that allowed his closeness to the divine to be pushed one stage further. The heroic dimension to ruler divinization is obvious here, as it is in the acclamations of Shulgi of Ur (r. 2092–2045 BCE), the strong man and "lion with terrifying eyes, born from a snake-dragon," who could run like a donkey between cities 200 km apart in one day.[8] It follows that a terrible defeat, as suffered by Sargon II of Assyria (r. 721–705 BCE), could be "a calamity for kingship" because it indicates an evident loss of divine favor.

There can be no better image of heroic kingship than the election of a ruler after they have won a duel at the Olympic Games, as in the case of Pittacus of Mytilene. Indeed, Lynette Mitchell's chapter is rich in illustrations of the play of charisma in ancient Greek kingship. At the same time—and perhaps accordingly—divinized kingship never became a stable hegemonic institution in Greece as it did in other ancient societies. This was the case, at least, until Alexander. He too is the archetype of heroic kingship, this "unconquered god" holding aloft the thunderbolt of Zeus after his victory over Porus in the Indus. His overwhelming achievements generated a charisma of such magnitude that it produced a structural breakthrough, establishing divinized kingship among the successor Hellenistic states and thereby allowing them to move into more cosmic forms.

Cosmic kingship, on the other hand, may be visualised through David Gellner's descriptions of the last Hindu kings of Nepal—the very last one was removed from office in 2007. These kings both received blessings from the gods and bestowed them on their subjects in turn through the annual cycle of festivals.[9] The narratives are uncannily similar to those of the very first Egyptian kings from several millennia ago. As Jan Assmann points out, the classic Eurasian iconography of kingship involving the sun and the eagle was set in motion by the Egyptian pharaoh as an avatar of Horus, who was the sun god and highest god of all, and "the terrestrial representation of solar power and cosmogonic energy."[10] Thus were the pharaohs identified with the all-encompassing deity, which Sahlins suggests lies at the top of all immanentist hierarchies, and granted a corresponding capacity to make the world hospitable for human society.

In fact, Horus as the sun god was thought to have formed a sacred marriage with Hathor, the goddess of love representing the land of Egypt. When we see that Horus symbolized the victorious chiefdom of Edfu, while his consort Hathor represented the cradle of pharaonic civilization, we see more than an echo of Sahlins's model of the stranger-king (associated with the sky, power, maleness) and the indigenes (associated with the earth, fertility, and femaleness). This clarifies why the phenomenon of stranger-kingship is prevalent in immanentist societies: it reflects the understanding that vitality and order arise from the movements between spatialized polarities. Thus, Gose tells us that sociopolitical organization across the Andean region was driven by distinctions between an "upper" moiety and a "lower" one, in which the former were typically defined "as intrusive conquerors who originated from Titicaca and the latter as conquered indigenous people who originated from the Pacific."[11] In addition, the former represented political dominion and the latter, priestly quietism. Diarchical patterns emerged too in the relationship between the Inca ruler (who claimed active power) and the high priest (who claimed ritual seniority). These dualisms were not static structural features; they produced rivalry and tension (which in turn led to conflicting diplomacy with the Spanish) and ensured that the inversion of their respective roles was a constant possibility.

The heroic and cosmic forms are not properties of stable systems but rather transient types thrown up by the churn of history. Puett maps their historicity onto Chinese dynastic cycles: the founder of a new dynasty who defeats the previous incumbents is the heroic figure, while their successors fashion a more cosmic form of kingship. It is significant that the equivalent to Alexander in China, the first emperor (August Thearch) of the Qin who unified China for the first time in 221 BC, set aside the cosmic form of kingship implied by the Mandate of Heaven principle and instead claimed to be a divinity rising above Heaven. The establishment of a new order required an act of transgression against the old.

Yet one reason why the heroic tends to congeal into the cosmic form was its susceptibility to the ritualization trap, typically elaborated by rival elite figures staking a claim to power or by successors of great nomadic conquerors as they endeavoured to preserve their sacred status in the face of inevitable sedentarization. Gellner sees this at work in the case of Nepalese kingship: from the late nineteenth century, the ruling dynasty was boxed into a ceremonial role by the prime ministers who took on the active function. Since the first prime minister took on explicitly royal stylings, we have diarchy once more.

TRANSCENDENTALISM, ZEAL, AND THE POLITICS OF RIGHTEOUSNESS

As chapter 1 noted, in certain core areas of Asia and the Mediterranean region, the immanentist worldview was cast into disarray during the Axial Age. Because the Axial Age concept is sometimes criticized for the liberal Christian biases of its original proponents, it is worth pointing out the possible political-economic foundations of this world historical shift in mentalities. The late David Graeber built upon the work of Richard Seaford and others to suggest that the idealism of the Axial Age took shape amid tyrannical new forms of materialism, namely, the market and the coercive state power that monopolized the issuing of money, that marked the Iron Age.[12] The call for righteous rule, no matter how unachievable in practice, can be understood as a desperate attempt to counter the cruelties of what Graeber called the military-coinage-slavery complex. This self-perpetuating complex had three interlocking components: new standing armies made up of freemen that had to be paid in coin; the need for coin, which generated a high demand for precious metal; and the need for metal, which was met via military campaigns to raid more temple treasuries and capture more slaves to work the mines. Aspects of what Max Weber called "prophetic religion" were shaped by a massive reaction to this oppressive political economy: enraged criticisms of the existing order, demands for social justice, and the codification of morality that enabled it to be preached as universal ethics. Puett's account of ancient China in this volume serves as a classic example of such a reaction to a new pan-Eurasian Iron Age order in which newly centralized states and their standing armies cast aside Bronze Age aristocracies.[13]

Far from Eurasia and the vicissitudes of the history that produced the Axial Age, the case of the Incas raises the question of how and whether a proto-transcendentalism might also emerge out of the immanentist dualisms described above. Peter Gose argues that this was obstructed by the way in which immanentist diarchy never settles down into a clean split between religious and political authority; among the Incas, the ritual function of rulers was so central that it precluded the establishment of a hereditary autonomous priestly class. Brisch's contrast between ancient Assyrian and Babylonian monarchies at particular stages in their development maps out a general spectrum within immanentist polities. In Assyria, as among the Incas, kings take on a ritual centrality and are closely associated with the highest deity; in Babylonia, priests take on key intercessory roles and are able to "tame" the king through ritual via the very explicit humiliations of the New Year festivals.[14] Gose suggests that what eventually allowed such divergences of functions to solidify, thus in turn allowing a sustained prophetic or literati critique of royal power, were the abstractions enabled by literacy and commodity exchange. If the Inca realm was one of pure immanence, it is surely germane that it also had no money and no real merchant class—the circulation of goods took place via the tributary system managed by the state—while the *khipu* system presumably placed real limits on the capacity to represent abstract thought. This rather strengthens the argument that key ingredients of Axial Age ferment include democratic forms of writing, Iron Age weaponry, and a money economy. Note, however, that the revolutionary new perspectives that emerged from this ferment were not developed by priests per se but by renouncers, philosophers, and prophets.

In a very general sense then, the Axial Age allowed the centrality of divinized kingship to become subject to new forms of critique that opened the possibilities of other visions of sociopolitical organization. This point needs to be handled with a great deal of subtlety, however. The model advanced in this volume by no means presupposes any essential correlation between democratic movements and transcendentalism. To take only the most obvious of points, many stateless non-Axial societies had far more egalitarian orders, while such was the power of sacred kingship that it reasserted itself upon the political order in societies where transcendentalist religions held sway. The recent and welcome move into the statistical examination of the Axial Age phenomenon by cliometricians will have to find a way of incorporating such complexities into their coding mechanisms.[15]

THE STANDOFF BETWEEN TRANSCENDENTALISM AND IMMANENTISM: INDIA AND CHINA

Hinduism and Confucianism in India and China, respectively, best demonstrate that transcendentalism never replaces immanentism; it instead becomes locked in a continual struggle to dominate it.[16] Both these traditions preserved extremely important lines of continuity with their immanentist origins, and both formed in dialogue with more emphatic expressions of transcendentalism or true counterreligions: Hinduism versus Buddhism and Jainism, and Confucianism versus Mohism and Daoism. Moreover, classical forms of Hinduism and Confucianism grew out of attempts to rationalize and speculate about ritual activity. It may be that the germ of many Axial Age movements lies in puzzling about ritual logic, contemplations that have no doubt arisen in many societies. Such may be suggested by the first millennium BCE Assyrian *Dialogue of Pessimism*, which appears to express a detached, ironic approach to ritual as if choosing whether to sacrifice could teach "your god to run after you like a dog."[17] Far more profound and sustained critiques of the immanentist logic of ritual developed among certain schools of thought in China, India, and Greece.[18] In both Hinduism and Confucianism, these critiques were incorporated or countered in a way that kept intact the primacy of ritual itself. In fact, Gellner suggests that Louis Dumont's interpretation of Hindu kingship exaggerated its transcendentalist element, given that brahmins largely functioned as ritual servants of a cosmic king.

Of course, Hinduism underlines, more emphatically than any other case, not just the survival of an immanentist notion of ritual purity but also its apotheosis. Nonetheless, if purity—as an embodied and concrete quality—was so deeply entrenched in the social order through the principle of caste, it was in part because it became inextricable from a transcendentalist insistence on soteriological purity as an abstract quality of the inner self. As nearly everywhere in the Axial Age, blood sacrifice was also problematized by the renouncer philosophies that Hinduism incorporated—even if the sacrifice of bulls in the Nepalese Dasain festival serve as an indicator of the limitations of that revolution and the enduring pluralism of religious behaviors bracketed under Hinduism.

A similar tense standoff between transcendentalism and immanentism shaped ancient China. Although human sacrifice, present in the Shang period, was abandoned, Confucianism retained sacrifice at the heart of ritual, and ritual at the heart of its practice. Yet after the Axial Age, the meaning of ritual would never be quite the same. Puett's chapter redefines the nature of China's Axial Age by clearly distinguishing several distinct manifestations, of which two are particularly important to note. The first was Confucianism, as discussed below, which did indeed come to dominate the nature of imperial authority, albeit never monolithically. Making up a second impulse were the Mohist and Daoist salvationist-millenarian movements, which often found expression as counterpoints to the state. Partly because of a tendency to define Chinese civilization in terms of Confucianism, scholarship has frequently missed the significance of this second manifestation, a form of transcendentalism fully equivalent to the Indic and especially monotheistic variants.

As Puett notes, the Celestial Masters movement, which began in 142 CE and became the origin of all later Daoist groups, was based on divine revelation issuing from the specific interventions of a historical prophet/god figure (Laozi). His teachings, considered as eternal truth and thus set down in scripture, told a narrative of the struggle between good and evil while set within an understanding of the universe as created by a fundamentally good deity who rewards moral conduct and must be approached with sincerity and faith. These were "offensive" revelations that are comparable to biblical religion's ban on idolatry leading to a devaluation of temple religion and sacrifice. In the case of the Celestial Masters, sacrificial ritual was not merely dismissed as irrelevant but as positively harmful; feeding the ghosts only made things worse. This was, more generally, an unmasking of ritual, as Puett underlines, interpreting its presuppositions with crushing literalism.

In one sense, Confucianism rejected this "reformed" perspective entirely by maintaining sacrificial ritual as its central form of practice, yet the meaning and purpose of ritual was drastically altered. The immanentist logic was quietly set to one side in a body of ritual theory that focussed instead on its capacity to create order and hierarchy through its disciplinary forms. Mencius, for example, understood ritual as an exercise in conveying civility (*ren*), as a tool of creating harmony through social and behavioral means rather than supernatural ones. For Xunzi:

> Rescuing the sun or moon from eclipse, praying [for rain] in time of drought, deciding great affairs only after reading cracks and casting stalks are not because one expects to get what he asks, but to manifest refined culture (*wen*). Hence, superior men consider these as refined culture, while the people consider these as dealing with deities. To consider them refined culture is auspicious, to consider them as dealing with deities is baleful.[19]

Undoubtedly, at a popular level, the immanentist understanding of ritual persisted essentially untroubled, but for the literati the worm of disenchantment had already started to uncoil. That Confucianism developed its own ethical and critical theory of ritual, which now found justification in its impact on the human subject rather than in wooing the favor of metapersons, reveals the effects of its engagement with the counterreligions of Mohism and Daoism. It is no coincidence that here, as everywhere affected by the Axial Age movements, human sacrifice was abandoned. Nevertheless, while Confucianism suppressed the more emphatic tendency toward self-divinization expressed by certain emperors, it did not question the moral or ritual primacy of kingship.[20] Other Axial Age movements exhibited a greater potential for a more profoundly critical stance toward monarchy.[21]

TRANSCENDENTALISM ASCENDANT: ISRAEL AND GREECE

Immanentist traditions could find ways of taming kings through ritual means: hence the Babylonian festival at which the king is pulled by the ear and slapped by the priest—subordinated to the gods and to the society they protect.[22] But transcendentalism attempts to limit the agency of rulers in a quite different way: by subordinating them to a higher soteriological-moral order. One way in which the community is protected from the egomaniacal tendencies and charismatic force of the leader is through the sanctification of the law above and beyond that of the sovereign. In historical terms, this took two forms. The first was an extreme manifestation of the transcendentalist subordination of kingship: the outright rejection of it in both the Judaic origins of monotheism as outlined by Assmann and its present-day manifestation in Islamic State of Iraq and Syria (ISIS) as described by Faisal Devji. In this starkly disembodied—or more pointedly, "bookish"—vision, it would not be the king who mediated between God and people but the law as outlined in scripture. The second form was the development of the law among the Greeks as a more autonomous principle of authority, sanctioned and protected by the gods but not monopolized by God as in the biblical case.

In ancient Egypt, the pharaoh had been the source of the law, and it was he who actively participated in the sphere of morality and social justice, not the gods.[23] The primary duty of the gods was to oversee the smooth operation of cosmos and nature, a task in which the pharaoh and his priests assisted by performing elaborate temple rituals. This ritual cooperation between the king and the gods was utterly rejected in the Hebrew Bible, which held up the pharaoh as the epitome of hubris and cruelty, rejecting his priestly duties as an attempt to take the place of God.

The covenantal theology of the Hebrew Bible is rooted in the story of the exodus of the Israelites from Egypt. The story ends in the Book of Deuteronomy, when Moses addresses his people at the entrance to the Promised Land and tells them to swear an exclusive oath of loyalty not to him but to their God. The radical innovation of Deuteronomic covenantal theology was not only its militant monotheism—that there was only one true God—but also its zealous rejection of monarchy with the insistence that it was only to God that an exclusive loyalty was due. It was a fundamental reconceptualization of religion without kingship. Indeed, it may be seen as a protodemocratic movement in which all could in theory have equal and unmediated access to God. In his chapter, Assmann even refers, for good reason, to equality and fraternity if not liberty.[24] In its devaluation of kingship, biblical religion was as radical as the violent rejection of monarchy in revolutionary France.

If the French revolution was an event of world historical importance, however, the biblical (Deuteronomic) revolution must be understood as an event of world literary significance. To be sure, the narrative frame of Deuteronomy was born out of a traumatic historical experience, the Israelite loss of temple and king during the time of Assyrian onslaught and Babylonian exile. Unsurprisingly then, its covenantal theology was modeled on a historical template, the oath of loyalty demanded by the Assyrian king of his conquered subjects. Nevertheless, its greatest significance lay in the fact that it produced a form of religion that was utterly dependent on writing. Biblical religion, as its name indicates, is founded on textual continuity or, more accurately, literary continuity. By contrast, temple religion—the immanentist religion of pharaoh, for example—had depended on ritual continuity. Indeed, biblical religion was the first religion of memory that violently rejected kingship (pharaoh as the epitome of injustice), a rejection that was created, preserved, and transmitted in a literary form in Deuteronomy and its covenantal theology. The gradual stabilization and eventual canonization of this literary narrative led to the recognition that this was indeed a new type of religion that could be abstracted from surrounding culture and used to create a new community—what the Qur'an would call "people of the book." For this reason—the ability for book religion to create a counterculture—Assmann calls it counterreligion.

Counterreligions could survive without temple, priest, and sacrifice as long as they had scripture, prophet, and law. What place could cosmic kingship have in this new-fangled religious form? Indeed, covenantal theology entailed a radical ban on the institution of stranger-kingship that was so widespread in immanentist societies.[25] For the latter, power must be harnessed from the sources beyond the domestic realm, creating the ceaseless back and forth of exchange across all the polarities discussed by Sahlins and Gose in this volume. Biblical religion, by contrast, did not locate vitalizing powers in the mundane beyond and so did not grant special intermediary status to alien humans. Instead, the whole people themselves were sanctified by their relationship with a transcendent and exclusive deity—"a kingdom of priests" (Exodus 19:6); "kings and priests unto God"

(Peter 2:9); and, "a chosen people, a royal priesthood" (Revelation 1:6). What became central in this scheme was the memory of the founding prophet and the divine law revealed to him. The only acceptable king in biblical religion was the one who swore to uphold this law and subordinate his sovereignty to prophetic revelation. This was righteous kingship in its most vehement form, but it was not the only possible form of transcendentalist politics, as the Greeks would demonstrate to the ancient world.

As Sahlins's discussion of the cosmic state implies, the decrees that would be passed by human lords had already been prefigured by the taboos and mandates issued by metapersons. Elites in immanentist societies frequently established their "laws" by declaring them to have issued from ancestors and gods and disclosed by revelation. Meanwhile, transcendentalism exhibited profound affinities not just with lawmaking but with *legalism*: that is, it did not merely endorse the discrete injunctions of hierarchs but rather the authority of the law as a coherent, autonomous, reified form of authority. Scriptural religions such as Christianity, Islam, and Buddhism codified their ethical laws into numbered lists, setting them down in texts that were granted an authority beyond the claims of any living human being, texts that could be interpreted only by a scholar-clerisy. In the case of Islam, we have the most complete identification of the "priestly" class and the functions of the scholar-jurist. In the writings of certain Ancient Greek philosophers, however, the law could be conceived in a way that detached it somewhat from religion: even if, for Plato and Aristotle, the law somehow remained "of god," this vague concept of justice overseen by divinity was far from that of "revealed" law in scriptural religions in which Divinity dictated law in codified form.

As Mitchell observes in her essay, the Greeks produced what was likely the first critical examination of the human and natural bases of *nomos* ("law"). It can be no coincidence that this happened among literate societies consciously experimenting with their own democratic and oligarchic constitutional arrangements and amid an intellectual culture that was driven by a vast respect for the potential of rational deliberation and written forms of thought. Yet just as Greek religion still remained essentially immanentist, so too Greek society still required, in practice, that political authority be established by reference to the divine. One solution was to turn the law into an abstract, transcendent, and somehow divine principle. Therefore, Heraclitus distinguished between human laws and the one divine law, with the former somehow derived from the latter (by divine inspiration if not divine dictation). On the one hand, this was a crucial step because it meant that the law was in theory situated above the ruler. On the other hand, it became difficult to conceive how this law was to be given effect.

We would suggest this was precisely because it was not rooted in a transcendentalist religious tradition: it was neither set down in scripture nor given agency through a clerisy. Perhaps this reflected the fact that the Greek city-states were relatively well protected in terms of geography from the reach of Iron Age empires. If the Persians had taken Athens and hauled off its elite into exile, perhaps it would have given birth to a Greek scriptural religion haunted by the memory of its lost temples! But this is not how history unraveled. The Greeks developed their own strong form of sacred kingship with Alexander, who embraced Persian ideals, and even went beyond Achaeminid concepts of sacred kingship to declare himself a god on earth and the very embodiment of the law. By then, however, the philosophers had already set the course for Greek transcendentalism.

In a sense, the philosophers tried to ethicize kingship by envisioning perfect philosopher-kings or at least rulers defined by their superior *aretē* or virtue.[26] It must be said here, however, that *aretē* seems to have been a principle of excellence that may be understood in terms of both heroic and ethical perfection. Note also that this phenomenon was a general product of Axial Age civilizations attempting to tame the charisma of heroic warriors, as it manifested itself in the post-Mongol moment in Islam, which also witnessed the rise of Neoplatonic conceptualization of the great ruler as both divinized and an embodiment of ethical perfection. For the Greek case, Mitchell tells us that Aristotle, after grappling with the idea of a *pambasileus* ("king of all") of incomparable virtue, "finally rejects the idea that this man should rule rather than law because a man always has passion which corrupts him, whereas law is reason without desire." It is as if Aristotle (who was Alexander's tutor) is pondering the possibility of a righteous king—an idealized incarnation of truth and morality—but because his reasoning does not proceed from the basis of a revealed tradition, a disenchanted understanding of human nature finally undermines the prospect. Others came to different conclusions, however, and the enduring understanding of rulership in terms of heroic charisma flared into life in the most striking way with Alexander, the very model of heroic divinized kingship. Sans scripture, how was law supposed to incarnate in a form that might reliably overmaster the accumulation of charisma?

"WORLD" RELIGIONS AND "UNIVERSAL" EMPIRES: ISLAM AND MONGOLS

The Axial Age took more than a millennium to affect Eurasia fully. The resulting amalgam can be described as one composed of world religions and universal empires, the former being a cult that could potentially spread over the entire world and the latter a form of polity in which the king could aspire to ruling over the entire world. It would be precise to call it an amalgam rather than a fusion because religion and kingship competed with one another or attempted to subsume the other to achieve their universal and global ambitions. The most well-known history of this competition and cooperation is that of biblical monotheism.

Even though the Book of Deuteronomy was composed—it is said to have been "discovered" during temple repair in Jerusalem—in the seventh century BCE, Islam was the first major religion that identified itself as a "community of the Book" more than a millennium later.[27] Islam's self-awareness in the seventh century CE as a scriptural religion has much to do with the fact that its two biblical predecessors, Christianity and Rabbinic Judaism, had settled on a scriptural canon a few centuries earlier, ushering in a new religious age in which temples and priests became optional or secondary, while preachers and teachers armed with a scriptural canon became the real soldiers of religion. This first happened in Christianity, which was transformed from an illegal and persecuted religious community into the official religion of a universal empire. In the process, Christian rulers began to be recruited as missionaries of monotheism. This did not mean, however, that transcendentalism won over immanentism or book religion overpowered temple religion once and for all. Rather, as examined in detail in *Unearthly Powers*, the spread of scriptural religion was characterized by the tense interaction between immanentism and transcendentalism.

The result at times could be thoroughly confusing, as it was in the case of the early caliphate discussed by Aziz Al-Azmeh in his chapter. The Qur'anic ideal of the caliph was supposed to produce a ruler thoroughly subordinated to scripture, a mere deputy of God. Indeed, the Qur'an calls David a "caliph on earth" but does not give him a ringing endorsement. In an echo of the Hebrew Bible, the Qur'an accepts sacred kingship begrudgingly and allows it only in a righteous doctrinal form, warning David not to follow his own whims because that would lead him astray and straight to terrible punishment on the Day of Judgment (38:26). Nevertheless, the caliph of Islam transformed, in the seventh and eighth centuries, into a sacred king who was both righteous and divinized.

Al-Azmeh aptly terms this phenomenon the immanence of transcendence, evident as a glissando, a gliding movement, between cosmic divinization and doctrinal righteousness. In many ways, the Qur'an itself was a product of such a dynamic, being a scripture (like the Hebrew Bible) that was "acutely monotheistic in its later portions, but was monolatrous and henotheistic at other points." The case of early Islam serves to remind us how transcendentalisms are rooted textually in the memory of an immanent act of sheer charisma. But scriptural canonization tames this charisma by banning its reinstantiation or delaying it until a far distant future, the Day of Judgment. The body of the sacred king, however, grates against these textual constraints on immanentism. The caliph, for instance, remained a master symbol of Islam four centuries after he had lost military, fiscal, and even doctrinal authority. From the ninth to the thirteenth century, practically no Muslim ruler would be accepted as a king without the caliph's pure touch. What this iconic caliphate retained was priestly authority.[28]

Caliphal immanence in Islam came to an end with the Mongol conquest and destruction of Baghdad, yet this destruction merely led to other creative acts of immanence, as Jos Gommans and Said Reza Huseini outline in their chapter on Neoplatonic kingship in post-Mongol Islam. The "pagan" Mongols had openly promoted heroic and cosmic forms of sacred kingship as a way of managing religious difference. They criticized scriptural religion for introducing strife and violence. This tendency toward immanentist religion did not end with the conversion of the Mongols to Islam over the fourteenth century. Rather, it unleashed a new type of political culture along with a revolution in philosophical thought where Neoplatonism became the dominant stream of intellectual culture across the eastern Islamic world. In effect, this intellectual culture cannot be unlinked from the culture of the Inner Asian warband that enabled Muslim kings to flout doctrinal constraints of transcendentalism openly.[29] By comparison, it would seem that Neoplatonism did not have the same political effect in Christian Europe because it remained geographically protected from Inner Asian conquests.

Even with the variance across Christian Europe and Muslim Asia in mind, it is worth suggesting that the principal historic function of Neoplatonism in Christian and Muslim cosmological thinking was to provide a bridge between immanentism and transcendentalism that could be crossed in either direction, by heroic conquerors and absolute rulers of Islam and Christianity divinizing themselves and by Muslim and Christian clerisies attempting to tame the charisma of such rulers by casting it as a product of ethical perfection. In the end, Plato and Platonists could not conceive of a means of making the transcendent immanent except through the agency of a single superlative individual—through a divinized king. As Gommans and Huseini argue, this was the divinization conferred upon the Mughal emperor Akbar in the "Millennial History," a unique work of post-Islamic history produced by a team of Muslim Neoplatonists assembled from across Iran, Central Asia, and South Asia. The Mughal Empire undertook this unique project because it contained various transcendentalist groups who would not be converted readily to one dispensation, necessitating some other mode of unification-via-sacralized-authority. This was not an attempt, however, to overthrow transcendentalist religions; it was a move to provincialize them all, including the king's own religion, Islam. Neoplatonism was appropriate for this context because, as Mitchell shows in her chapter, the Greeks had developed a philosophical transcendentalism that was not tied to a particular cult. In post-Mongol Islam, this Hellenistic transcendentalism was recast as universal wisdom and harnessed to the cult of cosmic kingship that developed in the wake of postnomadic sedentarization of the Inner Asian warbands.

Although none of the chapters in this volume deal with Christian Neoplatonism, it is worth a brief mention that, in Late Antiquity, Julian the Apostate (r. 361–363) had also tried to revive Platonism as a cosmology of sacred kingship in an attempt to undo the Christianization of the Roman Empire. Julian's Neoplatonism was clearly an interplay between transcendentalism and immanentism, but it demonstrated the difficulty in reverting to a pure immanentism once a culture has been exposed to a transcendentalist challenge. Overall, one could say that, even though Greek and Christian strands of transcendentalism thoroughly merged in Late Antiquity, the Greek philosophical inheritance served to stiffen Christian transcendentalism rather than make it more accommodating of religious difference, as would be the case in the Mughal Empire.

MODERN TRANSCENDENTALISM AND THE PROBLEM OF DISENCHANTMENT

By *disenchantment*, we simply mean the removal of immanent power from the world. If our starting point is Sahlins's cosmic polity, in which every aspect of social and political life was embedded in people's relations with the supernatural, in the modern era, we can really see how we stand on the other side of a watershed where priest-kings and collective fertility rituals are inconceivable as the major roles and acts of governance.[30] This is not to say that magic has been banished from our world but rather that the enchanted worldview is no longer the basis of a universal political order. The Thai king may still be venerated in a manner that recalls the divinized sovereigns of old, but it is the Thai prime minister who signs international treaties like ordinary mortals. While pacts between ancient Babylonians and Egyptians had to be sealed with oaths taken on the sun or moon gods, there is no place in the United Nations for such cosmic rites.

The long-term perspective taken in this volume reveals that we cannot simply tell the story of the disenchantment of rulership by beginning with Renaissance humanism or Enlightenment rationalism in the West. The origins of the humanization of kingship, its subordination to higher ethical principles, rational argument, and arbitration by subjects or clerisies, ultimately lie in the conceptual revolutions of a more broadly distributed Axial Age. This insight is made clear by the contributions of Assmann, Mitchell, Yelle and Devji on monotheism. Puett's chapter on China alludes to a somewhat different paradigm but one that also involved the ethicization of the emperorship, whose Mandate from Heaven depended on his virtue (a limitation on divinization), and the generation of countermovements to it. Yet it is entirely obvious that in the following millennia, neither secular rule nor serious restraints on monarchy was the result. First, in areas affected by the Axial Age, transcendentalist forms of sacred kingship increasingly took center stage. Second, as noted above in the discussion of Islam, there were many powerful forces at work that would ensure that the office of kingship was always subject to reenchantment, that is, to the lure of divinization.[31]

The impulse to divinize kings even in staunchly transcendentalist societies remained palpable far into what scholarship now increasingly refers to as the early modern period. Whatever the other merits of early modernity as a global paradigm, then, it cannot be extended to incorporate any significant disenchantment of authority. On the contrary, the huge Eurasian empires, constructed between 1500 and 1800, and the growing attempts on the part of emperors to gain control over the religious sphere only enhanced the appeal of divinized kingship in many areas. While in Christian Europe, more emphatically transcendentalist understandings of kingship and legitimate sovereignty began to take hold with the Reformation—a process with a weaker echo in the seventeenth- and eighteenth-century Islamic world—here too a form of sacred kingship remained in place.

Nevertheless, the divinized element of sacred kingship in Europe (already more muted in comparison to many other regions) was eventually rendered almost entirely unsustainable. Historians have long argued about the chronology and ultimate causes of the waning power of sacred kingship in Europe.[32] Appropriately alert to the dangers of teleology, they have also questioned grand narratives predicated on the coherence and radicalism of the scientific revolution and the Enlightenment. But these criticisms have yet to yield any alternative causal pathways that might help to explicate the momentous transformations that need explanation.[33] That is, from a truly global perspective, it will surely prove difficult to detach the process of the actual disenchantment of political authority from the long-term secularizing potential of movements in

European-Atlantic history, while its extension to other parts of the world was intimately bound up with the ascension of Western hegemony in all its guises. Questions abound. To what extent did the decentering of kingship from the political sphere and the unleashing of mass movements drive or reflect the secularization of political authority? What was the overall impact of European imperialism on monarchism?[34] This volume has not offered overview chapters on the shift into modernity, and so we will not attempt to answer these questions here. Still, it is an intriguing empirical starting point to note that it is precisely in three countries least affected by colonial interference—Thailand, Japan, and Nepal—that we see divinized kingship surviving most clearly in something like its premodern form.[35]

By contrast, in modern Europe, the impulse to divinize the ruler was eventually repressed. *Repression* is used here in a Freudian sense, which is to say that the divinization impulse was not so much suppressed as encrypted. It became an ideal that lay submerged beneath common knowledge but could not be well acknowledged, a type of public secret. Paradox attended every step of this journey. According to Robert Yelle's chapter, Thomas Hobbes founded modern political philosophy while invoking the archetypal divinized king, the pharaoh, as a model.

Hobbes's *Leviathan* (1651) was written during the civil war in Britain in which a combination of ultra-reformed transcendentalism in the shape of Puritanism and a resurrection of ancient classical ideas of liberty in republicanism had come together to help rebels briefly conceive of a society without kings. Thus, a certain potential lurking in the Greek and Jewish forms of the Axial Age came to fruition in the form of Charles I (r. 1625–49) being marched to the gallows after insisting upon his divine right. But in practice, it remained almost impossible to conceive of order without its personification in the figure of a sovereign.[36] And he implicitly understood the way in which divinized kingship, as epitomized by the Egyptian pharaoh, allowed for a far greater monopolization of the social power of the religion by the sovereign.[37] Yelle argues convincingly that Hobbes was surreptitiously upholding the pharaoh as a superior model of authority. We might add that he was moved by the disorder that may result when the transcendentalist subordination of sovereignty to the arbitration of the moral community of the faithful is allowed to run amok. The civil war and the previous European wars of religion had revealed as much.

In Hobbes's model, obedience to the state must come first. But his sovereign is only a righteous ruler in a most attenuated sense. The authority of the "mortal God" does not derive from his capacity to drive forward the communal pursuit of salvation. Instead, it famously derives from a social contract, which in turn is the only possible solution to the workings of the most basic laws of nature. Nor, however, is Hobbes really advocating a return to divinized kingship. The sovereign is only a "mortal God" in the most metaphorical of senses. He is defined by his possession of the same absolute authority that belongs to the immortal God, but God himself was subject to an unusual and extreme form of transcendentalization such that he became a profoundly unknowable and practically otiose First Mover, whose voice (scripture) was in effect submerged into that of the sovereign's.[38] If the sovereign stands in for him, this does not equate to any immanent power. He is certainly not credited with the supernatural capacities of fertility or cosmic regulation exhibited by the pharaoh. If it seems absurd to even point this out, it is no more than a measure of how different Hobbes's materialist ontology is to immanentism. Likewise, Hobbes radically innovated by leaving behind much of the traditional transcendentalist conception of kingship. The threat to sovereign authority from salvationist religion in particular—speaking to men's deepest fears about death—was immense, and it must be not only harnessed but neutered. Many have described his work as the birth of modern secularism; it certainly helped to disenchant politics while also suppressing the logic of righteous kingship.[39]

In an extremely abstract sense, what Hobbes's nascent political modernity and the Axial Age's religious modernity had in common was a shift toward intellectualization. Secular forms of politics and scriptural forms of religion attempt to circumvent the sacred body of the king and the ritual purity of the priest, respectively. This circumvention was surely intertwined with the development of new technologies of communication, including the spread of democratic forms of writing, and the rise of common literacy. These leaps in communicative power are a feature of both the Axial Age and modernity broadly conceived, the latter merely intensifying via the printing press and mass education what had begun in the former. The Axial Age had produced new types of philosophy and narrative literature that were surely enabled by writing—even if the case of India apparently bears witness to the capacity of traditions of oral disputations and mnemonic techniques to adduce similar results. The post–Axial Age canonization of texts and scholarly exegesis, meanwhile, is more straightforwardly associated with literacy. These new textual traditions brought an intense critical reflection to bear on the major conundrums of human existence. As Nicole Jerr shows, Henrik Ibsen's nineteenth-century play on the fourth-century Roman emperor Julian the Apostate is the epitome of such an intellectual and affective exercise.

In his impossibly long and anguished play—it would take eight hours to perform it on stage—Ibsen comes to term with a disenchanted post-Christian modern sense of self by examining the inner life of the first post-Christian Roman emperor. As Jerr puts it, Julian and the modern individual are both "beset by the anxieties symptomatic of an attempt to move beyond the Judeo-Christian worldview," repudiating Christianity yet deeply shaped by it nonetheless. In Ibsen's world, sacred kingship was already dead; it was now the self that was ostensibly sovereign—a legacy of transcendentalism that was also falling away. Just as Ibsen or the modern self is caught between transcendentalism and modernity, so Julian is caught between transcendentalism and immanentism. Both want to repudiate Christianity while not being free of it. Julian's neo-immanentism is not really a return to the status quo ante; the modern individual cannot operate as if transcendentalism never happened either. To put it plainly, for Ibsen, there is no going back even if one loses faith or if one finds secularism unbearably soulless. The world has changed irrevocably with the rise of monotheism/modernity.

Jerr's chapter leads us to the observation, more broadly, about the continuing impress of intellectualization from the Axial Age to modernity. Ibsen's lesson can be absorbed by modern individuals only via reading and lonely reflection. Who would sit together now in front of a stage for an eight-hour play? Consider, by contrast, the Greek tragedies, written amid the anxieties of the world's first experiment with democratic rule.[40] The Athenians enacted these plays from dawn to dusk, began the performance with a blood sacrifice to the gods, and required every voting male citizen to be present and share the affective burden. Despite being composed as written literature, Greek tragedies were consumed by their intended audience in a manner that was both physically and emotionally arduous. Surely, ancient Greece was much closer to the conundrum of politics without the king than modern Europe. Unlike the modern political citizen, whose imagination was moulded by print capitalism of the newspaper and the novel, the Greek citizen still had to participate communally and bodily in the emerging polity shaped by new forms of literature. In this sense, the Greek sensation of communal sovereignty was more deeply realized in their small city-states than in it would be in the democracies of vast modern states more than two millennia later. Nevertheless, the thread that ties the two cases together is the dependence on innovative literary forms.

Postcolonial political Islam, however, provides a sharply divergent case study to the end of kingship in modern times. In Devji's chapter on ISIS, transcendentalism roars back to life in an extreme form that attempts to cast aside not only sacred kingship but kingship per se, and not only kingship but even politics itself. The covenantal theology explored by Assmann in terms of its biblical origins is reanimated in a purist form in the guise of ISIS. If the Israelites were reduced to dispossession and kinglessness by exile, the Muslim world was stripped of its righteous kings by European colonialism. Both conditions yielded visions of people and God as unmediated by kingship, leaving only the transcendent law as the means by which the former may relate to the latter. In the case of Islam, the "massive compromise" with sacred kingship, as explored in the chapters by Al-Azmeh and by Gommans and Huseini, that had characterized much of premodern Islamic history was cast aside. Thus, the colonial destruction of Muslim kingship and the subsequent rise of the secular state cast Muslim majority populations into a situation in which the antipolitical strain could flourish as never before. Indeed, if secularism was produced by cleansing earthly politics not only of immanentist enchantment but also of righteous transcendentalism, then the fiercest opposition to it came from zealous proponents of the latter.

In keeping with some other Islamist movements, ISIS takes certain tendencies present within transcendentalism, especially its monotheistic form, to an extreme conclusion. These include taking up an ultra-"offensive" stance that is insistent on the fraudulent nature of other visions of reality—a zealous imposition of the Mosaic Distinction. ISIS ideology banishes all attempts to make the transcendent immanent, whether through mystical experience, reason, or supernatural presence—all, that is, except the law. By imposing a state of emergency, it creates what Assmann calls "total religion," that is, the direct and spoken will of God takes over all other aspects of culture, including the sphere of politics; the friend/foe distinction is aligned with divinity so that enemies of God become your enemy.[41]

Driven by a totalizing vision, ISIS completely rejects the territorial nation-state and its laws as an unacceptable return to paganism. It denies any claim of the nation and its land to be treated as sacred and set apart. It is no wonder then that ISIS took root precisely where the nation state had badly frayed. There is a genuine analogy to be pursued here with the tendency in Protestantism to reject all forms of accessing the transcendent except the written Word.[42] In general, radical "reform" movements tend to repudiate all forms of terrestrial sovereignty. Sometimes these take the form of millenarian movements in which the City of God will truly arrive on earth. In other words, if a mundane instantiation of the divine law is practically impossible, a millenarian vision allows it to become possible in the realm of the future.

In less totalizing instantiations, transcendentalist traditions have allowed rulers to become acceptable and even vital by rendering them righteous—by making them mere vehicles for scriptural truth and the societal quest for salvation. At first glance, ISIS appears to conform to this move by yielding a caliph figure. However, the ISIS caliph's role is relatively trivial and is overshadowed by the role accorded to the law itself. ISIS denies its caliph the possibility of acting as a kind of incarnation of the law or even a great protector of it. In one sense,

ISIS even denies the possibility of *righteous politics*, instead replacing it with *righteous society*. Nevertheless, such stark visions of transcendentalism render clearly the impossibility of institutionalizing politics without immanentist rites of embodiment and emplacement that all nation-states use to harness their citizens together to a common cause.

If sovereignty embodied in a ruler was torn away from the Islamic world in the colonial period, in Nepal, both sacred kingship and a remarkably immanentist version of Hinduism endured into the twenty-first century. Indeed, this case is so compelling because, in Nepal, the second great shift explored by this volume (the transition to the modern secular state) has only been accomplished in the last fifteen years. As noted earlier, Nepal might be usefully placed alongside Thailand to explore what happens when an embodied divinized sovereignty meets the forces of the modern world. Of course, there was also a nineteenth- and twentieth-century history to this encounter. Yet it was in the thirty years of the Panchayat regime (1960–1990) that the most significant tensions were generated. On the one hand, both the king's political centrality and his divinization were reasserted: at King Birendra's coronation ritual in 1975, he was rendered a "walking Vishnu." On the other hand, this was "the period when the foundations of Nepal's modernization were laid," when literacy shot up and a national infrastructure was constructed.[43]

Even when the Panchyat regime fell in 1990, the new constitution took for granted the foundational role of the monarchy, while the lines of the general public queueing up to receive blessings at the Dasain festival only increased in length. Yet from 1996, the country faced a modern secularism in its most revolutionary and violent incarnation through a Maoist insurgency, while an underlying dynamic of modernization was already producing "increasing denials and embarrassment around claims that the king is supposed to be viewed as a god."[44] The urgent question became: What to do about the physical presence of the king as the foundation stone of collective national life, his role in an annual ritual cycle, his magnified reality in the shape of the palace? Hurriedly the palace was transformed into a museum, and the president ushered in to take his place in the great national festivals.

Unlike in the ISIS case, two opposing dynamics were at work in modern Nepal. One was driven by Western forms of political disenchantment, colored by Protestant views of religion, which finally penetrated this region of the world. In this view, the divinity of the king became an embarrassing question, provoking awkward laughter, denial, apologies, and convoluted explanations from the Nepali political elite. For the West, the remnants of Nepali sacred kingship served as a form of Orientalist voyeurism, a fetishization of indigenous customs.

By deflecting the question of the divinity of their ruler, Nepali officialdom tried to downplay the cosmic and heroic aspects of Hindu kingship. Nonetheless, it is significant that these aspects could not be entirely done away with. At most, they could be mummified in the museum. This is due to the second dynamic at work in Nepal, the immanentist impulse to sacralize politics. This impulse continued among the wider population, making itself felt most strongly during large-scale festivals that required the country's president or some other functionary to serve as bodily replacements for the monarch. The last Nepali king may have abdicated, but the collective need for his sacred body lived on.

It is ultimately difficult to deny that, around much of the world, politics—if not modernity itself—has been shaped by certain processes of secularization, including the disenchantment of the public sphere. Yet this state of affairs is a blip on the scale of world history. It is so new that there is no consensus on whether to treat it as the beginning of a new era or as a passing fad that retreated within a century or so into postmodernity, postsecularism, the return of religion, and the reenchantment of politics. Our goal in this volume, then, was to pull ourselves out of these hypersensitive debates to view the world from afar so that, a bit like in Scipio's dream, humanity's immediate political and religious concerns appear small and manageable, if only for the duration of the dream. The perspective afforded by such distance allows one to see the newness of the modern age in light of the newness of the Axial Age. If modernity subordinated religion to politics, it was simply a twist on the Axial Age, which had invented religion as a new form of politics. Nonetheless, transcendentalism's victory was ever a partial one. Under its sign, ethicized religion and sacralized politics were destined to coexist in the manner of a single organism composed of genetically different material, separate yet inseparable, different but always together. This surreal chimera-like entity was not erased by modern secularism but repressed, which merely ensured its repeated return.

NOTES

1. As chapter 1 noted, current debates within political theology and critical treatments of secular politics tend to be anthropologically thin and temporally shallow. For a recent attempt to correct this imbalance, see https://tif.ssrc.org/2019/09/04/cfp-deprovincializing-political-theology/.

2. See Marshall Sahlins's chapter 2, this volume. Legitimation theory is described as necessary but insufficient in Alan Strathern, *Unearthly Powers: Religious and Political Change in World History* (Cambridge: Cambridge University Press, 2019), 110–14.
3. In and of itself, the latter is not then a feature particular to transcendentalisms. Luiz Costa and Carlos Fausto present Amazonia as conforming to a somewhat different model, seeing spirit masters as ill-accommodated within a pyramidal and nested hierarchy. Rather, they argue, hierarchical spiritual relations were a result of analogism and state construction. See Luiz Costa and Carlos Fausto, "The Enemy, the Unwilling Guest and the Jaguar Host," *L'Homme* 231–232 (2019): 195–226,
4. Strathern, *Unearthly Powers*, 31–33.
5. Peter Gose, chapter 3 this volume. "These distinctions (which on death became separations) were primarily material in nature and to that extent were immanent, not transcendental." Compare James Maffie's depiction of the Aztec worldview as pantheistic, insofar as power/*teotl* runs through it all, but also internally differentiated and thus productively interwoven. See James Maffie, *Aztec Philosophy: Understanding a World in Motion* (Louisville: University Press of Colorado, 2014), 513 on "*neplanta*."
6. Michael Puett, chapter 7.
7. As Gellner's chapter indicates with the remarkable assistance of opinion polls on the Nepalese monarchy, the divinity of the king may be something at once believed and disbelieved, although this may be the result of secularizing processes mentioned below. One longstanding way of comprehending this issue is through distinguishing the office from the mortal tenant, as Assmann tells us the ancient Egyptians did.
8. Note that the same strategy of divinizing him through kinship to the gods is still evident: he was, for example, "cared for by the goddess Nintur." See chapter 4 by Nicole Brisch in this volume.
9. Gellner notes the political misfortune attributed to neglect of the gods in these festivals. Kings were the lead sacrificers of their realms.
10. See chapter 5 by Jan Assmann in this volume.
11. See chapter 3 by Peter Gose in this volume.
12. David Graeber, *Debt: The First 5,000 Years* (Brooklyn: Melville House, 2011). Richard Seaford, *Money and the Early Greek Mind: Homer, Philosophy, Tragedy* (Cambridge: Cambridge University Press, 2004). Both Graeber and Seaford were present at the conference that led to this volume, the former as participant and the latter as an engaged audience member.
13. This topic is also explored in Michael Puett, "Early China in Eurasian History," in *A Companion to Chinese History*, ed. Michael Szonyi (Chichester: Wiley, 2017).
14. It may be that this monopolization of the religious sphere in Assyria can be related to both a more determined dynastic centralization of power and a more emphatic form of ruler divinization, conforming to the pattern noted in Strathern, *Unearthly Powers*, 213–6, but Nicole Brisch indicates that more research would be necessary here. See her chapter 4 in this volume.

15. The SESHAT initiative (http://seshatdatabank.info/) is a welcome attempt to provide greater rigor to the comparative method through the construction of a vast dataset that covers a much more diverse range of societies than theoreticians of the Axial Age normally attend to. Some of their proxies for axiality do indeed have an affinity with the points made about the political implications of axiality discussed here. Points 6–12 of their list are: (6) Equating Elites and Commoners, (7) Equating Rulers and Commoners, (8) Formal Legal Code, (9) General Applicability of Law, (10) Constraint on Executive, (11) Full-Time Bureaucrats, and (12) Impeachment. However, for reasons that we hope are clear from this volume, framed in this way and coded simply in terms of presence or absence, these attributes are unlikely to help us identify how and when societies were affected by the most distinctive features of the Axial Age. Indeed, the overall list of the proxies of the Axial Age would need fine-tuning. Hence it is not so surprising that they find the correlation between these proxies and the standard cases of the Axial Age to be weaker than is typically imagined (although still, in fact, correlated to some extent). See D. A. Mullins et al, "A Systematic Assessment of 'Axial Age' Proposals Using Global Comparative Historical Evidence," *American Sociological Review* 83 (2018): 596–626.
16. Chapter 1 did not explicitly address the way in which Hinduism or Confucianism might be inserted into the model; this is now undertaken in Alan Strathern, *Converting Kings: Kongo, Thailand, Japan and Hawaii Compared, 1450–1850* (Cambridge: Cambridge University Press, forthcoming the companion volume to *Unearthly Powers*. It is debatable whether the term *transcendentalism* can be stretched to include Confucianism, although it clearly is an important part of the wider family of Axial Age traditions.
17. See chapter 4 by Nicole Brisch, especially endnote 3, in this volume.
18. We would like to thank Richard Seaford for his insights on ritual, which he shared with us during the conference. See Richard Seaford, "The Interiorisation of Ritual in India and Greece," in *Universe and Inner Self in Early Indian and Early Greek Thought*, ed. Richard Seaford (Edinburgh: Edinburgh University Press, 2016), 204–219, which considers the way in which, in both Greece and India, the interiorization of cosmic rite of passage rituals, and their consequent implications for individualization, may have issued from monetization. Matylda Obryk shows how the Greek philosophical tradition, from Xenophanes onward, first shows forms of skepticism toward immanentist ritualism and then yields movements toward monotheistic-devotional forms of transcendentalism in a way that offers comparison with certain ancient Indian trends. Matylda Obryk, "On Affirmation, Rejection and Accommodation of the World in Greek and Indian Religion," in *Universe and Inner Self in Early Indian and Early Greek Thought*, ed. Richard Seaford (Edinburgh: Edinburgh University Press, 2016), 235–50.
19. Yuri Pines, *Foundations of Confucian Thought: Intellectual Life in the Chunqiu Period, 722–453 B.C.E* (Honolulu: University of Hawai'i Press, 2002), 55. Meanwhile, the effect of neo-Confucianism on China has been compared to the impact of Protestantism on northern Europe. See Victor Lieberman, *Strange Parallels: Mainland Mirrors: Europe, Japan, China, South Asia, and the Islands* (Cambridge: Cambridge University Press, 2009), 39, 95, 514–15, passim, following Phillip Gorski.

The argument is that, in both cases, a disciplinary revolution, inculcating an ethic of duty and emotional restraint, produced efficient economies and highly effective states.

20. The shared immanentist logic of the ritual function is what lies behind the comparability of the Chinese case and many African kingships, as noted by Jeroen Duindam, "The Court as a Meeting Point: Cohesion, Competition, Control," in *Prince, Pen, and Sword: Eurasian Perspectives*, ed. Jeroen Duindam and Maaike Van Berkel, vol. 15 (Leiden: Brill, 2018), 32–128, 91.

21. See chapter 1 in this volume, and Strathern, *Unearthly Powers*, 199–204.

22. Furthermore, where kings are held subject to divine punishment not simply for ritual failures (consider the accounts of the fall of Sennacherib or Naram-Sin) but for unethical behavior (note the warning of the *Advice to a Prince*, "If a king does not heed justice, his people will be thrown into chaos, and his land will be devastated") then this may be considered a step toward a more typically transcendentalist understanding. See Nicole Brisch's chapter in this volume and compare the Chinese Mandate of Heaven.

23. Jan Assmann, *The Price of Monotheism*, trans. Robert Savage (Stanford, CA: Stanford University Press, 2010). In Assmann's chapter 5n15, in this volume, Assmann does point to some intriguing ways in which the concept of Ma'at, an impersonal principle of truth, justice, and order, gestures toward the transcendent.

24. See Jan Assmann's chapter 5 in this volume.

25. This underscores the affinity between stranger-kingship and immanentism, although there are other elements of monarchical systems that give rise to stranger-kingship. See Alan Strathern, "The Digestion of the Foreign in Sri Lankan History, c. 500–1850 CE," in *Sri Lanka at the Crossroads of History*, ed. Zoltán Biedermann and Alan Strathern (London: UCL, 2017).

26. One can see this already prefigured in an ethicized understanding of the way in which the gods relate to rulers: in Hesiod, for example, misbehaving kings were subject to the chastisements of Zeus served by Justice.

27. By one argument, it was Mani who conceptualized the idea of Book religion but because Mani's religion did not survive the competition from Christianity, Islam, and Buddhism, he is rarely given credit for this idea. See Guy Stroumsa, *The Making of the Abrahamic Religions in Late Antiquity* (Oxford: Oxford University Press, 2015).

28. A. Azfar Moin, "Sovereign Violence: Temple Destruction in India and Shrine Desecration in Iran and Central Asia," *Comparative Studies in Society and History* 57, no. 2 (2015): 467–96.

29. This insight derives from Victor Lieberman's distinction between the exposed and protected zones of Eurasia in Lieberman, *Strange Parallels*, vol 2.

30. "Political" is in scare quotes precisely because our modern categories fail to describe what these offices were

31. Strathern, *Unearthly Powers*, 204–17, sketches out five of these forces.

32. There is a scholarly trend to argue against any profound desacralization of kingship throughout the eighteenth century in France and elsewhere, although note that this is not quite the same as a diminution of divinization per se. See Anne Byrne,

Death and the Crown: Ritual and Politics in France Before the Revolution (Manchester: Manchester University Press, 2020); Michael Schaich, *Monarchy and Religion: The Transformation of Royal Culture in Eighteenth-Century Europe* (Oxford: Oxford University Press, 2007). Jeroen Duindam has a brief and sensible summary of the longer-term picture. Jeroen Duindam, *Dynasties: A Global History of Power, 1300–1800* (Cambridge: Cambridge University Press, 2015), 310–14

33. Jonathan Sheehan, "Enlightenment, Religion, and the Enigma of Secularization: A Review Essay," *The American Historical Review* 108, no. 4 (2003): 1061–1080.

34. European empire itself could function as an agent of monarchism while also clearly undermining the political relevance of sacred kingship in certain ways. See Milinda Banerjee, *The Mortal God: Imagining the Sovereign in Colonial India* (Cambridge: Cambridge University Press, 2018.

35. Although, even here, of course, monarchy has been profoundly shaped by secularization. See the case of Japan in John Breen, "The Quality of Emperorship in 21st Century Japan: Reflections on the Reiwa Accession," *The Asia-Pacific Journal* 18 (2020): 1–24. For the influence of Western powers in nineteenth century Thailand, see Peter A. Jackson, "The Performative State: Semi-Coloniality and the Tyranny of Images in Modern Thailand," *Sojourn: Journal of Social Issues in Southeast Asia* 19, no. 2 (2004): 219–53.

36. Yelle's chapter 10 in this volume brings this out strongly. See also Kevin Sharpe, *Image Wars: Kings and Commonwealths in England, 1603–1660* (New Haven, CT: Yale University Press, 2010), 540–1.

37. Somewhat analogously to chapter 1, Hobbes proceeds from the psychological bases of religion to its Durkheimian utility as a kind of social cement. Thus, innate cognitive-emotional properties such as anxiety and curiosity were seeds nurtured by people, including "the founders of Commonwealths, and the lawgivers of the Gentiles" in order to make men "the more apt to Obedience, Lawes, Peace, Charity and civill society." See Thomas Hobbes, *Leviathan*, ed. R. Tuck, (Cambridge: Cambridge University Press 1996), 79.

38. Agostino Lupoli, "Hobbes and Religion Without Theology," in *The Oxford Handbook of Hobbes*, ed. A. P. Martinich and Kinch Hoekstra (Oxford: Oxford University Press, 2016). How this distant God was to be conceived, given Hobbes's materialist attack on superstitions regarding incorporeal spirits, was a conundrum. See Jon Parkin, "Hobbes and the Future of Religion" in *Hobbes on Politics and Religion*, ed. Laurens van Apeldoorn and Robin Douglass (Oxford: Oxford University Press, 2018), 196. For J. G. A. Pocock, Hobbes cleared a space for his radical reflections on sovereignty by confining God's kingdom to the past (when he spoke directly to Moses) and the future (the millennial kingdom): the present was the sovereign's time. See J. G. A. Pocock, "*Time, History* and *Eschatology* in the Thought of Thomas Hobbes" in *Politics, Language and Time: Essays on Political Thought and History* (Chicago: Chicago University Press, 1989), 148–201.

39. Mark Lilla, *The Stillborn God: Religion, Politics, and the Modern West* (New York: Knopf, 2007), 88. This is to reflect on the long-term effects of Hobbes rather than to describe what he thought he was doing or how his ideas related to contemporaries, although many of the latter were naturally disgusted. See Sarah Mortimer,

"Christianity and Civil Religion in Hobbes's *Leviathan*," in *The Oxford Handbook of Hobbes*, ed. A. P. Martinich and Kinch Hoekstra (Oxford: Oxford University Press, 2016), 515–6, and Parkin, "Hobbes and the Future of Religion."

40. The literature on Greek tragedy is vast. A succinct and engaging discussion for nonspecialists based on the work of Friedrich Nietzsche, Christiane Sourvinou-Inwood, and Christian Meier, among others, can be found in Robert Bellah, *Religion in Human Evolution: From the Paleolithic to the Axial Age* (Cambridge, MA: Belknap Press, 2011), 352–60.

41. Jan Assmann, "Total Religion: Politics, Monotheism, and Violence," in *From Akhenaten to Moses: Ancient Egypt and Religious Change* (Cairo: American University in Cairo Press, 2014), 113–29.

42. Note, however, that unlike Protestantism and in a somewhat contra-transcendentalist vein, the ISIS mode was to shift attention away from the self and on to sheer performance and observance.

43. See David N. Gellner's chapter 12 in this volume.

44. Gellner, chapter 12 in this volume.

Bibliography

"CFP: Deprovincializing Political Theology: Postcolonial and Comparative Approaches." *The Immanent Frame*. September 4, 2019. https://tif.ssrc.org/2019/09/04/cfp-deprovincializing-political-theology/.

"Seshat: Global History Databank." *Evolution Institute & Seshat Project*. Accessed April 17, 2021. http://seshatdatabank.info/.

"Video: Islamic state media branch releases 'The End of Sykes-Picot.'" July 1, 2014. *The Belfast Telegraph*. https://www.belfasttelegraph.co.uk/video-news/video-islamic-state-media-branch-releases-the-end-of-sykes-picot-30397575.html.

Abbasi, Rushain. "Did Pre-Modern Muslims Distinguish the Religious and the Secular? The *Dīn-Dunyā* Binary in Medieval Islamic Thought." *Journal of Islamic Studies* 31 (2020): 185–225.

Abercrombie, Thomas. *Pathways of Memory and Power: Ethnography and History among an Andean People*. Madison: University of Wisconsin Press, 1998.

Acosta, José de. *Historia natural y moral de las indias*. Madrid: Historia 16, 1590 [1987].

Adhikari, A. *The Bullet and the Ballot Box: The Story of Nepal's Maoist Revolution*. London: Verso, 2014.

Adhikari, I. *Military and Democracy in Nepal*. London: Routledge, 2015.

Aelian. *Varia Historia*. Ed. R. Hercher. Lipsiae: Aedibus B. G. Teubneri, 1866.

Agamben, Giorgio. *Homo Sacer: Sovereign Power and Bare Life*. Meridian: Crossing Boundaries. Trans. Daniel Heller-Roazen. Stanford, CA: Stanford University Press, 1998.

Agamben, Giorgio. "Stasis." In *The Omnibus Homo Sacer*, 247–92. Stanford, CA: Stanford University Press, 2017.

Alam, Muzaffar. *The Languages of Political Islam: India, 1200–1800*. Chicago: University of Chicago Press, 2004.

Alam, Muzaffar, and Sanjay Subrahmanyam. "Frank Disputations: Catholics and Muslims at the Court of Jahangir (1608–11)." *Indian Economic and Social History Review* 46, no. 4 (2009): 457–511.

Al-Azmeh, Aziz. "Al-Iṣlāḥīyūn al-nahḍawīyūn wa fikrat al-iṣlāḥ." *Al-Mustaqbal al-'Arabī* 455 (2017): 75–99.

Al-Azmeh, Aziz. *Arabic Thought and Islamic Societies*. New York: Routledge Library Editions, 2014.

Al-Azmeh, Aziz. *The Arabs and Islam in Late Antiquity*. Berlin: Gerlach Press, 2014.

Al-Azmeh, Aziz. "Chronophagous Discourse." In *The Times of History*, 139–64. New York: Central European University Press, 2007.

Al-Azmeh, Aziz. *The Emergence of Islam in Late Antiquity: Allah and His People*. New York: Cambridge University Press, 2014.

BIBLIOGRAPHY

Al-Azmeh, Aziz. "God's Caravan: Topoi and Schemata in the History of Muslim Political Thought." In *Mirror for the Muslim Prince: Islam and the Theory of Statecraft*, ed. Mehrzad Boroujerdi, 326–397. Syracuse, NY: Syracuse University Press, 2013.

Al-Azmeh, Aziz. "Monotheistic Monarchy." In *The Times of History*, 267–289. New York: Central European University Press, 2007.

Al-Azmeh, Aziz. *Muslim Kingship: Power and the Sacred in Muslim, Christian and Pagan Polities*. London: I.B. Tauris, 1997.

Albornoz, Cristóbal de. "Instrucción para Descubrir todas las Guacas del Piru y sus Camayos y Haziendas." *Journal de la Société des Américanistes* 56, no. 1 (1967): 8–39.

Al-i Davoud, Sayed Ali. *Tarikh-i Alfi: Tarikh-i Iran wa Kishvarha-yi Hamsaya dar Salha-yi 850–984H* (*Tarikh-i Alfi*: History of Iran and the Neighbouring Countries from 850–984H). Tehran: Intisharat-i Fikr-i Ruz, 1377/1999.

Allami, Abul Fazl. *Ai n-i Akbari*. Ed. H. Blochmann. 3 vols. Calcutta: Asiatic Society of Bengal, 1872.

Allami, Abul Fazl. *The History of Akbar*. Ed. and trans. Wheeler M. Thackston. 7 vols. Cambridge, MA: Harvard University Press/Murty Classical Library of India, 2017–21.

Allen, M. *The Cult of Kumari: Virgin Worship in Nepal*. Kirtipur: INAS, TU, 1975.

Al-Sammān, Muḥammad Ḥayyān, *Fī Tadbīr al-qadāsa: Adab al-Dukhūl ʿalā al-Sulṭān fī al-Turāth al-ʿArabī al-Islāmī*. Doha, Arab Centre for Research, 2018.

Al-Ṣābī, Hilāl. *Rusūm Dār al-Khilāfa* (*The Rules and Regulations of the ʿAbbāsid Court*). Trans. Elie A. Salem. Beirut: American University of Beirut, 1977.

al-Sammān, Muḥammad Ḥayyān. *Fī Tadbīr al-qadāsa: Adab al-Dukhūl ʿalā al-Sulṭān fī al-Turāth al-ʿArabī al-Islāmī*. Doha: Arab Centre for Research, 2018.

Alvi, M. A., and A. Rahman. *Shah Fathullah Shirazi: A Sixteenth Century Indian Scientist*. New Delhi: National Institute of Sciences of India, 1968.

Amanat, Abbas. "Persian Nuqṭawīs and the Shaping the Doctrine of 'Universal Conciliation' (*ṣulḥ-i kull*) in Mughal India." In *Unity in Diversity: Mysticism, and Construction of Religious Authority in Islam*, ed. Orkhan Mir-Kasimov, 367–93. Leiden: Brill, 2014.

Ambos, Claus. *Der König im Gefängnis und das Neujahrsfest im Herbst. Mechanismen der Legitimation des babylonischen Herrschers im 1. Jahrtausend v. Chr. und ihre Geschichte*. Dresden: ISLET Verlag, 2013.

Amir-Moezzi. Mohammad Ali. *The Divine Guide in Early Shi'sim*. Trans. David Streight. Albany: New York University Press, 1994.

Amir-Moezzi. Mohammad Ali, Maria de Cillis, Daniel De Smet, and Orkhan Mir-Kasimov, eds. *L'ésoterisme shi'ite, ses raciness et ses prolongements*. Turnhout, Belgium: Brepols, 2017.

Andani, Khalil. "Metaphysics of Muhammad: The Nur Muhammad from Imam Jaʿfar al-Sadiq (d.148/765) to Nasir al-Din al-Tusi (d.672/1274)." *Journal of Sufi Studies* 8 (2019): 99–175.

Anderson, Benedict. *Imagined Communities: Reflections on the Origin and Spread of Nationalism*. New York: Verso, 1990.

Annas, J. *Virtue and Law in Plato and Beyond*. Oxford: Oxford University Press, 2017.

Anonymous. "The Mystery of ISIS," *The New York Review of Books*. August 13, 2015. http://www.nybooks.com/articles/archives/2015/aug/13/mystery-isis/.

Anooshahr, Ali. "Dialogism and Territoriality in a Mughal History of the Islamic Millennium." *Journal of the Economic and Social History of the Orient* 55, no. 2–3 (2012): 220–54.

Anooshahr, Ali. "Shirazi Scholars and the Political Culture of Sixteenth-Century Indo-Persian World." *The Indian Economic and Social History Review* 51, no. 3 (2014): 331–52.

Arendt, Hannah. *On Revolution*. New York: Penguin, 1977.

Århem, Kaj, and Guido Sprenger, eds. *Animism in Southeast Asia: Persistence, Transformation and Renewal*. London: Routledge, 2016.

Aristotle. *Athenaion Politeia*. Ed. F. G. Kenyon. Oxford: Oxford University Press, 1920.

Aristotle. *Nicomachean Ethics*. Ed. I. Bywater. Oxford: Oxford University Press, 1894.

Aristotle. *Politics*. Ed. W. D. Ross. Oxford: Oxford University Press, 1957.

Arriaga, José de. *Extirpación de la Idolatría en el Perú*. In *Biblioteca de Autores Españoles*, vol. 209, 191–277. Madrid: Ediciones Atlas, 1621 [1968].
Ash-Shami, Abu Muhammad al-Adnani. "Indeed, Your Lord Is Ever-Watchful." In *Al-Qaeda 2.0: A Critical Reader*, ed. B. D. Holbrook and C. Moore, 154–67. New York: Oxford University Press, 2017.
Assmann, Jan. *Ägyptische Geheimnisse*. Munich: Wilhelm Fink Verlag, 2004.
Assmann, Jan. *From Akhenaten to Moses: Ancient Egypt and Religious Change*. Cairo: American University in Cairo Press, 2014.
Assmann, Jan. *Cultural Memory and Early Civilization: Writing, Remembrance, and Political Imagination*. Cambridge: Cambridge University Press, 2011.
Assmann, Jan. *Der König als Sonnenpriester: ein kosmographischer Begleittext zur kultischen Sonnenhymnik in thebanischen Tempeln und Gräbern*. Glückstadt: Verlag J. J. Augustin, 1970.
Assmann, Jan. *Of God and Gods: Egypt, Israel, and the Rise of Monotheism*. Madison: University of Wisconsin Press, 2008.
Assmann, Jan. *Herrschaft und Heil: Politische Theologie in Altägypten, Israel und Europa*. Munich: Hanser, 2004.
Assmann, Jan. *The Invention of Religion: Faith and Covenant in the Book of Exodus*, trans. Robert Savage. Princeton, NJ: Princeton University Press, 2018.
Assmann, Jan. "Königsdogma und Heilserwartung. Politische und kultische Chaosbeschreibungen in ägyptischen Texten." In *Apocalypticism in the Mediterranean World and in the Near East*, ed. D. Hellholm, 345–377. Tübingen: Mohr, 1983.
Assmann, Jan. *Ma'at: Gerechtigkeit und Unsterblichkeit im alten Ägypten*. Munich: C.H. Beck, 1990.
Assmann, Jan. *The Mind of Egypt: History and Meaning in the Time of the Pharaohs*. Cambridge, MA: Harvard University Press, 2003.
Assmann, Jan. *Moses the Egyptian: The Memory of Egypt in Western Monotheism*. Cambridge, MA: Harvard University Press, 1997.
Assmann, Jan. *Politische Theologie zwischen Ägypen und Israel*. 4th ed. Ed. Heinrich Meier. Munich: Carl Friedrich von Siemens Stiftung, 2017 [1992].
Assmann, Jan. *The Price of Monotheism*. Trans. Robert Savage. Stanford, CA: Stanford University Press, 2010.
Assmann, Jan. *Religion and Cultural Memory: Ten Studies*. Trans. Rodney Livingstone. Stanford, CA: Stanford University Press, 2005.
Assmann, Jan, Fritz Stolz, and Walter Burkert. *Funktionen und Leistungen des Mythos: drei altorientalische Beispiele*. Gottingen: Vandenhoeck and Ruprecht, 1982.
Bada'uni, Abd al-Qadir. *Muntakhab al-Tawarikh*. Ed. W. N. Lees and Munshi Ahmad Ali. 2 vols. Calcutta: Asiatic Society of Bengal, 1865.
Bajracharya, M., and A. Michaels. *History of the Kings of Nepal: A Buddhist Chronicle*. Vol. 1. Kathmandu: Social Science Baha and Himal, 2016.
Banerjee, Milinda. *The Mortal God: Imagining the Sovereign in Colonial India*. Cambridge: Cambridge University Press, 2018.
Barnes, Timothy D. *Ammianus Marcellinus and the Representation of Historical Reality*. Ithaca, NY: Cornell University Press, 1998.
Bashir, Shahzad. "Between Mysticism and Messianism: The Life and Thought of Muhammad Nurbakhsh (d. 1464)." PhD diss., Yale University, 1998.
Bataille, Georges. *The Accursed Share: An Essay on General Economy*. New York: Zone, 1988.
Beal, Timothy. *Religion and Its Monsters*. New York: Routledge, 2002.
Becker, Carl. *The Heavenly City of the Eighteenth-Century Philosophers*. New Haven, CT: Yale University Press, 1932.
Bellah, Robert. *Religion in Human Evolution: From the Paleolithic to the Axial Age*. Cambridge, MA: Belknap Press, 2011.
Bellah, Robert. "What Is Axial About the Axial Age?" *Archives Européens de Sociologie* 46 (2005): 69–89.

Ben-Dor Benite, Zvi, Stefanos Geroulanos, and Nicole Jerr, eds. *The Scaffolding of Sovereignty: Global and Aesthetic Perspectives on the History of a Concept*. New York: Columbia University Press, 2017.

Benjamin, Walter. *Reflections*. Ed. Peter Demetz. New York: Schocken, 1986.

Bennett, L. *Dangerous Wives and Sacred Sisters: The Social and Symbolic Roles of High-Caste Women in Nepal*. New York: Columbia University Press, 1983. Reissued by Kathmandu: Himal, 2004.

Bergeron, Katherine. "Melody and Monotone: Performing Sincerity in Republican France." In *The Rhetoric of Sincerity*, ed. E. van Alphen, M. Bal, and C. E. Smith, 44–59. Stanford, CA: Stanford University Press, 2009.

Berlekamp, Persis. *Wonder, Image, and Cosmos in Medieval Islam*. New Haven, CT: Yale University Press, 2011.

Beskow, Per. *Rex Gloriae: The Kingship of Christ in the Early Church*. Stockholm: Almqvist and Wiksell, 1962.

Betanzos, Juan de. *Suma y Naración de los Incas*. Madrid: Ediciones Atlas, 1551 [1987].

Bhattarai, B. *Monarchy vs Democracy: The Epic Fight in Nepal*. Delhi: Samkaleen Teesari Duniya, 2005.

Biedermann, Zoltán, Anna Gerritsen, and Giorgio Riella, eds. *Global Gifts: The Material Culture of Diplomacy in Early Modern Eurasia*. Cambridge: Cambridge University Press, 2018.

Biedermann, Zoltán, and Alan Strathern, eds. *Sri Lanka at the Crossroads of History*. London: UCL Press, 2017.

Binbaş, İlker Evrim. *Intellectual Networks in Timurid Iran: Sharaf al-Din ʿAlī Yazdī and the Islamicate Republic of Letters*. Cambridge: Cambridge University Press, 2016.

Black, Jeremy A. "The New Year's Ceremonies in Ancient Babylon: 'Taking Bēl by the Hand' and a Cultic Picnic." *Religion* 11 (1981): 39–59.

Black, Jeremy A., Graham Cunningham, Jarle Ebeling, Esther Flückiger-Hawker, Eleanor Robson, Jonathan Taylor, and Gabor Zólyomi. *The Electronic Text Corpus of Sumerian Literature*. Oxford: Oxford University Press, 1998–2006. http://etcsl.orinst.ox.ac.uk/.

Blackman, A. M. *The Story of King Kheops and the Magicians*. London: J.V. Books, 1988.

Blake, Stephen P. *Time in Early Modern Islam*. Cambridge: Cambridge University Press, 2013.

Bledsoe, B. "An Advertised Secret: The Goddess Taleju and the King of Kathmandu." In *Tantra in Practice*, ed. D. G. White, 195–205. Princeton, NJ: Princeton University Press, 2000.

Bloch, Maurice. *Prey into Hunter: The Politics of Religious Experience*. Cambridge: University of Cambridge Press, 1992.

Bloch, Marc. *Les rois thaumaturges: étude sur le caractère surnaturel attribué à la puissance royale particulièrement en France et en Angleterre*. Strasbourg: Istra, 1924.

Bloch, Marc. *The Royal Touch: Sacred Monarchy and Scrofula in England and France*. London: Routledge and Kegan Paul, 1973.

Blumenberg, Hans. *The Legitimacy of the Modern Age*. Trans. Robert M. Wallace. Cambridge, MA: MIT Press, 1983.

Boas, Franz. *The Central Eskimo*. Washington, DC: Government Printing Office, 1888.

Bodin, Jean. *On Sovereignty*. Ed. Julian H. Franklin. Cambridge: Cambridge University Press, 1992.

Bol, Peter K. "Emperors Can Claim Antiquity Too: Emperorship and Autocracy Under the New Policies." In *Emperor Huizong and Late Northern Song China: The Politics of Culture and the Culture of Politics*, ed. Patricia Buckley Ebrey and Maggie Bickford, 171–205. Cambridge, MA: Harvard University Asia Center, 2006.

Borre, O., S. R. Pandey, and C. K. Tiwari. *Nepalese Political Behaviour*. Delhi: Sterling, 1994.

Bosch-Puche, F. "The Egyptian Royal Titulary of Alexander the Great, I: Horus, Two Ladies, Golden Horus, and Throne Names." *Journal of Egyptian Archaeology* 99 (2013): 131–54.

Bosch-Puche, F. "The Egyptian Royal Titulary of Alexander the Great, II: Personal Name, Empty Cartouches, Final Remarks, and Appendix." *Journal of Egyptian Archaeology* 100 (2014): 89–109.

Bottéro, Jean. "The Dialogue of Pessimism and Transcendence." In J. Bottéro, *Mesopotamia. Writing, Reasoning, and the Gods*, 251–67. Chicago: University of Chicago Press, 1992.

Bourdieu, Pierre, and Jean-Claude Passeron. *Reproduction in Education, Society and Culture*. Trans. Richard Nice. London: Sage, 1977.
Bowersock, G. W. *Hellenism in Late Antiquity*. Ann Arbor: University of Michigan Press, 1990.
Bowersock, G. W. *Julian the Apostate*. Cambridge. MA: Harvard University Press, 1978.
Brack, Jonathan, "Theologies of Auspicious Kingship: The Islamization of Chinggisid Sacral Kingship in the Islamic World." *Comparative Studies in Society and History* 60 (2018): 1143–71.
Bredekamp, Horst. *Thomas Hobbes Der Leviathan: Das Urbild des modernen Staates und seine Gegenbilder, 1651–2001*. 4th ed. Berlin: Akademie Verlag, 2012.
Breen, John. "The Quality of Emperorship in 21st Century Japan: Reflections on the Reiwa Accession." *Asia-Pacific Journal* 18 (2020): 1–24.
Briant, P. *Antigone le Borgne. Les débuts de sa carrière et les problèmes de l'assemblée macédonienne*. Paris: Les Belles Lettres, 1973.
Brinkman, John Anthony. *Prelude to Empire. Babylonian Society and Politics, 747–626 B.C.* Occasional Publications of the Babylonian Fund, vol. 7. Philadelphia: University Museum, 1984.
Brisch, Nicole. "Changing Images of Kingship in Sumerian Literature." In *The Oxford Handbook of Cuneiform Cultures*, ed. K. Radner and E. Robson, 706–24. Oxford: Oxford University Press, 2011.
Brisch, Nicole. "Introduction." In *Religion and Power: Divine Kingship in the Ancient World and Beyond*, ed. Nicole Brisch, 1–11. Chicago: Oriental Institute of the University of Chicago, 2008.
Brisch, Nicole. "The Priestess and the King: The Divine Kingship of Šū-Sîn of Ur." *Journal of the American Oriental Society* 126 (2006): 161–76.
Brisch, Nicole, ed. *Religion and Power: Divine Kingship in the Ancient World and Beyond*. Chicago: Oriental Institute of the University of Chicago, 2008.
Brown, Alison. "Platonism in Fifteenth-Century Florence and Its Contribution to Early Modern Political Thought." *Journal of Modern History* 58 (1986): 383–413.
Brown, E. "Plato's Ethics and Politics in *The Republic*." In *The Stanford Encyclopedia of Philosophy*, ed. Edward N. Zalta, 2017. https://plato.stanford.edu/archives/fall2017/entries/plato-ethics-politics/
Browning, Robert. *The Emperor Julian*. Berkeley: University of California Press, 1976.
Brumbaugh, Robert. "The Rainbow Serpent in the Upper Sepik." *Anthropos* 82 (1987): 25–33.
Brunner, Hellmutt. *Die Geburt des Gottkönigs: Studien zur Überlieferung eines altägyptischen Mythos*. Wiesbaden: Harrassowitz Verlag, 1964.
Buc, Philippe. "Civil War and Religion in Medieval Japan and Medieval Europe: War for the Gods, Emotions at Death and Treason." *The Indian Economic and Social History Review* 57, no. 2 (2020): 261–87.
Buckler, F. W. "Firdausī's *Shāhnāma* and the *Genealogia Regni Dei*." Supplement 1, *Journal of the American Oriental Society* (1935): 1–21.
Buraselis, K., et al. "Einleitung: Terminologische Vorklärung" s.v. "Heroiserung und Apotheose." In *ThesCRA*, ed. K. Buraselis et al., vol. 2, 126–129. Los Angeles: J. Paul Getty Museum, 2004.
Burghart, F. *The Conditions of Listening: Essays on Religion, History and Politics in South Asia*, ed. C. J. Fuller and J. Spencer. Delhi: Oxford University Press, 1996.
Burke, Edmund. *A Philosophical Enquiry into the Sublime and the Beautiful*. London: Penguin, 2004.
Byrne, Anne. *Death and the Crown: Ritual and Politics in France Before the Revolution*. Manchester: Manchester University Press, 2020.
Cahen, Claude. "Mouvements populaires et autonomisme urbain dans l'Asie Musulmane du Moyen Age." *Arabica* 5 (1958): 225–50, and 6 (1959): 223–65.
Caillois, Roger. *L'Homme et le sacré*. 3rd ed. Paris: Gallimard, 1950.
Cannadine, David, and Simon Price, eds. *Rituals of Royalty: Power and Ceremonial in Traditional Societies*. Cambridge: Cambridge University Press, 1987.
Carboni, Stefano. *The Wonders of Creation and the Singularities of Painting*. Edinburgh: Edinburgh University Press, 2015.

Carnevero, M. "*Nomothesia* in Classical Athens: What Sources Should We Believe?" *Classical Quarterly* 63 (2013): 139–60.

Carney, E. D. *Women and Monarchy in Macedonia*. Norman: University of Oaklahoma Press, 2000.

Carrithers, M. "On Polytropy: Or the Natural Condition of Spiritual Cosmopolitanism in India: The Digambar Jain Case." *Modern Asian Studies* 34, no. 4 (2000): 831–61.

Chaniotis, A. "The Ithyphallic Hymn for Demetrios Poliorketes and Hellenistic Religious Mentality." In *More than Gods and Less Than Men: Studies on Royal Cult and Imperial Worship*, ed. P. P. Iossif, A. S. Chankowski, and C. C. Lorber, 157–95. Leuven: Peeters, 2011.

Chann, Naindeep. "In the Shadow of the Khan." In *Empires and Diversity: On the Crossroads of Archaeology, Anthropology, and History*, ed. Gregory E. Areshian, 231–249. Los Angeles: Cotzen Institute of Archaeology Press, 2013.

Charlesworth, Max, Howard Morphy, Diane Bell, and Kenneth Maddock, eds. *Religion in Aboriginal Australia*. St Lucua: Queensland University Press, 1984.

Cieza de León, Pedro de. *La Crónica del Perú*, Parts 1 and 2, in *Obras Completas*, vol. 1. Madrid: Consejo Superior de Investigaciones Cientificas, Instituto «Gonzalo Fernández de Oviedo», 1553 [1984].

Codrington, R. H. *The Melanesians: Studies in Their Anthropology and Folklore*. New York: Dover, 1881 [1972].

Cohen, D. *Law, Violence and Community in Classical Athens*. Cambridge: Cambridge University Press, 1995.

Conermann, Stephan. *Historiographie als Sinnstiftung: Indo-persische Geschichtsschreibung während der Mogulzeit (932–1118/1516–1707)*. Wiesbaden: Reichert Verlag, 2002.

Cook, David B. "Contemporary Martyrdom: Ideology and Material Culture." In *Jihadi Culture: The Art and Social Practices of Militant Islamists*, ed. T. Hegghammer, 151–70. Cambridge: Cambridge University Press, 2017.

Cooper, Jerrold S. *Reconstructing History from Ancient Inscriptions: the Lagash-Umma Border Conflict*. Sources from the Ancient Near East, vol. 2, fasc. 1. Malibu: Undena Publications, 1983.

Costa, Luiz and Carlos Fausto. "The Enemy, the Unwilling Guest and the Jaguar Host." *L'Homme* 231–232 (2019): 195–226.

Crielaard, J. P. "*Basileis* at Sea: Elites and External Contact in the Euboean Gulf Region from the End of the Bronze Age to the Beginning of the Iron Age." In *Ancient Greece: From the Mycenean Palaces to the Age of Homer*, ed. S. Deger-Jalkotzy and I. S. Lemos, 271–97. Edinburgh: Edinburgh University Press, 2006.

Cubelic, S., and R. Khatiwoda. "Nepalese Monarchy in an Age of Codification: Kingship, Patriotism, and Legality in the Law Code of 1854." In *Transnational Histories of the 'Royal Nation,'* eds. M. Banerjee, C. Backerra, and C. Sarti, 67–86. Cham, Switzerland: Palgrave Macmillan, 2017.

Cumont, Franz. *The Oriental Religions in Roman Paganism*. New York: Dover, 1956.

Daftary, Farhad. *The Isma'ilis: Their History and Doctrines*. Cambridge: Cambridge University Press, 1990.

Dagron, Gilbert. *Emperor and Priest. The Imperial Office in Byzantium*. Trans. Jean Birrell. Cambridge: Cambridge University Press, 2003.

Dallal, Ahmad S. *Islam Without Europe: Traditions of Reform in Eighteenth-Century Islamic Thought*. Chapel Hill: University of North Carolina Press, 2018.

Dangol, S. B. *The Palace in Nepalese Politics, with Special Reference to the Politics of 1951 to 1990*. Kathmandu: Ratna Pustak Bhandar, 1999.

Davidson, R. M. *Indian Esoteric Buddhism: A Social History of the Tantric Movement*. New York: Columbia University Press, 2002.

De Heusch, Luc. "Forms of Sacralized Power in Africa." In *The Character of Kingship*, ed. Declan Quigley, 25–37. London: Routledge, 2005.

D'Elia, Anthony F. *Pagan Virtue in a Christian World: Sigismondo Malatesta and the Italian Renaissance*. Cambridge, MA: Harvard University Press, 2016.

Demochares. *BNJ* 75, ed. S. Dmitriev. Accessed August 18, 2021. https://referenceworks-brillonline-com.uoelibrary.idm.oclc.org/entries/brill-s-new-jacoby/demochares-75-a75?s.num=31&s.start=20.
Demosthenes. *Orationes.* Ed. M. R. Dilts. Vol. 1. Oxford: Oxford University Press, 2002.
Dercksen, Jan-Gerrit. "The Silver of the Gods. On Old Assyrian *ikribū*." *Archivum Anatolicum* 3 (1992): 75–100.
Descola, Philippe. *In the Society of Nature: A Native Ecology in Amazonia.* Cambridge: Cambridge University Press, 1996.
Desmond, W. D. *Philosopher-Kings of Antiquity.* London: Continuum, 2011.
Devji, Faisal. *The Impossible Indian: Gandhi and the Temptation of Violence.* Cambridge, MA: Harvard University Press, 2012.
Devji, Faisal. "Islamism as anti-politics." *Political Theology Blog.* August 2, 2013. http://www.politicaltheology.com/blog/political-theology-and-islamic-studies-symposium-islamism-as-anti-politics/.
Devji, Faisal. *Landscapes of the Jihad: Militancy, Morality, Modernity.* Crises in World Politics. Ithaca, NY: Cornell University Press, 2005.
Devji, Faisal. *The Terrorist in Search of Humanity: Militant Islam and Global Politics.* New York: Columbia University Press, 2009.
Dhungel, S. P. S., B. Adhikari, B. P. Bhandari, and C. Murgatroyd. *Commentary on the Nepalese Constitution.* Kathmandu: DeLF, 1998.
Di Branco, Marco. "The 'Perfect King' and His Philosophers: Politics, Religion and Graeco-Arabic Philosophy in Safavid Iran: The Case of the Utūlūğiyā." *Studia Graeco-Arabica* 4 (2014): 191–218.
Diels, H., and W. Kranz. *Die Fragmente der Vorsokratiker.* 3 vols. Hildesheim: Weidmannsche, 2004.
Diodorus Siculus. *The Library of History.* Trans. C. H. Oldfather et al. 11 vols. Cambridge, MA: Harvard University Press/Heinemann, 1933–1957.
Diogenes Laertius, *Lives of the Eminent Philosophers.* Trans. R. D. Hicks. Cambridge, MA: Harvard University Press/Heinemann, 1972.
Dittenberger, W., and K. Purgold, eds. *Inschriften von Olympia.* Berlin: Verlag von A. Asher and Co, 1896.
Dougherty, C. *The Poetics of Colonization. From City to Text in Archaic Greece.* New York, Oxford: Oxford University Press, 1983.
Douglas, Mary. *Purity and Danger: An Analysis of Concepts of Pollution and Taboo.* New York: Praeger, 1966.
Douris of Samos, *BNJ* 76, Ed. F. Pownall. Accessed August 18, 2021. https://referenceworks-brillonline-com.uoelibrary.idm.oclc.org/entries/brill-s-new-jacoby/duris-of-samos-76-a76?s.num=7.
Downame, John, ed. *Annotations upon All the Books of the Old and New Testament.* London, 1645.
Downs, Brian W. *Ibsen: The Intellectual Background.* Cambridge: Cambridge University Press, 1948.
Doyle, Mary Eileen. *The Ancestor Cult and Burial Ritual in Seventeenth and Eighteenth-Century Central Peru.* Ann Arbor, MI: UMI Dissertation Services, 1988.
Drake, Harold A. *In Praise of Constantine: A Historical Study and New Translation of Eusebius' Tricennial Orations.* Berkeley: University of California Press, 1976.
Duggan, Christopher. *Fascist Voices: An Intimate History of Mussolini's Italy.* Oxford: Oxford University Press, 2013.
Duindam, Jeroen. "The Court as a Meeting Point: Cohesion, Competition, Control." In *Prince, Pen, and Sword: Eurasian Perspectives,* ed. Jeroen Duindam and Maaike Van Berkel, 32–128. Vol. 15 of Rulers & Elites. Leiden: Brill, 2018.
Duindam, Jeroen. *Dynasties: A Global History of Power, 1300–1800.* Cambridge: Cambridge University Press, 2015.
Duindam, Jeroen, and Martin Van Berkel, eds. *Prince, Pen, and Sword: Eurasian Perspectives,* Vol. 15 of Rulers & Elites. Leiden: Brill, 2018.
Dumézil, Georges. *L'héritage indo-européen à Rome.* Paris: Gallimard, 1949.
Dumézil, Georges. *Mitra-Varuna: An Essay on Two Indo-European Representations of Sovereignty.* New York: Zone, 1988.

Dumont, Louis. *Homo Hierarchicus: The Caste System and Its Implications*. Chicago: University of Chicago Press, 1980.

Dunbabin, T. J. *The Western Greeks: The History of Sicily and South Italy from the Foundation of the Greek Colonies to 480 B.C.* Oxford: Oxford University Press, 1948.

Duviols, Pierre. "Algunas reflexiones acerca de las tesis de la estructura dual del poder incaico." *Histórica* 4 (1980): 183–96.

Duviols, Pierre. "Camaquen, Upani: Un Concept Animiste des Anciens Péruviens." In *Estudios Americanistas*, eds. R. Hartmann and U. Oberam, vol. 1, 132–44. Bonn: Collectanea Instituti Anthropos, vol. 20, 1978.

Duviols, Pierre. *Cultura Andina y Represión: Procesos y Visitas de Idolatrías y Hechicerías, Siglo XVII*. Cuzco: Centro de Estudios Rurales Andinos «Bartolomé de las Casas», 1986.

Duviols, Pierre. "La Dinastía de los Incas: ¿Monarquia o Diarquia? Argumentos heurísticos a favor de una tesis estructuralista." *Journal de la Société des Américanistes* 66 (1979): 67–83.

Duviols, Pierre. "Huari y Llacuaz: Agricultores y Pastores. Un Dualismo Prehispánico de Oposición y Complementariedad." *Revista del Museo Nacional* 39 (1973): 153–91.

Duviols, Pierre. *La lutte contre les religions autochtones dans le Pérou coloniale (L'extirpation de l'idolatrie entre 1532 et 1660)*. Lima: Institut Français d'Etudes Andines, 1971.

Duviols, Pierre. "Un Symbolisme Andin du Double: La Lithomorphose de l'Ancêtre." *Actes du XLIIe Congrès International des Américanistes* 4 (1978): 359–64.

Ebstein, Michael, *Mysticism and Philosophy in Al-Andalus: Ibn Masarra, Ibn al-'Arabī and the Ismā'īlī Tradition*. Leiden: Brill, 2014.

Eilberg-Schwartz, Howard. *The Savage in Judaism: An Anthropology of Israelite Religion and Ancient Judaism*. Bloomington: University of Indiana Press, 1990.

Eisenstadt, S. N. "The Axial Age: The Emergence of Transcendental Visions and the Rise of the Clerics." *European Journal of Sociology* 23 (1982): 294–314.

Eisenstadt, Shmuel, ed. *The Origins and Diversity of Axial Civilization*. Albany: State University of New York Press, 1986.

Eisenstadt, Shmuel. "Introduction: The Axial Age Breakthroughs—Their Characteristics and Origins." In *The Origins and Diversity of Axial Civilization*, ed. Shmuel Eisenstadt, 1–25. Albany: State University of New York Press, 1986.

El Cheikh, Nadia Maria. "The Institutionalization of Abbasid Ceremonial." In *Diverging Paths? The Shapes of Power and Institutions in Medieval Christendom and Islam*, ed. John Hudson and Ana Rodriguez, 351–70. Leiden: Brill, 2014.

Elkin, A. P. "Mystic Experience: Essential Qualifications for Men of High Degree." In *Religion in Aboriginal Australia*, ed. Max Charlesworth, Howard Morphy, Diane Bell, and Kenneth Maddock, 281–91. St. Lucua: Queensland, Queensland University Press, 1984.

Elkin, A. P. "Rock-Paintings of North-West Australia." *Oceania* 1 (1930): 257–79.

Ellen, Roy. "Fetishism." *Man*, New Series, 23 (1988): 213–35.

Emmrich, C. "'All the King's Horses and All the King's Men': The 2004 Red Matsyendranāth Incident in Lalitpur." *Indologica Taurinensia* 32 (2006): 27–65.

Engelbach, R. "An Alleged Winged Sun-Disk of the First Dynasty." *Zeitschrift für Ägyptische Sprache* 65 (1930): 115–16.

Ernst, Carl W. *Refractions of Islam in India: Situating Sufism and Yoga*. New Delhi: Sage, 2016.

Ess, Josef. *Der Wesir und seine Gelehrten*. Wiesbaden: Abhandlungen für die Kunde des Morgenlandes XLV/4, 1981.

Euripides. *Fabulae*. Ed. J. Diggle. Vol. 2. Oxford: Oxford University Press, 1981.

Evans-Pritchard, E. E. *Nuer Religion*. Oxford: Clarendon, 1956.

Faraone, C. A., and F. S. Naiden, eds. *Greek and Roman Animal Sacrifice: Ancient Victims, Modern Observers*. Cambridge: Cambridge University Press, 2012.

Fausto, Carlos. "Too Many Owners: Mastery and Ownership in Amazonia." In *Animism in Rainforest and Tundra: Personhood, Animals, Plants, and Things in Contemporary Amazonia and Siberia*, ed. Vanessa Elisa Grotti and Olga Ulturgavsheva, 29–47. New York: Berghahn, 2012.

Filiu, Jean-Pierre. *L'Apocalypse dans L'Islam*. Paris: Fayard, 2008.

Firth, Raymond. *Tikopia Ritual and Belief*. London: Allen and Unwin, 1967.

Firth, Raymond. *The Work of the Gods in Tikopia*. London: Athlone, 1967.

Fischer, Johan. *The Halal Frontier: Muslim Consumers in a Globalized Market*. New York: Palgrave Macmillan, 2011.

Flatt, Emma J. *The Courts of the Deccan Sultanates: Living Well in the Persian Cosmopolis*. Cambridge: Cambridge University Press, 2019.

Fleischer, Cornell. "Royal Authority, Dynastic Cyclism and 'Ibn Khaldunism' in Sixteenth-Century Ottoman Letters." *Journal of Asian and African Studies* 18 (1983): 198–220.

Flood, Finbarr Barry. *The Great Mosque of Damascus*. Leiden: Brill, 2001.

Flower, M. "The Invention of Tradition in Classical and Hellenistic Sparta." In *Sparta: Beyond the Mirage*, ed. A. Powell and S. Hodkinson, 191–217. London: Classical Press of Wales, 2002.

Fortune, Reo. *Sorcerers of Dobu: The Social Anthropology of the Dobu Islanders of the WesternPacific*. New York: E.P. Dutton, 1965.

Foster, Benjamin R., *The Age of Agade. Inventing Empire in Ancient Mesopotamia*. London: Routledge, 2016.

Fowden, Garth. *Qusayr 'Amra: Art and the Umayyad Elite in Late Antique Syria*. Berkeley: University of California Press, 2004.

Frahm, Eckart. "Assyria and the South: Babylonia." In *A Companion to Assyria*, ed. E. Frahm, 286–98. Hoboken, NJ: Wiley, 2017.

Frahm, Eckart. "Hochverrat in Assur." In *Assur Forschungen. Arbeiten aus der Forschungsstelle "Edition literarischer Keilschrifttexte aus Assur" der Heidelberger Akademie der Wissenschaften*, ed. S. M. Maul and N. Heeßel, 89–139. Wiesbaden: Harrassowitz Verlag, 2010.

Frame, Grant. "Babylon: Assyria's Problem, Assyria's Prize." *Journal of the Canadian Society for Mesopotamian Studies* 3 (2008): 21–31.

Frame, Grant. "The God Assur in Babylonia." In *Assyria 1995. Proceedings of the 10th Anniversary Symposium of the Neo-Assyrian Text Corpus Project, Helsinki September 11–15, 1995*, ed. S. Parpola and R. M. Whiting, 55–64. Helsinki: Neo-Assyrian Text Corpus Project, 1997.

Frankfort, Henri. *Kingship and the Gods: A Study of Ancient Near Eastern Religion as the Integration of Society and Nature*. Phoenix, AZ: Oriental Institute of the University of Phoenix, 1978.

Frankfort, Henri, William A. Irwin, Thorkild Jakobsen, and John A. Wilson, eds. *The Intellectual Adventure of Ancient Man: An Essay on Speculative Thought in the Ancient Near East*. Chicago: University of Chicago Press, 1977.

Frayne, Douglas. *Pre-Sargonic Period (2700–2350 BC)*. The Royal Inscriptions of Mesopotamia, Early Periods, 1. Toronto: University of Toronto Press, 2008.

Frayne, Douglas. *Ur III Period (2112–2004 BC)*. The Royal Inscriptions of Mesopotamia, vol. 3/2. Toronto: University of Toronto Press, 1997.

Frazer, James G. *The Golden Bough: A Study in Magic and Religion*, 3rd ed, 12 vols. London: MacMillan, 1911–1915.

Fuchs, Simon Wolfgang. *In a Pure Muslim Land: Shi'ism Between Pakistan and the Middle East*. Chapel Hill: University of North Carolina Press, 2019.

Fulsås, Narve, and Tore Rem. *Ibsen, Scandinavia, and the Making of a World Drama*. Cambridge: Cambridge University Press, 2018.

Fulton, Thomas. "Toward a New Cultural History of the Geneva Bible." *Journal of Medieval and Early Modern Studies* 47, no. 3 (2017): 487–516.

Furet, François. *Penser la Révolution Française*. Paris: Gallimard, 1978.

Gaborieau, M. "Les rapports de classe dans l'idéologie officielle du Népal." *Purusartha* 6 (1982): 251–90.
Gaborieau, M. *Ni Brahmanes, ni Ancêtres: Colporteurs Musulmans de Népal.* Nanterre: Société d'Ethnologie, 1993.
Gagarin, M. *Early Greek Law.* Berkeley: University of California Press, 1986.
Gagarin, M. *Writing Greek Law.* Cambridge: Cambridge University Press, 2008.
García-Arenal, Mercedes. *Messianism and Puritanical Reform. Mahdīs of the Muslim West.* Trans. Martin Beagles. Leiden: Brill, 2006.
Gauchet, Marcel. *The Disenchantment of the World: A Political History of Religion.* Trans. Oscar Burge. Princeton, NJ: Princeton University Press, 1999.
Geertz, C. *Negara: The Theatre State in Nineteenth-Century Bali.* Princeton, NJ: Princeton University Press, 1982.
Gehrke, J.-H. "States." In *A Companion to Archaic Greece*, ed. K. A. Raaflaub and H. van Wees, 394–410. Malden, MA: Blackwell, 2009.
Gelasius I, *Duo sunt.* Trans. J. H. Robinson. Accessed October 27, 2021. https://sourcebooks.fordham.edu/source/gelasius1.asp.
Gellner, D. N. *The Anthropology of Buddhism and Hinduism: Weberian Themes.* Delhi: Oxford University Press, 2001.
Gellner, D. N. "Civilization as a Key Guiding Idea in South Asia." In *Anthropology and Civilizational Analysis: Eurasian Explorations*, ed. J. P. Arnason and C. Hann, 99–119. New York: SUNY Press, 2018.
Gellner, D. N. "Does Symbolism 'Construct an Urban Mesocosm'? Robert Levy's *Mesocosm* and the Question of Value Consensus in Bhaktapur." *Journal of Hindu Studies* 1, no. 3 (1997): 541–64. Republished as chapter 13 in D. N. Gellner, *The Anthropology of Buddhism and Hinduism: Weberian Themes*, Delhi: Oxford University Press, 2001.
Gellner, D. N. "The Emergence of Conversion in a Hindu-Buddhist Polytropy: The Kathmandu Valley, Nepal c. 1600–1995." *Comparative Studies in Society and History* 47 (2005): 755–80.
Gellner, D. N. "Himalayan Conundrum? A Puzzling Absence in Ronald M. Davidson's *Indian Esoteric Buddhism*." *Journal of the International Association of Buddhist Studies* 27, no. 2 (2004): 411–17.
Gellner, D. N. *Monk, Householder, and Tantric Priest: Newar Buddhism and Its Hierarchy of Ritual.* Cambridge: Cambridge University Press, 1992.
Gellner, D. N., S. L. Hausner, and C. Letizia, eds. *Religion, Secularism, and Ethnicity in Contemporary Nepal.* Delhi: Oxford University Press, 2016.
Gellner, D. N., and C. Letizia. "Hinduism in the Secular Republic of Nepal." In *The Oxford History of Hinduism: Modern Hinduism*, ed. T. Brekke, 275–304. Delhi: Oxford University Press, 2019.
Gellner, D. N., and C. Letizia. "Introduction: Religion and Identities in Post-Panchayat Nepal." In *Religion, Secularism, and Ethnicity in Contemporary Nepal*, ed. D. N. Gellner, S. L. Hausner, and C. Letizia, 1–32. Delhi: Oxford University Press, 2016.
Gellner, D. N., and C. Letizia. "Religion and Secularism in Contemporary Nepal." In *Routledge Handbook of South Asian Religions*, ed. K. Jacobsen, 335–54. Abingdon: Routledge, 2021.
Gellner, Ernest. *Spectacles and Predicaments: Essays in Social Theory.* Cambridge: Cambridge University Press, 1979.
Geréby, György. "Political Theology versus Theological Politics: Erik Peterson and Carl Schmitt." *New German Critique* 105 (2008): 7–33.
Geus, K. "Space and Geography." In *A Companion to the Hellenistic World*, ed. A. Erskine, 232–45. Malden, MA: Blackwell, 2003.
Godelier, Maurice. *The Mental and the Material.* Trans. Martin Thom. London: Verso, 2011.
Goldman, Irving. *The Mouth of Heaven: An Introduction to Kwakiutl Religious Thought.* New York: Wiley, 1975.
Gommans, Jos. "Cosmopolitanism and Imagination in Nayaka South India: Decoding the Brooklyn Kalamkari." *Archives of Asian Art* 70, no. 1 (2020): 1–21.
Gommans, Jos. *The Indian Frontier: Horse and Warband in the Making of Empires.* New Delhi: Manohar, 2018.

Gommans, Jos. *The Indian Frontier: Horse and Warband in the Making of Empires.* London: Routledge, 2017.

Gommans, Jos. *Mughal Warfare: Indian Frontiers and Highroads to Empire, 1500–1700.* London: Routledge, 2002.

Gommans, Jos. "The Neoplatonic Renaissance from the Thames to the Ganges." In *India after World History: Literature, Comparison, and Approaches to Globalization*, ed. Neilesh Bose. Leiden: Leiden University Press, forthcoming.

Gommans, Jos. *The Unseen World: The Netherlands and India from 1550.* Amsterdam: Rijksmuseum/Nijmegen: VanTilt, 2018.

Gommans, Jos, and Said Reza Huseini. "Neoplatonism and the Pax Mongolica in the Making of *Ṣulḥ-i Kull*: A View from Akbar's Millennial History." *Modern Asian History*, forthcoming.

González Holguín, Diego. *Vocabulario de la Lengua General de todo el Perú Llamado Lengua Qqichua o del Inca.* Lima: Imprenta Santa María, 1608 [1952].

Goodnick Westenholz, Joan. *Legends of the Kings of Akkade. The Texts.* Mesopotamian Civilizations, vol. 7. Winona Lake, IN: Eisenbrauns, 1997.

Goody, Jack. *Literacy in Traditional Societies.* Cambridge: Cambridge University Press, 1968.

Gose, Peter. "The Andean Circulatory Cosmos." In *The Andean World*, ed. L. Seligmann and K. Fine-Dare, 115–27. London: Routledge, 2019.

Gose, Peter. *Deathly Waters and Hungry Mountains: Agrarian Ritual and Class Formation in an Andean Town.* Toronto: University of Toronto Press, 1994.

Gose, Peter. *Invaders as Ancestors: On the Intercultural Making and Unmaking of Spanish Colonialism in the Andes.* Toronto: University of Toronto Press, 2008.

Gose, Peter. "Oracles, Mummies, and Political Representation in the Inka State." *Ethnohistory* 43, no. 1 (1996): 1–33.

Gose, Peter. "The Past Is a Lower Moiety: Diarchy, History, and Divine Kingship in the Inka Empire." *History and Anthropology* 9, no. 4 (1996): 383–414.

Gose, Peter. "Segmentary State Formation and the Ritual Control of Water Under the Incas." *Comparative Studies in Society and History* 35, no. 3 (1993): 480–514.

Gottwald, Norman. *The Tribes of Yahweh: A Sociology of the Religion of Liberated Israel, 1250–1050 BCE.* New York: Maryknoll, 1979.

Graeber, David. *Debt: The First 5,000 Years.* Brooklyn: Melville House, 2011.

Graeber, David. "Divine Kingship of the Shilluk: On Violence, Utopia, and the Human Condition." In *On Kings*, ed. David Graeber and Marshall Sahlins, 65–138. Chicago: HAU, 2017.

Graeber, David. "Notes on the Politics of Divine Kinship: Or, Elements for an Archaeology of Sovereignty." In *On Kings*, ed. David Graeber and Marshall Sahlins, 403–19. Chicago: HAU, 2017.

Graeber, David, and Marshall Sahlins. *On Kings.* Chicago: HAU, 2017.

Graeber, David, and Marshall Sahlins. "Theses on Kingship." In *On Kings*, ed. David Graeber and Marshall Sahlins, 7–9. Chicago: HAU, 2017.

Grobbel, Gerard. *Der Dichter Faiḍī und die Religion Akbars.* Berlin: Klaus Schwarz Verlag, 2001.

Gruendler, Beatrice, ed. and trans. *The Life and Times of Abū Tammām by Abū Bakr Muḥammad Ibn Yaḥyā l-Ṣūlī.* New York: New York University Press, 2015.

Guaman Poma de Ayala, Felipe. *Nueva Corónica y Buen Gobierno.* Paris: Université de Paris. 1615 [1936].

Gupta, S., and R. F. Gombrich. "Kings, Power and the Goddess." *South Asia Research* 6, no. 2 (1986): 123–38.

Guthrie, Stewart. *Faces in the Clouds: A New Theory of Religion.* New York: Oxford University Press, 1993.

Guthrie, W. K. C. *The Sophists.* Cambridge: Cambridge University Press, 1971.

Habicht, Christian. *Divine Honors for Mortal Men in Greek Cities: The Early Cases.* Trans. J. N. Dillon. Ann Arbor: Michigan University Press, 2017.

Hachhethu, K., and D. N. Gellner. "Nepal: Trajectories of Democracy and Restructuring of the State." In *Routledge Handbook of South Asian Politics*, ed. P. Brass, 131–46. London: Routledge, 2010.

Hallowell, Alfred Irving. "Some Empirical Aspects of Northern Salteaux Religion." *American Anthropologist* 36 (1934): 389–404.

Hanegraaf, Wouter J. *Esotericism and the Academy: Rejected Knowledge in Western Culture*. Cambridge: Cambridge University Press, 2012.

Hangen, S. I. "Boycotting Dasain: History, Memory, and Ethnic Politics in Nepal." *Studies in Nepali History and Society* 10 (2005): 105–33.

Hangen, S. I. *The Rise of Ethnic Politics in Nepal: Democracy in the Margins*. London: Routledge, 2010.

Hanne, Eric J. *Putting the Caliph in His Place: Power, Authority and the Late Abbasid Caliphate*. Madison, NJ: Fairleigh Dickinson University Press, 2007.

Hansen, Thomas Blom, and Finn Stepputat. "Sovereignty Revisited." *Annual Review of Anthropology* 35 (2006): 295–315. doi:10.1146/annurev.anthro.35.081705.123317.

Harris, Olivia. "The Dead and the Devils Among the Bolivian Laymi." In *Death and the Regeneration of Life*, ed. M. Bloch and J. Parry, 45–73. Cambridge: Cambridge University Press, 1982.

Harrison, Simon. *Stealing People's Names: History and Politics in a Sepik River Cosmology*. Cambridge: Cambridge University Press, 1990.

Hart, Vaughan. *Art and Magic in the Court of the Stuarts*. London: Routledge, 1994.

Hartenstein, Friedhelm, and Bernd Jankowski. *Psalmen: Biblischer Kommentar* (XV/1). Neukirchen-Vluyn: Neukirchener, 2012.

Hartmann, Angelika. *Al-Nāṣir li-Dīn Allāh (1180–1225): Politik, Religion, Kultur in der späten 'Abbāsidenzeit*. Berlin: Walter de Gruyter, 1975.

Hartung, Jan-Peter. *A System of Life: Maududi and the Ideologisation of Islam*. London: Hurst, 2014.

Hashim, Ahmed S. *The Caliphate at War: The Ideological, Organisational and Military Innovations of Islamic State*. London: Hurst, 2018.

Hassan, Mona. *Longing for the Lost Caliphate: A Transregional History*. Princeton, NJ: Princeton University Press, 2016.

Hegghammer, Thomas. *The Caravan: Abdallah Azzam and the Rise of Global Jihad*. Cambridge: Cambridge University Press, 2020.

Heidemann, Stefan. "The Evolving Representation of the Early Islamic Empire and Its Religion on Coin Imagery." In *The Qurʾān in Context*, ed. Angelika Neuwirth, Nicolai Sinai, and Michael Marx, 149–95. Leiden: Brill, 2010.

Hemmer, Bjørn. "Ibsen and Historical Drama." In *The Cambridge Companion to Ibsen*, ed. James McFarlane, 12–27. Cambridge: Cambridge University Press, 1994.

Henry of Huntingdon. *The History of the English People 1000–1154*. Trans. Diana Greenaway. Oxford: Oxford University Press, 2002.

Herodotus. *Historiae*. Ed. N. G. Wilson. 2 vols. Oxford: Oxford University Press, 2015.

Herodotus. *Histories*. Ed. A. D. Godley. Book 2. Cambridge, MA: Harvard University Press, 1920.

Hesiod. *Hesiod, the Homeric Hymns and Homerica*. Trans. H. G. Evelyn-White. Cambridge, MS: Harvard University Press/Heinemann, 1977.

Hesiod. *Opera*. 3rd ed. Ed. F. Solmsen, R. Merkelbach, and M. L. West. Oxford: Oxford University Press, 1990.

Hilāl al-Ṣābī, *Rusūm Dār al-Khilāfa (The Rules and Regulations of the 'Abbāsid Court)*. Translated by Elie A. Salem. Beirut, American University of Beirut, 1977.

Hirth, Kenneth, and Joanne Pillsbury. "Redistribution and Markets in Andean South America." *Current Anthropology* 54, no. 5 (2013): 642–7.

Hitch, S., and I. Rutherford, eds. *Animal Sacrifice in the Ancient Greek World*. Cambridge: Cambridge University Press, 2015.

Hobbes, Thomas. *Leviathan*. Ed. Edwin Curley. Indianapolis: Hackett, 1994 [1651].

Hobbes, Thomas. *Leviathan*. Ed. R. Tuck. Cambridge: Cambridge University Press, 1996.

Hocart, Arthur M. "Chieftainship and the Sister's Son in the Pacific." *American Anthropogist* 17 (1915): 631–46.

Hocart, Arthur M. *Kings and Councillors*. Chicago: University of Chicago Press, 1970.
Hocart, Arthur M. *Kingship*. Oxford: Oxford University Press, 1927, repr. 1969.
Hocart, Arthur M. *The Northern States of Fiji*. London: Royal Anthropological Institute of Great Britain and Ireland, 1952.
Hoem, Gunhild. "Emperor and Galilean: The Problem Child of Literary Scholars." In *Proceedings: IX International Ibsen Conference, Bergen 5–10 June 2000*, ed. Pål Bjørby and Asbjørn Aarseth, 309–14. Øvre Ervik, Norway: Alvheim and Eide Akademisk Forlag, 2001.
Höfer, A. *Caste Hierarchy and the State: A Study of the Mulukhi Ain of 1854*. Innsbruck: Universitätsverlag Wagner, 1979.
Höfert, Almut. *Kaisertum und Kalifat: Der Imperiale Monotheismus in Früh- und Hochmittelalter*. Frankfurt: Campus, 2015.
Hoffman, Michael A. *Egypt Before the Pharaohs: The Prehistoric Foundations of Egyptian Civilization*. London: Routledge and Kegan Paul, 1980.
Hölkeskamp, K.-J. "Written Law in Archaic Greece." *Proceedings of the Cambridge Philological Society* 38 (1992): 87–117.
Hölkeskamp, K.-J. "Arbitrators, Lawgivers, and the 'Codification of Law' in Archaic Greece." *Mètis* 7 (1992): 49–81.
Holy, Ladislav, ed. *Comparative Anthropology*. Oxford: Blackwell, 1987.
Homer. *Opera*. 3rd ed. Eds. D. B. Monro and T. W. Allen. 4 vols. Oxford: Oxford University Press, 1963.
Howe, T., and S. Müller, "Mission Accomplished: Alexander at the Hyphasis." *Ancient History Bulletin* 26 (2012): 21–38.
Humphreys, S. C. "Dynamics of the Greek Breakthrough: The Dialogue Between Philosophy and Religion." In *The Origins and Diversity of Axial Age Civilizations*, ed. S. N. Eisenstadt. Albany: State University of New York, 1986.
Humphreys, S. C. "'Transcendence' and Intellectual Roles: The Ancient Greek Case." *Daedalus* 104 (1975): 91–118.
Hunt, Rev. John. *Fiji Journals of John Hunt*, 1 Jan. 1839–29 July 1848. Wesleyan Methodist Missionary Society Collection, London, School of Oriental and African Studies, Box 5b.
Husain, S. A. "Hakeem Ali Gilani: A Commentator of Canon of Avicenna." *Bulletin of the Indian Institute for the History of Medicine* 27 (1997): 47–52.
Hutchins, F. G. *Democratizing Monarch: A Memoir of Nepal's King Birendra*. Kathmandu: Vajra, 2007.
Hutt, M., ed. *Himalayan 'People's War': Nepal's Maoist Rebellion*. London: Hurst, 2004.
Hutt, M. "The Last Himalayan Monarchies." In *Globalization in the Himalayas: Belonging and the Politics of the Self*, ed. G. Toffin and J. Pfaff-Czarnecka, 419–43. New Delhi: Sage, 2014.
Hutt, M. "Revealing What Is Dear: The Post-Earthquake Iconization of the Dharahara, Kathmandu." *The Journal of Asian Studies* 78, no. 3 (2019): 549–76.
Hutt, M. "Singing the New Nepal." *Nations and Nationalism* 18, no. 2 (2012): 306–25.
Hutt, M., and P. Onta, eds. *Political Change and Public Culture in Post-1990 Nepal*. Cambridge: Cambridge University Press, 2017.
Hyperides. *Minor Attic Orators*. Trans. J. O. Burtt. 2 vols. Cambridge, MA: Harvard University Press, 1962.
Ibn al-Zubayr. Aḥmad ibn al-Rashīd. *The Book of Gifts and Rarities*. Trans. Ghada Hajjawi al-Qaddumi. Cambridge, MA: Harvard University Press, 1996.
Ibn Khaldūn. *Al-Muqaddima*. Ed. ʿAbd al-Raḥmān Shaddādī. 3 vols. Casablanca: Bayt Dār al-Funūn wa'l-ʿUlūm wa'l-Ādāb, 2005.
Ibn Khaldūn. *Ibn Khaldun and Tamerlane*. Trans. with commentary by Walter J. Fischel. Berkeley: University of California Press, 1952.
Ibn Khaldūn. *Riḥlat Ibn Khaldūn*. Ed. Muḥammad b. Tāwīt al-Ṭanjī. Abu Dhabi: Dār Al-Suwaidī, 2003.
Ibn al-Zubayr, Aḥmad ibn al-Rashīd. *The Book of Gifts and Rarities*. Translated by Ghada Hajjawi al-Qaddumi. Cambridge, Mass., Harvard University Press, 1996.
Ibsen, Henrik. *Ibsen: Letters and Speeches*. Ed. Evert Sprinchorn. New York: Hill and Wang, 1964.

Ibsen, Henrik. *Letters of Henrik Ibsen*. Trans. John Nilsen Laurvik and Mary Morison. New York: Fox, Duffield and Company, 1905.

Ibsen, Henrik. *The Oxford Ibsen: Emperor and Galilean*, Vol 4. Eds. and trans. James Walter McFarlane and Graham Orton. London: Oxford University Press, 1963.

Ibsen, Henrik. *The Oxford Ibsen: John Gabriel Borkman*. Vol 8. Ed. and trans. James Walter McFarlane. London: Oxford University Press, 1977.

Ingram, Haroro J., Craig Whiteside, and Charlie Winter. *The ISIS Reader: Milestone Texts of the Islamic State Movement*. London: Hurst, 2020.

Jackson, Peter A. "The Performative State: Semi-Coloniality and the Tyranny of Images in Modern Thailand." *Sojourn: Journal of Social Issues in Southeast Asia* 19 (2004): 219–53.

Jacobsen Ben Hammed, Nora. "Knowledge and Felicity of the Soul in Fakhr al-Dīn al-Rāzī." PhD diss., University of Chicago, 2018.

Jakobsen, Thorkild. "Mesopotamia: The Cosmos as State." In *The Intellectual Adventure of Ancient Man: An Essay on Speculative Thought in the Ancient Near East*, ed. Henri Frankfort, William A. Irwin, Thorkild Jakobsen, and John A. Wilson, 125–84. Chicago: University of Chicago Press, 1977.

Jaspers, Karl. *The Origin and Goal of History*. Trans. Michael Bullock. New Haven, CT: Yale University Press, 1953.

Jenkins, Richard. "Disenchantment, Enchantment and Re-enchantment: Max Weber at the Millennium." *Max Weber Studies* 1 (2000): 11–32.

Jerr, Nicole. "Exit the King? Modern Theater and the Revolution." In *The Scaffolding of Sovereignty: Global and Aesthetic Perspectives on the History of a Concept*, ed. Zvi Ben-Dor Benite, Stefanos Geroulanos, and Nicole Jerr, 340–64. New York: Columbia University Press, 2017.

Jha, P. *Battles of the New Republic: A Contemporary History of Nepal*. London: Hurst, 2014.

Jimenez, Enrique. *The Babylonian Disputation Poems. With Editions of the* Series of the Poplar, Palm and Vine, *the* Series of the Spider, *and the* Story of the Poor, Forlorn Wren. Culture and History of the Ancient Near East, vol. 87. Leiden: Brill, 2017.

Johnston, Brian. *To the Third Empire: Ibsen's Early Drama*. Minneapolis: University of Minnesota Press, 1980.

Joshi, B. L., and J. Rose. *Democratic Innovations in Nepal: A Case Study of Political Acculturation*. Berkeley: University of California Press, 1966.

Junge F. "Die Welt der Klagen." In *Fragen an die altägyptische Literatur (Studien zum Gedenken an Eberhard Otto)*, ed. Jan Assmann, Erika Feucht, and Reinhard Grieshammer, 275–88. Wiesbaden: Reichert Verlag, 1977.

Kahn, C. H. *The Art and Thought of Heraclitus: An Edition of the Fragments with Translation and Commentary*. Cambridge: Cambridge University Press, 1979.

Kahn, Paul. *Political Theology: Four New Chapters on the Concept of Sovereignty*. New York: Columbia University Press, 2012.

Kalimi, Isaac, and Richardson, Seth, eds. *Sennacherib at the Gates of Jerusalem. Story, History and Historiography*: Culture and History of the Ancient Near East, vol. 71. Leiden: Brill, 2014.

Kamola, Stefan. *Making Mongol History: Rashid al-Din and the Jamiʿ al-Tawarikh*. Edinburgh: Edinburgh University Press, 2019.

Kantorowicz, Ernst. *The King's Two Bodies: A Study in Medieval Political Theology*. Princeton, NJ: Princeton University Press, 1957.

Katuwal, Rookmangud. *My Story*. Kathmandu: Nepalaya, 2016.

Keane, Webb. *Christian Moderns: Freedom and Fetish in the Mission Encounter*. Berkeley: University of California Press, 2007.

Keel, Othman, and Christoph Uehlinger. *Göttinnen, Götter und Gottessymbole*. Freiburg: Herder, 1992.

Keesing, Roger. *Kwaio Religion: The Living and the Dead in a Solomon Islands Society*. New York: Columbia University Press, 1982.

Khan, Shah Nawaz. *Ma'athir al-Umara*. Ed. Maulawi Abdur Rahim and Mirza Ashraf Ali. 3 vols. Calcutta: Bibliotheca Indica 112, 1888–91.

Kirkpatrick, Col. *An Account of the Kingdom of Nepal*. Delhi: Manjusri, 1969 [1811].

Kleeman, Terry F. *Celestial Masters: History and Ritual in Early Daoist Communities*. Cambridge, MA: Harvard University Asia Center, 2016.

Koch, Ebba. "Being Like Jesus and Mary: The Influence of the Jesuit Missions on Symbolic Representations of the Mughal Emperors Revisited." In *Transcultural Imaginations of the Sacred*, ed. Margit Kern and Klaus Krüger, 197–230. Munich: Fink Verlag, 2018.

Koch, Ebba. "The Intellectual and Artistic Climate of Akbar's Court." In *The Adventures of Hamza: Painting and Storytelling in Mughal India*, ed. John Seyller, 18–31. Washington, DC: Freer Gallery of Art and Arthur M. Sackler Gallery, 2002.

Korsten, Frans-Willem. "The Irreconcilability of Sincerity and Hypocrisy." In *The Rhetoric of Sincerity*, ed. E. van Alphen, M. Bal, and C. E. Smith, 60–77. Stanford, CA: Stanford University Press, 2009.

Krauskopff, G., and M. Lecomte-Tilouine, eds. *Célébrer le pouvoir: Dasai, une fête royale au Népal*. Paris: CNRS, 1996.

Kraut, R. "Aristotle's Ethics." *The Stanford Encyclopedia of Philosophy*, ed. E. N. Zalta. Summer 2018 edition. https://plato.stanford.edu/archives/sum2018/entries/aristotle-ethics/.

Krawulski, Dorothea. *The Mongol Īlkhāns and the Vizier Rashīd al-Dīn*. Frankfurt: Peter Lang, 2011.

Kuhrt, Amelie. "Usurpation, Conquest and Ceremonial: From Babylon to Persia." In *Rituals of Royalty: Power and Ceremonial in Traditional Societies*, ed. D. Cannadine and S. Price, 20–55. Cambridge: Cambridge University Press, 1987.

Lacroix, Stéphane, "Ḥākimiyya", in *Encyclopaedia of Islam, THREE*, Edited by: Kate Fleet, Gudrun Krämer, Denis Matringe, John Nawas, Everett Rowson. Consulted online on 20 February 2020 http://dx.doi.org/10.1163/1573-3912_ei3_COM_30217

Lacrosse, Joachim. "Plotin, Porphyre et l'Inde: Un ré-examen." *Le Philosophoire* 41 (2014): 87–104.

Lambert, Wilfred G. *Babylonian Creation Myths*. Mesopotamian Civilizations, vol. 16. Winona Lake, IN: Eisenbrauns, 2013.

Lambert, Wilfred G. *Babylonian Wisdom Literature*. Oxford: Clarendon, 1960.

Lane, George E. "Ṭusi, Naṣir-al-Din." *Encyclopaedia Iranica*. Accessed April 19, 2018. http://www.iranicaonline.org/articles/tusi-nasir-al-din-bio.

Lecomte-Tilouine, M. "The Fictional Kings of Nepal: An Exploration of the Monarch's Pluri-Selfhood." *Cahiers d'Extrême-Asie* 24 (2015): 211–29.

Lecomte-Tilouine, M. 2009. *Hindu Kingship, Ethnic Revival, and Maoist Rebellion in Nepal*. Delhi: Oxford University Press, 2009.

Lecomte-Tilouine, M. "Regicide and Maoist Revolutionary Warfare in Nepal: Modern Incarnations of a Warrior Kingdom." Trans. D. N. Gellner. *Anthropology Today* 20, no. 1 (2004): 13–19.

Lecomte-Tilouine, M., ed. *Revolution in Nepal: An Anthropological and Historical Approach to the People's War*. Delhi: Oxford University Press, 2013.

Lecomte-Tilouine, M. "The Transgressive Nature of Kingship in Caste Organization: Monstrous Royal Doubles in Nepal." In *The Character of Kingship*, ed. D. Quigley, 101–22. Oxford: Berg, 2005.

Lelyveld, David. *Aligarh's First Generation: Muslim Solidarity in British India*. Princeton, NJ: Princeton University Press, 1978.

Lepper, Verena M. *Untersuchungen zu pWestcar. Eine philologische und literaturwissenschaftliche (Neu-)analyse*. Wiesbaden: Harrassowitz Verlag, 2008.

Lesher, J. H. *Xenophanes of Colophon: Fragments—A Text and Translation with a Commentary*. Toronto: University of Toronto Press, 1992.

Letizia, C. "The Goddess Kumari at the Supreme Court: Divine Kingship and Secularism in Nepal." *FOCAAL—Journal of Global and Historical Anthropology* 67 (2013): 32–46.

Letizia, C. "Ideas of Secularism in Nepal." In *Religion, Secularism, and Ethnicity in Contemporary Nepal*, ed. D. N. Gellner, S. Hausner, and C. Letizia, 35–76. Delhi: Oxford University Press, 2016.
Letizia, C. "National Gods at the Court: Secularism and the Judiciary in Nepal." In *Filing Religion: State, Hinduism, and Courts of Law*, ed. D. Berti, G. Tarabout, and Raphaël Voix, 34–68. Delhi: Oxford University Press, 2016.
Letizia, C. "Shaping Secularism in Nepal." *European Bulletin of Himalayan Research* 39 (2011): 66–104.
Leuchtag, E. *With a King in the Clouds*. London: Hutchinson, 1958.
Levenson, Jon. "Exodus and Liberation." *Horizons in Biblical Theology* 13 (1991): 134–74.
Lévi, S. *Le Népal: Étude historique d'un royaume hindou*. 3 vols. Paris: Leroux, 1905. Reissued by Delhi: Asian Educational Services, 1991.
Levi-Strauss, Claude. *The Savage Mind*. Chicago: University of Chicago Press, 1966.
Levy, R., with K. Rajopadhyaya. *Mesocosm: Hinduism and the Organization of a Traditional Newar City in Nepal*. Berkeley: University of California Press, 1990.
Lieberman, Victor. *Strange Parallels: Southeast Asia in Global Context, c. 800–1830*. 2 vols. Cambridge: Cambridge University Press, 2003.
Lienhardt, R. Godfrey. *Divinity and Experience: The Religion of the Dinka*. Oxford: Clarendon, 1961.
Lilla, Mark. *The Stillborn God: Religion, Politics, and the Modern West*. New York: Vintage, 2007.
Lincoln, Bruce. *Myth, Cosmos, and Society: Indo-European Themes of Creation and Destruction*. Cambridge, MA: Harvard University Press, 1986.
Lindsay, T. H. "The 'God-Like Man' Versus the 'Best Laws': Politics and Religion in Aristotle's *Politics*." *Review of Politics* 53 (1991): 488–509.
Lingat, R. *The Classical Law of India*. Trans. J. D. M. Derrett. Berkeley: University of California Press, 1973.
Linssen, Marc J. H. *The Cults of Uruk and Babylon. The Temple Ritual Texts as Evidence for Hellenistic Cult Practices*. Cuneiform Monographs, vol. 25. Leiden: Brill, 2004.
Livingstone, Alasdair. *Court Poetry and Literary Miscellanea*. State Archives of Assyria, vol. 3. Helsinki: Helsinki University Press, 1989.
Locke, J. *Karunamaya: The Cult of Avalokitesvara–Matsyendranath in the Valley of Nepal*. Kathmandu: Sahayogi, 1980.
Locke, John. *Letter on Toleration*. 1689. Accessed April 10, 2021. http://www.let.rug.nl/usa/documents/1651-1700/john-locke-letter-concerning-toleration-1689.php.
Lombard, Denys. *Le sultanat d'Atjéh au temps d'Iskandar Muda, 1607–1636*. Paris: École Française d'Extrême-Orient, 1967.
Lommel, Andreas. *The Unambal: A Tribe in North West Australia*. Carnavon Gorge, Qeensland.: Takanaka Nowan Kas, 1997.
Lotman, Yuri M. *Universe of the Mind. A Semiotic Theory of Culture*. Trans. Ann Shukman. London: I.B. Tauris, 1990.
Lupoli, Agostino. "Hobbes and Religion Without Theology." In *The Oxford Handbook of Hobbes*, ed. A. P. Martinich and Kinch Hoekstra. New York: Oxford University Press, 2016.
MacDowell, D. M. *Spartan Law*. Edinburgh: Edinburgh University Press, 1986.
MacGaffey, Wyatt. *Religion and Society in Central Africa*. Chicago: University of Chicago Press, 1986.
Machinist, Peter. "On Self-Consciousness in Mesopotamia." In *The Origins of Diversity of Axial Age Civilizations*, ed. S. N. Eisenstadt, 184–91. Albany: State University of New York Press, 1986.
Maffie, James. *Aztec Philosophy: Understanding a World in Motion*. Louisville, CO: University Press of Colorado, 2014.
Maitland, Frederic William. "The Crown as Corporation." In *Selected Essays*, ed. H. D. Hazeltine, G. Lapsley, and P. H. Winfield, 104–27. Cambridge: Cambridge University Press, 1936.
Malagodi, M. *Constitutional Nationalism and Legal Exclusion: Equality, Identity Politics, and Democracy in Nepal (1990–2007)*. New Delhi: Oxford University Press, 2013.
Malcolm, Noel. "The Name and Nature of Leviathan: Political Symbolism and Biblical Exegesis." *Intellectual History Review* 17 (2007): 21–39.

Malcolm, Noel. "The Title Page of *Leviathan*, Seen in a Curious Perspective." In Noel Malcom, *Aspects of Hobbes*, 200–33. Oxford: Clarendon, 2002.

Malinowski, Bronislaw. *Magic, Science and Religion and Other Essays*. Boston: Beacon, 1948.

Mallat, Chibli. *The Renewal of Islamic Law: Muhammad Baqer as-Sadr, Najaf and the Shī'ī International*. Cambridge: Cambridge University Press, 1993.

Mandaville, Peter. "Post-Islamism as Neoliberalism." In *Islam After Liberalism*, ed. F. Devji and Z. Kazmi, 279–96. London: Hurst, 2017.

Maneck, Susan Stiles. *The Death of Ahriman: Culture, Identity and Theological Change Among the Parsis of India*. Bombay: K. R. Bed Oriental Institute, 1997.

Manow, Philip, Friedbert W. Rüb, and Dagmar Simon, eds. *Die Bilder des Leviathan: Eine Deutungsgeschichte*. Baden-Baden: Nomos, 2012.

Manu. *The Laws of Manu*. Ed. and trans. W. Doniger and B. K. Smith. London: Penguin, 1991.

Marchesi, Gianni. "Toward a Chronology of Early Dynastic Rulers in Mesopotamia." In *History and Philology*, ed. Walther Sallaberger and Ingo Schrakamp, Associated Chronologies for the Ancient Near East and the Eastern Mediterranean III, 139–56. Turnhout: Brepols, 2015.

Marcotte, Roxanne. "Suhrawardi." In *The Stanford Encyclopedia of Philosophy*, ed. Edward N. Zalta, Summer 2019 Edition. https://plato.stanford.edu/archives/sum2019/entries/suhrawardi/.

Martínez Cereceda, José Luis. *Autoridades en los andes, los atributos del señor*. Lima: Pontificia Universidad Católica del Perú, 1995.

Martinich, A. P., and Kinch Hoekstra, eds. *The Oxford Handbook of Hobbes*. New York: Oxford University Press, 2016.

Martinich, A. P. *The Two Gods of Leviathan: Thomas Hobbes on Religion and Politics*. Cambridge: Cambridge University Press, 1992.

Matienzo, Juan de. *Gobierno del Perú*. Lima: Institut Français d'Etudes Andines, 1567 [1967].

Maul, Stefan M. "*Den Gott Ernähren*. Überlegungen zum regelmäßigen Opfer in altorientalischen Tempeln." In *Transformations in Sacrificial Practices. From Antiquity to Modern Times*, ed. E. Stavrianopoulou, Axel Michaels, and Claus Ambos, 75–86. Berlin: LIT Verlag, 2008.

Maul, Stefan M. "Die Frühjahrsfeierlichkeiten in Aššur." In *Wisdom, Gods and Literature. Studies in Assyriology in Honour of W. G. Lambert*, ed. A. R. George and I. L. Finkel, 389–420. Winona Lake, IN: Eisenbrauns, 2000.

Maul, Stefan M. "Die tägliche Speisung des Assur (*ginā'u*) und deren politische Bedeutung." In *Time and History in the Ancient Near East. Proceedings of the 56th Rencontre Assyriologique Internationale, Barcelona, July 26–30, 2010*, ed. L. Feliu, J. Llop, A. Millet Albà, and J. Sanmartín, 561–74. Winona Lake, IN: Eisenbrauns, 2013.

Mauss, Marcel, "Essai sur le don: Forme et raison del'échanage dans les sociétés archaïques." In Marcel Mauss, *Sociologie et anthropologie*, 3rd ed., 167–8. Paris: Presses Universitaires de France, 1966.

Mavroudi, Maria. "Pletho as Subversive and his Reception in the Islamic World." In *Power and Subversion in Byzantium*, ed. Dimeter Angelov and Michael Saxby, 177–203. Farnham, Surrey: Ashgate, 2013.

Mazarakis Ainian. A. *From Rulers' Dwellings to Temples: Architecture, Religion and Society in Early Iron Age Greece (1100–700 BC)*. Jonsered: Paul Åströms Förlag, 1997.

McEvilley, Thomas. *The Shape of Ancient Thought: Comparative Studies in Greek and Indian Philosophies*. New York: Allworth Press, 2002.

McGlew, J. F. *Tyranny and Political Culture in Ancient Greece*. Ithaca, NY: Cornell University Press, 1993.

Medinaceli, Ximena. "Paullu y Manco ¿Una Diarquía Inca en tiempos de Conquista?" *Boletín del Instituto Francés de Estudios Andinos* 36, no. 2 (2007): 241–58.

Meiggs, R., and D. Lewis, eds. *Greek Historical Inscriptions to the End of the Fifth Century*. Oxford: Oxford University Press, 1988.

Melvin-Koushki, Matthew. "Early Modern Islamicate Empire: New Forms of Religiopolitical Legitimacy." In *The Wiley Blackwell History of Islam*, ed. Armando Salvatore and Roberto Tottoli, 353–75. Chichester: Wiley, 2018.

Melvin-Koushki, Matthew. "How to Rule the World: Occult-Scientific Manuals of the Early Modern Persian Cosmopolis." *Journal of Persianate Studies* 11 (2018): 140–54.

Melvin-Koushki, Matthew. "Powers of One: The Mathematicalization of the Occult Sciences in High-Persianate Tradition." *Intellectual History of the Islamicate World* 5 (2017): 127–99.

Menzel, Brigitte. *Assyrische Tempel. Band 1. Untersuchungen zu Kult, Administration und Personal*. Studia Pohl: Series Maior, vol. 10/1. Rome: Biblical Institute Press, 1981.

Metcalf, Barbara D. *Islamic Revival in British India: Deoband, 1860–1900*. Princeton, NJ: Princeton University Press, 1982.

Michaels, A. *Hinduism, Past and Present*. Trans. B. Harshav. Princeton, NJ: Princeton University Press, 2004.

Michaels, A. "The King and the Cow: On a Crucial Symbol of Hinduization in Nepal." In *Nationalism and Ethnicity in a Hindu Kingdom: The Politics of Culture in Contemporary Nepal*, ed. D. N. Gellner, J. Pfaff-Czarnecka, and J. Whelpton, 79–99. Amsterdam: Harwood, 1997. Reissued Kathmandu: Vajra, 2008.

Michalowski, Piotr. "Early Mesopotamia." In *The Oxford History of Historical Writing*, ed. A. Feldherr and G. Hardy, vol. 1, 5–28. Oxford: Oxford University Press, 2011.

Michalowski, Piotr. *The Lamentation over the Destruction of Sumer and Ur*. Mesopotamian Civilizations, vol. 1. Winona Lake, IN: Eisenbrauns, 1989.

Michalowski, Piotr. "Mortal Kings of Ur: A Short Century of Divine Rule in Ancient Mesopotamia." In *Religion and Power: Divine Kingship in the Ancient World and Beyond*, ed. Nicole Brisch, 33–45. Chicago: Oriental Institute of the University of Chicago, 2008.

Middleton, John. *Tribes Without Rulers: Studies in African Segmentary Systems*. London, Routledge and Kegan Paul, 1958.

Miller, Flagg. *The Audacious Ascetic: What Osama bin Laden's Sound Archive Reveals About Al-Qa'ida*. London: Hurst, 2015.

Mills, Kenneth. *An Evil Lost to View? An Investigation of Post-Evangelization Andean Religion in Mid-Colonial Peru*. Liverpool: Institute of Latin American Studies, 1994.

Mintz, Samuel I. "Leviathan as Metaphor." *Hobbes Studies* 2 (1989): 3–9.

Mitchell, L. G. "Alexander the Great: Divinity, and the Rule of Law." In *Every Inch a King: Comparative Studies in Ancient and Medieval Kingship*, ed. L. Mitchell and C. Melville, 91–107. Leiden: Brill, 2013.

Mitchell, L. G. *The Heroic Rulers of Archaic and Classical Greece*. London: Bloomsbury, 2013.

Mitchell, L. G. *Panhellenism and the War Against the Barbarian in Archaic and Classical Greece*. Swansea: Classical Press of Wales, 2007.

Mitchell, L. G. "Political Thinking on Kingship in Democratic Athens." *Polis* 36 (2019): 442–65.

Mitchell, Lynette G., and Charles Melville, eds. *Every Inch a King: Comparative Studies on Kings and Kingship in the Ancient and Medieval Worlds*. Leiden: Brill, 2013.

Mocko, A. T. *Demoting Vishnu: Ritual, Politics, and the Unraveling of Nepal's Hindu Monarchy*. New York: Oxford University Press, 2016.

Mohamedou, Mohammad-Mahmoud Ould. *A Theory of ISIS: Political Violence and the Transformation of the Global Order*. London: Pluto, 2018.

Moi, Toril. *Henrik Ibsen and the Birth of Modernism: Art, Theater, Philosophy*. Oxford: Oxford University Press, 2006.

Moin, A. Azfar. "Akbar's 'Jesus' and Marlowe's 'Tamburlaine': Strange Parallels of Early Modern Sacredness." *Fragments: Interdisciplinary Approaches to the Study of Ancient and Medieval Pasts* 3 (2013–2014): 1–21.

Moin, A. Azfar. "Challenging the Mughal Emperor: The Islamic Millennium According to 'Abd al-Qadir Badayuni." In *Islam in South Asia in Practice*, ed. Barbara Metcalf, 375–90. Princeton, NJ: Princeton University Press, 2009.

Moin, A. Azfar. *The Millennial Sovereign: Sacred Kingship and Sainthood in Islam*. New York: Columbia University Press, 2012.

Moin, A. Azfar. "Millennial Sovereignty and the Mughal Dynasty." In *Oxford Handbook of the Mughal World*, ed. Richard Eaton and Ramya Sreenivasan. Oxford: Oxford University Press, forthcoming.

Moin, A. Azfar. "The Politics of Saint Shrines in the Persianate Empires." In *The Persianate World: Rethinking a Shared Sphere*, ed. Abbas Amanat and Assef Ashraf, 105–24. Leiden: Brill, 2018.

Moin, A. Azfar. "Sovereign Violence: Temple Destruction in India and Shrine Desecration in Iran and Central Asia." *Comparative Studies in Society and History* 57 (2015): 467–496.

Molina, Cristóbal de (el almagrista). *Relación de muchas cosas acaescidas en el Perú*. In *Biblioteca de Autores Españoles*, vol. 209, 56–95. Madrid: Ediciones Atlas, 1553 [1968].

Momigliano, A. *Alien Wisdom: The Limits of Hellenization*. Cambridge: Cambridge University Press, 1975.

Monserrate, Antonio. *The Commentary of Father Monserrate, S.J., on His Journey to the Court of Akbar*. Trans. J. S. Hoyland. Annotated by S. N. Banerjee. London: Oxford University Press, 1922.

Morgan, K. *Pindar and the Construction of Syracusan Monarchy in the Fifth Century BC*. Oxford: Oxford University Press, 2015.

Mortimer, Sarah. "Christianity and Civil Religion in Hobbes's *Leviathan*." In *The Oxford Handbook of Hobbes*, ed. A. P. Martinich and Kinch Hoekstra, 515–16. Oxford: Oxford University Press, 2016.

Moses. *The Five Books of Moses*. Trans. Robert Alter. New York: Norton, 2008.

Mosko, Mark S. *Ways of Baloma: Rethinking Magic and Kinship from the Trobriands*. Chicago: HAU Books, 2017.

Mullins, Daniel Austin, Daniel Hoyer, Christina Collins, Thomas Currie, Kevin Feeney, Pieter François, Patrick E. Savage, Harvey Whitehouse, and Peter Turchin. "A Systematic Assessment of 'Axial Age' Proposals Using Global Comparative Historical Evidence." *American Sociological Review* 83 (2018): 596–626.

Munn, Nancy. "The Transformation of Subjects into Objects in WlabitiPitjantjara Myth." In *Religion in Aboriginal Australia: An Anthology*, ed. Max Charlesworth, Howard Morphy, Diane Bell, and Kenneth Maddock, 57–83. St. Lucia: University of Queensland Press, 1984.

Munn, Nancy. *Walbiri Iconography: Graphic Representation and Cultural Symbolism in Central Australian Society*. Chicago: University of Chicago Press, 1986.

Nachman, Alexander. "Outside of the Law: Khomeini's Legacy of Commanding Right and Forbidding Wrong in the Islamic Republic." *Sociology of Islam* 7 (2019): 1–21.

Naiden, F. S. *Smoke Signals for the Gods: Ancient Greek Sacrifice from the Archaic Through Roman Periods*. Oxford: Oxford University Press, 2015.

Necipoğlu, Gürlu. *Architecture, Ceremonial and Power: The Topkapı Palace in the Fifteenth and Sixteenth Centuries*. Cambridge, MA: MIT Press, 1991.

Needham, Rodney. "Dual Sovereignty." In *Reconnaissances*, 63–105. Toronto: University of Toronto Press, 1980.

Nelson, Eric. *The Hebrew Republic: Jewish Sources and the Transformation of European Political Thought*. Cambridge, MA: Harvard University Press, 2010.

Newell, W. R. "Superlative Virtue: The Problem of Monarchy in Aristotle's *Politics*." In *Essays on the Foundation of Aristotelian Political Science*, ed. C. Lord and D. O'Connor, 191–211. Berkeley: University of California Press, 1991.

Nizami, Azra. "Socio-Religious Outlook of Abul Fazl." In *Medieval India, A Miscellany*, vol 2. London: Asia, 1972.

Nur al-Din Muhammad Jahangir. *Tuzuk-i Jahangiri*. Ed. Muhammad Hashim. Tehran: Bunyadi-i Farhang-i Iran, 1980.

Oakley, Francis. *Kingship: The Politics of Enchantment*. Malden, MA: Blackwell, 2006.

Obryk, Matylda. "On Affirmation, Rejection and Accommodation of the World in Greek and Indian Religion." In *Universe and Inner Self in Early Indian and Early Greek Thought*, ed. Richard Seaford, 235–250. Edinburgh: Edinburgh University Press, 2016.

Oesterle, Jenny. *Kalifat und Königtum; Herrschaftsrepräsentation der Fatimiden, Ottonen und frühen Salier an religiösen Hochfesten*. Darmstadt: Wissenschaftliche Buchgesellschaft, 2009.

Olsthoorn, Johan. "The Theocratic Leviathan: Hobbes's Arguments for the Identity of Church and State." In *Hobbes on Politics and Religion*, ed. Laurens van Apeldoorn and Robin Douglass, 10–28. Oxford: Oxford University Press, 2018.

O'Meara, Dominic J. *Platonopolis: Platonic Political Philosophy in Late Antiquity*. Oxford: Oxford University Press, 2003.

Oosten, Jarich G. *The Theoretical Structure of the Religion of the Netsilik and Iglulik*. Groningen: Rijksuniversiteit de Groningen, 1976.

Orthmann, Eva. "Court Culture and Cosmology in the Mughal Empire: Humayūn and the Foundations of the Dīn-i Ilāhī." In *Court Cultures in the Muslim World: Seventh to Nineteenth Centuries*, ed. Albrecht Fuess and Jan-Peter Hartung, 202–21. London: Routledge, 2011.

Osborn, Joseph Warren. "Journal of a Voyage in the Ship *Emerald* owned by Stephen C. Phillips. . . . in the years 1833, 1834, 1835, and 1836." Pacific Manuscript Bureau 223. Original in Peabody Museum, Salem, MA.

Osborne, R. "Law and Laws: How Do We Join Up the Dots?" In *The Development of the Polis in Archaic Greece*, ed. L. G. Mitchell and P. J. Rhodes, 74–82. London: Routledge, 1997.

Ostovar, Afshon. "The Visual Culture of Jihad." In *Jihadi Culture: The Art and Social Practices of Militant Islamists*, ed. T. Hegghammer, 82–107. Cambridge: Cambridge University Press, 2017.

Ostwald, M. "Pindar, *Nomos*, and Heracles (Pindar, Frg 169 [Snell2]+POxy. No. 2450 Frg. 1)." *Harvard Studies in Classical Philology* 69 (1965): 109–38.

Otto, Eckart. *Das Gesetz des Mose*. Darmstadt: Wissenschaftliche Buchgesellschaft, 2007.

Ownby, David. "Chinese Millenarian Traditions: The Formative Age." *The American Historical Review* 104.5 (1999): 1513–30.

Pagani, Samuela. " « Roi ou serviteur »? La tentation de choix d'un modèle." *Archives des Sciences Sociales des Religions* 178 (2017): 43–68.

Papakonstantinou, Z. *Lawmaking and Adjudication in Archaic Greece*. London: Bloomsbury, 2008.

Parish, S. *Moral Knowing in a Hindu Sacred City: An Exploration of Mind, Emotion, and Self*. New York: Columbia University Press, 1994.

Parkin, Jon. "Hobbes and the Future of Religion." In *Hobbes on Politics and Religion*, ed. Laurens van Apeldoorn and Robin Douglass. Oxford: Oxford University Press, 2018.

Pausanias. *Description of Greece*. Trans. W. H. S. Jones, H. A. Ormerod, and R. E. Wycherley. 5 vols. Cambridge, MA: Harvard University Press/Heinemann, 1933.

Pease, Franklin. *Los ultimos Incas del Cuzco*. Lima: P. L. Villanueva, 1981.

Peel, J. D. Y. "History, Culture and the Comparative Method: A West African Puzzle." In *Comparative Anthropology*, ed. Ladislav Holy, 88–119. Oxford: Blackwell, 1987.

Pendrick, G. J. *Antiphon the Sophist: The Fragments*. Cambridge: Cambridge University Press, 2002.

Pettigrew, J. *Maoists at the Hearth*. Philadelphia: University of Pennsylvania Press, 2013.

Pfaff-Czarnecka, J. "A Battle of Meanings: Commemorating the Goddess Durga's Victory over the Demon Mahisa as a Political Act." *Kailash* 18, no. 3–4 (1996): 57–92.

Piccolomini, Enea Silvio (Pape Pie II). *Lettre à Mahomet II*. Trans. Anne Duprat. Paris: Editions Payot et Rivages, 2002.

Pindar. *Olympian Odes, Pythian Odes*. Trans. W. H. Race. Cambridge, MA: Harvard University Press/Heinemann, 1997.

Pines, Yuri. *Foundations of Confucian Thought: Intellectual Life in the Chunqiu Period, 722–453 B.C.E.* Honolulu: University of Hawai'i Press, 2002.

Pippin, Robert. *The Persistence of Subjectivity: On the Kantian Aftermath*. Cambridge: Cambridge University Press, 2005.

Pizarro, Pedro. *Relación del Descubrimiento y Conquista de los Reinos del Perú*. Lima: Pontificia Universidad Católica del Perú, 1571 [1978].

Plato. *Opera*. Ed. E. A. Duke, W. F. Hicken, W. S. M. Nicoll, D. B. Robinson, and J. C. G. Strachan. Vol. 1. Oxford: Oxford University Press, 1995.

Plato. *Opera*. Ed. J. Burnet. Vol. 5 Oxford: Oxford University Press, 1907.

Plato. *Respublica*. Ed. S. R. Slings. Oxford: Oxford University Press, 2003.

Platt, Tristan. "The Andean Soldiers of Christ. Confraternity Organization, the Mass of the Sun and Regenerative Warfare in Rural Potosí (18th–20th Centuries)." *Journal de la Société des Américanistes* 73 (1987): 139–92.

Plutarch. *Parallel Lives*. Trans. B. Perrin. Cambridge, MA: Harvard University Press/Heinemann, 1914–1926.

Pocock, J. G. A. *Politics, Language and Time: Essays on Political Thought and History*. Chicago: Chicago University Press, 1989.

Pocock, J. G. A. "Time, History and Eschatology in the Thought of Thomas Hobbes." In *Politics, Language and Time: Essays on Political Thought and History*, 148–201. Chicago: Chicago University Press, 1989.

Pollock, Sheldon. "The Divine King in the Indian Epic." *Journal of the American Oriental Society* 104, no. 3 (1984): 505–28.

Pollock, Sheldon. *The Language of the Gods in the World of Men: Sanskrit, Culture, and Power in Premodern India*. Berkeley: University of California Press, 2009.

Pollock, Sheldon. "Rāmāyaṇa and Political Imagination in India." *Journal of Asian Studies* 52, no. 2 (1993): 261–97.

Polo de Ondegardo, Jorge. *De los errores y supersticiones de los indios, sacadas del tratado y averiguación que hizo el Licenciado Polo*. In *Informaciones acerca de la Religión y Gobierno de los Incas*, ed. H. Urteaga, vol. 1, 3–43. Lima: Imprenta y Libreria Sanmarti, 1554 [1916].

Pomeranz, Kenneth. *The Great Divergence: China, Europe, and the Making of the World Economy*. Princeton, NJ: Princeton University Press, 2000.

Pomeranz, Kenneth, and David Segal. "World History: Departures and Variations." In *A Companion to World History*, ed. Douglas Northrop, 13–31. Chichester: Wiley-Blackwell Publishing, 2012.

Pongratz-Leisten, Beate. *Religion and Ideology in Assyria*. Studies in Ancient Near Eastern Records, vol. 6. Berlin: DeGruyter, 2015.

Popham, M. R., P. G. Calligas, and L. Hugh Sackett. *Lefkandi II: The Protogeometric Building at Toumba: Part 2, The Excavation, Architecture and Finds*. Athens: British School at Athens, 1993.

Postgate, J. Nicholas. "The Land of Assur and the Yoke of Assur." *World Archaeology* 23 (1992): 247–63.

Pradhan, R. "Domestic and Cosmic Rituals Among the Hindu Newars of Kathmandu, Nepal." PhD diss., Delhi School of Economics, 1986.

Pradhan, K. *The Gorkha Conquests: The Process and Consequences of the Unification of Nepal with Particular Reference to Eastern Nepal*. Calcutta: Oxford University Press, 1991.

Price, S. *Rituals and Power. The Roman Imperial Cult in Asia Minor*. Cambridge: Cambridge University Press, 1984.

Puett, Michael. *To Become a God: Cosmology, Sacrifice, and Self-Divinization in Early China*. Cambridge, MA: Harvard University Asia Center, 2002.

Puett, Michael. "Early China in Eurasian History." In *A Companion to Chinese History*, ed. Michael Szonyi, 89–105. Chichester: Wiley, 2017.

Puett, Michael. "Forming Spirits for the Way: The Cosmology of the *Xiang'er* Commentary to the *Laozi*." *Journal of Chinese Religions* 32 (2004): 1–27.

Puett, Michael. "Ghosts, Gods, and the Coming Apocalypse: Empire and Religion in Early China and Ancient Rome." In *State Power in Ancient China and Rome*, ed. Walter Scheidel, 230–59. Oxford: Oxford University Press, 2015.

Puett, Michael. "Human and Divine Kingship in Early China: Comparative Reflections." In *Religion and Power: Divine Kingship in the Ancient World and Beyond*, ed. Nicole Brisch, 207–20. Chicago: Oriental Institute of the University of Chicago, 2008.

Puett, Michael. "Life, Domesticated and Undomesticated: Ghosts, Sacrifice, and the Efficacy of Ritual Practice in Early China." *HAU: Journal of Ethnographic Theory* 9, no. 2 (2019): 439–60.

Puett, Michael. "The Offering of Food and the Creation of Order: The Practice of Sacrifice in Early China." In *Of Tripod and Palate: Food, Politics, and Religion in Traditional China*, ed. Roel Sterckx, 75–95. New York: Palgrave MacMillan, 2005.

Puett, Michael. "Ritual Disjunctions: Ghosts, Philosophy, and Anthropology." In *The Ground Between: Anthropologists Engage Philosophy*, ed. Veena Das, Michael Jackson, Arthur Kleinman, and Bhrigupati Singh, 218–33. Durham, NC: Duke University Press, 2014.

Puett, Michael. "Ritualization as Domestication: Ritual Theory from Classical China." In *Ritual Dynamics and the Science of Ritual, Volume I: Grammars and Morphologies of Ritual Practices in Asia*, ed. Axel Michaels, Anand Mishra, Lucia Dolce, Gil Raz, and Katja Triplett, 365–76. Wiesbaden: Harrassowitz Verlag, 2010.

Quigley, Declan, ed. *The Character of Kingship*. London: Routledge, 2005.

Radner, Karen. "Royal Decision-Making: Kings, Magnates, and Scholars." In *The Oxford Handbook of Cuneiform Cultures*, ed. K. Radner and E. Robson, 358–79. Oxford: Oxford University Press, 2011.

Radner, Karen. "The Trials of Esarhaddon: The Conspiracy of 670 BC." In *Assur und sein Umland. Im Andenken an die ersten Ausgräber von Assur*, ed. P. Miglus and J. Mª. Cordóba, 165–84. Isimu, vol. 6. Madrid: Universidad Autónoma de Madrid, 2003.

Rahman, Fazlur. "Islam and the Constitutional Problem of Pakistan." *Studia Islamica* 32 (1970): 275–87.

Rahman, Fazlur. "Islam and the New Constitution of Pakistan." *Journal of Asian and African Studies* 8, no. 3–4 (1973): 190–204.

Rappaport, Roy A. "Liturgies and Lies." *International Yearbook for Sociology of Knowledge and Religion* (1976): 75–104.

Rasmussen, Knud. *Intellectual Culture of the Iglulik. Report of the Fifth Thule Expedition, 1921–1922*, vol. 7. Copenhagen: Gvkkendalske Boghandel, 1929.

Ready, J. L. "Omens and Messages in the *Iliad* and *Odyssey*: A Study in Transmission." In *Between Orality and Literacy: Communication and Adaption in Antiquity*, ed. R. Scodel, 29–55. Leiden: Brill, 2014.

Redjala, Mohamed. "Un texte inédit de la *Muqaddima*." *Arabica* 22 (1975): 320–3.

Regmi, M. C. "Preliminary Notes on the Nature of the Gorkhali State and Administration" *Regmi Research Series* 10, no. 11: 141–7.

Reichel, Clemens. "The King Is Dead, Long Live the King: The Last Days of the Šū-Sîn Cult at Ešnunna." In *Religion and Power: Divine Kingship in the Ancient World and Beyond*, ed. N. Brisch, 133–55. Oriental Institute Seminars, 4. Chicago: Oriental Institute, 2008.

Rhodes, P. J., and R. Osborne. *Greek Historical Inscriptions 404–323 BC*. Oxford: Oxford University Press, 2003.

Riccardi, T. "The Royal Edicts of King Rama Shah of Gorkha." *Kailash* 5, no. 1 (1977): 29–65.

Rikala, Mia. "Sacred Marriage in the New Kingdom of Ancient Egypt: Circumstantial Evidence for a Ritual Interpretation." In *Sacred Marriages*, ed. M. Nissinen and R. Uro, 115–44. University Park: Pennsylvania University State Press, 2008.

Rizvi, Saiyid Athar Abbas. *Religious and Intellectual History of the Muslims in Akbar's Reign with Special Reference to Abu'l Fazl, 1556–1605*. New Delhi: Munshiram Manoharlal, 1975.

Robbins, Joel. "Transcendence and the Anthropology of Christianity: Language, Change, and Individualism (Edward Westermarck Memorial Lecture)." *Journal of the Finnish Anthropological Society* 37 (2012): 5–23.

Robinson, Francis. *The Ulama of Farangi Mahall and Islamic Culture in South Asia*. London: Hurst, 2001.

Robson, Eleanor. *Ancient Knowledge Networks. A Social Geography of Cuneiform Knowledge in First-Millennium Assyria and Babylonia*. London: UCL, 2019.

Robson, Eleanor. "Empirical Scholarship in the Neo-Assyrian Court." In *The Empirical Dimension of Ancient Near Eastern Studies*, ed. G. Selz, 603–29. Vienna: LIT Verlag, 2011.

Robson, Eleanor. *Mathematics in Ancient Iraq. A Social History*. Princeton, NJ: Princeton University Press, 2008.

Rochberg, Francesca. "The History of Science and Ancient Mesopotamia." *Journal of Ancient Near Eastern History* 1 (2014): 37–60.

Ross, Danielle. *Tatar Empire: Kazan's Muslims and the Making of Imperial Russia*. Bloomington: Indiana University Press, 2020.

Rostworowski de Diez Canseco, María. *Estructuras andinas del poder*. Lima: Instituto de Estudios Peruanos, 1983.

Rousseau, Jean-Jacques. *The Social Contract*. In *The Basic Political Writings*. 2nd ed. Ed. Donald A. Cress, 243–51. Indianapolis, IN: Hackett, 2011.

Rubio, Gonzalo. "On the Orthography of the Sumerian Literary Texts from the Ur III Period." *Acta Sumerologica* 22 (2000): 203–25.

Rumsey, Alan. "The Personification of Social Totalities." *Journal of Pacific Studies* 23 (1999): 48–70.

Rutter, K. *Greek Coinages of Southern Italy and Sicily*. London: Spink, 1997.

Sack, Ronald H. *Images of Nebuchadnezzar. The Emergence of a Legend. Second Revised and Expanded Edition*. Selinsgrove, NJ: Susquehanna University Press, 2004.

Sahlins, Marshall. *Islands of History*. Chicago: University of Chicago Press, 1985.

Sahlins, Marshall. "The Original Political Society." In *On Kings*, ed. David Graeber and Marshall Sahlins, 23–64. Chicago: HAU, 2017.

Sakya, Hemraj. *Samyak Mahadan Guthi*. Kathmandu: Jagatdhar Tuladhar, 1979.

Sallnow, Michael. *Pilgrims of the Andes*. Washington, DC: Smithsonian Institution Press, 1989.

Salomon, Frank. " 'The Beautiful Grandparents': Andean Ancestor Shrines and Mortuary Ritual as Seen Through Colonial Records." In *Tombs for the Living: Andean Mortuary Practices*, ed. Tom D. Dillehay, 315–53. Washington, DC: Dumbarton Oaks Research Library and Collection, 1995.

Salomon, Frank. *The Cord Keepers: Khipus and Cultural Life in a Peruvian Village*. Durham, NC: Duke University Press, 2004.

Salomon, Frank, and Jorge Urioste. *The Huarochirí Manuscript*. Austin: University of Texas Press, 1991.

Santillán, Hernando de. *Relación del Origen, Descendencia, Política y Gobierno de los Incas*. In *Historia de los Incas y Relación de su Gobierno*, ed. H. Urteaga, Colección de Libros y documentos referentes a la historia del Perú, vol. 9, 10–117. Lima: Imprenta y Librería Sanmartí, 1553 [1927].

Santner, Eric L. *The Royal Remains: The People's Two Bodies and the Endgames of Sovereignty*. Chicago: University of Chicago Press, 2011.

Santo Tomás, Domingo de. *Lexicon o Vocabulario de la Lengua General del Peru*. Lima: Universidad Nacional Mayor de San Marcos, 1560 [1951].

Sanyal, Usha. *Devotional Islam and Politics in British India: Ahmed Riza Khan Barelwi and His Movement, 1870–1920*. New Delhi: Oxford University Press, 1999.

Sarkar, B. *Heroic Shaktism: The Cult of Durga in Ancient Indian Kingship*. Oxford: Oxford University Press, 2017.

Sarmiento de Gamboa, Pedro. *Historia de los Incas*. Buenos Aires: Biblioteca Emecé, 1572 [1942].

Schaich, Michael. *Monarchy and Religion: The Transformation of Royal Culture in Eighteenth-Century Europe*. Oxford: Oxford University Press, 2007.

Schmitt, Carl. *The Leviathan in the State Theory of Thomas Hobbes: Meaning and Failure of a Political Symbol*. Trans. George Schwab. Chicago: University of Chicago Press, 2008.

Schmitt, Carl. *Political Theology: Four Chapters on the Concept of Sovereignty*. Ed. and trans. George Schwab. Chicago: University of Chicago Press, 2005.

Schofield, M. *Plato*. Oxford: Oxford University Press, 2006.

Schoorl, J. W. "Power, Ideology, and Change in the Early State of Buton." In *State and Trade in the Indonesian Archipelago*, ed. G. J. Schutte, 17–57. Leiden: KITLV, 1994.

Schulze, Reinhard. "Islam und Judentum im Angesicht der Protestantisierung der Religionen im 19. Jahrhundert." In *Judaism, Christianity and Islam in the Course of History: Exchange and Conflicts*, ed. Lothar Gall and Dietmar Willoweit, 139–64. Munich: Oldenbourg, 2010.

Scott, M. *Delphi and Olympia: The Spatial Politics of Panhellenism in the Archaic and Classical Periods*. Cambridge: Cambridge University Press, 2010.

Scott, Michael W. *Severed Snake: Matrilineages, Making Place, and a Melanesian Christianity in the Southeast Solomons*. Durham, NC: Carolina Academic Press, 2007.

Seaford, Richard. "The Interiorisation of Ritual in India and Greece." In *Universe and Inner Self in Early Indian and Early Greek Thought*, ed. Richard Seaford, 204–19. Edinburgh: Edinburgh University Press, 2016.

Seaford, Richard. *Money and the Early Greek Mind: Homer, Philosophy, Tragedy*. Cambridge: Cambridge University Press, 2004.

Seaford, Richard, ed. *Universe and Inner Self in Early Indian and Early Greek Thought*. Edinburgh: Edinburgh University Press, 2016.

Selden, John. *Titles of Honor*. London: 1614. 3rd ed., London: 1672.

"Seshat: Global History Databank." *Evolution Institute & Seshat Project*. Accessed April 17, 2021. http://seshatdatabank.info/.

Sever, A. *Nepal Under the Ranas*. Sittingbourne: Asia, 1993.

Shaha, R. *Essays in the Practice of Government in Nepal*. Delhi: Manohar, 1982.

Shaw, Wendy M. K. *What Is "Islamic" Art? Between Religion and Perception*. Cambridge: Cambridge University Press, 2019.

Sheehan, Jonathan. "Enlightenment, Religion, and the Enigma of Secularization: A Review Essay." *American Historical Review* 108 (2003): 1061–80.

Sheffield, Daniel. "The Language of Heaven in Safavid Iran: Speech and Cosmology in the Thought of Azar Kayvān and His Followers." In *There's No Tapping Around Philology*, ed. Alireza Korangy and Daniel Sheffield, 161–83. Wiesbaden: Otto Harrassowitz Verlag, 2014.

Shirazi, Qutb al-Din. *Sharh-i Hikmat al-Ishraq*. Ed. Mahdi Muhaqqiq and Abd Allah Nurani. Tehran: Anjuman-i Asar wa Mafakhir-i Farhangi, 1383/2004.

Shklar, Judith N. *Ordinary Vices*. Cambridge, MA: Belknap, 1985.

Shrestha, B. G. "The Death of Divine Kingship in Nepal: Nepal's Move from Autocratic Monarchy to a Fragile Republican State." In *Contesting the State: The Dynamics of Resistance and Control*, ed. A. Hobart and B. Kapferer, 195–223. Wantage: Sean Kingston, 2012.

Shrestha, S. "Maoist Defeat in Nepal: The Price of a Missed Opportunity." *Economic and Political Weekly* 49, no. 4 (2014): 13–16.

Shulman, D. *The King and the Clown in South Indian Myth and Poetry*. Princeton, NJ: Princeton University Press, 1985.

Sillander, Kenneth. "Relatedness and Alterity in Bentian Human-Spirit Relations." In *Animism in Southeast Asia: Persistence, Transformation and Renewal*, ed. Kaj Århem and Guido Sprenger, 157–80. London: Routledge, 2016.

Slusser, M. *Nepal Mandala: A Cultural Study of the Kathmandu Valley*. Princeton, NJ: Princeton University Press, 1982.

Smith, Jonathan Z. *To Take Place: Toward Theory in Ritual*. Chicago: University of Chicago Press, 1987.

Smith, William Robertson. *Lectures on the Religion of the Semites*. London: Adam and Charles Black, 1894.

Snell, B., ed. *Tragicorum Graecorum Fragmenta*. Vol. 1. Göttingen: Vandenhoeck and Ruprecht, 1971.

Sohn-Rethel, Alfred. *Intellectual and Manual Labour: A Critique of Epistemology*. London: MacMillan, 1978.

Sommerfeld, Walter. *Der Aufstieg Marduks in der babylonischen Religion des zweiten Jahrtausends v.Chr.* Alter Orient und Altes Testament, 213. Kevelaer: Butzen and Bercker, 1982.

Sommerfeld, Walter. "Marduk. A. Philologisch I. In Mesopotamien." *Reallexikon der Assyriologie*, vol. 7, 360–70. Berlin: DeGruyter, 1987–1990.

Speck, Frank. *Naskapi: The Savage Hunters of the Labrador Peninsula*. Norman: University of Nebraska Press, 1977.
Spengler, Oswald. *The Decline of the West*. 2 vols. New York: Knopf, 1932.
Springborg, Patricia. "Hobbes and Schmitt on the Name and Nature of Leviathan Revisited." *Critical Review of International Social and Political Philosophy* 12 (2010): 297–315.
Springborg, Patricia. "Hobbes's Biblical Beasts: Leviathan and Behemoth." *Political Theory* 23, no. 2 (1995): 353–75.
Stasavage, David. *The Decline and Rise of Democracy: A Global History from Antiquity to Today*. Princeton, NJ: Princeton University Press, 2020.
Stauffer, Devin. *Hobbes's Kingdom of Light: A Study of the Foundations of Modern Political Philosophy*. Chicago: University of Chicago Press, 2018.
Steadman, John M. "Leviathan and Renaissance Etymology." *Journal of the History of Ideas* 28 (1967): 575–6.
Stenerson, Anne. "A History of Jihadi Cinematography." In *Jihadi Culture: The Art and Social Practices of Militant Islamists*, ed. T. Hegghammer, 108–27. Cambridge: Cambridge University Press, 2017.
Stetkevych, Susanne. "Al-Akhtal and the Court of 'Abd al-Malik: The *Qasida* and the Construction of Umayyad Authority." In *Christians and Others in the Umayyad State*, ed. Antoine Borrut and Fred M. Donner, 129–55. Chicago: Oriental Institute, 2016.
Steymans, Hans Ulrich. "Die Literarische und historische Bedeutung der Thronfolgeregelung Asarhaddons." In *Die Deuteronomistischen Geschichtswerke*, ed. Jan Christian Gertz, Doris Prechel, Konrad Schmid, and Markus Witte, 331–49. Berlin: De Gruyter, 2006.
Stiller, L. *The Rise of the House of Gorkha: A Study in the Unification of Nepal, 1768–1816*. Delhi: Manjusri, 1973.
Strathern, Alan. *Converting Kings: Kongo, Thailand, Japan and Hawaii Compared, 1450–1850*. Cambridge: Cambridge University Press, forthcoming.
Strathern, Alan. "The Digestion of the Foreign in Sri Lankan History, c. 500–1850 CE." In *Sri Lanka at the Crossroads of History*, ed. Zoltán Biedermann and Alan Strathern, 216–38. London: UCL, 2017.
Strathern, Alan. "Drawing the Veil of Sovereignty: Early Modern Islamic Empires and Understanding Sacred Kingship." *History and Theory* 53 (2014): 79–93.
Strathern, Alan. "Transcendental Intransigence: Why Rulers Rejected Monotheism in Early Modern Southeast Asia and Beyond." *Comparative Studies in Society and History* 49 (2007): 285–383.
Strathern, Alan. *Unearthly Powers. Religious and Political Change in World History*. Cambridge: Cambridge University Press, 2019.
Strathern, Alan. "The Vijaya Origin Myth of Sri Lanka and the Strangeness of Kingship." *Past & Present* 203 (2009): 3–28.
Strathern, Andrew. "Great-Men, Leaders, Big-Men: The Link of Ritual Power." *Journal de la Société des Océanistes* 97 (1993): 145–58.
Strauss, Herman. *The Mi-Culture of the Mount Hagen People, Papua-New Guinea*. Pittsburgh, PA: University of Pittsburgh Press, 1990.
Strenski, Ivan. *Why Politics Can't Be Freed from Religion*. Malden, MA: Wiley-Blackwell, 2010.
Stroumsa, Guy. *The End of Sacrifice: Religious Transformations of Late Antiquity*. Chicago: University of Chicago Press, 2009.
Stroumsa, Guy. *The Making of the Abrahamic Religions in Late Antiquity*. Oxford: Oxford University Press, 2015.
Svendsen, Paulus. "Emperor and Galilean." In *Ibsen: A Collection of Critical Essays*, ed. Rolf Fjelde, 80–90. Englewood Cliffs, NJ: Prentice-Hall, 1965.
Tabassum, Rizwan. "Commemoration or Deification? Pakistanis Honor 'Martyred Queen' Benazir Bhutto." *NBC News*. January 2, 2013. http://worldnews.nbcnews.com/news/2013/01/02/16283955commemoration ordeificationpakistanishonormartyredqueenbenazirbhutto?lite.

Tadmor, Hayim. "Monarchy and the Elite in Assyria and Babylonia: The Question of Royal Accountability." In *The Origins of Diversity of Axial Age Civilizations*, ed. S. N. Eisenstadt, 203–24. Albany: State University of New York Press, 1986.

Tadmor, Hayim, Benno Landsberger, and Simo Parpola. "The Sin of Sargon and Sennacherib's Last Will." *State Archives of Assyria. Bulletin* 3 (1989) 3–52.

Tamanaha, B. Z. *On the Rule of Law: History, Politics, Theory*. Cambridge: Cambridge University Press, 2004.

Tambiah, Stanley. "On Flying Witches and Flying Canoes: The Coding of Male and Female Values." In *Culture, Thought, and Social Action: An Anthropological Perspective*, 287–315. Cambridge, MA: Harvard University Press. 1985.

Tareen, SherAli. *Defending Muhammad in Modernity*. Notre Dame, IN: Notre Dame University Press, 2020.

Taylor, Charles. *A Secular Age*. Cambridge, MA: Belknap, 2007.

Taylor, Gerald. "*Camay, Camac* et *Camasca* dans le Manuscrit Quechua de Huarochirí." *Journal de la Société des Américanistes* 63 (1974–1976): 231–44.

Taylor, Gerald. "Supay." *Amerindia* 5 (1980): 47–63.

Taylor, Jane. " 'Why Do You Tear Me from Myself?' Torture, Truth and the Arts of the Counter-Reformation." In *The Rhetoric of Sincerity*, ed. E. van Alphen, M. Bal, and C. E. Smith, 19–43. Stanford, CA: Stanford University Press, 2009.

Teitler, H. C. *The Last Pagan Emperor: Julian the Apostate and the War Against Christianity*. Oxford: Oxford University Press, 2017.

Tenney, Jonathan S. "The Elevation of Marduk Revisited: Festivals and Sacrifices at Nippur During the High Kassite Period." *Journal of Cuneiform Studies* 68 (2016): 153–80.

Thattavi, Qadi Ahmad, and Asaf Khan Qazvini. *Tarikh-i Alfi: Tarikh-i Hazar Sala-i Islam*. Ed. Ghulam Reza Tabatabai Majd. 8 vols. Tehran: Intisharat-i 'ilmi va Farhangi, 1382/2002.

Thomas, R. *Oral Tradition and Written Record in Classical Athens*. Cambridge: Cambridge University Press, 1989.

Thucydides. *Historiae*. Ed. H. S. Jones with revisions by J. E. Powell. Oxford: Oxford University Press, 1942.

Thucydides. *The Peloponnesian War*. Trans. Richard Crawley. New York: Dutton, 1910.

Toffin, G. *La fête-spectacle: Théatre et rite au Népal*. Paris: Editions de la Maison des Sciences de l'Homme, 2010.

Toffin, G. *Le palais et le temple: La function royale dans la vallée du Népal*. Paris: CNRS, 1993.

Toffin, G. *Société et religion chez les Néwar du Népal*. Paris: CNRS, 1984.

Toffin, G. "A Vaishnava Theatrical Performance in Nepal: The 'Kāttī-pyākhā' of Lalitpur City." *Asian Theatre Journal* 29, no. 1 (2012): 126–63.

Toynbee, Arnold. *A Study of History*. 12 vols. Oxford, Oxford University Press, 1951–1961.

Trilling, Lionel. *Sincerity and Authenticity*. Cambridge, MA: Harvard University Press, 1973.

Truschke, Audrey. *Culture of Encounters: Sanskrit at the Mughal Court*. New York: Columbia University Press, 2016.

Tugendhaft, Aaron. *The Idols of ISIS: From Assyria to the Internet*. Chicago: University of Chicago Press, 2020.

Uesugi, T. "Re-examining Transnationalism from Below and Transnationalism from Above: British Gurkhas' Life Strategies and the Brigade of Gurkhas' Employment Policies." In *Nepalis Inside and Outside Nepal: Social Dynamics in Northern South Asia Vol. 1*, ed. H. Ishii, D. N. Gellner, and K. Nawa, 383–410. Delhi: Manohar, 2007.

Unclassified Verbatim Transcript of Combatant Status Review Tribunal Hearing for ISN 10024.

Uspenskij, Boris A. "Tsar and Pretender: Samozvancestvo or Royal Imposture in Russia as a Cultural-Historical Phenomenon." In *"Tsar and Pretender" and Other Essays in Russian Cultural Semiotics*, ed. B. A. Uspenskij and Victor Zhivov, 113–52. Boston: Academic Studies, 2012.

Vacín, Ludek. "Šulgi of Ur. Life, Deeds, Ideology and Legacy of a Mesopotamian Ruler as Reflected Primarily in Literary Texts." PhD diss., University of London, 2011.
Vaidya, T. R. *Jaya Prakash Malla: The Brave Malla King of Kantipur*. New Delhi: Anmol, 2014.
Vaillant, George E. *Spiritual Evolution: A Scientific Defense of Faith*. New York: Broadway, 2008.
Valcárcel, Luis. "La Religión Incaica." In *Historia del Perú*, vol. 3, 75–202. Lima: Mejía Baca, 1980.
Valera, Blas. *Relación de las costumbres antiguas de los naturales del Pirú*. In *Biblioteca de Autores Españoles* vol. 209, 153–77. Madrid: Ediciones Atlas, 1590 [1968].
Valeri, Valerio. "Diarchy and History in Hawaii and Tonga." In *Culture and History in the Pacific*, ed. Jukka Siikala, 45–79. Helsinki: Finnish Anthropological Society, 1990.
Valeri, Valerio. *Kingship and Sacrifice: Ritual and Society in Ancient Hawaii*. Chicago: University of Chicago Press, 1985.
Van Apeldoorn, Laurens, and Robin Douglass, eds. *Hobbes on Politics and Religion*. Oxford: Oxford University Press, 2018.
Van Berke, Maaike, ed. *Crisis and Continuity at the Abbasid Court*. Leiden, Brill, 2013.
Van den Hoek, B. "Does Divinity Protect the King? Ritual and Politics in Nepal." *Contributions to Nepalese Studies* 17, no. 2 (1990): 147–55.
Van den Hoek, B. *Caturmāsa: Celebrations of Death in Kathmandu, Nepal*. Kathmandu: Vajra, 2014 [2004].
Van Driel, Govert. *The Cult of Aššur*. Assen: Van Gorcum, 1969.
van Ess, Josef. *Der Wesir und seine Gelehrten*. Wiesbaden: Abhandlungen für die Kunde des Morgenlandes XLV/4, 1981.
Vanessa, Elisa Grotti, and Olga Ulturgavsheva, eds. *Animism in Rainforest and Tundra: Personhood, Animals, Plants, and Things in Contemporary Amazonia and Siberia*. New York: Berghahn, 2012.
Van Laan, Thomas F. "Ibsen and Nietzsche." *Scandinavian Studies* 78, no. 3 (2006): 255–302.
Vernant, Jean-Pierre. "At Man's Table: Hesiod's Foundation Myth of Sacrifice." In *The Cuisine of Sacrifice among the Greeks*, ed. Marcel Detienne and Jean-Pierre Vernant, trans. Paula Wissing, 21–86. Chicago: University of Chicago Press, 1989.
Vesel, Živa. "The Persian Translation of Fakhr al-Din Rāzi's al Sirr al Maktūm ('The Occult Secret') for Iltutmish." In *Confluence of Cultures: French Contributions to Indo-Persian Studies*, ed. Françoise 'Nalini' Delvoye, 14–22. Delhi: Manohar, 1994.
Vicedom, Georg F., and Herbert Tischner. *The Mbowamb: The Culture of the Mount Hagen Tribes in East Central New Guinea*. 3 vols. Xerox manuscript. Canberra: Australian National University, 1943–1948.
"Video: Islamic State Media Branch Releases 'The End of Sykes-Picot.'" July 1, 2014. *The Belfast Telegraph*. https://www.belfasttelegraph.co.uk/video-news/video-islamic-state-media-branch-releases-the-end-of-sykes-picot-30397575.html.
Viveiros de Castro, Eduardo. *Cosmological Perspectivism in Amazonia and Elsewhere*. Manchester: HAU Network of Ethnographic Theory, 2012.
Viveiros de Castro, Eduardo. *From the Enemy's Point of View: Humanity and Divinity in Amazonia*. Chicago: University of Chicago Press, 1992.
Walbridge, John. *The Wisdom of the Mystic East: Suhrawardī and Platonic Orientalism*. Albany: State University of New York Press, 2001.
Walens, Stanley. *Feasting with Cannibals: An Essay on Kwakiutl Cosmology*. Princeton, NJ: Princeton University Press, 1981.
Wallraff, Martin. "Viele Metaphern—viele Götter? Beobachtungen zum Monotheismus in der Spätantike." In *Metaphorik und Christologie*, ed. Jörg Frei, Jan Rohls, and Ruben Zimmermann, 151–66. Berlin: Walter de Gruyter, 2013.
Walsh, E. H. *The Coinage of Nepal*. Delhi: Indological Book House, 1973.
Walzer, Michael. *Exodus and Revolution*. New York: Basic Books, 1985.
Waterhouse, Rev. Joseph. *The King and People of Fiji*. London: Wesleyan Conference Office, 1866.

Weber, M. *The Religion of India: The Sociology of Hinduism and Buddhism*. Ed. and trans. H. H. Gerth and D. Martindale. New York: Free Press, 1958.
West, M. L., ed. *Iambi et Elegi Graeci ante Alexandri Cantati*. Vol. 1. Oxford: Oxford University Press, 1971.
Westenholz, Joan Goodnick. *Legends of the Kings of Agade. The Texts*. Mesopotamian Civilizations, vol. 7. Winona Lake, IN: Eisenbrauns, 1997.
Whelpton, J. "The Ancestors of Jang Bahadur Rana: History, Propaganda and Legend." *Contributions to Nepalese Studies* 14, no. 3 (1987): 161–92.
Whelpton, J. *A History of Nepal*. Cambridge: Cambridge University Press, 2005.
Whelpton, J. "Political Identity in Nepal: State, Nation, and Community." In *Nationalism and Ethnicity in Nepal*, ed. D. N. Gellner, J. Pfaff-Czarnecka, and J. Whelpton, 39–78. Kathmandu: Vajra, 2008 [1997].
Whitehouse, Harvey. *Arguments and Icons: Divergent Modes of Religiosity*. Oxford: Oxford University Press, 2000.
Whitehouse, Harvey. "Implicit and Explicit Knowledge in the Domain of Ritual." In *Current Approaches in the Cognitive Study of Religion*, ed. Veikko Antonnen and Ilka Pyysiäinen, 133–52. London: Continuum, 2002.
Whitehouse, Harvey. "Modes of Religiosity: Towards a Cognitive Explanation of the Sociopolitical Dynamics of Religion." *Method and Theory in the Study of Religion* 14 (2002): 293–315.
Whitmarsh, B. "*Ganatantra Smarak* (Republic Memorial): The Politics of Memory." *Studies in Nepali History and Society* 24, no. 1 (2019): 171–216.
Whitmarsh, B. "The Narayanhiti Palace Museum: Memory, Power, and National Identity." Unpublished PhD diss., University of London, 2018.
Whitmarsh, B. "Staging Memories at the Narayanhiti Palace Museum, Kathmandu." *Himalaya* 37, no. 1 (2017): article 13. digitalcommons.macalester.edu/himalaya/vol37/iss1/13/.
Wildeberg, Christian. "Neoplatonism." In *The Stanford Encyclopedia of Philosophy*, ed. Edward N. Zalta, Summer 2019 edition. https://plato.stanford.edu/archives/sum2019/entries/neoplatonism/.
Willis, M. *The Archaeology of Hindu Ritual: Temples and the Establishment of the Gods*. Cambridge: Cambridge University Press, 2009.
Winter, Charlie. *The Terrorist Image: De-coding the Islamic State's Photo-Propaganda*. London: Hurst, 2021.
Wisnovsky, Robert. "On the Emergence of Maragha Avicennism." *Oriens* 46 (2018): 263–331.
Witzel, M. "The Coronation Rituals of Nepal, with Special Reference to the Coronation of King Birendra." In *Heritage of the Kathmandu Valley*, ed. N. Gutschow and A. Michaels, 415–67. Sankt Augustin, Germany: VGH Wissenschaftsverlag, 1987.
Wright, M. *The Lost Plays of Greek Tragedy: Volume 1: Neglected Authors*. London: Bloomsbury, 2016.
Xenophon. *Omnia Opera*. Ed. E. C. Marchant. Oxford: Oxford University Press, 1910–1963.
Yavari, Neguin. *Advice for the Sultan: Prophetic Voices and Secular Politics in Medieval Islam*. London: Hurst, 2014.
Yaya, Isabel. *The Two Faces of Inca History: Dualism in the Narratives and Cosmology of Ancient Cuzco*. Leiden: Brill, 2012.
Yelle, Robert A. "'An Age of Miracles': Disenchantment as a Secularized Theological Narrative." In *Narratives of Disenchantment and Secularization: Critiquing Max Weber's Idea of Modernity*, ed. Robert A. Yelle and Lorenz Trein, 129–48. London: Bloomsbury, 2020.
Yelle, Robert A. " 'By Fire and Sword': Early English Critiques of Islam and Judaism as 'Impostures' or Political and 'Unfree' Religions." *Patterns of Prejudice* 53 (2020): 91–108.
Yelle, Robert A. *Sovereignty and the Sacred: Secularism and the Political Economy of Religion*. Chicago: University of Chicago Press, 2019.
Yelle, Robert A. "Was Aśoka Really a Secularist Avant-la-Lettre? Ancient Indian Pluralism and Toleration in Historical Perspective." *Modern Asian Studies*, forthcoming.

Yılmaz, Hüseyin. *Caliphate Redefined. The Mystical Turn in Ottoman Political Thought*. Princeton, NJ: Princeton University Press, 2018.

Yoffee, Norman. *Myths of the Archaic State: Evolution of the Earliest Cities, States, and Civilizations*. Cambridge: Cambridge University Press, 2005.

Yoffee, Norman, and Andrea Seri. "Negotiating Fragility in Ancient Mesopotamia: Arenas of Contestation and Institutions of Resistance." In *The Evolution of Fragility: Setting the Terms*, ed. Norman Yoffee, 183–96. Cambridge: McDonald Institute for Archaeological Research, 2019.

Zaman, Muhammad Qasim. "The Sovereignty of God in Modern Islamic Thought." *Journal of the Royal Asiatic Society* 25, no. 3 (2015): 389–418.

Zgoll, Annette. "Königslauf und Götterrat. Struktur und Deutung des babylonischen Neujahrsfestes." In *Festtraditionen in Israel und im Alten Orient*, ed. E. Blum and R. Lux, 11–80. Veröffentlichungen der Wissenschaftlichen Gesellschaft für Theologie, 28. Gütersloh: Gütersloher Verlagshaus, 2006.

Ziai, Hossein. "Illuminationism." In *Encyclopædia Iranica*. Accessed January 9, 2020. http://www.iranicaonline.org/articles/kadimi-zoroastrian-sect.

Ziai, Hossein. "Source and Nature of Authority: A Study of Suhrawardi's Illuminationist Political Doctrine." In *The Political Aspects of Islamic Philosophy*, ed. Charles Butterworth, 304–44. Cambridge, MA: Harvard University Center for Middle Eastern Studies, 1992.

Zotter, A. "Conquering Navarātra: Documents on the Reorganisation of a State Festival." In *Studies in Historical Documents from Nepal and India*, ed. S. Cubelic, A. Michaels, and A. Zotter, 493–531. Heidelberg: Heidelberg University Publishing, 2018.

Zotter, A. "The Making and Unmaking of Rulers: On Denial of Ritual in Nepal." In *The Ambivalence of Denial: Danger and Appeal of Rituals*, ed. U. Husken and U. Simon, 221–56. Wiesbaden: Harrassowitz, 2016.

Zotter, A. "State Rituals in a Secular State? Replacing the Nepalese King in the Pacali Bhairava Sword Procession and Other Rituals." In *Religion, Secularism, and Ethnicity in Contemporary Nepal*, ed. D. N. Gellner, S. Hausner, and C. Letizia, 265–301. Delhi: Oxford University Press, 2016.

Zotter, A. "Who Kills the Buffalo? Authority and Agency in the Ritual Logistics of the Nepalese Dasaī Festival." In *Nine Nights of Power: Durgā, Dolls and Darbārs*, ed. U. Husken, V. Narayanan, and A. Zotter, 193–220. Albany: State University of New York Press, 2021.

Zuidema, R. Tom. *The Ceque System of Cuzco*. Leiden: Brill, 1964.

Index

Abu Mashar al-Balkhi, 211
Abul Fazl, 202, 203, 204, 206
Act of Supremacy, 226, 230
adverse sacralization, 16–17, 20
Agamben, Giorgio, 22
Age of Absolutism, 241
agriculture, 24, 43, 55, 61, 66, 138
Ainian, Mazarakis, 115
Akbar, 201: *Akbar Nama*, 192, 204–6; belief in Islam, 206–7; interpreting as Neoplatonic ruler, 192–222; imperial ideology, 195; legacy of, 207–10; magic powers of, 206; as millennial being, 202–4; ratio of, 205–7; sun and soul contributing to rule of, 210–14
Akhenaten, 237–38
Akhlāq, 200
al-Akhtal, 178
Alexander the Great, kingship of, 114, 117, 125–30
Andes, kingship in, 53–56; acting in place of Sun, 63–64; divine kingship in, 56–60; divisions in, 61–67; dualities, 61–67; hierarchical complementarity, 62, 65; moieties, 62–63, 65; stranger-kingship in, 56–60; timeline, 53; *vecochina*, 58–59; Wankas, 63; withdrawal/return pulse, 57–58
animists, 31, 41, 48, 57

Anne, Queen, 241
anthropology, 1–3, 33, 181, 240
apocalypse, peculiarity of, 316–17
Archilochus, 119
Arendt, Hannah, 315, 317–18, 322n32
aretē (excellence), 113–14, 116, 123–25, 129–30, 334
Arid Zone, 197
Aristotle, 113–14, 121, 123–25, 129–30, 181, 194, 196, 212, 333–34
Arrhidaeus, Philip, 117, 126
Assassin's Creed, 318
Assmann, Jan, 5, 224–29, 257; on monotheism, 10; on pharaonic kingship, 94–107; On Thomas Hobbes, 224–29, 237–42; wisdom tales, 8. *See also* counter-religion; Exodus; reversal of; Mosaic distinction
Assyria, 78, 83–85, 87, 332; contrasting Babylonia with, 79–82, 328; New Year's festivals in, 81–82; religious centralization in, 79–81
Assyriology, 73
Athens, 116, 120, 122–23, 126–27, 131n13
autognōmenes, 121
Axial Age, 5, 9, 20, 48, 67, 82, 138, 166, 224–25, 229; affecting Eurasia, 334–35, 338–41, 344; criticism of, 327–28; law constraint, 111–14; meaning of

Axial Age (*continued*)
ritual following, 329; Mesopotamia notions, 85–86; movements, 138, 142, 146, 158–59, 329–31; rejecting sacrifice, 158–59; relation to Confucius, 146, 155–56, 329–31; reversal of, 227, 241; South Asian religions, 271–72; term, 106n1; transformation from immanence to transcendence, 8

ayllu, 53, 56–59, 61, 67

Babylonia, 78–79, 337; Babylonian Epic of Creation, 79; Babylon-friendly politics, 84; contrasting Assyria and, 79–82, 328; honoring gods of, 85, 87; hostility to Jews, 232–33, 332; New Year's festivals in, 81–82, 85, 331; religious centralization in, 70–81; uprisings in, 84

Bada☒uni, Abd al-Qadir, 202–3, 206, 212
Baghdad, 162, 169–70, 181, 183, 200, 336
Bahadur, Jang, 278–79, 281–82
Bahuns, 276–79
basileis (rulers), 116–17, 119–20
Basileus, 163, 165, 170, 180–81
Behemoth, interpreting, 232. *See also* Leviathan
Bellah, Robert, 5
Bentian Dayak, 41
Bhutto, Benazir, 23
biblical iconoclasm, political meaning of, 102–7
Birendra, King, 280–82, 285
blessings, 40, 107, 278, 284–86, 300, 325, 343
Bloch, Marc, 3–4, 141, 149–50
Bodin, Jean, 177
Book of Rites, 147, 149, 151
Borsippa, 79–81
Bouldue, Jacques, 232
Bowersock, G. W., 251, 256
Brandes, George, 256
British East India Company, 277–78
Bronze Age, 137, 143, 150; kingdoms, 137–38, 143; sacrificial system, 147, 151

Buddhism, 12–13, 20, 138, 153, 185, 272, 275, 329, 333
Burke, Edmund, 165

Caliphate, 162–67; common assertion regarding, 169–70; cosmological vacuum left by, 170–71; culture of, 180–85; Mohammadomimesis, 184; legal definition of, 169; preternatural sovereignty of, 171–76; revived version of, 170; therapeutic form of, 167–71; self-referential sovereignty, 176–79; typology in, 180–81
Capac, Huayna, 64
Carpet of Mirth, 212
Castro, Viveiros de, 47
celeritas, 16, 140
Celestial Masters, 138, 151–55, 158, 330
China, 9, 48, 157–60; Axial Age movements in, 145–46; dynastic cycle in, 143–45; empire in, 150–51; historical dynamics in, 154; immanentism practices, 143–45; millenarian movements in, 151–53; rejecting sacrifice, 137–39; sacrificial system in, 143–45; sovereignty rituals in, 153–54; transcendental movements in, 145–46; transcendental unmaskings in, 154–59; Warring States period, 150. *See also* sovereignty; vitality
Christianity, 13, 20, 107, 138, 153, 256–58; Christian Hebraism, 231; Emperor and Galilean, 256–59, 263, 265; Greek sacrifice lens, 150; inventive Andean Christianity, 68n1; millenarian movements and, 151–53; Reformation Christianity, 166–67; transcendental sovereignty, 142–43
Church, 12, 18, 225–26
clerisy, 12, 18, 179, 333–34
Codrington, Bishop, 41–2, 44–45
cognition, 6, 9–11
Cold War, 304, 310
Confucius, 138, 146, 151, 153, 155, 159
Constantine, 165–66, 174, 180–81, 184, 255

constitutionalism, move toward, 121–22
cosmic divination, 15, 335
cosmic kingship, 15, 23, 28n64, 140, 332, 337; in Mesopotamia, 81; Neoplatonism, 197–98, 202, 205, 213
cosmic polity, 1, 31–32, 34, 37–38, 323, 327
Cubelic, Simon, 279
Cumont, Franz, 181
Curse of Agade, 84–85
Cuthean Legend, 84–85
Cyrus the Younger, 123

dead, 32, 35; components of, 59–60; integration into ancestral communities, 58–59; *Ma'at*, 101; mummifying, 56–57; presence of, 37–38. *See also* ghosts; spirits
Decalogue, 103
deity; creator deity, 142, 145, 151–52, 154, 158; higher deity, 143; patron deity, 74, 78, 80; sovereign deity, 30n80, 47; term, 165–66
Deuteronomy, 102, 105–6
al-Dhubyani, al-Nabigha, 176
Di, 144
diarchy, 54–56, 278, 327; Andean diarchy, 62–63, 66; integrating distinctions, 61–66. *See also* Andes, kingship in
Dinka, 36, 40
Diodorus, 118–19
disenchantment, 337–44
divination, 82, 85, 87; divine gifts, 74–76; dynastic cycle, 143–45; experts, 83; science of, 206; subtypes of, 14–21. *See also* Mesopotamia, kingship in: preliminaries
divine kingship, 16; core of, 54; dark side of, 54–55; fundamental premise of, 65–66
divinity, humanization of, 31–32; austere transcendentalism, 48–49; hegemons, 37; hierarchy, 36–39, 43–46; highest gods, 37; hubris, 39–41; human finitude, 32–34; power, 41–43; powers, 36–39; precedent of political action, 46–48; spiritual multitude, 32–34

divinization, 14; cosmic, 15, 335; forms of, 17, 20; heroic dimension to, 325, 345n14; self-divinization, 145, 151–53, 158, 331
divinized kingship, 193, 198, 272, 324, 338–40; centrality of, 328; cosmic form of, 325–27; heroic form of, 325–27, 334; immanentist mode, 15, 19
doctrinal kingship, 19, 22, 143, 153
domestication, rituals, 147–50
Dreros, 112, 120
dual sovereignty, 225, 241, 264–65, 278
Duindam, Jeroen, 16
Dumézil, Georges, 54–55, 139–40, 154
Dumont, Louis, 274–75
dynastic cycle, 143–45, 151, 153–54, 158, 326. *See also* China

E'annatum, 75, 325
egalitarian peoples, 35
Egypt, pharaonic kingship in, 8, 94–102; duality, 94–95; incarnation, 97–101; representing Horus, 95–97; tasks of king on earth, 101–2. *See also* Exodus, reversal of
elder-rulers *(kurakas)*, 57
emanationism, 194. *See also* Neoplatonism: defining
empathy, harnessing, 6–7
Emperor and Galilean (Ibsen), 249–50, 249–51; aesthetic priorities of, 253–57; bridge between works and, 251–53; dramatic inventions in, 261–63; modern currents in, 264–67; sovereign conversion, 258–60. *See also* Julian (*Emperor and Galilean*)
emperors, 20, 179–81, 338; Mughal, 192, 206; Roman, 177, 184, 194–95, 249, 340–41; term, 165–66
empire: emergence of, 150–51; gunpowder empires, 169; universal, 192, 210, 334–37. *See also* Neoplatonism; sovereignty
Enlil, 78
epic, law in, 111–15
Erastianism, 224, 229–30
Erastus, Thomas, 229–30

Ernst, Carl, 210
Esarhaddon of Assyria, 83–84
ethics, 10–11, 13, 17, 165, 184, 327
Euripides, 122
Eusebius, 165, 180, 184
Evans-Pritchard, E. E., 35
Exodus, reversal of, 240–42; democratic revolution, 236–40; identifying Leviathan, 232–36; Mortal God figure, 223, 227, 230–31, 234–35, 239; reducing religion to politics, 229–32; sacred kingship exodus, 223–29; state fetishism, 227

Faizi, 203, 204, 210, 212
al-Farabi, 195
al-Farazdaq, 176
Fath Allah Shirazi, Shah 202–3, 206
Fiji, tribal kingship in, 44–46
Firth, Raymond, 38
Foley, Jim, 305
Frankfort, Henri, 48
Frazer, James G., 3, 40, 46, 53–54, 323
Freud, Sigmund, 324

Gandhi, Mohandas, 302, 304
Geertz, Clifford, 275–76
Gelasius, Pope, I, 225–26
Gellner, Ernest, 12
Geneva Bible, 232–34
geographical separation, 60
gerousia, 121
ghosts, 33, 37, 145, 147, 150–52, 155, 157; ghostly authority, 230, 236, 240–41
Gilgamesh, 77
glissando, 164–65, 170, 178–85
God, Israel, 102–7. *See also* Israel
Godelier, Maurice, 178–79
Goldman, Irving, 39
Gommans, Jos, 20, 192, 336, 342
Gose, Peter, 16, 324
Gottwald, Norman, 239
Graeber, David, 3, 16, 18, 23, 116, 223
Grand Conjunction, 167–68, 172
gravitas, 16, 140

Great Divergence, 2
Great Peace movement, 138, 151–53. *See also* China
Greece, 9; first known written law in, 120–21; hero-cult, 117–18, 126; heroic nature of ruling, 116–17; immanentist kingship in, 115–19; king as god and law, 125–30; Olympic Games, 116, 118, 325; rule of law in, 111–15; transcendentalism in, 119–25
Gupta Empire, 275
Gurung, Dhan Bahadur, 281
Gyanendra, King, 282–83

Hagen people, 32
Hakim Ali Gilani, 202
Hakim Humam, 202
Halbertal, Moshe, 239
Hammurabi of Babylon, 79
Han Empire, 151
Haravi, Nizam al-Din Ahmad, 202
Harrison, Simon, 32–33
Hebrew Bible, 226, 228, 233, 235, 239, 247n80; alignment, 261; transcendentalism and, 331, 335. *See also* Exodus, reversal of
heroes: divination, 14–15, 151, 334; kingship, 15, 19–20, 140, 197, 325; hubris and, 39–41
heroic kingship, 15, 19–20, 140, 197, 325
Heroön, 116, 132n24
Hesiod, 117, 119, 131, 150
Hieron, 118–19
hijaba, 183
Hindu kingship, 271–74; classic theories of, 274–76; Dasain festival, 285–86; Laws of Manu, 272; in Malla period, 276–79; monarchy decline, 282–84; post-1951 monarchy, 280–81; post-kingship modernization, 286–89; Rana period, 278–79; ritualization trap, 278; in Shah period, 276–79; tantras, 275
Hinduism, 271–73, 275, 328–29; Tantric, 272, 275
Hobbes, Thomas, 223–24, 302; reducing religion to politics, 229–32

INDEX   385

Hocart, A. M., 3, 10, 14, 44–45, 47, 162, 178, 231, 323
hoi tuchontes, 121
Holmes, Stephen, 239
hubris, 46–48, 168; Caliphal hubris, 182–83; descent as kind of, 44; divinized kingship as form of, 324; heroes and, 39–41; pharaoh and, 331; Philosopher King and, 124; sovereign hubris, 183
Huizong, Emperor, 154
humanization, 31, 338. See also China
Humphreys, Sally, 113–14
Hunt, John, 45
hypocrite (*munafiq*), 314, 317. See also Islamic State of Iraq and Syria (ISIS), sovereignty of: hypocrisy

Ibn ʿArabi, 171, 198–99
Ibn Khaldun, 172, 209–10
Ibn Qasi, 172
Ibsen, Henrik: aesthetic priorities, 253–57; bridging works of, 251–53; dramatic inventions in work of, 261–63; inspiration of, 249, 251, xiv; modern currents, 264–67; sovereign conversion, 258–60
Illuminationism, 199–200, 205, 210, 217n26
immanence, 6–9, 109n16, 197, 328; Andes as case of, 53–71, 324; Axial Age transformation, 8; divine kingship as core of, 54; kingship types and, 19; makeup of, 14; plays of Ibsen, 257; predominance of ritual in, 7–8; sacred kingship between, 19; of transcendence, 162–85, 335–36; world history, and, 14–21
immanentism, 5, 7–9, 26n24, 48, 67, 163–66, 271; Andean immanence, 57, 60, 324; between transcendentalism and, 166, 257, 335–36; of Caliphal, 175; enchanting politics, 323–24; idealizing cosmic kingship, 17–18; Maʿat and, 109n16; mentality accompanying, 27n38; politics of righteousness, 327–28; production, 324; royal accountability,

82–87; shift to transcendentalism, 224–25, 227; term, 138; traditions, 14, 21; transcendentalism *vs.*, 328–31
Incas, 16, 53–54, 328; diarchy of, 63–64; regaining autonomy from, 62–63; secessionist rebellions, 65; Upper/Lower Cuzco relation, 63
India, 9, 302–4; Axial Age India, 27n44; Hindu kingship and, 272–73, 275, 277, 283, 285, 289; installation rituals, 139; Neoplatonism in, 202–3, 208, 212–14, 217n28; transcendentalism vs. immanentism, 328–31. See also Kathmandu Valley
Inuit, 39–40
Islam, 20, 138, 142, 153; anarchist/neoliberal views of, 303; ghostly appearance of, 303–4; Hajj, 13; Shia version, 308–9
Islamic State of Iraq and Syria (ISIS), sovereignty of, 166, 299–301, 322n32, 331, 341–43; absent sovereign, 315–19; criticizing modern state, 301–4; *ghayr muqallid*, 306; hypocrisy, 312–15; logic of mirrors, 304–9; militancy surface, 311–12; *qiyas*, 306; secrecy emphasis, 309–11
Israel, 9; divine sonship in, 106–7; rejection of images in, 102–7; role of God in, 102–7. See also Exodus, reversal of; Hebrew Bible

Jacobsen, Thorkild, 31
Jamiʿ al-Tawarikh (Compendium of Histories), 200
Jatra, Bhoto, 284
joy, harnessing, 6–7
Judaism, 27n45, 107, 166, 225, 335; Torah, 102, 104. See also Exodus, reversal of; Hebrew Bible
Julian (*Emperor and Galilean*), 249–50, 337, 340–41; aesthetic priorities regarding, 253–57; coloring events surrounding, 261–63; in history, 250–51, 253; modern currents, 264–67; sovereign conversion, 258–60

Julian the Apostle, 193
Jupiter, 167, 192, 204
Justinian, 180

ka'ba, 13
kamaqnin, 59–60
Kathmandu Valley, 272, 276–78, 284, 286. *See also* Hindu kingship; Nepal, kingship in
al-Katib, 'Abd al-Hamid ibn Yahya, 182
kava rites, 38, 45–46
Khalid Sheikh Mohammed, 313
khalifa, 18
Khan, Chinggis, 207–10
Khan, Ghazan, 205, 208–9
Khan, Naqib, 202
Khan, Ögedei, 208
Khatiwoda, Rajan, 279
kingship: accepting diversity, 207; breaking down divinized form of, 325–27; congeniality to immanent nature of, 179; defining, 1–2; *dharma*, 274; *dharma-raja*, 272–73; in dynastic cycle, 144–45; ending kingship, 271–98; forms of, 76, 166, 275, 326; idea of, 97, 107, 273; inbetween-ness of, 14; king as god, 279; kings before; 31–49; kingless societies, 323–24; *ksatra*, 274; *maharaja* title, 278; modernization following, 286–89; Mesopotamian, 73–74, 87; Mortall God, 178; Muslim, 168–69, 171, 175, xiii; Neoplatonism, 192–222; pharaonic kingship, 94–102; preliminaries of, 74–79; principal functions, 104; recent conquest and, 197; sonship and, 106–7; transmission, 179; types of, 16, 19, 164, 195–96. *See also* cosmic kingship; divine kingship; divinized kingship, doctrinal kingship, heroic kingship, righteous kingship, sacred kingship, stranger-kingship; zealous kingship
Kirkpatrick, Colonel, 272
Kitab al-Milal wa al-Nihal (The book of sects and creeds), 211

Kitchmanitoci, 35
knotted cord literacy, 67
Koirala, B. P., 280
Koirala, Girija, 283–84

Lagash-Umma border conflict, 74–75
Lamentation over the Destruction of Sumer and Ur, 73–74
Laozi, 153–54
Late Intermediate Period, 53, 65
law: ancestral law, 123–25; divine law, 112, 122, 134n75, 308, 310, 333, 342; eternity of, 121; rule of, 111, 113–14; sacred law, 196, 301–2, 304, 308–19, 313; written laws, 112–13, 120–25, 131n13
Lecomte-Tilouine, Marie, 277
Lévi-Strauss, Claude, 15, 324
Lévi, Sylvain, 272–73
Leviathan (Hobbes), 223, 236; chapter 29 of, 230; civil and ecclesiastical powers, 237; describing Commandments, 238; as esoteric text, 231; frontispiece of, 232; works cited in, 235
Leviathan, identifying, 226–27, 230–31; interpreting term, 234–35; as Pharaoh, 232–36
Levy, Robert, 271–72, 277
Lienhardt, 40
Lincoln, Bruce, 155
lineage *(numaym)*, 43–44
literati, 82
Locke, John, 224–25
locum tenens, 45

Ma'at, political concept, 101–2. *See also* Egypt, pharaonic kingship in
al-Ma'mun, Caliph 193
Mahendra, King, 280, 287
Malcolm, Noel, 232
Malinowski, Bronislaw, 33
mallki, 60. *See also* dead
mana, 34, 36, 38–39, 41–42, 47
Mandate of Heaven, 144–45, 326
Maneck, Susan, 199
manitou, 47

Männerbunde, 170
Martabat Tujuh, 201
Maududi, Abul Ala, 301–3
Maul, Stefan, 80
Mauss, Marcel, 34
al-Mawardi, 184
Mehmet II, 193
Melville, Charles, 3
Mesopotamia, kingship in, 72–74; Axial-Age notions of accountability, 85–86; Lagash-Umma border conflict, 74–75; preliminaries, 74–79; rituals, 79–82; royal accountability, 82–88
metahumans, 33; powers, 32, 37–39, 42, 47; sources, 37, 41, 47
metapersons, 1, 6–12, 14, 16, 57, 72, 162, 324, 330, 333; hierarchy and, 36–37; Neoplatonism and, 196; spirit owners/masters, 34–35; term, xii, 24n1, 31, 49n4, 88n2
metempsychosis, 212–13
Michaels, Axel, 280–81
Michalowski, Piotr, 85
millenarian movements, 151–53
Mir Yahya, 202
mirabilia, 185
Mitchell, Lynette G., 3
mnemohistory, 228, 237–38
Mocko, Anne T., 278–79, 283–86
modern drama, 249, 252–53, 268n14, 269n53
modernity, 223–24, 231, 285, 301, 338–41; arrival of, 21–24
Mohists, 138, 146, 151–53, 155, 158, 228, 237–38
Moin, A. Azfar, 197–98, 224, 304
Molina, Cristóbal de, 63–64
Mongols, 196, 198–200, 205: universal peace defined by, 207–10
morality, 8–13, 178, 249, 272, 327, 334
Mosaic Distinction, 12, 193, 342; *Emperor and Galilean*, 257; Exodus, 224, 227–29, 237–41; *Tarikh-i Alfi*, 207
Mosaic Law, 102
Mosko, Mark, 37

Mount Sinai, 103–4
Mozi, 145–46
Mu'awiya, 183
Muda, Iskander, 201
Mughal Empire, 201, 205, 336–37
Muhammad, 167, 180–81, 183; preternatural sovereignty, 173–76; self-referential sovereignty, 176, 179
Mulla Omar, 167
Muslims, 13, 202, 285, 301, 312, 316; mythological time, 37

Naram-Sin of Agade, 75–76, 85
Narayanhiti Palace Museum, 287–88
Needham, Rodney, 225
Neoplatonic kingship, 192, 195, 202, 336. *See also* kingship: Neoplatonism
Neoplatonism, 192–93; appeal of, 196–98; authorship, 202–4; defining, 193–96; Eastern presence of, 198–202; Illuminationism, 199–200, 205, 210; *lex animata*, 195; *philosophia perennis*, 196; signatures of, 201; in time and space, 193–204; universal peace defined by, 205–10; world history, 204–14
Nepal, kingship in, 271–74; classic theories, 274–76; Dasain festival, 285–86; Malla period, 276–79; monarchy decline, 282–84; post-1951 monarchy, 280–81; post-kingship modernization, 286–89; Rana period, 278–79; ritualization trap, 278; Shah period, 276–79
New Guinea Highlands, 32–33
Nichoria, 115–16
nomocratic politics, 184
Nuqtavis, 203–4, 207

O'Meara, Dominic, 195
Obama, Barack, 23
On Kings (Sahlins), 3

Paleo-Islam, 173–76
pambasileus, 123–24, 129, 334
Panchayat, 279–80, 282, 285, 287, 343
paqarikuq, 58

paqarinas, 56
Pariaqaqa, 61
participation, 11, 82, 146, 180–81
Pasikhani, Mahmud, 203–4
Peel, J. D. Y., 4
Perses, 119. *See also* Hesiod
Pharaoh, biblical deconstruction of, 94–107; interpreting, 223–42. *See also* Egypt, pharaonic kingship in; Exodus, reversal of
Plato, 112–15, 123–25, 195–96, 203, 206, 212
play, term, 6–7
Pletho, Georgios Gemistos, 196
Plotinus, 135n99, 194
polis, 113–14, 120, 126
politics: enchantment of, 323–24; mystification of, 230–31; prophetic, 227, righteousness, 327–28; secular, 223–42; theologizing, 228
polygyny, 177–78
Pongratz-Leisten, Beate, 85
Postgate, Nicholas, 80
powers (*nawalak*), 43–44
Prakash, Jaya, 278
Prometheus, 141
prophets, 8–10, 35, 47; Arab prophetic model, 193; distinguishing, 207; Israeli prophetic opposition, 102–7; politics, 227; prophetic religion, 327; replacing, 205; source of, 213
Puett, Michael, 4, 324
purity, 7–8, 10

al-Qadir, Caliph 170
al-Qaeda, 166, 304–7, 309, 311, 315–16, 318–19
Qur'an, 17–18, 168, 172–73, 175, 178, 181
Qutb al-Din Shirazi, 201

Rashid al-Din, 200–201
Razi, Fakhr al-Din, 201, 212
real abstraction, 55, 67
Redfield, Robert, 272
Regmi, Mahesh Chandra, 279

religion: avoiding as category of analysis, 2–3; biblical, 330, 332–33; civil, 224, 227, 241; counter-religion, 224, 227; as *Doppelgänger*, 240; establishing coherent definition of, 5–14; forms of, 103, 224, 227, 229, 240, 275, 332; goal of, xii; immanentist, 7, 72, 88n3, 332, 336; invisible, 6; and politics, 224–27, 240–42; salvationist, 138–39, 142, 158–59, 340; scriptural, 7, 27n44, 333–36; transcendentalist, 18, 88n3, 114, 328, 337. *See also* Buddhism; Christianity; Islam; Judaism; Sufism
Renaissance, 196, 200–201, 338
righteous kingship, 17, 115, 143, 167, 308, 319, 333, 340; transcendentalist righteous kingship, 197; under transcendence, 19
rituals, 179; coronation ritual, 100, 280–81, 283; Dasain, 285–86; deities, 79–80; domestication, 147–50; Hindu kingship and, 208, 276–79, 285; immanentist practices, 143–45; installation rituals, 139, 142; millenarian movements, 151–53; practices, 159, 161n24; public, 273, 283–84, 289; reinforcement ritual, 283–86; ritual statements, 145–46; ritualization trap, 16, 28n64, 278, 326; sacrifice, 137–39, 143, 149, 155, 159; theory, 146–47, 149, 151, 156, 330; transcendental movements, 145–46; vitality, 140–42. *See also* sacrifice
Robbins, Joel, 5
Roko Tui Bau, 45
rule of law, principle, 111, 113–14, 124

sacred kingship, 1, 40, 94, 104, 213, 343; Alexander the Great and, 334; between immanence and transcendence, 14–21, 19, 93n66; compromise with, 342; death of, 341; divinized element of, 338; entering modernity, 21–24; exodus from, 223–29, 239–41; immanentist approach to, 15–16, 197; kings before, 31–52; Mesopotamian type of, 108n7;

modal hybridity approach, 20–21; persistence of, 23–24; in Qur'an, 335; religion-politics relationship, 223–42; synthesizing, 323–344; transcendentalist approach to, 17–21, 328; types of, 19, 22–23, 239, 336, 338; world history and, 2–5, 249

sacrifice, 7, 237–38, 251; blood, 329, 341; critiquing, 154–59; domestication rituals, 147–50; human sacrifice, 17, 146, 329–30; millenarian movements and, 151–53; rejection of, 137–39; self-sacrifice, 12, 257, 265; sovereignty and, 153–54. *See also* rituals; sovereignty

Sahlins, Marshall, 1, 3, 16, 31 139–40, 162, 196, 223, 323–24. *See also* divine kingship; kingship: kings before; metahumans

salvation, 10–11, 17, 124–25; salvationist religions, 138–39, 142, 158–59, 340. *See also* doctrinal kinship

Sargon II of Assyria, 83–84

Sarhindi, Haji Ibrahim, 202–3, 219n42

Saturn, 167, 192, 204

Sayyid Qutb, 301

Schmitt, Carl, 18, 22, 102, 103, 226, 308

secularization, 5, 18, 22, 149, 224, 229, 275, 339, 344

self-divinization, 145, 151–53, 158, 331

Sennacherib, 82–84, 87

Shah, Prithvi Narayan, 273, 278, 280, 281

shariʿa, 166, 168, 178–79, 179, 182, 306, 313, 318–19

Shaykh Abu Muhammad al-Adnani ash-Shami , 313–14, 317

Shulgi of Ur, 76–77

Shulman, David, 275–76

"Sin of Sargon, The," 82–84, 87; interpretating, 85

Smith, William Robertson, 172–73

soul, transmigration of, 210–14

sovereignty: absence of, 315–19; ambiguity of, 22; assumption of, 182; being beyond judgment, 178–79; caliphal form of, 162–85; comparative forms of, 139–40; concept of, 163, 181, 249, 250–51, 254–55, 266, 301–2; counter-sovereignty, 227, 237; dual sovereignty, 225, 241, 264–65, 278; forms of, 139–40, 143, 146, 150, 159, 166, 305; ghostly authority, 230; human sensibility, 177; individualization of, 304–5; indivisibility of, 237, 241; ISIS, 299–319; Millennial Sovereignty, 201; preternatural, 171–76; pronouncements, 1–2; reserving, 299–319; rituals of, 153–54; sacrifice rituals, 137–39; secrecy, 309–11; self-referential, 176–79; social reciprocity, 183–85; transcendental, 141–43; ultimately arbitrary power, 223

spirits, 1, 38, 348n38; Axial Age, 145–46; in China, 143, 150, 152–53, 155–58; in *Emperor and Galilean*, 259, 262; evil spirits, 36–37; hierarchy, 43, 45; hubris, 39–41; owners/masters, 34–35; powers, 33, 35, 39, 41–42, 47, 230; sacrifices, 43

stranger-kingship, 54–55, 139–40; diarchy and, 61–67; diarchy emerging from, 55–56; prevalence of, 326, 332, 347n25

Strathern, Alan, 14, 43, 48, 53, 138, 155, 168–69, 197–98, 271, 304

Strauss, Leo, 38, 226

Sufism, 169–71, 169–72, 195, 198–200

Suhrawardi, Shihab al-Din, 198–202, 211–12

Suleyman the Magnificent, 168

sulh-i kull 193, 205; *see also* universal peace

Sumerian Kingslist, 78–79

sun: acting in place of, 63–64; worshipping, 210–14

Tadmor, Hayim, 82–83, 85

taqiyya, 309, 314

Tarikh-i Alfi; authorship of, 202–4; commissioning creation of, 192–93; source of, 200–202; sun worship, 210–13; *tanāsukh*, 212; as world history, 204–10

Taskhir al-Kawakib (The possession of stars), 211

Taussig, Michael, 227

Taylor, Charles, 21

Teitler, H.C., 250, 257
Ten Commandments, 238–39
Third Dynasty of Ur, 73–74; aftermath of fall of, 76–79
Third Empire, 251, 263–64, 269n53
Three Dynasties, 143, 150–51
Timurids, 167–68, 172, 201
Toynbee, Arnold, 173
transcendence, 9–14, 48, 62, 165, 167, 335; Axial Age transformation, 8; "Dialogue of Pessimism" in context of, 86; in *Emperor and Galilean*, 257; Hindu kingship and, 271–72; idealizing, 12; immanence of, 162–85; ISIS and, 301–3, 310, 316, 318; makeup of, 14; morphological opportunities for, 66; realm of play, 11; relation to immanence, 53–54; royal id in, 163–64; sacred kingship between immanence and, 19; sun worship and, 109n16; world history, 14–21. *See also* Caliphate; Hindu kingship; immanence; Islamic State of Iraq and Syria (ISIS), sovereignty of
transcendentalism, 5, 23, 48–49, 253, 256, 263; in Andes, 53–55, 62, 64, 66–67; ascendant forms of, 331–34; austere transcendentalism, 48–49; in Caliphate, 163, 166, 174, 179, 181; challenging, 54; in China, 328–31; contemplative prayer, 11; defining, 9–14; in Egypt, 224, 227, 241; in Greece, 113, 115, 119–25, 129, 331–34; immanentism vs., 328–31; in India, 328–31; in Israel, 331–34; in Mesopotamia, 86, 88n3; modernity, 337–44; monism, 27n45; proto-transcendentalism, 120, 327; term, 138–39; transcendentalist righteous kingship, 197; in world history, 17–21; writing as part of push toward, 121; and universal empires, 334–37. *See also* immanentism; Islamic State of Iraq and Syria (ISIS), sovereignty of
Trobriands, 33, 37, 40
Two Kingdoms doctrine, 225–26, 229–30, 240–41

Ulama (also Ulema), 12, 18, 164, 169, 175, 179, 184–85, 203
Umayyads, 173–78, 182–83
universal peace, 205–7; Mongol model of, 207–10
upani, 59–60

Vaihinger, Hans, 165
Venkata II, 201
vitality, 140–42

Walzer, Michael, 226, 234
Waterhouse, Joseph, 45
welfare (*maslahat*), 308–9
Whelpton, J., 279
Whitehouse, Harvey, 173
Whitmarsh, Bryony R., 287
willaq umu, role of, 64–65
Works and Days (Hesiod), 119–20
world history, 2–5, 22, 88, 137, 249, 344; constructing, 204; Neoplatonic kingship, 198–202; Neoplatonic project of, 204–13; sacred kingship in, 14–21
world religion, 2, 48–49, 334–37

Xavier, Jerome, 202–3
Xenophanes, 122, 346
Xenophon, 113, 123, 125, 129

Yazdi, Sharaf al-Din Ali, 205
YHWH, 105–6
Yoshimitsu, Ashikaga, 170

al-Zarqawi, Abu Musab, 308
Zayn al-Abidin, 208
zealous kingship, 18–19, 143, 198
Zeus, 37, 180, 257, 325; equal standing with, 127, 129–30; immanentist cosmological structure, 116–18, 124; origin of law, 112–13, 120
Ziai, Hossein, 211
Zotter, Astrid, 283
Zuidema, R. Tom, 65

GPSR Authorized Representative: Easy Access System Europe, Mustamäe tee 50, 10621 Tallinn, Estonia, gpsr.requests@easproject.com

www.ingramcontent.com/pod-product-compliance
Lightning Source LLC
Chambersburg PA
CBHW031229290426
44109CB00012B/216